Child Rights in India

LAW, POLICY, AND PRACTICE

Second Edition

ASHA BAJPAI

OXFORD
UNIVERSITY PRESS

YMCA Library Building, Jai Singh Road, New Delhi 110 001

Oxford University Press is a department of the University of Oxford. It furthers the University's objective of excellence in research, scholarship, and education by publishing worldwide in

Oxford   New York

Auckland Cape Town Dar es Salaam Hong Kong Karachi Kuala Lumpur
Madrid Melbourne Mexico City Nairobi New Delhi Shanghai Taipei Toronto

With offices in

Argentina Austria Brazil Chile Czech Republic France Greece Guatemala
Hungary Italy Japan Poland Portugal Singapore South Korea Switzerland
Thailand Turkey Ukraine Vietnam

Oxford is a registered trademark of Oxford University Press
in the UK and in certain other countries

Published in India by Oxford University Press, New Delhi

© Oxford University Press 2003, 2006

The moral rights of the author have been asserted
Database right Oxford University Press (maker)

First published in 2003
Second Edition (Oxford India Paperback) 2006
Third Impression 2009

All rights reserved. No part of this publication may be reproduced, or transmitted in any form or by any means, electronic or mechanical, including photocopying, recording or by any information storage and retrieval system, without permission in writing from Oxford University Press. Enquiries concerning reproduction outside the scope of the above should be sent to the Rights Department, Oxford University Press, at the address above

You must not circulate this book in any other binding or cover
and you must impose this same condition on any acquirer

ISBN 13: 978-0-19-567082-0
ISBN 10: 0-19- 567082 5

Typeset in A Garamond Regular 8/10
By Jojy Philip New Delhi 110 015
Printed in India by De unique, New Delhi 110 018
Published Oxford University Press
YMCA Library Building, Jai Singh Road, New Delhi 110 001

To my father
RAM MANOHAR BAJPAI
my source of inspiration and strength

Preface to the Second Edition

For some time now, I have been aware of the need to make some additions to this book so that developments since its original publication may be taken into account. The decision to bring out a paperback edition has presented an ideal opportunity to do. I have, therefore, written an extensive introduction outlining the major changes in the law and policy, as well as significant court decisions. Some information, I felt, belonged to particular portions of the text itself. Each such place has been marked with an asterisk (✽) and the new material added in an Addendum at the end.

August 2006   ASHA BAJPAI
Mumbai

Contents

Foreword by N.R. Madhava Menon	xi
Introduction to the Second Edition	xiii
Abbreviations	lxviii
Acknowledgements	lxx
Preface	lxxii

1	RIGHTS OF THE CHILD—AN OVERVIEW	1
	Introduction	1
	The Legal Definition of a Child	2
	Present Legal Framework	6
	Policies and Action Plans	10
	International Law on the Rights of the Child	14
	Children and Courts	24
	Government Programmes and Schemes	27
	Interventions and Strategies by Non-Governmental Organizations (NGOs)	28
	Challenges Ahead...	29
2	RIGHT TO FAMILY ENVIRONMENT: ADOPTION AND OTHER NON-INSTITUTIONAL SERVICES	33
	Adoption in History, Mythology, and Religion	33
	Indian Adoption Laws	42
	Critique of Laws and Practice Relating to Adoptiom	52
	Adoption Practice	52
	Important Judgments Relating to Adoption	61
	Recommendations for Law Reform	72
	Interventions and Initiatives for Providing Non-institutional Services	74
	International Legal Policies and Practices	75
	A Comparative Study of International Law	82
	Towards a Common Secular Law on Adoption	87

3 RIGHT TO PARENTAL CARE: CUSTODY AND GUARDIANSHIP — 92

- Historical Evolution — 92
- The Present Legal Regime — 94
- Major Reported Judicial Decisions — 113
- Analysis of Case Laws — 123
- Law Reform in the Best Interest of the Child — 128
- A Comparative Survey of International Laws — 131
- Some Legal Developments and Trends of Comparative Law — 141
- Discussion — 144

4 RIGHT AGAINST ECONOMIC EXPLOITATION—CHILD LABOUR — 148

- What is Child Labour? — 148
- Laws to Prohibit and Regulate Child Labour in India — 158
- The National Policy on Child Labour — 168
- Laws Relating to Bonded Child Labour — 172
- Critique of the Laws — 173
- Enforcement of the Child Labour and Bonded Child Labour Legislation — 178
- Judicial Response to Child Labour—Important Case Law — 180
- Some Significant Court Rulings Related to Bonded Child Labour — 183
- Non-governmental Organizations' (NGOs) Interventions — 185
- Government Initiatives and Schemes — 192
- International Legal Interventions, Strategies, and Movements — 193
- Conclusion — 203

5 RIGHT TO PROTECTION AGAINST SEXUAL ABUSE AND EXPLOITATION — 207

- Introduction — 207
- Part A: Child Sexual Abuse in India — 211
- Introduction — 211
- The Present Legal Regime — 216
- Child Marriages — 220
- Judicial Trends — 227
- Law Reform — 232
- International Legal Initiatives — 241
- Role Played by NGOs and the Government in Child Sexual Abuse Cases — 246
- Part B: Commercial Sexual Exploitation and Trafficking of Children — 247
- Introduction — 247
- The Indian Scenario — 252

	Indian Laws Dealing with Commercial Sexual Exploitation of Children and Trafficking	253
	Judgments on Trafficking	256
	Law Reform	262
	International Instruments	265
	International Initiatives to Prevent Child Pornography on the Internet	270
	Government/NGO Interventions in the Area of Exploitation and Trafficking	271
	Whose Child Next?	275
	Handling Child Sexual Abuse in Future	275
6	JUVENILE JUSTICE: ADMINISTRATION AND IMPLEMENTATION	277
	Introduction	277
	The Juvenile Justice Act 1986	282
	Administration and Implementation of the Juvenile Justice Act 1986	287
	Government Schemes and NGO Interventions in the Juvenile Justice System	295
	What Needs to be Done	296
	The Juvenile Justice (Care and Protection of Children) Act 2000 (J J Act 2000)	299
	Significant Changes Brought about by the Juvenile Justice Act 2000	306
	Critique of the Juvenile Justice (Care and Protection of Children) Act 2000	307
	Trends of Judicial Response to Juvenile Justice	309
	International Law and the Administration of Juvenile Justice	316
	Mission of Juvenile Courts for the Twenty-first Century	323
7	RIGHT TO DEVELOPMENT	327
	Elementary Education—The Right of Every Child	327
	Laws Relating to Child Education in India	334
	Educational Policy and Planning in India	342
	Judgments	345
	Government Schemes and Programmes in the Field of Elementary Education in India	347
	NGO Interventions in Elementary Education	350
	The Global Context of Basic Education	354
	Some International Initiatives	364
	Right to Play and Recreation	365

Future Challenges	367
8 RIGHT TO SURVIVAL: HEALTH, NUTRITION, AND SHELTER	374
Right to Health	374
International Human Rights Law	375
International Campaigns on Health	378
Law and Policy on Health in India	379
Children's Health Scenario in India	383
Rights of Unborn Child and Rights during Early Childhood	385
Medical Termination of Pregnancy Act 1971 (MTP Act 1971)	394
Amendments to the Medical Termination of Pregnancy Act 1971, and the Prenatal Diagnostic Techniques (Regulation and Prevention of Misuse) Act, 1994	396
The Pre-natal Diagnostic Techniques (Regulation and Prevention of Misuse) Amendment Bill 2002 (PNDT 2002)	397
Rights during Early Childhood	399
Rights of the Child and Working Mothers	407
Relevant Provisions of the Maternity Benefit Act 1961	408
Government Programmes and Schemes for Child Health and Development	412
NGO Initiatives	414
Special Health Issues Relating to Children	415
Children and Disability	419
Children as Victims of Drugs	427
Children's Right to Shelter/Housing	428
Towards Right to Survival for All	435
9 MAKING CHILD RIGHTS A REALITY	437
The Paradigm Shift	437
Initiatives by the Government of India	439
Major Concerns and Obstacles in Realizing the Rights of the Child	449
Conclusion	476
Select Bibliography	479
Index	488
Addendum	505

Foreword

Children constitute over 400 million of the one billion plus population of India. It is indeed an important factor in shaping the future of the nation if childhood can be endowed with the minimum requisites for healthy growth and development. Unfortunately, it is not happening today despite some of the key initiatives of the government and a number of significant interventions of the judiciary and international as well as civil society organizations.

Is the problem with the numbers, or with the institutions, or with the policies themselves? Or is it the lack of adequate social/political will and low priority in the scheme of governance? In the beginning of the Republic one could blame it all on poverty and illiteracy; but today the country is registering 8 to 10 per cent growth and is claiming to become a world economic power by 2020. Can it sustain this goal with 30 per cent of its child-citizens under-nourished, illiterate, neglected, and forced into unproductive pursuits? Should the fact that they have no clout in electoral politics blind policy planners and decision-makers in the Planning Commission and HRD Ministry at the Centre and in the States to the plight of underprivileged children in India now subjected to some of the most dastardly crimes of exploitation and abuse?

Asha Bajpai, a long-time colleague of mine has spent a substantial part of her professional life in pursuing the development of child rights and juvenile justice administration primarily in Mumbai and other cities. The volume in hand, first published in 2003, is testimony to her scholarship on the subject. There have been a number of important legislative initiatives in the recent past, which deserve to be looked into, to assess policy goals and prospects. Has the Constitutional Amendment making the right to education a fundamental right made any difference to the child in the matter of access to education at the ground level? Is the establishment of the Child Rights Commission as structured in the proposed Bill going to improve the quality of life for the neglected children? Does the new Child Offences Act ensure adequate protection to children against exploitative and abusive behaviour of parents, relatives, and strangers? These are important issues waiting to be addressed by the government and civil society organizations working in the field of child welfare and child rights. In preparing them to undertake the challenges ahead, Bajpai's book will be of immense value. Of course, it will continue to be a textbook for students pursuing studies in law, social work, psychology, and public administration.

I am delighted to write this note for the second edition of a scholarly publication by a child-friendly activist and teacher, already popular among those concerned with the subject.

Trivandrum
August 2006

N.R. Madhava Menon
former director,
National Judicial Academy, Bhopal

Introduction to the Second Edition

There have been some significant changes in the indicators since this book was first written. Also, some efforts have been made by the law and policymakers for the protection of child rights. There have been several new policy documents, laws, and some significant court rulings. A few bills are pending on issues relating to child marriage, child sexual abuse and exploitation, children with HIV/AIDS, child labour, right to education, juvenile justice, and reproductive rights. This introduction highlights some important changes in the law, policy, and law reform in the area of child rights.[1]

Given below are a few current indicators relating to Indian children.[2] These indicators are significant as they help in measuring the state of a nation's children and consequently also human, as well as, economic progress of the country.

- Under 5 mortality rate[3] (2004) 85 per thousand live births[4]
- Infant mortality rate (under 1) (2004) 62 per thousand live births[5]
- Net primary school enrolment/attendance (1996–2004) 77 per cent[6]

---

[1] I would like to acknowledge the assistance and inputs of Karandikar, Kabir Duggal, Susan Alexander, and Devendra Shanghari for this introduction.

[2] The State of the World's Children 2006, UNICEF, New York.

[3] The under 5 mortality rate is chosen by UNICEF as its single most important indicator of the state of a nation's children.

[4] Probability of dying between birth and five years of age expressed per thousand live births.

[5] Probability of dying between birth and one year of age expressed per thousand live births.

[6] National Household survey. Derived from net primary school enrolment rate as reported by UNESCO/UIS and from National Household survey reports of attendance at primary school or higher. The net primary attendance ratio is defined as the percentage of children in the age group that officially corresponds to primary schooling who attend primary school or higher.

- Percentage of infants with low birth weight (1998–2004) 30[7]
- GDP per capita average annual growth rate (1990–2004) 7 per cent[8]
- Child Labour (5–14 years) (1999–2004)[9]

Male:	14 per cent
Female:	15 per cent

- Child marriage (1996–2004)[10]

Urban:	26 per cent
Rural:	55 per cent
Total:	46 per cent

- Birth registration (1999–2004)[11]

Urban:	54 per cent
Rural:	29 per cent
Total:	35 per cent

- Population using improved drinking water sources (2002): 88 per cent[12]
- Population using adequate sanitation facilities (2002): 30 per cent

The National Charter for children, adopted on 9 February 2004, emphasizes commitment to children's right to survival, development, and protection. It also stipulates the duties of the state and the community towards children and emphasizes the duties of children towards family, society, and the nation.

The National Plan of Action for Children 2005 was introduced in the

---

[7] Infants who weigh less than 2,500 grams.

[8] Gross domestic product (GDP) is the sum of value added by all resident product taxes (less subsidies) not included in the valuation of output plus net receipts of primary income (compensation of employees and property income) from abroad. GN per capita in US dollars is converted using the World Bank Atlas method

[9] Percentage of children aged 5 to 14 years involved in child labour activities at the moment of survey. A child is considered to be involved in child labour activities under the following classification:
(a) children 5–11 years of age who, during the week preceding the survey did at least one hour of economic activity or at least 28 hours of domestic work and (b) children 12–14 years of age that during the week preceding the survey did at least 14 hours of economic activity or at least 42 hours of economic activity and domestic work combined.

[10] Percentage of women 20–24 years of age who were married or in union before they were 18 years old

[11] Percentage of children less than five years of age who were registered at the moment of the survey.

[12] Use of improved drinking water sources and adequate sanitation facilities—UNICEF, World Health Organisation (WHO), Multiple Indicator Cluster Surveys (MICS) and Demographic and Health Surveys (DHS).

Parliament to provide a roadmap for steps to be taken for improvement in the lives of Indian children.[13] The Plan 2005 is divided into four sections:

- child survival
- child development
- child protection
- child participation

The guiding principles of the Plan are:

- to regard the child as an asset and a person with human rights
- to address issues of discrimination based on gender, class, caste, race, religion, and legal status to ensure equality
- to accord utmost priority to the most disadvantaged, poorest of the poor, and least-served child in all policy and programme interventions
- to recognize the diverse stages and settings of childhood and fulfil basic needs and rights.[14]

The Plan[15] has identified twelve key areas keeping in mind the priorities and the intensity of challenges that require utmost and sustained attention in terms of outreach, programme, interventions and resource allocation, so as to achieve the necessary targets and ensure the rights and entitlements of children at each stage of childhood. It has set up very ambitious goals:

- Reducing Infant mortality rate (below 30 per 1000 live births by 2010)
- Reducing Maternal Mortality rate(below 100 per 100,000 live births by 2010)
- Reducing malnutrition among children. (To reduce under five malnutrition and low birth weight by half by 2010)
- Achieving 100 per cent civil registration of births(to achieve 100 per cent registration of births , deaths, marriages and pregnancies by 2010)
- Universalization of early childhood care and development and quality education for all children achieving 100 per cent access and retention in schools, including pre-schools. (Universal retention by 2010)
- Complete abolition of female foeticide, female infanticide and child marriage and ensuring the survival, development, and protection of the girl child. (To eliminate child marriages by 2010)

---

[13] National Plan of Action for Children, 2005, Government of India, Ministry of Human Resource Development, Department of Women & Child Development, New Delhi, India, 2005.

[14] Ibid.

[15] Department of Women and Child Development, Ministry of Human Resource Development, Government of India.

- Improving Water and Sanitation coverage both in rural and urban areas. (Universal equitable access to and use of safe drinking water and improved access to sanitary means of excreta disposal by 2010)
- Addressing and upholding the rights of children in difficult circumstances. (Implementation of the Juvenile Justice Act and adherence to international standards of care and protection)
- Securing for all children legal and societal protection from all kinds of abuse, exploitation and neglect. (To ratify UN Protocol to Prevent, Suppress and Punish Trafficking in persons, especially women and Children by 2007)
- Complete abolition of child labour with the aim of progressively eliminating all forms of economic exploitation of children. (To this end it has been decided to request the Census of India 2011 to enumerate the number, gender, caste, religion, occupation, and ages of children engaged in all kinds of child labour)
- To rescue and remove children below 10 years of age from the workforce by 2010
- Monitoring, Review and Reform of policies, programmes and laws to ensure protection of children's interests and rights. (To develop new laws and strengthen existing legal instruments especially relating to child sexual abuse and exploitation))
- Ensuring child participation and choice in matters and decisions affecting their lives.(To take measures to enable participation of children in the monitoring of the National Plan of Action (NPA) and preparation of the CRC report by supporting local, state, and national consultations with children and young persons)

Right to Free and Compulsory Education

The 86th Constitution Amendment Act 2002 added Article 21A affirming that every child between the ages of 6 and 14 years has the right to free and compulsory education.

There have been some significant rulings under this Article. It has been held that imparting of education is a sovereign function of the state, and Article 21A of the Constitution of India envisages that children of the age group 6 to 14 have a fundamental right to education. The ruling further stated that clause 3 of Article 15 of the constitution envisages special protection and affirmative action for women and children.[16] Article 21A

---

[16] *State of Bihar* v. *Project Uchcha Vidya, Sikshak Sangh and Ors*, Judgment dtd. 3 January, 2006.

would cover primary as well as secondary education and people, by approaching the court, can claim the benefit of Part III of the constitution as well.[17]

In another case, it was held that the expression 'education' must be given a broader meaning having regard to Article 21A of the constitution as also the Directive Principles of State Policy. There is a need to look into the governing power, subject to the fundamental constitutional limitations, which requires an expansion of the concept of state action.[18] It has also been clarified, however, that Article 21A not only covers the right to primary education, but also includes the right to quality education.[19]

The Right to Education (Draft) Bill 2005

It was after a long struggle that the constitutional amendment to make the right to education a fundamental right was made in 2001. State laws have still to be drafted. The Government of India has prepared a Draft Bill on the right to education. The Right to Education Bill seeks to give effect to the 86th constitutional amendment.[20]

Some of the highlights of the draft bill are:

- Every child who has attained the age of 6 years shall have the right to participate in full-time elementary education and to complete it, and to this end, be admitted to a neighbourhood school.[21] Government schools shall provide free education to all admitted children. There is a right of transition to a child till the completion of elementary education.[22]
- The state shall ensure a school in every child's neighbourhood, within a period of three years. If there is no such school, the state shall provide free transportation to the nearest school.[23] Every child who completes elementary education shall be awarded a certificate.[24]

---

[17] *State of Maharashtra* v. *Sant Dnyaneshwar Shikshan Shastra Mahavidyalaya and Ors.*, Judgment dtd. 31 March 2006, JT 2006 (4) SC 201.

[18] *Zee Telefilms Ltd and Anr* v. *Union of India and Ors* AIR 2005 SC 2677.

[19] *Binod Vikash Manch and Anr* v. *State of Jharkhand and Ors* 2003 (4) JCR 710 (Jhr).

[20] The preamble of the draft Bill states that it is to put into effect the 'Right to Free and Compulsory Education' for all children in the age group of 6 to 14 years.

[21] Right to Education (Draft) Bill, 2005, Section 2 (aa) defines neighbourhood as such areas around the residence of a child.

[22] Ibid., Section 4.

[23] Ibid., Section 5.

[24] Ibid., Section 30.

- Every school shall conform to certain minimum standards defined in the Bill.[25] Norms and standards for schools are set in the schedule to the Bill.
- Private schools shall admit at least 25 per cent of children from weaker sections; no fee shall be charged from such children.[26]
- Screening tests at the time of admission and capitation fees are prohibited for all children.[27] Admission to schools to be done generally at the time of commencement of the academic year, but in case of a child admitted to a neighbourhood school, such a child should not be denied admission at any time of the year.[28]
- Government schools will be managed by School Management Committees (SMCs), mostly composed of parents, teachers, the community, and representatives of the local authority. Such SMCs shall be constituted for every state school and aided school.[29]
- Teachers of state schools to be a school-based cadre. Teachers will be assigned to a particular school; there will be no transfers.[30]
- The National Commission for Elementary Education shall be constituted to monitor all aspects of elementary education, including quality,[31] and recommend corrective measures wherever necessary.
- Under this Bill, in Section 2(tt), a working child means a child who works for wages whether in cash or in kind or works for her own family in a manner which prevents her from participation in elementary education. Further, Section 48 provides that no person shall prevent a child from participating in elementary education. There is a proviso to this section that states that no person shall employ a child that renders her a working child .

Some experts criticize the Bill for not implementing the 'common school system' whereas others believe that even the 25 per cent free seats required of private schools is not justifiable. There is a concern that assigning teachers to a specific school will affect their chances of promotions and job security.

The Bill appears to be ambiguous on its applicability to schools administered by minorities. It has not specified clearly the rights of children with disabilities and how these will be implemented. There is mixed evidence on

[25] Ibid., Section 18.
[26] Ibid., Section 14.
[27] Ibid., Section 15.
[28] Ibid., Section 16.
[29] Ibid., Section 22.
[30] Ibid., Section 23.
[31] Ibid., Section 33.

the ability of SMCs in improving quality of schools and learning outcomes of children. It has been recently reported that the Centre has decided to ask all states to include and amend all laws to make the right to education a fundamental right. This has, perhaps, been done to pass the expenditure incurred to the states.

Child Marriages or Early or Forced Marriages

Child marriages are still rampant in India. The National Family Health Survey of 1998–1999 found that 65 per cent of girls are married by the time they are 18. Child marriage is a violation of human rights, compromising the development of girls and often resulting in early pregnancy and social isolation, with little education and poor vocational training reinforcing the gendered nature of poverty.[32] Child marriages are also responsible for the rise in trafficking of women.

The Child Marriage Restraint Act 1929 continues to recognize child marriages as valid, thus violating Article 16(2) of the Convention on the Elimination of all forms of Discrimination Against Women (CEDAW), which lays down that 'the marriage of a child shall have no legal effect'. It also violates Articles 19 and 34 of the Convention on the Rights of the Child 1989 requiring the child to be protected from all forms of physical or mental violence and all forms of sexual exploitation and abuse. It is also in breach of Article 16 of the Universal Declaration of Human Rights, which requires that marriage shall be entered into only with the free and full consent of the intending parties. It is also a violation of a girl's right to life under Article 21 of the Constitution of India.

India has, therefore, still not complied with its obligations under the constitution and the major international human rights instruments, the International Covenant on Civil and Political Rights (ICCPR) 1966, the International Covenant on Economic, Social and Cultural Rights (ICESCR), Convention on Elimination of All Forms of Discrimination Against Women (CEDAW), and the Convention on the Rights of the Child (CRC) 1989.

There have been some significant judgments on child marriage. It has been held that Muslims are not exempted from the Child Marriage Restraint Act 1929. If the marriage of a Muslim girl is performed during her minority, the marriage is not void but the persons who participated in the marriage are not immune from punishment, which is provided under Sections 4, 5, and

---

[32] UNICEF, *Early Marriage: A Harmful Traditional Practice, A Statistical Exploration*, New York, USA, 2005.

xx *Introduction*

6 of the Act of 1929. However, a Muslim girl can marry on attaining the age of puberty and her marriage cannot be declared void because she is below the age of 18, as per the Act of 1929.[33] Raising the age of consent for sexual intercourse to 18, consistent with the stipulations in the saner subsequent enactments, appears to be the unavoidable imperative before the system.[34] The supreme court, on 14 February 2006, made it mandatory for all marriages to be registered and directed authorities across the country to amend rules so that its order could be implemented within three months. This judgment could have a significant effect on child marriages. The court was of the view that one way of curbing the practice of child marriages was to make it mandatory for everyone to register their marriages to ensure that people record their ages at the time of marriage. The supreme court asked the central government to give wide publicity to this order. The central and state governments will have to incorporate appropriate provisions for the consequences of non-registration as well as false documentation during the registration of marriages. The court also made it clear that the rules should specifically contain a provision for appointment of an officer for this purpose.[35]

A petition was filed in the supreme court on the ground that child marriages continued despite there being a legislation in force which prohibited child marriages.[36] When this matter was called out for hearing, the Additional Solicitor General appearing on behalf of the Union of India produced before the court a copy of the Bill known as the Prevention of Child Marriage Bill, 2004, which had been presented in parliament, and objections were invited from the general public. The court hoped and trusted that, in the meantime, the Collectors and Superintendents of Police of all the districts in the states would endeavour to prevent child marriages as far as possible, and more so events where mass marriages took place.

The Prevention of Child Marriage Bill, 2004

The Government of India drafted 'The Prevention of Child Marriage Bill, 2004' which when passed will repeal the Child Marriage Restraint Act, 1929. The preamble to the Bill states that it provides for the prevention of

---

[33] *Muzaffar Ali Sajjad and Ors.* v. *State of Andhra Pradesh*, 2002, CriLJ 1068.
[34] *Joseph* v. *S.I. of Police*, 2005 (2) KLT 269.
[35] *Times of India*, Mumbai, 15 February 2006.
[36] *Forum, Fact Finding Documentation and Ors.* v. *Union of India and Ors.*, Writ Petition (Civil) No. 212/2003.

Introduction xxi

solemnization of child marriages. Under the Bill, a child means a person, who, if a male has not completed twenty-one years of age, and if a female has not completed eighteen years of age.[37] Child marriage is a marriage in which either of the contracting parties is a child.[38]

Some of the salient features of the Bill are:

- Child marriages are made voidable at the option of the contracting party who is a child provided that, the petition for annulling may be filed at the district court only by a contracting party who was a child at the time of the marriage. The petition may be filed before the child filing the petition completes two years of attaining majority.
- While granting a decree of nullity, the district court shall make an order directing both parties and their parents or guardians to return to the other party the money, valuables, ornaments, and other gifts received on the occasion of marriage or an equivalent amount.[39]
- Provision of providing maintenance and residence to the female contracting party to the child marriage until her remarriage.[40]
- The quantum of maintenance to depend on the needs of the child, lifestyle enjoyed and means of income.[41]
- Where there are children born of child marriage, the district court shall make appropriate order for the custody of such children taking into consideration the best interests of the child.[42]
- Regarding the legitimacy of such children, the Bill provides that the children will be deemed to be legitimate notwithstanding that the child marriage has been annulled under Section 3.[43]
- The punishment has been enhanced under the new Bill. If a male adult above eighteen years contracts a child marriage, he shall be punishable with simple imprisonment up to two years or with fine which may extend to one lakh rupees or both.[44]
- Persons who do any act to promote child marriage or permit it to be solemnized, including participating in it, are also punishable. Unless the contrary is proved, it will be presumed that the person having

---

[37] The Prevention of Child Marriage Bill, 2004, Section 2 (a).
[38] Ibid., Section 2 (b).
[39] Ibid., Section 3 (4).
[40] Ibid., Section 4 (1).
[41] Ibid., Section 4 (2).
[42] Ibid., Section 5.
[43] Ibid., Section 6.
[44] Ibid., Section 9.

charge of such minor has negligently failed to prevent the marriage from being solemnized.[45]
- The Bill provides for three circumstances wherein the marriage of a minor child is void.[46] Those are:
  » a) where a child is taken or enticed out of the keeping of a lawful guardianship, or
  » b) where a child has been by force compelled, or by deceitful means induced, to go from any place, or
  » c) where a child is sold for purposes of marriage and made to go through a form of marriage after which the child is trafficked or used for immoral purposes.
- The court of Judicial Magistrate First Class or the Metropolitan Magistrate may take *suo motu* cognizance on the basis of any reliable report or information.[47]
- The court has been given power to issue an interim injunction in case of an emergency to prevent child marriages, without giving any notice.[48] Any marriage solemnized in contravention of interim or final injunction shall be void *ab initio*.[49]
- All offences under this Act are cognizable and non-bailable.[50]
- The state will appoint Child Marriage Prevention Officers to prevent solemnization of child marriages, collect evidence for effective prosecution, advise or counsel the residents of the locality, create awareness, sensitize the community, furnish periodical returns and statistics.[51]

The Bill has some lacunae, which need to be removed. It is silent on the registration of marriages. There is no provision for punishment of officials for allowing child marriages. No incentives have been provided for traditional communities engaging in child marriages, and there is no reference to state laws or court judgments on the issue of child marriages.

Child Custody and Guardianship

There have been some important judgments on the issue of custody, guardianship, and maintenance of children. In one case, the court would not

---

[45] The Prevention of Child Marriage Bill, 2004, Section 11.
[46] Ibid., Section 12.
[47] Ibid., Section 13.
[48] Ibid., Section 13 (6).
[49] Ibid., Section 14.
[50] Ibid., Section 15.
[51] Ibid., Section 16.

Introduction xxiii

compel a girl, though she was a minor, to stay with her father or husband if she could decide what was in her interest on her own.[52] Another ruling stated that orders related to the custody of a minor are not final but interlocutory in nature and subject to modification at any future time upon proof of change in circumstances.[53] In a custody suit, where the minor lived with the mother, the place of jurisdiction was the mother's residence and not the residence of the father.[54]

Children of Void and Voidable Marriages

Though a child born out of marriage which is null and void under Section 16 is legitimate, yet Sub-section (3) of Section 16 restricts his rights in, or to the property of, any person, other than the parents, in any case where, but for the amendment Act, such child would have been incapable of possessing or acquiring any such rights by reason of his not being the legitimate child of his parents.[55]

Right to compassionate appointment is not a right to property of the deceased employee. The parents of a child referred to under Section 16 (3) are his parents who have entered into a void or voidable marriage. Such a child does not have a right to property of any person other than his parents. He, therefore, cannot claim compassionate appointment, which is a statutory right of the family of the deceased. There are other reasons for reaching the same conclusion. There can be a conflict of interest between wife and her children from first valid marriage, and the child whose legitimacy is protected under Section 16 of the Hindu Marriage Act 1955.[56] It was held that the Family Court has no jurisdiction to grant declaratory relief as to legitimacy of the child.[57]

Children's Testimony

Regarding validity of a child's testimony, the courts have held that while the law recognizes the child as a competent witness, a child, particularly at the

---

[52] *Krishna Prasad Paul* v. *State of West Bengal,* 2005 (4) CHN 308.

[53] *R.G. Bhuvanesh* v. *G. Usha Rani* 2004 (5) CTC 179; *Leeladhar Kachroo* v. *Umang Bhat Kachroo* 2005 (82) DRJ 609; *Jai Prakash Khadria* v. *Shyam Sunder Agarwalla* AIR 2000 SC 2172.

[54] *Ranubala Moharana and Anr.* v. *Mina Mohanty and Ors* JT 2004 (5) SC 377.

[55] *Ramesh Chand* v. *Executive Engineer, Electricity Distribution Division-II, Uttar Pradesh Power Corporation Ltd. and Ors* (2004), 1 UPLBEC 794.

[56] Ibid.

[57] *Renubala Moharana and Anr.* v. *Mina Mohanty and Ors.* JT 2004 (5) SC 377.

tender age of six years, who is unable to form a proper opinion about the nature of the incident because of immaturity of understanding, cannot be considered to be a witness whose sole testimony can be relied upon without other corroborative evidence. The evidence of a child is required to be evaluated carefully because he is an easy prey to tutoring. Therefore, the court always looks for adequate corroboration of his testimony.[58]

Further, Section 118 of the Evidence Act envisages that all persons shall be competent to testify, unless the court considers that they are prevented from understanding the questions put to them or from giving rational answers to these questions, because of tender years, extreme old age, disease—whether of mind, or any other cause of the same kind. However, a child of tender age can be allowed to testify if he has intellectual capacity to understand questions and give rational answers thereto.[59]

The Pre-Conception and Pre-Natal Diagnostic Techniques (Prohibition of Sex Selection) Act, 2003 (PCPNDT)[60]

The National Population Policy, 2000 of the Government of India aims at gender-balanced stabilization but also underscores the need for addressing issues such as child survival, maternal health and contraception, while increasing the provision and outreach of education, extending basic amenities such as sanitation, safe drinking water, and housing, besides empowering women and enhancing their employment opportunities.

The child sex ratio has deteriorated across the country over the last decade. In the Indian context, there is a strong preference for a son. This preference is influenced by many socio-economic and cultural factors, such as the son being responsible for carrying forward the family name and occupation. Sons are desired because they are considered a source of support during old age and for performing the religious rites at the time of cremation and subsequently. The practice of dowry and daughters being viewed as '*paraya dhan*' ('to be married and sent away' literally 'another's wealth') is yet another reason why sons are preferred to daughters. In the recent past, pre-natal diagnostic centres became very popular and their growth was tremendous. These centres were misusing the techniques for female foeticide.

---

[58] *Bhagwan Singh and Ors.* v. *State of M.P.* AIR 2003 SC 1088.
[59] *Ratansinh Dalsukhbhai Nayak* v. *State of Gujarat* AIR 2004 SC 23.
[60] Amended by the Pre-Natal Diagnostic Techniques (Regulation and Prevention of Misuse) Amendment Act, 2002.

Introduction xxv

The Pre-Natal Diagnostic Techniques (Regulation and Prevention of Misuse) Amendment Act, 2002, came into force with effect from 14 February 2003. The Pre-Natal Diagnostic Techniques (Regulation and Prevention of Misuse) Act, 1994 (PNDT) has now been renamed 'The Pre-Conception and Pre-Natal Diagnostic Techniques (Prohibition of Sex Selection) Act, 2003 (PCPNDT). The PCPNDT Act provides for the prohibition of sex selection, before or after conception, and regulates the use of pre-natal diagnostic techniques for the purpose of detecting genetic abnormalities or other sex-linked disorders in the foetus. Under the PCPNDT Act no person shall conduct or cause to be conducted any pre-natal diagnostic techniques including ultra sonography for the purpose of determining the sex of a foetus.[61]

Important changes brought in by the PCPNDT Act are:

- New definitions have been included relating to conceptus,[62] embryo,[63] foetus,[64] pre-natal diagnostic procedures,[65] pre-natal diagnostic test,[66] and sex-selection.[67]
- Prohibition of Sex Selection:[68] The PCPNDT Act prohibits the use of

---

[61] Preamble to the PCPNDT Act 1994.

[62] 'Conceptus' means any product of conception at any stage of development from fertilization until birth including extra embryonic membranes as well as the embryo or foetus; Ibid., Section 2 (ba).

[63] 'Embryo' means a developing human organism after fertilization till the end of eight weeks (fifty-six days); Ibid., Section 2 (bb).

[64] 'Foetus' means a human organism during the period of its development beginning on the fifty-seventh day following fertilization or creation (excluding any time in which its development has been suspended) and ending at birth. Ibid., Section 2 (bc).

[65] 'Pre-natal diagnostic procedures' means all gynaecological or obstetrical or medical procedures such as ultrasonography, foetoscopy, taking or removing samples of amniotic fluid, chorionic villi, blood or any tissue of a pregnant woman for being sent to a Genetic Laboratory or Genetic Clinic for conducting pre-natal diagnostic test, Ibid., Section 2 (i).

[66] 'Pre-natal diagnostic test' means ultrasonography or any test or analysis of amniotic fluid, chorionic villi, blood or any tissue of a pregnant woman conducted to detect genetic or metabolic disorders or chromosomal abnormalities or congenital anomalies or haemoglobinopathies or sex-linked diseases, Ibid., Section 2 (k).

[67] 'Sex-selection' includes any procedure, technique, test or administration or prescription or provision of anything for the purpose of ensuring or increasing the probability that an embryo will be of a particular sex, Ibid., Section 2[2(o).

[68] No person including a specialist or a team of specialists in the field of infertility, shall conduct or cause to be conducted or aid in conducting by himself or by any other person, sex selection on a woman or a man or on both or on any tissue embryo, conceptus, fluid or gametes derived from either or both of them, Section 3A PCPNDT Act, 1994.

any pre-natal diagnostic procedures[69] and tests[70] except for the purposes specified below:[71]

(i) chromosomal abnormalities;
(ii) genetic metabolic diseases;
(iii) haemoglobinopathies;
(iv) sex-linked genetic diseases;
(v) congenital anomalies;
(vi) any other abnormalities or diseases as may be specified by the Central Supervisory Board,[72]

and after satisfying any of the conditions as under:[73]

(i) age of the pregnant woman is above thirty-five years;
(ii) the pregnant woman has undergone two or more spontaneous abortions or foetal loss;
(iii) the pregnant woman had been exposed to potentially teratogenic agents such as drugs, radiation, infection, or chemicals;
(iv) the pregnant woman or her spouse has a family history of mental retardation or physical deformities such as spasticity or any other genetic disease; and;
(v) any other condition as may be specified by the Board.

However, the person conducting ultrasonography on a pregnant woman is required to keep complete record thereof in the clinic, and any deficiency or inaccuracy found would amount to contravention of the provisions of Sections 5 or 6 unless the contrary is proved by the person conducting such ultrasonography.[74]

---

[69] 'Pre-natal diagnostic procedures' means all gynaecological or obstetrical or medical procedures such as ultrasonography, foetoscopy, taking or removing samples of amniotic fluid, chorionic villi, embryo, blood or any other tissue or fluid of a man, or of a woman before or after conception, being sent to a Genetic Laboratory or Genetic Clinic for conducting any type of analysis or pre-natal diagnostic tests for selection of sex before or after conception. Ibid., Section 2 (i).

[70] 'Pre-natal diagnostic test' means ultrasonography or any test or analysis of amniotic fluid, chorionic villi, blood or any tissue or fluid of a pregnant woman or conceptus, conducted to detect genetic or metabolic disorders or chromosomal abnormalities or congenital anomalies or haemoglobinopathies or sex-linked diseases. Ibid., Section 2 (k).

[71] Ibid., Section 4 (2).

[72] 'Board' means the Central Supervisory Board constituted under Ibid., Section 7.

[73] Substituted by Pre-Natal Diagnositc Techniques (Regulation and Prevention of Misuse) Amendment Act 2002 (14 of 2003) w.e.f 14.02.2003.

[74] Section 4 (3) proviso PCPNDT Act 1994.

Introduction xxvii

- Prohibition on sale of ultrasound machine, etc., to persons, laboratories, clinics etc., not registered under the Act.[75]
- Several offences and penalties have been included in the Act. Any medical geneticist, gynaecologist, registered medical practitioner or any person who owns a genetic clinic[76] and contravenes any of the provisions of the Act can be punished with imprisonment for a term which may extend to three years and with a fine which may extend to ten thousand rupees, and on any subsequent conviction, with imprisonment which may extend to five years, and with a fine which may extend to fifty thousand rupees.[77] The name of the registered medical practitioner shall be reported and there may be suspension of the registration if the charges are framed by the court, and if convicted, his name may be removed from the register of the Medical Council for a period of five years for the first offence, and permanently for the subsequent offence.[78] Even a person, who seeks the aid of any such genetic clinic for the purpose of sex-selection of the foetus, may be punished for a term of three years and a fine up to fifty thousand rupees for the first offence and for a term of five years and a fine upto one lakh rupees for subsequent offences.[79] Under the Act, even a company or the director, manager, secretary or other officer of the company may be punished, if found guilty of contravening the provisions of this Act,[80] unless it is proved that the offence was committed without the knowledge of such director, manager, secretary, or other officer or that he exercised all due diligence to prevent such an offence.[81] Every offence under this Act shall be cognizable, non-bailable, and non-compoundable.[82]

---

[75] No person shall sell any ultrasound machine or imaging machine or scanner or any other equipment capable of detecting sex of foetus to any genetic counselling centre, genetic laboratory, genetic clinic, or any other person not registered under the act, Section 3B, PCPNDT Act, 1994.

[76] 'Genetic Clinic' means a clinic, institute, hospital, nursing home or any place, by whatever name called, which is used for conducting pre-natal diagnostic procedures. Ibid., Section 2 (d).

[77] Ibid., Section 23 (1).
[78] Ibid., Section 23 (2).
[79] Ibid., Section 23 (3).
[80] Ibid., Section 26 (1).
[81] Ibid., Section 26 (1) proviso.
[82] Ibid., Section 27.

Directions by Supreme Court for Implementation of PCPNDT Act 1994—'CEHAT Judgement'

In order to implement the provisions of the Act more rigorously, the supreme court, in a landmark judgment,[83] has issued a number of guidelines for the central government, the central supervisory board, and the state governments. The important directions are:

I. Directions to the Central Government

1. The central government is directed to create public awareness against the practice of pre-natal determination of sex and female foeticide through appropriate releases/programmes in the electronic media.

II. Directions to the Central Supervisory Board (CSB)

1. Meetings of the CSB will be held at least once in six months. The supreme court hoped that this power would be exercised so as to include those persons who can genuinely spare some time for implementation of the Act.
2. The CSB shall review and monitor the implementation of the Act.
3. The CSB shall issue directions to all states/urban territories and appropriate authorities to furnish quarterly returns to the CSB giving a report on the implementation and working of the Act. These returns should *inter alia* contain specific information about:

    (i) Survey and registration of bodies specified in the Act.
    (ii) Action taken against non-registered bodies.
    (iii) Complaints received by the appropriate authorities under the Act and action taken pursuant thereto.
    (iv) Number and nature of awareness campaigns conducted and results flowing therefrom.

4. The CSB shall examine the necessity to amend the Act keeping in mind emerging technologies and difficulties encountered in implementation of the Act, and to make recommendations to the central government.
5. The CSB shall lay down a code of conduct to be observed by persons working in bodies specified therein, and to ensure its publication so that the public at large can know about it.
6. The CSB will require medical professional bodies/associations to create

---

[83] *Centre for Enquiry into Health and Allied Themes (CEHAT) and Ors.* v. *Union of India and Ors.* AIR 2003 SC 3309.

awareness against the practice of pre-natal determination of sex and female foeticide and to ensure implementation of the Act.

III. Directions to State Governments/UT Administrations

1. All state governments/Union Territory (UT) administrations are directed to appoint by notification, fully empowered appropriate authorities at district and sub-district levels and also advisory committees to aid and advise the appropriate authority in discharge of its functions by such persons who can devote some time for the work assigned to them.

2. All state governments/UT administrations are directed to publish a list of the appropriate authorities in the print and electronic media in its respective state/UT.

3. All state governments/UT administrations are directed to create public awareness against the practice of pre-natal determination of sex and female foeticide through advertisement in the print and electronic media by hoarding and other appropriate means.

4. All state governments/UT administrations are directed to ensure that all state/UT appropriate authorities furnish quarterly returns to the CSB giving a report on the implementation and working of the act. These returns should *inter alia* contain specific information about:

    (i) Survey of bodies.
    (ii) Registration of bodies.
    (iii) Action taken against non-registered bodies operating in violation of the Act, inclusive of search and seizure of records.
    (iv) Complaints received by the appropriate authorities under the Act and action taken pursuant thereto.
    (v) Number and nature of awareness campaigns conducted and results flowing therefrom.

5. a) For effective implementation of the Act, information should be published by way of advertisements as well as through the electronic media. This process should be continued till there is awareness in public that there should not be any discrimination between male and female child.

    b) Quarterly reports by the appropriate authority, which are submitted to the supervisory board, should be consolidated and published annually for information of the public at large.

    c) Appropriate authorities shall maintain the records of all the meetings of the advisory committees.

d) The National Monitoring and Inspection Committee constituted by the central government for conducting periodic inspection shall continue to function till the Act is effectively implemented. The reports of this committee be placed before the central supervisory board and state supervisory board for any further action.

e) As provided under Rule 17 (3), public would have access to the records maintained by different bodies constituted under the Act.

IV. Directions to Appropriate Authorities

1. Appropriate authorities are directed to take prompt action against any person or body who issues or causes to be issued any advertisement in violation of Section 22 of the Act.
2. Appropriate authorities are directed to take prompt action against all bodies specified in Section 3 of the Act as also against persons who are operating without a valid certificate of registration under the Act.
3. All state/UT appropriate authorities are directed to furnish quarterly returns to the CSB a giving report on the implementation and working of the Act. These returns should *inter alia* contain specific information about:

   (i) Survey of bodies specified in Section 3 of the act.
   (ii) Registration of bodies specified in Section 3 of the Act including bodies using ultrasound machines.
   (iii) Action taken against non-registered bodies operating in violation of Section 3 of the Act, inclusive of search and seizure of records.
   (iv) Complaints received by the appropriate authorities under the Act and action taken pursuant thereto.
   (v) Number and nature of awareness campaigns conducted and results flowing from them.

First Conviction under PCPNDT Act 1994

The first conviction came in the case of *State, through District Appropriate Authority-cum-Civil Surgeon, Faridabad* v. *Dr. Anil Sabhani, Kartar Singh and M/s Dr. Anil Ultrasound, Faridabad.*[84] In this case, the district appropriate authority-cum-civil surgeon, Faridabad, filed a complaint against the accused on the ground that M/s Dr. Anil Ultrasound Centre, Faridabad—a registered genetic clinic, was engaged in illegal sex determination in

---

[84] Case No. RBT-298/2 of 2001 decided on 25.3.2006 in the Court of Sub-Divisional Judicial Magistrate, Paliwal.

violation of the Act. A doctor and a decoy patient visited the clinic with marked currency notes. The doctor accompanying the decoy patient as her attendant carried a hidden tape recorder, while other members waited outside for the signal. While performing the ultrasound on the patient, the doctor prompted that he could also disclose the sex of the foetus for an additional payment. On payment of the required amount, the doctor performed ultrasonography on her without any written consent and orally conveyed that it was a female foetus. No receipt for payment or any written report of sex determination was issued by the accused, except a routine ultrasound report. After getting the signal, the entire team entered the clinic and took into custody all files and records. The accused admitted to disclosing the sex of the foetus, which was video-recorded. On the basis of the above circumstantial and corroborative evidence, the accused were held guilty and convicted.

Amendment to the Infant Milk Substitutes, Feeding Bottles and Infant Foods (Regulation of Production, Supply and Distribution) Amendment Act, 2003[85]

The following activities are prohibited under the Infant Milk Substitutes, Feeding Bottles and Infant Foods (Regulation of Production, Supply and Distribution) Amendment Act, 2003:[86]

- Prohibition of advertising, or taking part in publication of any advertisement.[87]
- To give an impression or create a belief in any manner that feeding of infant milk substitutes and infant foods are equivalent to, or better than, mother's milk;[88] or
- To take part in the promotion of infant milk substitutes, feeding bottles or infant foods.[89]

The penalty for contravening this provision is imprisonment for a term which may extend to three years, or with fine which may extend to five thousand rupees, or with both.[90]

---

[85] Infant Milk Substitutes, Feeding Bottles and Infant Foods (Regulation of Production, Supply and Distribution) Amendment Act (38 of 2003).

[86] Ibid.

[87] To advertise, or take part in the publication of any advertisement, for the distribution, sale or supply of infant milk substitutes, feeding bottles or infant foods Ibid., Section 3 (a).

[88] Ibid., Section 3 (b).

[89] Ibid., Section 3 (c).

[90] Ibid., Section 3 (1).

xxxii *Introduction*

- Prohibitions relating to incentives for the use or sale of infant milk substitutes or feeding bottles.[91]

  The penalty for contravening this provision is imprisonment for a term which may extend to three years, or with fine which may extend to five thousand rupees, or both.[92]

- Prohibition relating to donations of infant milk substitutes or feeding bottles or equipment or related materials.[93]

- Any informational or educational equipment or material relating to infant milk substitutes, feeding bottles or infant foods cannot be donated or distributed except through the health-care system.[94]

  The penalty for contravening this provision is imprisonment for a term which may extend to three years, or with fine which may extend to five thousand rupees, or both.[95]

Information to be Supplied on Containers and Labels of Infant Milk Substitutes or Infant Foods

- Before producing, supplying or distributing infant milk food or substitutes, the containers and labels should be provided with certain particulars in a clear, conspicuous, easily readable and understandable manner:[96]

---

[91] For the purpose of promoting the use or sale of infant milk substitutes or feeding bottles or infant foods, the Infant Milk Substitutes, Feeding Bottles and Infant Foods (Regulation of Production, Supply and Distribution) Amendment Act 2003 prohibits: (1) supply or distribution samples of infant milk substitutes or feeding bottles or infant foods or gifts of utensils or other articles; (2) contact with any pregnant woman or the mother of an infant; or (3) inducement of any other kind Ibid., Section 4 (a) (b) (c).

[92] Ibid., Section 20 (1).

[93] Donation or distribution of infant milk substitutes or feeding bottles or infant foods can only be made to an orphanage unless the donation is by an institution or organization engaged in health care for mothers, infants or pregnant women, or to a mother who cannot resort to breastfeeding and who cannot afford to purchase infant milk substitutes or feeding bottles Ibid., Sections 5 (a), 8 (4).

[94] Ibid., Section 5 (b).

[95] Ibid., Sections 20 (1). Section 6 (1), (a)–(i).

[96] (1) The words 'IMPORTANT NOTICE' written in capital letters in a prescribed language; (2) a statement 'MOTHER'S MILK IS BEST FOR YOUR BABY' written in capital letters; (3) a statement that infant milk substitutes or infant food should be used only on the advice of a health worker; the health worker should advise on the need for its use and the proper method of its use; (4) a warning stating that infant milk substitutes or infant food is not the sole source of nourishment for an infant; (5) the instructions for preparing it appropriately and a warning against the health hazards of its inappropriate preparation; (6) the ingredients used; (7) the storage conditions required; (8) the batch

Introduction xxxiii

The punishment for contravening provisions is imprisonment for a term, which shall not be less than six months but which may extend to three years and with fine, which shall not be less than two thousand rupees.[97] The court may, for any adequate and special reasons, impose a sentence of imprisonment for a term which must not be less than three months but which may extend to two years and with fine which shall not be less than one thousand rupees.[98]

- Certain kinds of information or pictures should not be supplied on containers and labels of infant milk substitutes or infant foods.[99]

The punishment for contravening this provision is an imprisonment for a term which shall not be less than six months but which may extend to three years and with fine, which shall not be less than two thousand rupees.[100] The court may, for any adequate and special reasons, impose a sentence of imprisonment for a term which must not be less than three months but which may extend to two years and with fine which shall not be less than one thousand rupees.[101]

- Certain particulars must be printed on the covers of educational and other materials relating to feeding of infants. Every educational or other material including advertisements or material relating to promotion of infant milk substitutes, feeding bottles and infant foods, whether audio or visual, dealing with pre-natal or post-natal care or with the feeding of an infant, and intended to reach pregnant women or mothers of infants must include clear information relating to (1) the benefits and superiority of breastfeeding; (2) the preparation for, and the continuance of, breastfeeding; (3) the harmful effects on breastfeeding due to the partial adoption of bottle feeding; (4) the difficulties in reverting to breastfeeding of infants after a period of feeding by infant milk substitute; (5) the financial and social implications in making use

---

number, date of its manufacture and the date before which it is to be consumed, taking into account the climatic and storage conditions of the country and other prescribed particulars; (9) the composition or analysis—Infant Milk Substitutes, Feeding Bottles and Infant Foods (Regulation of Production, Supply and Distribution) Amendment Act 2003 Section 6 (1) (a)–(i).

[97] Ibid., Section 20 (2).
[98] Ibid., Section 20 proviso.
[99] (1) no pictures of an infant or a woman or both or pictures or other graphic material or phrases designed to increase the saleability of infant milk substitute or infant food; (2) use on it the word 'humanized' or 'maternalized' or any other similar word or such similar particulars on the labels and containers—Ibid., Section 6 (2) (a)–(d).
[100] Ibid., Section 20 (2).
[101] Ibid., Section 20 proviso.

xxxiv *Introduction*

of infant milk substitutes and feeding bottles; (6) the health hazards of improper use of infant milk substitutes and feeding bottles; (7) the date of printing and publication of such material and the name of the printer and publisher; and anything else which may be prescribed:[102]

The penalty for contravening this provision is imprisonment for a term which may extend to three years or with fine which may extend to five thousand rupees, or both.[103]

Use of Health-care System

- For dissemination of information on infant milk substitutes, foods or feeding bottles, the health-care system should not be used for the display of placards or posters relating to, or for the distribution of materials for the purpose of promoting the use or sale of infant milk substitutes or feeding bottles or infant foods.[104] However, the health-care system can be used for the dissemination of information to a health worker about the scientific and factual matters relating to the use of infant milk substitutes or feeding bottles or infant foods.[105]
- Any person who works in the health-care system cannot be paid by any producer, supplier, distributor or seller of infant milk substitutes, feeding bottles or infant foods, for promoting the use or sale of such substitutes or bottles or foods.[106]

The punishment for violation of the above conditions is imprisonment for a term which may extend to three years or with fine which may extend to five thousand rupees, or both.[107]

- Only a health worker is permitted to demonstrate feeding with infant milk substitutes or infant foods to the mother of an infant or to any member of her family.[108] The health worker must also clearly explain to such mother or such other member the hazards of improper use of infant milk substitutes or feeding bottles or infant foods.[109]
- No person, other than an institution or organization, engaged in health care for mothers, infants or pregnant women is permitted to distribute

---

[102] Infant Milk Substitutes, Feeding Bottles and Infant Foods (Regulation of Production, Supply and Distribution) Amendment Act 2003, Section 7 (a)–(g).
[103] Ibid., Section 20 (1).
[104] Ibid., Section 8 (1).
[105] Ibid., Section 8 (1) (b).
[106] Ibid., Section 8 (2).
[107] Ibid., Section 20 (1).
[108] Ibid., Section 8 (3).
[109] Ibid., Section 8 (3).

Introduction xxxv

infant milk substitutes or feeding bottles to a mother, who cannot resort to breastfeeding and who cannot afford to purchase infant milk substitutes or feeding bottles.[110]
- A producer, supplier, distributor or seller of infant milk substitutes, feeding bottles or infant foods cannot offer or give, directly or indirectly, any financial inducements or gifts to a health worker or to any member of his family for the purpose of promoting their products.[111] No producer, supplier or distributor referred to above can offer or give any contribution or pecuniary benefit to a health worker or any association of health workers, including funding of any seminar, meeting, conference, educational course, contest, fellowship, research work or sponsorship.[112]

The penalty for contravening this provision is imprisonment for a term which may extend to three years or with fine which may extend to five thousand rupees, or both.[113]

Exemption for Orphanages
- Exemption from restrictions regarding infant milk substitutes, feeding bottles and related equipment: Infant milk substitutes or feeding bottles or infant foods can be donated to orphanages.[114]
- An orphanage may purchase infant milk substitutes or feeding bottles at a price lower than their sale price.[115] Such purchases will not amount to an inducement for promoting the use or sale of infant milk substitutes or feeding bottles.[116]

Remuneration of Employees
- Remuneration of employees of person who produces, supplies, distributes or sells infant milk substitutes: The remuneration of a person who produces, supplies, distributes or sells infant milk substitutes or feeding bottles or infant foods should not be fixed on the basis of the volume of sale of such substitutes or bottles or foods made by such employees,

---

[110] Infant Milk Substitutes, Feeding Bottles and Infant Foods (Regulation of Production, Supply and Distribution) Amendment Act 2003, Section 8 (4).
[111] Ibid., Section 9 (1).
[112] Ibid., Section 9 (2).
[113] Ibid., Section 20 (1).
[114] Ibid., Section 5 (a).
[115] Ibid., Section 8 (5).
[116] Ibid., Section 8 (5) exception.

nor should any commission be given to the employee on the basis of the volume of sale of such substitutes or bottles or foods.[117]

If this provision is violated, such violation is punishable with a term which may extend to three years or with fine which may extend to five thousand rupees, or both.[118]

Standards of Infant Milk, Feeding Bottles and Foods

- Standards of infant milk substitutes, feeding bottles or infant foods: Infant milk substitute or infant food have to conform to the standards specified for such substitute or food.[119,120]

    Any person who violates this provision shall be punishable with imprisonment for a term, which shall not be less than six months but which may extend to three years and with fine, which shall not be less than two thousand rupees.[121]

- The feeding bottle containers should conform to the standard mark specified by the Indian Bureau of Standards and such mark should be affixed on the containers.[122]

    Any person who violates this provision shall be punishable with imprisonment for a term which may extend to three years or with fine which may extend to five thousand rupees, or both.[123]

- Powers of entry, search, seizure, and confiscation:[124] The Act also provides the power to confiscate suspect items if the provisions of the Act are contravened.[125, 126, 127, 128]

---

[117] Infant Milk Substitutes, Feeding Bottles and Infant Foods (Regulation of Production, Supply and Distribution) Amendment Act 2003, Section 10 (1).

[118] Ibid., Section 20 (1).

[119] Under the Prevention of Food Adulteration Act, 1954 (37 of 1954), and should have the relevant Standard Mark specified by the Bureau of Indian Standards, Ibid., Section 11 (1).

[120] Where no standards have been specified for any infant milk substitute or infant food under the Prevention of Food Adulteration Act, 1954, the approval of the Central Government has to be taken before it is sold or distributed, Ibid., Section 11 (1).

[121] Ibid., Section 20 (2).

[122] Ibid., Section 11 (2).

[123] Ibid., Section 20 (1).

[124] If any food inspector or authorized officer has reason to believe that in respect of any infant milk substitute or feeding bottle or infant food or container thereof, the specified standards are not being conformed to, then he can enter, search the relevant premises and seize infant milk food substitutes, feeding bottles or infant foods or their containers, Ibid., Sections 12 and 13.

[125] Ibid., Section 14.

- Notice to the owner of the seized infant milk substitute or feeding bottle or infant food or container.[129, 130]

Amendment to the Juvenile Justice (Care and Protection of Children) Act, 2000

In a public interest litigation (Civil Writ Petition No. 3447 of 2001), certain provisions of the Juvenile Justice Act were challenged before the High Court of Delhi. During the course of the hearings, the High Court observed that some of the provisions of the Act merited re-consideration. Keeping in view these observations, it was proposed to carry out amendments to Sections 32, 33, 56, 57 and 59 of the Act.[131]

An Amendment Bill was introduced in the Lok Sabha on 29.8.2005[132] called the 'the Juvenile Justice (Care and Protection of Children) Amendment Bill, 2005'.

The following amendments were introduced to the Act and made applicable to all cases involving detention, prosecution or sentence on imprisonment of juveniles under any such law:

- 'juvenile in conflict with law' means a juvenile who is alleged to have

---

[126] The court has the power to give the owner the option to pay costs in lieu of confiscation—Infant Milk Substitutes, Feeding Bottles and Infant Foods (Regulation of Production, Supply and Distribution) Amendment Act 2003, Section 15.

[127] No confiscation made or cost ordered to be paid under the Act will be a bar to other punishments under it or any other act, Ibid., Section 16.

[128] Any order adjudicating confiscation or directing payment of costs will be made only after giving the owner notice in writing and giving him a reasonable opportunity to defend himself, Ibid., Section 18.

[129] Before any order adjudicating confiscation or directing payment of costs is made, the owner of the infant milk substitute or feeding bottle or infant food or container has to be given a notice in writing, informing him of the grounds on which it is proposed to confiscate his goods and then giving him an opportunity of making a representation in writing, within a reasonable time, Ibid., Section 18 (1).

[130] If no such notice is given within a period of 90 days from the date of the seizure of the infant milk substitute or feeding bottle or infant food or container, such substitute or bottle or food or container shall be returned after the expiry of that period to the person from whose possession it was seized, Ibid., Section 18 (1) proviso.

[131] Accordingly, an Amendment Bill was introduced in the Lok Sabha on 28.7.2003. The Lok Sabha referred the said Bill to the Parliamentary Standing Committee on Labour and Welfare for examination and report. Before the Standing Committee submitted its report, the Lok Sabha was dissolved and the said Bill lapsed.

[132] Bill No. 124 of 2005.

committed an offence and has not completed eighteen years as on the date of commission of such offence.
- Whenever a claim of juvenility is raised before any court or a court is of the opinion that an accused person produced before it was a juvenile on the date of commission of the offence, the court shall make an inquiry, take such evidence as may be necessary (but not an affidavit) so as to determine the age of such person, and shall record a finding whether the person is a juvenile or a child or not, stating his age as nearly as may be.
- An important provision is that a claim of juvenility may be raised before any court and it shall be recognized at any stage even after disposal of the case in terms of the provisions. If the court finds a person to be juvenile on the date of commission of the offence, it shall forward the juvenile to the Board.[133]
- As soon as a juvenile in conflict with law is apprehended by the police, he shall be placed under the charge of a special juvenile police unit or the designated police officer, who shall produce the juvenile before the Board without any loss of time but within a period of twenty-four hours of his apprehension, excluding the time necessary for the journey from the place where the juvenile was apprehended, to the Board. Under the amendment, the juvenile can be placed with or without surety, and can also be placed in a fit institution.[134]
- An order can be made directing the juvenile to be sent to a special home for a period of three years or until he ceases to be a juvenile, whichever is later.[135]
- It has been provided that no report in any newspaper, magazine, newssheet or visual media of any inquiry regarding a juvenile in conflict with law or a child in need of care and protection under this Act shall disclose the name, address of the school, or any other particulars calculated to lead to the identification of the juvenile or child, nor shall any picture of any such juvenile or child be published.[136] The authority holding the inquiry may permit such disclosure, if in its opinion such disclosure is in the interest of the juvenile or the child. This has to be given in writing.
- It has been clarified in the amendment that the child shall be produced

---

[133] The Juvenile Justice (Care and Protection of Children Amendment) Act 2005, Section 7A.

[134] Ibid., Section 12 (g).

[135] Ibid., Section 15 (1).

[136] Ibid., Section 21.

before the Committee without any loss of time but within a period of twenty-four hours excluding the time necessary for the journey.
- There is no need to make a report to the police under the amended Act.
- The police is not supposed to conduct any inquiry. In Section 33 of the principal Act:
    (a) in sub-section (1), the words 'or any police officer or special juvenile police unit or the designated police officer' shall be omitted:
    (b) for sub-section (3), the following sub-section shall be substituted, namely:

'(3) After the completion of the inquiry, if the Committee is of the opinion that the said child has no family or ostensible support or has continued need of care and protection, it may allow the child to remain in the children's home or shelter home until suitable rehabilitation is found for him or till he attains the age of eighteen years.'

In Section 39 of the principal Act, for the *Explanation,* the following *Explanation* shall be substituted, namely:

'*Explanation*: For the purposes of these Sections 'restoration of and protection of a child' means restoration to:

(a) parents;
(b) adopted parents;
(c) foster parents;
(d) guardian;
(e) fit person; or
(f) fit institution.'

In Section 41 of the principal Act:
(i) for sub-section (2), the following sub-section shall be substituted, namely:

'(2) Adoption shall be resorted through such mechanisms as may be prescribed for the rehabilitation of children who are orphaned, abandoned, neglected, and abused.'

(ii) for sub-section (6), the following sub-section shall be substituted, namely:

'(6) The Board may allow a child to be given in adoption:

(a) to a single parent;
(b) to parents to adopt a child of same sex, irrespective of the number of living biological sons or daughters; or
(c) to childless parents.'

(iii) after sub-section (6), the following sub-section shall be inserted, namely:

'(7) No adoption under this Section shall be allowed unless the child and the parents are citizens of India.'

'57. The State Government may direct any child or the juvenile to be transferred to any children's home or special home or institution of like nature with the prior intimation to the Committee or the Board, as the case may be, and such order shall be deemed to be operative for the competent authority of the area to which the child or the juvenile is sent.'

In Section 64 of the principal Act, the following shall be inserted, namely:

'provided that the State Government or as the case may be, the Board may, for any adequate and special reason to be recorded in writing, review the case of the juvenile undergoing such sentence, who has ceased to be so on or before the commencement of this Act, and pass appropriate order in the interest of the juvenile.

Explanation: In all cases where a juvenile in conflict with the law is undergoing a sentence of imprisonment at any stage on the date of commencement of this Act, his case including the issue of juvenility, shall be deemed to be decided in terms of the provisions contained in this Act and the rules made thereunder, irrespective of the fact that he ceases to be juvenile on or before such date and accordingly he shall be sent to the special home or a fit institution, as the case may be, for the remainder of the period of the sentence.'

Age Determination

Age determination is a very complex issue. There have been some recent judgments on this issue. The supreme court has held that on the point of proof of age, school leaving certificate is the best evidence and so far as the medical certificate is concerned, the same is based on estimate, and possibility of error cannot be ruled out.[137] However, regarding date of birth, the secondary school certificate is not to be taken to be correct unless corroborated by parents who got the same entries made.[138]

---

[137] *Bhoop Ram* v. *State of U.P.* AIR 1989 SC 1329; *Rajan and Ors.* v. *State of Rajasthan* 2002 CriLJ 3152; *Ram Sanehi Pandey* v. *U.P. Rajya Vidyut Parishad and Ors* 2004 (2) AWC 1211; *Pratap Singh* v. *State of Jharkhand and Anr* AIR 2005 SC 2731.

[138] *Biradmal Singhvi* v. *Anand Purohit* AIR 1988 SC 1796; *Tara Devi* v. *Sudesh*

Thus, it can easily be said that the best evidence for determination of age is the birth certificate or the school certificate and in case it is available, that would be considered the best evidence, and so far as the medical evidence is concerned, since it has margin of error, it would be taken into consideration only when primary evidence which is found in the birth certificate or school certificate is not available.[139]

If it is not clear as under what provision of law, the school register is maintained, the entries made in such a register cannot be taken as a proof of age of the person concerned for any purpose.[140] In a supreme court judgment, it has been held that entries in birth register made by the official concerned in discharge of his official duties are admissible evidence under Section 35 of the Indian Evidence Act.

The following are some points that have been decided in cases under the Juvenile Justice (Care and Protection of Children) Act 2000

1) When the school leaving certificate shows the age of the child as below 18 years, but arrest memo shows it as 18 years, the court should first enquire about the current age of the child. The order of rejecting the bail without such inquiry in respect of the age in Narcotic Drugs and Psychotropic Substances Act is improper.[141]
2) If the age of the accused during the recording of the statement under Section 313 of the Criminal Procedure Code is 22 years, but was 'juvenile' at the time of commission of the offence, he must be treated as 'juvenile' for sentencing purposes.[142]
3) When there are various dates in various documents of the accused, viz., two sets of school certificates, ration card, voters list and medical report, the concurrent finding of the fact by both the courts (that the accused is above 16 years is in the instant case, arisen on the Juvenile Justice Act 1986) based on the material on record cannot be disturbed.[143]
4) If any proceeding is pending on the date of enforcement of the new Act, that proceeding shall be concluded under the provisions of the old Act.

Choudhary AIR 1998 Raj 54 (DB); *Ram Sanehi Pandey* v. *U.P. Rajya Vidyut Parishad and Ors* 2004 (2) AWC 1211.

[139] *Rajan and Ors.* v. *State of Rajasthan* 2002 CriLJ 3152.
[140] *Ramdeo Chauhan* v. *State of Assam* AIR 2001 SC 2231.
[141] *Manoharlal* v. *State of Rajasthan* 2002 CriLJ 394.
[142] *Chandrika Kumar and Ors.* v. *State of Bihar* 2002 CriLJ (NOC) 38 (Patna) (2001) 1 BLJ 614.
[143] *Mehmood Khan* v. *The State* 2002 CriLJ 2123.

However, Section 20 of the new Act provides that in case the court finds that the accused was juvenile and he committed the offence, the court shall record its finding, but shall not pass any sentence and send the juvenile to the Board for appropriate orders. The sending of juvenile before the Board would arise after the conclusion of the trial and finding that the accused had committed the offence. But it is clear that except the said procedure, the provisions of the new Act would not be applicable to the above proceeding.[144]

5) The Additional Chief Judicial Magistrate in the state of Bihar is competent to hold an enquiry under Section 4 of the new Act for the purpose of determining the age of the juvenile.[145]

6) The new Act is not applicable to pending cases, only if trial is pending on the date of enforcement of the Act, which is 1 April 2001. Even though persons between the ages of 16 and 18 have been brought within the definition of 'juvenile' under the new Act, a person who has not been held to be juvenile under the old Act being above 16 years, cannot be treated as a juvenile under the new Act even if he is below 18 years.[146] Bail cannot be refused to the juvenile merely because he has been charged with having committed a heinous offence triable exclusively by a court of sessions.[147]

7) Court should not guess about the existence of grounds for refusal of bail. Those grounds should be substantiated by some evidence on record.[148]

8) Plea of juvenility can be taken anytime even before the appellate court.[149]

9) Conduct of trial of 'juvenile' by the sessions court without first enquiring his age in order to ascertain as to whether he is 'juvenile' or not is not proper and Rajasthan High Court directed the sessions judge first to conduct an enquiry about the age of the accused and if he is found juvenile, then to forward the relevant record to the competent court, and if found otherwise, to decide sessions case as per the law.[150]

10) The provisions of the Act would be applicable even to those cases

---

[144] *Lallan Singh* v. *State of U.P. and Anr* 2002 CriLJ 1242.
[145] *Abhishek Singh* v. *State of Jharkhand* 2002 CriLJ 3801.
[146] *Vijay Singh and Anr.* v. *State of U.P* 2003 CriLJ 3461.
[147] *Vikky alias Vikram Singh* v. *State of U.P. and Ors* 2003 CriLJ 3457.
[148] Sanjay State of U.P. 2003 CriLJ (NOC) 252; 2003 AllLJ 2378 (reasons are necessary for refusing the bail).
[149] *Munshi Khan* v. *State of Rajasthan* 2004 CriLJ 3465 (Rajasthan).
[150] *Ratanlal alias Ram Ratan* v. *State of Rajasthan* 2004 CriLJ 734.

Introduction xliii

initiated and pending for offences committed under the Act of 1986 provided the offender has not completed 18 years of age as on 1 April 2001.[151]

11) The reckoning date for determination of age of juvenile offender is the date of offence and not the date when he is produced before the court/competent authority.[152, 153, 154]

12) Considering the difficulty of transportation of juveniles from far-off places for trial and considering the fact that only 5 Juvenile Justice Boards were constituted to deal with the entire state of Karnataka, the high court directed the state government to consider the necessity of establishing one Board for each district.[155]

13) The Board has exclusive power to deal with trial of juveniles in conflict with law. To that extent, jurisdiction of any court including that of session's court or fast track court is barred.

14) A juvenile was not presented before the court on various dates. The copy of order of the court declaring the petitioner to be juvenile and directing to shift him to observation board was misplaced by the jail authorities. So, the juvenile had to remain in an adult jail for 25 months. The juvenile was granted compensation of rupees one lakh.[156] In the same case, the Bombay High Court had directed the sessions court and magistrates courts to get compliance report of their orders in 6 weeks in all cases where bail is granted to avoid such incidents.

15) The sessions courts cannot refuse to make enquiry for purpose of determination of the age of alleged juvenile offender on the sole ground that a Board is constituted.[157] If the accused had admittedly opened an account in a bank, his contention that he was a minor at the time of the commission of the offence cannot be accepted because he could not have an open account, had it been so.[158]

16) While dealing with the question of determination of age of the accused, for the purpose of finding out whether he is a juvenile or not, hyper-technical approach should not be adopted while appertaining the

---

[151] *Pratap Singh* v. *State of Jharkhand and Anr* 2005 CriLJ 3091; see also *Bijender Singh* v. *State of Haryana* 2005 CriLJ 2135.
[152] *Pratap Singh* v. *State Jharkhand and Anr* 2005 CriLJ 3091.
[153] *Nasir Ali* v. *State of Punjab* 2005 CriLJ (NOC) 180 (P&H) 2005 1 Rec CriR 576.
[154] *Arnit Das* v. *State of Bihar* 2000 CriLJ 291 is overruled.
[155] *State of Karnataka* v. *Harshad* 2005 CriLJ 2357.
[156] *Master Salim Ansari and Anr.* v. *Officer-in-Charge Borivali Police Station Mumbai and Ors* 2005 CriLJ 799.
[157] *Pankaj and Anr* v. *State of U.P. and Anr* 2005 CriLJ 3683.
[158] *Om Prakash alias Raja* v. *State of Uttaranchal* 2003 CriLJ 483.

evidence adduced on behalf of the accused in support of the plea that he was a juvenile in borderline cases.[159]
17) Proper care is expected from all the agencies, institutions and the government to ensure that necessary effort is made to take appropriate and prompt steps to provide necessary infrastructure and opportunity for reformation of juvenile and not to allow them to become hardened criminals.[160]

Rights of Minor Children living with Convicted Mothers

Children living with convicted mothers in prisons and institutions are a cause of concern. In a recent judgment, the supreme court[161] has brought to light the existing provisions in various state prisons to care for female pregnant convicts and female convicts with small children.

Directions by the Supreme Court

Based on the affidavits of various state governments, union territories, union of India and submissions made, the court has also issued the following guidelines:

1. A child shall not be treated as an undertrial/convict while in jail with his/her mother. *Such a child is entitled to food, shelter, medical care, clothing, education, and recreational facilities as a matter of right.*
2. *Pregnancy*
    a. Before sending a pregnant woman to jail, the concerned authorities must ensure that the jail in question has the *minimum basic facilities for child delivery as well as for providing pre- natal and post-natal care for both mother and child.*
    b. When a woman prisoner is found or suspected to be pregnant at the time of her admission or at any time thereafter, the lady medical officer shall report the fact to the superintendent. As soon as possible, arrangement shall be made to get such prisoner medically examined at the female wing of the district government hospital for ascertaining the state of her health, pregnancy, duration of pregnancy, probable date of delivery, and so on. After

---

[159] *Rajinder Chandra* v. *State of Chattisgarh and Anr* (2002) 2 SCC 287.
[160] *Rahul Sharma* v. *State of Maharashtra and Anr* 2005 AllMR (Cri) 1973.
[161] *R.D. Upadhyay* v. *State of A.P. and Ors.* (2001) I SCC 437.

ascertaining the necessary particulars, a report shall be sent to the Inspector General of Prisons, stating the date of admission, term of sentence, date of release, duration of pregnancy, possible date of delivery, and so on.

c. *Gynaecological examination of female prisoners shall be performed in the district government hospital.* Proper pre-natal and post-natal care shall be provided to the prisoner as per medical advice.

3. Childbirth in prison

   a. *As far as possible and provided she has a suitable option, arrangements for temporary release/parole (or suspended sentence in case of minor and casual offender) should be made to enable an expectant prisoner to have her delivery outside the prison.* Only exceptional cases constituting high security risk or cases of equivalent grave descriptions can be denied this facility.

   b. Births in prison, when they occur, shall be registered in the local birth registration office. But the fact that the child has been born in the prison shall not be recorded in the certificate of birth that is issued. Only the address of the locality shall be mentioned.

   c. As far as circumstances permit, all facilities for the naming rites of children born in prison shall be extended.

4. Female prisoners and their children

   a. Female prisoners shall be allowed to keep their children with them in jail till they attain the age of 6 years.

   b. No female prisoner shall be allowed to keep a child who has completed the age of 6 years. Upon reaching the age of 6 years, the child shall be handed over to a suitable surrogate as per the wishes of the female prisoner or shall be sent to a suitable institution run by the Social Welfare Department. As far as possible, the child shall not be transferred to an institution outside the town or city where the prison is located in order to minimize undue hardships to both mother and child due to physical distance.

   c. Such children shall be kept in protective custody until their mother is released or the child attains such age as to earn his/her own livelihood.

   d. Children kept under the protective custody in a home of the Department of Social Welfare shall be allowed to meet the mother at least once a week. The Director, Social Welfare Department, shall ensure that such children are brought to the prison for this purpose on the date fixed by the Superintendent of Prisons.

e. When a female prisoner dies and leaves behind a child, the Superintendent shall inform the District Magistrate concerned and he shall arrange for the proper care of the child. Should the concerned relative(s) be unwilling to support the child, the District Magistrate shall either place the child in an approved institution/home run by the State Social Welfare Department, or hand the child over to a responsible person for care and maintenance.

5. *Food, clothing, medical care, and shelter*

   a. Children in jail shall be provided with adequate clothing suiting the local climatic requirement for which the state/urban territory government shall lay down the scales.
   b. State/urban territory Governments shall lay down dietary scales for children keeping in view the calorific requirements of growing children as per the medical norms.
   c. A permanent arrangement needs to be evolved in all jails, to provide separate food with ingredients to take care of the nutritional needs of children who reside in them on a regular basis.
   d. Separate utensils of suitable size and material should also be provided to each mother prisoner to use while feeding her child.
   e. *Clean drinking water must be provided to the children.* This water must be periodically checked.
   f. Children shall be regularly examined by the lady medical officer to monitor their physical growth and shall also receive timely vaccination. Vaccination charts regarding each child shall be kept in the records. Extra clothing, diet, and so on may also be provided on the recommendation of the medical officer.
   g. In the event of a woman prisoner falling ill, alternative arrangements for looking after any children falling under her care must be made by the jail staff.
   h. Sleeping facilities that are provided to the mother and the child should be adequate, clean, and hygienic.
   i. Children of prisoners shall have the right of visitation.
   j. The prison superintendent shall be empowered in special cases and where circumstances warrant, to admit children of women prisoners to prison without court orders provided such children are below 6 years of age.

Introduction xlvii

6. *Education and recreation for children of female prisoners*
   a. The children of female prisoners living in jails shall be given proper education and recreational opportunities and while their mothers are at work in jail, the children shall be kept in creches under the charge of a matron/female warder. This facility will also be extended to children of warders and other female prison staff.
   b. There shall be a crèche and a nursery attached to the prison for women where the children of women prisoners will be looked after. Children below 3 years of age shall be allowed in the creches and those between 3 and 6 years shall be looked after in the nursery. The prison authorities shall preferably run the said creches and nursery outside the prison premises.
7. In many states, small children are living in sub-jails that are not at all equipped to keep small children. Women prisoners with children should not be kept in such sub-jails, unless proper facilities can be ensured which would make for a conducive environment there, for proper biological, psychological, and social growth.
8. The stay of children in crowded barracks amidst women convicts, undertrials, offenders relating to all types of crimes including violent crimes, is certainly harmful for the development of their personality. Therefore, children deserve to be separated from such environments on a priority basis.
9. *Diet*

   Exclusive breastfeeding on the demand of the baby, day and night is recommended.[162] If, for some reason, the mother cannot feed the baby, undiluted fresh milk can be given.

   The court recommends the following portions for children from the ages of 6–12 months, 1–3 years and 4–6 years, respectively: Cereals and Millets—45, 60–120 and 150–210 grams respectively; Pulses—15, 30, and 45 grams respectively; Milk—500 ml (unless breastfed, in which case 200 ml); Roots and Tubers—50, 50, and 100 grams respectively; Green Leafy Vegetables—25, 50, and 50 grams respectively; Other Vegetables—25, 50, and 50 grams respectively; Fruits—100 grams; Sugar—25, 25, and 30 grams respectively; and Fats/Oils (Visible)—10, 20, and 25 grams respectively. One portion of pulse may

---

[162] Dietary scale for institutionalized infants/children prepared by Dr. A.M. Dwarkadas Motiwala, MD (Paediatrics) and Fellowship in Neonatology (USA) has been submitted by Mr. Sanjay Parikh.

be exchanged with one portion (50 grams) of egg/meat/chicken/fish. It is essential that the above food groups be provided in the portions mentioned in order to ensure that both macronutrients and micronutrients are available to the child in adequate quantities.
10. Jail Manual and/or other relevant rules, regulations, instructions, etc. shall be suitably amended within three months so as to comply with the above directions. If in some jails, better facilities are being provided, the same shall continue.
11. Schemes and laws relating to *welfare and development of such children shall be implemented in letter and spirit.* State legislatures may consider passing of necessary legislations, wherever necessary, having regard to what is noticed in this judgment.
12. The State Legal Services Authorities shall take necessary measures to periodically inspect jails to monitor that the *directions regarding children and mother are complied with in letter and spirit.*
13. *The Courts dealing with cases of women prisoners whose children are in prison with their mothers are directed to give priority to such cases and decide their cases expeditiously.*
14. Compliance report stating steps taken by the union of india, state governments, union territories and state legal services authorities shall be filed in four months whereafter matter shall be listed for directions.

Classroom Violence against School Children

- *8-year-old beaten up by teacher for making noise in class*
- *Standard X student beaten up by a rulerpaddle*
- *I was not allowed to go to bathroom*
- *I was locked in a closet or small room*
- *I was slapped*
- *Classroom horror haunts students*
- *Students exposed to sexual harassment*
- *Student ends life*

The above are some of the newspaper headlines of growing classroom violence of sexual/physical/mental abuse of minors in schools, which just represents the tip of the problem as many cases are hardly reported.

Throughout the country there have been newspaper reports about children being brutally and violently beaten up in schools by teachers. This affects the physical and mental health of children. It affects the psyche of the children for their entire life and makes them prone to psychological abnormalities.

Introduction xlix

Children have limited protection from violence and abuse under the Penal Code (1860, with amendments) and the Juvenile Justice (Care and Protection of Children) Act (2000). Corporal punishment is unlawful as a sentence for crime under the Juvenile Justice (Care and Protection of Children) Act, 2000, which prohibits torture and other cruel, inhuman or degrading treatment or punishment and does not list corporal punishment among permitted sanctions.[163]

There is no national prohibition in law of corporal punishment in schools. The government has issued instruction to states to stop its use in schools and the National Policy on Education (1986, modified 1992) states in Section 5.6 that 'corporal punishment will be firmly excluded from the educational systems'. A draft Free and Compulsory Education for Children Bill which proposes prohibiting corporal punishment in schools, applicable to the whole of India, is under discussion (April 2005).

Some states have prohibited corporal punishment in schools. In 2003, the Andhra Pradesh government imposed a ban on corporal punishment in all educational institutions by amending Rule 122 of the Education Rules (1966), violations of which should be dealt with under the Penal Code. Corporal punishment was prohibited in Tamil Nadu in June 2003 through an amendment of Rule 51 of the Tamil Nadu Education Rules prohibiting the infliction of mental and physical pain during 'corrective' measures. In February 2004, the Calcutta High Court ruled that caning in state schools in West Bengal was unlawful, and it was prohibited in Chandigarh in the 1990s. In December 2000, the Delhi High Court ruled that provisions for corporal punishment in the Delhi School Education Act (1973) were inhumane and detrimental to the dignity of children.

Recommendations of the Committee on the Rights of the Child[164]

'In respect of Article 37 (a) of the Convention, the Committee is concerned by numerous reports of routine ill-treatment, corporal punishment, torture, and sexual abuse of children in detention facilities, and alleged instances of killings of children living and/or working on the streets by law enforcement officials.

'Amendment to the Juvenile Justice Act is recommended to provide for complaints and prosecution mechanisms for cases of custodial abuse of children. In addition, the Committee recommends the amendment of Section 197 of the Code of Criminal Procedure, which requires government

---

[163] Juvenile Justice (Care and Protection of Children) Act, Section 21.
[164] 26 February 2004, CRC/C/15/Add.228, Concluding observations on second report, paras 44 and 45.

1 Introduction

approval for prosecution of law enforcement officials when complaints of custodial abuse or illegal detention are alleged; and Section 43 of the Police Act, so that the police cannot claim immunity for actions while executing a warrant in cases of illegal detention custodial abuse.

'In the light of Articles 19 and 39 of the Convention, the Committee is concerned at the widespread ill-treatment of children in India, not only in schools and care institutions, but also within the family.

'The Committee recommends that the State party take legislative measures to prohibit all forms of physical and mental violence, including corporal punishment and sexual abuse of children in the family, schools, and care institutions. The Committee recommends that these measures be accompanied by public education campaigns about the negative consequences of ill-treatment of children. The Committee recommends that the State party promote positive, non-violent forms of discipline as an alternative to corporal punishment, especially in the home and schools. Programmes for the rehabilitation and reintegration of abused children need to be strengthened, and adequate procedures and mechanisms established to receive complaints, monitor, investigate, and prosecute instances of ill-treatment. In the light of alarming and brutal proportion of this problem, these recommendations need to be adopted immediately.'

Child Sexual Abuse and Exploitation and Law Reform

The laws dealing with sexual offences do not specifically address child sexual abuse. It is disconcerting but true; the India Penal Code 1860 does not recognize child abuse. Only rape and sodomy can lead to criminal conviction. Anything less than rape as defined by the law, amounts to 'outraging the modesty'. The word 'rape' is too specific; this does not even include abuse on 'boys'.

The Immoral Trafficking (Prevention) Act (ITPA), has to be broadened to cover the trafficking of children to beaches, hotels, and guesthouses, and their subsequent sexual abuse. First of all, it does not define trafficking. It distinguishes between child and a minor.

In the leading case of *Sakshi* v. *Union of India*,[165] the court gave the following directions in holding a trial of child sex abuse or rape:

(i) a screen or some such arrangement may be made where the victim or witnesses (who may be equally vulnerable like the victim) do not see the body or face of the accused;

[165] AIR 2004 SC3566.

(ii) the questions put in cross-examination on behalf of the accused, in so far as they relate directly to the incident should be given in writing to the Presiding Officer of the court who may put them to the victim or witnesses in a language which is clear and is not embarrassing;
(iii) the victim of child abuse or rape, while giving testimony in court, should be allowed sufficient breaks as and when required.

Goa Children's Act, 2003

This is a legislation against child sexual abuse, especially those related to sex tourism. The legislation has specifically made all cases of abuse of such nature, a non-bailable offence under Section 2 (a) of the Criminal Procedure Code, 1973. The fines and jail terms are also severe; one lakh rupees with imprisonment between 1 to 3 years for sexual assault and incest, and two lakh rupees with 7 to 10 years jail term in case of a grave sexual assault. The setting-up of a Children's Court to try all offences against children is a bold step prescribed by this law. A child-friendly court will help to minimize the double trauma that abused children are subject to in courts, which even adults find awesome and terrifying.

According to the Goa Children's Act 2003, there lies a lot of onus on establishments like hotels, airports, and rentals to prevent child trafficking and child sexual abuse in the form of sale and procurement of children. Any form of soliciting or publicizing or making children available to any adult or even other children by hotels, for purposes of commercial exploitation, is prohibited. This includes hosting websites, taking suggestive or obscene photographs, providing materials, soliciting customers, guiding tourists and other clients, appointing touts, using agents, or any other form which may lead to abuse of a child.[166] Airport authorities, border police, railway police, and traffic police are required to report any suspected case of trafficking of children or an adult travelling with a child under suspicious circumstances.[167] Sale of children is also prohibited under this Act.[168] Sale of children would include:

(a) when there is trading, that is, selling children;
(b) when a pregnant mother executes an affidavit of consent for adoption for a consideration;
(c) when a person, agency, establishment or child-caring institution

---
[166] Goa Children's Act, 2003, Section 8 (12).
[167] Ibid., Section 8 (15).
[168] Ibid., Section 16.

recruits women or couples to bear children for the purposes of child trafficking;

(d) when a doctor, hospital, or clinic official or employee, nurse, midwife, local civil registrar, or any other person creates birth records for the purpose of child trafficking; or

(e) when a person engages in the act of finding children among low-income families, hospitals, clinics, nurseries, day-care centres, or other child-caring institutions, who can be offered for the purposes of child trafficking.

The Act also envisages the government's role in making sure that all child prostitutes are removed from their existing place of exploitation, and in ensuring that they are rehabilitated and integrated into society.[169] The Act further provides that, the state shall provide for the setting-up of one or more Victim Assistance Units, which shall facilitate the child to deal with the trauma of abuse and assist the child in processes involved with appearing as a witness before any court or authority handling a case of abuse of a child.[170] The state is also expected to carry out child sensitization programmes for police officers at all levels which shall include an orientation on child rights laws. Child rights laws and methods of handling child abuse related cases shall also be specifically included in the Police Training School curriculum.[171] The State shall undertake child sensitization training for those involved in healing and rehabilitation and other assistance programmers for children who are victims and promote programmes of information support and training for such children.[172]

According to a recent state legislation,[173] whosoever commits any sexual assault[174] against a child,[175] can be punished with imprisonment for a term that may extend to 3 years and shall also be liable to fine of one lakh rupees,

---

[169] Goa Children's Act, 2003, Section 9 (2).

[170] Ibid., Section 19.

[171] Ibid., Section 20.

[172] Ibid., Section 21.

[173] Ibid.

[174] 'Sexual Assault' covers sexual touching with the use of any body part or object, voyeurism, exhibitionism, showing pornographic pictures or films to minors, making children watch others engaged in sexual activity, issuing of threats to sexually abuse a minor, verbally abusing a minor using vulgar and obscene language. Ibid., Section 2 (y) (ii).

[175] 'Child' means any person who has not completed eighteen years of age unless any other law in force specifies otherwise or unless otherwise indicated in specific provisions in this Act. Ibid., Section 2 (d).

and whoever commits any grave sexual assault[176] shall be punished with imprisonment for a term that shall not be less than 7 years but which may extend to 10 years, and shall also be liable to a fine of two lakh rupees. In such cases, testimony of the child victim shall be treated on par with the testimony of a child rape victim.[177] Any person who exploits a child for commercial sexual exploitation shall be liable to pay a penalty which may extend to one lakh rupees and simple imprisonment of 1 year.[178] Any person who abets the performance of any ceremony or any act for dedicating[179] a minor girl child as a *devadasi* can be, on conviction, punished with imprisonment for a term which may extend to 3 years and with fine which may extend to two thousand rupees.[180] Any person who employs, aids, or abets in the trafficking, including by employment of such trafficked children shall be penalized with a fine of fifty thousand rupees and/or imprisonment of either description of not less than 3 months.[181]

Child Pornography

Child Pornography is the fastest growing crime against children. In India, there are provisions in Section 61 of the Information Technology Act, 2000, which deals with publishing of information which is obscene in electronic form. Section 61 states that whoever publishes or transmits or causes to be published in electronic form, any material which is lascivious, or appeals to the prurient interest, or if its effect is such as to tend to deprave and corrupt persons who are likely, having regard to all relevant circumstances, to read, see, or hear the matter contained or embodied in it, shall be punished on first conviction with imprisonment of either description for a term which may extend to 5 years and with fine which may extend to one lakh rupees, and in the event of a second or subsequent conviction with imprisonment of either description for a term which may extend to 10 years and also with fine which

---

[176] 'Grave Sexual Assault' which covers different types of intercourse: vaginal, oral, anal, use of objects, forcing minors to have sex with each other, deliberately causing injury to the sexual organs, making children pose for pornographic photos or films. Goa Children's Act, 2003, Section 2 (y) (i).

[177] Indian Penal Code, 1860 Section 375.

[178] Goa Children's Act, 2003, Section 9 (4).

[179] 'Dedication' means the performance of any act or ceremony by whatever name called, by which a girl child is dedicated to the service of any deity, idol, object of worship, temple, other religious institutions or places of worship. Ibid., Section 2 (n).

[180] Ibid., Section 9 (7).

[181] Ibid., Section 7 (9).

may extend to two lakh rupees.[182] This provision is inadequate and a more stringent law is required for this grave offence.

Pedophilia—Landmark Judgment

Child sex tourism is a frighteningly well-organized operation and police enforcement in India has been notoriously lax. A decade or so ago, the Interpol has listed Goa as an organized hub of such activities and other states too have been known to attract such offenders.

On 18 March 2006, the Additional Sessions Judge P.S. Paranjpe delivered a verdict convicting two men to a sentence of 6 years of rigorous imprisonment for offences related to unnatural sex and abuse of children. The two men have been fined twenty thousand pounds each, of which five lakh rupees will go towards the rehabilitation of the two boys who were residents of Anchorage and whose testimony in court was crucial to the case. The court also held William Micheal D'Souza (manager of the Shelter Home) guilty for aiding and abetting the crime and assaulting the children. He has been sentenced to 3 years of imprisonment.

This judgment in the Anchorage shelter case where two foreigners, Duncan Grant and Allen Walters, were sentenced for pedophilia crimes is a strong indictment of this heinous crime, and also an unambiguous signal that India will not become another spot on the world sex tourism map. In fact, the judge in the case said as much when he sentenced the duo.

This was run on money sent in by well-meaning foreign donors. Those exploited often had no one to turn to since they were either orphans or beggars from the harsh streets of Mumbai. Not only was pedophilia rampant at the shelter — it was also brazen. The place is a few minutes walk from the police station. It is only the courage of two boys, who stood by their testimony in spite of threats and bribe offers, which put the duo behind bars.

The judgment is an indication that India is at last waking up to the horrors of pedophilia which is fast spreading its tentacles in some important tourist spots in the region.

Judge Paranjpe said that he intended the verdict to send a clear message to pedophiles all over the world that India is not a destination for them. He hoped that the sentence would go a long way in wiping India off the map of international sex tourism.[183]

---

[182] Information Technology Act, 2000 s 61.
[183] www.hindu.com/2006/03/19/stories/2006031904371000.htm.

Offences against the Child Bill, 2006[184]

An important step towards consolidating the various laws relating to children is the 'Offences against the Child Bill 2006', that has been drafted and is under discussion.

Some of the salient features of the Bill under consideration are:[185]

- Under the draft Bill some of the important definitions include:
- '*Child*': A child shall mean any person who has not completed the eighteenth year of age unless a separate age has been provided in this Bill.[186]
- '*Children's Courts*' shall mean a court as constituted under the Commissions for Protection of Child Rights Act, 2005.[187]
- '*Child Neglect*' shall mean the omission on the part of the caregiver of a child to provide for the developmental needs of a child in all spheres, and shall include health, education, mental well-being, emotional development, nutrition, shelter, and safe living conditions, in the context of resources reasonably available to such caretakers and causes or is likely to cause harm or present danger to the child's life, health, development, dignity or esteem.[188]
- '*Offence*' shall denote a thing made punishable by this Bill or any other law for the time being in force.[189]

Guiding principles for implementation laid down in the draft Bill:

Every stakeholder imposed with a duty of implementation of this Bill shall follow such procedures and practices as may be prescribed, provided that the procedures and practices so prescribed shall be *child-friendly* and shall be deemed to include the following:

---

[184] The preamble to the Bill states that all offences against children are being consolidated in a separate Code bearing in mind international and regional standards, directives provided by the Supreme Court of India, other good practices relating to children, and learning from the experiences of other countries.

[185] Some of the comments in the footnotes are of Kabir Duggal, UNICEF, Maharashtra.

[186] There are many laws in India that have different ages for defining a child.

[187] Sections 25 and 26.

[188] This definition is modelled on the WHO definition of Neglect.

[189] Similar to Section 40 of the IPC and Section 2 (p) of the Juvenile Justice (Care and Protection of Children), Act 2000; since this term is used often, it was felt necessary to define the same.

(1) *Principle of Best Interest of a Child*[190]
(2) *Principle of 'Protection' of a Child*[191]
(3) *Principle of Equality and Non Discrimination—'Leave no Child behind'*[192] *Principle of Individuality and Participation*[193]
(4) *Principle of Privacy and Confidentiality*[194]
(5) *Principle of Non-Stigmatizing Semantics, Decisions, and Actions*
(6) *Principle of Avoidance of Harm*[195]
(7) *Principle of Non Criminalization of a Child*[196]

Chapter III of the bill deals with sexual offences against a child. The offences included are:

1. Sexual Assault of a Child[197]

The definition of sexual assault is widened to include all forms of sexual assault on children. A person is said to commit 'Sexual Assault of a Child' when that person, with or without the consent of the child:

(1) penetrates the vagina (which shall include the *labia majora*), the anus, or the urethra of any child with:
   a. any part of the body of that person or of any other person; or
   b. an object manipulated by another person.
(2) manipulates any part of the body of a child so as to cause penetration

---

[190] The Convention on the Rights of a Child, 1989, Article 3.
[191] Ibid., Article 19.
[192] Ibid., Article 2.
[193] Ibid., Article 12.
[194] Ibid., Article 16.
[195] Ibid., Article 6.
[196] This principle has been introduced considering the fact that children from brothels or from labour situations are often treated as criminals, when they are actually the victims of the process.
[197] For any such section to be effective, an amendment would be needed to Sections 375, 376 and 377 of the IPC. No matter what the provision/age be, an amendment would be required to the IPC, considering the fact we have decided to make the age consistent with international age and remove all inconsistencies, making the age of consent 18 years (as opposed to the existing 16 years).

Counter view: This point needs some consideration because some groups are of the opinion that with advancing puberty and tendency to engage in sexual activity earlier, probably the age of consent should be reduced, some groups even suggest the age to be 12 years.

of the vagina (which shall include the *labia majora*), the anus, or the urethra of the person by any part of the child's body;
(3) commits the act of fellatio, on or by a child;
(4) commits the act of cunnilingus, on or by a child;
(5) commits the act of analingus, on or by a child.[198]

Explanation: Penetration to even the *slightest* extent is sufficient to constitute penetration for the purpose of this Section.[199] It is not necessary that the hymen is ruptured or semen is emitted to constitute sexual assault.[200]

The punishment for sexual assault of a child[201] is rigorous imprisonment for a term which shall not be less than 10 years but can extend to life, and shall also be liable to a fine p*rovided that*, the court may, for adequate and special reasons, record in writing and only in the rarest of rare circumstances, impose a sentence of less than 10 years. In all cases, where the penalty shall be less than 10 years, no such sentence shall be executed, unless it is confirmed by the High Court.[202]

---

[198] Sub-sections (3) to (5) involve penetration by the tongue/use of mouth. Considering the fact that penetration by the penis may not be possible in children, these forms are more common. It is necessary that we criminalize them as 'sexual assault' as well. Further, see the 172nd Law Commission Report, which states that, 'In a vast majority of child sexual abuse cases the penetration is *other than penile-vaginal*. Such penetration causes lasting psychic damage to the child. In such a situation, a restrictive meaning attached to penetration is likely to prove inadequate.' (*Emphasis supplied*)

See also, The 156th Report of the Law Commission, which has recommended that penile/oral penetration and penile/anal penetration be covered by Section 377 IPC, and that finger penetration and object penetration into vagina or anus can be adequately covered under Section 354 with a more severe punishment. This recommendation requires reconsideration. Such a restrictive view fails to take into consideration several forms of child abuse and the further fact that very often the sexual abuse of children is by persons known to them.' *Available at*: Law Commission of India, One Hundred and Seventy Second Report on: 'Review of Rape Laws March, 2000', D.O. No. 6 (3) (36)/2000_LC (LS, *at*: http://www.lawcommissionofindia.nic.in/ rapelaws.htm (March 27, 2006).

[199] *See*: *Ranjit Hazarika* v. *State of Assam* 1998 (8) SCC 635.

[200] We need to articulate this because the police machinery usually looks at the emission of semen or rupturing of hymen as signs for rape.

[201] The sexual offences against children are broadly being classified into 3 categories, this classification is done keeping in mind the gravity of the offence and accordingly providing different penalties. In simple terms, these offences would include: (a) sexual offences involving 'penetration' (termed as 'sexual assault'); (b) sexual offences involving contact but without penetration; (c) sexual offences without contact.

[202] An alternative on sexual experiment can be included as an exception, if required:

lviii *Introduction*

2. Aggravated Forms of Sexual Assault of a Child

A. Aggravated sexual assault occurs, if sexual assault of a child is committed under any of the following circumstances,

(1) the child is killed as the result of the assault;
(2) physically incapacitates the child or causes the child to become insane or mentally unfit to perform regular tasks;
(3) commits sexual assault with more than one person ('*gang sexual assault*');
(4) is related by blood or adoption, legitimately or illegitimately or as per the personal laws, is within the prohibited degrees of consanguinity or affinity (*incest*);[203]
(5) makes the child pregnant as a consequence of the sexual assault;
(6) inflicts the child with HIV/AIDS or any other life threatening disease or infection;
(7) commits sexual assault on a person less than 12 years of age;

B is committed by:

(1) a public servant as defined under Section 21 of the Indian Penal Code, 1860;
(2) a police officer, while on duty, taking advantage of one's official position;
(3) a medical officer, while on duty, taking advantage of one's official position;
(4) the staff or the management of any of the children's institutions, while on duty, taking advantage of one's official position;
(5) the school management, teachers, principal or any other staff of the educational institution while on duty, taking advantage of one's official position.

The accused who has committed aggravated sexual assault shall be liable to rigorous imprisonment for a term which shall not be

---

(2) *Provided that*, where both persons are below 18 years of age and above 16 years of age and it appears *prima facie* that they have entered into a consensual act involving penetration stated above, the matter will be decided by the Juvenile Justice Board and will be decided as per Section 15 of the Juvenile Justice (Care and Protection) of Children Act, 2000.

In these cases of sexual experimentation among children, the offence remains the same but considering the age of the children, the penalty has been reduced.

[203] This would effectively cover the situation of 'incest'.

Introduction lix

less than 14 years[204] but can extend to death[205] and shall also be liable to fine.[206]

If the sexual assault takes place in any children's institution (whether run by the state or by NGOs), in addition to the penalty referred to above, the state or the NGO, as the case may be, will be liable to pay the child a fine to be provided to the child, on the completion of his/her eighteenth year.[207]

Other examples of aggravated sexual assault are unlawful sexual contact[208] and non contact based sexual offences with a child.[209]

---

[204] *State of A.P.* v. *Polamala Raju alias Rajarao*, 2000 (7) SCC 75, '9, imposition of grossly inadequate sentence and particularly against the mandate of the legislature not only is an injustice to the victim of the crime in particular and the society (as a whole) in general, but also at times encourages a criminal.' It goes further to say, '12 ... protection of society and deterring the criminal is avowed object of law and that is required to be achieved by imposing an appropriate sentence...commensurate to the gravity of the offence.'

[205] *See. Laxman Naik* v. *State of Orissa*, 1994 (3) SCC 381, '28 .... a calculated, cold-blooded and brutal murder of a girl of a very tender age after committing rape on her would undoubtedly fall in the category of rarest of rare cases attracting no punishment other than the capital punishment.'

[206] This Section also provides that, (1) the court may, for adequate and special reasons, record in writing and only in the rarest of rare circumstances, impose a sentence of penalty less than 14 years. In all cases, where the penalty shall be less than 14 years, no such sentence shall be executed, unless it is confirmed by the High Court.

[207] This provision seeks to create state accountability for abuses in institutions. Considering the rise in offences of this nature, it is imperative to penalize the same.

[208] If there is an intention to achieve sexual gratification and a person commits any of the following with a child:
(1) fondling the genitalia or other parts of the child;
(2) making the child fondle the genitalia or other parts of the body of any person;
(3) kissing the child on the lips;
(4) any other act, which involves a physical contact but no penetration, as required under Section(9).

(such person) shall be liable to simple imprisonment for a term which shall not be less than 3 years but can extend to 14 years and shall also be liable to a fine.

[209] Whoever, with an intention to achieve sexual gratification, commits any of the following with a child:
(a) exposing the genitalia to the child (*voyeurism*) or making the child do so (*exhibitionism*);
(b) masturbating in the presence of the child or making the child do so;
(c) showing pornography to the child, in any form or media;
(d) exposing the child to sexual contact between any two persons;
(e) using sexually explicit and inappropriate language, according to the age of the child;

Introduction

The Bill also deals with offences relating to trafficking.[210] For the purposes of this Bill, the offence of trafficking shall mean, 'the recruitment, transportation, transfer, harbouring, or receipt of persons, by means of threat or use of force or other forms of coercion, of abduction, of fraud, of deception, of the abuse of power, or of a position of vulnerability, or the giving or receiving of payments or benefits to achieve the consent of a person having the control over another person, for the purposes of exploitation' and shall include:

(1) Selling a child for the purposes of prostitution as defined under Section 12;
(2) Buying a child for purposes of prostitution;
(3) Procuring, inducing or taking a child for the sake of prostitution; and
(4) Dedicating a child.

The proposed Bill deals with the following offences relating to economic exploitation of children and child labour.

- The use of a child under 14 for any form of employment, process or labour
- Employment of child under 14 as domestic help
- Employment of a child for begging
- Exploitation of a child employee

Chapter VII deals with offences relating to a child's body.
The proposed offences under this chapter are:

- Cruelty to a child;
- Corporal Punishment on a child;
- Punishment for corporal punishment on a child;
- Ragging of a child in an institution;

(f) undertaking any other acts intended to outrage the modesty of a child; shall be liable for simple imprisonment which shall extend to 2 years and shall also be liable to fine. (Section 9 of the Offences Against the Child Bill, 2006)

Explanation: The question involving '*intention to achieve sexual gratification*' and '*acts intended to outrage the modesty of a child*' is a question of fact.

[210] *See*. Articles 34 and 35 of the Convention on the Rights of a Child. Further, India has now ratified Optional Protocol II to the Convention on the Rights of the Child: 'Sale of children, child prostitution and child pornography.' Further, the National Plan of Action for Children 2005 states in Clause 14.1.1 'Goal: To stop sale of children and all forms of child trafficking, including for sexual purposes, marriage, labour, adoption, sports, and entertainment, and illegal activities like organ trade, begging and drug peddling.'

- Acts intended to intimidate a child;
- Giving a child intoxicating liquour, narcotic drug or psychotropic substance;
- Using a child for vending, peddling, carrying, supplying or smuggling any intoxicating liquor, narcotic drug or psychotropic substance;
- Offences relating to the sale of the child's organs;
- Offences relating to kidnapping and abduction;
- Offences relating to wrongful restraint and wrongful confinement;
- Pre-determination of sex;
- Offence of foeticide and infanticide;
- Using a child or children for pornographic purposes and possession of any pornographic material involving a child or children.

In Chapter XII there are provisions for punishment for 'committing, attempting to, abetting the commission of offences'. Giving false complaints or false information is also punishable. An important provision in the proposed Bill is that offences committed on disabled children will be subjected to double the punishment. The other significant features of the proposed Bill are:

- 'Child Trauma and Counselling Centre' for medical care and attention;
- Formation of the Emergency Response Team;
- All court hearings and proceedings[211] in which a child is involved shall be completed within 4 months;[212]
- Procedural safeguards for the Child;
- While conducting the court hearing, the following shall be adopted:
  (1) All judicial proceedings must be conducted in an 'in camera' trial;[213, 214]
  (2) The identity of the victim child must be protected at all times during the judicial proceedings;[215]
  (3) The presiding judge shall be a female in cases of a single bench or in cases of a larger bench, at least one of the presiding judges shall be a female;[216]

---

[211] *State of Punjab* v. *Gurmit Singh* 1996 SCC (CR) 316, p. 384, 'The Courts, therefore, shoulder a great responsibility while trying an accused on charges of rape. They must deal with utmost sensitivity'.

[212] Section 54, Offences against the Child Bill 2006.

[213] These provisions should extend to all cases of children (and not merely to sexual offences).

[214] *State of Punjab* v. *Gurmit Singh*, 1996 SCC (CR) 316.

[215] *See*: Beijing Rule 8 (1) and (2).

[216] *State of Punjab* v. *Gurmit Singh*, 1996 SCC (CR) 316.

lxii *Introduction*

(4) Such cases shall be taken up as a priority and hearings shall be held on a day-to-day basis, as far as possible. The entire proceeding shall be concluded within 4 months;

(5) The presiding judges shall ensure that no more than three adjournments shall be allowed in the entire proceedings to avoid unnecessary delay. Adjournments shall be allowed only in the most unavoidable situations.

Child Labour

A comprehensive law to address and combat the gigantic problem of child labour is required. One important case relates to the applicability of the Workmen's Compensation Act to child labourers. It was held that the scheme of the Workmen's Compensation Act nowhere states that there is a prohibition against employing a child. In view of Section 3 and in the absence of any specific prohibition under the Workmen's Compensation Act, it can be very well held that a child can be employed to carry out the work provided this work does not come under the Parts A and B of the Schedule of the Child Labour (Prohibition and Regulation) Act, 1986, and the child is entitled to all compensations.[217] Child Labour (Prohibition and Regulation) Act, 1986, only prohibits employment of child labour in certain industries set out in Part A and Part B of the Schedule. But in respect of industries other than Parts A and B, the Act permits a child to be employed. Any employer who violates the provisions of the Act is liable to be punished. The right to get compensation is traceable to the provisions of the Workmen's Compensation Act and not the Child Labour (Prohibition) Act, and the same is not controlled by the Child Labour (Prohibition and Regulation) Act, 1986.[218]

The directions given by the Supreme Court for rehabilitation of children employed as labourers[219] have still to be implemented.

Children and Domestic Violence

The Protection of Women from Domestic Violence Act, 2005 (43 of 2005) covers even adopted and foster child since in this Act 'child' means any person below the age of 18 years and includes any adopted, step, or foster child.

[217] *The Oriental Insurance Company Limited, Bangalore* v. *Smt. Rathnamma and Anr* 2001 ACJ 231I.
[218] Ibid.
[219] *M.C. Mehta* v. *State of Tamil Nadu and Ors* AIR 1997 SC 699.

Domestic violence [220] has been defined as any act that:

- Harms, injures, or endangers the health, safety, life, limb or well-being, whether mental or physical, of the aggrieved person or tends to do so, and includes causing physical abuse, sexual abuse, verbal and emotional abuse, and economic abuse.[221]
- Harasses, harms, injures, or endangers the aggrieved person with a view to coerce her or any other person related to her to meet any unlawful demand for any dowry or other property or valuable security.[222]
- Has the effect of threatening the aggrieved person or any person related to her by any conduct.[223]
- Otherwise injures or causes harm, whether physical or mental, to the aggrieved person.[224]

An order of protection of children from domestic violence can be obtained under this Act.[225] Under this Act, the magistrate may, on being *prima facie* satisfied that domestic violence has taken place, or is likely to take place, pass a protection order in favour of the aggrieved person[226] and prohibit the respondent from entering, if the person aggrieved is a child, his school or any other place frequented by the aggrieved person.[227] Thus, protection to children may be granted even in anticipation of domestic violence being caused. The magistrate may further impose any additional conditions or pass any other decision which he may deem reasonably necessary to protect or to provide for the safety of the aggrieved person or any child of such aggrieved person.[228]

Further the Act provides that, notwithstanding anything contained in any other law for the time being in force, the magistrate may, at any stage of hearing of the application for protection order or for any other relief under this Act grant temporary custody of any child or children to the aggrieved

---

[220] Protection of Women from Domestic Violence Act (43 of 2005) Section 2 (g).
[221] Ibid., Section 3 (a).
[222] Ibid., Section 3 (b).
[223] Ibid., Section 3 (c).
[224] Ibid., Section 3 (d).
[225] Ibid., assented on 13 September 2005.
[226] 'aggrieved person' means any woman who is, or has been, in a domestic relationship with the respondent and who alleges to have been, subjected to any act of domestic violence by the respondent. Protection of Women from Domestic Violence Act (43 of 2005) Section 2 (a).
[227] Ibid., Section 2 (b).
[228] Ibid., Section 2 (b).

person or the person making an application on their behalf and specify, if necessary, the arrangement for visit of such child or children by the respondent, provided that if the magistrate is of the opinion that any visit of the respondent may be harmful to the interest of the child or children, the magistrate shall refuse to allow such visit.[229] Thus, the person who is likely to cause harm to the child may be disallowed to meet the child if it is believed that such meeting may cause harm to the child.

The magistrate may further direct the respondent to pay monetary relief to meet the expenses incurred and losses suffered by the aggrieved person and any child of the aggrieved person as a result of domestic violence, and such relief may include the maintenance for the aggrieved person as well as her children,[230] if any, including an order under or in addition to an order of maintenance.[231]

Adoption of Children

At present, there is a huge gap in India between the number of children who need to be adopted and the number who are adopted every year. It is estimated that there are nearly 12.5 million orphaned children in the country and millions of others who are neglected, abused, and/or abandoned. There are thousands of non-Hindus who wish to adopt but barring those who agree take a child home under Guardianship and Wards Act, the majority of them end up dissuaded and decide not to do so since the Indian law does not permit them to adopt and they do not wish to take the child as mere wards.

Many of these millions of children, who are deprived of their right to life in any sense of the term, could get adopted into loving and caring families and find a home for themselves which would, in turn, open the doors of life to them.

There is an urgent need to enact a special enabling law for adoption which can be availed of by any person irrespective of his/her religion for adoption of child of any religion/sex. The issue of adoption is beyond political, religious, and patriarchal issues. This legislation would ensure justice to the child, and provide all the rights and privileges to the adopted child, as those available to a child born in legal wedlock.

The case for such a law arises because:

---

[229] Protection of Women from Domestic Violence Act (43 of 2005) Section 2 (b).
[230] Ibid., Section 2 (b).
[231] Under Section 125 of the Code of Criminal Procedure, 1973.

1. Under Article 32 of the Constitution of India, seeking the recognition and implementation of the right to adoption and right to family, of all children, as part of the fundamental right to equality and life, under Articles 14 and 21 of the Constitution of India, and also as per the numerous international instruments to which India is a signatory, which urge for recognition of right of every child to family, and to be adopted.
2. A special law which would be optional, while not impinging on the religious sentiments of any faith, would provide a legal option of adoption for all persons to take advantage of, irrespective of the religion of the adoptive parents or of the adopted child. Similar to the model of the Special Marriage Act, such a law would have no compulsive effect forcing anyone to act contrary to his religious tenets; it would be merely an enabling legislation for those who desire to adopt and should anyone feel that adopting would be contrary to his religion, s/he would be free not to adopt.
3. To ensure throughout the country the effective and uniform implementation of Section 41 of the Juvenile Justice (Care and Protection of Children) Act 2000, which is an existing enabling provision for adoption across, and irrespective of religions, towards the rehabilitation and social reintegration of children in need of care and protection. At present, the said provision is not being utilized for the purpose of adoption due to some lacunae in the Act as would be explained later hereunder.

Trial of Children under NDPS Act

The earlier position of the courts was that the said provision contained in Section 37 of the Narcotic Drugs and Psychotropic Substances Act would over-ride the earlier general provision of Section 18 (now Section 12) of the Juvenile Justice Act and consequently, a juvenile delinquent being accused of commission of an offence under the former Act cannot be released unless the pre-conditions contained in Section 37 of the former Act are complied with.[232]

However, under the new position, the provisions of Juvenile Justice Act override the provisions of NDPS Act, that irrespective of Section 36A of NDPS Act, a juvenile has to be dealt with under Juvenile Justice Act.[233] When the Juvenile Justice (Care and Protection) Act is a beneficial act meant

---
[232] *Antaryami Patra* v. *State of Orissa* 1993 CriLJ 1908.
[233] *Matadin* v. *State of M.P.* 1994 (3) CRIMES 510.

lxvi *Introduction*

to benefit the juvenile children, the provisions contained therein will have an over-riding effect over the provisions contained in the NDPS Act. If a juvenile is accused of an offence under the provisions of the NDPS Act, he is certainly entitled to the necessary benefits under the special enactment, namely Juvenile Justice Act.[234]

When that is the case, there is no reason for refusing to invoke the first proviso under Section 437 (1) of the Criminal Procedure Code 1973. The intention of the legislature in having incorporated the stringent provisions under Section 37 of the Narcotic Drugs and Psychotropic Substances Act, is obviously in the greater interest of the society, that a person accused of an offence under the Act shall not ordinarily be let off, so that he may not again perpetrate such offence on the society, but certainly it is not the intention of the legislature that under any circumstances that person cannot be let off.[235]

Conclusion

It is a matter of concern that the rehabilitation of child victims is still to be incorporated in various legislations. The initiative taken by the Government of India to enact The Commissions for Protection of Child Rights Act, 2005 is an important milestone in translating commitments into action. The Act received the assent of the President on 20 January 2006. The Act provides for the constitution of a National Commission and State Commissions for Children for the protection of child rights and children's courts for providing speedy trial of offences against children, or of violation of child rights.[236] This commission must work.

There have been regional attempts to protect victims and witnesses of trafficking. A Regional Victim Witness Protocol has been drafted to protect such victims.[237] SAARC Convention on Preventing and Combating Trafficking in Women and Children for Prostitution was signed on 5 January 2002 and ratified on 2 September 2003. SAARC Convention on Regional Arrangements for the Promotion of Child Welfare in South Asia was signed on 5 January 2002 and ratified on 2 September 2003. At the international level, Optional Protocol on the Sale of Children, Child Prostitution, and Child Pornography was ratified on 15 November 2004.

---

[234] *Gopu Ilaiah and Ors.* v. *The State of A.P. rep. by Public Prosecutor* Crl. P. Nos. 4247, 4340, 4341,4398, 4399, 4400 and 4446 of 2001, MANU/AP/1212/2001.
[235] Ibid.
[236] The preamble to the Act.
[237] At the initiative of Sariq.

We are moving towards the standards set by international laws. Now, what is important is that we monitor and enforce the laws. What is required now is that the spirit of the laws is inculcated among the lawmakers and civil society so that children get justice and these laws do not simply remain on paper.

Selected Abbreviations used in Foreign Cases

AC	Appeal Cases
ACL	Australian Current Law
AJIL	American Journal of International Law
ALJ	Australian Law Journal
ALL	Australian Law Librarian
All ER (D)	All England Reports (Digest)
All ER (EC)	All England Law Reports, European Cases
All ER Rep	All England Law Reports, Reprint
All ER Rep Ext	All England Law Reports, Reprint, Extension Volumes
All. E.R.	All England Reporter
ALR/AR	Argus Law Reports
ALR	American Law Reports
BYIL	British Year Book of International Law
C.A	Court of Appeals
CAL	California Supreme Court Reports
Cal 2d	California Reports, 2nd Series
Cal 3d	California Reports, 3rdSeries
Cal 4th	California Reports, 4thSeries
Cal App 2d	California Appellate Reports, 2nd Series
Cal Rptr	California Reporter
Cal Rptr 2d	California Reporter, 2nd Series
CalApp	California Appellate Reports
CalApp 2d	California Appellate Reports, 2ndSeries

Selected Abbreviations used in Foreign Cases

CalApp 3d	California Appellate Reports, 3rdSeries
CalApp 4th	California Appellate Reports, 4thSeries
Ch.	Chancery
F.L.R.	Family Law Reports
ICLQ	International and Comparative Law Quarterly
ILM	International Legal Materials
ILR	International Law Reports
KB	King's Bench
Moo &P	Moore & Payne's Common Pleas Reports
Moo &S	Moore & Scott's Common Pleas Reports
MooIndApp	Moore's Indian Appeal Cases
MooPC	Moore's Privy Council Cases
MooPCCNS	Moore's Privy Council Cases, New Series
Mos	Moseley's Chancery Reports
P	Law Reports Probate
P&D(UK)	Probate & Divorce Division, United Kingdom (1865-1875)
PC	Privy Council
QB	Queen's Bench
SE	South Eastern Reporter (USA)
SE 2d	South Eastern Reporter, Second Series (USA)
SW	South Western Reporter (USA)
SW 2d	South Western Reporter, 2ndSeries (USA)
SW 3d	South Western Reporter, 3rdSeries (USA)
U.K.H.L.	United Kingdom House of Lords
US Rep	United States Reports
USCA	United States Court of Appeal
USLW	United States Law Week
WLR	Weekly Law Reports

Acknowledgements

My professional interest in the issue of children began at the National Law School of India University, Bangalore, where I could research, teach, train, intervene, and interact with child rights professionals and NGOs on issues relating to children. This provided me with the opportunity to begin thinking about the scope of law differently. Thanks to Professor Chhaya Datar, head, unit for women's studies, the interest was furthered by the opportunities I received at TISS, Mumbai. UNICEF, Maharashtra, assigned me a study on the implementation and administration of the Juvenile Justice Act 1986 in Maharashtra. I was also involved in drafting the Maharashtra rules for the JJA 1986 as well as 2000 Acts for the department of women and child development, Government of Maharashtra. The appointment in the Mumbai High Court expert committee to survey the conditions of children's institutions all over the state of Maharashtra gave me insights into the status of child rights on the field. I am grateful to Hon. Justice A.P. Shah of the Mumbai High Court for giving me this opportunity. I must express my special thanks to Professor N.R.M. Menon, vice chancellor, National University of Juridical Sciences, Kolkata, and Professor S.P. Sathe, honorary director, Institute of Advanced Legal Studies, Pune, for their constant encouragement. I would like to especially acknowledge the kindness and cooperation of my colleague at TISS, Professor Sivaraju, who excused me from a routine task at a crucial stage so that I could concentrate on this book. The moral support of Padma Velaskar and Leena Abraham, my colleagues at TISS, was always there.

I received help initially in arranging the source material from Meenakshi. My sincere thanks are due to Binoy Job for conscientiously assisting me in data conversion, organizing, and retyping the material. His commitment to the work helped me in completing the final manuscript. Several libraries have helped me in locating material—TISS, SNDT, UNICEF, National Law School of India University, Banglore, and National University of Juridical Sciences, Kolkata. I thank them all. I appreciate the many acts of kindness of the staff of the library at TISS, in particular, Kiran, Shyamla,

Malikarjun and 'Mama'. Laksmi and Nita from the unit of women's studies library were always ready and willing to help. I would like to express my gratitude to Mr Gopi Menon and Malthi Pillai of UNICEF, Maharashtra, for helping me with the information, material, and documentation whenever required

My heartfelt thanks go to many children in difficult circumstances whom I came across during my work and who confided in me.

I appreciate the support of my family which provided the space and tolerated the 'mess' of books and papers all over during the completion of the manuscript. And in the end, on a personal note, I would like to thank my mother whose encouragement, warmth, and motivation enabled me to complete this book.

Preface

This book is an attempt to integrate the law in theory and field practice. It provides the important legislation and judgments on the subject, along with the initiatives for legal reform, interventions by some non-governmental organizations (NGO), and international legal trends. The approach is multidisciplinary and each chapter contains the constitutional provisions and statutory and decisional law; highlights various relevant regional and international mechanisms and international standards of behaviour towards children; examines and recognizes the inadequacies in laws and procedures; and looks at some examples and approaches of current NGO interventions and strategies in the field to enhance and protect the rights of the child. It shares the knowledge of experimental efforts that have worked. And finally it focuses on some legal strategies and law reform recommendations to be carried at all levels—from local and national, to regional and international.

The issues addressed in this book include child custody and guardianship, adoption, child labour, child sexual abuse and trafficking, juvenile justice, education, health and nutrition of children, and their right to play and recreation. The book also contains important findings from many research studies, articles, and field experiences. The focus of this book is on law—its enforcement, implementation, and reform. The range of topics covered in this book should be of broad interest to professionals working in the field of child rights. It is intended for legal personnel, including judicial officers, police, lawyers, and public prosecutors. It is hoped that legal personnel, policy makers, researchers, NGOs, policy planners, administrators, students of law and social work, persons and organizations working with children or who come in contact with children, and all those who are interested in the development of children will find useful guidance in these pages. It could also reach out further to the paralegal workers, social and legal activists, and workers at the grass roots who already have some idea of law and legal institutions. Ultimately, children should benefit.

The recognition of children as a discrete group with identifiable rights and needs is now increasingly accepted as a legal principle which underlies much of the relevant international human rights and humanitarian law. Arguments for the special treatment of children usually rely on two main factors: the particular vulnerability of children and the fact that they are the new generation to be cherished as they represent the future. In international law the idea that special treatment should be granted to the child is found, for example, in the guiding norm that 'mankind owes the child the best it has to give' (first set out in the 1924 Declaration of the Rights of the Child). Later it has been reiterated in almost all the international instruments which are to some extent concerned with the entitlements of children.

It has now become increasingly clear that many children suffer from multiple types of maltreatment, sometimes by several perpetrators including the legal system. Charles Dickens said in *Great Expectations*: 'In their little worlds in which children have their existence, there is nothing so finely perceived and so finely felt, as INJUSTICE.' Access to justice is the primary need and right of every human being including children. The legal system of a country is part of its social system and reflects the social, political, economic, and cultural characteristics of that society. Children as a class need the support of law. Of course, the government has the major responsibility through its courts, law enforcement agencies, and the legal aid apparatus. Voluntary organizations and the media play an important role in advocacy and dissemination and in creating awareness. There is a need to develop a comprehensive policy on children, which should look at the whole child and not compartmentalize issues. Multiple strategies need to be developed since no unitary law or scheme can provide a solution. All the laws relating to children need to be reviewed. The content as well as modalities and infrastructure for implementation of laws, policies, and schemes need to be relooked and harmonized with the Convention on the Rights of the Child (CRC).

Education is one of the most important investments that any developing country can make for its future. Education is the most effective tool for empowerment and human development. Today, education appears to be high on the national agenda. Elementary education in India has been a saga of broken promises. It has been characterized by neglect of education of urban disadvantaged children, the girl child; and disabled children, and by low budgetary allocation. While presenting the ninety-third Constitutional Amendment Bill, the Union human resource development minister informed the Lok Sabha that there are forty-two million children in the age group of 6–14 years, who are not getting access to basic education. As a result of continuous and persistent advocacy campaign, the Parliament passed the ninety-third Constitutional Amendment Bill 2001 to make education a fundamental right in India (Lok Sabha passed the amendment in the winter session of 2001 and the Rajya Sabha in the budget session 2002). Education should not be confined to mere literacy. It is much more. It includes all that completes the personality of an well-informed and cultured person. Curriculum should not only include knowledge but also skill development that would result in change in attitude and behaviour which is more tolerant and value based and which promotes equality, diversity, and respect for human dignity. Educating children through quality methods irrespective of socio-economic backgrounds is imperative.

Democracy implies equality of opportunity. Child labour can never contribute to this democratic goal. Children must go to school. It is time to take hard policy decisions. Banning child labour will involve an expense but in the interest of the nation we must bear the cost. There has to be an end to the intolerable exploitation of children through child labour. There are, however, fundamental issues which need to be addressed with regard to the policy and measures which need to be taken up by the government to abolish child labour. Poverty can no longer be an excuse for child labour. Poverty, as one of the causes of child labour, needs to be urgently addressed. Child labour is not the concern of the labour ministry alone but is an issue that equally concerns the ministry of human resource development, that is, the departments of women and child development, education, welfare, and environment. Accordingly, the problem has to be tackled interdepartmentally.

A comprehensive national policy which has a multidisciplinary and interdepartmental approach should form the basis of any law on child labour. The standards are prescribed by the UN Convention on the Rights of the Child. Guidelines in the national policy on child labour must include constitutional directions on land reforms, ILO Convention No. 138, Minimum Wages Act, employment generation , fair minimum wages to parents, and free and compulsory education which must be taken into consideration while drafting any law on child labour. Judgments of the Supreme Court and the High Courts must form part of the law on child labour. The ILO Convention on the Worst Forms of Child Labour which calls for an end to the intolerable and persistent exploitation of children in slave-like and bonded conditions in hazardous and arduous work, in prostitution, pornography, etc., needs to be considered. Child domestic work is an intolerable form of child labour. This group of child workers trapped in exploitative or hazardous working conditions are the most difficult to reach because of cultural insensitivity and the dilemma of respecting the privacy of the home. As outlined in the ILO Convention, other types of 'worst forms of child work' that 'endanger the health, safety or morals of children' may also be identified through a broad process of consultation.

For juvenile justice, the real choice today is mounting a serious, large-scale effort to rebuild weak families. In the context of the CRC and the Global Movement of Children, it is important to change our perspective from needs to development, from welfare to rights, from institutional care to holistic care. We ought to try to improve our performance on both prevention and punishment effort, but we have a long way to go before that. By prevention it is meant intervening in a person's life before he or she has become a serious or high-rate 'offender'. Families need to be strengthened. Strategies, policies, and programmes which strengthen the families will reduce the vulnerability of children and provide a supportive and healthy environment to children. Community-based alternatives to traditional juvenile prisons must exercise very close supervision if they are to be effective. Amidst horror stories of infants being kidnapped and sold for adoption, it is heartening to note that legal adoption is slowly gaining acceptance in society. It has also been reported that the Government of India is in the process of ratifying The Hague Convention on international adoptions. This will be a significant step towards strengthening non-institutional services like adoption.

The Juvenile Justice (Care and Protection) of Children Act 2000, reinforces the role of the state as the guardian of any child in its custody. It is a move towards inclusion and mainstreaming, getting children's participation and finding alternatives in the form of family and community for these children. Institutional care should be the last option for children. The institutional care should be improved with the help of monitoring/supervision/support to ensure the minimum standards in child care. Quality institutional care for children and minimum standards need to be laid down. The SOS villages model need to be adopted.

As rightly put, sexual abuse degrades the very soul of the victim. Children are particularly vulnerable to sexual abuse and exploitation—both commercial and non-commercial. The commercial sexual exploitation of girls is a global, multi-million dollar industry, pouring money into the hands of private citizens, governments, and the police. Trafficking in persons is an issue of growing concern in the international community. The human rights of trafficked persons must be kept in mind as trafficked persons are revictimized in the remedial process. There has to be a shift in the working paradigm from one of criminal sanction to human rights protection. The Protocol to Prevent, Suppress, and Punish Trafficking in Persons, especially Women and Children, supplementing the UN Convention against Transnational Organized Crime adopted in October 2000 is the recent international instrument that focuses specifically on trafficking. Trafficking is defined for the first time in international law in the Protocol.

A significant aspect of child sexual abuse is child pornography which is the depiction of minors engaged in various kinds of sexual acts. Real children are depicted in computer-manipulated images of sexual acts. The provision of the Indian Penal Code and the Information Technology Act 2000 (IT Act) restrict but do not specifically deal with exploiting children for pornographic purposes. There should be specific laws targeting child pornography that not only shield children from viewing pornographic material but also protect them from being depicted in them.

Techniques for interviewing child victims of sexual abuse need to be developed. There is still much to be done to reduce the harrowing and difficult experiences in the courts. The courts have shown inconsistency in dealing with rape cases. Courts cannot remain silent spectators to insensitive cross-examination. Many physicians are unfamiliar with the medical examination procedure of sexual assault victims. The trend among doctors is to do cursory examinations which is one of the reasons for a low rate of conviction in sexual assault cases The medical examination of rape victims further traumatizes her. The doctor's role and attitude immediately after the sexual abuse are a vital factor in the victim's family to go through the legal action. Besides, while forensic doctors and consultants are available in cities, the medical fraternity is ill equipped in the rural areas and small towns.

Health is a low-cost, high-return investment that can give a boost to every aspect of child development and also to a nation's overall progress and prosperity. Addressing the neglect of children's health care is a challenge for health care providers. The special needs of the disabled child must be considered. The human immunodeficiency virus (HIV) has created a generation of orphan children. Children are both infected and affected by the virus. There are more and more children on the streets who are abused and exploited and are becoming particularly vulnerable to HIV and other sexually transmitted diseases. India is a signatory to the Declaration of Commitment on HIV/AIDS of the Twenty-sixth United Nations General Assembly Special Session (UNGASS) on HIV/AIDS held in June 2001. This document has laid down a time-bound programme for nations to follow in their commitment to prevent the spread of HIV and for care and support.

Protecting the girl child is an issue of major concern. The issues of eliminating female foeticide and infanticide, reducing early marriage, and ensuring that girls go to school should be immediately addressed. With increasing advances in reproductive technologies and the mushrooming of

IVF clinics across the country there is a need for greater regulation of medical technology. Recently, the Parliament passed the amended version of the Prenatal Diagnostic Techniques (PNDT) Act which expands the ban on sex determination tests to include pre-conception sex selection techniques. Since pre-selection was not covered by any legislation, several clinics were openly offering sex selection services. Sadly, medical associations have failed to check any form of malpractice in the profession. The associations need to be proactive in educating their members on the implications of such malpractice and need to take harsh decisions. The PNDT (Amendment) Bill 2003 asks the state authorities to create public awareness about the issue. It also provides for the possibility of further amendments which may be needed to deal with changes in technology and social conditions.

It is a matter of concern that the international community has taken scant notice of the hazards and violation of child rights during armed conflict, economic and international sanctions against any country, natural disasters, and terrorist attacks. This harm is not limited to death and injury alone. It also includes illness, long-term disability, deprivation due to family impoverishment, separation from families, missed schooling, displacement from home, torture, arrest and detention, sexual and physical abuse, abduction, and distortion of values by exposure to violence. Many of these may not have immediate effects but long-term ones.

Children are the potential beneficiaries who stand to make the greatest gains from sustainable development. There must be urgent steps by everyone of us including governments, civil society, and the private sector to assure the well-being and security of the future generations by safeguarding the environment at global, national, and local levels.

Enforcement of laws would require a very effective and efficient system for providing economic relief, support services, and social education. Further liberalizing the principle of locus standi would strengthen the enforcement of the laws relating to children. Monitoring of judgments and decisions of the courts have to be undertaken. The State Monitoring Committee on Juvenile Justice in Maharashtra set up by the Mumbai High Court is one such example. It is strongly proposed that NGOs working with children, trade unions, and the panchayats be part of the monitoring. Academic institutions, especially colleges of law, medicine, and social work, could be included in enforcement of laws and judgments. Monitoring enables ongoing support. Professionals often think of professionals to provide services to families and children overlooking informal helps from family friends and support from families who are resistant to interventions from a public agency.

Lack of sensitization, commitment, enforcement mechanism, and trained personnel is the major obstacle in providing child rights. Besides these, there is the lack of political will of the policy makers, indifference of the administrative machinery, lack of budgetary commitment, and lack of awareness. Children are not aware of their rights.

There is a need for a comprehensive law on children that integrates the CRC 1989 and the four sets of civil, political, social economic, and cultural rights of every child—their right to survival, protection, development, and participation. The Indian Parliament will reportedly bring in the National Commission on Children Bill during the budget session of 2003–04. But laws alone cannot bring about the rights of children. There has to be a political commitment and will to protect and promote the rights of children in India. We have to move from a sectoral and departmental approach to a holistic integrated approach in which the services for children must be convergent linking the allied systems. Participation is the key. Children must be involved. Children must be made aware of their rights. There is a need for community understanding, willingness, and participation to advance the whole process of development. An opportunity to empower local communities to control the critical resources affecting their livelihoods and family well-being has been offered by the seventy-third Constitutional Amendment, the Local Government or Panchayati Raj Act of 1992, and the equivalent seventy-fourth Amendment for urban local bodies. Panchayati Raj offers a unique opportunity for community involvement. This opportunity needs to be tapped.

Advocacy is much needed at different levels: the individual, child, parent, family, community, and society. Several child rights have been the result of persistent advocacy campaigns emerging out of the efforts of social action groups at the grass roots, social movements, people's organizations, advocacy organizations, and regional and national coalitions. The process of advocacy—persuading, arguing, winning over influencing opinion formers and policy makers—can give a much needed boost to any programme initiative. There has to be change in perspective both in approach and attitude.

The challenges ahead are creating awareness, increasing stakeholder participation, and finally and more importantly, mobilizing resources. Continuous efforts are to be made to re-educate the people who control the lives of children, in whichever capacity—as parents, teachers, community workers, professionals, and elected representatives. Ongoing training of all functionaries working with children has been found to be an effective tool and strategy in raising awareness, providing understanding of and developing critical analysis on issues. Training intervention could be used as a means to respond to the needs of the trainees for exchange of information, mobilization, documentation, and developing strategies around issues confronting children. Some of the relevant service agencies and other service providers who can be approached to cooperate in this effort are the government departments dealing with health/medical institutions and personnel—doctors, nurses, and other health professionals; legal institutions including the judiciary, private lawyers, government prosecutors, and judges; law enforcement personnel—the police including the civil and immigration officials, and NGO advocates; women's organizations, human and civil rights activists, and others.

There have been the usual constraints of space. But, I have tried to make this book as comprehensive as possible and to ensure the accuracy of the subject matter. Nevertheless, there still may remain imperfections and inaccuracies. Besides, during the time that has elapsed between writing of this book and its final printing, there may also have been a number of significant developments relevant to the subject matter.

I hope this book will be of some significance to all those who are interested in child development and empowerment through law and the formulation of a child-friendly legal system in India that will eventually bring about the desired social change and lead to more productive interventions and policies to support the growth and well-being of children. It is further hoped that it will transcend the division between law in theory and law in practice and serve the intended objectives and help as a guide to building an advocacy strategy to address the issue of empowering and protecting children. There is a need to go beyond formal rights and laws as far as children are concerned and a more active role for children themselves in inacc.

Laws concerning children—like most laws—will inevitably remain flawed, inadequately observed, and in need of constant revision. Clearly, children do not receive 'the best that mankind has to offer' but they can be shielded from the worst. There is the strong evidence of the existence of a well-established legal principle—set out in various human rights and humanitarian legal instruments and constitutions—that children as such are entitled to special treatment. The governments of the world have made a commitment to put children first. Their rights are non-negotiable. However, it is not only governments that must put children FIRST. It is up to to all of us to ensure that this promise of the FIRST CALL becomes a reality.

Mumbai
February 2003

Asha Bajpai

1
Rights of the Child—An Overview

Introduction

The law, policy, and practice of child welfare have undergone a significant change from a historical perspective. Before 1839, there was the concept of authority and control. It was an established common law doctrine that the father had absolute rights over his children. After this, the welfare principle was reflected in the dominant ideology of the family. The Victorian judges, who developed the welfare principle, favoured one dominant family form. The Indian traditional view of welfare is based on *daya*, *dana*, *dakshina*, *bhiksha*, *ahimsa*, *samya-bhava*, *swadharma*, and *tyaga*. The essence of which were self-discipline, self-sacrifice, and consideration for others. It was believed that the well-being of children depended on these values.

Children were recipients of welfare measures. It was only during the twentieth century that the concept of children's rights emerged. This shift in focus from the 'welfare' to the 'rights' approach is significant. Rights are entitlements. They also imply obligations and goals. The rights approach is primarily concerned with issues of social justice, non-discrimination, equity, and empowerment. The rights perspective is embodied in the United Nations Convention on the Rights of the Child 1989, which is a landmark in international human rights legislation. India ratified the Convention on the Rights of the Child in December 1992.

There are around 380 million children below the age of fourteen years in India[1] and 157,863,145 children in the age group of 0–6 years.[2] Children with disabilities are approximately thirty-five million and the proportion of girls marrying below the legal age of eighteen years is 39 per cent. There are around 36,528 children living in institutions and the number of children

---

[1] Written replies by the Govt. of India to the Committee on the Rights of the Child, (CRC/C/Q/IND/1) CRC/C/28/ADD.10, Govt. of India. Report 117/12/99.

[2] Census of India 2001.

living in streets is around 5,000,000.[3] The projected child population in India by age group upto 2016 is presented in Table 1.1

Table 1.1: Projected child population by age group in India from 1996 to 2016

Sr. No.	Year	\multicolumn{4}{c}{Child Population in the age group (Years)}
		0–4	5–9	10–14	0–14
1	1996	119,546	123,686	109,545	352,777
2	2001	108,494	116,145	122,905	347,544
3	2006	113,534	105,744	115,488	334,766
4	2011	119,530	110,968	105,206	335,704
5	2016	122,837	117,099	110,461	350,397

Source: Census of India 1991.

The Legal Definition of a Child

All cultures share the view that the younger the children, the more vulnerable they are physically and psychologically and the less they are able to fend for themselves. Age limits are a formal reflection of society's judgment about the evolution of children's capacities and responsibilities. Almost everywhere age limits formally regulate children's activities: when they can leave school; when they can marry; when they can vote; when they can be treated as adults by the criminal justice system; when they can join the armed forces; and when they can work. But age limits differ from activity to activity and from country to country.[4] In India, the Census of India defines persons below the age of fourteen as children. While making use of standard demographic data, social scientists include females in the age group of fifteen to nineteen years under the category of the girl child. Most of the government programmes on children are targeted for the age group below fourteen years.

The legal conception of a child has thus tended to vary depending upon the purpose. According to Article 1 of the United Nations Convention on the Rights of the Child 1989, 'a child means every human being below the age of eighteen years unless, under the law applicable to the child, majority is attained earlier'. The Article thus grants the discretion to individual countries to determine by law whether childhood should cease at 12, 14, 16, or whatever age they find appropriate. In India, the age at which a person ceases

---

[3] Written replies by the Govt. of India to the Committee on the Rights of the Child, (CRC/C/Q/IND/1) CRC/C/28/ADD.10, Govt. of India. Report 117/12/99.
[4] The State of the World's Children, UNICEF, 1997.

to be a child varies in different laws. Some of the provisions relating to age are as follows:

The Indian Majority Act 1875

The Indian Majority Act 1875 was enacted in order to bring about uniformity in the applicability of laws to persons of different religions.[5] Unless a particular personal law specifies otherwise, every person domiciled in India is deemed to have attained majority upon completion of eighteen years of age. However, in case of a minor for whose person or property, or both, a guardian has been appointed or declared by any court of justice before the age of 18 years, and in case of every minor the superintendence of whose property has been assumed by the Court of Wards before the minor has attained that age, the age of majority will be twenty-one years and not eighteen [The Indian Majority Act 1875, Section 3]. The Hindu Minority and Guardianship Act (HMGA) 1956, in Sec. 4(a) defines a 'minor' as a person who has not completed the age of eighteen years. The age of majority for the purposes of appointment of guardians of person and property of minors according to the Mohammedan law is also completion of eighteen years.[6] Christians[7] and Parsis[8] also reach majority at eighteen. The age of marriage is twenty-one years for males and eighteen years for females.[9]

For purposes of criminal responsibility, age limit is seven [Sec. 82] and twelve [Sec. 83] under the Indian Penal Code 1860 (IPC). For purposes of protection against kidnapping, abduction, and related offences, age is fixed at sixteen in the case of boys and eighteen in the case of girls.[10] Under the Child Labour (Prohibition and Regulation) Act 1986, child means a person who has not completed his fourteenth year of age.[11] For purposes of special treatment under the Juvenile Justice Act 1986, the age prescribed was sixteen years for boys and eighteen years for girls.[12] Now under the Juvenile Justice (Care and Protection of Children) Act 2000, the age is eighteen for both boys and girls.[13] Ages prescribed for majority under various legislations are presented in Table 1.2.

[5] Indian Majority Act 1875, see preamble.
[6] The Dissolution of Muslim Marriage Act 1939.
[7] The Indian Divorce Act 1860.
[8] The Parsi Marriage and Divorce Act 1936.
[9] Child Marriage Restraint Act 1929.
[10] IPC deals with kidnapping from lawful guardianship, Section 361.
[11] Child Labour (Prohibition and Regulation) Act 1986. Section 2(ii).
[12] Juvenile Justice Act, 1986. Section 2(h).
[13] Juvenile Justice (Care and Protection of Children) Act 2000. Section 2(k).

Table 1.2: Age prescribed for majority under variouw laws*

Legislation	Provision
Indian Penal Code 1860	Nothing is an offence which is done by a child under the age of seven years [Sec 82 IPC]. The age of criminal responsibility is raised to twelve years if the child is found to have not attained the ability to understand the nature and consequences of his/her act [Sec 83 IPC]. Attainment of sixteen years of age for a girl is necessary for giving sexual consent. In case she is married, the prescribed age for sexual consent is not less than fifteen years.
Child Marriage Restraint Act 1926	Child means a person who, if a male, has not completed twenty-one years of age and, if a female, has not completed eighteen years of age.
Apprentices Act 1961	A person is qualified to be engaged as an apprentice only if he is not less than fourteen years of age and satisfies such standards of education and physical fitness as may be prescribed.
Juvenile Justice (Care and Protection of Children) Act 2000	'Juvenile' or 'child' means a person who has not completed eighteenth year of age.
Factories Act 1948	A child below fourteen years of age is not allowed to work in any factory. An adolescent between fifteen and eighteen years can be employed in a factory only if he obtains a certificate of fitness from an authorized medical doctor. A child between fourteen and eighteen years of age cannot be employed for more than four-and-a-half hours.
Mines (Amendment) Act 1952	No person below eighteen years of age shall be allowed to work in any mine or any part thereof.
Army Head Quarters Regulations	The age of recruitment in the army is from sixteen to twenty-five years. Persons, who are recruited at the age of sixteen years, undergo basic military training for up to two-and-a-half years from the date of enrolment and are then inducted into regular service.
Indian Contract Act 1870	A person below the age of eighteen years has no capacity to contract.

Constitution of India (Ninety-third Constitution-Amendment)	Article 21 (a) of the Constitution states that the state shall provide free and compulsory education to all children of the age of six to fourteen years in such manner as the state may by law determine. Article 45 of the Constitution states that the state shall endeavour to provide early childhood care and education for all children until they complete the age of six years. Article 51(k) lays down a duty that the parents or guardians should provide opportunities for education to his child/ward between the age of six and fourteen years.

The word 'child' has been used in various legislations as a term denoting relationship, as a term indicating capacity, and as a term of special protection. Underlying these alternative specifications are very different concepts about the child. These include viewing children as a burden which invokes rights to maintenance and support; regarding children as undergoing temporary disabilities making for rights to special treatment and special discrimination; treating children as specially vulnerable for ensuring rights to protection; and recognizing children as resources for the country's development necessitating their nurturing and advancement.

There does not appear to be any criteria or scientific parameters. For instance, in some laws as in the Child Marriage Restraint Act 1929, there is a difference between the age of the boy and that of the girl. The minimum age of marriage for girls is eighteen but the age of sexual consent under the rape laws is sixteen and it is fifteen if she is married. The *Mines Act* defines children as those below eighteen years and the various state Shops and Establishment Acts define the age between twelve and fifteen years. It is necessary that the definition of 'child' be brought in conformity with the Convention on the Rights of the Child, viz., below eighteen years of age. Though one may like to have a uniform age limit legally prescribed for the status of childhood, it may perhaps not be possible or even desirable. Nevertheless, some rationalization is possible or some norms can be laid down, as some of the age limits in the laws appear to be arbitrary or based on socio-cultural perceptions. If the best interests of child interpretation were to be adopted, one can err on the side of a higher age limit for protective care and a lower age limit in respect of civil and cultural matters. The question of review of the definition of 'child', in the light of Article 1 of the Convention on the Rights of the Child has been referred to the Law Commission of India for consideration while undertaking a comprehensive review of the Code of Criminal Procedure, the Indian Evidence Act, and the Indian Penal Code.

Present Legal Framework

It is evident that legislation is one of the main weapons of empowerment of children. Even though appropriate legislation may not necessarily mean that the objectives of the legislation will be achieved, its very existence creates an enabling provision whereby the state can be compelled to take action. Legislation reflects the commitment of the state to promote an ideal and progressive value system. The notion of duty also applies to the state.

India follows an adversarial legal system with an in-built bias in favour of the accused who is presumed innocent till proved guilty. The Constitution of India, the fundamental law of the country, came into effect on 26 January 1950. It provides a protective umbrella for the rights of children. These rights include right to equality [Art. 14], right to freedom including the freedom of speech and expression [Art. 19(1)(a)], personal liberty, right to due process of law [Art. 21], right against exploitation [Art. 23], religious, cultural, educational rights [Art. 29], and right to constitutional remedies [Art. 32].

In addition to these basic rights, there are certain fundamental rights especially for children. These rights are necessary because of their physical and mental immaturity; the children are especially vulnerable and need special protection. Article 15 of the Constitution prohibits discrimination of citizens on the grounds only of religion, race, caste, sex, place of birth, or any of them. But subsection 3 adds: 'Nothing in this Article shall prevent the state from making any special provision for women and children.' Therefore, laws can be made giving special protection to children. These rights are included in Part III and Part IV of the Constitution. The fundamental rights in Part III are enforceable in courts whereas the directive principles of state policy in Part IV are guidelines and principles that are fundamental to the governance of the country. It is the duty of the state to apply these principles in making laws. If the fundamental rights are violated, a writ petition can be filed in the Supreme Court or the High Court [Arts. 32 and 226].

Under the Constitution, it is the duty of the state to secure that children of tender age are not abused and forced by economic necessity to enter vocations unsuited to their age and strength [Art. 39 (9)(e)] and to ensure that children are given opportunities and facilities to develop in a healthy manner and in conditions of freedom and dignity [Art. 39 (f)]. The directive principles provide for maternity relief [Art. 42]. Rights provided under Part IV (directive principles) of the Constitution can be read into the fundamental rights provided in Part III and hence enforceable in courts. Because of judicial interpretation, many of the directive principles have now become enforceable through legal actions brought before the courts (for example, the right to education). There are certain aspects relating to children that are dealt with in the state and concurrent lists of the Constitution of India.[14]

It is estimated that there are more than 250 Central and state statutes under which the child is covered in India. Some of the important, special legislations that deal with children are the following:

The Guardian and Wards Act 1890

This Act deals with the qualifications, appointment, and removal of guardians of children by the courts and is applicable to all children irrespective of their religion.

The Child Marriage Restraint Act 1929

This Act as amended in 1979 restrains the solemnization of child marriages by laying down the minimum age of marriage for both boys and girls. This law is applicable to all communities irrespective of their religion.

Hindu Adoption and Maintenance Act 1956

This codifies the law relating to adoption and maintenance among Hindus.

The Hindu Minority And Guardianship Act 1956

This provides for the appointment of guardians of minors among Hindus.

Young Persons Harmful Publications Act 1956

This Act prevents the dissemination of certain publications that are harmful to young persons.

Probation of Offenders Act 1958

This law lays down the restrictions on imprisonment of offenders under twenty-one years of age.

---

[14] List II—State list in Entry 4 includes prisons, reformatories, borstal institutions, and other institutions of a like nature and persons detained therein; arrangements with other states for the use of prisons and other institutions.

List III—Concurrent list, Entry 5: Marriage and divorce, infants and minors, adoption, wills, intestacy and succession, joint family and partition, all matters in respect of which parties in judicial proceedings were immediately before the commencement of this Constitution subject to their personal law.

Entry 30: Vital statistics including registration of births and deaths.

Entry 41: Custody, management, and disposal of property (including agricultural land) declared by law to be evacuee property.

The Orphanages and Other Charitable Homes (Supervision And Control) Act 1960

This Act provides for the supervision and control of orphanages and homes for children.

Apprentice Act 1961

This lays down qualifications for persons above fourteen years of age to undergo apprenticeship training in any designated trade.

The Medical Termination of Pregnancy Act 1971

This law stipulates when pregnancies may be terminated by registered medical practitioners.

The Child Labour (Prohibition And Regulation) Act 1986

This Act prohibits the engagement of children in certain employment and regulates the conditions of work of children in certain other employments.

The Children (Pledging of Labour) Act 1933

This prohibits pledging the labour of children.

The Infant Milk Substitutes, Feeding Bottles and Infant Foods (Regulation of Production, Supply and Distribution) Act 1992

This Act regulates the production, supply, and distribution of infant milk substitutes, feeding bottles, and infant feeds with a view to the protection and promotion of breastfeeding and ensuring the proper use of infant feeds and other incidental matters.

The Pre-Natal Diagnostic Technique (Regulation and Prevention of Misuse) Act 1994

This provides for the regulation of the use of prenatal diagnostic techniques for the purpose of detecting genetic or metabolic disorders or chromosomal abnormalities or certain congenital malformations or sex-linked disorders, and for the prevention of the misuse of such techniques for the purpose of prenatal sex determination leading to female foeticide.

The Juvenile Justice (Care and Protection of Children) Act 2000

This Act deals with the law relating to juveniles in conflict with law and children in need of care and protection, by providing for proper care, protection, and treatment by catering to their development needs, and by adopting a child-friendly approach in the adjudication and disposition of matters in the best interest of children, and for their ultimate rehabilitation through various institutions established under the Act.

Besides the above special legislations that deal with children, there are provisions that concern children in various general statutes. Provisions relating to children have also developed in the areas of criminal law, family law, employment law, and other aspects of childcare and welfare. There are also specific rules which apply to minors engaged in civil or criminal proceedings or commercial matters. The Code of Criminal Procedure 1973 lays down various procedures to be followed in a criminal trial and provides for the machinery for the punishment of offenders. The Code of Civil Procedure 1908 lays down the procedure to be followed in civil trials. The Indian Evidence Act 1872 deals with the competency of the witness and the value of evidence given by children [Sec. 112].

Several criminal laws give special protection to children. These statutes include the Indian Penal Code 1860, the Evidence Act 1872, and the Code of Criminal Procedure 1973. The Indian Penal Code 1860 defines various categories of offences and the punishment for such offences. It has special provisions relating to the causing of miscarriages and injuries caused to the unborn child [IPC Secs. 312–318]. In case of child rape, consent cannot be a defence where the child is below sixteen years of age. Marital rape is recognized only if the wife is below fifteen years [IPC Secs. 375, 376]. There is an enhanced punishment in cases of rape by public servants and custodial rape [IPC Sec. 376 (a) (b) (c) (d)], including rape of children in institutions. There are provisions for kidnapping, abduction, and buying of minors for the purposes of prostitution, slavery, and forced labour [IPC 358–374]. The Immoral Traffic (Prevention) Act 1956, which was amended in 1987, tries to curb trafficking in young persons, both boys and girls. There are provisions relating to children in the Cable Television Network (Regulation) Act 1995 and the Prevention of Illicit Traffic in Narcotic Drugs and Psychotropic Substances Act 1988.

In the area of family law, the personal laws are religion based. The rights of children born to Hindus are governed by the Hindu Marriage Act 1955 and the Hindu Succession Act 1956. Christian children are governed by the Indian Divorce Act 1860 and the Indian Succession Act 1925. In matters of marriage, maintenance, custody, guardianship, adoption, succession, and inheritance, the Muslim children are governed by the Muslim personal law. The Parsi children are governed by the Parsi Marriage and Divorce Act 1936 and the Indian Succession Act 1925. An important provision in the Criminal Procedure Code (CrPC) 1973 is the order for maintenance of children [Sec. 125].[15]

---

[15] CrPC Section 125 provides for an order of maintenance of the legitimate or illegitimate child (not a married daughter) who has attained majority. Such a child, by reason of any physical or mental abnormality or injury is unable to maintain itself.

10 *Child Rights in India*

There are provisions relating to employment of children in the Factories Act 1948, the Minimum Wages Act 1948, the Plantations Labour Act 1951, the Mines Act 1952, the Merchant Shipping Act 1958, the Motor Transport Workers Act 1961, the Payment of Bonus Act 1965, the Beedi and Cigar Workers (Conditions of Employment) Act 1966, the Bonded Labour System (Abolition) Act 1976, the Trade Unions Act 1926, and the various state Shops and Establishment Acts. The Contract Act 1872, the Indian Partnership Act 1932, and the Indian Trust Act 1882, contain provisions relating to civil and commercial rights and liabilities of minors.[16]

Policies and Action Plans

A number of policy initiatives, plans, and programmes relating to children have been undertaken in India. The policy documents are reference points available for planning and other interventions. Some major policy and plan documents are the following:

- National Policy for Children 1974
- National Policy on Education 1986
- National Policy on Child Labour 1987
- National Plan For SAARC Decade of the Girl Child 1991–2000
- National Plan of Action for Children 1992
- National Nutrition Policy 1993
- National Population Policy 2000
- National Health Policy 2001

These are discussed in brief in the following paragraphs.

National Policy for Children 1974

India is one of the very few States that has a written National Policy for Children. The Policy declares the nation's children as a supremely important asset and states that children's programmes should find a prominent place in our national plans for the development of human resources. The objectives to be attained through this policy were as follows:

- To provide adequate services to children, both before and after birth and through the period of growth.
- To ensure their full physical, mental, and social development.
- To progressively increase the scope of such services so that within a reasonable time, all children in the country enjoy optimum conditions for their balanced growth.

[16] The enactments use the term minor and minority is defined as below eighteen years.

Salient Features of the Policy

Some of the salient features of the National Policy for Children 1974 are:

- A comprehensive health programme will cover all children.
- Programmes will be implemented to provide nutrition services with the object of removing deficiencies in the diet of children.
- Programmes will be undertaken for the general improvement of their health and for the care, nutrition, and education of expectant and nursing mothers.
- Free and compulsory education will be provided to all children up to the age of fourteen years.
- There will be provision for non-formal education.
- Physical education, games, sports, and other types of recreational as well as cultural and scientific activities will be promoted in schools, community centres, and such other institutions.
- Equality of opportunity to all children will be ensured.
- Facilities for education, training, and rehabilitation of socially disadvantaged and physically, emotionally, and mentally retarded children will be provided.
- Children are to be protected against neglect, cruelty, and exploitation.
- No child under fourteen is to be engaged in any hazardous occupation.
- Children are to be given priority for protection and relief in times of distress or natural calamity.
- Special programmes will be taken up to encourage and assist gifted children.
- Laws are to be amended so that in all legal disputes the interests of children are given paramount consideration.
- Family ties are to be strengthened.
- National Children's Board will be constituted for meeting the needs of children.
- Adequate resources will be provided for child welfare programmes of voluntary organizations.

The above policy is now outdated as at it does not conform to the standards laid down in the United Nations Convention on the Rights of the Child which India has ratified and in conformity of which it is obliged to make laws.

National Policy on Education 1986 (Modified in 1992)

In several developed and developing countries, universal education was seen as a main factor in the development of a modern nation. The National Policy

12 *Child Rights in India*

on Education in India was modified in 1992. Thereafter, Parliament approved a programme of action which sought to launch the National Elementary Education Mission—Education for All—in 1993 and the District Primary Education Programme launched in 1994. Currently the emphasis is on universal primary education.

National Policy on Child Labour 1987

The National Child Labour Policy was formulated with the basic objective of suitably rehabilitating the children withdrawn from employment and reducing the incidence of child labour in areas where there is a known concentration of child labour. The policy consists of three main ingredients: the legal action plan, focusing of Central government programmes, and project-based plan of action.

National Plan for SAARC Decade of the Girl Child 1991–2000

In 1992, the Government of India prepared a separate National Plan for the Girl Child for the period 1991–2000. This plan identified three major goals:

- Survival and protection of the girl child and safe motherhood
- Overall development of the girl child
- Special protection for vulnerable girl children in need of care and protection.

National Plan of Action for Children 1992[17]

India joined the comity of nations in the successive reaffirmations of global commitment to the cause of children in 1989–90. The UN Convention on the Rights of the Child (CRC) in November 1989, the World Conference on Education for All at Jomtien (Thailand) in March 1990, the Global Consultation on Water and Sanitation in September 1990, the World Summit on Children in the autumn of 1990, and the SAARC Summit on Children were all part of this re-affirmation process which transcended national barriers. India is a signatory to the World Declaration (September 1990) on the Survival, Protection, and Development of Children and the Plan of Action for implementing it.[18] The NPA is a follow-up of the promises made by the global fraternity at the World Summit for Children. The plan of action

---

[17] Ministry of Human Resources Development, Government of India, New Delhi, 1992.

[18] National Plan of Action, A Commitment to the Child, Government of India, Department of Women and Child Development, New Delhi, 1992.

identifies quantifiable targets in terms of major as well as supporting sectoral goals. Some of the major goals for 1990–2000 were:
- Reduction of infant mortality rate to less than ten.
- Reduction of maternal mortality rate by half.
- Reduction in severe and moderate malnutrition among under-5 children by half.
- Universal access to safe drinking water and improved access to sanitary means of excreta disposal.
- Universal enrolment, retention, minimum level of learning, reduction of disparities, and universalization of effective access of schooling.
- Achievement of adult literacy rate of 80 per cent in the age group of 15–35, with emphasis on female literacy.
- Improved protection of children in especially difficult circumstances.
- Assistance to children affected by one or more disabilities, having no access to proper rehabilitative services and especially upliftment of the status of those most marginalized.
- Removal of gender bias and improvement in the status of the girl child.
- Conservation and protection of the environment for the well-being of children.
- Promotion of advocacy and people's participation for the child.

National Nutrition Policy 1993

The National Nutrition Policy reflects the understanding that malnutrition is not simply a matter of 'not enough food', but is most frequently caused by a combination of factors, including lack of time and attention to childcare, inadequate feeding of the child especially in the first year of life, poor health, unhygienic conditions as well as the lack of purchasing power of poor families. A National Plan of Action on Nutrition was formulated in 1995.

National Population Policy 2000

The crux of the policy rests on denying state representation to Parliament based on their population. In other words, the essence of the population policy is that by taking away the democratic rights of those states whose population is growing too fast, these states will somehow find a way of controlling their population. It simultaneously addresses the issues of child survival, maternal health, and contraception.

The National Health Policy 2001

The National Health Policy 1983 has now been revised and a new National Health Policy 2001 has been drafted. The main objectives of NHP 2001 are to achieve an acceptable standard of good health amongst the general population of the country. The approach would be to increase access to the decentralized public health system by establishing new infrastructure in deficient areas, and by upgrading the infrastructure in the existing institutions. Broadly, NHP-2001 will endeavour to achieve time-bound goals in the areas of Infant Mortality Rate (IMR), Maternal Mortality Rate (MMR), etc.

These laws and policies tend to work in isolation. The right to education, for instance, is linked to issues of child labour, juvenile justice, child marriages, health, and nutrition. Second, the policy perspectives relating to children and childhood are confused. On one hand you have the ninety-third Constitutional amendment stating that it is a fundamental right of children between six and fourteen years to be in school, and on the other hand you have the Child Labour (Prohibition and Regulation) Act 1986 laying down that children below fourteen years can work in non-hazardous occupations and processes. Further, there is a Child Marriage Restraint Act 1928, setting a minimum age of marriage but not declaring the marriage void. The Persons with Disabilities (Equal Opportunities, Protection of Rights and Full Participation) Act 1995 is totally alienated from the education, health, and nutrition policies and the children in need of care and protection under the Juvenile Justice (Care and Protection of Children Act 2000. The JJ Act 2000 has attempted to bring in adoption of children under the Act. But it is not clear about adoption of children whose personal laws do not 'permit' adoption. The current criminal provisions are not adequate to deal with cases of child sexual abuse. Laws in India have yet to evolve clear legal definition for child sexual abuse. The National Policy on Children 1974 is now outdated. It has to be more children-oriented and rights-based in order to be effective. Besides, the rights of children are inalienable and indivisible. They cannot work in isolation. The laws relating to children also have to be interlinked. Perhaps, a single code on children can best protect the interests of the child. The laws and the policies now have to conform to the international standards laid down in the CRC which India has ratified. The interpretation and enforcement of laws is not always in the best interest of the child.

International Law on the Rights of the Child

Law in the form of international conventions can contribute considerably. International instruments stress 'participation' as a core value along with survival, protection, and development. Laws and legal strategies must be devised to encourage these values. In a recent judgment, the Supreme Court held that 'once signed, any international Treaty or Convention will be treated as a part of law unless otherwise stated'. The Indian government is thus bound in its obligation to implement any convention or treaty that is signed. India has ratified the United Nations Convention on the Rights of the Child and the Convention on All Forms of Discrimination against Women.

Since the beginning of the twentieth century, the development of international law on the rights of the child has paralleled, in part, the development of the general body of international human rights law. The first stage was the recognition by the international community that all individuals, including children, were the objects of international law requiring legal protection. The second stage, which is still evolving, is the granting of specific substantive rights to individuals including children. The third stage, which is also still developing, is the acknowledgement that in order to ensure that individuals are able to enjoy the exercise of their fundamental rights they must be acknowledged to possess the necessary procedural capacity to exercise and claim these rights and freedom.[19]

Human Rights Instruments Specific to the Rights of the Child

The Declaration of the Rights of the Child 1924, adopted by the fifth Assembly of the League of Nations, can be seen as the first international instrument dealing with children's rights.[20] The Declaration establishes the claim that 'mankind owes to the child the best it has to give'. The five principles that are enumerated are:

- The child must be given the means requisite for its normal development, both materially and spiritually.
- The child that is hungry must be fed; the child that is sick must be nursed; the child that is backward must be helped; the delinquent child must be reclaimed; and the orphan and the 'waif' must be sheltered and succoured.
- The child must be the first to receive relief in times of distress.
- The child must be put in a position to earn a livelihood, and must be protected against every form of exploitation.
- The child must be brought up in the consciousness that its talents must be devoted to the service of its fellow men.

This Declaration is important as it highlights the social and economic entitlements of children and establishes internationally the concept of the

[19] Geraldine Van Bueren, *The International Law on the Rights of the Child*, Netherland: Kluwer Academic Publishers, 1995.

[20] Records of the Fifth Assembly, 1924. Supplement no. 23, League of Nations Official Journal.

rights of the child, thereby laying the foundation for setting future international standards in the field of children's rights.[21]

DECLARATION OF THE RIGHTS OF THE CHILD 1959

The preamble describes the principles as enunciating rights and freedom, which governments should observe by legislative and other measures progressively taken. The Declaration of the Rights of the Child makes reference in its preamble to both the United Nations Charter and the Universal Declaration of Human Rights. The preamble also refers to the special safeguards and care, including appropriate legal protection needed by children, and recalls the original recognition of those needs by the Declaration of the Rights of the Child 1924 and in the statutes of specialized agencies and international organizations concerned with children. It reiterates the pledge that, 'mankind owes to the child the best it has to give', and it places a specific duty upon voluntary organizations and local authorities to strive for the observance of these rights. The role of voluntary organizations is highlighted because of their instrumental role in persuading governments of the need for international legal protection of children's rights and of their recognized impartial expertise in the formulation of these rights.[22]

In accordance with the Declaration, a child is entitled to a name and nationality [Principle 3, Declaration of the Rights of the Child (DRC)], to adequate nutrition, housing, recreation, and medical services [Principle 4 DRC]. Attention is paid to the special needs of physically, mentally, and 'socially handicapped' children [Principle 5 DRC], and to children who are without a family [Principle 6 DRC]. The right to education is included, as is the right to play and recreation [Principle 7 DRC]. A noticeable departure from the principles of the 1924 Declaration is that the earlier Declaration specified that 'children must be the first to receive relief', whereas the 1959 Declaration lays down that children shall be 'among the first' to receive protection and relief. This is a more realistic approach taking account of situations where more children's lives would be saved if relief is administered first to an appropriate adult such as a doctor.

The Declaration of the Rights of the Child enshrines the principle that children are entitled to 'special protection' and that such special protection should be implemented by reference to 'the best interests of the child', which 'shall be the paramount consideration' [Principle 2 DRC]. The Declaration also contains a broad non-discrimination clause [Principle 2 DRC].

---

[21] Geraldine Van Bueren, *The International Law on the Rights of the Child*, Netherland: Kluwer Academic Publishers, 1995.

[22] UN Doc E/CD, 5/111 17.

Convention of the Elimination of All Forms of Discrimination against Women 1979 (CEDAW)

Article 5 (b) of this Convention obligates states to take all appropriate measures to ensure that family education includes a proper understanding of maternity as a social function and the recognition of the common responsibility of men and women in the upbringing and development of their children, it being understood that *the interests of the children is the primordial consideration in all cases*. Article 16 (1)(d) of the same Convention provides that in all matters relating to marriage and family relations, *the interests of the children shall be paramount*.[23] This Convention seems to restrict the best interests principle in family relations and matters. The scope is not wide. But today, the principle needs wider applicability than custody and family matters.

Convention on the Rights of the Child 1989 (CRC)

The United Nations Convention on the Rights of the Child (CRC) represents a turning point in the international movement on behalf of child rights. This comprehensive document contains a set of universal legal standards or norms for the protection and well-being of children. The range of rights can be summarized as the three Ps: provision, protection, and participation. Children have a right to be provided with certain services ranging from a name and nationality to heath care and education. They have a right to be protected from certain acts, such as torture, exploitation, abuse, arbitrary detention, and unwarranted removal from parental care and children have the right to participate in the decisions affecting their lives.

The CRC gives children their basic human rights—civil, economic, social, cultural, and political—which enable children to achieve their full potential.[24] The *civil rights* of children include right to a name and a nationality, protection from torture and maltreatment, special rules governing the circumstances and conditions under which children may be deprived of their liberty or separated from their parents, etc. The *economic rights* under the CRC include the right to benefit from social security, the right to a standard of living adequate to ensure proper development and protection from exploitation at work. The *social rights* include the right to the highest attainable standard of health services, the right to social care for handicapped

---

[23] In all matters relating to the placement of a child outside the care of the child's own parents, the best interests of the child, particularly his or her need for affection and right to security and continuing care, should be the paramount consideration.

[24] This is another way of classifying the rights under the Convention on the Rights of the Child.

children, protection from sexual exploitation and abduction, and the regulation of adoption. Right to education, access to appropriate information, recreation and leisure, and participation in artistic and cultural activities are included in the *cultural rights* of the children under the CRC. It is unusual among human rights treaties because it is not only concerned with the granting and implementing of rights in times of peace, but is also concerned with the regulation of armed conflicts as they affect children as civilians and combatants.[25]

Broadly the civil, political, social, economic, and cultural rights of every child can be grouped into the following four classes.

THE RIGHT TO SURVIVAL

This includes the right to life, the highest attainable standard of health and nutrition, and adequate standards of living. It also includes the right to a name and a nationality.

THE RIGHT TO PROTECTION

This includes freedom from all forms of exploitation, abuse, inhuman or degrading treatment, and neglect, including the right to special protection in situations of emergency and armed conflicts.

THE RIGHT TO DEVELOPMENT

This includes the right to education, support for early childhood development and care, social security, and the right to leisure, recreation, and cultural activities.

THE RIGHT TO PARTICIPATION

This includes respect for the views of the child, freedom of expression, access to appropriate information, and freedom of thought, conscience, and religion.

The UN Committee on the Rights of the Child has identified a thematic clustering of child rights. The clustering is as follows:

- *General measures of implementation* are laid down in Articles 4, 42, and 44 of CRC. This highlights the need to constantly review the relevance of reservations and the importance of bringing national legislation in conformity with the Convention.

---

[25] Geraldine Van Bueren, 'Special Features of the Assistance and Protection of Children', in Frits Karlshoven (ed.), *Assisting the Real Victims of Armed Conflict and Other Disasters*, 1989.

- *Definition of child*: Article 1[26] gives the definition of the age of the child. No minimum age is defined.[27]
- *General principles, civil rights, and freedoms*: In this theme, Articles 2, 3, 6, and 12 of CRC give the four general principles of the Convention, i.e. non-discrimination, best interests of the child, right to survival and development, and respect for the views of the child. Whereas, Articles 7, 8, 13–17, and 37(a) specify the civil rights and freedoms which include the right to a name and nationality, freedom of expression and peaceful assembly, right not to be subjected to torture, etc.
- The theme on *family environment and basic health* includes Articles 5, 9–11, 18, 19, 21, 25, and 27 that deal with parental guidance and responsibilities, illicit transfer and non-return, unaccompanied minors and adoption, psychosocial recovery, and reintegration. It also includes articles that address health, standard of living, and facilities for treatment and rehabilitation in Articles 6, 18, 23, 24, 26, and 27.
- The theme on *education, leisure, and special protection* stresses the importance of education including vocational training and guidance, and also protection of refugee children, children in emergencies, children in the juvenile justice system, and children in danger of exploitation. In Articles 28, 29, and 31, it is laid down that education should be child-friendly, and leisure and culture should be provided. Physical and psychological recovery as well as social integration for children is given in Articles 22, 32–36, and 37–40.

The CRC is guided by the principle of a *first call for children*—a principle that the essential needs of children should, at all times, be given priority in the allocation of resources at all times. The Convention is derived from a core set of human values and ethical premises that recognize the inherent dignity and the equal and inalienable rights of all members of the human family as the foundation of freedom, justice, and peace in the world. Accordingly, the Convention states that the rights shall be extended to all children without discrimination of any kind, irrespective of the child's or his or her parents' or legal guardian's race, nationality, colour, sex, language, religion, political or other opinion, social origin, property, disability, and birth or other status.[28] The Convention also draws particular attention to the fact that such

---

[26] For the purpose of the present Convention, a child means every human being below the age of eighteen years unless under the law applicable to the child, majorities attained earlier.

[27] This was done to avoid debate over abortion, which could have threatened the acceptance of the Convention.

[28] *The Right to Be a Child*, UNICEF, New Delhi, India, 1994.

children need special consideration. It advocates measures for the protection and harmonious development of the child that are consistent with the traditions and cultural values of different peoples. By providing safeguards against economic and other policies that have a negative effect on the well-being of children, the Convention reaffirms a commitment to promote social progress that will ensure a better quality of life and greater freedom for people in general and children in particular. It also underscores the importance and potential of international cooperation for promoting and improving the living conditions of children in every country.[29]

Therefore there are four general principles enshrined in the Convention. These are meant to help with the interpretation of the Convention as a whole and thereby guide national programmes of implementation. The four principles are formulated, in particular, in Articles 2, 3, 6, and 12.[30] These are:

- *Non-discrimination* (*Art. 2*): State parties must ensure that all children within their jurisdiction enjoy their rights. No child should suffer discrimination. The essential message is equality of opportunity. Girls should be given the same opportunities as boys. Refugee children, children of foreign origin, or children of indigenous or minority groups should have the same rights as all others. Children with disabilities should be given the same opportunity to enjoy an adequate standard of living.
- *Best interests of the child* (*Art. 3*): When the authorities of a state take decisions which affect children, the best interests of children must be a primary consideration. The principle relates to decisions by courts of law, administrative authorities, legislative bodies, and both public and private social-welfare institutions.
- *The right to life, survival, and development* (*Art. 6*): The term 'development' in this context should be interpreted in a broad sense, adding a qualitative dimension—not only physical health but also mental, emotional, cognitive, social, and cultural development.
- *The views of the child* (*Art. 12*): Children have the right to be heard and to have their views taken seriously, including any judicial or administrative proceedings affecting them.

An analysis of the Convention on the Rights of the Child reveals that it attempts to accomplish five goals. It creates new rights under international

---

[29] Ibid.
[30] The Rights of the Child, Fact Sheet No. 10, United Nations, Geneva, 1996.

law for children where no such rights existed, including the child's right to preserve his or her identity and the right of indigenous children to practise their own culture [CRC Arts. 8 and 30]. Second, the Convention on the Rights of the Child enshrines rights in a global treaty which had until the Convention's adoption only been acknowledged or refined in case law under regional human rights treaties; for example, a child's right to be heard either directly or indirectly in any judicial or administrative proceedings affecting that child, and to have those views taken into account [CRC Art. 12]. Thirdly, the Convention also creates binding standards in areas which, until the Convention's entry into force, were only non-binding recommendations. These include safeguards in adoption procedures and the rights of mentally and physically disabled children [CRC Arts. 21 and 23].

The Convention also imposes new obligations in relation to the provision and protection of children. These include the obligation on a state to take effective measures to abolish traditional practices prejudicial to the health of children (although not mentioned expressly, this includes female circumcision) and to provide for rehabilitative measures for child victims of neglect, abuse, and exploitation [CRC Arts. 28(3) and 39]. Finally, the Convention adds an additional express ground by which states are under a duty not to discriminate against children in their enjoyment of the Convention's rights [CRC Art. 2(1)].*

Global Human Rights Instruments and the Rights of the Child

The Constitutional document establishing the United Nations is the Charter of the United Nations which came into force in 1945. It is clearly not a human rights instrument but it does contain provisions relevant to international human rights law. There is no express provision relating to children.

UNIVERSAL DECLARATION OF HUMAN RIGHTS 1948

The Universal Declaration of Human Rights 1948 proclaims a catalogue of human rights which apply to all human beings and therefore implicitly to children [CRC Art. 1]. It contains only two articles, which expressly refer to children. Article 25 (2) on special care and assistance and Article 26 on education.

Article 25, emphasizes the rights of children to special care and assistance and it provides this through the direct protection of the rights of the child and indirectly through the protection of motherhood. Article 26 deals both with access to and the aims of education.

This is a non-binding resolution of the General Assembly but it helped in laying down certain common standards for children world-wide.

INTERNATIONAL COVENANT ON ECONOMIC, SOCIAL, AND CULTURAL RIGHTS 1966

It applies to all 'men and women' and therefore by implication to children.[31] The preamble recognizes that all human rights are interlinked and of equal importance. The Covenant stresses that children 'deserve special measures of protection and assistance'.

The Covenant specifically refers to children in Articles 10 and 12. In Article 10, the states recognize the family as the 'natural and fundamental group unit of society' and therefore accord the widest possible protection and assistance to the family. Article 10(3) contains a broad ambit of protection.

Special measures of protection and assistance should be taken on behalf of all children and young persons without any discrimination for reasons of parentage or other conditions. Children and young persons should be protected from economic and social exploitation.

The International Covenant on Economic, Social, and Cultural Rights also enshrines in Article 13(1) the right of everyone to education and provides that primary education should be compulsory and free to all. States undertake to implement all the rights in the Covenant. This Covenant implicitly helped to raise the status of children in the resource allocation of the various countries.[32]

INTERNATIONAL COVENANT ON CIVIL AND POLITICAL RIGHTS 1966 (ICCPR)

The International Covenant on Civil and Political Rights 1966 complements the Economic, Social, and Cultural Covenant.[33] Children are implicitly entitled to benefit from all relevant rights contained in the Covenant and in addition there are specific provisions for children. Article 14(1) provides an express exception to the right to a hearing in public, when it is in the interests of the juveniles or where it concerns the guardianship of children.

Article 14(3)(f) provides that criminal proceedings should take account of juveniles' age and their 'desirability of promoting their rehabilitation'. The Covenant prohibits the imposition of death penalty for crimes

---

[31] See Kabuta, 'Protection of Children's Rights', *International Review of Criminal Policy*, United Nations, Vol. 39–40, 1989, No. 108.

[32] Geraldine Van Bueren, *The International Law on the Rights of the Child*, Martinus Nijhoff Publishers, Netherlands, 1995.

[33] See Henkin (ed.), The International Bill of Human Rights: The Covenant on Civil And Political Rights, 1981.

committed by persons under eighteen years of age.[34] The Covenant obliges states to separate accused juveniles from accused adults and bring them as speedily as possible for adjudication[35] and accord them treatment according to their age and legal status [ICCPR Art. 10 (3)].

The family is recognized as being the natural and fundamental unit of society and as such is entitled to state protection [ICCPR Art. 23]. Under the Covenant, states are obliged to respect the liberty of parents to ensure the religious and moral education of children in accordance with their beliefs and, in the event of a dissolution of the marriage, provision shall be made for the protection of any children [ICCPR Art. 18(4) and 24(4)]. In addition to these specific rights, the International Covenant on Civil and Political Rights incorporates a specific article on children [ICCPR Art. 24].

Regional Instruments for the Protection of Children

There are regional human rights instruments, for the protection of children, adopted by the* Council of Europe, the Organization of American States (OAS), and the Organization of African Unity (OAU).*

EUROPEAN CONVENTION ON HUMAN RIGHTS 1950

The Convention adopts the term 'everyone' and children have successfully brought cases either on their own behalf or as co-applicants with their parents. The Convention has thus been used as a valuable instrument for children. The Council of Europe has also adopted the European Social Charter 1961. The Charter contains a number of specific references to children. Part I enshrines the basic principle: *'Children and young persons have the right to special protection against the physical and moral hazards to which they are exposed.'*

Enforcement of International Instruments in India

The Government of India has ratified the Convention on the Rights of the Child on 12 November 1992.* It has also endorsed the twenty-seven survival and development goals for the year 2000 laid down by the World Summit for Children. Article 73 of the Constitution states: 'Subject to the provisions of this Constitution, the executive power of the Union shall extend to the matters with respect to which Parliament has power to make laws; and to the exercise of such rights, authority and jurisdiction as are exercisable by the Government of India by virtue of any treaty or agreement.' Article 253 of the Constitution states that 'Parliament has power to make any law for the

---

[34] UN Doc A/C 3/L 650. This was done at the initiative of Japan.
[35] This was a result of a proposal from Sri Lanka.

whole or any part of the territory of India for implementing any treaty, agreement to Convention with any other country or countries or any decision made at any international conference, association or other body.' Therefore, international conventions like CRC can be enforced in Indian courts without a statute. Any international convention consistent with the fundamental rights and in harmony with its spirit must be read into the provisions of the Constitution. Therefore, the provisions of the CRC in consonance with the fundamental rights can be enforced without a statute.

This was clearly laid down in the case of Mayanbhai Ishwarlal Patel v Union of India.[36] Again in the case of Vishaka v State of Rajasthan,[37] the Supreme Court reiterated the principle that in the absence of a domestic law the contents of international conventions and norms are relevant for the purpose of interpretation of the fundamental rights.

It is significant to note that with the exception of the UN Convention on the Rights of the Child 1989, there is no other child-centred approach and second, the Asia region, which has the highest proportion of the world's children, does not have any similar regional human rights or child rights instrument. All the countries have ratified the UN Convention on the Rights of the Child, subject to Reservations/Declarations.

Children and Courts

Rights are of limited value unless they can be asserted. One very significant structure of the legal system is represented by the courts. Courts are a body that is in authority to take decisions. Provisions in various laws, which are presently in practice, guide these decisions. Children in India can come in direct contact with the courts and the legal system in various contexts, for example, as offenders and witness to crimes. Also, family matters like divorce, separation, adoption, guardianship, etc., can bring a child to the courts. There are the ordinary civil and criminal courts based on the adversarial model. The system uses formal procedural justice to obtain binding decisions and remedies. The main laws that govern the criminal and civil justice systems include the Code of Civil Procedure 1908, the Indian Evidence Act 1872, the Indian Penal Code 1860, and the Code of Criminal Procedure 1973. Besides these ordinary courts and legal procedures, there are specialized courts. Two most commonly accessed courts by children are the juvenile courts or the Juvenile Justice Boards[38] and family courts.

[36] AIR 1969 SC 783.
[37] (1997) 6 SCC 241.
[38] Juvenile courts have been replaced by the Juvenile Justice Boards under the new Juvenile Justice (Care and Protection of Children) Act 2000 for dealing with children in conflict with law.

Conciliation, counselling and individualized treatment based on casework approach with expertise and inputs from law, psychiatry, and social work have been envisaged for these courts. Simplicity, informality, and flexibility have been attempted in these courts.

Children are unable by definition to petition the courts themselves, they have had to rely on the *parens patriae* role of the state. The courts have on several occasions responded to the needs of children through public interest litigation, especially in the areas of improvement of conditions of children in institutions, prisons, illegal confinement, treatment of physically and mentally disabled children, child labour, adoption, juvenile justice, prevention of trafficking of young girls, welfare of children of prostitutes, prohibition of corporal punishment in schools, and sex selection tests. Several of these issues were raised before the courts by social activists, journalists, or newspaper reports, or taken up *suo motu* by the courts. Some of the landmark decisions are:

M.C. Mehta v State of Tamil Nadu[39]
This judgment passed elaborate directions to stop child labour in hazardous occupations and processes.

Sanjay Suri v Delhi Administration[40]
The court ordered transfer of some guilty officers and laid down rules to protect children in jails.

Lakshmikant Pandey v Union of India[41]
These were a series of decisions in which the Supreme Court laid down directions for inter-country adoption of children.

Gaurav Jain v Union of India[42]
The Supreme Court held that segregating the children of prostitutes would not be in their interest.

Peoples Union for Democratic Rights (PUDR) v Union of India[43]
Employment in construction work was held to be hazardous for children.

Vishal Jeet v Union of India[44]
Several directions were issued to end sexual exploitation of children.

---

[39] AIR 1997 SC 699
[40] AIR 1986 SC 414
[41] AIR 1984 SC 469; AIR 1986 SC 272; AIR 1992 SC 118
[42] AIR 1990 SC 292
[43] AIR 1982 SC 1473
[44] AIR 1990 SC 1412

Dukhtar Jahan v Mohammed Farooq[45]
The Supreme Court asked the husband to pay maintenance to the child even though he had divorced the wife. The allegation of the husband that the child was illegitimate was rejected.

Sheela Barse v the Secretary, Children's Aid Society & Ors[46]
The petition was filed in public interest with regard to improper functioning of childcare institutions in Mumbai. The Supreme Court directed that in no case should a child be kept in jail and a central law must be enacted to bring uniformity in juvenile justice system.

Delhi Domestic Working Women's Forum v Union of India & Ors[47]
The Supreme Court directed the setting up of the Criminal Injuries Compensation Board to award compensation to rape victims.

Sarita Sharma v Sunita Sharma[48]
The court helt that in the issue relating to custody of children, paramount consideration should be given to the welfare of the children.

Shantistar Builders v Narayan Khimlal Totame[49]
The case dealt with the concept of suitable accommodation for a child.

Kishen Pattnayak v State of Orissa[50]
Poor people were forced to sell children to buy food. The Orissa government was compelled to take several welfare actions.

Unnikrishnan J.P. & Others v State of Andhra Pradesh[51]
The court held that the right to education is implicit in the right to life.

The epistolary jurisdiction of the court, by which the Supreme Court entertains writs even on the basis of letters, has increased the access to courts. By liberalizing the principles of locus standi, the court has enabled social activists, journalists, academicians, lawyers, and child welfare organizations to approach the highest court for redressal of injustice to children. During the past one decade or so, affirmative action has been taken by the Supreme

---

[45] AIR 1987 SC 1049
[46] AIR 1987 SC 656
[47] (1995)1 SCC 14
[48] (2000)3 SCC 14
[49] AIR 1990 SC 630
[50] AIR 1989 SC 677
[51] AIR 1993 SC 2178

Court and the High Courts to protect children's rights. There have been persistent efforts on the part of jurists and social activists to make law and legal system a tool for social change.

Recently, in a case of an 'unwanted child' being born due to the doctor's negligence in performing the sterilization operation, the Supreme Court passed a judgment upholding that the woman was entitled to claim damages for bringing up the child. The Delhi High Court upheld the death sentence on a couple for murdering a one-and-a-half-year-old girl during a witchcraft ritual. In another significant judgment, the Supreme Court held that the children of a Hindu father, born out of his illegal second marriage, were entitled to equal share in the property and assets left behind by him.

From the decisions of the courts it is significant that the child's interests are primarily the perceptions of the adults and in cases of family disputes, the competing adult claimants. The Convention on the Rights of the Child lays down two principles of interpretation in international law, namely, the best interests of the child and the evolving capacities of the child. The manner of application of the best interests principle[52] has transformed it from the traditional concept of welfarism. This is an umbrella provision for actions concerning children. The scope has been widened much beyond the custody area alone. Where judicial discretion is exercised, an understanding of the framework of rights can stimulate dynamic interpretations of law that will give the child access to justice through the court system and other methods of dispute settlement.[53] The courts in India have ensured the implementation of progressive laws and the interpretation of restrictive laws in the best interest of the child. The courts in public interest litigation including *suo motu* petitions and in adversarial litigation have passed orders in the interest of the child.

Government Programmes and Schemes

There are several government documents, campaigns, and schemes that reaffirm the Government of India's commitment to the cause of children. Some of these programmes and schemes are also in cooperation with the

---

[52] Article 3 of the United Nations Convention on the Rights of the Child 1989 states that 'In all actions concerning children, whether undertaken by public or private social welfare institutions, courts of law, administrative authorities or legislative bodies, the best interests of the child shall be a primary consideration.'

[53] Savitri Goonesekere, 'Children and justice integrating international standards into the national context', *The Child and the Law*, Papers from the International Conference on Shaping the Future by Law Children, Environment and Human Health, UNICEF, New Delhi, 1994.

NGOs. These programmes and schemes focus on child labour, non-institutional services, health, nutrition, education, street children, children in institutions, child prostitutes, and disabled children. The Government of India is implementing about 120 schemes and programmes for the welfare and development of children and women through more than thirteen ministries and departments.[54] These schemes include: the Reproductive and Child Health Programme for providing integrated quality health to women and children and the Integrated Child Development Services programme which delivers health, nutrition, and pre-school services through a single window. Two schemes under the latter programme are detailed below:

Integrated Child Development Services (ICDS)

This programme is a vehicle for achieving major nutrition, health, and education goals to nearly twenty-eight million children throughout the country (since 1975). A network of *Anganwadi* centres,[55] literally courtyard play centres, provide basic health, nutrition, and early childhood care and development services to address the interrelated needs of children below the age of six, adolescent girls, and expectant and nursing mothers from the disadvantaged communities.

National Initiative for Child Protection (NICP)

This is a campaign initiated by the Ministry of Social Justice and Empowerment through the National Institute of Social Defence (NISD) and Childline India Foundation (CIF). NICP aims at building partnerships with the allied systems such as the police, the health care system, the judicial system, the juvenile justice system, the education system, the transport system, the labour department, the media, the department of telecommunications, the corporate sector, social workers, and elected representatives. NICP hopes to achieve this by using advocacy and creating awareness and by involving children in making decisions that will directly affect their lives.

A point of significant concern is that there are various different ministries dealing with the issues of children.

Interventions and Strategies by Non-Governmental Organizations (NGOs)

NGOs have played a significant role and have been in the forefront providing services to children. There has been a shift from the welfare approach to thrust on development and empowerment in the interventions for

---

[54] India Report on the World Summit for Children 2000, Department of Women and Child Development, Ministry of Human Resource Development, Government of India.

[55] Centres for delivering the ICDS services to women and children.

children. The NGOs have developed several strategies based on child rights perspective to intervene on behalf of children and protect their rights. Many NGOs and grass-roots organizations have intervened with various approaches. Some of the interventions have been in the following kinds of activities:

- Research and documentation
- Advocacy of all levels to bring about structural and policy changes
- Preparing alternative reports on status of child rights
- Promoting networking and coordination among NGOs to jointly advocate on issues which affect the rights of the child
- Awareness building
- Mobilization of public opinion
- Intervening in special cases of violations
- Providing a platform for expression of children's concerns
- Direct action like raids and liberation of children in servitude
- Building pressure groups
- Capacity building (building in the necessary skills, structures, attitudes, and knowledge) required to work better
- Lobbying with the government to review existing schemes towards being more child-oriented
- Running field action projects to reach out to children
- Direct work with children and their communities.

Role of International Organizations

Several international organizations like UNICEF (United Nations Children's Fund), UNDP (United Nations Development Programme), UNIFEM (United Nations Development Fund for Women), WHO (World Health Organization), ILO (International Labour Organization), FAO (Food and Agriculture Organization), UNESCO (United Nations Educational, Scientific, and Cultural Organization), UNFPA (United Nations Fund for Population Activities), CARE (Cooperative for Assistance and Relief Everywhere), Save the Children, Canada, and the IBRD (International Bank for Reconstruction and Development) are actively involved in the development and protection of child rights. Some other important agencies, including Human Rights Watch, Defence for Children International (DCI), International Society for the Prevention of Child Abuse and Neglect (ISPCAN), and End Child Prostitution in Asian Tourism (ECPAT), work towards promoting the rights of the child.

Challenges Ahead . . .

Like many developing countries, India faces problems of infant mortality, child marriage, maternal mortality, and the phenomena of child widows, sex tourism, and child trafficking even across national borders for prostitution, child abuse, and child labour. There are several challenges ahead. Child marriages are still on in spite of the Child Marriage Restraint Act 1928. There is abuse and exploitation of children through international trafficking, through sex tourism, and even as instruments of amusement. The Act itself is very weak and dilatory. Child marriages are valid even though there is a prescribed minimum age of marriage. The procedures to prevent child marriages are very cumbersome and time consuming. Illiteracy and orthodoxy of the people have proved to be other stumbling blocks. There is a need for a uniform law of adoption so that the children of all religious communities can be adopted. Child sexual abuse needs a sensitive law. The disabled child needs special protection. Problems of street children need to be tackled. HIV/AIDS, drug abuse, and environmental concerns place a huge obstacle in the way of children's rights to survival and development.

Liberalization has also aggravated emergency situations in rural and urban areas, which disrupt the major support systems of children such as family and school, exposing them to several vulnerabilities. Globalization has also led to expansion of international organized crime, enlarging the scope for exploitation of children.[56] Children are also victims of war, terrorism, poverty trap, environmental disasters, displacement due to development, and globalization.

Of all the demographic groups, the girl child is probably the most socially disadvantaged. At every stage of her life cycle—from conception to adulthood—she is especially vulnerable to human rights abuses. In India, where every study points out the low utilization of health services, low coverage of antenatal and post-natal care, and low levels of institutional deliveries, the utilization of the sophisticated modern technology for sex detection of the foetus on a large scale is a big surprise and a matter of concern. The Census 2001 has revealed some interesting and worrying features with regard to sex ratios, which calls for some explanation. For example, the overall improvement in sex ratio in favour of females may be explained by the fact that female death rates have become lower than the male death rates. But the sex ratio at birth (SRB) becoming more favourable to males has, however, influenced the overall sex ratios in Punjab and Haryana, especially with the adverse sex ratio at birth pointing towards rampant practice of female foeticide along with a certain amount of infanticide in these two states. The fact that both Uttar Pradesh and Uttaranchal have registered an improvement in overall

---

[56] Murli Desai, Child Protection Current Status and Recommendations of Strategies for the India Country Programme for 2003–2007: A Consultancy Report for UNICEF India Country Office, New Delhi, December 2001.

sex ratio between 1991 and 2001, but with the child sex ratio declining sharply requires a detailed probing. Interestingly, all the states that have shown large declines in child sex ratio between 1991 and 2001—Punjab, Haryana, Himachal Pradesh, Gujarat, Maharashtra, Chandigarh, and Delhi—are economically well developed and have recorded a fairly high literacy rate.[57]

A child-focused culture has to be developed. The legal system should interpret the laws in the context of the rights and standards given in the CRC. This will give the child access to justice through the court system. There has to be child-centred focus in legal proceedings. All the children's legislations need to be reviewed in the context of CRC and its standards and there has to be linkages between them. The Indian legal system has to evolve a great deal for securing the rights of the child and providing justice to the child.

Some initiatives have been taken. The Draft National Policy and Charter for Children 2001 states that its intent is to remove the structural causes related to the issues affecting children's rights in the wider societal context and to awaken the conscience of the community to protect children from violation of their rights, while strengthening the family, society, and above all, the nation. The Children's Code Bill 2000 (Draft) has been formulated by the Government of India to give effect to the Convention on the Rights of the Child and to provide for the constitution of national and state commissions for children for better protection and enforcement of the rights of children, and to do all such things as are necessary to promote and preserve the general all-round development, safety, and welfare of children. The 172 Law Commission Report has recommended laws to protect children from sexual abuse. The ninety-third Constitutional Amendment Bill has been recently passed by the Indian Parliament.[58] This amendment covers the age group of children between six and fourteen years and makes it a fundamental duty the state to provide free and compulsory education to all children in the age group of 6–14 years. Legislation will now have to be made to enforce this amendment. The infrastructure is yet to be provided to make this amendment work, though it has made it a fundamental duty of parents to send their children to school. The Juvenile Justice (Care and Protection of Children) Act 2000 provides for non-institutional services.

Legal reform alone cannot bring justice to the child. Inter-agency structures and systems need to be worked out laying great emphasis on prevention. Undoubtedly, the most effective prevention measure is awareness of

---

[57] Mahendra K. Premi, 'The Missing Girl Child', *Economical and Political Weekly*, 26 May 2001.

[58] After Article 21, a new Article 21A has been inserted.

such possible abuse and how to deal with it amongst the various service providers—the doctors, teachers, lawyers, judges, police, volunteers, parents, trade unions, and social workers—so that they can significantly reduce the risk of abuse, if it does occur, by responding appropriately. Rights are of limited value unless they can be effectively asserted. Advocacy and lobbying in support of proposals for legal reform will also be necessary. Non-governmental organizations have assumed a significant role and they perform crucial tasks in the struggle for the realization of the rights of the child—a struggle in which law and rights prove to be important resources.

Resource allocation for legislative and regulatory mechanisms to ensure the proper delivery of services is as much part of the legal reform as law. The development of the human person is the essence of development. If rights of the child are to be taken seriously, they must include rights to resource allocation for effective programmes on the education and cultural development of the child. Such resource allocation should be accompanied by the creation of participatory delivery mechanisms for the effective utilization of such resources through development processes which are humane and which foster self-reliance, dignity, and participation. The child's right to development is crucial, both to safeguard the right to a future as well as the rights of future children.[59]

This will require creative interaction between judges, lawyers, lawmakers, policy planners, law enforcers, intellectuals, government officials, social work groups, child activists, children's organizations, and child victims. It is also essential that issues relating to the rights of the child in the Third World have to be viewed not in isolation but within the context of development. And it is essential that the child is placed high on the political agenda of development.

These challenges have to be rapidly addressed. And above all, the core value of the universal legal principle that policies be made, structures and processes be established, and actions be taken that are always and invariably in the best interests of the child should be followed. The struggle for the realization of the rights of the child is indeed going to be a long journey.

---

[59] Clarence Dias, 'The Child in the Developing World: Making Rights a Reality', Report of a Seminar on Rights of the Child, National Law School of India University, Bangalore, 1990.

2

Right to Family Environment: Adoption and Other Non-Institutional Services

Adoption in History, Mythology, and Religion[1]

Adoption is the act of establishing a person as parent to one who is not in fact or in law his child. Thus adoption signifies the means by which a status or legal relationship of parent and child between persons who are not so related by nature is established or created.[2] The very purpose of any adoption proceedings is to effect this new status of relationship. As a result of a decree of adoption, the child, to all intents and purposes, becomes the child of the adoptive parent. Adoption is also defined as a process by which people take a child who was not born to them and raise him or her as a member of their family.[3]

Adoption is so widely recognized that it can be characterized as an almost worldwide institution with historical roots traceable into antiquity. Mythology also expresses the deepest needs of adoptive parent to make the adopted child the same as if it were born to them. As quoted in James Frazer's *Golden Bough*, Diodorus Siculus describes Hera adopting Hercules:

The Goddess got into bed and clasping the burly hero to her bosom, pushed him through her robes and let him fall to the ground in imitation of real birth.[4]

Primitive tribes continue this practice to the present time.[5]

---

[1] Asha Bajpai, *Adoption Law and Justice to the Child*, National Law School of India University, Bangalore, India, 1996

[2] Britannica Inc., *The New Encyclopaedia Britannica*, Vol. I, Fifteenth Edition, 1991, p. 105.

[3] World Book Inc., *The World Book Encyclopedia*. Chicago, Illinois, 1988, Vol. I, p. 66.

[4] T.G. Frazer, *The Golden Bough*, New York: Macmillan, 1922.

[5] S.B. Presser, *The Historical Background of the American Law of Adoption*, Journal of Family law, II, 443–516, 1972.

Four thousand years ago, his/her tongue would be cut out if an adoptee dared to openly say that he/she was not born to his/her parents. And if he/she went further in search of his/her biological family he/she would be blinded in punishment. The Code of Hammurabi, a part of Babylonian Law, was clear in its strictures governing adoption:

If a man takes a child in his name, adopts and rears him as a son, then the grown-up son may not be demanded back. If a man adopts a child as his son after he has taken him, he transgresses against his foster-father, that adopted son shall return to the house of his own father.[6]

The meaning of the blood tie was so strong that the only acceptable method of initiating non-relatives was to make them 'artificially blood relatives' by adoption. Adoption into a group, therefore, meant complete severance from one's original family or group with the promise of allegiance and total loyalty to the new family. To seek one's origins or to question one's true identity was seen then as dangerous, ungrateful, and disloyal.[7]

The Egyptians and the Hebrews knew of adoption and chronicled the most famous example of all times. The daughter of the Pharaoh adopted a foundling as a son and called him Moses. And it was the young adult Moses who returned to 'his people', the Jews, and led them out of their Egyptian bondage to their homeland. This was where he felt he truly belonged.[8]

Adoption in Hindu Mythology

Hindu mythology contains several 'visions' concerning adoption. Anthropologically and historically speaking, they represent attitudes and value systems of human history. They may not be adoptions but they represent the 'concept of adoption', i.e. of bringing up someone else's child as one's own.

The myth of Shakuntala, found originally in the *Mahabharata* and later on artistically changed to suit the needs of Kalidasa, is among the most popular in this genre. The following is the conversation between Shakuntala and King Dushyant who falls in love with her:

Who art thou a fairest one? The bright-eyed one answered: 'I am the daughter of the holy high-souled Kanwa.' Said the king, 'But Kanwa is chaste and celibate, nor can he have broken his rigid vow. How come is it that thou were the daughter of such a one?'

---

[6] I. Kocourek, and P. Wigmore, *Evaluation of Law, Sources of Ancient and Primitive Laws*, Encyclopaedia Britannica, Vol. II, 1947, p. 135.

[7] L.A. Huard, 'The Law of Adoption, Ancient and Modern', *Vanderbilt Law Review*, 1956, 9.743–63.

[8] Ibid.

Then the maiden, who was Shakuntala, narrated to the king sage the secret of her birth. She revealed that her real sire was Vishwamitra, the holy sage who had been a Kshatriya and was made a Brahmin in reward for his austerities. It was said that Indra became alarmed at his growing power. So Indra commanded Menaka, the beautiful *apsara*, to disturb the meditation of the holy sage. . . . In time Menaka became the mother of a baby girl whom she left in the forest. Now the forest was full of lions and tigers, but a large bird protected her from harm. . . . Then Kanwa found and took pity on the child. He said: 'she will be mine, my own daughter'.[9]

The myth of Shakuntla assumes importance because it may be regarded as a case of female adoption, which was not much in favour in later times. It can be considered as a parable of humanity and fellow feeling.

Another myth relates to the origin of Agni and is found in a hymn from the Vedas. Matariyan brought Agni to Bhrigu as a gift, precious like wealth. Since this hymn relates to the *Rig Veda*, it is among the earliest sources in which the myth of miraculous origin is found. Here 'adoption' itself is an inference, strongly borne out by the reference to double birth. First is the birth as god, and second is the fact of Bhrigu establishing him among the clan of Ayu.

A myth relates to the birth of the mother of the *Pandavas*, Kunti, (referred to as Pritha). King Pandu had two wives, Pritha and Madri. Pritha was of celestial origin, for her mother was a nymph and her brother (Vasudeva) was the father of Krishna. When she was a baby she had been 'adopted' by the Raja of Shuranyena, whose kingdom was among the Vindhya mountains. She was of pious heart and always showed reverence to holy men. The myth of Karna, found in the Mahabharata, is a tale of 'adoption' and the consequent duties of a son. A classic example of foster care is that of Lord Krishna who was the son of Devaki but was brought up by Yashoda.

The object of adoption was mainly to secure performance of funeral rites and to preserve the continuance of one's lineage.[10] A *Dattak Homam* made the relationship valid and gave full rights to name and inheritance to the son.[11] It has to be noted that adoption was a parent-oriented practice that mostly took place between families whereby the natural parents physically gave the child in adoption to the adopting couple, usually some kith or kin. Boys were given in adoption and a female could not take a child in adoption

---

[9] Mackenzie A. Donald (1985). *India—Myth and Legend*, London: Mystic Press, p. 159.
[10] *Inder Singh v Kartar Singh*, AIR 1966 Punj 258.
[11] Manu, Chapter IX, 16.

excepting a widow who could adopt a boy in the name of her late husband.[12] Adoption was a custom applicable to the Hindus. Christians, Muslims, Jews, and Parsis were out of its purview, though the Church accepted adoption as part of its canon law and gave the adopted child the full status of a biological child. On 21 December 1956, this custom of adoption among the Hindus was given a legal status through the enactment of the Hindu Adoption and Maintenance Act 1956.

Adoption and Parsis

The laws of the ancient Zoroastrians are in the twenty-one *nasks* or holy books that were part of the Avesta.[13] During the *Kirnian* period[14] childlessness was considered the greatest calamity for a couple.

The Prophet sanctified childhood. Ahura Mazda holds the father of a family far above him who is childless. Sons were valued more than daughters as they were permanent economic assets and they commemorated the departed ones of their family. They also carried on the family line and perpetuated the father's name. A son could be adopted in case a man had none born to him.[15]

Chapter IX[16] of the *Digest of a Thousand Points of Law* deals with adoption of children and states that an instance of the concern of the ancient Iranians to see that no father neglected his natural duties towards his child or palmed them off on another individual, is to be seen in the law which allows a father to give his only minor child in adoption to some person. The father could appoint a guardian over his minor child, apparently to safeguard his interests in case of his death, but he could withdraw such guardianship whenever he found a proper reason for doing so.

This digest also mentions about 'partial adoptions'. It has been pointed out that children were adopted not always because the adoptive parents had none of their own, for people having legitimate living children were also allowed to adopt children. This probably happened owing to people's desire to admit into their family more intelligent, more desirable, or more useful persons. From a review of the ancient texts, the concept of adoption occupies a very important place in the religion of fire worshippers. The objective appears to be purely religious, i.e. to deliver the father to the next world.

---

[12] This principle is responsible for the doctrine of relation back.
[13] Sohrab Jamshedjee Bulsara, *The Laws of the Ancient Persians*, 1937, p. 38.
[14] 2000 BC–700 BC.
[15] Manekaji Nussurwanji Dhall, *Zoroastrian Civilisation*, 1992, p. 38.
[16] Bulsara Sohrab Jamshedjee, *The Laws of the Ancient Persians* as in the Digest of A Thousand Points of Law, Hosing Anklshwaria, Mumbai, 1937, IX, pp. 56–7.

There is no legislation for the adoption of children by Parsis in India. The Parsis today recognize under their custom adoption in the forms of *Palukaputra* and *Dharamaputra*. The *Palukaputra* form of adoption is purely contractual and is determined at the option of either of the parties. A son or daughter can be adopted and created as their own and can be given certain property, i.e. rights of inheritance or of performing religious ceremonies.[17]

When the Adoption of Children Bill 1980 was introduced in Parliament, some members of the Parsi Zoroastrian community formed a special committee, known as the Bombay Zoroastrian Jashan Committee, which declared that a very large part of their community was against the application of the Bill to the Parsis in India, and they wanted the Parsi community to be exempted from the application of this bill.

Some members of the Parsi community who favoured this Bill said that the Zoroastrian religion enjoins conversion. They quoted the statement of Justice Davar in his judgment.[18] Today, there appears a vast change among the Zoroastrian followers in India. It is now believed by many that any person, Zoroastrian or otherwise, is sent to heaven or hell solely on the basis of the balance of good deeds and bad deeds. Only Ahura Mazda decides the relative weights attached to the deeds committed. No funeral rites and ceremonies can affect the final judgment. Therefore, it is not absolutely necessary for a person to have a son or a descendant to perform his religious ceremonies.

In practice it appears that adoption among Parsis is a question of personal preference. Nowadays, usually a childless couple brings up the child of some relative. When it comes to distribution of property, a person's last words are usually respected. There are instances when certain priests have performed *Navjot* ceremony on children whose only one parent is a Parsi.

The concept of adoption, i.e. looking after the welfare of someone else's child can thus be regarded as prevalent among Parsis. Regarding providing such a child's security, many are of the view that a will made in his favour may prove sufficient.

Adoption and Muslims

Islam emerged in Arabia when the Iranian civilization was breathing its last. Islam gave the concept that the Almighty, the Creator of the universe, was supreme and man was his deputy on earth.

---

[17] Paras Diwan, *Indian Personal Law II, Law of Adoption, Minority and Guardianship and Custody*, Wadhwa and Co., Allahabad, India, 1993, 2nd Edition, p. 4.
[18] (1909) Bom LR 95.

There is a story that Zaid was Prophet Mohammed's freedman and adopted son. Prophet Mohammed had seen and admired Zaid's wife Zainab and her husband at once offered to divorce her. Prophet Mohammed's marriage with Zainab occasioned much scandal among his contemporaries.[19]

During the time when this event took place, the Arabs used to consider their adopted children in the same light as real children of their body. In *Surat*[20] XXXIII (Medinah) of the Koran in the chapter on confederates, Prophet Mohammed forbade this practice and thus legalized his marriage with Zainab, the divorced wife of his freedman Zaid who was also his adopted son.

There are certain Koranic injunctions relating to orphans:[21] *Hedaya*[22] contains very elaborate instructions for the faithful. The books of the *Hedaya* contain the laws relating to the rights of destitute children. *Lakeet*, in its primitive sense, signifies anything lifted from the ground: the term is chiefly used to denote an infant abandoned by some person on the highway.

It would, therefore, clearly appear that adoption in Islam would be permissible only if:

- The true identity of the child is disclosed to him where it is known.
- The rights of inheritance of the natural heirs are not disturbed.

To provide security to the adopted child one of the following methods or a combination of them could be adopted:

- Provide *kafala* (maintenance) for the child.
- Make a gift (always permissible under Muslim law) in favour of the child.[23]
- Bequeath up to one-third of the property in his favour[24] (also permissible under Muslim law).

---

[19] The Holy Koran, revised and edited by the Presidency of Islamic Researchers, IFTA, Call of Guidance, 123.
[20] Verse.
[21] K.A. Majid (compiled), *Quaranic Injunctions Do and Do Not: The Code of Salvation*, extracts from the translation of A. Yusuf Ali, Do and Don't Publishers, North Nizamabad, Karanchi, Pakistan, 1990, p. 21.
[22] *Hedaya* (guide) was translated from the original Arabic by four Maulvis or Mohammedan lawyers and from Persian into English by Charles Hamilton by order of Warren Hastings when he was Governor General of India.
[23] Under Mohammedan law a testamentary disposition is limited to one-third of the net estate.
[24] A Mohammedan cannot by will dispose of more than one-third of the surplus of his State after payment of funeral expenses and debts. Bequests in excess of the legal third

Today, some Muslims do adopt children in India but since there is no law[25] to make their adoption legal, the adoption remains informal. In some Islamic countries such as Pakistan, Iran, Tunisia, and even some Arabic countries, substantial changes have been made in personal laws. Therefore, an attempt could be made again in India in the cause of justice to the destitute and orphaned child or *lakeet*s.

Adoption and Christians

Christians have not had any particular opposition to adoption. The very religion seems to have the 'concept of adoption' deeply embedded in it. If you look into the whole scheme of the Bible there are several instances of adoption. The very birth of Jesus Christ took place in the following way.[26] It is said that when his mother Mary had been betrothed to Joseph before they came together, she was found to be with the child of the Holy Spirit, and her husband Joseph being a just man, unwilling to put her 'to shame', resolved to divorce her quietly. But as he considered this, an angel of the Lord appeared to him in a dream saying. 'Joseph, Son of David, do not fear to take Mary, your wife for that which is conceived in her is of the Holy Spirit. She will bear a son and you shall call his name Jesus for he will save his people from their sins.' The reference to adoption in the canon law[27] of the Christians is in C-689 C3 which says that an adopted child can be baptized in the church and C-110 which says that children who are adopted in accordance with the civil laws are to be considered the children of that person or persons who have adopted them.

Therefore, the canon law does not bar or prohibit Christians from adopting a child. But since there is no law on adoption for Christians in India, they have to resort to the Guardians and Wards Act 1890. The guardian has a

---

cannot take effect unless the heirs consent thereto after the death of testator. Law allows a man to give away the whole of his property during his lifetime but only one-third of it can be bequeathed by will.

[25] The Joint Committee of the Parliament introduced the Indian Adoption Bill in the Rajya Sabha in 1976. This Bill was opposed by the Muslims on the ground that adoption was against the Koran. Another Bill was introduced in the Lok Sabha on 16 December 1980. This Bill exempted Muslims from its operation. This is Section 3(1) of 'The Adoption of Children Bill 1980: No adoption order shall be made in respect of a Muslim child or for adoption by a Muslim of any child, whether a Muslim or not, under this Act'. This Bill also lapsed when Parliament was dissolved in 1984.

[26] Mathew 1:18–23, The New Testament.

[27] The word 'canon' in its proper sense means a 'measuring rod'. But here it may be defined as the organized body of laws by which the pastoral ministry of the Church is guided and structures of church defined.

fiduciary relationship with the child and this relationship would cease to exist on the death of the guardian, the marriage of the minor, or when the minor becomes a major.

A non-governmental organization had come up with a bill on adoption known as the Christian Adoption Bill 1988. The main features of this bill were the following:
- Adoption can be of children of either sex.
- Adoption should be without court intervention.
- Single males could also adopt; if adopting a girl, the age difference should be twenty-one years. The girl should not have completed the age of fifteen years.

The Present Status of Adoption

The traditional approach for adoption was institutionalization of destitute, neglected, marginalized children and children in especially difficult circumstances. This approach resulted in the child being separated from the family environment. The trend today is towards non-institutional services. During the last few decades the significant role that a family plays in a child's nurture and his/her physical, psychological, mental, and social growth and development has been increasingly realized. The non-institutional approach to children in crisis situation is upheld globally as it meets the child's right to a family.[28] Every child has a right to a family. This can be achieved by strengthening the family as a unit, by providing counselling and support services. When the child's own family cannot look after him/her, substitute family-based care should be arranged. The final objective is towards deinstitutionalization of the child. Some of the common family-based non-institutional services are, adoption, foster care, and sponsorship programmes.

The concept and practice of adoption in India have changed significantly from the past. Adoptions in the earlier times were 'parent-centred'—the needs of the parents being the primary consideration. The practice was to adopt children from within the family or kinship group. Beginning from the 1960s changes have taken place at the social, legal and practice levels of adoption. The traditional practice of institutional care being offered to an increasing number of orphaned, destitute children was replaced by non-institutional approaches of finding family-based alternatives. Adoption is considered the best alternative for children deprived of biological families. The practice of placing unrelated children in adoption through agency

---

[28] Article 9 of the United Nations Convention on the Rights of the Child states that the child should be ideally brought up in a family environment that is secure, nurturing, and protects its rights.

intervention began in the early seventies. National and international instruments influenced this change, namely the National Policy for Children 1974, the United Nations Declaration on the Rights of the Child 1959, and most significantly, the United Nations Convention on the Rights of the Child 1989. Article 20 of the UNCRC states that children deprived of family environment be provided with alternative family care or institutional placement. The focus of adoption has now clearly shifted from the needs of parents to the rights of a child to a family.

Of the several million homeless children only a few find homes through in-country and inter-country adoption, as the data presented in Tables 2.1 and 2.2 indicate.

Foster care provides temporary substitute care for children. It is different from adoption where the child severs all ties with his own natural parents. In foster care, the child is placed in another family for a short or extended period of time depending on the circumstances. The child's own parents usually visit regularly and eventually after the rehabilitation the child may return home. When the family is undergoing a temporary crisis (like the death of a parent or sudden illness), children experience a lot of stress and tension. They may need to be removed from their natural home to prevent their neglect. These children can be placed in foster families till the crisis is over. Unwed mothers, and single parents can also be helped through foster care. Services like foster care, though family-based, can be effectively implemented even while faced with large-scale natural calamities like earthquake or cyclone. The foster care scheme must provide adequate financial support to the foster family in order to care for the child as well as support to the natural parents towards rehabilitation so that they may take the child back, when possible.

Table 2.1: Estimated number of adoptions through recognized agencies in India (1996–2000)

Year	In-country adoptions	Inter-country adoption	Total
1996	1623	990	2613
1997	1330	1026	2356
1998	1746	1406	3152
1999	1558	1293	2851
2000	1870	1364	3234

Source: Central Adoption Resource Agency (CARA), Ministry of Social Justice & Empowerment, Govt. of India.

Table 2.2: State-wise data (Inter-country Adoptions) (1 January to 31 December 2000)

S. No.	State	Male	Female	Total
1.	Andhra Pradesh	34	183	217
2.	Delhi	42	174	216
3.	Goa	1	1	2
4.	Gujarat	10	17	27
5.	Haryana	0	0	0
6.	Karnataka	17	43	60
7.	Kerala	18	23	41
8.	Maharashtra	200	317	517
9.	Orissa	6	30	36
10.	Pondicherry	1	2	3
11.	Tamil Nadu	13	33	46
12.	Uttar Pradesh	2	8	10
13.	West Bengal*	n.a.	n.a.	162*
14.	Special Needs Children	n.a.	n.a.	27
	Total	344	831	1364*

*This includes NRI and special needs children.

Source: Central Adoption Resource Agency (CARA), Ministry of Social Justice & Empowerment, Govt. of India.

Sponsorship provides supplementary support to families who are unable to meet educational and other needs of their children. The sponsorship assistance enables the family to send the child to school, provide medical aid, and at the same time remain in touch with the family of birth.

Indian Adoption Laws

The laws concerning adoption and guardianship of children in vogue in India are the following:

Hindu Adoption and Maintenance Act 1956 (HAMA)

It is the only statute in force governing adoption of children and its ambit is confined to Hindus in India. [Sec. 2 of The Hindu Adoption and Maintenance Act 1956 defines who are considered Hindus for the application of this act].[29] There is a legal vacuum as regards adoption by or of other communities in India.

[29] The Hindu Adoption and Maintenance Act 1956 Section 2.

The Juvenile Justice (Care & Protection) of Children Act 2000 (JJA 2000)

The JJ Act 2000 contains provisions relating to rehabilation and social integration of children (Chapter IV). It provides that the rehabilitation and social integration of a child shall begin during the stay of the child in a children's home or special home by adoption, foster care, sponsorship, and sending the child to after-care organization.

The Guardians and Wards Act 1890 (GWA)

This Act is indirectly invoked by other communities also to become guardians of children during minority. The statute does not deal with adoption as such but mainly with guardianship, and is to be read along with the respective personal laws, or as ancillary/corollary to the latter. It may be indirectly invoked, in certain cases, to confer legal guardianship of children during their minority. But the process is not equivalent to adoption; it would only consider the child as the ward.

The Hindu Minority and Guardianship Act 1956 (HMGA)

This Act reforms and codifies the Hindu law relating to guardianship of minors.

The Hindu Succession Act 1955 (HSA) and the Indian Succession Act 1925 (ISA)

These two Acts govern succession and inheritance rights.

Basic Features of Laws Relating to Adoption

Some of the basic features of these laws relating to adoption are:

- The HAMA drastically amended the pristine law of adoptions among Hindus, and unified several forms of adoption which prevailed earlier like *Dattaka, Kritrima*, etc.,[30] into a single form.
- Under the HAMA, in-country adoption is even now a private act between the natural and the adoptive parents, not requiring scrutiny or permission of the court except when a person other than the natural guardian is giving the child in adoption.[31]
- A married man, a widow, a widower, a single woman, or a divorced or a deserted woman has the capacity to adopt, if they are Hindus [HAMA 1956 Section 8].

---

[30] For the forms of adoption under ancient law, see 'Adoption in History, Mythology and Religion' at the beginning of this chapter.

[31] HAMA 1956, Section 9: Persons capable of giving in adoption.

- The father has a prior right to give in adoption but he can do so only with the consent of his wife, i.e. the mother of the child [HAMA 1956 Section 7]. An adoption made without her consent is void.[32] The mother may give the child in adoption if the father is dead or has completely and finally renounced the world or has ceased to be a Hindu.
- Both sons as well as daughters can be adopted.[33] Any Hindu child, whether relative or not of the adoptive parent can now be adopted. Sister's son, daughter's son, or son of any woman whose mother the adopter cannot marry in her maiden state can also be taken in adoption.[34] Adoption of any child, eldest child, youngest child, or middle child is valid. Legitimate as well as illegitimate children, whom their parents have abandoned or whose parentage is not known, can now be adopted. Caste or sub-caste of the child is no bar; the only condition is that the child should be a Hindu. Adoption of physically and mentally disabled children is also valid.
- No Hindu male or female can adopt a son if he or she already has a Hindu son, son's son, or son's son's son living at the time of adoption. Similarly, he or she has no right to adopt a female child if he or she has a Hindu daughter or son's daughter living at the time of adoption (Section 11, HAMA).
- The HAMA abrogates all pre-Act customs and usages pertaining to adoption for which provision has been made in the Act.[35] Custom is preserved in the following two areas:
  - A married child can be adopted, if custom permits such an adoption, and
  - A child of fifteen years or above can be adopted if custom permits such an adoption.
- To prevent sexual abuse, the HAMA provides that there shall be an age difference of twenty-one years between the adoptive parents and the adopted child whenever they are of opposite sex (Section 11, HAMA).
- All adoptions under the HAMA are secular, so much so that even a

[32] The consent is waived only in cases where the mother has completely and finally renounced the world or has ceased to be a Hindu or, has been declared by a court of competent jurisdiction to be of unsound mind.

[33] *Chettiar v Chettiar* (1978), 3 SCC 55.

[34] The *Virudha Sambandha* rule which prohibited a man from taking a child, whose mother he could not have married in her maiden state such as daughter's child, sister's child, etc., is no more valid.

[35] HAMA 1956, Section 4: Overriding effect of the Act, *Kartar Singh v Surjan Singh*, (1974) 2 SCC 359.

religious ceremony like *Dattaka Homa* is not necessary. The child to be adopted must actually be given and taken in adoption by the parents or the guardians concerned—or under their authority—with the intent to transfer the child from the family of its birth (or in case of an abandoned child whose parentage is not known from the place or family where it has been brought up) to the family of its adoption. The performance of the ceremony of giving and taking can be delegated to any person but the power or right to give and take a child in adoption cannot be delegated (Section 11, HAMA).

- The adopted child is deemed to be the child of the adopter for all purposes and is in the same position, for all intents and purposes, as that of a natural born child, having the same privileges and obligations in the adoptive family.[36] The adopted child has the right of collateral succession both on his adoptive mother's side and adoptive father's side. All persons are entitled to succeed him as if he is a natural born child of that family and the Hindu Succession Act 1955 will be applicable. He can claim maintenance against his adoptive parents and he is also liable to maintain all those persons whom a natural child has an obligation to maintain (Section 12, HAMA).
- If in the natural family some property was vested in the child before adoption that will remain vested in him and he cannot be divested of it just because he has gone to another family on adoption. It has been held that the coparcenary interest is a vested interest and even on adoption it remains vested in him (Section 12, HAMA).
- The child retains *sapinda* relationship and degrees of prohibited relationship in his natural family for the purpose of marriage (Section 12, HAMA).
- The adoption of the same child by more than one person simultaneously is not permitted (Section 11, HAMA).
- Once an adoption is made, it is final and irrevocable (Section 15, HAMA).
- The Muslims, Christians, and Parsis have to appoint themselves as guardians under the Guardians and Wards Act 1890. This Act applies to all communities and castes though in appointing or declaring a person as guardian of the minor, the court will take into consideration the personal law of the minor. But once a person is appointed or declared as guardian of a minor, irrespective of the fact whether the minor is

---

[36] In fact the adoptive son's position is now better under the Act than earlier. On inheritance he takes an equal share with a subsequently born *aurasa*. But his share was much less under the pristine law.

Hindu, Muslim, Christian, or Parsi, such a guardian is subjected to the Guardians and Wards Act 1890.
- The Guardians and Wards Act deals only with the guardians of the person and property of the minor. In appointing or declaring the guardian of a minor, the court shall be guided by what appears in the circumstances of the case to be for the welfare of the minor and consistent with the law to which the minor is subject. Among the various factors to be considered by the court in the matter, the welfare of the child is one of the considerations. [Guardians and Wards Act, Section 17].
- Mother has been recognized as the natural guardian of her illegitimate children. The putative father is the natural guardian of his illegitimate children after the mother.[37] (His obligation to maintain them has now been given statutory recognition under the Hindu Adoption and Maintenance Act 1956).
- Chapters II and III of Part V of the Indian Succession Act 1925 deals with wills. Schedule III to the Act states that the words 'son', 'child', 'children', in the will, will be deemed to include the adopted son, child, or children.[38]
- Under HAMA, an adoption does not deprive the adoptive father or mother of the power to dispose of his or her property by transfer inter vivos or by will [HAMA 1956 Section 13].
- Rehabilitation and social integration of a child is an important part of the Juvenile Justice Act 2000. Chapter IV of the Act lists adoption, foster care, sponsorship, and sending of the child to an after-care organization to achieve the goal of rehabilitation and social integration [JJ Act 2000, Sections 40, 42, 43]. It also states that the primary responsibility for providing care and protection to children shall be that of his family [Sec. 41(1), JJ Act 2000]. This Act deals with adoption for a special category of children and for a special purpose. The JJ Act 2000 is silent on the question of religion.
- The Juvenile Justice Act 2000 defines a child as a person who has not completed the age of eighteen years [Sec. 2(k)]. Under Hindu Adoption and Maintenance Act 1956, the age for adoption of children is up to fifteen years.
- The Juvenile Justice Act 2000 empowers the Juvenile Justice Board to give a child in adoption and also carry out such investigations as are required for giving children in adoption in keeping with the provisions

---

[37] See Hindu Adoptions and Maintenance Act 1956, Section 21(viii) and (ix).
[38] Schedule III, Indian Succession Act 1925.

of the various guidelines for adoption issued from time to time by the state governments [Sec. 41(3)].
- A child can be offered in adoption under the JJ Act 2000, only after two members of the Child Welfare Committee declare the child legally free for placement, in the case of abandoned children, and till the two months' period for reconsideration by the parent is over in case of surrendered children [Sec. 41(5)].
- The JJ Act 2000 requires that the child's consent be taken into account before the adoption is completed if the child can understand and express his consent [Sec. 41(5)].
- The JJ Act 2000 allows parents to adopt a child of the same sex irrespective of the number of living biological sons or daughters [Sec. 41(6)].

Inter-country Adoption

There is no legislation providing for the adoption of an Indian child by a foreign parent The only way in which a foreigner parent can take an Indian child in adoption is by becoming a guardian of the child under the Guardians and Wards Act 1890. But a Hindu, even if he is a foreigner, i.e. a national of another country, may nevertheless adopt a Hindu child in India in accordance with the provisions of HAMA 1956.

The Guardians and Wards Act 1890 applies to all minor children of any caste and creed, though in appointing or declaring a person as guardian the court will take into consideration the personal law of the minor.[39] But once a person is appointed or declared as guardian of a minor, irrespective of the fact whether the minor is a Hindu, or a Muslim, or subject to any personal law, such a guardian will be subject to the provisions of the Guardians and Wards Act 1890.

Section 7 of the Guardians and Wards Act deals with the powers of the court to appoint or declare a person as guardian. The procedure under the Guardians and Wards Act 1890 is as follows: Any person who claims or desires to be the guardian of the minor, or who is a relative or friend of the minor, or the collector [Section 8 of the Guardians and Wards Act] of the district, shall make an application to the district or family court where the minor ordinarily resides [Section 9 of the Guardians and Wards Act]. On receipt of the application of a person if the court comes to the conclusion that

---

[39] In effect, the procedural law regarding the appointment or declaration of the person as a guardian is laid down in the Guardians and Wards Act yet the substantive part is still the personal law. Paras Diwan, *Law of Adoption*, Minority, Custody and Guardianship, Wadhwa and Co., Allahabad, India, 1989, p. 345.

it would be for the welfare of the child to appoint a guardian of the person of the minor, it can appoint the guardian.[40]

In considering what will be the welfare of the minor, the court shall take into account the age, sex, and religion of the minor, the character and capacity of the adopter, and the wishes of the deceased parent. If the minor is able to form an intelligent opinion, the court will consider his/her preference also.

Therefore, the personal law of the minor has to be taken into consideration at this time, along with the welfare of the child. The judicial attitude is fairly well settled that the welfare of the minor has been given greater significance than the rights of the parties under the personal law in deciding the question of guardianship under the Act. When the court is satisfied that the appointment is for the welfare of the minor, an order appointing a guardian may be made in any one of the three forms:[41]

- A simple order where no security is asked for;
- An order appointing a person as guardian and asking him to furnish security within a specified time; and
- An order appointing a guardian on the condition that he should furnish security.

An order appointing a person as guardian under Section 7 amounts to the termination of the guardianship of all persons who have the care of the child, his person, or property, as the case may be. In passing the order for guardianship, the court may order or issue directions in respect to collateral matters also.

A foreigner therefore wishing to take an Indian child for adoption has to use the above very circuitous way under the Guardians and Wards Act 1890. The order will appoint the person as guardian of the child with leave to move the child out of India and take him/her to his own country for the purpose of adopting him/her, in accordance with the law of his country.

The procedure led to a lot of malpractice by social organizations and voluntary agencies engaged in the work of facilitating the adoption of Indian children by foreign parents. When the Supreme Court of India received

---

[40] See Guardians and Wards Act 1890, Section 17.
[41] *Tuminra Khatun v Ghariya Bibi*, AIR 1942 Cal. 281, *Mir v Munji*, AIR 1952 Mad.280, AIR 1983 J&K 70, *Bholanath v Sharda Devi*, AIR 1954 Pat 489, *Smt Bhagwat Devi v Muralidhar Sahu*, AIR 1943 PC106. In all these cases the court has stated that the principle matter to be considered is the welfare of the minor irrespective of the personal law of the child.

a letter complaining of these malpractices and found that there was no legislation enacted by the Parliament for laying down the principles and norms which must be observed, and the procedure which must be followed in giving an Indian child in adoption to foreign parents, a writ petition was initiated on the basis of the letter. After hearing several social organizations and voluntary agencies engaged in placement of children in adoption, an exhaustive judgment was delivered formulating the normative and procedural safeguards to be followed by other judgments[42] clarifying and supplementing the above norms and procedures.

The procedure for inter-country adoptions laid down by these judgments can be summarized as follows:

The Supreme Court judgments, described as model public interest litigations, have acknowledged inter-country adoption as a means to rehabilitate abandoned children. These guidelines have put a stop to private adoptions. All inter-country adoptions are adoptions directly by foreign parents through governments recognised by them in both sending and receiving countries. The judgments attempt to make every party in the adoption process accountable. There are certain regulating agencies recommended in the judgment like the Scrutinizing Agency, the Voluntary Coordinating Agency, the Central Adoption Resource Agency, and the recognized Child Welfare Agency (Placement Agency). The Child Welfare Agency processing the applications of the foreign parent must place sufficient material before the Court to satisfy it that the child is legally free for adoption.[43]

Role of Scrutinizing Agencies

The Supreme Court has recognized the Indian Council for Child Welfare and the Indian Council for Social Welfare as the agencies for the purpose of scrutiny of adoption cases.[44] Scrutinizing agencies are appointed by the court to facilitate the processing of applications as well as related documents with regard to the children being given in in-country and inter-country adoption. The scrutinizing agency has to ascertain and verify the following points:[45]

- Whether the giving institution is recognized by the Government of India to place children in foreign countries.

[42] AIR 1984 SC 469; AIR 1986 SC 272; AIR 1987 SC 232;1990 4 SCC 513; AIR 1992 SC 118.
[43] For details see 'Important Judgments Relating to Adoption' on p. 57.
[44] AIR 1986 SC 272.
[45] D. Paul Chowdhry, *Inter-country Adoption: Social and Legal Aspects*, Indian Council For Child Welfare, New Delhi, 1988, pp. 80–1.

- Whether the institution processing the cases in the receiving country has recognition from the Government of India.
- Whether the child is legally free for adoption.

The Role of the Voluntary Coordinating Agency (VCA)

The VCA was established basically with the singular objective of promoting in-country adoption. The Supreme Court has directed in its judgment that regarding placement of the children, first and foremost priority is given to Indian families. The scrutizing agency has to ensure that at the time of scrutinizing the case, the VCA has issued a clearance certificate for inter-country adoption.

The Role of Central Adoption Resource Agency (CARA)

CARA, initially set up under the ministry of welfare, Government of India, has now become an autonomous body concerned with regulating adoption matters. Adoption guidelines were formulated in 1989 with regard to adoption of Indian children internationally. The ministry of social justice and empowerment, Government of India, subsequently revised these in 1995 to include both domestic and foreign adoptions.[46] The guidelines provide the framework within which adoption has to be carried out within and outside the country. They also provide the system of licensing/recognizing agencies in India and abroad for placement of Indian children in adoption as well as of other regulatory bodies, namely, the scrutiny agencies and VCAs. This has introduced professional accountability for the first time. Adoptions can now be done only through recognized adoption agencies. Placements done directly by individual doctors and hospitals (of unrelated children) are not permitted. For all inter-country placements a no objection certificate (NOC) has to be obtained from CARA. Agencies desirous of processing inter-country adoption cases must seek recognition from CARA.

Enlistment of Indian and Foreign Agencies

The state government shall maintain a list of children's homes and adoption agencies working in the state. The request from foreign agencies for enlistment for the purpose of inter-country adoption will be considered by CARA.

---

[46] Adoption of Indian children is presently governed by the Supreme Court guidelines and the Government of India 'Revised guidelines on inter-country adoption of Indian Children 1995'.

Other Directions of the Supreme Court

- The Government of India should enter into bilateral agreement with countries which are receiving children from India for the purpose of adoption.
- In case of inter-country adoption it came to be said[47] that the Indian citizenship should not continue until the adopted child attains the age of majority and is legally competent to opt as this would hinder the need of quick assimilation and may often stand as a barrier to the requirements of the early cementing of the adoptee child into the adoptive family.
- Birth certificate of the adopted child should be obtained on the basis of the application of the society sponsoring the adoption.[48]
- A bond may be taken from the recognized placement agency which is processing the application. Such placement agency may in turn take a corresponding bond from the sponsoring social or child welfare agency in the foreign country.
- The judgment[49] also laid down a scale of expenses to be recovered by the agency offering placement from the adoptive parents for maintaining the child.[50] It also provided for escalation of expenses by 30 per cent to be reviewed once in three years.[51]
- In order to facilitate the implementation of these norms, principles, and procedures, the Government of India, ministry of welfare adopted a resolution which also provided for the violation of guidelines.[52]
- Adoption of Indian children placed with Indians living abroad will be treated as in-country placement. However, such Indians would have to follow the same procedure of sending applications, documents, etc., through an enlisted foreign agency in that country as in the case of inter-country adoption.
- On adoption of the child by the foreign parent according to the law of the land, the child would acquire the same status as a natural born child

---

[47] (1984)2 SCC 244.
[48] AIR 1992 SC 118.
[49] AIR 1986 SC 236.
[50] AIR 1985 Supp. SCC 701.
[51] AIR 1992 SC 118.
[52] *Guidelines to regulate matters relating to adoption of Indian Children.* Resolution No. 13–33/85-CHR(AC), Government of India, Ministry of Welfare, New Delhi, 4 July 1989.

within wedlock with the same rights of inheritance and succession and the same nationality as the foreign parent adopting the child.

Critique of Laws and Practice Relating to Adoption[53]

The issue of 'gender injustice' is also evident in the practice of adoption. 'Childlessness' is not seen as a human problem, and the stigma of 'infertility' is attached only to the woman. The man is often forced to remarry and the male infertility factor is never under question. Patriarchal religious values are evident and implicit in the social practice of adoption as well as in the law of adoption. Research on parliamentary debates show that the objections raised by various religions towards the acceptance of a uniform adoption law are also based on the issue of succession, inheritance, and property rights. Considerable social consciousness bereft of any religious dogma among the masses and the social reformers and lawmakers is required for the evolution of a proper adoption law and its trouble-free practical implementation.

Adoption Practice

The practice of adoption is based on the enactments, directions, resolutions, and guidelines along with social work inputs to protect the rights of the child to family care and inheritance. The documentation required for adoption is presented below as well as the interventions and initiatives by the non-governmental organisations and the government.

Documents Required for Indian Adoption[54]

PRELIMINARY ESSENTIAL DOCUMENTS

- Birth certificate (photocopies) of the adoptive couple and the child, if any.
- Marriage certificate (photocopies) of the adoptive couple.
- Health certificate of the couple and the child, if any.
- Gynaecological report: Infertility should be mentioned, if applicable. This report must include the line of treatment the couple is undergoing

---

[53] Asha Bajpai, *Adoption Law and Justice to the Child*, National Law School of India University, Bangalore, India, 1996.

[54] Information provided by the Indian Association for Promotion of Adoption and Child Welfare, Mumbai. The procedure and documentation may differ for other agencies in India.

or has undergone, the period of treatment, an opinion or a reason for childlessness, and the chances of the couple having a biological child in future, whether nil, remote, or fair.
- A recent postcard size colour photograph of the adoptive family (five copies).
- Three letters of recommendations from persons who know the family well enough to recommend them as a married couple, as persons, and as prospective adoptive parents. Two of these letters should be from parents or immediate relatives of each spouse.
- Property statement: A statement on the value of the property owned by the family, including other assets like bonds, shares, policies, fixed deposits, etc., and liabilities.
- Employment certificate: Income certificate from the employer indicating gross and net salary, designation, and also the length of service of the husband and the wife, in case the wife is also employed.
- Bank reference indicating the current bank balance of the adoptive family.
- Childcare arrangements: If both husband and wife are working, a joint statement expressing what childcare arrangements they foresee when they have a child.
- Undertaking from a family member expressing their willingness to look after the child in any short or long-term eventuality. In case of couples who are above forty years of age, a younger relative should provide this undertaking.

ADDITIONAL DOCUMENTS, IF APPLICABLE
- In cases where couples have a biological and/or adopted child/children and such children—biological or adopted are old enough, they will be required to express their thoughts on paper to convey their reactions to their parents' decision to adopt a child/children again.
- A copy of the adoption decree/s, if the couple have adopted child/children earlier.
- Divorce decree in case one or both of the spouses were earlier divorcees.

HOME STUDY REPORT OF THE ADOPTIVE PARENTS

Once these documents are submitted and the couple registers with the agency, the social worker will arrange to start the home study of the family. The home study report aims at giving a brief profile of the financial status, reason for adoption, and so on.

A suitable child will be identified for the couple only after all the required documents mentioned above are received and approved. If the child is approved, the child study form, the medical report, and the photograph of the child will have to be countersigned by the parents. In case of children over three years, an IQ report will be given to the couple for their approval.

Documents Required for Processing an Inter-country Adoption Case[55]

There are similar documents required before identification of a child for inter-country adoption. The home study report in these cases must be prepared by a trained social worker of a licensed social welfare agency of the country. The agency must be recognized by the ministry of social welfare, Government of India. The agency must give an undertaking to send periodic follow-up reports in the following pattern.

In the case of children taken in adoption under the Hindu Adoption and Maintenance Act of 1956, follow-up reports must be sent quarterly for the first year and half-yearly for the second year. In the case of children taken in guardianship under the Guardians and Wards Act of 1890, quarterly follow-up reports for the first two years and half-yearly for the subsequent three years should be sent. The adoptive parents must similarly give an undertaking to send periodic follow-up reports of the child. Approval of the government or of a competent authority from the adopting couple's country, approving the adoption and the adoptive parents, has to be obtained for the purpose of adoption.

After identification of the child, a joint declaration in guardianship matters indicating approval of the child will also be sent to the couple. This should be duly filled and returned after the approval and selection of a child. If a couple desires that legal procedures be initiated/legislation be completed in their absence, they will be required to give a specific power of attorney to persons whose names will be communicated later.

The expenses for completing the various adoption formalities will be estimated approximately including service charges and registration fees, the legal fees for the advocate and for the scrutinizing body for adoption, and other incidental expenses for courier, telephone, telegram, etc. The couple will be required to bear costs for foster care, if the child selected by them has been in foster care and/or had received medical treatment.

Parents residing abroad are expected to adopt the child according to the laws of the country in which they reside. In certain cases, when the court passes the final order in favour of the adoptive parents/guardians, it is

---

[55] Information provided by the Indian Association for Promotion of Adoption and Child Welfare, Mumbai. The procedure and documentation may differ other agencies in India.

expected, in the interest of the child, that a certain amount of money be deposited in the child's name.

The only adoption law prevalent in India (HAMA 1956) is not a child-oriented legislation, but rather parent-oriented. It is a religion-based law applicable only to Hindus. It is also not child-centred, since it is not a response of the society to the destitute, orphan, or abandoned child, in an attempt, provide a 'home to the homeless'.

The Hindu Adoption and Maintenance Act 1956 is an attempt to de-emphasize the religious significance of adoption and put it on a secular basis. The performance of the religious ceremony *Dattaka Homa* is no longer essential.[56] But the physical act of giving and taking by the parties concerned is essential for its validity [Section 11(iv). Hindu Adoption and Maintenance Act 1956]. Second, all the parties concerned, viz., the natural parents, the adoptive parents, and the child must be Hindus.[57]

Even today it is necessary to establish the religion of the child as Hindu if it is to be given or taken validly in adoption under the HAMA. Section 2(bb)[58] added in 1962 to cover abandoned children states that such abandoned children shall be 'brought up' as Hindus. What it means to 'be brought up' as Hindus is still not very clear and needs to be defined. Such lack of clarity may give rise to contentious issues like the following:

- A Hindu male or female could have been allowed under the Act to adopt a non-Hindu child also. And since on adoption the adopted child 'shall be deemed to be the child of his adoptive father or mother for all purposes', the child would then be a Hindu by religion.
- Section 2(bb) further states that if a child has been abandoned by his father and mother, it is necessary that irrespective of whether the child is legitimate or illegitimate both the parents will have to abandon. This provision leads to a lot of problems in cases of illegitimate children where the father is missing and cannot be found or does not give his consent and the mother wants to relinquish the child. The provision is an obstacle to the adoption of abandoned children. The consent of such a father should be done away with.

[56] In *Madhusudhan Das v Narayanibai*, SC 114, 1983, it was held that for a valid adoption the ceremony of giving and taking is an essential requisite on all adoptions, whatever the caste.

[57] Therefore Hindus could be by religion, by birth, and by negative definition, i.e. by explaining who are not Hindus. Persons capable of giving and taking in adoption lose their capacity if they cease to be Hindus.

[58] See Hindu Adoptions and Maintenance Act 1956, Section 2(bb).

- Under the HAMA, the court gets jurisdiction only in cases when a guardian other than the parents give the child in adoption. When the father or mother gives his/her child in adoption they need not go through the courts. This may lead to abuse and exploitation by the parents due to poverty and other causes. Therefore, all cases of adoption, whether by parents or guardians, should be through courts so that all in-country adoptions can be regulated and monitored.
- Under the Hindu Adoption and Maintenance Act 1956, when an unmarried person or a widow/widower or divorcee adopts a child and subsequently marries, the other spouse is only the stepfather/stepmother of the child.[59]

However, in other situations, for instance when a divorcee adopts a child, there will be no relationship between the child and the divorced spouse as after the divorce, the marital links between the two spouses have come to an end. Even though a widow can now adopt, as a widow is allowed to adopt a child in her own capacity,[60] there has been a lot of controversy over this. Several decisions of the High Courts and the Supreme Court have applied to the *doctrine of relation back*. Accordingly, the child adopted by a widow remains the child of her deceased husband[61] on the assumption that the

---

[59] Hindu Adoption and Maintenance Act 1956, Section 14. Also see *Sitabai v Ramchandra* (1969)2 SCC544, wherein it was held that when a widower or bachelor adopts a child and he gets married subsequent to the adoption, his wife becomes the stepmother of the adopted child. In case of there being two wives, the child becomes the adopted child of the senior wife in marriage and the junior wife becomes the stepmother of the adopted child.

[60] See HAMA 1956, Section 8.

[61] The question came up before the Mumbai High Court in *Ankush v Jenabai* (AIR 1966 Bom. 174) where a Hindu, N, died leaving behind two widows L and T and a daughter J from L. The senior widow L died in 1938. The junior widow T adopted the plaintiff as her son in 1957. The plaintiff filed a suit for the recovery of the possession of all the properties of N including those alienated by the widows, on the plea that he was not merely the adopted son of T but also of N. It was held by the Mumbai High Court that an adopted child of the widow was absorbed in the adoptive family to which the widow belonged, i.e. the family of her deceased husband.

The question came up again before the Supreme Court in *Sawan Ram v Kalawati* (AIR 1967 SC 1761). The Supreme Court reiterated the *doctrine of relation back* and declared that adoption by widow relates back to the deceased husband and the child is an adopted son of such deceased husband too. Analysing Section 4(1) of the Hindu Adoption and Maintenance Act 1956, the learned judge said that the section envisages two kinds of adoptions: (I) an adoption by a Hindu and (II) an adoption to a Hindu, i.e. instances where there is an adoption by a female whose husband is dead, or has completely and

husband's family is the family of the widow. The reasons seem to be past legal notions and social values.[62] Hindu law has always maintained that on marriage, the girl completely passes from the family of her father to the family of her husband.

However, in the cases decided by the High Courts and the Supreme Court where *the doctrine of relation back* was applied, the issue of divesting of widow's property did not arise, and therefore the adopted son was allowed to take the property of the deceased husband, in preference to other heirs/reversionists. But where the issue of divesting of property on adoption was involved before the High Courts, the adopted child was not allowed to do so.[63] The ruling in *Sawan Ram v Kalavati* still remains valid and binding. Hence, even today the child adopted by a widow remains the child of her deceased husband.

This appears to be against the statement of objects and reasons of the HAMA 1956 which states that the adoption made by a Hindu widow will be in her right. Second, the law should provide that the stepparent might ratify the adoption affected by the other spouse after marriage so that the child has a father rather than a stepfather.

Section 11(1) of the HAMA lays down that when a Hindu male or female desires to adopt a son, he or she can do so only when he or she has no Hindu son or son's son living at the time of adoption whether by legitimate blood relation or by adoption. Similarly, no Hindu can adopt a daughter, if he or she already has a Hindu daughter or son's daughter living at the time of adoption. This provision seems to be discriminatory to illegitimate children and needs to be remedied. This means that the existence of an illegitimate son/

---

finally renounced the world, or has been declared to be of unsound mind by a court of competent jurisdiction, or has ceased to be a Hindu by converting to another religion. In these cases the adopted son of the Hindu female will also be a son of her deceased, sanyasi, insane, or non-Hindu husband. This argument was further fortified by Section 12. It was further held that on marriage, the family of a Hindu female is the family of her husband and therefore, the child adopted by her must belong logically to the same family. Therefore, on adoption by a widow, the adopted son is deemed to be a member of the family of the deceased husband of the widow and he would obtain rights in the capacity of a member of that family as an adopted son of the deceased husband of the widow. In another case, *Sitabai v Ramachandra*, 1969, 2Sa 544, the *doctrine of relation back* was reiterated that the child adopted by the widow is the child of her deceased husband.

[62] Paras Diwan, *Law of Adoption, Minority Guardianship and Custody*, Wadhwa and Company, 1989, p. 81.

[63] In *Hirabai v Babu* (AIR 1980 Bom 315) it was held that divesting of properties already vested in others before adoption of the child was not allowed with the intention of safeguarding the interests of others.

daughter is no bar irrespective of the fact whether the adoption is by a male or female. In other words, if a woman has an illegitimate son, she can also make an adoption of a son and if a Hindu male has an illegitimate son he too can make an adoption of a son. There could be a provision in the adoption law that the putative father can, by declaration before the proper legal forum, adopt his child as legitimate.[64]

Adoption is a specialized childcare service and needs to be handled by specialized courts, for instance, adoption cells in family courts could be established for this purpose rather than civil courts.

The child, if he is capable of understanding, should be involved in the adoption process. There is no provision in the Act for it. The desire of the child should be ascertained before an adoption is made. The child should be counselled so that he/she is prepared to enter a new home.

The requirement under Section 10 of the HAMA 1956 that the adoptee must not have completed the age of fifteen years does not appear to be reasonable. A minor child, who has completed that age, may still be in as much need of being adopted as one below that age.

Under Section 9 of the HAMA, if the father changes his religion he loses his right to give his child in adoption and the right stands transferred to the mother, and if the mother changes her religion she loses her right to be consulted and to prevent her child from being given in adoption without her consent. Thus, there is discrimination between a father and mother continuing to be Hindus and a father or mother ceasing to be a Hindu based solely on religion which violates Article 15 (1) of the Constitution.[65]

According to the succession laws of India, an illegitimate child cannot inherit its father even if the genetic father is known. A father cannot cease to be a father simply because he is not lawfully wedded to the mother of the child. Therefore, an illegitimate child should be allowed to inherit the property of his putative/genetic father.

The adoptive parents are the natural guardians of their adopted minor child, first the father and then the mother. If the adopted child is less than five years, the adoptive mother will have preferential claim to the custody of the child.[66] This section should be amended as per the Law Commission

---

[64] M.P.P. Pillai, *The Law of Adoption in India: Need for a Fresh Approach*, Rights of the Child, NLSIU, Bangalore, India, 1990.

[65] Article 15 Constitution of India: Prohibition of discrimination on grounds of religion, race, caste, sex, or place of birth.

1) The State shall not discriminate against any citizen on grounds only of religion, race, caste, sex, place of birth, or any of them.

[66] The provision contained in Section 6(a) of the Hindu Minority and Guardianship Act 1956.

recommendations. Mother should have the same and equal rights vis-à-vis father and the custody of the minor who has not completed twelve years of age shall ordinarily be with the mother.[67] This will be in the interest of the child.

The Hindu Minority and Guardianship Act 1956 provides that a Hindu parent 'ceasing to be a Hindu' shall not 'be entitled to act as the natural guardian [Section 7]. This provision has therefore classified Hindu children into two categories—children whose parents continue to be Hindu and children whose parents have ceased to be Hindu—and has discriminated against the latter by providing for them the loss of their natural guardian. It is not at all fair and just to disrupt the parental home of the child solely because one of the parents has chosen to renounce his religion. This provision should be amended as it violates Article 15 of the Constitution.[68]

Under the Hindu Adoption and Maintenance Act 1956, inheritance of property is automatic. Muslims, Christians, Parsis, and Jews have to resort to the Guardians and Wards Act 1890. The guardian-ward relationship does not have the force of law beyond the time when the child reaches the age of majority. The child does not gain automatically the privileges of permanent family linkages such as the name, religion, properties, inheritance, etc., as in a legal adoption. This is again discrimination against children solely on the grounds of religion and hence violates Article 15 of the Constitution.[69]

---

[67] Some of the recommendations are: 'Mother' should have same and equal (and not inferior) rights vis-à-vis 'father'.

The provision contained in Section 6(a) of the Hindu Minority and Guardianship Act 1956 (HMG Act for short), constituting the father as a natural guardian of a Hindu minor's person as well as in respect of his property in 'preference' to the mother, should be amended so as to constitute both the father and the mother as being natural guardians 'jointly and severally', having equal rights in respect of the minor. There is no justification for according a superior and preferential treatment to the father vis-à-vis the mother of the minor and because it violates the spirit and conscience of Article 15 of the Constitution of India.

The custody of a minor who has not completed twelve years of age shall ordinarily be with the mother.

The proviso to Subsection (a) of Section 6 of the HMG Act deserves to be amended so that the custody of a boy or an unmarried girl who has not completed the age of twelve years (instead of the age limit of five years as prescribed at present) shall ordinarily be with the mother. Law Commission of India, *One Hundred Thirty-third Report on Removal of Discrimination against Women in matters relating to guardianship and custody of minor children and elaboration of the welfare principle 1986.*

[68] Article 15(1): The State shall not discriminate against any citizen on grounds only of religion, race, caste, sex, place of birth, or any of them.

[69] For all practical purposes, however, guardianship placements are also treated like adoption. The child takes the guardian's family name and religion. With respect to a share

The definition of a 'child' varies under different legislations. The HAMA 1956 defines the child as not older than fifteen years of age, and GWA 1890 defines the child as not older than eighteen years of age unless it is a ward of the state. In the latter case, the age limit extends to twenty-one years. There should be uniformity regarding the minority of the child.

Any discrimination against the adopted child should be punishable by law. There is no provision regarding this under the Hindu Adoption and the Maintenance Act 1956.

Disparity in the rights of men and women, legal inequality, and disabilities based on sex persist in the matter of adoption and succession. There is only a 'notional' equality after the codification of Hindu personal laws. Patriarchal values have been implicit in the Hindu adoption law prior to codification and to some extent even after codification, as evident from the following:[70]

- The main purpose of the law is to provide a male heir, a 'son to the sonless', for the purpose of inheritance and funeral rites.
- The law is inextricably related to succession and inheritance. Prevention of adoption of a male, if there is already a male child, is definitely a reflection of the desire to prevent disinheritance of biological heirs in the main line.
- The focus of the adoption law is on the transfer of property, not on having a child, nor on enjoying parenthood.
- That adoption and maintenance matters are incorporated together under one law is also reflective of patriarchal biases.
- A girl child could not be adopted prior to the codification of the law in 1956.
- A woman could not adopt prior to the codification of the law.
- After codification, a single woman could adopt unto herself. A married woman could not adopt, but only be a consenting party.*
  - In view of express religious prohibition, the courts leave it to interpretation whether Juvenile Justice Act 2000 can give rights of adoption.
  - The Juvenile Justice Act 2000 is silent on the issue of inter-country adoption.
  - The functionaries in the juvenile justice system need training to carry out the provisions of the Act in its true spirit.

---

in the family property, the guardian or any family member may make a will in favour of the child. Nevertheless, a guardianship placement will not stand the test of a legal challenge of adoption.

[70] Nilima Mehta, *The Adoption Agenda in India*, Horizons, Gender Just Laws Bulletin, India Centre for Human Rights and Law, Vol. 2, No. 2, July 1999.

- Finally, there should have been a specific provision to make democratic institutions like *Zila Parishads*[71] or Municipalities or Panchayati Raj[72] institutions responsible for the welfare of children.[73]

Important Judgments Relating to Adoption

Lakshmi Kant Pandey v Union of India[74]

FACTS

This writ petition was initiated on the basis of a letter addressed by one Lakshmi Kant Pandey, an advocate, complaining of malpractices indulged in by social organizations and voluntary agencies engaged in the work of offering Indian children in adoption to foreign parents. The petitioner accordingly sought relief restraining India-based private agencies 'from carrying out further activity of routing children for adoption abroad' and directing the Government of India, the Indian Council for Child Welfare, and the Indian Council for Social Welfare to carry out their obligations in the matter of adoption of Indian children by foreign parents. This letter was treated as a writ petition and by an order, the court issued notice to the Union of India, the Indian Council for Child Welfare, and the Indian Council for Social Welfare to appear in answer to the writ petition and assist the court in laying down principles and norms which should be followed in determining whether a child should be allowed to be adopted by foreign parents and if so, the procedure to be followed for that purpose, with the object of ensuring the welfare of the child.

HELD

In the absence of a law providing for adoption of an Indian child by a foreign parent, the only way in which such adoption can be effectuated is by making it in accordance with the law of the country in which the foreign parents reside. Therefore, the only way in which a foreign parent could take an Indian child in adoption was by making an application to the court under whose jurisdiction the child ordinarily resided, for being appointed guardian

---

[71] District level administrative structures.
[72] Village level administrative structures.
[73] In England, according to the provisions of the Children Act 1980, in the case of any person under eighteen years who is a subject of a court order, it will be the duty of every local authority to make available such advice, guidance, and assistance as may promote the welfare of children.
[74] (1984) 2 SCC 244.

of the person of the child under the Guardians and Wards Act 1890, and with leave to remove the child out of India and take it to his own country for the purpose of adopting it in accordance with the law of his country. It was opined that such inter-country adoption should be permitted after exhausting the possibility of adoption within the country by the Indian parents.

The concern in this case was not the cases of adoption of children living with their biological parents, for in such class of cases, the biological parents would be the best persons to decide whether to give their child in adoption to foreign parents. It was only in those cases where the children sought to be taken in adoption are destitute or abandoned or are living in social or child welfare centres that it was necessary to consider that normative and procedural safeguards should be forged for protecting their interest and promoting their welfare.

The requirements to be insisted upon, so far as a foreigner wishing to take a child in adoption is concerned, were laid down. A summary of the requirements is as follows:

- Every application from a foreigner desiring to adopt a child must be sponsored by a social or child welfare agency recognized by the government of the country in which the foreigner is resident and every application for taking a child in adoption must be accompanied by a home study report, prepared by a professional social worker, and other documents.
- The Government of India shall prepare a list of social or child welfare agencies licensed or recognized for inter-country adoption by the government of each foreign country where the children from India are to be taken in adoption, and the list shall be prepared after getting the necessary information from the government of each foreign country and the Indian diplomatic mission in that foreign country.
- If the biological parents are known, they should be properly assisted in making a decision about relinquishing the child for adoption, by the institution or Centre or home for childcare or social or child welfare agency to which the child is being surrendered. It was also pointed out that the biological parents should be induced or encouraged or even permitted to take a decision in regard to giving a child in adoption before the birth of the child or within a period of three months from the date of birth.
- But where the child is an orphan, destitute, or abandoned child and its parents are not known, the institution or centre or home for childcare

or social or child welfare agency in whose care the child has come, must try to trace the biological parents of the child. If the biological parents can be traced and it is found that they do not want to take back the child, the adoption process may continue. But if for any reason the biological parents cannot be traced, there can be no question of taking their consent or consulting them.
- Every recognized social or child welfare agency must maintain a register with the names and particulars of all children proposed to be given in inter-country adoption through it. The recognized social or child welfare agency must prepare a child study report through a professional social worker giving all relevant information in regard to the child so as to help the foreigner to come to a decision whether or not to adopt the child, and to understand the child if he decides to adopt it; as also to assist the court in coming to a decision whether it will be for the welfare of the child to be given in adoption to the foreigner wishing to adopt it.
- The Government of India should set up a Central Adoption Resource Agency with regional branches at a few centres, which are active in inter-country adoptions. Such an agency can act as a clearing house of information in regard to children available for inter-country adoption, and all applications by foreigners for taking Indian children for adoption can then be forwarded by the social or child welfare agency in the foreign country to the Central Adoption Resource Agency and the latter can in turn forward them to any of the recognized social or child welfare agencies in the country.

Lakshmi Kant Pandey v Union of India & Another[75]

FACTS

This writ petition was initiated on the basis of a letter addressed by the petitioner complaining of malpractices indulged in by social organizations and voluntary agencies engaged in the work of offering Indian children in adoption to foreign parents.

HELD

- The scrutinizing agency appointed by the court for the purpose of assisting it in reaching the conclusion whether it would be in the interest of the child to be given in adoption to foreign parents must not in any manner be involved in placement of children in adoption.

[75] AIR 1985 Supp SCC 701.

- The social or child welfare agency sponsoring the application must undertake that in case of disruption of the family of the foreigner before adoption can be effected, it will take care of the child and find a suitable alternative placement for it with the approval of the social or child welfare agency concerned in India, and report such alternative placement to the court handling the guardianship proceedings and such information shall be passed on both by the court as also by the social or child welfare agency concerned in India to the secretary, ministry of social welfare, Government of India.
- In the event of disruption of the family of the foreigner before adoption can be affected, the agency shall give intimation of this fact to the Indian Embassy or High Commission, as the case may be, and the Indian Embassy or High Commission shall also be kept informed about the whereabouts of the child so that they can take the necessary steps for ensuring that the child is properly taken care of and a suitable alternative placement for it is found. The primary responsibility for ensuring that the child is legally free for adoption must be that of the social or child welfare agency processing the application of the foreigner for guardianship of the child.
- No court in a state will entertain an application for appointment of a foreigner as guardian of a child which has been brought from another state, and if there is a social or child welfare agency in that other state which has been recognized by the Government of India for inter-country adoption. If there is no recognized social or child welfare agency in the state where the child is found or obtained, the child shall be transferred to a recognized social or child welfare agency at the nearest place in the immediate neighbouring state.
- Progress reports shall be submitted by the social or child welfare agency sponsoring the application of the foreigner until adoption is effected.
- A foreign social or child welfare agency having a representative in India, should have such a representative who is an Indian citizen with a degree or diploma in social work coupled with experience in child welfare.
- The execution of a bond would ordinarily be sufficient. The bond should be by way of security for repatriation of the child to India in case it becomes necessary to do so as also for ensuring adoption of the child within a period of two years.
- Where it is not possible for the foreigner to complete the adoption process within two years, an application should be made to the court for extension of time for making the adoption and the court may grant appropriate extension of time.

- Notice of the application for guardianship of a child should in no case be published in the newspapers, because then the biological parents would come to know who is the person taking the child in adoption.
- The recognized social or child welfare agency processing the application must also be entitled to recover from the foreigner who is sought to be appointed guardian of the child, costs incurred in preparing and filing the application and processing it in court.
- The court recommended the setting up of such Voluntary Coordinating Agency in each state and if circumstances so require, there may even be more than one Voluntary Coordinating Agency in a state. Where there is a Voluntary Coordinating Agency or any other centralized agency which maintains a register of children available for adoption as also a register of Indian adoptive parents, it would be enough to wait for a period of three to four weeks.

Lakshmi Kant Pandey v Union of India & Others[76]

In this judgment further directions were given regarding the adoption of children by foreign parents:

- It was not agreed that Indian citizenship should continue until the adopted child attains the age of majority and is legally competent to opt. Such a step would run counter to the need of quick assimilation and may often stand as a barrier to the requirements of the early cementing of the adopted child into the adoptive family. In regard to the issue of the birth certificate of the adopted child, it was opined that such certificate should be obtained on the basis of application of the society sponsoring adoption. In most of these cases the registration of birth may not be available because that would not have been done.
- The licensing authority should ordinarily ensure that the registered agency has proper childcare facilities.
- An escalation of 30 per cent was allowed for expenses to be recovered by the agency offering placement for maintaining the child from the adoptive parents. But the escalation of 10 per cent each year was not agreed to. The matter would be reviewed once in three years so far as escalation of expenses was concerned.
- About the transfer of children from statutory homes to recognized agencies for placement, it was directed that as and when such a request

[76] 1991 (2) Scale, Order dated 14 August 1991 in Criminal Misc. Petition Nos. 3352, 3475, 2045, 5704, 8661, 8842, 9122 of 1990, and 2838 of 1991 in Writ Petition (Criminal) No. 1171 of 1986.

is received from recognized agencies, the juvenile court or the board set up under the Act may consider the feasibility of such transfer and make appropriate order keeping the interests of the child in view, the possibility of an adoption within a short period, and the facilities available in the recognized agency, as also other relevant factors.

Re Manuel Theodore D'souza and Mrs. Lourdes D'souza[77]

FACTS

This was a matter of appointment of guardian of a female minor. Two couples who were Indian citizens and professing the Christian faith applied to the Mumbai High Court for being appointed as guardians under the Guardians And Wards Act. In the course of the proceedings, they amended their petition to seek a prayer that the child be given to them in adoption.

The main issues before the Court were:

- In the absence of legislation, whether the court has powers of giving an abandoned, orphaned, or destitute child in adoption.
- Does an abandoned, orphaned, or destitute child has a right to a family, a name, and nationality as a part of the right to life.
- Is the right of being adopted a fundamental right guaranteed to a child by Article 21 of the Constitution.
- Can the state deny to an orphaned or destitute child the right to be adopted because of its constitutional failure to enact legislation to give effect to Entry 5 of List III of the Seventh Schedule to the Constitution of India.
- Whether a married, childless couple has the fundamental right to adopt a child.
- Is adoption purely a part of personal law.
- If the right to adopt is a fundamental right, can civil courts enforce this right in the absence of legislation and/or administrative instructions having the force of law.
- Can this court in exercise of the power conferred on it under Clause 17 of the amended letters patent, give a child in adoption.

HELD

It was held by the court that the abandoned, orphaned, destitute, or a similarly situated child has a right to be adopted as a part of his fundamental right to life as embodied in Article 21 of the Constitution. The fundamental

---

[77] 2000 (3) BCR, 243.

right to life of these children includes the right to be adopted by willing parent/parents and to have a name and nationality. The right to be adopted therefore is an enforceable civil right which is justiciable in a civil court.

In the absence of any legislation setting out who can adopt, a person or persons who has or have taken a child in guardianship under the Guardians and Wards Act will have the right to petition the courts to adopt the child.

As jurisdiction to pass orders on guardianship is in the district court and/or a High Court having jurisdiction under its letters patent, pending legislation, it will be these courts which will have the right to give the child in adoption by way of a miscellaneous application in the petition for guardianship.

The court, before giving the child in adoption, must satisfy itself that it is in the best interest of the child that the person or persons seeking the guardianship of the child is or are suitable parent or parents.

A period of two years must elapse before the court considers the petition for adoption from the date the court passes the order of guardianship. Before making an order of adoption, the following conditions will have to be satisfied:

- A home study should be available which must contain, amongst other information, the following:
  - The financial status of the adoptive parent or parents and their capacity to look after the needs of the child.
  - The health and the medical report of the adoptive parent/parents.
  - The opinions formed by the interviewer after interviewing the parent/parents and the child, if possible.
  - Progress report of the child after having been given in guardianship, including state of health.
- The cost of preparing the report shall be borne by the adoptive parent/parents.
- Before passing final orders on the petition, the views of the Indian Council of Social Work (ICSW) shall be heard. The costs of ICSW will be borne by the adoptive parent/parents. The adoptive parent/parents will have to deposit a sum of Rs 500/- initially. Any additional expenses will be reimbursed by the adoptive parent(s).

As a child can be given in guardianship to person/persons eligible under the Indian Guardians and Wards Act and as they also have been given the right to adopt, the issue whether a childless couple has a fundamental right to adopt need not be answered, though prima facie it may be possible to arrive at that conclusion.

A guardian/guardians who has/have been appointed by courts in the post and whose guardianship continues, can apply for adoption if the period of two years has elapsed since the date of order of appointment of guardianship.

The legal consequences of an order of adoption will be that the personal law of the adoptive parent(s) would be applicable to the child whose right of inheritance will be the same as that of a natural born child.

As a consequence of adoption, the adoptive parent(s) will have the right to apply and get rectified the register of births showing the adoptive parent/parents as parents of the adopted child and bearing their name and surname, if so desired, by the adoptive parents.

The court held these directions binding and they were issued to all state governments and authorities in the states and Union Territories within the territorial jurisdiction of the Mumbai High Court under Articles 225 and 226 of the Constitution of India as *parens patriae*.

Re Jay Kevin Salerno[78]

FACTS

In this petition Pooja, a minor, was abandoned by her natural mother in the care of Bal Asha Trust, an institution. This institution is not recognized for inter-country adoption. Hence the secretary of the trust requested St Joseph's Home and Nursery to admit the minor to that institution for the purpose of inter-country adoption. After the child was accepted and registered at St Joseph's Home, she was kept in a private nursing home for better care. The child was thus not physically kept at St Joseph's Home. As per the direction of the Supreme Court, a child has to be in the custody of a recognized agency for at least a month. This was to prevent a recognized institution from acting merely as a post office or conduit pipe.

It was held that the term 'custody' cannot be interpreted as actual physical custody. Interpreting the Supreme Court direction given in the case of Lakshmikant Pandey too literally would also cause harm to a child in a given case, e.g. it may not be desirable to move the child physically from familiar surroundings to another place for a period of one month merely for the preparation of a child study report. The custody, therefore, of a recognized institution should be broadly interpreted to mean not physical custody but custody in the sense of supervision and control over the child so that the institution can arrange for a child's individual care or medical treatment (whenever required).

---

[78] Misc. Petition No. 490 of 1987 (Bom. Original Side). Decided 7 October 1987.

Bengt Ingmar Eriksson v Jamnibai Sukharya Dhangda[79]

FACTS

One J and her husband, labourers of a village in Bassein *taluka* had two minor daughters G and L. Returning home late one evening, J found both the minor daughters missing from home, and unable to trace them till next morning lodged a missing report at Bassein police station. Next evening two minor girls were found crying on the street in Bombay city and at night both these girls were sent to a remand home at Dongri. The metropolitan magistrate, after receiving a report that it was not possible to trace the parents of the minor girls at Bassein, detained the girls in the observation home. One Mrs M, a representative of the Family Association for Inter-country Adoption incorporated in Sweden, approached the juvenile court for permission to ascertain whether any child in the remand home could be considered for being given in foreign adoption and thereafter as a constituted attorney of one Mr E, a national of Sweden, filed two miscellaneous petitions on the original side of the Bombay High Court for appointment as guardian of girls G and L, in accordance with the provisions of Section 9 of The Guardians and Wards Act 1890. One petition in respect of girl G was dismissed by the High Court on the ground that G and L were siblings and they could not be separated and thereafter the petition in respect of L was withdrawn. Prior to the disposal of the said petitions, the juvenile court had passed an order declaring both the girls G and L to be destitute under Section 45 of the Bombay Children Act 1948. Later Mrs M, as constituted attorney of E, the national of Sweden, again filed one miscellaneous petition for appointment of E as guardian of both minor girls G and L. After completion of other formalities, a notice of the application was given by the High Court to representatives of the Indian Council of Social welfare and after receiving their representation, the High Court allowed the petition and granted leave to remove both the girls G and L to Sweden. On application to the juvenile court to hand over custody of the two girls G and L, the custody was handed over to Mr E and his wife in February 1981. In July 1981, a court in Sweden granted permission for adoption of both the girls in favour of their national E and his wife and that decree of adoption became final. Swedish citizenship was thereafter granted to the adopted children and they were given Swedish names. J, the mother, who was making inquiries for over two years made an application in February 1982, claiming custody of the girls G and L to the

---

[79] Decided 8 June 1987. Notice of Motion No. 1738 of 1985 in Misc. Petition No. 570 of 1980 (Bom. Original Side).

juvenile court but it disposed these applications expressing inability as the two girls had already left for Sweden in pursuance of the orders of the High Court. After about two years, J addressed a letter through her advocate to the Indian Council of Social Welfare seeking information about the two girls G and L. A year later, J took out a notice of motion, claiming that she should be added as a party, a respondent to the miscellaneous petition in which E was appointed as guardian and was permitted to take the two girls G and L to Sweden for adoption. J further prayed for reopening the case and setting aside the order passed in favour of E. The principal relief she claimed was directing E to produce and hand over the two girls to her as their mother and natural guardian and by way of interim relief sought a direction that the two girls G and L be brought back to Bombay for meeting the natural parents. J also took out a motion of notice for contempt proceedings against Mr E and his constituted attorney in India, Mrs M.

HELD

- That the submission that the natural mother had a legal right to the custody of the children and that right could not be deprived for any reasons whatsoever was totally untenable. It was well settled that whenever a question pertaining to custody of a minor child arose before a court, the matter had to be decided not on consideration of legal rights of parties but on the sole and predominant criteria of what would best serve the interest and welfare of the minor.[80]
- That having regard to all the circumstances in the case including the time interval, it was in the interest and welfare of girls G and L that they should continue to have their status of adopted children and to live in Sweden in their adoptive homes.
- That in spite of the sympathy one might feel for the natural mother, the effect of removing the girls G and L from the care and control of the adoptive parents would lead to disastrous consequences which must be avoided and that it was not in the interest of the children to grant any relief sought in the motion.

This decision laid down several directions relating to the adopted children:

- The principle that the best interest of the child was of paramount consideration was reiterated.

[80] *Mrs Elzabeth Dinshaw v Arvand M. Dinshaw*, AIR 1987 SC 3; *J v C*, 1967 Ch. Div. 761; re E(D)1970 AC 669.

Right to Family Environment

- It was also not possible to grant the relief because the two girls G and L were no longer Indian nationals but had acquired Swedish nationality after passing of the adoption decrees by the Swedish court. An adopted child must be treated in law as if it had been born to the adopters in wedlock and since an adoption affected the status traditionally, the law of the domicile had a paramount controlling influence over the creation of status. Consequently, on adoption decree being passed, the law of their domicile would determine the rights of care and custody in respect of the two girls and that was the Swedish law. In view of these developments it was not possible for the High Court to have any control over the two girls and it was not permissible to pass any order directing Mr E, a Swedish national, to bring back the two girls who were also Swedish nationals.

- The undertaking given to the High Court at the time of passing of the order appointing Mr E as guardian that the minor girls would be repatriated to India as and when it became necessary could not be availed of after passing of the decree of adoption by the Swedish court. Once the girls became Swedish nationals and were duly adopted, the undertaking to repatriate them came to an end and could not be enforced.

- Irrespective of the fact whether a child was adopted in a foreign country or in India, the court should be extremely reluctant and slow in either setting aside the adoption or in ignoring it as it would lead to serious consequences both to the adopter and to the adopted child. The Court might exercise the jurisdiction in exceptional cases, where it was established that the adoption was secured by fraud or misrepresentation and such fraud or misrepresentation was at the instance of the adopter.

- No directions could be issued to the adoptive parents in respect of upbringing of the daughters G and L and making them learn any Indian languages and it would be appropriate to leave it to the good sense of the adoptive parents to determine whether the girls should maintain any contact with the natural parents in India and if so, in what form.

- More precautions were required to be taken before declaring a child as a destitute. It was desirable that the state government should immediately issue the following instructions to the police so that such occasions would not be repeated when, in spite of a complaint having been lodged about a missing child, the police authorities fail to give any assistance to the unfortunate parents:
  – A separate register of missing children should be maintained at each police station.

72 Child Rights in India

- An entry should be made immediately on production of any missing child at the police station and the child's photograph kept in the register.
- Copies of the entries in the register with the copies of the photograph should be forwarded at the end of each month by each police station to the commissioner of police in Greater Bombay and a central register should be maintained in the office of the commissioner of police. In the rural areas, copies should be forwarded to the office of the district superintendent of police and a central register should be maintained at each district headquarters.
- The state government should give wide publicity to the fact of recovery of missing children in local newspapers, on the radio, and on the television. This publicity should be given within a period of fifteen days from the date of production of the child before the juvenile court.

Recommendations for Law Reform[81]

The first and the most important recommendation is the enactment of a common or special adoption law that will be applicable to all people of India, irrespective of their religion. This would be an enabling legislation and ensure the best interests of the child. Till a law gets enacted, a modification in the existing HAMA should be sought which will take care of the existing lacunae in the law.

It is also very essential that enquiries are conducted in an expeditious manner for declaring the child destitute under the Juvenile Justice Act so that the child can be suitably rehabilitated without undue delay.

A set of 'norms and criteria' must be evolved by NGOs to assess the suitability of placement with Indian or foreign parents, so that there is uniformity in practice among agencies and there is no indiscriminate placement.

The role and functions of the following agencies involved in adoption work must be clearly defined and delineated to avoid ambiguities and misinterpretations:

- CARA.
- Placement Agencies.
- Scrutinizing Agencies.

[81] N. Mehta, K. Telang, A Paper on *Family Environment and Alternate Care*, for The Maharashtra State Level Workshop on the Convention on the Rights of the Child, 18–19 January 2001.

- VCA (should actually be called ACA—Adoption Coordinating Agency, because the nomenclature of the term 'voluntary' causes confusion). These agencies must also be licensed for adoption work.

The major role and function of CARA should be to regulate inter-country adoptions and facilitate in-country adoptions. All its functionaries must be clear about this role and should not in any way take a contrary stand of promoting inter-country adoptions over in-country adoptions.

The government must undertake projects/programmes for promotion of in-country adoption through its various media and also support NGOs in their efforts for promotion of Indian adoptions.

A regular, annual meeting of all adoption agencies must be held under the auspices of CARA so that there is a platform and an opportunity available for discussion of common issues.

There should be a separate licensing system from the state government for agencies involved in in-country adoption work just as there is a licence for inter-county adoption work from the Central government. The government must lay down a set of eligibility criteria for adoption agencies.

Agencies receiving funds from affiliated agencies abroad should ensure that such assistance is not linked with an obligation to send a certain number of children for foreign adoptions.

The government/CARA should introduce more schemes and programmes for giving grants and funds and incentive to adoption agencies for promoting in-country adoption.

A birth certificate as a form of identification is the basic right of every child. The adopted child must receive a birth certificate like any natural born child.

Leave benefits like 'maternity leave' should also be available to the adoptive parents. It could be called 'child care leave' when they adopt a child.

A national-level forum of NGOs involved in adoption work should be set up so that they can discuss issues on a common platform.

All adoption agencies must take a more holistic view of child welfare and evolve preventive, community-based, non-institutional services for children and families at risk.

Supporting and empowering of communities to reach out to and protect a child in distress need to be considered as a way to help the ever increasing number of children who need these services.

Group foster homes[82] with families should be encouraged as an alternative to institutionalization.

---

[82] Group foster care in foster homes on the SOS model brings together 8–10 children

An orientation programme must be undertaken for all the functionaries of the juvenile court, welfare boards, city civil courts, High Courts, and district courts that deal with destitute children and adoption. A module must be evolved to address all the issues.

Interventions and Initiatives for Providing Non-institutional Services

Foster Care Schemes

The state of Maharashtra, in joint initiative with UNICEF, took a lead in introducing *Bal Sangopan Yojana (BSY)* in February 1995. This was followed in Karnataka mainly for de-institutionalization of children, *Mamta Grihas* in Orissa, and foster family care in Gujarat.[83] The primary objective of the *Bal Sangopan Yojana* of Maharashtra is to prevent institutionalization of orphan, destitute, and single-parent children by providing financial assistance for care of children in a substitute family. In case of single-parent children, the child's own biological parent is also eligible for assistance under this scheme. The scheme offers Rs 250 per month to the substitute family or the single parent for the care of a child. Besides counselling and emotional support, motivation and encouragement are also provided to the families. BSY plays a vital role in avoiding displacement of a child from a familiar environment and ensures continuity in a child's upbringing. The Indian Association for the Promotion of Adoption and Child Welfare (IAPA)[84] was one of the organizations identified to implement the scheme in Mumbai since April 1995.

Association of Adoptive Families

There are adoptive parents' organizations coming together, like the National Association of Adoptive Families (NAAF)[85] founded by committed groups of parents who have adopted children. NAAF has been formed with the exclusive objective of promoting the concept of child adoption in a vigorous and sustained manner. It is the firm conviction of NAAF that adoption is not merely a personal, need-fulfilling solution for childlessness, but in a wider

---

of varying ages and under the care of a house mother/father. This family unit could be located within the community or in the larger campus of the institution.

[83] Telang K., *Sharing*, A newsletter of the Indian Association for Promotion of Adoption and Child Welfare, April–June 2001, Vol. II, No. 4.

[84] IAPA is a registered voluntary organization established in 1970 in Mumbai and working in the field of child welfare.

[85] A non-governmental organization in Mumbai.

and more rational perspective, an eminently desirable social crusade. It observed the first year of the new millenium, i.e. 2001, as the Year of Adoption.

National Initiative for Child Protection has been launched by the National Institute of Social Defence (NISD) in collaboration with the Central Adoption Resource Agency (CARA). The objective is to train and sensitize various people involved in adoption. The programmes are being organized region-wise. The target group for training include: functionaries of placement agencies, VCAs, Scrutinizing agencies, CARA functionaries at all levels, the state authorities (directors of welfare, police, Juvenile Welfare Board members), NGOs, and officials of allied services (passport officers, municipal corporators, and medical professionals).[86]

International Legal Policies and Practices

Children are on the international agenda today in a way that they have never been before. There are now some universally accepted basic rights which are essential to any child's harmonious and full development even if there is a diversity of the nations' socio-economic, religious, and cultural perceptions of childhood and the child's role in the family and society at large.

Inter-country or international adoptions, that is adoptions in which the adopter and the adoptee are of different nationality or different domicile are becoming increasingly frequent in the modern world. Many countries, particularly in Europe and America, no longer have a sufficient number of children available for adoption. Conversely, countries in which there are numerous children who may be adopted rarely have a large number of prospective adopters.[87]

Every state has the right to regulate the manner in which an adoption may be effected and there are therefore a great many ways in which a person may be adopted. However, there are some international conventions that attempt to harmonize national rules regarding adoptions. The needs for special safeguards and care, including appropriate legal protection for a child, have been stated in the Geneva Declaration of the Rights of the Child 1924.[88] This declaration stated that 'mankind owes to the child the best that

---

[86] *Sharing*, A newsletter produced by the Indian Association for Promotion of Adoption and Child Welfare, Vol. II, No. 1, July–October 2000.

[87] Delupis I. *International Adoptions and the Conflict of Laws*, Almqvist & Wiksell, Uppsala, 1975, p. 11.

[88] It was drafted by the Save the Children International Union, a non-governmental organization established by Eglantyne Jebb to respond to the needs of children during the aftermath of World War I. The declaration was adopted by the League of Nations in 1924.

it has to give'. This declaration was the first step towards protecting children's rights in the broadest sense.

United Nations Instruments Relating to Adoption

In 1959, the United Nations gave official recognition to the human rights of children by adopting the Declaration of the Rights of the Child 1959, a ten principle document. The Declaration set out certain principles relating to the rights of a child to a name and nationality and to be protected from practices which may foster religious discriminations.[89]

Besides, there were several general declarations, covenants, and conventions, which stated the rights of children.[90] The Declaration of Social and Legal Principles, relating to the protection and welfare of children with special reference to foster placement and adoption nationally and internationally 1986, also recognized that the primary aim of adoption is to provide the child who cannot be cared for by his or her own parents with a permanent family. It can be stated that foster placement should also be regulated by law.[91]

The various declarations on the rights of the child were not binding on the governments of the world. Therefore, an idea emerged about drafting a treaty between the governments on the rights of the child which would be more binding. Second, it was realized that the interests of children were not necessarily identical with those of their guardians. The project to draft a Convention started within the UN Commission of Human Rights; a special working group was set up for the purpose under that body.[92]

---

[89] Every child, without any exception whatsoever, shall be entitled to these rights, without distinction or discrimination on account of race, colour, sex, language, religion, political or other opinion, national or social origin, property, birth or other status, whether of himself or of his family. *Principle 1, United Nations Declaration of the Rights of the Child 1959.*

The child shall be entitled from his birth to a name and a nationality. *Principle 3, United Nations Declaration of the Rights of the Child 1959.*

The child shall be protected from practices which may foster racial, religious, and any other form of discrimination. He shall be brought up in a spirit of understanding, tolerance, friendship among people, peace, and universal brotherhood, and in full consciousness that his energy and talents should be directed to the service of the fellow men. *Principle 10, United Nations Declaration of the Rights of the Child 1959.*

[90] Universal Declaration of Human Rights, the International Covenant on Economic, Social, and Cultural Rights, the International Convention on the Elimination of All Forms of Racial Discrimination, and the Convention on the Elimination of All Forms of Discrimination against Women.

[91] Article 10: ibid.: Foster placement should be regulated by law.

[92] It was in commemoration of the twentieth anniversary of the Declaration of the

During the second reading of the draft Convention, four areas emerged as what might be called highly controversial issues. These were the rights of the unborn child, the right to foster care and adoption, freedom of religion, and the minimum age for participation in armed conflict.[93]

Objections to the freedom of religion and to adoption and foster care were launched by the Islamic delegations, which found articles relating to them in conflict with the Koran and with their national legislations.[94] The final text of the articles guaranteeing freedom of religion and the right to adoption and foster care is the result of very difficult and delicate negotiations.[95]

The principles that children have equal values as human beings, that the best interest of the child should be of primary consideration, that due weight should be given to the child's opinion, and that each child has rights are all of great importance.[96]

The Convention has also recognized the right of a child to have an identity and to grow up in a family environment. It also states that the parties to the Convention that permit the system of adoption must ensure that the best interests of the child shall be the paramount consideration. The Convention also provides that there should be no discrimination of any kind irrespective of the child's or his/her parents' or legal guardian's race, colour, sex, language, religion, birth, or other status.

Rights of the Child 1959, that 1979 was designated as the International Year of the Child (IYC). As part of this celebration, Poland proposed that an international treaty be drafted which would put into legally binding language the principles set forth in the 1959 Declaration. The working group established by the Commission in 1979 completed its first draft of the Convention in February 1988.

[93] C.P. Cohen, *United Nations: Convention on the Rights of the Child*, 28 ILM 1448, 1989.

[94] According to Islamic law it is not possible for a child to be able to choose a religion or to change his or her religious faith. This is a privilege available only to adults. Similarly, the Islamic religion does not recognize the right to adoption. In part, this position is based on a concept of consanguinity and inheritance within the interrelated extended family, which cannot and should not be altered or affected by the act of bringing an outsider into the family structure. Instead, the Islamic countries substitute the concept of *Kafala* as a method of caring for abandoned or orphaned children. Under *Kafala*, a family may take a child to live with them on a permanent legal basis, but that child is not entitled to use the family's name or to inherit from the family. The practice of *Kafala* would seem to be somewhat akin to permanent foster care.

[95] I.A. Huard, *The Law of Adoption, Ancient and Modern*, Vanderbilt Law Review, 1956, (ix), 243–63.

[96] T. Hammerberg, 'Making Reality of the Rights of the Child', Legal Perspectives, File No. 33, 1993, p. 9.

Under the Convention, a committee is established to monitor the implementation and all state parties have to submit their first report to the committee within two years of ratification. There is also a link between reports by the states and discussions about assistance. On 11 December 1992, India ratified the Convention[97] and acquired an obligation to ensure that the rights enshrined under the Convention are protected in the country. It is the Government of India that is responsible for ensuring that the norms laid down in the Convention are adhered to in actual practice by enacting laws. International treaties do not automatically become part of the national law. They have to be incorporated into the legal system by appropriate law.[98] Article 4 of the Convention provides that the state parties should review its legislation and ensure that the laws are consistent with the Convention.[99]

Therefore, we now have to make laws for adoption of all children without any discrimination. The various rights under the Convention are not ranked in order of importance but the Convention has an integrated approach and they interact with one another to form part of the same wholeness.

India has also become a signatory to the Declaration of the World Summit for Children setting up goals for survival and child development for the year 2000. The survival and development goals of the World Summit for Children provide substance to the commitment to implement the provisions of the Convention.[100]

The Convention on Protection of Children and Cooperation in Respect of Inter-country Adoption was adopted at the seventeenth session of the Hague Conference on Private International Law. India was also a participant at the deliberations.[101] The Convention is to cover all inter-country adoptions between countries becoming parties to it, whether those adoptions are

---

[97] By the end of 1992, 117 countries have ratified the Convention on the Rights of the Child 1989. By 1996 it was raised to 185. Recently Somalia also ratified. Only USA has non ratified as of now.

[98] The Constitution of India Article 253: Parliament has the power to make any law for the whole or any part of the territory of India for implementing any treaty agreement or Convention with any other country.

[99] See CRC Article 4.

[100] The National Plan of Action for the Child formulated by the Government of India incorporates immediate as well as long-term goals for the year 2000 and outlines a time-bound strategy for achieving the targets.

[101] This conference was convened at the Hague on 10 March 1993 at the invitation of the Government of Netherlands and was attended by government delegates of nearly sixty-nine countries including India. At the conclusion of the seventeenth session of the Hague Conference the participating states adopted the final text of the subject Convention.

partly parent-initiated or arranged by public authorities, adoption agencies, or by private providers of adoption services. The Convention sets a framework of internationally agreed minimum norms and procedures that are to be complied with in order to protect the children involved and the interests of their parents and adoptive parents. Contracting states are free to maintain or impose requirements and prohibitions additional to those set out in the Convention.

Summary of the Convention's Provisions

The Convention's preamble recognizes that the child, for the full and harmonious development of its personality, should grow up in a family environment and that inter-country adoption may offer the advantage of a permanent family to a child for whom a suitable family cannot be found in its state of origin.

OBJECT OF THE CONVENTION

The Convention's objects are as follows:[102]

- To establish safeguards to ensure that inter-country adoptions take place in the best interests of the child and with respect to its fundamental rights.
- To ensure a system of cooperation among contracting states so that the safeguards are respected and thereby there is a prevention of abduction, sale, or traffic in children, and to secure the recognition of adoptions made in accordance with the Convention. The Convention is to apply to all adoptions between contracting states that create a permanent parent-child relationship.[103]

Requirement for inter-country adoptions are set out in Articles 4 and 5 of the Convention. The Convention also requires every contracting state to establish central authorities and accredited bodies related to inter-country adoptions. The procedural requirements in inter-country adoptions are set out in the Convention.

Article 14 of the Convention requires that prospective adoptive parents, habitually resident in one contracting state and wishing to adopt a child habitually resident in another, must apply to the central authority in the state of their habitual residence or by reason of Article 22 to an accredited agency in that state. Under Article 22 (5), the home study report on the prospective adoptive parents, finding them eligible and suited to adopt and the report

---

[102] Article 1 of the Convention.
[103] Article 2 of the Convention.

on the child, are to be prepared 'under the responsibility of the respective state's Central Authority or other public authority or an accredited body'. Chapter V of the Convention deals with the recognition and effects of adoption. It ensures that adoptions certified as made in accordance with the Convention shall be recognized by operation of law in other contracting state.

Chapter VI contains a number of provisions of general application. Articles 30 and 32 deal with the preservation of information concerning the child's origin, identity of its parents, and its medical history. Article 33 deals with the reporting of actual or possible responsibility for ensuring that appropriate measures are taken. No reservations are permitted under Article 40 of the Convention. The seventeenth session, unable in the available time to fit the adoption of refugee and internationally displaced children into the structure of the Convention, determined that further study and possibly the elaboration of special instrument supplementary to the Convention were necessary on these issues and therefore requested the Hague Conference Secretary General in consultation with the United Nations High Commissioner for Refugees to examine the issue of refugee and internationally displaced children.

Significance and Relevance of the Hague Convention to India

The objectives and provisions of the Convention reiterate and elaborate what is clearly contained in the Constitution of India, the National Policy for Children 1974, the United Nations' Convention on the Rights of the Child 1989, and the Supreme Court guidelines for inter-country adoption laid down in the Laxmikant Pandey judgments[104] and Guardians and Wards Act 1890. For instance, Article 4 of the Hague Convention states that an adoption within the scope of the Convention will take place only after the possibilities for placement of the child within the state of origin of the child have been given due consideration. It also provides for consent of the child where possible, and counselling of the child and the parents, and ensures that such consent has not been induced by payment or compensation of any kind.

As per the Supreme Court guidelines followed in India, first priority is given to in-country adoption and where this is not possible inter-country adoption may be resorted to in the interest of the child. If the biological parents are known, they should be properly assisted by the social or child welfare agency in making decision about relinquishing the child. The Supreme

---

[104] *Laxmikant Pandey v Union of India*, AIR 1984 SC 4699; AIR 1986 SC 273; AIR 1987 SC 232.

Court also imposes a duty upon the recognized social or child welfare agency through which the foreigner wants to adopt a child to make sure that the child is free for adoption. It also provides that for children above seven years, their wishes may be ascertained if they are in a position to indicate any preference.

Article 6 of the Hague Convention states that there should be designated a central authority to discharge the duties which are imposed by the Convention. In India, the Central Adoption Resource Agency (CARA) has also been set up with similar functions.[105] The CARA guidelines have been formulated to ensure what has been stated in Articles 7, 8, 9, 16, 18, 19, 20, 21, 22, and 23 of the Hague Convention.

Articles 10, 11, 12, and 13 of the Hague Convention provide for accreditation to the competent bodies and norms for registration of agencies for inter-country adoptions. Under the prevalent Supreme Court guidelines, directions have been given to the ministry of social welfare of the Government of India and of the states to recognize and license suitable agencies within the country. These could be further streamlined to ensure that the right kinds of agencies are involved.

Every application from a foreigner desiring to adopt a child from India must be sponsored by a social worker or child welfare agency recognized or licensed by the government of the country in which the foreigner is resident.[106] Article 15 of the Hague Convention provides what we call the home study report, which has to accompany every application of the foreigner. There are similar provisions laid down in the Supreme Court guidelines and the guidelines of the task force.

Article 24 of the Hague Convention states that the recognition of adoption may be refused in a contracting state only if the adoption is manifestly contrary to its public policy taking into account the best interests of the child. This clause is the general escape clause, which allows any of the Convention's provisions to be disregarded when observance would be manifestly contrary to the public policy. This clause probably adds little to a power of exception which any of the contracting states would already have under the general rules of public policy, which operate over and above the framework of the Convention.

India should accede to this Convention, as it will oblige India to formulate legislation on inter-country adoption.[107] It will ensure that the child will not be abused in the receiving country, as we will be sending our children

---

[105] Refer to the role of the CARA on p. 51
[106] The Hague Convention, 1993. Article 14.
[107] The Hague Convention, Article 28, allows the enactment of law.

to those countries which are parties to this Convention. Besides, the Convention does not intervene in the personal laws of the country.[108]

In an era when a pro-children development strategy has been adopted by the government, the accession of this Convention—which conforms to our Constitutional mandate[109] and our national norms and procedures for inter-country adoption—is desired. This Convention is compatible with Indian laws both in letter and spirit and therefore needs to be ratified so that we have a law on inter-country adoption that will contribute to the international legal regime on adoption and in the cause of justice to the child.

A Comparative Study of International Law

Comparative studies of the laws of some developing countries reveal that:

- Generally, it is the orphan, destitute, and abandoned children who can be adopted.
- In the Philippines the age of the adoptive parents is not specified (though in practice the adoptive agencies have set up some age limits) but in other developing countries the age limit is between 25–40 years.
- Several countries do not specify the age difference between parents and adopted child but countries like Columbia, the Philippines, and Thailand give it as fifteen years or more, whereas India and Kenya give it as twenty-one years or more.
- The average age of the child to be adopted is 0–14 years. In Indonesia, for inter-country adoption the age of the child is 0–6 years only.
- In Nepal there is no foreign adoption. Customary adoptions are carried on in India and Kenya. Thailand, Ethiopia, Indonesia, Columbia, and the Philippines carry it through government recognized adoption agencies and courts.

A comparative study of adoption practices in some developed countries reveals that:

- The system of adoption is a highly professionalized childcare service.
- Most of the countries allow adults to adopt, i.e. twenty-one years of age for the adoptive parents.
- Both married as well as single persons are allowed to adopt.
- The age of the child is normally under eighteen years of age.
- Adoptions are regulated by legislations.
- There are special procedures for legitimizing children under the various legal systems.

---

[108] See the Hague Convention, Article 37.
[109] See The Constitution of India, Articles 15(3), 23, 24, 39, 45, and 46.

- The consent of the child is relevant in several states.
- The child is given all rights as a natural born child, including inheritance rights.
- Adoptions can be revoked under certain circumstances.
- Maternity benefit and compensation are normally extended to adoptive parents.

Some of the features present in international practices in adoption that need to be highlighted and could be amended suitably and incorporated in the common law of adoption are as follows:

- In several countries adoption laws have been founded upon broad humanitarian principles.
- The tendency of modern statutes is to confer upon adopted children the right to inherit not only from the adoptive parents but also through the adoptive parents and from the adoptive parents' next of kin and to take away from the adopted child, rights of inheritance not only from its natural parents but from all blood relations of natural parents.
- The right to custody of an illegitimate child is with its mother and most statutes recognize this right and require the consent of the mother for adoption of her child.
- The fact that the mother is a minor does invalidate her consent.
- In the absence of any acknowledgement of paternity by the father of an illegitimate child and his marriage with the mother, the consent of the father of an illegitimate child to its adoption by another is not essential and he is not entitled to the notice of adoption proceedings.
- An important contribution by the United States of America in the field of child welfare is the role of child advocacy which professionals are encouraged to play. Children's rights have to be campaigned for because child welfare is an important issue for socio-economic development as an investment in children is an investment in the nation's future.
- In connection with inter-country adoption in the UK, four main services have to be provided:
    - Counselling and preparation of anyone considering adoption from abroad.
    - Assessment, including a home study report of suitability of prospective adopters to adopt from overseas.
    - Providing supervision and support to child and family pending the making of an adoption order.
    - Post-adoption services: In Britain, courses for those wishing to adopt have been developed by Bury Social Services and by Childlink. In

both cases the preparation is linked to assessment and, in these respects, follows a well-established tradition of using group sessions in selecting adoptive and foster parents.
- In the Netherlands, it is now compulsory for all prospective adoptive parents to attend the information and preparation programme. Research studies have shown that 'well-prepared parents seem more able to cope with problems'.
- In Sweden, the National Board has produced a number of publications providing general information about adoption. Group meetings are recommended before the assessment process starts. Adoption agencies such as the Adoption Centre in Stockholm also offer preparation courses. The course involves 10–14 evening sessions offered in the applicants' home area (two weekends in more sparsely populated areas) covering a whole range of issues and a full day *take-off* course for those who have been approved and are soon to have a child placed with them.
- The need for better post-adoption services is recognized in several countries. A central feature of post-adoption work is helping adapted children/adults wishing to find more about their birth parents.
- Taking a child from a set of parents and placing him/her with another set, who pretend that the child is born to them, disrupts a basic natural process. The need to be connected with one's biological and historical past is an integral part of one's identity formation. The search and ultimate reunion between adopters and the adopted child's birth parents provide the means for bringing together the broken connections from the past. The adopter's need to search for birth parents and true identity has always existed. Reunions are now more widespread and techniques of searching more sophisticated. Adoption agencies no longer guarantee secrecy and anonymity. They now advise adoptive parents that their children may want to meet their birth parents.
- While the rule of strict construction is stated in many cases, modern authorities, recognizing that adoption statutes tend to conserve the best interests of the society and the State, are more and more inclined to abandon the old rule of strict construction, with a view of sustaining the assumed relationship,[110] particularly against collateral attacks by strangers to the proceedings.[111] Therefore, the prevailing tendency in many jurisdictions is in the direction of liberal construction and many of the adoption statutes are by their terms to be liberally construed.[112]

[110] Re Frazier, 180 or 232, 170 AR 729.
[111] Re Mckeag's Estate, 141 Cal 403.
[112] *Cofer v Scroggins*, 980 ALR 342.

- The right of a grandparent to adopt grandchildren is recognized. It is not usually a requirement that a person seeking to adopt another be married, although many statutes require in the case of adoption by a married person either a joint petition by the husband and wife or the consent of the other spouse.
- It is generally recognized in American law that one who is legally competent to adopt another as his child may enter into a valid and binding contract to do so and, according to most but not all authorities, if such a contract is not performed by the promisor during his lifetime, it may be enforced in equity against his estate at the instance of the intended adopter. Such agreements are to be distinguished from contracts whereby a parent bargains away, for pecuniary gain, the custody of his child to another person. To be valid, a contract to adopt must be between parties who are competent to contract and the contract must be based upon a valid consideration. In America, it has been held that the consideration necessary to support a contract to adopt may be any consideration sufficient to support an ordinary contract. The consideration to support the adoption contract may be to the detriment of the party surrendering the child, or the change in the domestic status of the child, or the benefits in the love and affection accruing to the adopting party[113] or the society, and the companionship and filial obedience of the child or the surrender of natural ties by the parent, and the sacrifice of the parent in giving up the child. For the most part, executory contracts or agreements for adoption have been presented to the courts for examination and enforcement only after the death of the promisor and for the purpose of recovering from the estate of the promisor a portion of the property claimed to be due to the child by reason of a promise expressed in or implied from the contract to adopt.[114] Such a contract or agreement does not, in and of itself, create a status of parent and child between the child and the promisor or make the child the heir of the promisor. That can be done only by compliance with the statutory method prescribed, which usually requires a decree of a designated court in a proceeding held for that purpose, although under some statutes, a legal adoption may be effected by a written and duly recorded declaration or deed. Breach of a valid contract to adopt may give rise to an action for damages,[115] and a suit for damages for breach of a contract to adopt may be maintained by the prospective adoptive parent when

---

[113] *Foster v Creek*, 212 GA 821, 96 SE 2d 545.
[114] *Lyan v Hockaday*, 162 No.111, 61 SW 885.
[115] Re Carroll's Estate, 219 Pa 440, 68.

the other party fails to perform the agreement. But while a court of equity may, at the death of the foster parent, enforce rights of the child in property to the extent of decreeing that he is entitled to share in the property of the deceased foster parent, a court of equity will not decree specific performance of a contract to adopt and compel performance of the agreement by the promisor in his lifetime. Thus, it is held that the child cannot maintain a suit for specific performance or a suit to compel its adoption, since there would have been no mutuality of remedy to enforce the contract against the child, because personal services on its part would be involved. Other factors that preclude a decree of specific performance of contract to adopt are the intimate and personal relationship of parent and child, and the necessity of determination of the best interests of the child.

- While there is some difference of opinion, most courts, which have considered the effect of an agreement to adopt, hold that an agreement clear and complete in its terms, entered into by parties capable of contracting, which has been fully and faithfully performed on the part of the child so that relief is required as a matter of justice and equity, will be enforced in equity to the extent of decreeing that the child occupy in equity the status of an adopted child, and be entitled to the same rights of inheritance in intestate property of the promisor to which he would have otherwise been entitled had the intended adoption proceedings been legally consummated. Such a suit may be and usually is brought by the child in its own name, although not a party to the contract.
- The courts merely enforce a contract, which has been fully performed on one side; they do not undertake to change the status of either party, or to decree that the child is entitled to the right of inheritance as an heir. The relief which equity grants is the equivalent of the property rights the child would have received had the adopter performed his contractual obligation to formally and legally adopt the child.[116]
- Principles of estoppel have also been applied to preclude privities of the adoptive parent from denying the status of the child when the parent has received the benefits of performance on the part of the child and privileges accruing from such performance, and by his representations has induced such performance under the belief of the existence of the status of an adopted child.[117]

---

[116] Re Grace's Estate, 83 Cal App 2d 956, 200 P 2d 189.
[117] *Roberts v Roberts* (CAB Mo) 223 F 775 Cert der 239, US 639 60.

- As indicated above, the basis of doctrine of recognition of a foster child and enforcement of his claim to share in the estate of the deceased foster parent who had agreed to adopt him is that it is inequitable and unjust to allow the parent to escape obligations of an adoptive parent by his failure to comply with the agreement made with the parent or custodian of the child.[118] There is no absolute right to demand enforcement; the matter rests in the discretion of the court and will be granted only if to do so would not be unfair, inequitable, or unjust.[119]
- The doctrine of equitable adoption will not be applied to enforce rights in the estate of the deceased promisor where the contract was made; to do so would be contrary to the fundamental basis of the doctrine, and open the door to fraudulent claims.[120]

Towards a Common Secular Law on Adoption

Religion has played a very dominant role in India and religion is the basis of various personal rights including adoption. The fact today is that a Hindu child is being governed by the Hindu Adoptions and Maintenance Act 1956 and has the opportunity of being taken in adoption under the Act only because he is a Hindu by religion. The Muslim child, the Christian child, and the Parsi child are denied this opportunity only because they are Muslims, Christians, and Parsis by religion. Many of these orphan, destitute children do not have the historical or social background, educational or cultural outlook, and way of life or thought common to the community. Therefore the discrimination of the children is solely on the grounds of religion. Therefore Article 15 of the Constitution forbidding discrimination on the ground of religion alone would strike down all these provisions as unconstitutional and ultra vires.

The Constitution has itself recognized the existence of various personal laws in operation in our country. When the Constitution was being adopted and enacted, it had in Article 44 directed that the state shall endeavour to secure for the citizens a uniform civil code throughout the territory of India. In 1949, when this article was enacted, we already had uniform codes covering every aspect of legal relationship excepting only those matters in which we were governed by the various personal laws. The laws of contracts, of

---

[118] *Thompson v Moseley*, 344 Mo 240, 125 SW 2d 860.
[119] 11 ALR 819.
[120] See *Roberts v Roberts* (CAB Mo) 223 F 775 Cert der 239, 4563960.

transfer of property, of sale of goods, partnership, companies and negotiable instruments, of civil procedure, arbitration, and limitation of crimes and criminal procedures, and a host of other statutory laws were uniform civil codes applying throughout the country. As Dr B.R. Ambedkar observed during the debates in the Constituent Assembly on the draft Article 35 (subsequently enacted as Article 44), the only area which was not covered by any uniform civil code was marriage and succession, and it was the intention of those who enacted Article 44 as part of the Constitution to bring about that change. In fact, Article 44 could have only the different personal laws in view, the rest of the areas having mostly been covered by uniform civil codes. The Article therefore appears to be a demonstration of the conviction on the part of its framers that the existence of the different religion-oriented personal laws of ours is not in tune with egalitarian philosophy.

About Article 44 in particular, it has been observed by Chief Justice Gajendragadkar that 'in any event, the non-implementation of the provisions contained in Article 44 amounts to a grave failure of Indian democracy and the sooner we take suitable action in that behalf, the better'. In 1985, the Supreme Court regretted in the unanimous decision of the five-judge Bench in the Shah Bano case that Article 44 of our Constitution has remained a dead letter and that 'a beginning has to be made if the Constitution is to have any meaning'. In another decision in that year a two-judge Bench of the Supreme Court relied on these observations and reiterated that 'the time has come for the intervention of the Legislature in these matters to provide for a uniform code'.

The comments of Dr K.M. Munshi in the Constituent Assembly Debates still hold good today in the interest of social justice to the child. Dr Munshi pointed out that as regards the right to freedom of religion guaranteed under Article 25 of the Constitution, it was subject to reasonable restriction by the state, and the Parliament could make laws regulating and restricting . . . any secular activity which may be associated with religious practices. Hence, if a religious practice or secular activity falls within the field of social welfare, it would be open to Parliament to make laws about it and such a law would not violate any fundamental rights. The object of this provision, he said, was that as and when the Parliament thinks proper, an attempt may be made to unify the personal laws of the country. Dr Munshi, talking about the argument relating to minority rights, pointed out that even in the most advanced Islamic countries, the personal law of each minority has not been recognized as so sacrosanct as to prevent the enactment of a uniform civil code. He said, 'When you want to consolidate a community, you have to take into consideration the benefit which may accrue to the whole community and not to the customs of a part of it.'

Article 44 is contained in Part IV of our Constitution captioned 'Directive Principles of State Policy' and Article 37 declares that though the provisions contained in Part IV are not enforceable in or by any court as the provisions relating to fundamental rights in Part III are, yet 'the principles therein laid down are nevertheless fundamental in the governance of the country and it shall be the duty of the State to apply these principles in making laws'. Therefore the provisions of Part IV are mandatory in letter and spirit and if that is so, the non-implementation of these provisions would deviously amount to a breach of trust with which we have entrusted ourselves by our Constitution.

The question of uniform civil code has again sprung into prominence because of the judgment delivered by Justice Kuldeep Singh and Justice Sahai in the case of *Sarla Mudgal v Union of India*, on 10 May 1995.

The main issues involved were:

- Whether a Hindu husband married under the Hindu law, by embracing Islam can solemnize a second marriage,
- Whether such a marriage without having the first marriage dissolved under the law would be valid, and
- Whether the converted husband would be guilty of bigamy under Section 494 of the Indian Penal Code.

It was held by the Supreme Court that the second marriage of the Hindu husband after embracing Islam violates the principles of justice, equity, and good conscience and would be void on the ground of natural justice.

While delivering the judgment, the Supreme Court requested the government to have a 'fresh look' at Article 44 of the Constitution of India and 'retrieve Article 44 from the cold storage' where it is lying since 1949. The Court also observed that successive governments till date had been wholly remiss in implementing Article 44.

The Court stated that Article 44 is based on the concept that there is no necessary connection between religion and personal law in a civilized society. Article 25 guarantees religious freedom whereas Article 44 seeks to divert religion from social relations and personal law. Marriage, succession, and like matters of a secular character cannot be brought within the guarantee enshrined under Articles 25, 26, and 27.

This judgment generated a renewed debate on the Uniform Civil Code. The oral observation on 11 August 1995 of Justice Kuldeep Singh (Justice Sahai had already retired) that their observations on the Uniform Civil Code were obiter dicta and not binding, were perhaps meant to stem the debate under judicial restraint. The oral observation from the Bench does not and in law cannot value away the direction of the two judges to the Union government.

On 9 August 1995, the Maharashtra Legislative Assembly passed a bill called the Maharashtra Adoption Act 1995 to provide for adoption of children, which applied to every person adopting a child in the state of Maharashtra, irrespective of the person's religion, caste, race, and sex. The Government of Maharashtra declared that this legislation was for giving effect to the policy of the state towards securing the principles specified in Article 44 of the Constitution of India.

Some of the salient features of the proposed Act were:

- The age of the person adopting the child has to be twenty-five years or more.
- A married Hindu woman whose husband is alive will be able to adopt with her husband's consent.
- Twins will be able to be adopted at the same time.
- Adoption will be done in the jurisdiction of the district courts in which the person adopting the child resides.

This bill did not receive the presidential assent. An attempt has also been made in Kerala for a uniform law on adoption. The proposed bill envisages giving full legal status to the adopted children at par with the biological children, irrespective of the religious status of the adoptive parents.[121]

But, whatever the controversy, adoption of children is not an issue of Hindu law or Muslim law or any other theological system, but an issue of justice to the child and the best interests of the child. If the Maharashtra bill had in its preamble stressed on the aspect of the justice to the child rather than the uniform civil code, it would perhaps have had a better chance of being enacted into a law. The proposed common secular law on adoption would perhaps be acceptable to all communities if its main focus is on the welfare of the destitute and orphan child and it does not interfere with the inheritance laws, which are of divine origin in some communities. But, for the safety and security of the adopted child, the following could be considered;

- All the parents who have adopted a child would have deemed to have willed away one-third of their property to their adopted child out of love and affection, unless a wish to the contrary has been expressed in writing, along with reasons, to be recorded which would facilitate the application of the mind and prudence of the court.

---

[121] *Sharing*, Newsletter of the Indian Association for the Promotion of Adoption, Vol. II, No.1, July–October 2000.

- In case there is no property, usufructary rights and other heritable rights like tenancy, cultivation, etc. could be shared at least to the extent of one third of the property.
- In case of joint Hindu family property/ *Wakf* property/Parsi, Jewish, or Christian trusts, the adopted child should become a beneficiary in the corpus of the property to the extent of one-third of the property.
- Perhaps, a form of contract could be provided which gives the rights and duties of the adoptive parents and adopted children along with a remedy of breach of specific performance.

3

Right to Parental Care: Custody and Guardianship

Historical Evolution

The legal relationship of parent and child is composed of rights and duties. Parents have parental rights by virtue of being natural guardians of their children. The term 'guardianship' in its fullest sense embraces a 'bundle of rights' or to be more exact a 'bundle of powers' which a parent has over his child, i.e. the full parental rights which constitute the parent-child relationship. These normally include the right to determine the child's upbringing 'as regards religion, education, and other matters'. The word 'custody' is normally used in India to denote the right to physical possession of the child, i.e. charge of the minor's person. In Hindu law, the concept of guardianship appears to date back to the time of the Vedic age, when for all practical purposes, the Hindu family was a patriarchal one, with considerable powers resting with the head of the family. Infants were considered as the property of the father. Acquisition or holding of independent separate property was not possible for them and the properties belonged to the father.[1] Gradually, the son's right to separate self-acquired property was recognized by law.

The ancient Hindu law vested the supreme guardianship of all in the broad principle of the king as *parens patriae*.[2] Sage Narada[3] mentioned father and mother as guardians. The minor children mostly lived in the joint family and were always under the protection of the *karta* or the head of the family. Even if the child did not belong to a joint family but if he belonged to the first three varnas, he had to go to a guru's ashram to study and was under the protection of the guru.[4] Thus there was no need for the law of guardianship of the person.[5] The question of guardianship of minor's property would have

[1] A.N. Saha, *Guardians and Wards Act*, Eastern Law House, 13th edition, 1998.
[2] Manu Smriti, VII 27, *Gautama* 10, 48.
[3] Narada Smriti, XIII (28–9).
[4] Teacher.
[5] Paras Diwan, *Modern Hindu Law*, Allahabad Law Agency, 1992, p. 239.

arisen only in those cases where the child was not a member of any joint family and had no parents. In respect of such children, the king was the supreme guardian who protected all such children and their property.[6]

In the ancient texts, the following are the references to the custody and guardianship. A text of Manu[7] states: 'The king shall protect the inherited (and other) property of a minor until he has returned (from his teacher's home) or until he has passed his minority.' Sage Gautama[8] also declared: 'The king should protect till he has attained majority or has completed his education.' According to Vasishtha:[9] 'The king might entrust others with the minor's affairs.' Narada stated: 'The father has the first claim and after him comes the elder brother. His powers as guardian will be determined as may be deemed justly required for the benefit of the infant.'[10]

It is significant here that the concept of benefit of the minor was prevalent even in Narada's text. It is also to be noted that with the exception of Narada, who alone mentions the father, the mother, and the elder brother as guardians, all other sages merely declare the king to be the guardian of minor's[11] property. But none of the ancient text writers have spoken of the guardianship of the person of the minor. All of them mention about the guardianship of the property of the minor. It seems that the guru or the teacher was the guardian of his pupil and because of joint family system, the children in the family were under the protection of the *karta* or the head of the joint family property. Under Hindu law, since the joint family was like a perpetual corporation, after the death of the father or *karta* the issue of guardianship did not arise at all.[12]

Till the passing of the Hindu Minority and Guardianship Act 1956, the traditional Hindu Law remained in force throughout British India and most of the Indian states.[13] The main feature that emerged in these laws was the predominant position of the father in respect of guardianship. The Hindu Minority and Guardianship Act 1956 reformed and codified the Hindu law of guardianship and minority. Under the Act, the supremacy of the paternal right during the lifetime of the father remained intact. So long as he was alive,

---

[6] Paras Diwan, *Modern Hindu Law*, Allahabad Law Agency, 13th edition, 1998.
[7] Manu Smriti, VII, 27.
[8] Gautama Smriti, 10, 48.
[9] Vasishtha Smriti, 16, 7–8.
[10] Narada Smriti, XIII, 28–9.
[11] Diwan Paras, *Law of Adoption, Minority, Guardianship of Custody*, Universal Law Publishing Co. Pvt. Ltd., Delhi, 2000.
[12] Ibid.
[13] Ibid.

he was the sole guardian and after his death or if he was unfit, the mother was the natural guardian of her minor children.

During the British period, the courts developed the law of guardianship. The Guardians and Wards Act (GWA) was passed in 1890 and conferred on the district courts the power of appointing guardians of minor children belonging to any community. A guardian is thus a person who has rights and duties with respect to the care and control of a minor's person or property. Guardianship includes the right to make decisions about the minor's upbringing, disposal of his/her property, etc.[14] The word used in defining guardian is 'care'. 'Care' indicates looking after in wider senses than 'custody' which is simply 'physical keeping'. Custody refers to the physical care and control of a minor. Custody is thus the right to the physical presence of the child. It includes the right to take day-to-day decisions regarding the child's education, medical treatment, and general movement. Custody can only be of the person of the minor but not of its property.[15]

The Present Legal Regime

The law of guardianship and custody of minors is governed by:

- The Guardians and Wards Act 1890 (GWA).
- The Hindu Minority and Guardianship Act 1956 (HMGA) and the unmodified Muslim law of custody and guardianship.
- The personal laws of Hindus, Parsis, and Christians which lay down the principles relating to the custody and guardianship of children during matrimonial proceedings.

The Guardians and Wards Act 1890 (GWA)

The Guardians and Wards Act 1890 was among the earliest statutes enacted by the British Indian legislature relating to minors. The charters of the High Courts and the High Court Act of 1861 conferred special jurisdiction on the High Courts in regard to minor children. Before 1890, there were scattered statutes and regulations enacted by the Presidencies of Madras, Bombay, and Bengal.[16] The Guardians and Wards Act, 1890 was a consolidating and amending statute. All the provisions of the earlier scattered statutes have

---

[14] Section 4(2), Guardians and Wards Act 1890.
[15] Lawyers' Collective, *Legal Aid Handbook 2, Custody and Guardianship of Minors*, Lawyers Collective and Kali for Women, New Delhi, 1995.
[16] Paras Divan, *Law of Adoption, Minority, Guardianship and Custody*, Universal Law Publishing Co. Pvt. Ltd., Delhi, 2000.

been consolidated under the present Act. It is a complete code defining the rights and remedies of guardians and wards. All matters relating to guardianship, their rights and obligations, the removal and replacement of the guardian, and remedies available to the wards are regulated by the provisions of the Act. This Act applies to all minor children of any caste and creed, though in appointing or declaring a person as guardian of the minor, the court will take into consideration the personal law of the minor. The Guardians and Wards Act deals with the guardian of the person and property of the minor. When an application is made to the court for the appointment or declaration of a person as guardian, the court is required to take into consideration the personal law of the minor [Sec. 19]. But once a person is appointed or declared as guardian of a minor, irrespective of the fact whether the minor is a Hindu, a Muslim, or subject to any other personal law, such guardian will be subject to the provisions of the Act. Once a certificated guardian is appointed or declared, the powers of natural or testamentary guardian under the personal law stands suspended.[17] But if the personal law is not in conflict with any provision of the Act, the personal law will apply.[18]

Courts have exercised the power of appointing guardians from a very early time. Whenever a matter of guardianship or custody of a child is brought before it, the courts assume the charge of the child and endeavour to see that the child is brought up in the same manner as natural parents should have done. The guardian court usually discharges the function by appointing a suitable guardian. A guardian appointed by the court is under the supervision and control of the court and he cannot take any steps except the routine ones, without the prior permission of the court. The court may be called upon to appoint a guardian of the person of the minor or of his property or of both. The procedure for appointing guardians is prescribed under this Act.

The natural guardian of a minor is the person who is legally presumed to have a natural right of guardianship over it and consequently is presumed to make ultimate decisions about his/her welfare. The natural guardian has the legal right to act as a minor's guardian, unless that right is taken away by a court in a proceeding under the GWA or unless a testamentary guardian has been properly appointed by will. The natural guardian does not have to go to court to be appointed guardian. A person cannot surrender to another party his or her duty to act as a guardian although custody of a minor may be given to another.

---

[17] *A.R. Krishnan Chetty v Valliachani*, AIR 1914 Mad 648.
[18] *Siddigunnisa Bibi v Nizamuddin*, AIR 1932 All 215.

96 Child Rights in India

Under Section 20 of the GWA, the relationship between a guardian and the ward is a fiduciary relationship. This means that guardians cannot profit from their guardianship and must act only with the wards' welfare in mind. There are two types of guardians: of the minor's person and of the minor's property. A guardian of a minor's person is expected to take custody of the minor and is obliged to provide financial support, health care, and education. If a court has appointed the guardian of the person, he or she is not permitted to remove the ward from the jurisdiction of that court without the court's permission.

Guardians of property have an obligation to deal with the minor's property as if it were his or her own and can act to protect or enhance the property. Guardians of property who are appointed by the court cannot mortgage, transfer, or dispose of immovable property, or lease it without prior approval from the court. Transfer in violation of this restriction is void. Generally, the powers of guardians that are appointed by a will can be further restrained by the will, and the powers of guardians of property are contained in the GWA.

Welfare of the Child under the Guardians and Wards Act 1890

Section 7(1) of the Guardians and Wards Act, 1890, deals with the power of the Court to appoint or declare a person as guardian. Whenever the court on the application of a person comes to the conclusion that it would be for the welfare of the child to appoint a guardian of the person or property or both of the minor, it can appoint a guardian.

Section 17 of the Guardians and Wards Act 1890 deals with the power of the court to appoint or declare a person as guardian. Whenever the court, on the application of a person, comes to the conclusion that it would be for the welfare of the child to appoint a guardian of the person or property or both of the minor, it can appoint a guardian. Section 17 lays down the various factors which would help the court in finding out the welfare of the child.

Section 7(1) lays down the cardinal rule in the matter of guardianship and custody of children. It states that the court should appoint a guardian only when it is satisfied that the appointment of guardian is necessary for the welfare of the child. In considering what will be for the welfare of the minor, the following factors have been mentioned, all of which are contained in Sec. 17(2):

- Age of the minor;
- Sex of the minor;

- Religion of the minor;
- The character and capacity of the proposed guardian;
- Nearness of kin to the minor;
- Wishes, if any, of the deceased parent;
- Any existing or previous relations of the proposed guardian with the minor or his property; and
- If the minor is old enough to form an intelligent preference, the court may consider that preference.

These are the guiding factors laid down by the Guardians and Wards Act 1890 to determine the welfare of the child. Section 7 read with Section 17 can be interpreted as stating that the welfare of the minor should be consistent with the personal law of the minor. It is significant to note that the personal law of the minor is a very important consideration.

Second, Section 17(5) states that the court shall not appoint or declare any person to be a guardian against his/her will. This means that the guardian appointed by the court must accept his/her appointment. His/Her will appears to be more important than the welfare of the child. Even if he is the most suitable person for the welfare of the child, if he does not accept his appointment, he cannot be appointed. This provision clearly subordinates the welfare of the child as the paramount consideration. From the wordings of the provision of the Guardians and Wards Act, it thus appears that the welfare of the minor should conform to the personal law of the minor and the willingness of the guardian.

The other considerations like age, sex, character, and capacity of the guardian, nearness of kin, and the wishes of the deceased parent, and the wishes of the child may help the court in determining the welfare of the child. From the reading of Sections 7(1) and 17 of the Guardian and Wards Act, it has not been specifically mentioned that the *welfare of the child is the paramount consideration*. The principle of the best interests of the child has not been actually laid down. But decisions of the Supreme Court and High Courts have interpreted that the welfare of the child should be the paramount consideration.

Under Section 7, the district court or the family court has the power to appoint or declare a person as guardian of a minor's person or property and once it decides to make such an appointment or declaration, Section 17 comes into operation, as the court would appoint a guardian after considering these factors. These factors assist the court in determining what is for the welfare of the child.

The Hindu Minority and Guardianship Act 1956 (HMGA)

Under the Hindu Minority and Guardianship Act 1956 the father is the natural guardian of the person and property of legitimate children and after him[19] the guardianship vests in the mother[Sec. 6]. The Supreme Court has now made the mother also the natural guardian.[20] The undivided share of the minor in the joint family property is excluded from the purview of guardianship. The father cannot now deprive the mother of guardianship after his death by appointing a guardian by will. Even during the lifetime of the father, the mother is entitled to the custody of her children below the age of five years. It is suggested that this age needs to be increased.

Under the Act, mother is the natural guardian of her illegitimate children and after her death, the putative father is the natural guardian. The adoptive father, and after him the adoptive mother, is the natural guardian of an adopted child. Under the HGMA, both the parents have been given power of appointing testamentary guardians. Parents have power of testamentary appointment in all those cases where they are competent to act as natural guardians.

However, a Hindu father cannot appoint a guardian of his minor illegitimate children, even when he is entitled to act as their natural guardian. The guardianship of a minor girl comes to an end on her marriage and it cannot be revised even if she becomes a widow during her minority. In that event, the guardianship would belong to the nearest *sapinda* (near kinsmen) of her husband.

QUALIFICATIONS REGARDING NATURAL GUARDIANS

Although Section 6(a) of the Hindu Minority and Guardianship Act 1956 declares that in the case of a boy or an unmarried girl, the natural guardians of Hindu minor are the father, and after him, the mother, that proposition is subject to two qualifications as enumerated below:

- The proviso to Section 6 lays down that the custody of a minor who has not completed the age of five years shall ordinarily be with the mother; and
- Section 13(1) lays down that in the appointment or declaration of any person as guardian of a Hindu minor by a court, the welfare of the minor shall be the paramount consideration. By Subsection (2) of the same Section, it is provided, inter alia, that no person is entitled to

---

[19] For the latest interpretation of 'after him' see *Githa Hariharan & Another v Reserve Bank of India and Another and Vandana Shiva v Jayanta Bandhopadhyaya & Another*, 99(2)SCC, 228.

[20] See *Githa Hariharan v Reserve Bank of India*, 99(2)SCC, 228.

guardianship by virtue of the provisions of this Act, if the court is of the opinion that his or her guardianship will not be for the welfare of the minor.

It is thus fairly clear that if the case comes before the court, the court must look to the welfare of the minor and not merely to the legal provisions relating to guardianship. In this sense, Section 6 is subject to Section 13 whereby welfare of the minor is to be of paramount consideration [HMGA, Section 13]. This is the legal position under the Hindu Minority and Guardianship Act which is supplemental to the Guardians and Wards Act as regards Hindu children. The provisions for the appointment or declaration of guardians are given in the Guardians and Wards Act.

Section 13(1) makes the welfare of the minor as paramount or the sole consideration in the appointment and declaration of the guardian. Section 13(2) says that no person is entitled to guardianship by virtue of the provisions of this statute or any other law if it is not for the welfare of the child. Thus all guardians, natural, testamentary, certificated, or marriage guardians are subject to the principle of paramountcy of the welfare of children.

CUSTODY AND GUARDIANSHIP DURING MATRIMONIAL PROCEEDINGS

The matrimonial courts/family courts may be called upon to decide questions of passing orders relating to custody, education, and maintenance of children at any one of the following stages of matrimonial proceedings:

- Pending matrimonial proceedings, i.e. between the period of filing of the petition and final disposal of the petition. These orders are known as interim orders or temporary orders.
- At the time of the passing of the decree granting the petition. These are known as permanent orders.
- Subsequent to the passing of the decree granting the petition. At this stage the question may come up in either of the following two ways:
  – When in the matrimonial proceedings, no application was made for custody, etc., of children and therefore, after the decree, an altogether fresh petition may be made for custody, education, and maintenance of children.
  – When the court had already passed a permanent order of custody, etc., an application may be made to get that order modified, rescinded, or changed.

Section 26 of the Hindu Marriage Act 1955[21] deals with custody of the children. Section 38 of the Special Marriage Act 1954 is substantially the

---

[21] Hindu Marriage Act 1955, Section 26.

same as Section 26 of the Hindu Marriage Act. Dealing with the same subject, Section 49 of the Parsi Marriage and Divorce Act 1936[22] is slightly differently worded. The difference between the two provisions is in two respects:

- Under the former statute, the age of children for whom such orders can be made is eighteen years, while under the latter the age is sixteen, i.e. the ages of children in regard to whom such orders can be made should be below the age of eighteen years under the Parsi Marriage and Divorce Act.
- Under the Hindu Marriage Act and the Special Marriage Act, the wishes of children are to be considered, but there is no such provision under the Parsi Marriage and Divorce Act, though in practice the courts do consult the wishes of the children if they are intelligent enough to express the same, (though the courts are not bound to follow them).

The Indian Divorce Act deals with the subject in Part XI (Sections 41 to 44) under the title 'Custody of Children'. Interim matters relating to custody, education, and maintenance of children are dealt with in Section 41 (judicial separation proceedings) and Section 43 (nullity and divorce proceedings), while matters relating to permanent custody, etc., are dealt with in Section 42 (judicial separation proceedings) and Section 44 (nullity and divorce proceedings). In fact the provisions are substantially the same as under the Parsi Marriage and Divorce Act. The Indian Divorce Act does not deal with the question of custody, maintenance, and education of children in restitution proceedings. The age of children is their minority, i.e. below the age of eighteen years under the Indian Divorce Act. In the interest of children it is recommended that under all the statutes this provision should be uniformly incorporated. Further, the age of children in respect of whom orders of custody, maintenance, and education can be made should be the age of minority.[23]

JURISDICTION OF THE COURT

Permanent orders for custody, etc., can be made only if the court passes a decree granting the relief. If the petition is dismissed, the proceedings relating to children also fall through and the court has no power to make any orders for custody, etc., of children. Thus, in matters relating to custody, maintenance, and education of children the court exercises jurisdiction only if it has jurisdiction in the main petition.

[22] Parsi Marriage and Divorce Act 1938, Section 49.
[23] Paras Diwan, *Law of Adoption, Minority, Custody and Guardianship*, New Law Publishing Co. Ltd., New Delhi, 2000.

The question relating to custody, etc., of children may come before the court in any one of the following situations:

- Interim orders for custody, etc., of children, i.e., an order may be passed at any time from the date of filing of the proceedings and before the final disposal of the proceedings.
- Permanent orders of custody, etc., of children. Such orders my be passed:
  - At the time of passing of the decree granting the relief in a matrimonial cause.
  - Subsequent to the passing of the decree in a matrimonial cause. The question may come up in the following two situations:
    - If at the time of the passing of the decree or earlier no prayer was made for custody, etc., of children, a fresh application by petition may be made subsequently at any time after the passing of the decree.
    - When orders for custody, etc., have already been made, an application may be made for revoking, suspending, or varying such orders.

In these matters, the court is invested with a very wide discretion and broad powers. In the welfare of children it has power to pass any order. It is now a very well-established principle that in all proceedings in respect of children, their welfare is the paramount consideration, though the court may also take into consideration such matters as age, sex, and wishes of the child, and the fitness of the parent to whom custody is to be committed.

The court has power to revoke, suspend, or vary any order of custody, etc., of children at any time subsequent to making of the order, whenever the circumstances of the case require it to do so. This applies to both interim and final orders of custody, education, maintenance, and access. For variation of the order, the party seeking to do so must establish a case justifying revocation, suspension, or rescinding of the order.

Muslim Personal Law of Custody and Guardianship

The Muslim law of custody and guardianship is based on certain verses in the Koran[24] and a few *Hadis*.[25] These verses speak of the guardianship of the

---

[24] The following verses in the Koran are considered to be the foundation of the law of guardianship:
Give unto orphans their substance and give them not the bad in exchange for the good and devour not their substance by adding it to your own substance. Verily that would be a great sin. Give not unto the weak of understanding, the substance which God has appointed you to preserve for them but provide them therewith and clothe them and speak to them with kindly speech. Provide orphans until they attain the age of marriage,

property of the minor but very little has been said about the guardianship of the person of the minor.[26]

On the failure of the natural guardian and testamentary guardian, the matter is governed by the Guardians and Wards Act 1890. The power of appointing or declaring any person as guardian is conferred on the district court. The district court may appoint or declare any person as guardian of a minor child's person as well as property whenever it considers it necessary for the welfare of the minor, taking into consideration the age, sex, wishes of the child, and the personal law of the minor.[27]

Section 2 of the Muslim Personal Law (Shariat) Application Act 1937 includes guardianship among the issues where the Muslim personal law (Shariat) will apply. Under Muslim law, guardians are of three types:[28]

- Natural guardians,

---

then if ye perceive that they are able to manage their affairs well, then deliver unto them their substance and devour it not wastefully or hastily for they are growing up. Let him that is rich abstain generously (entirely from taking the property of orphans) and that who is poor let him take thereof in reason. And when ye deliver up their substance unto orphans, have (the transaction) witnessed in their presence.

—The Koran IV, 2,5,6

Another verse runs as under:

'Come not near the wealth of the orphans save with that which is better, till he comes to strength.'

—The Koran XVIII, 34; iv, 153.

The Koran permits a guardian of property of minor to take reasonable recompense for the trouble of looking after the affairs of an infant (iv, 5).

[25] The following *Hadis* trace the history of the obligation and liability of guardians of minor children:

When these revelations came down, viz., meddle not with the substance of the orphan, otherwise than for improving thereof and surely they who devour the possessions of the orphans unjustly, shall swallow down nothing but fire into their bellies and shall broil in ragging flames, all those who have orphans in their care went home and they separated their own food from orphans and also their water, fearful lest they might be mixed. Then when the orphans left any of their meat or drink, it was taken care of for them to eat afterwards. Then this method was unpleasant to the orphans, and they mentioned it to the Prophet, the God sent down this revelation, of Mohammed, they will ask concerning the orphans, answer to deal righteously with them is best and if ye mix your things with theirs, verily, they are your brethren. Then they mixed their meat and drink together.

—Misccat ul-Messabib, Book XIII, Chapter XVII, Part 3

[26] Paras Diwan, *Law of Adoption, Minority, Custody and Guardianship*, Universal Law Publishing Co. Ltd. Delhi, 2000.

[27] See Guardians and Wards Act 1890, Section 17.

[28] Paras Diwan, *Law of Adoption, Minority, Custody and Guardianship*, New Law Publishing Co. Ltd., New Delhi, 2000.

- Testamentary Guardians, and
- Guardians appointed by the Court.

Natural Guardians

The father's right of guardianship is recognized in all schools of Muslim law. Even when the custody is with the mother or any other female entitled to custody, the father's right of general supervision and control exists.[29]

Testamentary Guardian

The father as natural guardian has full powers of appointing a guardian by his will for his children. In the absence of the father and his executor, the grandfather can also appoint a guardian by his will. A mother can be appointed as a testamentary guardian or executor of the person as well as of the property of her minor children. But the Muslim mother has no power to appoint testamentary guardian of the property of her minor children.

Guardians can be Appointed by Court:

Under the procedures prescribed in Guardians and Wards Act 1890.

Hizanat (Custody)—Right of the Mother

All Muslim authorities recognize the mother's right of *hizanat*. According to the *Rudd-ul-Muhtar*, 'the right of the mother to the custody of her child is recognized whether she be a *mosalman*, or a *kitabia* or a *majoosia*, even though she be separated from her husband. But it does not belong to one who is an apostate.'[30] The *Fatwai Alamgiri* puts it thus: 'The mother is of all persons the best entitled to the custody of her infant children during connubial relationship as well as after its dissolution.'[31] The term *hizanat* is applied to the woman to whom belongs the right of rearing up a child.

Of all the persons, the first and foremost right to have the custody of children belongs to the mother, and she cannot be deprived of her right so long as she is not found guilty of misconduct.[32] Mother has the right of custody and care of children during the period laid down in Muslim law. *Hizanat* is recognized in the sense that it can be enforced against the father or any other person. But it is a right to which obligations are attached. The mother's right of *hizanat* is, in fact, a right of rearing up of children. If she is not found

---

[29] Father's right to control the religion of his children is recognized even if the mother is a non-Muslim. He has also the right to control the education, general upbringing, and movements of his children. In the absence of the father, the same right can be exercised by the grandfather or executor, whoever is entitled to guardianship.

[30] The *Rudd-ul-Muhtar*, 11, 1041.

[31] The *Fatwai Alamgiri*, I.728.

[32] *Md Shafi v Shamim*, AIR 1979, Bom 16.

suitable to bring up the child, or her custody is not conducive to the physical, moral, and intellectual welfare of the child, she can be deprived of it.

Since Muslim law considers the right of *hizanat* as no more than the right of rearing up the children, it terminates at an early age of the child. In this regard Muslim law makes a distinction between the son and the daughter. According to the *Fatwai Alamgiri*, the mother is entitled to the custody of a boy until he is independent of her care, that is, until he is seven years old.[33] According to the *Hanafis*, it is an established rule that the mother's right of *hizanat* over her son terminates on the latter's completing the age of seven years.[34]

The Shias hold the view that the mother is entitled to the custody of her son until he is weaned[35] (this is considered to be on the completion of two years) and that during this period the mother cannot be deprived of the custody of her son under any circumstances whatever, except with her own consent.[36] On the completion of the age of two by the son, the mother's right of custody terminates.

According to the Malikis, the mother's right of *hizanat* over her son continues till the child attains puberty.[37] The rule among the Shafis and the Hanbalis is the same as among the Hanafis. But these schools hold the view that on completion of the age of seven years, the child is given a choice of living with either parent. But in every case, the father is entitled to the custody of his son when it attains puberty.[38]

Among the Hanafis, the mother is entitled to the custody of daughters till they attain the age of puberty.[39] Among the Malikis, the Shafiis and the Hanbalis, the mother's right of custody over her daughters continues till they are married.[40] On the other hand, under the Ithana Ashari law, the mother is entitled to the custody of her daughters till they attain the age of seven.[41] In all the schools of Muslim law, the mother has the right to the custody of her married daughter below the age of puberty in preference to the husband.[42]

[33] Baillie I, 435, See also *Imtiaz v Masood*, AIR 1979, All 25.

[34] *Farjanb v Aynu*, AIR 1989, Bom 357.

[35] See the *Sharaya-ul-Islam*.

[36] *Sherkhan v Ajbhoi*, 11 Bom LR 75.

[37] *Sautayra*, 1, 348.

[38] The *Fatwai Alamgiri*, I. 730; The *Fatwai Kazi Khan*, I. 478. For details see Paras Diwan, *Law of Adoption, Minority Custody and Guardianship*, Universal Law Publishing Co., Ltd., Delhi,, 2000.

[39] Ibid. For details see Paras Diwan, *Law of Adoption, Minority Custody and Guardianship*, Universal Law Publishing Co., Ltd., Delhi, 2000.

[40] The *Rudd-ul-Muhtar*, II. 1054.

[41] Baillie, II. 95.

[42] In the matter of Khatija Bibi ILR (1870) 5 Bom LR 557; In the matter of Mohim Bibi (1874) 13 BLR.

Right to Parental Care

The mother has the right of her children up to the ages specified in each school, irrespective of the fact whether the child is legitimate or illegitimate.

OTHER FEMALES ENTITLED TO *HIZANAT* (CUSTODY)

Among the Hanafis, the following females are, after the mother, entitled to *hizanat* of the minor children of the age up to which the mother is entitled to it:[43]

- Mother's mother, howsoever high.[44]
- Father's mother, howsoever high.[45]
- Full sister.
- Uterine sister.
- Consanguine sister.[46]
- Uterine sister's daughter.
- Consanguine sister's daughter.
- Full sister's daughter.
- Maternal aunts, in like order as sisters.
- Paternal aunts, in like order as sisters.[47]

Under the Shia school, after the mother, the *hizanat* belongs to the father. In the absence of both the parents, or on their being disqualified the grandfather is entitled to the custody.[48] Among the Malikis the following are entitled to the custody of a minor in the absence of the mother:

- Maternal grandmother.
- Maternal great grandmother.
- Maternal aunt and grand-aunt.

---

[43] Tayabji and Ameer Ali give a different list. The rule is that among the females, the nearer excludes the remoter.

[44] *Fatima v Shaik Peda*, AIR 1941, Mad 944; *Nur Begum v Begum*, AIR 1934, Lah 274; In re Ghulam Md, AIR 1924, Sind 154.

[45] *Boocha v Elahi Bux*, ILR 11, Cal 574.

[46] In the *Hedaya* and the *Fatwai Alamgiri* the consanguine sister is not mentioned. Mulla holds the view that the omission is purely accidental, since the paternal aunt is expressly mentioned. Ameer Ali puts her after full sister's daughter and uterine sister's daughter (II 253.). See Paras Diwan, *Law of Adoption, Minority, Custody and Guardianship*, Universal Law Publishing Co. Ltd., Delhi 2000.

[47] Paras Diwan, *Law of Adoption, Minority, Custody and Guardianship*, Universal Law Publishing Co. Ltd., New Delhi, 2000.

[48] Authorities are not clear as to who is entitled to the custody after the grandfather. Some Shia authorities have laid down certain rules of preference on the basis of which the textbook writers have compiled a list of persons who are entitled to the custody of minor children in the absence of the grandfather. Ameer Ali holds the view that after the grandfather, *hizanat* belongs to the grandmother, after her it belongs to the ascendants, then to collateral's within the prohibited degrees, the nearer excluding the remoter. For

- Full sister.
- Uterine sister.
- Consanguine sister.
- Paternal aunt.

All the schools of Muslim law recognize the right of the father to the custody of his minor children in the following two cases:

- On the completion of the age by the child up to which the mother or other females are entitled to its custody.
- In the absence of the mother or other females who have the right to *hizanat* of minor children.

The father cannot be deprived of the right of *hizanat* of his male child of seven years if he is not found to be unfit.[49]

The cardinal principle of *hizanat* in Muslim law is also the welfare of the child. This is the reason why Muslim law gave preference to mother over the father in the matter of custody of children of tender age. The Muslim law of *hizanat* states that every other consideration is subordinated to the welfare of the child. A woman who is unworthy of credit may still retain the custody of the child, if welfare of the child so requires.

Custody and Guardianship of Children in Family Courts

Marriage dissolution leaves many problems to be resolved and family disputes, especially custody disputes, by their very nature, call for solutions which must be arrived at with speed and simplicity, and at low cost, guided mainly by conciliation proceedings. A suit or proceedings in relation to the guardianship of the person or custody of, or access to, any minor is dealt by family courts or by district courts where there are no family courts.[50] The family court has provided for the association of family counsellors, conciliators, and social service organizations in the process of settlement of disputes through conciliation. Thus the family court is a specialized court.[51] In any matrimonial conflict which is heading towards a divorce or separation inevitably, questions of custody and maintenance of children will arise. In such situations, the family courts are required to make a decision based on the best interests of the child.

---

details see Paras Diwan, *Law of Adoption, Minority, Custody and Guardianship*, Universal Law Publishing Co. Ltd., Delhi, 2000.

[49] Paras Diwan, *Law of Adoption, Minority, Custody and Guardianship*, Universal Law Publishing Co. Ltd., Delhi, 2000.

[50] Section 2 of the Family Courts Act 1984.

[51] Section 6 of the Family Courts Act 1984.

A review of the petitions/orders passed by the family courts in Mumbai in which children's interests were involved reveal that:[52]

- Children's concerns are never the primary or major concerns in any petition. The facts always concentrate on the matrimonial disputes and children are merely mentioned for an ancillary relief along with the parents.
- There is no follow-up of the orders relating to children.
- There is no set of standards/guidelines laid down to deal with children in family courts.
- The judges, lawyers, counsellors, and other court personnel are not trained to adopt a 'child-centred approach'.
- The orders depend on the perception of individual judges as to what constitutes the 'best interest of the child'. Some judges interview the child personally; others leave it to the counsellors.

Children find the atmosphere of a family court intimidating when they are brought to the court for an interview. They are bewildered and confused. The judges' chambers do not have 'child-friendly' environment. Children are often the least considered. Children also need behavioural expertise and services. Associations between marital conflict and adjustment problems in children are now well established. Children's distress and behavioural disregulation increase due to marital conflict. In fact, marital conflict is related to the children's negative outcomes in homes that are characterized as disturbed for other reasons. There is no direct provision in the Family Courts Act for the psychological recovery and social reintegration of the child. The links with social service agencies and childcare professionals are inadequate. The workload in the family courts is so high that in many instances it is not possible to consider the child's special concerns and needs.

A child's perceptions are very different. The jurisprudence of rights and obligations developed in the conventional mould is not appropriate for the delivery of justice to the child. Children by themselves are unable because of a physical and mental immaturity to avail of legal rights and entitlements.

There are several legal, social, and ethical issues involved. Several rival considerations compete for recognition while dealing with the welfare of the child within a legal regime. There are independent power centres, the courts, the police and the social services that are involved in an ad hoc manner and without any coordination between the various agencies.

The voices of children need to be heard in the family courts. A guardian ad litem or a representative or a counsel in the family court should aid the

[52] Asha Bajpai, *A Study of Children and Courts in Mumbai*, sponsored by BRS, TISS, 1999.

child. This service should have absolute freedom from hierarchical and functional interference. It has to be able to promote the child's interest authoritatively. Human behavioural scientists and experts should necessarily be associated whenever a child is involved. This service must also have a direct link between the children and the courts and become the ultimate point of reference. This can be provided for within the existing framework of the Family Courts Act. Training has to be provided to the judges, lawyers, police, and counsellors and other court personnel to develop child-centred competencies.[53]

Children and women of minority communities should also get the benefits of counselling and informal forum and speedy settlements of disputes in family courts. When the Family Courts Act transferred the jurisdiction of the district court to family court, the FCA, did not expressly transfer the matrimonial jurisdiction of the High Court to the family court. Whereas under the Indian Divorce Act 1869, the Guardians and Wards Act 1890, the Parsi Marriage and Divorce Act 1936, the Dissolution of Muslim Marriages Act 1939, and for matrimonial issues concerning the Jewish community, the jurisdiction continues to be with the High Court. This needs to be rectified so that all children get the benefit of the FCA 1984.[54]

Areas of Concern

The court is invested with a very wide discretion and broad powers in matters of custody, etc., of children. The expression generally used in the matrimonial statutes is 'if the court thinks fit'. Although the matrimonial statutes do not directly mention that in these proceedings the welfare of children is of paramount consideration, the courts have always taken the welfare of the children as the paramount consideration in determining matters relating to custody of children. The custody is given to a person only if it is for the welfare of the child. The court may look into other matters such as age, sex, or wishes of the child, but the welfare of the child will override all these considerations.

An area of concern is that if the court dismisses the matrimonial proceedings, proceedings relating to children terminate automatically. The court exercises jurisdiction over children only if it has jurisdiction in the main petition.

Orders in respect of children, whether temporary or permanent, are never final. The court may, on the application of either party, alter, rescind, or

---

[53] See Asha Bajpai, *Towards Equity and Empowerment of Children, 1989–1999, A Decade of Family Court*, Family Court Bar Association Mumbai, 1999.
[54] Flavia Agnes, *Contesting Rights Over Children, Custody and Guardianship in Matrimonial Disputes*, Manushi, No.114.

modify any order at any stage of the proceedings, or subsequently at any time after the passing of the decree till the child attains majority.

When parents separate from each other, the court gives custody of children to one of the parents and access to the other parent is usually allowed so that children grow up under the full awareness and affection of both parents.

While deciding what is best for the child, many varying factors need to be considered by the courts: the child itself, the parents, the relationship between child and parents, the surroundings of the family, educational possibilities, the future prospects of the children and their parents, wishes of parents and children, and so on. When studying the orders of the family courts it was evident that the concept of the best interests of the child or the welfare of the child is not at all mentioned in the decisions.[55] The best interest of the child may have been considered but there was no evidence. The courts do not give any information about the factors they have considered or the reasons for awarding custody. The orders just mention whom the custody was given to in a particular case. If the case is dismissed for any reason, the custody issue is also dismissed without looking at the welfare of the child. It all appears to be a question of 'negotiations'. The party who can 'negotiate' well will get the decision tilted in his/her favour. The courts have neither the time nor the resources to evaluate the various factors. It is also important to understand the additional factors that lead to the custody decision rather than just the surface problems as stated by the parties and try to find a solution that is truly in the child's best interests.

In fact, it appears that orders relating to children are just disposed of as secondary matters. Judges in family courts in many cases depend on the counsellors to understand the dynamics of family relationship and children's wishes. Judges need multi-disciplinary social help in making decisions based on both legal social and psychological principles. The services of mental health experts and childcare experts are not used in the family courts in all custody cases. The judges in the family courts are not sufficiently trained to be aware of the psychological pitfalls implicit in making children choose and reject a parent.[56]

Judicial interviews with children in chambers can be traumatic. The child's wish may also be a result of deliberate or subconscious influence on the part of one of the parents. It may also be difficult to prove what the child really wants. The child may be in the middle of conflicting loyalties and will not want to hurt either of the parents. Each custody decision has to be a concrete evaluation of the facts of the particular case. But in practice the

---

[55] Asha Bajpai, *The Legal System and the Principle of the Best Interest of the Child*, Empirical Study, 1998, Mumbai (Unpublished).
[56] Ibid.

family courts are not equipped to determine the best interests of the child. Judges and other personnel handling a large number of assigned cases obviously have less time to hear each case. They suffer due to high caseloads, lack of specific training and experience, rapid turnover, and low status.

The divorce proceedings are turned into a 'battleground' by parents to settle scores with each other and often the children are turned into instruments. One of the easiest ways to poison a child's mind is to malign the mother and label her as 'adulterous' and 'promiscuous'. The child may not know what it means, but she/he is scared. Instigated in several cases by the father and his relatives, she/he rejects the mother even without knowing her. A teenaged girl instigated by her grandparents screamed at her widowed mother for being friendly with a man. The daughter was convinced that her mother had committed a 'sin'.[57]

In order to have an upper hand, a lawyer or adviser may advise one of the spouses to strike when the other is most vulnerable. In one case, the husband served the petition when the wife was in the seventh month of pregnancy. Due to the trauma, the wife delivered prematurely, which endangered the child's life. In another case, the wife served the petition on her husband during the daughter's annual examination. The father took it well but the daughter's performance in the examination was affected. Making the child the centre of legal battles always affects the very core of the child. A husband will find a new wife and a wife will find a new husband but the child will lose the parents and will never find 'new' parents.[58]

The parents play upon the child's psyche and pass on their own prejudices regarding their spouses to the child. It is impossible for 'warring' parents to accept that even while one spouse has failed the children, he/she could be a good parent to them. Hurt by their spouse they put venom in the mind of their children about the other parent. They fail to comprehend as to what extent it would affect the child's personality. Not only is the child deprived of the other parent's association but is also tutored to view the other parent through a tinted glass. A distorted image of the other parent is projected while their emotions may pull them in the opposite direction. This dichotomy of emotions carries through the adult life. The changes in the child are slow, subtle, and silent. Most parents put the blame on the other parent and abdicate their responsibility. Nobody tries to heal the scars of this child torn between two warring parents.

[57] Gheewalah (1999), *Towards Equity and Empowerment of Children, 1989–1999: A Decade of Family Court*, Family Court Bar Association, Mumbai.
[58] Ibid.

The phenomenon of the father/mother not possessing any resources or income to provide for the child is very common. Clearly, it is obvious that when the parent appears before the family courts, there is 'nothing in their name'. This adversely affects the child.

The trauma of the child is never taken into consideration. The parents are busy taking care of their own interests. Even within a conflicting situation of divorce, it is necessary for the parents to examine their motives and assess the consequences of their actions on their children. Sometimes the parent does not see the child for years nor contribute anything towards the child's upkeep. Then all of a sudden, when the child is well settled in the new surroundings, the parent may come to stake a claim and assert ownership over the child without pausing to question the implications of such a move upon the child. Is remarriage of the spouse disturbing them? Are they consumed by jealousy? Is it hurting their ego? Why in the first place did they not see the child for years? What pleasure would they get by shattering the secure life of the child? In custody 'battles' it is necessary to set limits on the demands of parents, examine their motives closely, and evaluate their contributions towards the child before consenting to any rights. The time has come for parents to realize that the child is not their 'property' for exercising their ownership rights.

There is no legal representation of the child's interests in the family courts. The husband and wife may know what they want and be able to hire lawyers to help them get it, but no one speaks for the children, even though they have at least as much at stake in the divorce as do their parents. The adults are most likely to be preoccupied with their own problems and to be in a position where what is best for them is not necessarily best for the children. Moreover, the emotional stress during the last days of a dying marriage can be such that the parents do not really know what is best for themselves, let alone for anyone else.

Almost by default the courts have been given the responsibility to see that children are not the innocent casualties of matrimonial warfare. If the children have been injured by conflict between their parents, the court is expected to heal the wounds. Unfortunately, it rarely does, nor does it have the expertise or resources to do it.

In family courts much effort is being made these days in saving marriages. But what has to be saved is not solely the form of marriage but its spirit. A marriage can be saved at too great a cost especially for children. It is the children who pay the heaviest price, for they pay not only in present unhappiness but also in future maladjustment and perhaps also in their own marriages to come. Child's interests should be represented by a counsel or a representative.

In the best interests of the child it is absolutely necessary that experienced and able judges preside over the family courts. They ought to have some training in handling the delicate matters and be child-friendly.

When everybody is trying to save time in view of pendency of large number of litigations in various courts, it is a sad commentary that even in joint petitions under Section 13-B of the Hindu Marriage Act 1955, the parties are sent to marriage counsellors and a lot of time is wasted. In such cases only the best interests of the child need to be looked into when children are involved.

Not only in regard to the matrimonial petitions but also in all litigations, wherever they are pending, much time is consumed by the unnecessary procedure of filing affidavit of documents, giving inspection, etc. It is common knowledge that unless the last stage is reached, this formality is not to be complied with. Consequently, there is much avoidable delay. Particularly in case of family courts which are constituted for quick and speedy disposal of such matters, any application, however complicated, should not be allowed to be on the file of the family court for more than a couple of years.

The judge should take the help of experts in every child custody matter. Family courts must be equipped with legal, social, economic, medical, and psychological experts. Section 9 of the Family Courts Act contemplates the judges' role as one of assistance and persuasion to settle the matter. For that purpose the court may follow such procedure as it may deem fit. The same power is repeated in Section 10(3) of the Act where the scope is wider, in as much as the procedure can be devised for arriving at the truth of the facts alleged by one and denied by the other. But in the absence of clear rules laid down by the High Court in these regards, the judges very often hesitate to experiment with any innovative procedure. The result is that the cases are handled in a routine way, to avoid any criticism or censure when the matter goes to the High Court in appeal.

Under the law, appeals from the family court go the High Court. Very often judges who have no experience whatsoever of dealing with family disputes in a humane and child-friendly way deal with the matter. In the interests of the child, the High Court should be able to have the same special approach to deal with the case in a humane way, as is supposed to be done in the family court, as appeals should also follow the same standards. It is therefore necessary that there should be a separate division in the High Court where children's issues are dealt with in a sensitive manner. Another alternative could be a second appeal in the family court itself before a Division Bench.

Other issues that call for consideration in this regard include the following:
- The family courts should also have a supervisory role.
- In cases of mutual consent, the judge/counsellors should strike down those clauses which are against the welfare of the child.
- There should be proper follow-up of orders relating to children and the family courts must carry on the consequences of the decisions.
- Decisions of the family court reflect the own stereotyped beliefs of the judges and counsellors about what is in a child's best interests. These beliefs may or may not fit with the empirical findings. The court needs expertise from various fields.

In the family court the principles of law, the conscience of the community, and the social sciences, particularly those dealing with human behaviour and personal relationships, must work together.

Major Reported Judicial Decisions

While interpreting the principle of the best interest of the child in family courts, several legal, social, and ethical issues are involved. Several rival considerations compete for recognition while dealing with the welfare of the child or the best interests of the child. This principle of the welfare of the child or the best interests of the child has been applied largely in relation to family affairs especially relating to disputes concerning custody, adoption, and maintenance. This principle guides decisions at present generally in custody cases. An underlying assumption in social policy is that parents or their surrogates in the families are responsible for their own children. Recently, there have been a well-documented increase in the divorce rate in India and the largest number of circumstances in which the law of child custody applies is on the divorce of child's parents. The presence of children adds to the family complexity and complicates a divorce considerably. Child-related issues such as custody, visitation, and child support appear to be particular catalysts for litigation. The custody orders may nevertheless also be passed in cases of judicial separation of parents, restitution of conjugal rights, nullity of marriages, etc.[59]

The principle of child's welfare reflects a modern belief that while parents may choose divorce for themselves and must face the consequences of their own decisions, children need legal protection against their parents' actions.

[59] Asha Bajpai, *The Principle of the Best Interest of the Child and the Indian Legal System* (unpublished).

The legal justification for the fundamental intrusion into parental autonomy in the interests of the children is on the premise that children will be 'damaged' by their parent's divorce and that it is the responsibility of the courts to protect them against such 'damage'.

The child's welfare depends entirely on the current understanding (of adults) of what is best for children. The posing of the issue as a choice between parents is itself problematic, since although the ultimate decision dictates such a choice, the process of decision-making involves other direct or indirect considerations. The welfare of the child holds the central position in the custody disputes. Whatever the practice, the laws place the child's protection or nurturance philosophy at the centre of the decision-making process and whatever interpretations are given to the welfare principle, nowadays, the prominence of the child-centred approach receives universal support. Every case involves different facts and circumstances; therefore, previous decisions could only provide guidelines or indicators as to what was regarded as the best interests of the child.

Review and Analysis of Some Reported Major Judicial Decisions[60]

GOHAR BEGUM V SUGGI ALIAS NAZMA BEGUM[61]

The child was the illegitimate daughter of the appellant who was a Muslim woman. The mother was the mistress of the father who was then living with the respondent. The father had sworn an affidavit acknowledging the paternity of the child and undertaking to bring her up properly. He had sufficient means. The appellant applied for the custody of the daughter under Section 491 of the CrPC (illegal detention by the respondent).

The High Court held that the child was not illegally and improperly detained by the respondent. It held that it was not the functions of the court in an application under Section 491 to record findings on such controversial facts like paternity of the child and that the mother should apply under GWA for custody. The court held that it did not appear to be in the interest and welfare of the minor to grant custody to the mother. It did not give any reason for this view. On appeal, the Supreme Court held that the mother was entitled custody of the child. The fact that the mother had a right under GWA to recover custody of the child is no justification for denying rights under Section 491 CrPC.

---

[60] Asha Bajpai, *The Principle of the Best Interest of the Child and the Indian Legal System* (unpublished).
[61] AIR 1960 SC 93.

The court held that under Mohammedan law, the custody of an illegitimate child, no matter who the father is, should be with the mother. With respect to a child under guardianship for nurture, the child is supposed to be unlawfully imprisoned when unlawfully detained from the custody of the guardian and when delivered to him, the child is supposed to be set at liberty.

The technicalities of the law appear to come in the way of the best interest of the child. It is to be noted with concern that the concept of illegitimacy of children is still prevalent in the Indian laws.

JIJABAI GAJRE V PATHAN KHAN AND ORS[62]

The father and the mother of the appellant Jijabai lived separately. The appellant had obtained properties from her father under a gift deed dated September 1944. She served notice dated 31 March 1962 on the tenant to terminate his tenancy and to surrender possession or in the alternative to be allowed to recover at least half of the land. The tenant pleaded that the appellant was a minor and her claim barred by limitation. As the father was alive notice by the mother on behalf of the minor was invalid.

The 'Naib Tehsildar' held that as the father of the appellant was alive and was, in law, her natural guardian, the lease executed was not legal and valid, as the mother was not entitled to represent her.

The High Court held the mother to be considered the natural guardian, as the father was not interested.

The Supreme Court held that the father was alive but was not taking any interest in the affairs of the minor and it was as good as if he was non-existent so far as the minor was concerned. Therefore, in this case, the mother can be considered as the natural guardian of the minor daughter.

A prolonged litigation had to be carried on, which itself was against the interest of the child. In this case the Tehsildar's court just looked at the technicalities of law.

ROSY JACOB V JACOB A[63]

The Supreme Court considered a Christian father's application to obtain custody of his children under Section 25 of the GWA. The court was entrusted with a judicial decision to order return of the ward to the custody of the guardian. The court held that Section 25 of the GWA is attracted only if a ward leaves or is removed from custody of a guardian of his person and the court is empowered to make an order for the return of the ward to his

---

[62] (1970) 2 SCC 717.
[63] AIR 1973 SC 2090.

guardian if it is of the opinion that it will be for the welfare of the ward to return to the custody of his guardian.

Under the Indian Divorce Act 1869 [Section 3(5)], the sons of native fathers cease to be minors on attaining sixteen years of age and their daughters cease to be minors on attaining thirteen years of age. The court held that Section 25 of the GWA contemplates not only actual physical custody but also constructive custody of the guardian, which includes all categories of guardians. It was further held that Section 25 of the GWA demands reasonable and liberal interpretation. The court also held that the discretion under Section 25 is to be exercised judiciously.

The court went on to pronounce the presumption that a minor's parents would do their very best to promote the child's welfare and would not grudge any sacrifice of their own personal interest. The father's fitness is to be considered, determined, and weighed in terms of the welfare of the minor. If the custody of the father cannot promote the welfare of the child equally or better than the custody with the mother, the father cannot claim indefeasible right to custody under Section 25 of the GWA.

The court stated that in disputes between a mother and a father a 'just and proper balance' must be struck between the child's welfare and the parents' rights, even though the child's welfare must ultimately be considered more important. In considering this application, the court declared that 'the controlling consideration governing the custody of the children is the welfare of the children concerned and not the rights of their parents'.

THRITY HOSHIE DOLIKUKA v H.S. DOLIKUKA[64]

In this case both the parents were working and the child was with the father. The mother wanted to remove the child from the father's home and place her in a boarding school.

The High Court had refused custody of the daughter to the mother mainly on the ground that the mother was a 'working girl'. The Supreme Court held that the father cannot be considered to be a fit person to be given the custody of the child. The mother was given the custody of the minor daughter till she reached the age of sixteen years. The child was allowed to continue her education in the boarding school. The parents were given liberty to meet the daughter alternately in accordance with the rules and regulations of the school. The father was given the first opportunity.

During vacations, the girl would live with the father for the first half and with the mother for the second half. After the vacation, the girl had to be

[64] AIR 1982 SC 1276.

taken back to the boarding school and entrusted to the custody of the principal.

The court stated that there was no duty or obligation of the court to send for the minor and interview her to ascertain her wishes, before deciding the question of her custody. The father was obsessed with the idea of obtaining exclusive control of the daughter and keeping the daughter with him in his house. The mother had no self-interest or obsession and had the best interest and welfare of the daughter in mind and was prepared to make any necessary sacrifice for the daughter. Custody was given to the mother.

BHAGYALAKSHMI V K. NARAYANNA RAO,[65]
THRITY HOSHIE DOLIKUKA V HOSHIAM S. DOLIKUKA,[66] AND
JASWANT KAUR V MANJIT SINGH[67]

In the first case the wife left the husband and took with her three minor children aged fourteen, twelve, and nine. After three years the father sued for custody. In the second case the eleven-year-old girl was with the father. In the third case the mother gave birth to the child at her parent's house and the child remained in their custody. When the boy was ten, the father sued the maternal grandparents for custody. In all these three cases the issue involved custody of growing children.

The court granted custody to the father in the first case, viewing the minors' welfare including material as well as spiritual well-being. The father was better off financially, while the mother's father was in debt. Besides, a fourteen-year-old son needed his father's advice, hence the father was given custody. In the second case, the eleven-year-old daughter needed her mother's guidance, hence the mother was given custody (partly on this ground). A ten-year-old boy needed his father's 'control', hence the father was given custody in the third case despite the fact that the child had been in the continuous care of his grandparents. The court viewed the minor's welfare including material as well as spiritual well-being. Importance was given to the financial capacity of the father.

SUMITRA DEVI V BHIKAN CHOUDHARY[68]

Application for maintenance under Section 125 of the CrPC was filed by a woman for herself and her minor daughter. She asserted that the child was

[65] AIR 1983 Mad 9.
[66] AIR 1982 SC 1277.
[67] AIR 1985 Del 159.
[68] AIR 1985 SC 765.

from her marriage but the husband denied this. She alleged that the husband was already married once and that was not known to her at the time of marriage. The husband alleged that she was already three months pregnant at the time of their marriage and therefore the marriage was void on the grounds of fraud. He also said that there were no religious rites. After ten years of marriage, the relationship strained on these grounds and she sought maintenance from her husband. The magistrate granted maintenance both to her and to her child. The sessions judge reversed the order. The Patna High Court approved the sessions court order. So the mother appealed to the Supreme Court.

The Supreme Court chastised the lower courts for not examining the witnesses properly. The case was remanded to the magistrate for a proper examination within three months, as already a lot of time was lost due to the improper conduct of the case by her lawyers and the courts. The SC reminded the magistrate that under Section 125 of the CrPC even an illegitimate minor child was entitled to maintenance. The SC said the lawyers and magistrates had not devoted proper attention to the case. The lower courts did not refer to the fact that the couple were living together for ten years and their names appeared in the voters' list as 'husband and wife'. Witnesses also confirmed it. The evidence regarding the religious ceremonies were not complete. Therefore, the case was remanded for a fresh enquiry. The Supreme Court said that the role of the Court in this type of cases is not that of a silent spectator or of a passive agency. It must take genuine interest to find out the truth. If the right questions were put to the witnesses, facts would have come out and the prolonged litigation could have been avoided.

Elizabeth Dinshaw v Arvand Dinshaw[69]

The petitioner and her husband were living in the USA. They were divorced and the child (minor) continued to live with the mother pursuant to a divorce decree. The father was given visitation rights on weekends and was specifically directed in the decree that if the father wished to travel with the minor child outside the territorial limits of the USA he shall bring a petition to the court, setting forth the conditions under which he intends to leave the country with the minor child.

Taking advantage of the weekend visitation rights granted to him by the above decree, the father picked up his minor son and secretly left the USA not intimating to the court about the intention to take him out of the

[69] (1987) 1 SCC 42.

country; nor had he given the slightest indication to the petitioner about his intention to leave the USA permanently for India. The conduct of the father in taking the child from the custody of the person to whom it had been entrusted by the court was undoubtedly most reprehensible.

The Court, after going into the facts and circumstances of the case, looked into what would best serve the interest and welfare of the minor and opined that in the interest and welfare of the child, he should return to the USA and continue his education there under the guardianship and custody of the mother to whom the guardianship and custody have been entrusted by a competent court. The court held that the minor child should go back with his mother to the USA and continue there as a ward of the concerned court having jurisdiction in the state of Michigan. The father had tendered an unconditional apology for this illegal act.

The court further held that the father cannot claim advantage of the wrongful act of abduction. Whenever a question arises before the court pertaining to the custody of a minor child, the matter is to be decided not on the considerations of the legal rights of the parties but on the sole and predominant criterion of what should serve the interest and welfare of the minor. The court was satisfied that the petitioner who is the mother was full of genuine love and affection for the child and could solely be trusted to look after him, educate him, and attend to his proper upbringing in every possible way.

POONAM DATTA V KRISHNLAL DATTA[70]

On the death of the minor's father, the mother was living separately from her in-laws. Money received from the employer of the deceased father was kept in a fixed deposit in a bank. The minor was studying in a school in which his mother was a teacher. The grandfather wanted custody of the child.

The court directed the child to be kept in custody of her mother and to continue to study in the same school. But the grandfather was permitted to take the child and keep him in the company of his family every weekend. Money was to remain in deposit and the interest thereof payable to the mother and the grandfather in equal share. This arrangement was to continue until either of the parties moves for the appropriate guardianship proceedings and gets a declaration. The case was under Section 6 of the HMGA 1956 and Sections 12 and 17 of the GWA 1890. The court directed the parties to consider interest of the child as paramount.

---

[70] 1989 Supp (1) SCC 587.

Kirtikumar Maheshankar Joshi v Pradipkumar Karunashankar Joshi[71]

After the unnatural death of their mother, the children were living with their maternal uncle. The father was facing charge under Section 498 IPC. Before the Supreme Court, the children expressed their willingness to remain with their maternal uncle, who, according to them, was looking after them very well. In the interest and welfare of the children, custody was handed over to the maternal uncle instead of the father. In the welfare of the child, the legal rights were superceded.

Chandrakala Menon v Capt Vipin Menon and another[72]

The appellant married the respondent. A girl was born to them in 1985 and two years thereafter both went to the USA leaving the girl with her maternal grandparents at Bangalore. Two years thereafter the girl went to live in the USA and was sent back to live with her maternal grandparents a year later. Differences arose between the husband and the wife and they filed a joint petition for divorce by mutual consent. While the girl was residing with her maternal grandparents at Bangalore, the respondent came to see the daughter and took her away to Bombay. A case of kidnapping was registered against the respondent. The High Court held the respondent being a natural guardian of the girl, could not be charged with the offence of kidnapping. This appeal by Chandrakala was against the order of the High Court.

The Supreme Court dissolved the marriage by mutual consent under Section 13B of the Hindu Marriage Act 1955. Regarding custody of the child, the judges gathered her wishes and sentiments in their chambers and found that she had ample love and affection for both her parents and also her maternal grandparents. The court granted custody to the mother Chandrakala and the father was given visitation rights.

The principle reiterated in this case is that the question regarding the custody of a minor child cannot be decided on the basis of the legal rights of the parties. The custody of the child has to be decided on the sole and predominant criterion of what would serve the interest and welfare of the minor.

Pannilal v Rajinder Singh[73]

Land owned by the respondents was sold, while they were still minors, by their mother acting as their guardian. On attaining majority, the respondents sued Pannilal for possession on the ground that the sale was made

---

[71] (1992) 3 SCC 573.
[72] (1993) 2 SCC 6.
[73] (1993) 4 SCC 38.

without permission of the court though the sale deed was signed by the mother and attested by the father.

The trial court held that there was no reliable evidence on record to show that the alienation in dispute had been made for the legal necessity or for the benefit of the minors.

The High Court held that there was no evidence to show that the father of the respondents was not taking any interest in their affairs or that they were in the keeping and care of the mother to the exclusion of the father. The sale by the mother was held to be void. The Supreme Court also held that there was no evidence to show that the father was not taking an interest in their affairs. Sale by the mother was not sale by the father who was the natural guardian.

Anjali Anil Rangari v Anil Rangari[74]

This writ petition was filed by the appellant—a mother of two minor children, a daughter and a son, aged nine and five years respectively. The father averred in the application before the Chief Judicial Magistrate's (CJM) court that the mother left the matrimonial home along with two children for Delhi, where her parents reside, without informing him as well as his parents. The children were in illegal custody and were in wrongful confinement by the mother. The Nagpur police went to Delhi and fetched the children from the custody of the mother and produced them before the CJM who passed an order directing that custody be given to the father. The Supreme Court held that the custody of the children with the mother was neither unlawful nor were they wrongfully confined by the mother in Delhi. The father was directed to hand over the custody of both the children to the mother.

Dhanwanti Joshi v Madhav Unde[75]

The respondent married the appellant (who was then in the USA) in 1982 in the USA. On 19 June 1982, a separate marriage ceremony as per Hindu rituals was performed. Nine months later, a boy was born to them in the USA. The appellant left the respondent when the child was thirty-five days old. The respondent continued to live in the USA and the appellant and her son were living in India. The parties have been involved in civil and criminal litigation both in the USA and in India for fourteen years.

The petition was filed for custody and divorce. The Family Court granted custody to the father. The High Court held that the custody is to be given to the father who has acquired citizenship in America and will provide a comparatively superior upbringing.

---

[74] (1997) 10 SCC 342.
[75] 1997(9) *Judgements Today* 220.

The Supreme Court gave the custody to the mother and visitation rights to the father when he is in India. Whatever may be the disputes between the parties, the courts have to consider, in proceedings under the Guardianship Act, what is in the interest of the minor child. The paramount interest of the boy aged fourteen years of age is definitely his future education and career. The further education of a boy aged fourteen years of age will be comparatively superior (High Court).

Both the Family Court and the High Court based their decisions on the sole circumstance, i.e. the financial capacity of the father to give better education to the boy in USA. The welfare of the child is not to be measured by money alone, nor by physical comfort only. The word 'welfare' must be taken in its widest sense. The moral and religious welfare must be considered as well as the physical well-being. Nor can the ties of affection be disregarded (refer Lindley L.J. in Re v Mc Grath 1893 (1) Ch. 143). More important are the stability and the security, the loving and understanding care and guidance, the warm and compassionate relationship that are essential for the full development of the child's own character, personality, and talents (Hardy Boys J of New Zealand court in *Walker v Walker and Hanuson* 1981 NZ Recent Law 257 cited by British Law Commission Working Paper No.96— quoted by the Supreme Court).

GITHA HARIHARAN & ANOTHER V RESERVE BANK OF INDIA AND ANOTHER AND VANDANA SHIVA V JAYANTA BANDHOPADHYAYA & ANOTHER[76]

The petitioner Githa Hariharan applied to the Reserve Bank of India (RBI) in 1984 for 9% Relief Bond to be held in the name of her minor son, along with an intimation that the mother would act as the natural guardian for the purposes of investment. The application was sent back by RBI advising her to produce the application signed by the father and in the alternative, the Bank informed that a certificate of guardianship from a Competent Authority would be necessary.

The Writ Petition (WP (c) 1016 of 1991) by Vandana Shiva was a prayer for custody of the minor son who was staying with the mother. The father had shown total apathy towards the child and was not interested in the welfare and benefit of the child, excepting the right to be natural guardian without however discharging any corresponding obligation.

Both the petitions prayed for the declaration of the provision of Sec. 6(a) of the HMGA read with Sec. 19(b) of the GWA as violative of Articles 14 and 15 of the Constitution. The father and mother are natural guardians in terms of the provisions of Sec. (6) read with Sec. 4(c) of the HMGA.

[76] AIR 1999 SC 1149.

The court held that Sec. 6(a) itself recognizes that both the father and mother ought to be treated as natural guardians and the expression 'after' should be read and interpreted in a manner so as not to defeat the true intent of legislature.

The word 'after' in Sec. 6 of the HMGA, shall have to be given a meaning which would serve the need of the situation, viz., the welfare of the minor. The word 'after' does not necessarily mean after the death of the father. On the contrary, it depicts an intent so as to ascribe the meaning as 'in the absence of, be it temporary or otherwise, or total apathy of the father towards the child, or even inability of the father by reason of ailment or otherwise, and it is only in the event of such a meaning being ascribed to the word 'after' as used in Section 6, the same would be in accordance with the intent of the legislation, viz., welfare of child. A rigid incidence of strict statutory interpretation may not be conducive to the growth of the child and welfare being the predominant criterion, it would be a plain exercise of judicial power of interpreting the law so as to be otherwise conducive to a fuller and better development and growth of the child. The whole tenor of the HMGA 1956 is to protect the welfare of the child and as such any interpretation ought to be in consonance with the legislative intent.

S.N. Nirmala v Nelson Jayakumar[77]

The Division Bench of the Gujarat High Court denied the mother visiting rights to her minor daughter while dismissing her appeal against the single judge's order conferring custody to the father. The Supreme Court held that the mother should not be denied visiting rights in relation to minor daughter in the custody of the father without adequate justification.

Analysis of Case Laws

From the survey of rulings of the High Courts and the Supreme Court in India, some of the trends and issues that affect the custody decision are discussed below:

Restoration of Minor to Lawful Custody by a Writ of Habeas Corpus

A habeas corpus proceeds on the fact of illegal restraint. Article 226 of the Constitution[78] is frequently resorted to in order to obtain the custody of the child from a person who has unlawfully detained him/her, as it is a speedy remedy. The underlying principle of every writ of habeas corpus in reference

---

[77] (1999) 3 SCC 126.
[78] Article 226 of the Constitution of India empowers High Courts to issue orders, directions, etc., in the nature of certain writs.

124 Child Rights in India

to the child has been to ensure the protection and well-being of the child brought before the court under the writ.[79]

Tender Years Doctrine

In the interest of the child, a special provision for children of tender years has been made. Section 6(a) of the HMGA lays down that ordinarily the custody of children of tender years will be with the mother. The tender age is considered to be up to five years. This is a mandatory provision. But the courts have considered children from birth upto the age of thirteen years to be of 'tender years'.

The Courts have laid down the following:

- A child of tender years should be in the custody of the mother.[80]
- A boy of seven years would be much better off living with his mother than with his father.[81]
- If the mother is a suitable person to take charge of the child, it is quite impossible to find an adequate substitute for a child of tender years.[82]
- The mother's lap is 'God's own cradle' for a child of this age.[83]
- The conversion of a mother[84] or her being outcaste[85] does not matter. A non-Hindu mother of a Hindu child of tender age is entitled to its custody. It is significant to note that in these cases the religion of the parties is not a factor. The same views have been expressed by the courts irrespective of the fact whether the parties were Hindus, Muslims, Christians, or Parsis. (Also see *Rajkumar Gupta v Barbara Gupta*, AIR 1989 Cal 165).

It appears to be now a universally recognized rule that a parent cannot be deprived of the custody of his/her children merely because he/she happens to be poor.[86] Many court decisions have given custody to the party who has taken care of the child even if he/she is financially/economically less well off than the other. This trend has favoured women as custodians and if a mother is financially/economically less well off than the father, courts still consider

---

[79] See Paras Diwan, *Law of Adoption, Minority, Guardianship and Custody*, Wadhawa and Company, 1993.
[80] *Ahmed v Dehnatton* (1917) 40 IC 1070.
[81] *Tara Bai v Mohan Lal*, AIR 1932 Bom 405.
[82] *Saraswatibai v Sripad*, AIR 1941 Bom 103.
[83] Re Kamal Rudra ILR (1949) 2 Cal 374.
[84] *Budhan v Bahadur Khan*, AIR 1942 Pesh 41.
[85] *Kaulesra v Jorai Kasudhan*, ILR, (1905) 28 AII 233.
[86] Paras Diwan, *Law of Adoption, Minority, Guardianship and Custody*, Wadhwa and Co., 1993, p. 444.

giving her custody on the grounds that the father can be ordered to pay her maintenance.[87]

Abdication and Abandonment

In a case where the father had given custody of his three children to their grandfather under an agreement and then after seven years asked for their custody, the court held that the father must be held to have lost his right to the guardianship of his children, not merely because he allowed them to be maintained and educated by the grandfather, but also because at this stage to alter the course of their life would be detrimental to their interest.[88]

Mother also a Natural Guardian

The Supreme Court has held that[89] the mother is also the natural guardian of her minor child, in the absence of father. The landmark judgment is hailed as historic as no longer will women live in fear of losing custody of their children on the ground that they are not the natural guardians of their children. The validity of any transaction cannot now be called into question on the ground that it has been entered into by the mother and not the father. Local bodies like schools, banks, passport offices, immigration officials, and government institutions will be obliged to enter into transactions with the mother without insisting that the father alone can apply on behalf of the child. Clearly, this judgment is in the interest of the child. But the court has unfortunately stopped short of giving equal status to the mother as a natural guardian.

Paternal Rights and Welfare of Children

Section 19 of the Guardians and Wards Act 1890 provides for the supremacy of paternal rights whereas Section 17 provides for the welfare of the child. In many cases, the courts have to decide between these two contending issues.

Before 1950, the courts have generally given importance to the father's right as the natural guardian and legal guardian. The courts have held in several cases that before the father can be deprived of the custody of the child it must be established that he is unfit to act as a guardian because of any act

---

[87] Lawyers Collective, *Legal Aid Handbook 2, Custody and Guardianship of Minors*, Lawyers Collective and Kali for Women, Delhi, 1995.
[88] *Baldeo v Dhannaram*, AIR 1927 Nag 314.
[89] See *Githa Hariharan & Another v Reserve Bank of India and Another and Vandana Shiva v Jayanta Bandhopadhyaya & Another*, AIR 1999.

or conduct.[90] From 1950 onwards, there appears a general change in judicial thinking,[91] and in a series of a cases the Madras High Court held that the welfare of the child is paramount and the father can be deprived of custody even though he is not found unfit, if circumstances show that in the welfare of the child, the custody should be given to someone else.

Wishes of the Child

This is an important factor to be taken into consideration by the courts. The Indian courts have in some cases given effect to the wishes of children of ten years and in some others, they have declined to give them effect. Whereas, in some cases, the court has gone against the wishes of a child of sixteen years. As is evident, some courts take the orthodox view that the father's right of custody being an absolute right is enforceable against the wishes of the children whatever be their age. Under the present law, in many cases, the courts have disregarded the wishes of older children who are capable of expressing their preference whenever the courts were of the view that the wishes of the children must be disregarded for their own welfare.

Two questions can be raised here:

- Is it in the interest of the child to stay with somebody with whom he does not wish to stay?
- Do children actually give their own preferences to the courts? Do their custodian's interests and wishes influence their wishes?

At present judges and courts are not equipped and trained to determine the actual wishes of the child and see through the other external influences, etc. But in the best interests of the child, they have to be equipped to deal with such issues. There are scientific evaluation techniques available.

Critique of the Present Law

It is thus evident from the analysis of the case laws that the welfare principle has quite often not been properly appreciated or has been overlooked by the trial court and the mother has had to approach the higher court at considerable cast of time and money. Many cases do not reach the higher courts for lack of resources and in these cases the interest of the child suffers. Secondly, due to long legal battles, the custody of the child remains with a person with

---

[90] See *Queen v Nisbet, Perry* OC 103; re: Callor Nariuswamy, Mayne's PCS, 391; re: Hanumath Boe; *Reade v Krishna* ILR (1886). Mad 391; re: *Andiappa v Nallendrian* ILR (1915) 39 Mad 473.

[91] Paras Diwan, *Law of Adoption, Minority, Guardianship and Custody*, Universal Law Publishing Co. Ltd., Delhi, 2000.

whom it should perhaps not remain. The right of the child to speedy trial is also violated. The trial courts have to be sensitized to the rights of the child and to be more child-friendly. Besides, these are the following lacunae:

- The personnel working in family courts are not sensitive to child rights.
- There are no provisions for follow-up of cases after the court has given custody and access to parents.
- The prevailing assumption in the present custody and guardianship laws is that the child's interests are identical to those of the parent's interest but this may not always be true. Children may have interests independent of their parents.
- There has to be provision for legal counsel in every case where children are involved.
- There is no enforcement of child maintenance and support orders. There has to be enforcement mechanism/body.
- The child in these contests does not have full party status. They are not regarded as independent third parties. This has to be provided.
- There is no concept of available alternatives/options for the child while determining the orders.
- In matrimonial proceedings the question of custody is treated as ancillary proceedings. When matrimonial proceedings are filed between the parties, the relationship is usually strained and the home is virtually broken. The parties may not be living together. The position in law is that if the main proceedings are dismissed, the proceedings in respect of children are not continued. The children have to go back to the tense environment. There is a need to protect the interests of children at this stage. Even if the main petition fails, arrangements need to be made in the best interests of the child.
- There is no law on parental responsibility. There is a need for such a law.
- After the Githa Hariharan Case, the mother has been given the status of natural guardian in the HMGA but in all other laws, the father still has the superior position as a natural guardian. This is discrimination against children as a class.
- Tender years of child are generally till five years. It needs to be reviewed. The Law Commission recommendations in the eighty-third and 133rd reports need to be considered.
- The maintenance orders need to be enforced stringently.
- The non-custodial parent in many cases should not automatically be given access or visitation rights.

- The children are often shuttled back and forth from parent to parent on a regular basis.
- Orders are passed without making adequate arrangements for children.
- There is no provision to understand or handle the trauma that a child is undergoing during the custody battle between the parents.
- The concept of illegitimacy of children is still prevalent in laws. This outdated concept needs to be removed.

Law Reform in the Best Interest of the Child

The welfare of the child being the sole consideration or paramount consideration is the principle found at present only in the substantive laws on custody and guardianship. The other substantive and procedural laws are silent on this issue In fact, the best interest principle should be included in all the substantive and procedural laws including the matrimonial laws, the Civil Procedure Code, and the Criminal Procedure Code.

There is a lot of emphasis on the age of the child, which in many legislations are arbitrarily fixed. The best interest interpretation needs to be adopted on this issue and one can err on the side of higher age limit for protective care and lower age limit for special rights in respect of civil and cultural matters as the courts and the enforcement authorities are at present interpreting it very technically and narrowly.

To determine the best interests of the child demands that medical justice, educational justice, recreational justice, nutritional justice, and participatory justice are included. The courts need new institutional arrangements and involvement of professional services, before passing an order.

The 133rd Law Commission Report[92] made several recommendations in the existing laws relating to custody and guardianship of children. These amendments need to be incorporated in the laws relating to custody and guardianship. A summary of the recommendations is as follows:

- *The mother should have same and equal (and not inferior) rights vis-à-vis father.*
  The provision contained in Section 6(a) of the Hindu Minority and Guardianship Act 1956 constituting the father as a natural guardian of a Hindu minor's person as well as in respect of his property in preference to the mother should be amended so as to constitute both the

---

[92] Government of India, Ministry of Law, Justice and Company Affairs, The 133rd Law Commission Report, Removal of discrimination against women in matters relating to guardianship and custody of minor children, New Delhi, 1989.

father and the mother as being natural guardians 'jointly and severally' having equal rights in respect of the minor, because there is no jurisdiction for according a superior and preferential treatment to the father *vis-à-vis* the mother of the minor and besides; it violates Article 15 of the Constitution of India.

- *The custody of a minor who has not completed twelve years of age shall ordinarily be with the mother.*

The proviso to subsection (a) of Section 6 of the HMGA needs to be amended so that the custody of a boy or an unmarried girl who has not completed the age of twelve years (instead of the age limit of five years as prescribed at present) shall ordinarily be with the mother.

- The third amendment lays down some important considerations in the application of the welfare principle.

The welfare principle projected in Section 13 of the HMGA and Section 17 of the Guardians and Wards Act needs to be amplified and spelt out so as to make it explicit that:

– Where the father has remarried, the custody of the minor, irrespective of the minor's age, shall ordinarily be with the mother. The minor should not be obliged to live with his or her stepmother unless there are exceptional circumstances which shall be recorded in writing.

– Where the mother has remarried, a female child should not be made to live with her stepfather in order to guard against possible sexual abuse and harassment. The court may consider whether the paternal or maternal grandparents should be entrusted with the custody of the female child on merits.

– Where the mother has remarried but the father has not, ordinarily the minor, even if a male child, should not be made to live with the stepfather.

– Where both the father and mother have remarried, the court may determine whether to entrust the guardianship and/or custody to the father, the mother, the grandparents, depending on what the court considers to be conducive to the maximum welfare of the minor in the light of the facts of each case.

– A mother shall not be denied the custody of the minor merely on the ground that the father is in more affluent circumstances or that the mother's economic circumstances are not as good as those of the father.

– In applying the welfare principle, the court shall have due regard to the fact that the minor needs emotional support and warmth of the

mother who is ordinarily better equipped than the father to impart such emotional support and warmth which are essential for building up a balanced personality.
- *Grandparents shall have equal claim in the matter of appointment of guardian of a minor irrespective of whether they are paternal grandparents or maternal grandparents.*

In considering the question of appointment of guardian of the person and the property of a minor and entrustment of the custody of a minor, the circumstances whether the grandparents are from the paternal side or maternal side should be disregarded. The paternal grandparents on the one hand and maternal grandparents on the other hand shall be treated at par having equal claim to be appointed in this behalf subject to the paramount consideration regarding the welfare of the minor.
- *It should be recognized that both father and mother have a claim to the exclusion of others to be appointed a guardian of a minor unless considered unfit by the court.*

Section 19(b) of the Guardians and Wards Act of 1890, which inter alia provides that the court will be authorized to appoint the guardian of the person of a minor whose father is living and is not, in the opinion of the court, unfit to be the guardian of the person of the minor, deserves to be amended so as to accord equal treatment to the mother by incorporating a reference to mother along with that to the father. It should be provided that the court will not be authorized to appoint the guardian of the person of a minor whose *father or mother* is living and is, in the opinion of the court, not unfit to be the guardian of the person of the minor, for there is no rational basis for discriminating between the father of a minor on the one hand and the mother of a minor on the other in the context of this provision. A consequential amendment also needs to be made in Section 41(e) by substituting the words 'father or mother' in place of the word 'father' wherever it occurs therein.
- *Section 7 of the the Hindu Minority and Guardianship Act relating to guardianship of an adopted son should be amended.*

As at present, Section 7 of the Hindu Minority and Guardianship Act 1956 is applicable in the context of natural guardianship of an adopted son. In view of the enactment of Hindu Adoptions and Maintenance Act which now enables a daughter also to be adopted, the above provision requires to be recast so as to be made applicable also to the guardianship of an adopted daughter who is a minor. So also the phrase 'to the adoptive father and after him to the adoptive mother' needs to be substituted by the phrase 'to the adoptive father and the adoptive mother jointly and severally' for the sake of removing the discrimination against women.

The laws have to clearly state that the guardianship and custody are not to be looked at from the point of view of anybody's right; they have to be looked at from the point of view of the welfare of the child and his best interest. In every case, irrespective of age, sex, religion, caste, etc., the best interest of the child shall prevail and shall be the only and the sole criterion overriding all other considerations.

A Comparative Survey of International Laws

Australian Law

Under The Family Law Act 1975, the family court was set up to administer the law. It was envisaged as a 'helping court' and was to operate as a 'closed court' with limited formality, simplified procedures, and with the assistance of specialist counselling and welfare staff.

The Act directed that in custody and other proceedings concerning children, the paramount consideration should be the welfare of the child. The main innovations in custodial matters were: provision for parents to attend conferences with welfare officers to discuss the welfare of children and endeavour to resolve differences; provision for the wishes of children concerned to be ascertained and observed; and an attempt to provide more effective enforcement procedures.

PARAMOUNT CONSIDERATION—THE WELFARE OF THE CHILD

In common law a father had sole custody of his legitimate children. By the Family Law Act the father and the mother, *subject to any court order, have joint custody of children of the marriage under the age of eighteen.* In exceptional circumstances the family court may order that the disputing parents have joint custody with care and control to one party. The most common order is a grant of sole custody to one parent with the other parent given access to the child.

The concern of the legislation in this area is to promote the interests of the child, which may often be overlooked by the parents themselves, embroiled as they may be in a bitter dispute. The Act states that in custody proceedings the court shall regard the welfare of the child as the paramount consideration. This test was also applied under the Matrimonial Causes Act 1959. There are no principles of law providing a decisive test as to the welfare of the child. Rather *this is a question to be determined from case to case on the particular and unique facts.*

The Wishes of the Child

In addition to emphasizing the welfare of the child, the Act directs that except in special circumstances the court shall not make a custody order contrary to the wishes of any child of fourteen or over. If the child is under fourteen, the court may take into account his or her wishes.

The Japanese Law—The Family Court in Japan and the Best Interests of the Child

The family court in Japan is a specialized court dealing with family affairs cases and juvenile delinquency cases. Through its basic objectives of maintaining the welfare of families and seeking the sound upbringing of juveniles, it tries to answer the modern demand for justice fitted to the needs of society. It is a court in which the principles of law, the conscience of the community, and the social sciences, particularly those dealing with human behaviour and personal relationships, work together. Practically, the function of the court is to deal, within the scope defined by law, with actual problems of families and delinquent juveniles.

Jurisdiction of the Family Court

The family court has a very broad jurisdiction encompassing all disputes and conflicts within the family as well as all related domestic affairs, which are of legal significance.

The juvenile division of the family court handles cases involving delinquent juveniles under twenty years of age and adults who have in some way brought about an injury to the welfare of juveniles. 'Delinquent juveniles' include not only minors who have committed criminal offences under the penal laws but juveniles whose tendencies indicate that they might commit offences in future as well. The court has primary jurisdiction in regard to all juvenile offences, whether they are felonies such as homicides or arsons, or misdemeanours such as traffic offences and violations of administrative control laws. Thus, all criminal cases concerning minors primarily are sent to the family court for investigation and hearing.

Jurisdiction over Adult Criminal Cases

Adults who have committed acts injurious to the welfare of juveniles are also subject to the family court's jurisdiction. Various specific offenses are set down in the Child Welfare Law, the Labour Standards Law, and the School Education Law, etc. Such offences as the inducement of obscene acts, cruel treatment, and employment of children at extremely late hours are examples. The foundation of the jurisdiction over the offences is the protection of juveniles and the maintenance of their basic human rights. However, neither desertion nor neglect of the duty of support by parents or guardians constitutes an offence justifying the jurisdiction of the family court in Japanese juvenile law. Support is considered to be a family law problem and therefore is subject to determination and conciliation procedure of the family affairs division, while desertion, if sufficient to constitute an offence under the penal code, is handled by a regular criminal court.

The French Legal System Relating to Custody of Children

The court, which has exclusive jurisdiction on matters of divorce and its consequences, is the Tribunal de Grande Instance. One of the judges of the Tribunal is appointed to deal with matrimonial matters. *He is especially in charge of the duty of safeguarding the interest of minor children.* He is also exclusively competent to decide on the custody of children and on the modification of the alimony whatever the ground for divorce. The trial on the grounds or consequences of divorce and the interim relief are held in camera.[93]

CONSEQUENCES OF DIVORCE ON THE CHILDREN

The general principle is that divorce leaves intact the rights and duties of the father and mother with regard to their children. However, the custody of the children is given to either of the spouses. In exceptional cases such custody may be given to a third person chosen preferably among the relatives or, when this is not possible, to an educational institution.

The spouse who has been deprived of the custody of the children has the right to watch the way in which they are brought up and educated. He/she also has the duty to contribute, proportionately to his/her income, to the expenses. He/she has also the right to visit and to receive them in his/her residence. Such a right can be denied only for grave reasons. Notwithstanding the normal provisions to the contrary, in law, the spouse who is denied the custody of the children may be entrusted with the task of administering, under judicial control, all or part of the estate of the children, if the interest of a good administration of such estate so requires.

The decision on the grant of the custody of the children and on the mode of exercise of parental authority is taken at the request of one of the spouses or of a member of the family or of the *Procureur de la Republique*. For reaching a decision the judge has to take into account:

- the agreements entered into between the spouses;
- the information collected during the inquiry and counter-inquiry; and

---

[93] See David J. Annoswamy, *The French Legal System and its Indian Connection*, Institute Of Compartive Law, NLSIU, Bangalore, 1996.

- the feelings expressed by the minor children. They will be heard if it appears necessary and when no inconvenience is likely to be caused to them.

The spouse who has been denied the custody of the children will contribute for their maintenance and education in the form of alimony paid to the person who has been entrusted with their custody. The form of such alimony and the guarantee for its payment are fixed by the judgment or in case of divorce on joint request by the agreement between the spouses as approved by the judge.

When the nature and the assets of the spouse liable to pay permits, the liability for alimony may be discharged, in whole or in part:

- by depositing certain amount of money with an accredited organization with a charge to pay to the children a periodical allowance indexed to the cost of living;
- by granting usufructuary right over some properties; or
- by allotting some income yielding properties.

When the capital thus constituted becomes insufficient to cover the needs of the children, the person who has the custody may ask for grant of supplement in the form of alimony. The parent who is mainly in charge of the major children, who are unable to provide themselves for their needs, may ask the other spouse to pay him a contribution for their maintenance and education.

The Law in the United States of America (USA)

In USA, the interests of the child, the parents, and the state balance delicately. The natural rights of parents have a constitutional basis in American law and cover such areas as control over religious training, medical decisions, and mental health. Parental rights are not absolute. The child's interests are protected by the state through the *parens patriae* power. The state uses *guardians' ad litem and special child advocates* to protect many children whose parents' rights are questioned. Each advocate is appointed individually to act, often in a voluntary capacity, to represent children in court or to make recommendations to the court that are in the best interest of the child. The principle of the best interest of the child is the basic guideline governing civil cases involving children. In broad terms, it means that a court must operate in such a manner as to further justice while at the same time promoting the welfare and well-being of the child. The best interest principle is used in a variety of situations in the US: mental health commitments; delinquency hearing; abuse, neglect, or dependency hearings; and custody determination following a divorce. In cases wherein the parents' rights and responsibilities are balanced against the child's best interest, above all other considerations, the child's interests in the eyes of the judge are paramount. But to enforce the rights of the child above those of the parents, the parents' rights first must be overcome.

THE BEST OR LEAST WORST INTEREST OF THE CHILD

The term *best interest* also refer to the goal of the judicial determination in abuse, neglect, and dependency actions in juvenile court. The courts are charged with discovering and putting into place dispositions that will meet the child's best interest. This phrase, though neither advocated nor invented by the courts, came into popular use after publication of the series of books by Professor Joseph Goldstein, Dr Anna Freud, and Dr Albert Solnit: *Beyond the Best Interest of the Child* (1973), *Before the Best Interest of the Child* (1979), and *In the Best Interest of the Child* (1986). These books are an examination of information derived from the Yale University Child Study Center and the Hampstead Child Therapy Clinic. In these books, the authors question the value and ability of any person's attempts to determine and put into effect the best interest of a child. The case goal that is offered by these authors to supplant the so-called best interest goal is 'the least detrimental harm'.

Another author, Professor Ane Coyne (1992) of the University of Nebraska at Omaha, has used a different phrase—'finding the least worst solution'. Although the least worst solution may not be readily apparent to the lawyers and the judge in a particular case, focusing on the least worst solution, Professor Coyne says, will force the lawyers or judge to confront the perils in the other choices available, thereby avoiding or mitigating them. A more productive goal than seeking the best interest, which may be unknowable, is to seek the least worst solution, which would help the professionals involved in the case avoid doing greater harm to a child who is already the subject of an abuse, neglect, or dependency action.

The need for reform in the United States was expressed earlier. In the early nineteenth century, the view of families as patriarchal entities gave way to the newer ideal of democracies populated by individuals with inalienable rights and obligations.[94]

By 1830, a Maryland court was ready to give open support to the notion that a child had an important interest in remaining in his or her mother's care. In *Helms v Franciscus* (1830), the court gave custody of a child of tender years to the mother after she had been granted a legal separation on the basis

---

[94] Walker, Brooks, Wrightsma, *Children's Rights in the United States*, Sage Publication, New Delhi, 1999.

that her husband had been living in open adultery with another woman. The innocent injured spouse received custody of the infant of the marriage, but again the father's right to the older children was upheld despite the fact that the man was an adulterer. The right of a father to ownership of his children was recognized, but the court acknowledged that the laws of nature require that a child not be snatched from a mother in infancy. A child should stay with the breastfeeding mother. Here, the emphasis is not on a woman's right to companionship of her child, but rather on the tender years interests of a breastfeeding child.

The tender years rule was the first appearance of legal consideration of the needs of very young children; as such, it was a best interest standard. Once the tender years rule was fully accepted by the US divorce courts, fathers found the tables completely turned. For almost a century, the only way a father could gain custody over the children of the marriage, on legal separation or divorce, was to prove the mother's unfitness. During the peak of the tender years rule, the law was as gender-biased against men as it had been in favour of them before.

The gender bias was declared unconstitutional by many states in the wake of the first gains of the women's movement. In *Ex parte Devine* (1981), for example, the Alabama Supreme Court declared the gender-based 'tender years rule' over when it found the doctrine to be unconstitutional. Similarly, a few years earlier, in *State ex rel. Watts v Watts* (1973), New York's highest court, its Court of Appeals, found that any legal presumption against fathers was unconstitutional.

Other courts have found otherwise. Oklahoma's Supreme Court, in *Gordon v Gordon* (1978), upheld that state's statutory preference for maternal custody 'other things being equal'; in that case, the US Supreme Court refused to hear an appeal against the state court's ruling (1978), in effect refusing to disapprove the state court's decision.

West Virginia's High Court, however, has held the tender years rule to be constitutional on the basis of the following:

- Men and women are not similarly situated when it comes to parenting, at least when the child is very young (e.g. breastfeeding).
- The presumption in favour of mothers may be an appropriate offset to the historic disadvantages they suffered (*J.B. v V.B.*, 1978).

As state courts dropped the tender years rule and its explicit preference for mothers, they retained the spirit of it in the name of 'the best interest of the child standard'. In essence, the tender years doctrine, which was aimed at meeting the needs of children, became gender-neutral without losing the goal of appropriately addressing children's needs. Currently, the courts are asked to carry out evaluations about the child's best welfare. A judge is not required to follow the psychologist's recommendations. In fact, judges' decisions may reflect their own stereotyped beliefs about what is in a child's best interests, beliefs that may or may not fit in with empirical findings.[95]

The Uniform Marriage and Divorce Act (UMDA 1979), which has had a significant impact on the statutory reforms of many states, describes the following as among the factors a judge may consider in reaching a custody decision:

- The mental and physical health of all individuals involved;
- The child's adjustment to home, school, and community;
- Each parent's ability to provide food, clothing, medication, and other remedial care and material benefits to the child;
- The interaction and interrelationship of the child with parents or other individuals who might affect the child's best interests (thus, in a general sense, the parent's lifestyle and the child's individual needs);
- The wishes of the parents and the child.

It is with respect to the last factor that children's rights to self-determination are beginning to emerge. At least twenty states permit children beyond a specified age to state which parent they prefer for custody. Some states specify age, typically twelve or fourteen; others consider the maturity of the child's cognitive or emotional development. For instance, in the case *In re Marriage of Rosson* (1986), the court concluded that a child of a sufficient age and capacity to reason well enough to form an intelligent custody preference does have the right to have that preference seriously considered. But consensus is lacking on how much weight is to be given to the child's preferences.

Laws in the United Kingdom

The term 'child' means a person, who has not reached his or her eighteenth birthday. This broad definition grants agencies and courts great discretion when dealing with young people. In English law, the word 'custody' has been used in a wider sense so as to include practically all the rights of guardianship as well as in a narrow sense as to include only 'care and control'. The history of the law in United Kingdom relating to the custody of a child shows two important trends as will be evident from the following.

The Guardianship of Minors Act 1971 repealed the Guardianship of Infants Act 1925. It made no changes in the substantive law.

---

[95] Walker, Brooks, Wrightsma, *Children's Rights in the United States*, Sage Publication, New Delhi, 1999.

GENERAL PRINCIPLES

A dispute over custody may take one of the two forms: it may be a dispute between the father and the mother; or it may be a dispute between one parent and a stranger, for example, a testamentary guardian appointed by the other parent, or a person who has obtained *de facto* control of the child either with the parent's consent or as a result of his having abandoned it.

As the House of Lords held in *J. v C.*,[96] the principle laid down in Section 1 of the Guardianship of Minors Act 1971, that the welfare of the child is to be regarded as the first and paramount consideration, applies equally whether the dispute is between the parents, or between one or both parents and a stranger. In this case, however, the wishes of an unimpeachable parent stand high among the remaining considerations: to give effect to the blood tie will itself normally be for the child's benefit and usually he should be with his natural parents. But there is no presumption that the natural parents should have custody; in the words of Lord Macdermott:[97]

> ... when all the relevant facts, relationships, claims and wishes of parents, risks, choices and other circumstances are taken into account and weighed, the course to be followed will be that which is most in the interests of the child's welfare as that term has now to be understood.

If all considerations are equal, however, the court will give effect to this relationship and grant custody to a parent rather than to a stranger. This was not the case in *J. v C.* The parents of the child were Spanish nationals resident in Spain, but the child, who was then aged ten years, had spent the whole of his life except for eighteen months with foster parents in England. He had been brought up as an English boy, spoke little Spanish and scarcely knew his natural parents. The House of Lords refused to interfere with the order of the trial judge who left custody, care, and control with the foster parents and refused to give it to the natural parents on the ground that they 'would' be quite unable to cope with the problems of adjustments or with consequential maladjustment and suffering and that the father's character would inflame the difficulties' if the boy were to go to live with them in Spain.

The one statutory exception to this rule is to be found in Section 3 of the Custody of Children Act 1891. This section provides that where a parent has abandoned or deserted his child or allowed it to be brought up by, and at the expense of, another person, school, institution, or local authority, in such circumstances as to show that he was unmindful of his parental duties, no

---

[96] (1969), All E.R.788.
[97] Ibid., p. 821.

order is to be made giving him the custody of the child unless he proves that he is a fit person to have it. But in order to bring this section into play, the parent's conduct must show some degree of moral turpitude. If he relinquishes control temporarily because this is the best that he can do for the child in the circumstances, the court ought not, on this ground alone, to deprive him of custody. In practice, this section is rarely invoked.

POWER OF APPELLATE COURTS

It will be seen that the court must always be guided by the interests of the child and, as the House of Lords emphasized in *J. v C.*,[98] a court of first instance has a discretion with which no appellate court will interfere unless it is satisfied that the lower court has clearly acted under a misapprehension of fact, or gave weight to irrelevant or unproved matters, or failed to take relevant matters into account.[99] On the other hand, an appellate court is not entitled to allow an appeal and substitute its own discretion merely because it would have come to a different conclusion on the evidence.[100] Difficulty arises because in some cases appellate courts are so convinced that the lower court exercised its discretion wrongly that they will reverse the decision even though the latter purported to apply the right principles in reaching it.[101] On hearing an appeal, a court is apparently entitled to consider the relative weight which the lower court attached to the various facts which it had to take into account and to conclude that the court acted on the wrong principles if it disagrees with the weighting.[102]

Children's Act 1989, Section 1 provides: 'When a court determines any question with respect to

- upbringing of a child or
- the administration of the child's property or the application of any income arising form it, the child's welfare shall be the court's paramount consideration.'

The welfare principle in Section 1 applies only to courts, but parents, local authorities, and children themselves must also have regard to children's welfare. Decisions by parents which conflict with welfare may be reviewed by the courts and thus it has been said that parents must apply the welfare

---

[98] As *in Re Thin*, [1926], Ch. 676, C.A.
[99] See *Re O'Hara*, [1900]2I.R. 232 at pp. 238, 243, 251; *Re Carroll*, [1931]1 K.B. 317, 360-3, CA; *R.v Bolton Union*, (1892),36 Sol.J.255.
[100] [1969]t All E.R. 788, H.L.;[1970] A.C.668.
[101] *B.(B.) v B. (M)*, [1969] I All E.R. 891,961;[1969] P.103, 115.
[102] If evidence is available to the appellate court which was not before the lower court.

principle. The same could be said of children.[103] Local authority decisions, which do not require court approval, are generally immune from review on the merits but local authorities are under a duty to safeguard and promote the welfare of children in need and those they are looking after.[104] The word 'first' was thought by the Law Commission to suggest that the child's welfare should be balanced with other factors.[105]

The leading case on the welfare principle is *J. v C,*[106] where the courts considered whether a ten-year-old boy should be returned to his parents (Spanish nationals resident in Spain) or remain with English foster parents who had looked after him for all, except eighteen months, of his life. The House of Lords upheld the decision of the trial judge and the Court of Appeal that he should stay in England. Lord Macdermott stated that paramountcy of welfare means:

the child's welfare is to be treated as the top item in a list of items relevant to the matter in question. [The words] connote a process whereby, when all the relevant facts, relationships claims and wishes of parents, risks, choices and other circumstances are taken into account and weighed, the course to be followed will be that which is most in the interests of the child's welfare as that term is now understood. . . . [It is] the paramount consideration because it rules upon or determines the course to be followed.[107]

The boy's welfare necessitated that he remain with the parent figures he was attached to, the more so since his natural parents would have been unable to cope with his consequent maladjustment. Against these considerations the claims of 'unimpeachable' natural parents could not prevail. The court came to a different conclusion in a similar case in 1996.

The Children's Act 1989 did not create a unified family court but it reformed the magistrate's court, renaming the domestic court the 'family proceedings court' and giving it jurisdiction over all civil matters concerning the upbringing of children.

The Act created four orders relating to children. These are:
- residence order which states where the child should live,
- the contact order which requires a carer to allow someone to have contact with the child,

---

[103] *Re O* (1971) 2 WLR 784 C.A.
[104] *Cf. Re O* (1962) 2 All. E.R 10 C.A.
[105] Law Com 96 para 6,9. Law Com No. 172, Review of Child Law Guardianship and Custody (1988) HC 594 para.
[106] 1990 AC 668.
[107] Ibid., at 710–11.

- the prohibited steps order which restricts the exercise of parental responsibility, and
- the specific issue order which determines how parental responsibility is to be exercised.

Together exercised, these are known as the 'Section 8' orders.

Some Legal Developments and Trends of Comparative Law

When the needs of children cannot be met by those responsible for their care, the state recognizes its responsibility to intervene and assure their care, development, and safety. A survey of comparative legal interventions in custody and guardianship proceedings reveal that the practice of democratic legal systems has accepted, on a wide front, the challenge of individualization. Wide powers have been given to the courts to make decisions based on the welfare of children during marital proceedings.

- Growth of the child welfare professions and the desire to reach better and more justifiable decisions in children's cases have shifted the reasoning in these cases towards arguments based on theories of child development. The courts rely on the evidence of experts and reports from welfare officers. But the 'child welfare science' is reconstructed by the legal process.
- As a general rule children are represented by a next friend or guardian ad litem. A child who wishes to proceed without a guardian *ad litem* must seek leave of the court.
- The definition of the child in developed countries is a person who is under the age of eighteen.
- The opinion of the minor is considered in deciding custody. In Hong Kong, the age is above ten years and in Australia it is fourteen years or over.
- The welfare principle applies not only to courts but also to parents, local authorities, and children themselves.
- Evaluators get involved in a family's legal dispute and the custody and visitation of the family's minor children. The evaluators help the courts understand the family dynamics in a way that will allow for the development of an appropriate plan for custody and visitation of minor children.
- In developed countries it is a well-settled law that the religion of the minor is not at all a relevant factor in determining the custody of the

child. In developing countries, the law is still to be settled. Though the trends are changing through case laws.
- The law imposes duty on children to support and assist their parents.
- Acceptance of arbitration awards by courts.
- Representation of child's interests in matrimonial disputes.
- The Arbitration option is given to the parties in dispute.
- Conciliation counselling in an attempt to bring about an agreement.
- Mediation has become an important option.
- The utilization of alternative dispute resolution (ADR) techniques in custody disputes.
- Unified family courts that bring together under one court custody and guardianship dispute as well as juvenile justice matters.
- Strong evidence needed to justify a change of custody.
- Third parties, relatives, and friends may stand as sureties for the implementation of schemes relating to children.
- The maintenance amount for children can be deposited with an accredited organization with a charge to pay to the children a periodical allowance.
- Finding the least or worst solution will force the lawyers and judges to confront the perils in other choices available.
- The gender-based tender years doctrine found unconstitutional by some US courts but it was retained in the best interest of the child.
- In the tender years doctrine, the emphasis is not on women's rights to companionship of her child but on the tender years interest of a breast-feeding child.
- Consensus is lacking on how much weight is to be given to the child's preference.
- Scientific evaluations of child custody decisions are carried out.
- A continuing conflict-riddled relationship between parents can be determinant in joint custody arrangement.
- Today, custody mediations are being questioned because of their 'non-legal' character.
- In-service training to develop professional ability and skill.
- Family court clinic is an auxiliary organ of the court for scientific examination and diagnosis of parties and juveniles.
- Involving senior citizens and volunteers from the public.
- Attendants as defence counsel for a child.
- One of the judges of matrimonial court exclusively appointed to take charge of safeguarding the interests of minor children.
- Child's wishes presented in an affidavit.

- Access is a right of the child, which promotes its welfare and should be denied only in exceptional circumstances.
- Use of casework method to diagnose the cause of a particular trouble and to prescribe a reasonable remedy.
- Supervisory role of the court for the protection of the welfare of families.
- Judges and probation officers to use wide professional skills in the field of medicine, psychology, pedagogy, sociology, and other sciences related to human beings.
- Welfare conferences to discuss the welfare of the child.
- Judicial interviews should be sparingly used.
- Child's counsel to make submissions on the welfare of the child and put forward the wishes of the child.
- Paramountcy of welfare is a principle whereby all the relevant facts, relationships, claims and wishes of the parents, risks, choices, and other circumstances are taken into account and weighed.
- A list of factors of the welfare checklist from various countries include:
  – The mental and physical health of all individuals involved.
  – Age of the child.
  – Sex of the child.
  – Mental sturdiness of the child.
  – The child's adjustment to home, school, and community.
  – Each parent's ability to provide food, clothing, medication, and other benefits to the child.
  – Parent's lifestyle.
  – Wishes of the child.
  – Needs of the child.
  – Separation of siblings.
  – Moral guilt of parents.
  – Characteristics of parents.
  – Continuity principle.
  – Housing conditions.
  – School situation.
  – Playmates for the child.
  – Remarriage of parents.
  – Wishes of the parents.
  – Religion or faith of parents.
  – Views of experts.
  – Representation of child's interests.
  – Health or financial difficulties of parties.

- Priority to party who can no longer have any children.
- Parent who lives with the child longer than the other parent and where a clearly negative impact would be experienced by the child as a result of change of environment.
- Healthy growth of the child.
- The relations between the child and parents.
- Lifestyle of parents (conventional morality).
- Religious convictions.
- Detailed future scheme which would be put into action to ensure the maintenance and education of children along with sureties for its implementation.
- Consequences of the court's decision.
- Least detrimental solution.

Legislations include a duty to minimize delay because of the damage the uncertainty of litigation could do to children and the existence of a legal culture where delay was acceptable. Decision-making processes should take account of the child's sense of time. The paramountcy of the child's welfare and the speed with which young children develop attachments mean that delay often benefits one of the adults and harms the child.

Above all, the trend is to view the family divorce through the eyes of children, understand how children feel, what they fear and wish, and what makes conflict resolution difficult to be achieved. We need to stay focused on the needs of the children who have the most to lose and finally we must reduce the pain for the children—the real pawns in the game of their parents' divorce.

Discussion

It is clear that rulings granting custody are affected by issues like poverty, character adultery, immorality, religion, sex, age, abandonment, remarriage, wishes of parents and children, and nearness of kin.[108] These are the factors that are taken into account by the courts while determining the best interests of the child.

There are no hard and fast rules or precedents, in fact there cannot be. Decisions are based on the facts and circumstances of each case. Courts often prefer not to disturb the status quo and generally place the child in the custody of the person who has already exercised custody at the time of petition. Courts have also in recent times rejected the arguments of working women and economic well-being, but in some cases orthodox views still persist.

[108] Paras Diwan, *Muslim Law in Modern India*, Wadhwa and Co., Delhi, 1987, pp. 128, 129.

Issues like child abuse and cruelty to children have not come up frequently. Child's interests are fashioned primarily on the perspective, needs, and wishes of competing adult claimants, or to protect the general policies of childcare, or what the adults perceive to be the best interest of the child. Wherever possible, the courts have taken the wishes of children into account but many children can be easily tutored by the undue influence of the non-custodial parent against the absentee parent.

Clearly, the best interest standards give judges tremendous discretion. The background of judges and their understanding as to what is the best interest of the child play an important role. It is still a question of 'proved' and 'not proved' based on the facts presented before the courts. There also appears to be tension between the apparent meaning of the best interest standard and its construction in legislative and court decisions. There are also risks to the child due to delays and adjournments that are a regular feature of the legal system.

Since the child is not represented in the Indian courts, it is upto the judge to ensure that the child's interests are not harmed or negated. The judges are not trained or sensitized to be friendly. Besides, even in those cases where the courts have managed to determine the best interests of the child, the social, administrative, and enforcement machinery is not sensitive enough to implement them.

Child sexual abuse cases have now started coming up before courts in custody matters. Orders granting custody of children to one parent are invariably accompanied by an order granting visitation rights to the non-custodial parent. Courts are of the view that it is essential for the healthy emotional development of the children to have continued contact with the non-custodial parent. But the visitation rights to the non-custodial parent do not always serve the best interest of the child. There is now a need for the non-custodial parent to justify and the courts to determine whether visitation rights and access is in the best interest of the child. The non-custodial parent could interfere with the quality of relationship between the child and the custodial parent.

Some courts recognize joint custody. Joint legal custody entitles both parents to share equally in all decisions relating to the child's upbringing, medical care, and attention. However, the quality of the child-parent relationship appears to be a function of the degree of conflict rather than the custody arrangement, the ex-partners displaying the most bitterness also have the most conflictual relationship with their children, even when the children are in joint custody.[109]

---

[109] P.R. Amato, and S.J. Rezac, 'Contact with non-residential parents, interparental conflict, and children's behaviour', in *Journal of Family Issues*, 15, 191–207 (1994).

Assessing the 'Parent-child Goodness of Fit'

Children constitute an arena for parental power struggles. The toughest part of custodial decisions occurs in assessing this parent-child goodness of fit. It involves gathering of data from several sources—interviews, reports, psychological testing, projective techniques, and direct observation of each parent, both individually and with children. After gathering the data, it has to be integrated and assigned weights to the relative meaning of each fact before making a responsible, fact-based decision. It is a unique and speculated skill at extrapolating meaningful recommendations from a decision-making strategy that combines data from a variety of sources along a variety of different behavioural dimensions into a coherent whole. This requires the involvement of several experts along with the judge. In the superior courts, there have been instances as in *Thrity Dolikukas* case, where the Supreme Court has appointed independent experts, but at the trial courts level there is no such instance. Many of the trial courts and even High Courts have erred in their decision making and the child has to go through unnecessary trauma and further litigation. No court has looked into the lifelong trauma of the child. There can never be any compensation for such trauma but a provision to this effect can go a long way in creating awareness on this aspect. There is also a need for follow-up of the custody decisions.

The courts have considered the wishes of the child but children whose parents are separated or are in conflict situations may be predicated to demonstrate some behaviours of distress or confusion more often than many children in intact families. The wishes expressed to the court may not always be their own. They may not want to 'hurt' the feelings of the custodial parent or their wishes can be 'influenced' by several factors, which may not have come up before the court.

How can courts make routine decisions in cases of custody? Custody cases have to be treated differently. It is a parental tug of war in which each parent claims his or her legal rights while tearing the child apart. Rarely is it a simple process to evaluate both parents and the child and determine the best interests of the child. And finally, it is undoubtedly true that the best parenting is achieved with two parents.

Originally, unless the father was unfit, the father had an absolute 'right to the custody and control' of a child. Later, the decisions swung to the presumption that a child of tender years should be placed with the mother.

In the legal process the courts usually consider children through a paternalistic discourse. Whether the talk is of 'needs', 'welfare', or 'best interest' of the child, *it is adults who interpret this*. Analysis of the process reveals that the focus of law is inevitably drawn to competing adults. This is so whether they are seeking possession of the child as object or are engaged in a power struggle over the child. The discourse of judges and lawyers who claim to take into account only the interest of the child (as opposed to the interests of each of the parents) can be countered by showing that when they speak of the child, they are inevitably speaking of something else—the father, the mother, the family. Courts also rested the issue of custody solely on the welfare of the child.

4
Right Against Economic Exploitation— Child Labour

What is Child Labour

Child labour is a complex and a controversial issue. Unfortunately, it is a global phenomenon. In almost all societies, children work in some way, though the types of work they do and the forms of their involvement vary. But many millions of children work under abusive and exploitative conditions that are clearly dangerous to them. They are found in the following situations among others:

- In agriculture, performing heavy work and exposed to the many hazards associated with the introduction of modern machinery and chemicals.
- In dangerous industries and occupations, such as glass making, construction, mining, and carpet weaving.
- In domestic service, carrying out arduous work under conditions of isolation, over excessively long hours and with physical and sexual abuse.
- In the streets, working as rag pickers, vendors, and child prostitutes, often under threat of violence from street gangs and the police, and with exposure to life-threatening diseases.
- In small industrial workshops and service establishments.
- At home, tending younger children or helping in family farms and business, working such long hours that it is impossible to play or attend school.
- As bonded labourers in outright slavery.
- In predominantly exports industries, such as textiles, clothing, carpets, and footwear.

Child labour includes children prematurely leading adult lives, working long hours for low wages, under conditions damaging to their health and to their physical and mental development, sometimes separated from their families, frequently deprived of meaningful education and training opportunities that could open up for them a better future.[1] Child labour is therefore all work that places children at risk.[2]

When the business of wage earning or of participation in self or family support conflicts directly or indirectly with the business of growth and education, the result is child labour.[3] Any non-school-going child is a child labourer.[4] A recent International Labour Organization (ILO) report on child labour used the term 'child labour' to cover all economic activities carried out by persons less than fifteen years of age, regardless of their occupational status (wage earners, own-account workers, unpaid family workers, etc.), but not household work performed by them in their parents' home, except where such work can be assimilated to an economic activity as for example, when a child must devote his or her entire time to the work so that his or her parents can be employed outside the home and is, therefore, deprived of the possibility of going to school.

This includes children working in any sector, occupation, or process, including the formal and non-formal, organized and unorganized, within or outside the family.[5] Child labour also includes:

- Child labour in bondage,
- Child labour within and with families (including domestic child labour),
- Girl child labour,
- Child labour separated from families, and
- Child labour which is itinerant.

Child labour can be broadly classified into the following categories:

- Child labour covered by legislation,
- Child labour falling outside the legislative framework,
- Agriculture and allied activities, and
- Informal, unorganized, semi-urban, and urban sector.[6]

[1] The International Labour Organization, 1983.
[2] Report of the Director General of the International Labour Organization, 1983.
[3] Encyclopedia of Social Sciences.
[4] Some voluntary groups.
[5] Campaign Against Child Labour (CACL)—A network of over 5400 anti-child labour groups spread over twelve States in India.
[6] Public Hearing and Second National Convention of Child Labourers: Reference Kit, CACL, March 1997.

Magnitude of Child Labour

The estimates on the magnitude of child labour vary due to multiplicity of definitions, different methods of computation, and the collection of data at different points of time. Statistics on child labour are, therefore, elusive not only because of the special and practical difficulties involved in the design and implementation of child surveys but also because of differences in perception about what constitutes a child, or child work, or child labour. Despite these shortcomings certain figures and estimates have been produced and these highlight a very concerning global scenario. The evidence reveals a problem found throughout the world, especially in Africa, Asia, and Latin America.

Earlier estimates based on very limited statistical information obtained from about a hundred countries indicated that there were seventy-three million working children between ten and fourteen years of age in these countries in 1995. However, recent experimental surveys carried out by the International Labour Organization's (ILO's) Bureau of Statistics in a number of countries indicate that this figure is a gross underestimation. They further indicate that even children below ten years of age are at work in substantial numbers. The Bureau now estimates that, in the developing countries alone, there are at least 120 million children between the ages of five and fourteen who are fully at work, and more than twice as many (or about 250 million) if those for whom work is a secondary activity are included. Of these, 61 per cent are found in Asia, 32 per cent in Africa, and 7 per cent in Latin America. Although Asia has the largest number of child workers, Africa has the highest incidence at around 40 per cent of children between five and fourteen years old. Though primarily a developing-country problem, child labour also exists in many industrialized countries and is emerging in many East European and Asian countries, which are in transition to a market economy.[7]

One of the most visible forms of child labour in big cities in many countries is that performed by street children. This applies to countries such as Brazil in South America, Kenya in Africa, and India in Asia.[8] The numbers of street children are increasing in the former communist countries of eastern Europe. However, in large cities, many child workers are hidden from public view, such as the children who help out in small workshops and garages in

---

[7] International Labour Organization, *Child labour: Targeting the intolerable—The problem*, Geneva, 1996, p. 7.

[8] Sandy Hobbs, Jim McKechnie, and Michael Lavalette, *Child Labour: A World History Companion*, MPG Books Limited, Bodmin, Cornwall, Great Britain, 1999.

Cairo, Egypt, or those who scavenge in the garbage dumps outside Lima, Peru.[9]

Most of the countries of Latin America, Africa, and Asia have similar economic problems. They have been agricultural communities in the past, but the pressures to industrialize are great. Child workers are found both in traditional work and in modern industrial production. Children fish in Indonesia and herd animals in Zimbabwe. They also work in the coal mines of Colombia and garment factories of Morocco.[10] Western countries have their own child labour problems, although on the whole the scale is smaller in North America and western Europe than elsewhere in the world. A good deal of the work performed by Western children is part-time and does not interfere with their attending school.[11]

Child Labour in India

The 1991 census of India put the figure of child labour as 11.28 million; the survey conducted by the National Sample Survey Organization (NSSO) in 1993–4 estimated 13.3 million child labour out of which 10.1 million were estimated to be employed full-time. The ILO, according to the data collected in 1996 put the figure at 23.17 million, out of which 12.67 million were employed full-time. According to the NSSO, child workers constitute 3.4 per cent of the total labour force and agriculture accounts for more than 75 per cent of the total employment of child labour. Table 4.1 shows the participation rate and percentage of children in the total labour force according to the various surveys of the NSSO. The latest NSSO study showed that the agriculture sector is the dominant employer of the child workers; and most of the child labourers are either self-employed or are casual wage labourers.[12]

Table 4.1: Child Labour in India as Percentages of Total Labour Force and Total Population

Year	Total Number	Percentage of Total Labour Force	Percentage of Total Labour Population
1977–8	19.4	11.0	7.0
1983	20.6	10.9	6.7
1987–8	17.7	8.8	5.2
1993–4	13.3	6.2	3.4

Source: NSSO Data.

[9] Ibid.
[10] Ibid.
[11] Ibid.
[12] K. Sharma, *Child Labour in India*, The Lawyers Collective, November 1999.

Table 4.2 shows the magnitude of child labour in India from various sources:

Table 4.2: Child Labour in India

Source	Year	Millions
Census of India	1971	10.7
	1981	13.0
	1991	11.3
NSS India	1987–8	17.6
	1993–9	13.5
ILO	1975	15.1
	1996	23.2

Source: Sekar Helen, *Ensuring Their Childhood*, V.V. Giri National Labour Institute, New Delhi, 2001.

Besides, there are about 74.4 million children, who are neither enrolled in schools nor accounted for in the labour force, who come under the category of 'nowhere' children.[13]

Major Sectors where Children Work

Children work in all the sectors of the economy, i.e. the agrarian, the manufacturing, and the service sectors. Census enumerates only those workers who are engaged in economically productive work and only such working children are counted as part of labour force.[14] One very common feature of child labour is its concentration in unskilled and simple routines which offer little opportunity for transfer to other more remunerative, safer, or more interesting occupations.[15] Among the male child workers, though about 78 per cent are concentrated in the agricultural sector, their presence seems to be quite considerable in the non-agricultural sector worth over 20 per cent. Among the female working children, about 52 per cent are agricultural labourers and in total about 83 per cent are in the agricultural sector. Thus concentration of female child workers in the agricultural sector is more than that of male child workers. As an implication of this, their presence in non-agricultural sector is only 12.16 per cent. The overall picture reveals that more and more female children are engaged in low-paid jobs as compared

[13] Helen Sekar, *Ensuring Their Childhood*, V.V.Giri National Labour Institute, New Delhi, 2001.
[14] Ibid.
[15] Aseefa Bequele and Jo Boyden (eds), *Combating Child Labour*, International Labour Office, Geneva, 1988.

Right Against Economic Exploitation 153

to male children. Though the figures given here indicate the incidence of child labour and their occupational classification for the whole country, there is a great variation of the incidence and classification across the states in India.[16] The distribution of male and female child workers in different categories of occupation throughout India is presented in Figures 4.1 and 4.2.

Figure 4.1: Category-wise Percentage of Male Child Workers
Source: Census of India, 1991.[17]

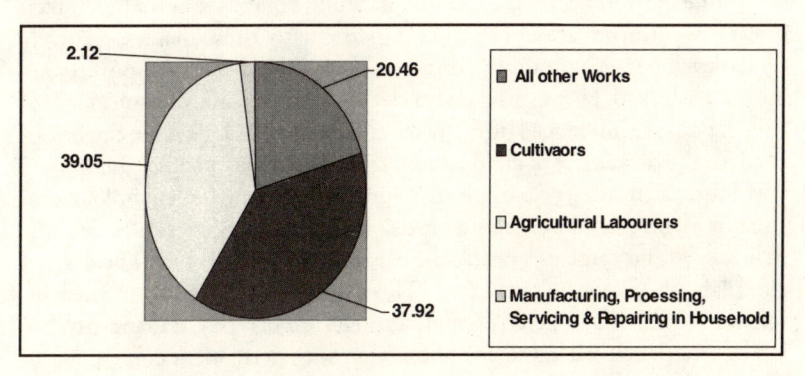

Pie chart values: 2.12, 20.46, 39.05, 37.92
- All other Works
- Cultivaors
- Agricultural Labourers
- Manufacturing, Proessing, Servicing & Repairing in Household

Figure 4.2: Category-wise Percentage of Female Child Workers
Source: Census of India, 1991[18]

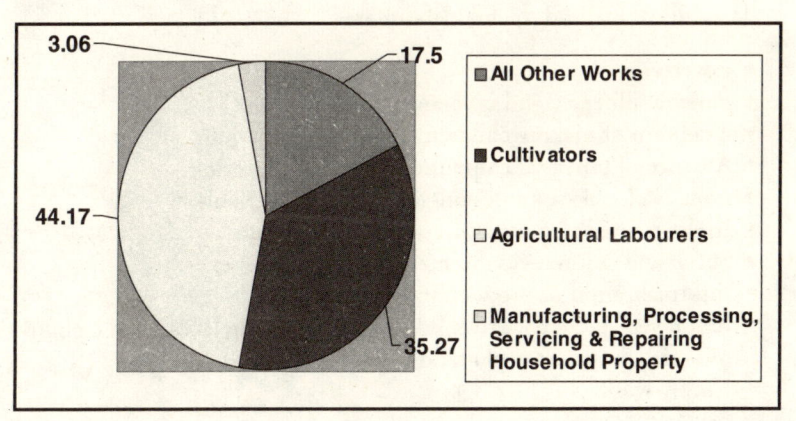

Pie chart values: 3.06, 17.5, 44.17, 35.27
- All Other Works
- Cultivators
- Agricultural Labourers
- Manufacturing, Processing, Servicing & Repairing Household Property

---

[16] Helen Sekar, *Ensuring Their Childhood*, V.V. Giri National Labour Institute, New Delhi, 1999.

[17] R. Vidhyasagar, *Child Labour in India: An Analysis of 1991 Census*, Mimeo, 1998, pp. 4 and 5.

[18] Ibid.

The state with the highest child labour population in the country is Andhra Pradesh that has 1.95 million working children as per the 1981 census. Other states where child labour population is more than one million are Bihar, Karnataka, Madhya Pradesh, Maharashtra, Rajasthan, and Uttar Pradesh.

Causes and Consequences of Child Labour

It is often assumed that the nature and extent of poverty in a country determine the number of its child labour. Studies that have been undertaken in various countries around the world, particularly those that are relatively underdeveloped economically, do show that child labour and poverty are intimately linked. However, it is also clear that the specific circumstances of child labour are influenced by many other factors. No single cause can be isolated for the prevalence of child labour. It is a combination of several factors. It is inherent in the cycle of poverty, unemployment, underemployment, and low wages caused by inequitable distribution of resources and economic policies. But no cause can justify the existence of child labour. The costs of child labour cannot be overstated. There is the complete loss of their invaluable childhood. There is an impairment of both physical and psychological health at a critical stage of life, often with permanent consequences. There is also the permanent damage to social development of the child. Lack of education condemns children to the worst employment prospects as adults and pushes them into the army of low wage earners.

The causes that lead to child labour are:[19]

- Poverty
- Parental illiteracy and ignorance
- Tradition of making children learn the family skills
- Absence of universal compulsory primary education
- Non-availability of and non-accessibility to schools
- Irrelevant and non-attractive school curriculum
- Social and cultural environment
- Informalization of production
- Employers' preference to children for their cheap labour and inability to organize against exploitation
- Family work
- Level of technology
- Apathy of trade unions

[19] Helen Sekar, *Ensuring Their Childhood*, V.V. Giri National Labour Institute, New Delhi, 2001.

- Ineffective enforcement of the legal provisions pertaining to child labour.

Child labour often creates a vicious circle of poverty, as a child coming from an impoverished family surviving harsh conditions becomes an unskilled, debilitated adult who is not employed even in the industry that exploited him/her earlier. Furthermore, child labour receives a low, negligible income and often no wages at all. They have no rights as workers and may not join trade unions. Child labour also depresses adult labour and keeps adults unemployed.[20]

Girl Child Labour[21]

The girl child requires a special mention in the context of child labour. Although the labour of young children of both sexes is exploited, the plight of the girl child labourers is worse off. She is a child, a girl, and a labourer, and she faces discrimination on all counts, in almost all areas—rural and urban. There are many reports of girls being allocated tasks that are more tedious or arduous, more damaging to education, less well paid, and requiring a fairly longer working day than boys.[22] The girl child labour is prevalent in the following areas:

- *Household work*: Girls between the ages of six and eleven sweep, wash, collect water and firewood, and mind younger siblings and livestock.
- *Agriculture work*: Young girls work long hours in the fields.
- *Home-based piece-rate work*: Girls toil in this kind of work. Her existence as an economic entity is rarely known to anybody. Large numbers of home-based girls are employed in rolling beedis,[23] carpet industry, lock making, and gem polishing. Poverty forces them to work but cultural tradition prevents them from seeking work in the organized sector. Therefore, in their case there is no legal protection at all. Her work is seen as part of her mother's labour. The patriarchal value system that operates in the family justifies the unequal labour of boys and girls.
- *Bonded labour*: During drought, famine, or natural calamities, they may be given away as bonded labour to moneylenders or sold into beggary or prostitution. The red light areas of India's major cities are

[20] Vikas Adhyayan Kendra, *Facts Against Myths*, Vol. III, 8, 1996, p. 2.
[21] Asha Bajpai, Recommendations given to The National Commission for Women, New Delhi, for amending the Child Labour (Prohibition and Regulation) Act 1986 (unpublished).
[22] Assefa Bequele and Jo Boyden (eds), *Combating Child Labour*, International Labour Office, Geneva, 1988.
[23] Tobacco rolled in leaves for smoking.

full of female child prostitutes who have been sold by families or lured away. Some communities institutionalize prostitution by dedicating their young girls as devadasis.
- *Domestic servants*: Girl children are forced to work for long duration, without wages, or on low wages. In return they have no opportunity for acquiring any skill. They have to face rampant and systematic physical and sexual exploitation.

Therefore, the significant characteristics of the girl child labour are:

- Invisible work—not recognized as economic activity. They do not come under the purview of law.
- No identifiable employer.
- Long working hours and poor conditions that prevent them from attending any school.
- No skill formation.
- Low pay and low status.
- Physical abuse.
- Sexual harassment and abuse.

Domestic Child Labour

Here are a few real-life instances of inhuman torture and exploitation of domestic child labour:

- Nirmala, a thirteen-year-old maid working with a couple, was beaten with iron rods for having broken a glass. This incident brought to light many such cases of violence against domestic workers in Delhi.
- Nayaagamma witnessed the torture of her thirteen-year-old daughter Kaveri, a domestic servant, by the local police. She was suspected of having stolen some jewellery from her employer's house. Unable to bear the shame and sight of the brutal torture of her innocent daughter, she committed suicide in Bangalore on 29 April 1997.
- Mary Gracy Ekka, twenty-five, was murdered on 24 July 1995 inside the kitchen of the home she worked in, in broad daylight in Bandra, one of the busiest suburbs of the city of Mumbai. The certificate permitting burial stated in one simple sentence. . . 'shock and haemorrhage, due to injuries to vital organs'.

Such testimonies as above are endless.[24]

There is a growing phenomenon of rampant and systematic exploitation of children in domestic work in urban areas. In many cases, such children

---

[24] The Hidden 'Live-In' Slaves, The Domestic Workers—May Day Message 1998 (Excerpts), the RALLY, April 1998.

have been forced to work for long durations, without food, and/or have worked for very low wages. Many of the live-in domestic workers are in a situation of near slavery. With the violation of their human rights, not only are there sub-human living and working conditions but even blatant injustice of non-payment of wages as well as criminal acts of physical, sexual, and psychological violence amounting to torture have been documented. A task force was set up by four NGOs/networks working with child labourers and on child rights issues and domestic work in Mumbai, primarily to obtain first-hand detailed information on the causes of death of three child workers, Cherry, Radha, and Asha. The interim fact-finding report of the task force has pointed out the following common features derived from all the three cases:

- The employers have been inflicting injuries and battering them repeatedly, over weeks and months.
- The employers have amply demonstrated the extent of their disturbed mentality, going by the gruesome third-degree battering of the children.
- The employers are all professionals, two among them being government employees, who have been treated leniently by the respective government departments.
- The child domestic workers have had no recourse to help or were working in conditions of absolute bondage and slavery.
- These children constitute a force that is predominantly invisible and silent, and hence subject to a higher degree of exploitation and abuse.
- The children were continuously locked in the homes and had no opportunity to share/express their anguish and pain, and this proved to be a critical psychological hazard.
- The employers do have their own children who have been well protected, which clearly demonstrates that the employers have exploited the class background of the domestic workers to abuse them.

Even though the children have been in conditions of extreme exploitation and abuse, the legislation permits the employment of children in this domestic sector.

Even though the Child Labour (Prohibition and Regulation) Act 1986 does not define domestic child labour as 'hazardous', the nature of the work, as is amply clear, is extremely hazardous and in fact detrimental to the life of the children, whose very fundamental right to life[25] has been denied.[26]

---

[25] The Constitution of India, Article 21, states that no person shall be deprived of his life or personal liberty except according to the procedure established by law. According to the Supreme Court, the right to life includes a right to live in dignity.

[26] Task Force Against Domestic Child Labour, Interim Fact Finding Report.

Bonded Child Labour

Bonded child labour refers to the phenomenon of children working in conditions of servitude in order to pay off a debt that binds them to their relatives or guardians—usually a parent. The creditors-cum-employers offer 'loans' to destitute parents in an effort to secure the labour of a child, which is always cheap, but even cheaper under a situation of bondage.[27] The parents, for their part, accept the loans. Bondage is a traditional worker-employer relationship, and the parents need the money, perhaps to pay for the costs of a medical treatment, perhaps to provide a dowry to a marrying child, or perhaps—as is often the case—to help put food on the table.[28] The children who are sold to these bond masters work long hours over many years in an attempt to pay off these debts. Due to the astronomically high rates of interest charged and the abysmally low wages paid, they are usually unsuccessful.[29] As they reach maturity, some of them may be released by the employer in favour of a newly-indebted and younger sibling, back to their parent, or even to their own children.[30]

Laws to Prohibit and Regulate Child Labour in India

The Constitution[31] of India has laid down that no child under the age of fourteen years shall be employed in any mine or engaged in any other hazardous employment [Article 24] and any contravention of this provision shall be an offence punishable in accordance with law. The directive principles of state policy in Article 39(e) provide that the health and strength of workers, men and women, and the tender age of children are not abused and that citizens are not forced by economic necessity to enter avocations unsuited to their age or strength. Article 39(f) directs that the children are given opportunities and facilities to develop in a healthy manner and in conditions of freedom and dignity and that childhood and youth are protected against exploitation and moral and material abandonment. It has been made a duty

---

[27] Human Rights Watch Children's Rights Project, *The Small Hands of Slavery, Bonded Child Labour in India*, Human Rights Watch, USA, 1996.
[28] Ibid.
[29] Ibid.
[30] Ibid.
[31] See the Constitution of India, Parts III and IV. The fundamental rights are embodied in Part III of the Constitution and the directive principles are in Part IV of the Constitution.

of the state to raise the level of nutrition and the standard of living and to improve public health.

Legislation to control and regulate child labour in India has existed for several decades. A resume of the history of legislation relating to child labour and some salient features are presented below:[32]

The Factories Act 1881

- Minimum age (seven years);
- Successive employment (employment in two factories on the same day) prohibited;
- Duration of employment (working hours not to exceed nine hours a day and at least four holidays to be given in a month);
- Factories employing one hundred or more persons were covered by this Act.

The Factories Act 1881 was revised in 1891 with respect to the following matters:

- Minimum age (increased to nine years);
- Hours of work (maximum seven hours per day, with prohibition of work at night between 8 p.m. and 5 a.m.).

The Mines Act 1901

This Act prohibited employment of children under twelve years of age.

The Factories Act 1911

This Act provides:

- Work between 7 p.m. and 5.30 a.m. prohibited;
- Work in certain dangerous processes prohibited;
- Certificate of age and fitness required.

The Factory (Amendment) Act 1922

To implement the ILO Convention (No. 5) 1919, the amendment provided for changes such as:

- Minimum age (fifteen years in general);
- Working hours (maximum six hours, and also an interval of half an hour if children are employed for more than five-and-a-half hours);

---

[32] A.P. Varma, 'Child Labour in India: An Overview', Awards Digest: Journal of Labour Legislation Vol. XX, Nos. 7–12, July–Dec., 1994, National Labour Institute, Deep Printers, New Delhi.

- Establishments employing twenty or more persons with mechanical processes were covered under this Act with power vested in the local government to exclude the applications of provisions to premises employing ten or more persons;
- Prohibition of employment of children below eighteen and women in certain processes;
- Provision for medical certificate and also certificate of re-examination for continuing work.

The Indian Mines Act 1923

This Act raised the minimum age for employment from twelve to thirteen years.

The Factories (Amendment) Act 1926

This Act imposed certain penalties on the parents and guardians for allowing their children to work in two separate factories on the same day.

The Indian Ports (Amendment) Act 1931

This Act laid down twelve years as the minimum age that could be prescribed for handling goods in ports. The report of the Royal Commission on Labour (1931) had an impact on legislation pertaining to child labour during the period between 1931 and 1949.

The Tea Districts' (Emigration Labour) Act 1932

This was passed to check migration of labourers to districts in Assam. It provided that no under-age child is employed or allowed to migrate unless the child was accompanied by his or her parents or adults on whom the child was dependent.

Children (Pledging of Labour) Act 1933

This Act prohibited pledging of children, i.e. taking of advances by parents and guardians in return for bonds, pledging the labour of their children—a system akin to the bonded labour system. The Royal Commission noticed this practice of pledging of labour of children in areas such as Amritsar, Ahmedabad, Madras, etc., and in carpet and beedi factories. The children in these situations were found to be working under extremely unsatisfactory conditions.

The Factories (Amendment) Act 1934

This Act had elaborate provisions for regulating the employment of children of various age groups in the factories, such as:

- Employment of children between twelve and fifteen years were generally prohibited in certain areas;
- Employment of children under twelve and fifteen years restricted to five hours a day in other areas;
- For employment of children between fifteen and seventeen years, certain restrictions were imposed.

The Mines (Amendment) Act 1935

This also introduced divisions of children according to age groups and the position which emerged was as follows:

- Employment of children less than fifteen years in mines was prohibited.
- Underground employment was permitted only on production of certificate of physical fitness granted by a qualified medical practitioner for persons between fifteen and seventeen years.
- Working time restricted to a maximum of ten hours a day and fifty-four hours a week for work above the ground and nine hours a day for work underground.

The Employment of Children Act 1938

This Act was passed to implement the Convention adopted by the twenty-third session of ILO (1937) which inserted a special article on India:

- Children under the age of thirteen years shall not be employed or work in the transport of passengers, or goods, or mails, by rail, or in handling of goods at docks, quays, or wharves, but excluding transport by hand. Children under the age of fifteen years shall not be employed or work . . . in occupations to which this Article applies which are scheduled as dangerous or unhealthy by the competent authority.

This Act:

- Prohibited employment of children under fifteen years in occupations connected with transportation of goods, passengers, and mails, or in the railways;

- Raised the minimum age of handling goods on docks from twelve to fourteen years;
- Provided for the requirement of a certificate of age.

The Factories Act 1948

This Act raised minimum age for employment in factories to fourteen years.

Employment of Children (Amendment) Act 1949

This Act raised the minimum age to fourteen years for employment in establishments governed by the Act.

Employment of Children (Amendment) Act 1951

As a result of the ILO Convention relating to night work of young persons this Act prohibited the employment of children between fifteen and seventeen years at night in the railways and ports and also provided for requirement of maintaining a register for children under seventeen years.

The Plantations Labour Act 1951

This Act prohibited the employment of children under twelve years in plantations.

The Mines Act 1952

This Act prohibited the employment of children less than fifteen years in mines. The Act stipulates two conditions for underground work:

- Requirement to have completed sixteen years of age; and
- Requirement to obtain a certificate of physical fitness from a surgeon.

The Factories (Amendment) Act 1954

This included prohibition of employment of persons under seventeen years at night. ('Night' was defined as a period of twelve consecutive hours which included hours between 10 p.m. and 7 a.m.).

The Merchant Shipping Act 1958

This prohibits children under fifteen to be engaged to work in any capacity in any ship, except in certain specified cases.

The Motor Transport Workers Act 1961

This Act prohibits the employment of children less than fifteen years in any motor transport undertaking.

The Apprentices Act 1961
This prohibits the apprenticeship/training of a person less than fourteen years.

The Beedi and Cigar Workers (Conditions of Employment) Act 1966
This Act prohibits:
- The employment of children under fourteen years in any industrial premises manufacturing beedis or cigars;
- Persons between fourteen and eighteen years from working at night between 7 p.m. and 6 a.m.

Employment of Children (Amendment) Act 1978
This Act prohibited employment of a child below fifteen years in occupations in railway premises such as cinder picking or clearing of ash pit or building operations, in catering establishments and in any other work which is carried on in close proximity to or between the railway lines.

The Child Labour (Prohibition and Regulation) Act 1986
The Child Labour (Prohibition and Regulation) Act 1986 (CLARA) is an outcome of various recommendations made by a series of committees.[33] From a reading of the recommendations made by various committees, there was a national consensus in favour of a uniform comprehensive legislation, to prohibit the engagement of children in certain other employment. To achieve this goal, Parliament enacted the Child Labour (Prohibition and Regulation) Act 1986 which came into force on 23 December 1986.

Legislative history in India has traversed a long way since 1881 by progressively extending legal protection to the working children. Provisions relating to child labour under various enactments have concentrated mainly on aspects such as minimizing working hours, increasing minimum age, and prohibition of employment of children in occupations and processes detrimental to the health and welfare of children of tender age.[34] The Employment of Children Act 1938, which was the first enactment on child labour, was repealed by the Child Labour (Prohibition and Regulation) Act 1986.

---

[33] The National Commission on Labour 1969, the Committee on Child Labour 1979, the Gurupadswamy Committee on Child Labour 1976, and the Sanat Mehta Committee 1984.

[34] *Awards Digest: Journal of Labour Legislation* (Vol. XX, Nos. 7–12).

Objectives of CLPRA

The objectives of the Child Labour (Prohibition and Regulation) Act 1986 are:

- Banning the employment of children, i.e. those who have not completed their fourteenth year, in specified occupations and processes;
- Laying down procedures to decide modifications to the schedule of banned occupations or processes;
- Regulating the conditions of work of children in employment where they are not prohibited from working.

Significant Provisions of the CLPRA

The preamble to the Act states that it is an Act to prohibit the employment of children in certain employment and to regulate the conditions of work of children in certain other employment. The Act prohibits the employment of any person who has not completed his fourteenth year of age[35] in occupations and processes set forth in Part A[36] and Part B[37] of the Schedule of the Act.

The Act thus classifies all establishments in two categories:

- Those in which employment of child labour is prohibited, and
- Those in which the working conditions of child labour shall be regulated.

The Central Government has the power to amend the schedule [CLPRA 1986, Section 4]. The Central government may by notification in the official

---

[35] CLPRA 1986, Section 3: 'No child shall be employed or permitted to work in any of the occupations set forth in Part A of the Schedule or in any workshop wherein, any of the processes set forth in Part B of the Schedule is carried on.'

[36] Part A lists out the occupations connected with: (1) transport of passengers, goods or mails by railway; (2) cinder picking, clearing or an ash pit or building operation in the railway premises; (3) work in a catering establishment at a railway station, involving the movement of a vendor or any other employee of the establishment from one platform to another or into or out of a moving train; (4) work relating to the construction of a railway station or with any other work where such work is done in close proximity to or between the railway lines; (5) a port authority within the limits of any port; (6) work relating to selling of crackers and fireworks in shops with temporary licences; (7) abattoirs/slaughter houses; (8) automobile workshops and garages; (9) foundries; (10) handling of toxic or inflammable substances or explosives; (11) handloom and power loom industry; (12) mines (underground and underwater) and collieries; and (13) plastic units and fibre glass workshops.

[37] Part B lists out the following processes:
Beedi making; carpet weaving; cement manufacture, including bagging of cement;

gazette constitute an advisory committee called the Child Labour Technical Advisory Committee for the purpose of addition of occupations and processes to the Schedule [CLPRA 1986, Section 5]. Several occupations and processes have been added. More have to be added. For instance, domestic child labour, and work in artistic performances like clubs, circuses, etc., present a risk of serious damage to the health or morals of young persons.

The prohibition of employment of children is not applicable to any workshop wherein any process is carried on by the occupier with the aid of his

---

cloth printing, dyeing, and weaving; manufacture of matches, explosives, and fireworks; mica cutting and splitting; shellac manufacture; soap manufacture; tanning; wool cleaning; building and construction industry; manufacture of slate pencils (including packing); manufacturing of products from agate; manufacturing process using toxic metals and substances such as lead, mercury, manganese, chromium, cadmium, benzene, pesticides, and asbestos; hazardous processes as defined in Section 2(cb) and 'dangerous operations' as notified in rules made under Section 87 of the Factories Act 1948 (Act 63 of 1948); printing as defined in Section 2(k) (iv) of the Factories Act 1948 (Act 63 of 1948); cashew and cashewnut desiccating and processing; soldering processes in electronic industries; *agarbatti* manufacturing; automobile repairs and maintenance including processes incidental thereto, namely, welding, lathe work, dent beating and painting; brick kilns and roof tiles units; cotton ginning and processing and production of hosiery goods; detergent manufacturing; fabrication workshops (ferrous and non-ferrous); gem cutting and polishing; handling of chromate and manganese ores; jute textile manufacture and coir making; lime kilns and manufacture of lime; lock making; manufacturing processes having exposure to lead such as primary and secondary smelting, welding and cutting of lead-painted metal constructions, welding of galvanized or zinc silicate and polyvinyl chloride, mixing (by hand) of crystal glass mass, sanding or scraping of lead paint, burning of lead in enamelling workshops, lead mining, plumbing, cable making, wire patenting, lead casting, type founding in printing shops, store type setting, assembling of cars, shot making and lead glass blowing; manufacture of cement pipes, cement products, and other related work; manufacture of glass, glassware including bangles, fluorescent tubes, bulbs, and other similar glass products; manufacture of dyes and dye stuff; manufacturing or handling of pesticides and insecticides; manufacturing or processing and handling of corrosive and toxic substances; metal cleaning and photo engraving and soldering processes in electronic industry; production of burning coal and coal briquettes; manufacturing of sports goods involving exposure to synthetic materials, chemicals, and leather; moulding and processing of fibreglass and plastic; oil expelling and refinery; paper making; potteries and ceramic industry; polishing, moulding, cutting, welding, and manufacture of brass goods in all forms; processes in agriculture where tractors and threshing and harvesting machines are used, and chaff cutting; saw mill—all processes; sericulture processing; skinning, dyeing, and processing for the manufacture of leather and leather products; stone breaking and stone crushing; tobacco processing including manufacture of tobacco and tobacco paste and handling of tobacco in any form; tyre making, repairing, retreading, and graphite benefaction; utensils making, polishing, and metal buffing; *zari* making (all processes).

family, or to any school established by or receiving assistance or recognition from government [CLPRA 1986, Proviso to Section 3].

Part III of the Act provides for regulation of conditions of work of children in establishments in which none of the occupations or processes referred to in the Schedule are carried out. It provides for the hours and period of work and weekly holidays for the children. The period of work of the child on each day shall be so fixed that no period shall exceed three hours and that no child shall work for more than three hours before he has had an interval for rest for at least one hour.[38] The total period of work inclusive of the interval for rest should be not more than six hours. The child is not permitted to work between 7 p.m. and 8 a.m. or overtime. The double employment of a child is banned.[39] The Act also empowers the appropriate government to make rules for the health and the safety of the children employed or permitted to work in any establishment or class of establishments[CLPRA 1986, Section 13].

PROCEDURE FOR PROSECUTION OF OFFENCES

The procedure laid down in the Act relating to the prosecution of offences is as follows:

- Any person, police officer, or inspector may file a complaint of the commission of an offence under this Act in any court of competent jurisdiction.
- Every certificate as to the age of a child which has been granted by a prescribed medical authority shall, for the purposes of this Act, be conclusive evidence as to the age of the child to whom it relates [CLPRA 1986, Section 10].
- No court inferior to that of a metropolitan magistrate or a magistrate of the first class shall try any offence under this Act.

PENALTIES UNDER THE ACT

The penalties under this Act are relatively more stringent than the earlier Acts and violating the provisions relating to child labour in certain other Acts results in a penalty under this Act [CLPRA 1986, Section 15].

The penalties[40] under this Act are as follows:

- Whoever employs any child or permits any child to work in any hazardous employment shall be punishable with imprisonment for a term

[38] CLPRA 1986, Section 7(1) (2) (3) (4) (5) (6).
[39] Ibid.
[40] CLPRA 1986, Section 14.

which shall not be less than three months but which may extend to one year, or with fine which shall not be less than ten thousand rupees but which may extend to twenty thousand rupees, or with both.[41] For a repeat offence, the punishment is imprisonment for a term which shall not be less than six months but which may extend to two years.[42]
- For failing to give notice to the inspector as required by Section 9, or failing to maintain a register as required by Section 11, or making any false entry in the register, or failing to display an abstract of Section 3,[43] or failing to comply with any other provisions of this Act or rules, the punishment is imprisonment which may extend to one month, or with fine which may extend to ten thousand rupees, or both.[44]

It is to be noted that the Act provides for both fines as well as imprisonment. But in practice, in those few instances where the employer is prosecuted, he is generally fined.

POSITIVE FEATURES OF THE ACT

- It increases and makes more stringent the penalties for employing child labour in violation of the law for factories, mines, merchant shipping, and motor transport [Section 15(1) and (2)].
- It defines 'family' and thereby makes it more explicit, thus precluding the possibility of its abuse.
- It empowers the Union government to bring into force provisions that regulate conditions of work of children in non-hazardous employment and also empowers state governments to make rules for further regulation. It provides the machinery, i.e. the Child Labour Technical Advisory Committee, for adding to the list of occupations and processes in which the employment of child labour is prohibited. (This was not possible in the Employment of Children Act 1938).
- It permits any person, besides a police officer or inspector, to file a complaint against anyone employing or permitting a child below fourteen in the prohibited occupations and processes.

[41] CLPRA 1986, Section 14(1).
[42] CLPRA 1986, Section 14(2).
[43] 'Every railway administration, every port authority, and every occupier shall cause to be displayed in a conspicuous and accessible place at every station, its railway or within the limits of a port or at the place of work, as the case may be, a notice in the local language and in the English language containing an abstract of Sections 3 and 14' Section 12, CLPRA 1986.
[44] CLPRA 1986, Section 14(3).

- It makes the display of Sections 3 and 14 of CLPRA a mandatory requirement for the railway administration, the port authority, and the occupier.

The National Policy on Child Labour

The National Policy on Child Labour[45] is a landmark endeavour in the progressive elimination of child labour in India. *A National Policy on Child Labour has been formulated in conjunction with the legal measures to address the socio-economic issues having a bearing on child labour and to provide a framework for a concrete programme of action.* The policy attempts to deal with the situation where the children work, or are compelled to work, on a regular or a continuous basis to earn wages for themselves and/or their families, and where their conditions of work result in their being severely disadvantaged and exploited, and where abuses connected with such factors impacting on wage-employed children need to be given close attention by the state for rectification, amelioration, and regulation through specific legal and administrative instruments and measures. The policy encompasses action in the fields of education, health, nutrition, integrated child development, and employment.[46] Figure 4.3 details the evolution of the policy on child labour in India.

Figure 4.3: The Evolution of Child Labour Policy in India

Sr. No.	Event	Date	Details
1	Ratification of ILO, Night Work of Young Persons (Industry), Convention 1919 (No. 6).	July 1921	Night work by young persons in any public or private industrial undertaking prohibited.
2	Ratification of ILO, Minimum Age of Trimmers and Stokers Convention, 1921 (No. 15).	November 1922	Employment of young persons as trimmers and stokers in vessels or ports prohibited.
3	Ratification of ILO, Medical Examination of Young Persons (Sea) Convention 1921 (No. 16).	November 1922	Compulsory medical examination of children and young persons employed at sea provided for.
4	Enactment of Children (Pledging of Labour) Act 1933.	February 1933	Pledging of labour of children prohibited and penalty for parents/guardians and pledging of

[45] National Policy on Child Labour 1987, Government of India.
[46] Ashok Narayan, *Child Labour Policies and Programmes: The Indian Experience*, Government of India, Ministry of Labour, New Delhi, 1988.

			child labour prescribed. Employment of children below fifteen years prohibited in certain occupations.
5	Enactment of Employment of Children Act 1938.	February 1938	Employment of children below fifteen years prohibited in certain occupations.
6	Adoption and Enactment of the Constitution of India Act by the Constituent Assembly.	1949	Prohibition of employment of children below fourteen years of age in factories, mines, and hazardous employment in terms of a fundamental right; and directive principles laid down against the abuse of the tender age of the children and for free and compulsory education for children up to fourteen years of age.
7	Ratification of ILO, Night Work of Young Persons (Industry) Convention (Revised) 1948 (No. 90).	July 1950	Night work by children and young persons abolished.
8	Ratification of ILO, Minimum Age (Industry) Convention 1919 (No. 5).	September 1955	Employment of children under fourteen years of age in public or private industrial undertaking prohibited.
9	Report of the National Labour Commission.	1969	Recommended combination of work with education and flexible employment hours, which would not inhibit education.
10	Ratification of ILO, Minimum Age (Underground Work) Convention 1965 (No. 123).	March 1975	Employment of persons below sixteen years of age for work underground in mines prohibited.
11	Report of Gurupadaswamy Committee.	1979	Recommended setting up of Child Labour Advisory Board; fixation of minimum age of entry to any establishment; strengthening of enforcement machinery; formulation of effective educational policy with emphasis on integration of educational requirements with local crafts.

12	Establishment of the Central Child Labour Advisory Board with labour minister as chairman.	March 1981	To review implementation of existing laws; to suggest legislative and welfare measures for working children; and to recommend industries where child labour should be eliminated.
13	Enactment of Child Labour (Prohibition and Regulation) Act 1986.	December 1986	Employment of children below fourteen years of age prohibited in specific occupations and processes; procedure for modification of schedule of banned occupations or processes laid down; regulation of working conditions for children in non-prohibited employment provided for; penalties for violation of the law provided for; and uniformity in definition of 'child' in related laws provided for.
14	Adoption of the National Child Labour Policy 1987.	August 1987	Provided for a legislative action plan; focusing of general development programmes for the benefit of working children as well; and formulation of project-based action plain in areas of high concentration of child labour.
15	Report of the Task Force on Child Labour set up by the Child Labour Adisory Board under the Chairmanship of Dr L.M. Singhvi.	December 1989	Recommended amendments to child labour laws and National Policy on Child Labour.
16	Report of the National Commission on Rural Labour.	July 1991	Recommended enactments of compulsory Primary Education Acts by states; creation of non-formal education centres; enhancement of outlays for elementary education guaranteed; wage employment

			for parents of working children; universal prohibition of child labour; media publicity against child labour.
17	Report of the study group on women and children of the II National Commission on Labour	2002	Recommended the enactment of Child Labour (Prohibition and Education Bill 2000

The National Policy on Child Labour is set under the following three heads:

- The Legislative Action Plan.
- Focussing of general programmes for benefiting child labour wherever possible.
- Project-based plan of action in areas of high concentration of child labour engaged in wage/quasi-wage employment.

Legislative Action Plan

Under the Legislative Action Plan, emphasis is laid on strict and effective enforcement of the provisions of the Child Labour (Prohibition and Regulation) Act 1986, the Factories Act 1948, the Mines Act 1952, the Plantation Labour Act 1951, and other Acts containing provisions relating to the employment of children.

Focussing of General Programmes for Benefiting Child Labour

Various national development programmes exist in the areas of education, health, nutrition, integrated child development, and income and employment generation for the poor. These programmes will be utilized to create socio-economic conditions in which the compulsions to send the children to work diminish and the children are encouraged to attend school rather than take up wage employment.

Project Based Plan of Action in Areas of High Concentration of Child Labour

This involves launching of projects for the welfare of working children in areas of high concentration of child labour. These projects withdraw children from hazardous employment and ensure their rehabilitation through education in special schools. According to government sources, ninety-one

172 Child Rights in India

child labour projects have been sanctioned till 2000 for rehabilitating nearly 0.19 million children in the most endemic areas and 145,725 children have already been enrolled in the special schools.[47]

Laws Relating to Bonded Child Labour

Article 23 of the Constitution of India prohibits the practice of debt bondage and other forms of slavery, both modern and ancient.[48] Along with the Child Labour (Prohibition and Regulation) Act 1986 and other labour laws, the following laws provide legal protection to bonded child labourers.

Bonded Labour System (Abolition) Act 1976

In this Act, bonded labour system is defined in Section 2(g) as the system of forced, or partly forced, labour which a creditor extracts from a debtor by virtue of an agreement between the two. The Bonded Labour System (Abolition) Act purports to abolish all debt agreements and obligations. It is the legislative fulfilment of the Indian Constitution's mandate against *begar* and forced labour.[49] It frees all bonded labourers, cancels any outstanding debts against them, prohibits the creation of new bondage agreements, and orders the economic rehabilitation of freed bonded labour. It also prescribes a penalty of up to three years in prison and rupees two thousand in fin for any violators.[50]

Children (Pledging of Labour) Act 1933

This Act predates independence but remains in force. It is rarely used and rarely mentioned in discussions of bonded labour and child labour, probably because the more recent laws carry penalties that, while lenient themselves, are none the less stiffer than those of the Children (Pledging of Labour) Act.

The Act calls for penalties to be levied against any parent, middleman, or employer involved in making or executing a pledge of child's labour. Such a pledge is defined as an 'agreement written or oral, express or implied, whereby the parent or guardian of a child, in return for any payment or

---

[47] India Report on the World Summit for Children, Department of Women and Child Development, Ministry of Human Resource Development, Government of India, 2000.

[48] *People's Union for Democratic Rights v Union of India* [Asiad Workers' Case], AIR 1982 SC 1473, paragraph 1486.

[49] Consequently, post-act social action litigation on behalf of bonded labours is brought under both the Bonded Labour System (Abolition) Act and the Constitution of India. For a discussion of cases, see Reddy, *Bonded Labour System in India*, chapter 4.

[50] The Bonded Labour System (Abolition) Act 1976, Secs. 4, 5, 6, and 14.

benefit received or to be received by him, undertakes to cause or allow the services of the child to be utilized in any employment.'[51] Lawful labour agreements are limited to those made in consideration of reasonable wages and terminable at seven days' or less notice. The fines for violating this law are fifty rupees against parent and two hundred rupees against either the middleman or employer.

Critique of the Laws and Law Reform

The CLPRA 1986 needs to be amended for better implementation and enforcement. The following are the areas of concern that need legal reform:

- CLPRA covers only 10 per cent of the total working children. Moreover, the agricultural sector, which constitutes more than 75 per cent of the child employment is not covered by the Act. The CLPRA is not easy to enforce in the unorganized sector because the units are numerous and unregistered. The employer-employee relationship is continuously changing, and frequently the unit is a tiny family-based one. Most of these units spring up and disappear overnight and are very difficult to keep track of in the absence of any requirement of registration.
- Section 3 of the CLPRA[52] keeps the occupation, work, or process that is carried on by the occupier with the aid of his family out of the purview of the Act. The intention of the Act is to exempt a family enterprise in which all or several of the members of the family are involved. It was not intended to exempt farmed out, piece-rate work, where the home merely replaces the factory premises. This proviso is abused by employing children in respect of families and work experience acquired by children. This provision helps employers to 'pose as family members' of the children working in their premises and thus continue to exploit the children. When any action is taken against any employer for employing a child, the excuses given are that 'the child is a relative and is helping in housework' or 'the child is being trained for a family trade' and so on. Therefore, there is a need to add to the provision that 'it shall be presumed that occupier is also the employer for the purpose of the Act and the onus to prove that the child is a member of his or her family would rest on the occupier'.

[51] The Children (Pledging of Labour) Act 1933, Sec. 2. 'Child' is a person less than fifteen years old.

[52] Sec. 3 proviso: Provided that nothing in this Section shall apply to any workshop wherein any process is carried on by the occupier with the aid of his family or to any school established by or receiving assistance or recognition from Government.

- In the Child Labour (Prohibition and Regulation) Act 1986, definition of 'workshop'[53] in Section 2(x) is to be amended to include all places of work/occupation in which children are employed. Section 3 of the Child Labour Prohibition and Regulation Act 1986 should be amended to include the factories as registered under the Factories Act 1948 and the Mines Act.
- The word 'occupier'[54] in Section 2(vi) is not clearly defined and, therefore, it may not have check on the employers' agents and the contractors who play a vital role in the employment of children.

The word 'hazardous' is not clearly defined and it is left to the Technical Advisory Committee [CLPRA, Section 4] to define hazardous occupations and processes. The word at present appears to take into consideration only the physical harm to the children. The emotional and psychological aspects have also to be taken into consideration. In fact there should be prohibition of all forms of child labour since all occupations are hazardous to children. as they affect the development of the child If *the child is denied primary, elementary education because of the need to work, it is a hazard.*[55] Besides, there are occupations that are not included in the hazardous list but these children are subject to the grossest forms of physical, emotional, and sexual abuse within the four walls of a home. Even though in agricultural processes, the child comes into direct contact with harmful pesticides and fertilizers, the agricultural sector is kept out of the purview of the Act. The definition of 'hazardous' process in the Factories Act could be considered.[56] There should be a provision for public mechanisms and participation in the functioning of the Technical Advisory Committee. Children in hazardous employment should be given top priority in all developmental efforts.

[53] CLPRA, Sec. 2(x), Workshop means any premises(including the precincts thereof) wherein any industrial process is carried on, but does not include any premises to which provisions of Section 67 of the Factories Act 1948 for the time being apply.

[54] CLPRA, Sec. 2(vi) defines 'occupier' in relation to an establishment or a workshop as the person who has the ultimate control over the affairs of the establishment or workshop.

[55] Ossie Fernandes, Towards Amendments/Restructuring of the Child Labour Prohibition and Regulation Act 1986, a draft note prepared on behalf of the Legal Working Group, Campaign Against Child Labour (CACL).

[56] Factories Act Section 2(cb) defines hazardous process as any process or activity in relation to an industry specified in the First Schedule where, unless special care is taken, raw materials used therein or the intermediate or finished products, by-products, wastes, or effluents thereof would cause material impairment to the health of the persons engaged in or connected therewith, or result in the pollution of the general environment. The First Schedule of the Factories Act contains a list of industries involving hazardous processes.

A bill known as the Child Labour in Hazardous Employment (Abolition, Rehabilitation and Welfare) 2000 has been prepared[57] for abolishing employment of children, bonded or otherwise, in hazardous employment, rehabilitation of those children who are employed, and for welfare measures for them. Under Section 2(d) 'hazardous employment' means engagement in a job, occupation, or enterprise, in a situation where the worker is exposed to hazards to life or serious accident, chronic diseases, depravity or degeneration in life, and risk of grievous hurt, and which would include engaging children in begging or collection of alms or in immoral and criminal acts including prostitution or those having direct impact on the moral character of the child, and other hazardous employment as prohibited under the Child Labour (Prohibition and Regulation) Act 1986. Under this draft bill any employer[58] who employs child labour in hazardous employment shall be punished with imprisonment which shall not be less than three years and with fine which shall not be less than twenty-five thousand rupees:
But if the child employed is:

- a girl child,
- a bonded child labourer, or
- engaged in.
  - begging,
  - prostitution,
  - jobs involving crime and moral turpitude, or
  - work having direct impact on the morality and character of the child,

the employer shall be punished with imprisonment which shall not be less than five years and with fine which shall not be less than fifty thousand rupees but may extend to one lakh rupees in case where the child is employed as sex worker, in smuggling, or as carrier in espionage and other heinous crimes. Every employer who employs a child in non-hazardous job shall arrange free education and vocational training for the children employed in his workshop, establishment, or household and shall also provide adequate facilities for games, sports, and recreation after working hours, or otherwise, in such manner, as may be prescribed.

Under this draft Bill, the appropriate government has been asked:

- To conduct a census of child labour within its territorial jurisdiction and to rehabilitate the child labour found, under Section 5. If a police

[57] Draft prepared by Kanti Singh, practising in the Supreme Court of India.
[58] Under Section 2(c) 'employer' means a person who engages a child in any job or occupation and if the employer is a company or a corporate body, the chairman, managing director, or an executive head of such body or company.

officer responsible for registering cases under his territorial jurisdiction refuses to register a first information report for an offence under this act, or otherwise aids or abets the commission of such offence, he shall be punished with imprisonment for a term which shall not be less than two years and with fine which shall not be less than twenty thousand rupees.
- To declare a comprehensive list of hazardous employment and jobs being carried out within its territorial jurisdiction.

The provisions of this Bill appear to have been based on the landmark Supreme Court judgment.[59]

The existing law also needs review and improvement on the following points:

- The present definition of establishment has considerable scope for extension and enlargement.[60]
- CLPRA does not specify the minimum age of employment of children in the occupations and processes other than the prohibited ones. Most laws and legal provisions relating to child labour specify the minimum age entry for employment to be fourteen years. Nevertheless, the United Nations Convention on the Rights of the Child gives in Article 1 the standard concerning the definition of a child that a child means every human being below the age of eighteen, unless, under the law applicable to the child, majority is attained earlier. This standard age of the child should be adhered to in all legislations including the CLPRA.
- Determining the age of the child is a big problem. In a country like India, many children do not have birth certificates. This procedure needs to be simplified. Besides, it is recommended that till such time as age is determined, the benefit of doubt should be in favour of the child.
- There is no provision for the education of working children. In many countries, compulsory education laws usually precede child labour laws and their enforcement substantially reduces or eliminates child labour.[61] There should be mandatory provisions in the Act for education, vocational training, and other welfare measures.

[59] M.C. Mehta v State of Tamil Nadu and others, AIR 1997 SC 699.

[60] CLPRA, Sec. 2(iv) defines establishment as a shop, commercial establishment, workshop, farm, residential hotel, restaurant, eating house, theatre, or other place of public amusement or entertainment.

[61] Myron Weiner, *The Child And State in India*, Oxford University Press, Delhi, 1991.

- There is no specific provision in the 1986 Act for applying the provisions of other laws like the Industrial Disputes Act, the Shops and Commercial Establishments Act, the Minimum Wages Act, etc. A child who has a dispute relating to his wages, salaries, and other employment benefits in the permissible areas of work has to approach the adult dispute resolution mechanism. The child labourers in the prohibited areas of work cannot even approach the adult dispute settlement machinery as their employment is 'illegal' under the Act.[62] There should be a provision in the Act for a dispute resolution mechanism for the protection of wages or other employment benefits. Special courts could be set up for a speedier and more effective trial of violations under this Act.
- Elimination of child labour should be statutory on the part of all local self-government bodies, both rural and urban. There should be a provision for elimination of child labour, whether directly or indirectly, immediately in all government organizations.
- Establishment of an in-depth monitoring agency at the state and national levels to oversee enforcement of the Bonded Labour System (Abolition) Act 1976. For full implementation of the Act, this body should be statutorily empowered to receive and address complaints of Act violations and complaints of official misconduct. In the Bonded Labour System (Abolition) Act 1976, there should be more provisions for rehabilitation of children and needs of children are to be specifically addressed.
- The rules relating to the CLPRA in various states need to be immediately amended for better implementation of the CLPRA Act.
- District magistrates—called district collectors or deputy commissioners in some states—are responsible for the enforcement of the Bonded Labour System (Abolition) Act 1976. The district magistrate is to constitute and participate in the functioning of a district-level 'vigilance committee'. Very few such vigilance committees have been formed or are operative.
- References to rehabilitation of freed bonded labourers occur twice in the Bonded Labour System (Abolition) Act 1976—once in reference to the district magistrate's duty to 'secure and protect the economic interests' of the bonded labourer [Section 11] and once in stipulating

---

[62] Ossie Fernandes, A Critique: Towards Amendments/Restructuring of the Child Labour (Prohibition and Regulation) Act 1986, A Note prepared on behalf of the Legal Working Group, CACL.

the vigilance committees' duty to provide for the 'economic and social rehabilitation' of the bonded labourers [Section 14]. The Act itself does not specify what this rehabilitation should consist of and has left the implementation to the state governments.

- The extent to which the bonded labourers have been identified, released, and rehabilitated by the government officials is negligible.[63]
- The Children (Pledging of Labour) Act 1933 is outdated and needs to be amended. The penalty provided under the Act for a serious action like making an agreement to pledge the labour of a child is as meager as Rs 200 [Section 6].

Enforcement of the Child Labour and Bonded Child Labour Legislation

In spite of the laws, child labour continues to exist in prohibited industries and areas of employment and is subject to very little regulation and control in non-prohibited industries and areas of employment Table 4.3 shows the position regarding the number of prosecutions and convictions under the Child Labour (Prohibition and Regulation) Act 1986 from 1992 to 1999.[64]

The table clearly shows that out the number of convictions is very low. Even if the employer is convicted, he is normally let off with a fine. It has never been heard that any employer has undergone imprisonment for

Table 4.3: Prosecutions and Convictions under CLPRA during 1992–9

Year	No. of Inspections	No. of Violations	No. of Prosecutions	No. of Convictions
1992–93	28,183	1,890	1,890	163
1993–94	16,904	1,308	1,826	265
1994–95	63,728	4,961	2,496	1,532
1995–96	23,349	543	3,146	18
1996–97	35,886	458	1,868	18
1997–98	8,42,497	1,749	2,329	743
1998–99(Part)	30,455	1,235	789	761

Position regarding the enforcement of the Child Labour Act 1986

Source: Awards Digest, Journal of Labour Legislation.

[63] Human Rights Watch, Children's Rights Projects, *The Small Hands of Slavery, Bonded Child Labour in India*, Human Rights Watch, USA, 1996.

[64] Meena Gupta, 'Special Problems of Enforcement of Child Labour Laws and Regulations', *Awards Digest, Journal of Labour Legislation*, Vol. XX, Nos. 7–12.

violating the CLPRA 1986. Studies in child labour reveal that enforcement of child labour legislation faces a number of problems. Broadly, the difficulties fall into the following categories:[65]

- *Enforcement of social legislations*: Social legislations are often difficult to enforce, as the law enforcers do not understand the spirit of the law. Neither the employers of child labour, nor the parents, nor the law enforcers perceive child labour as an undesirable thing.
- *Informalization of child labour*: Due to 'informalization of child labour', viz., work involving child labour moving out of the factories and large establishments into small cottage and home-based units, from out of the organized sector to the unorganized sector, it has become difficult to enforce the Act. This requires a large increase in the labour enforcement machinery. Other labour laws are applicable only to the organized sector. Besides, no records are maintained of the child workers.
- *No successful conviction*: Where an inspector manages to find children working in an establishment, in violation of the law, the prosecution does not lead to successful conviction. The reasons for acquittal in many cases are:[66]
  – Delay in filing the case: Courts rely on evidence and the inspectors fail to produce evidence in courts. Many employers, especially from small units, are often let off because they claim that the children were their family members. The proviso to Section 3 of the CLPRA helps them in this claim.[67] In larger units, the employers generally claim that the children had come to meet their parents or to provide lunch to their parents and were not working there.[68] There is, therefore, no evidence that the child was working in the premises and the courts let off the employers. The offence should be made cognizable. The burden of proof should be shifted on the employer.
  – Another reason for failure of prosecution is due to lack of evidence relating to the age of the child. The child's age has to be proved in the

[65] Meena Gupta, 'Special Problems of Enforcement of Child Labour Laws and Regulations', Awards Digest: *Journal of Labour Legislation*, Vol. XX: Nos. 7–12.
[66] E. Illamathian, '*Micro-Lab on Case Studies*,' paper presented at the workshop on 'Enforcement of child Labour Laws in match and Fireworks in Tamilnadu' organized by Tamilnadu Institute of Labour Studies, 8–9 December 1992.
[67] 'Provided that nothing in this section shall apply to any workshop wherein any process is carried on by the occupier with the aid of his family.'
[68] Meena Gupta, 'Special Problems of Enforcement of Child Labour Laws and Regulations', *Awards Digest: Journal of Labour Legislation*, Vol. XX: Nos. 7–12.

courts. Usually, in rural areas the children do not have a birth certificate. There is therefore no reliable evidence to prove the age of the child. In such cases, the inspector is supposed to get the child medically examined at the expense of the employer. This leads to further delay. There should be severe punishment for giving wrong certificates. In case of certain groups the statement of the mother regarding the age of child should be valid.
 - Courts tend to pass lighter sentences in child labour matters. This is also due to the insensitivity of the judiciary.
 - The implementation of child labour legislation is entrusted to inspectors of factories. The inspectors are overburdened and the enforcement of the CLPRA is not their 'priority'. It is commonly believed that there is rampant corruption in the enforcement machinery. Besides, the inspectors are not sensitized towards the problem of child labour. They have no responsibility for implementing the Act. Even in a progressive State like Maharashtra, no inspector appointed under the CLPRA has been punished or even asked to explain why he did not implement the Act. Community participation and accountability have to be introduced.

Official statistics relating to the enforcement of the Bonded Labour System (Abolition) Act are difficult to obtain. Up to 1988, there were 7000 prosecutions under the Act throughout India, of which only 700 resulted in convictions.[69] The main obstacles to enforcement are:

- Apathy among government officials. Vigilance committees, which form the core of the enforcement of the Act, have to be functional. Collectors are too overburdened to implement the Act.
- There is corruption and lack of accountability and a caste and class bias in the enforcement.
- There are no linkages between the various applicable Acts.

Judicial Response to Child Labour—
Important Case Laws

The judiciary in the country has shown its great concern for the working children by bringing occupations or processes under the judicial scrutiny by directly applying the constitutional provisions relating to children.

In *People's Union for Democratic Rights v Union of India*[70] the court held: But apart from the requirement of ILO Convention No. 59, we have Article

---

[69] Y.R. Hargopal Reddy, *Bonded Labour System in India*, p. 171.
[70] AIR 1982 SC 1480.

24 of the Constitution which even if not followed up by appropriate legislation must operate *proprio vigore* and construction work being plainly and undoubtedly a hazardous employment, it is clear that by reason of constitutional prohibition no child below fourteen years can be allowed to be engaged in construction work. There can, therefore, be no doubt that notwithstanding the absence of specification of construction industry in the Schedule to the Employment of Children Act 1938, no child below fourteen years can be employed in construction work and the Union of India as also every state government must ensure that this constitutional mandate is not violated in any part of the country.

The Supreme Court has suggested that it is the duty of the government to ensure education of children of parents who are working in construction sites.

Labourers Working on Salal Hydro Project v State of Jammu and Kashmir and Others[71]

The Supreme Court directed that whenever the Central Government undertakes a construction project which is likely to last for a considerable period of time, it should ensure that children of construction workers who are living at or near the project site are given facilities for schooling. The Court also specified that this may be done either by the Central Government itself or if the Central Government entrusts the project work or any part thereof to a contractor, necessary provision to this effect may be made in the contract with the contractor.

Rajangam, Secretary, District Beedi Workers Union v State of Tamil Nadu and others[72]

The Supreme Court opined that tobacco manufacturing was indeed hazardous to health. Child labour in this trade should therefore be prohibited as far as possible and employment of child labour should be stopped either immediately or in a phased manner that is to be decided by the State Government but it should be within a period not exceeding three years.

M.C. Mehta v State of Tamil Nadu and Others[73]

In this case the Supreme Court allowed children to work in a prohibited occupation like fireworks. According to Justice Ranganath Mishra and Justice M.H. Kania, the provision of Article 45 in the Directive Principles of State Policy still remained a far cry and though according to this provision

---

[71] 1983 Lah I.C. 542.
[72] (1992) 1 SCC 221.
[73] 1991 SC 283.

all children upto the age of fourteen years are supposed to be in school, economic necessity forces grown-up children to seek employment. Children can, therefore, be employed in the process of packing of fireworks but packing should be done in an area away from the place of manufacture to avoid exposure to accident.

M.C. Mehta v State of Tamil Nadu and Others[74]

When news about an accident in one of the Sivakasi cracker factories was published in the media wherein several children were reported dead, the court took *suo motu* cognizance of it. The court gave certain directions regarding the payment of compensation. An Advocates' Committee was also constituted to visit the area and report on the various aspects of the matter.[75]

A three-judge Bench of the Supreme Court comprising Justice Kuldip Singh, Justice B.L. Hansaria, and Justice S.B. Majumdar delivered a landmark judgment on 10 December 1996. This judgment is of considerable important and is a progressive advancement in public interest litigation and child jurisprudence. The decision has attempted to tackle the problem of child labour.

M.C. Mehta, a lawyer, filed a writ under Article 32 of the Constitution of India, as the fundamental right of children against exploitation (Article 24) was being grossly violated in the match and fireworks industries in Sivakasi where children were employed. The Court then noted that the manufacturing process of matches and fireworks is hazardous, giving rise to accidents including fatal cases. Therefore, keeping in view the provisions contained in Articles 39(f) and 45 of the Constitution, it gave directions as to how the quality of life of children employed in the factories could be improved.

Social action through law and the struggle for children's rights got a new impetus with the passing of the above directions. This ruling has certainly succeeded in generating a lot of enthusiasm relating to the elimination of child labour amongst the agencies concerned and State Governments. Since labour is on the concurrent list of the Constitution, there has to be coordination between both the Central and the State Governments. Besides the labour ministry, the education ministry also needs to be involved as more schools, teachers, and staff will be required. Teachers and staff will have to be oriented and mobilized to integrate child labourers entering their schools. It requires an inter-sectoral action. Massive additional funds will be required

---

[74] AIR 1997 SC 699.

[75] The Committee consisting of Shri R.K. Jain, a senior advocate, Indira Jaisingh, another senior advocate, and Shri K.C. Dua, advocate, submitted its report on 11 November 1991.

to comply with the judgment. Rules will have to be immediately framed by the State Governments for implementing the directions of the Court.

Child labour has been made expensive and thereby deterrent to both the employer and the government. An important dimension is the award of compensation granted to the affected parties, i.e. the children. This implies that it is the obligation or a social duty of the state to protect the fundamental rights of children.

A tremendous responsibility has been placed on the inspectors appointed under the Child (Labour Prohibition and Regulation) Act, 1986. But many of these inspectors are themselves responsible for the tardy implementation of the Act. there is a need for orientation and training of these inspectors and the other staff concerned. A question that arises is how these inspectors will ensure that, in non-hazardous industries, the child receives education for at least two hours each day at the cost of the employer.

Certain aspects that need to be considered are:

- Greater involvement of voluntary agencies concerned with child welfare.
- Access to adequate schooling facilities as, in our country, in many areas, schools are simply not available.
- Accountability of enforcement officers involved.
- Review and amendment of the Child Labour Act, the Primary Education Act, the Juvenile Justice Act, and the rules made under them.
- The invisibility of the girl child, especially those who work as helpers of adult workers.

The judgment certainly holds out hopes for the future. These hopes should turn out to be true in the cause of justice to the child and they should not become another 'lucrative' option for the enforcement officials and parents. Perhaps, an independent enforcing body can monitor the enforcement of this judgment.

Some Significant Court Rulings Related to Bonded Child Labour

Bandhua Mukti Morcha[76] *v Union of India and Others*[77]

The court emphasized that when the allegations revealed that the workers were being held in bondage without basic amenities like shelter, drinking,

---

[76] *Bandhua Mukti Morcha* is an organization working for the release of bonded labourers.

[77] AIR 1984 SC 802; (1984) 3 SCC 161.

water, or two square meals a day, it was a violation of the fundamental rights as in this country everyone has a right to live with dignity and free from exploitation. The court also ruled that its power under Article 32 is very wide and it can adopt any 'appropriate' proceedings.

People's Union for Democratic Rights v Union of India[78]

The Supreme Court in this case provided a rule to determine what situations constitute forced labour. The court held: 'Where a person provides labour or service to another for remuneration which is less than the minimum wage, the labour or service provided by him clearly falls within the scope and ambit of forced labour.'

Neeraja Chaudhary v State of Madhya Pradesh[79]

This case was on behalf of a group of bonded quarry workers in the early 1980s. A letter was sent to the Supreme Court referring to an article written by the petitioner. The reporter had visited three of the villages in Madhya Pradesh where released bonded labourers were returned after the Court had ordered their release in a case filed by *Bandhua Mukti Morcha*.[80] All the seventy-five released bonded labourers from these villages were from tribal communities and they had not been rehabilitated six months after their release. The Supreme Court stated that it was imperative that the freed bonded labourers are properly rehabilitated after their identification and release. The Supreme Court also ruled that 'it is the plainest requirement of Articles 21 and 23 of the Constitution that bonded labourers must be identified and released and on release they must be suitably rehabilitated. Any failure of action on the part of the State Government(s) in implementing the provisions of the Bonded Labour System (Abolition) Act would be the clearest violation of Article 21 and Article 23 of the Constitution.'

Bandhua Mukti Morcha v Union of India[81]

In this judgment the court directed the Central Government to convene a meeting of the concerned ministers from different states to evolve policies for the progressive elimination of child labour. Some of the areas pointed out were compulsory education of children, vocational training, health check-ups, and nutritious food.

---

[78] (1982)3 SCC 235.
[79] 3 SCC 243, 1984.
[80] See *Bandhua Mukti Morcha v Union of India and others.*
[81] AIR 1997 SC 2218.

Non-Governmental Organizations' (NGOs) Interventions

Non-government organizations have played an active and vital role in making child labour visible, raising levels of public concern, and protecting the working children. They have monitored the conditions in which the children work and helped launch the long, indispensable process of changing public attitudes, providing alternatives, and access to justice. A number of NGOs have taken up the issue of child labour and bonded labour and carried out programmes to throw light on this issue. The interventions are in the areas of counselling, awareness raising, social mobilization, encouraging community participation, releasing children from work, providing vocational training, enrolling children in schools and ensuring their retention, monitoring the functioning of schools, bringing children into the formal mainstream schooling system, preparing educational kits, and facilitating interaction between the various stakeholders like government officials, teachers, employers, etc. Some such interventions are presented below:

- The South Asian Coalition on Child Servitude (SACCS)[82] works with government officials in raiding sites where children are known to be working in intolerable circumstances. SACCS takes credit for being either directly or indirectly involved in the release of some twenty-nine thousand children since its inception.
- Several rallies have been organized by children to raise the concerns. A rally of around two thousand children was taken out in a town of Palamau district, then in Bihar, on 30 April 1994. The rally demanded the strict implementation of laws prohibiting child labour and provision of alternatives to child labourers released from bondage. The rally also demanded facilities for appropriate education for child workers with relevant vocational training. These demands were specifically targeted to the authorities of the district collectorate of Palamau.[83]
- Two thousand child labourers in Kolkata undertook a three-kilometre walk through important areas of the city on the Child Labour Day,

---

[82] It has been observed that child servitude is not peculiar to India; it exists in the entire South Asian Region. This observation mobilized some NGOs in India, Pakistan, Nepal, Bangladesh, and Sri Lanka to link up and work against the exploitation of children. The South Asian Coalition on Child Servitude (SACCS) was formed in 1989 with more than sixty member NGOs from these countries.

[83] CACL Update, 1 May 1994.

highlighting the vulnerability of child labourers. This rally[84] was led by children who were tea stall workers, vendors, battery cleaners, rag pickers, motor garage mechanics etc. They, along with some important citizens appealed to all people to actively join them in the struggle against exploitation of child labourers and to restore their right to childhood. The issue of forming child labour unions as well as the inadequate implementation of the Juvenile Justice Act was also raised.[85]

- Five hundred child workers expressed their ideas and feelings in a colourful way in a public action programme, organized on 29 April 1994, the eve of the Child Labour Day. These works were then put up for exhibition on the same day. The objective was highlighting the rights of the child and the evils of child labour. To demonstrate their protest against child labour, the five hundred children formed a human chain on the streets of Chennai. Later the children also addressed a press gathering.[86]

- The *Bal Majdoor* Union[87] comprising fifty children, most of them below fifteen years, was formed on 24 August 1994 with the help of Butterflies.[88] On approaching the registrar they were informed that the Trade Union Act of 1926 did not allow children below fifteen to form a trade union. In February 1995, the 'Union' filed a writ petition in the Delhi High Court, challenging the decision of the registrar. The court refused to admit the petition as it found no merit in it. The 'Union' then went to the Supreme Court, which issued notices to the Centre, the registrar of trade unions, and the lieutenant governor of Delhi, but finally rejected the petition. The petition stated that there were eighteen million child labourers in India and highlighted that they were not organized, there were no proper rules, working hour limits and health facilities. It lamented the discrimination between adult and child labourers.[89]

- A *panchayat*[90] level convention of 200 child labourers from Botalma panchayat, Khurda district in Orissa was held on 24 August 1995.[91]

---

[84] Organized by NGO Forum for Street and Working Children.

[85] CACL Update, 1 May 1994.

[86] CACL Update, 3 May 1994. This programme was organized jointly by some NGO representatives, some social activists, trade unionists, and organizations like the UNICEF.

[87] Child Labour Union.

[88] A registered society working nationwide for the cause of street children and child labourers.

[89] *Child Labour in India—A Dossier*, Compiled by CACL.

[90] Village council.

[91] Arranged by CACL Orissa's member organizations of the area.

These child labourers (almost 50 per cent of the total work force) were working in the *beedi* manufacturing units of the village. The Convention was a culmination of a three-month project initiated to collect the basic information on the issues influencing the phenomenon of child labour in the village. The programme envisaged the enrolment of working children full-time into school and monitoring mechanisms that would ensure their continual attendance. The convention involved local leaders, the *Sarpanch*[92] of every *panchayat*, active members of youth organizations, ward members, women's groups, enthusiastic individuals, and others to eradicate child labour from the beedi units in the village.[93]

- All the political parties were called upon[94] to accord primary importance to children in 'all future policy decisions, budgetary allocation, and legislation'. The 'Children's Manifesto' was released on 3 February 1998 and it demanded that child labour be totally banned 'in all factories, establishments, and occupations, including household-based employment before the year 2000'. It stated that steps should also be taken to ensure employment with adequate living wages for their parents, which should be periodically revised. It further stated that children should not be taken to police stations on any ground and harassment of children should also be stopped. This was especially so for the children who lived on the streets. The manifesto wanted punishment for the policemen who commit crimes against children. To provide security and employment to street children, they should be provided shelter homes with health care, education, recreation, and skill-training facilities. The manifesto also highlighted the need to ensure that benefits of programmes aimed at children reach them in full measure, and for increased importance to the issues relating to children, and making special provisions for disabled children.[95]

- Street plays were organized[96] on 5 February 1998, targeted at the contestants of the forthcoming polls. Addressing the gathering, the performing slum children demanded basic amenities, abolition of child labour, and recognition of primary education as a fundamental right.[97]

---

[92] Village head.
[93] CACL Update, Sept.–Oct. 1995.
[94] CACL, Tamilnadu.
[95] CACL Update, 1 February 1998.
[96] The Shishu Milap, Vikas Jyot, Centre for Social Justice, Vikas Centre for Development, and the Baroda Citizens Council (BCC) were the organizers.
[97] CACL Update, 1–2 February 1998.

- Campaign against domestic girl child labour was organized in Mumbai[98] with the main objective of providing visibility to the girl child labourer and creating awareness about the seriousness of the issue so that it is included in the prohibited sector of the Child Labour Act. This campaign included a ten-day performance of street plays in Mumbai, a two-day convention where the children expressed their views on 'me and my work, my stand on child labour and my future'. It also included a public meeting where government officials and media heard the views of the domestic girl child labourer. Seventy-five domestic girl child labourers from all over Maharashtra participated in this programme. It is significant to note that since there was no access to full-time domestic girl child workers, only two full-time workers participated. The rest were part-time domestic girl child workers.

- Many NGOs, including the People's Union for Civil Liberties and the Campaign Against Child Labour, have initiated several cases against child labour and thus played a significant role in the struggle against child labour. In a much-awaited judgment of the Shiva Murugan murder case, the hotel owner who killed the child labourers was sentenced to death. In Gujarat, a PIL for and on behalf of young children engaged or employed by the Municipal Corporation in road construction in Ahmedabad was filed by CACL. The Gujarat High Court issued a notice consequently, in reply to which the Ahmedabad Municipal Corporation took an undertaking not to use children and abide by the law of the land.

- An organization[99] in Hyderbad aims at motivating parents and children to utilize the formal education school as a medium for advancement of the child. Based on the belief that 'every child out of school is a child labourer', the programme does not make any distinction between one form of child labour and another. Propelled by a set of non-negotiable principles[100] that guide the programme, its one-point agenda is to ensure that no child works and all children go to school. The strategy adopted is essentially based on age and gender. Older children (9–14 years) are put through a bridge course, which equips them to catch up with the regular school-going children. Younger children are directly

---

[98] During 23–30 April 2001, organized by Campaign Against Child Labour, Maharashtra, and CCVC Mumbai.

[99] MV Foundation, Hyderbad.

[100] The non-negotiables are:
- All children must attend full-time formal day schools.
- Any child not at school is a child labour.

admitted to schools. There is a detailed follow-up programme, which ensures a minimum dropout rate, and makes the education system more accessible to the working children. Very often, this involves addressing issues such as getting birth certificates, ensuring hostel admissions, and so on. Education activists under the programme are trained to identity and resolve every possible impediment in the way of converting a child labour to a full-time student. This includes handling such sensitive issues as age at marriage for girls. The programme has demonstrated that parents, irrespective of their economic status, have a great desire to educate their children and give them a better future. Once they are assured that their child will be looked after at school, they are willing to make enormous sacrifices in terms of time and money to ensure that the child stays in school.

There have been other spin-offs of this project. The village community feels greater pride in their children, and greater sense of responsibility towards their rights. Issues such as the age at marriage for girls have come under scrutiny, with several girls insisting on remaining in school. In agriculture, it has meant a change in cropping pattern for the employers, and to the adult labourer, a greater bargaining power. Above all, with the community owning up the programme, schools have become vibrant institutions where children's rights are protected.

This perspective and strategy on child labour and education have also been adopted by several voluntary organizations in India. Their initiatives to withdraw children from work have been relevant and effective in situations varying from urban areas to remote tribal pockets, cutting across regions and cultures.

- There was a national public hearing on child labour held in Delhi on 31 March 1997. The jury comprised eminent judges, advocates, journalists, and senior government officials. Several child labourers deposed before the jury. On the basis of the depositions by child labourers and other information, the jury made several recommendation for eliminating the practice of child labour. Some of the recommendations are:

    – The Child Labour (Prohibition and Regulation) Act 1986 should be amended to prohibit the employment of children up to the age of fourteen in all sectors, including employment in private dwelling

---

- All work/labour is hazardous, and harms the overall growth and development of the child.
- There must be total abolition of child labour.
- Any justification perpetuating the existence of child labour must be condemned.

houses or employment carried on with the aid of the family, and generally to fulfil India's commitment under international instruments.
- The recent Supreme Court judgment in *M.C. Mehta v the State of Tamil Nadu*[101] should be strictly enforced and citizens' groups be actively involved.
- The distinction between hazardous and non-hazardous occupations in the 1986 Act and in the Government of India policy should be done away with, as all employment of children is *per se* hazardous to the well-being of the child.
- An adequate and effective social security system should be put in place as a measured step towards preventing children from being driven into child labour.
- The Government of India and the State Governments should undertake a comprehensive survey of child labour in all sectors, organized an unorganized, and this should lead to the early formulation of a comprehensive policy to end child labour.
- There should be community involvement in the measures for the development of the child and the elimination of child labour at the level of the panchayats.[102]

Child Workers Opportunities Project[103]

The CWOP aims to work towards the elimination of damaging and exploitative forms of child work and for providing developmental opportunities for 9100 (5200 girls and 3900 boys) child workers in three states[104] of India. The CWOP has adopted a multi-pronged strategy with multiple interventions which complement and reinforce each other. The action areas are as follows:

- Opportunities for participation in non-formal and formal education;
- Opportunities for participation in vocational training;
- Provision of alternative support such as short-stay homes, health services, and recreational facilities;
- Provision of income generation opportunities for families of the child workers from needy households;

---

[101] AIR 1997 SC 699.
[102] Village councils.
[103] Executing Agency: Save the Children Canada.
[104] Maharashtra, Rajasthan, and Gujarat.

- Raising awareness and changing the attitudes of employers, parents, and children regarding the social acceptability of child work;
- Advocacy at both the local and national levels for the rights of the child as defined in the UN Convention; and
- Capacity building of the partner organizations to manage and implement child-focused development programmes.

Project for the Rehabilitation and Prevention of Working Children from Abattoirs in Parbhani (Maharashtra)

The main objective of the project was to eliminate child labour in slaughterhouses. However, in order to achieve this the short-term objectives were primarily to ensure that all children were in school and achieved basic levels of literacy and numeracy.

The specific objectives of the project were:

- To provide educational opportunities for children by bringing them into the mainstream formal schools system as well as offering alternative learning support systems.
- To liase with the primary school system and District Primary Education Programme (DPEP) to ensure joyful and child-centred learning in the classrooms.
- To mobilize women through self-groups to enable them to address issues concerning themselves and their families.
- To establish linkages with the government health system in order to provide continuous preventive and promotive health care for the community.
- To mobilize youth from the community as peer educators and social mobilizers to create awareness about child labour and to ensure that all children are in school.
- To forge enduring partnerships with representatives other NGOs and academic institutions.

The outcomes of this project were:

- Five hundred fifty-one children are now in school.
- Twenty Self Help Groups (SHGs) of 400 women have been formed.
- Sanitation and personal hygiene camps for children have led to visible improvement.
- Two hundred forty-seven children are attending Balwadis. Five teachers have been loaned by the DPEP to the programme.
- *Prerana*, an NGO, has organized classes for adolescent girls on life skills training.

- Regular health check-ups were conducted by the civil hospital.
- Inter-sectoral convergence with the municipal council, district administration as in the collectorate and the police, district rural administration and programmes as in the zilla parishad and through them the District Primary Education Programme (DPEP), civil hospital, Muslim religious leaders. The state government department that supports income generation activities through vocational training, the college of home science, and all training programmes conducted by other organizations like Academy for Mobilizing Rural Urban Action through Education (AAMRAE), demonstrates how minimum funds can extract support from the sectors concerned through effective mobilization.

Government Initiatives and Schemes

Besides the NGO initiatives mentioned earlier, certain initiatives have been taken and schemes formulated by the governments, both at the Centre and at the States. Some of these are:

- The National Child Labour Projects were started in 1988 to withdraw and rehabilitate children working in hazardous trades and industries in various states. The rehabilitation of child labourers included freeing them from their employers and providing them with relevant education. Also free uniforms and incentives to the families of the child labourers were provided to lure them to join schools.[105]
- The Karnataka Shops and Commercial Establishments (Amendment) Bill 1997, which was passed in September 1997, increased the age limit for being considered as child from twelve years to fourteen years and also increased the period of renewal of registration of shops/commercial establishments from one year to five years. It was punishable under the new legislation to employ children below the age of fourteen years. Those between the age group of 12–18 years were defined as 'young persons' as against the earlier 12–15 years age limit.[106]
- A three-day collaborative social audit of interventions against Child Labour since the last fifteen years[107] examined the set objectives, approaches, effectivity, learnings, and shortcomings of interventions

[105] CACL Update, 3 February 1998.
[106] CACL Update, 6 February 1998.
[107] This was organized by CACL and the central trade unions such as the Hind Mazdoor Sabha (HMS), Centre of Indian Trade Unions (CITU), and United Trade Union Council (UTUC), in New Delhi between 27 and 29 November 2001.

made by NGOs. International NGOs (INGOs), multilateral and bilateral agencies, trade unions, employers organizations and the government since the enactment of the CLPRA 1986. The following resolutions were passed:
- Work against economic policies that create economic conditions which perpetuate child labour.
- National efforts on commitment to eliminate child labour on a long-term basis be strengthened and consolidated.
- Government be urged to ratify the ILO Convention No. 138 on minimum age of employment.
- Employers be looked on as partners for the elimination of child labour and to engage in a dialogue with those employers, who are directly involved in child labour concentration areas like builders, owners' associations, merchants' associations and beedi workers associations.
- Political parties be sensitized about child labour.
- Government should review the ninety-third constitutional amendment and the issue should be taken to the village *panchayats*.
- A significant issue of concern is that the majority of the children in institutions in India are child labourers. Government schemes and programmes do not reach these children. Any scheme dealing with child labour should also include the institutionalized children.

International Legal Interventions, Strategies, and Movements

The International Labour Organization's policy has the abolition of child labour as the objective based on the recognition that total abolition will take a long time and that a start has necessarily to be made. To this end it has defined priority areas. It has launched a global project, the International Programme on the Elimination of Child Labour. The United Nations Children Fund (UNICEF) acknowledges the need to tackle the problem of child labour in order to implement the Convention on the Rights of the Child 1989. International standards, especially those laid down by the International Labour Organization and the United Nations have had its impact on our law-making process. One of the most important tools available to the ILO and the UNO for improving the legislation and international standards concerning child labour is the set of large numbers of international treaties, declarations, covenants, and conventions. Some of them relating to child labour are as follows:

1919: Minimum Age (Industry) Convention No. 5

Adopted at the first session of the ILO and ratified by seventy-two countries, the Convention established fourteen years as the minimum age for children to be employed in industry. It was the first international effort to regulate children's participation in the workplace and was followed by numerous ILO instruments applicable to other economic sectors.

1930: Forced Labour Convention No. 29

This Convention provides for the suppression of the use of forced or compulsory labour in all its forms. The term 'forced or compulsory labour' is considered to mean all work or service exacted from any people under the threat of penalty and for which they have not offered themselves voluntarily.

1966: International Covenant on Civil and Political Rights

Adopted by the UN General Assembly in 1966 and entered into force in 1976, it reaffirms the principles of the Universal Declaration of Human Rights (1948) with regard to civil and political rights and commits state parties to take action to realize these rights. Article 8 states that no one should be kept in slavery or servitude or be required to perform forced or compulsory labour.

1966: International Covenant on Economic, Social, and Cultural Rights

Adopted by the UN General Assembly in 1966 and entered into force in 1976, it reaffirms the principles of the Universal Declaration of Human Rights with regard to economic, social, and cultural rights. Article 10 enjoins state parties to protect young people from economic exploitation and from employment in work likely to hamper their morals, their health, or their lives, or likely to hamper their normal development. It also commits state parties to set age limits below which the paid employment of child labour should be prohibited and punishable by law.

1973: ILO Minimum Age Convention No. 138

This supersedes prior instruments applicable to limited economic sectors. The Convention obliges member states to pursue a national policy designed to ensure effective abolition of child labour. In this connection, it establishes that no child can be employed in any economic sector below the age designated for the completion of compulsory schooling—and not less than fifteen years. The minimum age for admission to any work likely to jeopardize health, safety, or morals is eighteen years.

1973: Minimum Age Recommendation No. 146

This calls on states to raise the minimum age of employment to sixteen years. While not legally binding, it nonetheless is a strong call to action on the part of member states. Convention No. 138 and this recommendation are regarded as the most comprehensive international instruments and statements on child labour.

1989: UN Convention on the Rights of the Child

This enshrines as interdependent and indivisible the full range of the civil, political, economic, social, and cultural rights of all children that are vital to their survival, development, protection, and participation in the lives of their societies. Because of this connection between children's rights and the survival and development, virtually all the Convention's articles address issues—such as education, health, nutrition, rest and relaxation, social security, the responsibilities of parents—that are related to child labour and its effects on children. One of the tenets of the Convention is that in all actions concerning children, their best interests should be taken fully into account. Article 32 recognizes children's right to be protected from work that threatens their health, education, or development and enjoins state parties to set minimum ages for employment and to regulate working conditions.

1999: Convention No. 182 Concerning the Prohibition and Immediate Action for the Elimination of the Worst Forms of Child Labour[108]

On 17 June 1999, this ILO Convention was adopted. The new Convention defines for the first time what constitutes the 'worst forms of child labour', and includes a ban on forced or compulsory recruitment of child soldiers. It calls for international cooperation on social and economic development, poverty eradication, and education to realize its terms, and provides for broad consultations among governments, workers, and employers—the 'social partners' in the ILO's tripartite structure. It defines the worst forms of child labour as:

- All forms of slavery or practices similar to slavery, such as the sale and trafficking of children, debt bondage, serfdom, and forced or compulsory labour;
- Forced or compulsory recruitment of children for use in armed conflict;

---

[108] Adopted by the General Conference of the International Labour Organization at its eighty-seventh Session, Geneva, 17 June 1999.

- Use of a child for prostitution, production of pornography or pornographic performances;
- Use, procuring or offering of a child for illicit activities, in particular for the production and trafficking of drugs; and
- Work which is likely to harm the health, safety, or morals of children.

The Convention requires ratifying States to 'design and implement programmes of action' to eliminate the worst forms of child labour as a priority and to 'establish or designate appropriate mechanisms' for monitoring implementation of the Convention, in consultation with employers' and workers' organizations. It also says that the ratifying States should 'provide support for the removal of children from the worst forms of child labour, and their rehabilitation; ensure access to free basic education or vocational training for all children removed from the worst forms of child labour; identify children at special risk; and take into account the special situation of girls'.

An accompanying recommendation defines 'hazardous work' as 'work which exposes children to physical, psychological or sexual abuse; work underground, under water, at dangerous heights or in confined spaces; work with dangerous machinery or tools, or which involves heavy loads; work in unhealthy environments which may expose children to hazardous substances, temperature, noise or vibrations; and work under particularly difficult conditions such as long hours, during the night or where a child is confined to the premises of the employers'.[109]

Strategies for Effective Implementation of International Conventions[110]

All Conventions so far have paid very little heed to the 'strategies' and this is the gap that needs to be urgently filled. Any new Convention, no matter how narrow or focused the area of intervention may be, will fail if sufficient attention is not paid to the operational aspects.

The urgent need is to focus energies and resources on preparing a well-defined plan of action, which clearly identifies each actor and his responsibilities. These actors are first and foremost accountable to working children and their immediate communities. Viable alternatives should be evolved on the basis of the following principles:

- All actions should be child-centred and in the best interest of working children. Interventions should have a positive short-term and long-term effect on the children themselves, first and foremost.

[109] International Labour Conference (1999), *World of Work*, 30, 5.

[110] The Concerned for Working Children, *Child Labour—The New ILO Convention, A Position Paper*, Bangalore, India.

- All interventions should improve the quality of life of the children, their families, and their communities.
- Organized representation of working children and their protagonism has to be recognized and respected. No decisions or actions, which have an impact on working children, should be taken without consulting them.[111]
- The immediate and long-term impacts of all actions on 'working children' have to be monitored and assessed. It should be mandatory that the monitoring mechanisms should include working children and NGOs.
- A comprehensive strategy has to be designed to address the basic causes that create and perpetuate child labour. An action plan—that identifies a set of specific interventions that will have an impact on the basic causes of child labour and create alternatives that improve the quality of life of child workers and their communities—will have to be formulated. This will have a spin-off effect on working children outside the target group as well.
- All strategies should place special emphasis, not only on the problems of girls but also of all marginalized groups including backward castes and tribes.
- Short-term strategies should always be steps toward long-term goals and not limit themselves to removing the scum from the top of a boiling pot. Long-term strategies should concern themselves with the root causes of child labour and its perpetuation. These strategies should recognize that policies such as globalization, structural adjustment, and General Agreement on Tariffs and Trade (GATT) have further marginalized large sections of our societies. A strategy to successfully address child labour has to include mechanisms to counter policies which are anti-poor and anti-children.
- The implementation of the Convention has to be monitored by children and local communities who are nearest to the reality at the grass roots and who are the first ones to experience the real impact of the convention on children. The authority to ensure implementation and monitoring of relevant instruments should be decentralized and vested with local authorities/governments. Local task forces should be formed to monitor the implementation of the intervention and these should mandatorily include working children and NGOs. Such a body should be primarily concerned with monitoring and evaluating the short-term and long-term impacts on the working children themselves.

---

[111] This point received special mention in the Amsterdam Child Labour Conference.

International Legislation

Child labour was sharply reduced in Western countries at the beginning of the twentieth century in part by combining legislation and its enforcement with compulsory primary education. Other important factors included a rise in family incomes and technological improvements that made children's labour less useful to employers. But legislation had an undeniable impact far beyond deterrence. It set new standards and changed attitudes across society. These in turn provided, and still provide, the best insurance against a return to high levels of child labour in industrialized countries.[112] Hong Kong, which is completely urban and has a thriving economy, has provided a notable success story having eliminated child labour through:

- Regular and persistent inspections by the labour department,
- Special annual campaigns to detect child employment,
- Requiring all young workers to carry identity cards with their photographs, thus facilitating enforcement, and
- Introducing welfare benefits, especially social assistance, to poor families, which assured a minimum income and removed the need to rely on child labour.[113]

Child labour legislation can also be a means of educating people and promoting debate on the issue. An example of legislation being used in this educative way comes from Brazil where children working on the street were considered a social welfare or public security problem and deemed 'delinquents'. Child-centred policies were developed and street children began to be seen as active and responsible agents of their own destinies.[114]

The new Article of the Constitution of Brazil[115] states that it is the duty of the family, of society, and of the State to assure children and adolescents, with absolute priority, the right to life, health, nutrition, education, recreation, vocational preparation, culture, dignity, respect, liberty, and family and community solidarity, over and beyond making them safe from neglect, discrimination, exploitation, cruelty, and oppression.[116] This was followed by the passing of the statute on children and adolescents in July 1990, which

---

[112] UNICEF, *The State of the World's Children*, 1997.
[113] Ibid.
[114] Jo Boyden and Willliam Myers, *Exploring Alternative Approaches to Combating Child Labour: Case Studies from Developing Countries*, Innocenti Occasional Papers, Child Rights Series No. 8, UNICEF International Child Development Centre, Florence, 1995, p. 20.
[115] Passed by the Brazilian Congress in October 1988.
[116] Ibid., p. 20–3.

set child labour in the context of child rights by clearly stating that the welfare of the child must take precedence over all competing interests, including those of the family. The principle established is 'children first'.

International Movements

One of the most striking developments in the last decade and a half is the emergence of a worldwide movement against child labour. In 1986, UNICEF gave impetus to the cause through its programme on children in especially difficult circumstances. The body of international law and ILO instruments was given added momentum. With the adoption in 1989, of the UN Convention on the Rights of the Child, child labour has now shot to the top of the global agenda and consumer concerns in both developing and industrialized countries. Corporations are reacting to consumer and other pressure in rich countries demanding corporate responsibility from manufacturers to respect human rights, including the ILO Convention and workers rights and child labour. World-renowned manufacturers such as Levi, Strauss, Reebok, Sears, and others in the supporting goods industry are now looking into conditions under which their products are being manufactured. In Europe, a number of established stores have decided not to sell products such as carpets unless they are certified as being made without child labour. Some have agreed to establish a code of conduct to help abolish child labour. The world's football governing body, the Federation of International Football Association (FIFA), has agreed upon the content of the code of labour practice in production of goods licensed by FIFA with the International Confederation of Free Trade Unions (ICFTU), the International Textile, Garment, and Leather Workers' Federation (ITGLWF), and the International Federation of Commercial, Clerical, Professional, and Technical Employees (FIET). The code contains a specific provision prohibiting the use of child labour in producing FIFA-licensed goods; only workers above the age of fifteen years are allowed, in accordance with ILO Convention No. 138.

These very powerful movements by consumers and manufacturers alike have been accompanied by perhaps even more powerful efforts on the legislative and trade fronts:

- The European Union (EU) has reached agreement on a new Generalized System of Preferences (GSP). The GSP, while providing reduced tariffs on the import of many products from developing countries, requires a ban on goods produced by prison and slave labour, respect for trade union rights, and the prohibition of child labour, as defined by ILO Conventions. Countries, which provide proof of compliance will receive privileged access to EU markets.

- The United States has also introduced provisions into its legislation linking the granting of trade privileges to foreign countries with their respect for minimum workers' rights. The GSP includes references to workers' rights in the exporting country. In the United States, Senator Tom Harkin has introduced a bill, not yet enacted, banning the import of products from industries using child labour.
- At the international level, there has been considerable discussion as to whether global competition rules should require the implementation of certain basic international standards, including the progressive elimination of child labour. In the ILO, the question of linkage of trade and labour standard has been the subject of sharply divergent views. But there has been wide agreement on the need for intensified action against child labour with an immediate attack on the worst abuses.
- This change in attitude has led to some remarkable changes in the behaviour of the major actors, particularly governments. In the past, the illegality of child labour and the political sensitivity of governments were such a barrier to national action that there was not one single technical cooperation project which the ILO could implement.
- Many governments have embarked on a review and updating of national legislation on child labour and have adopted practical policies and programmes on child labour (Brazil, India, Indonesia, Kenya, Nepal, Pakistan, the Philippines, the United Republic of Tanzania, Thailand, and Zimbabwe). The ILO's International Programme on the Elimination of Child Labour (IPEC) is now operational in more than twenty-five countries.[117]

Labour Clauses, The WTO, and Child Labour

The recent acceleration in the process of economic globalization has induced widespread concern that governments and labour organizations may no longer be able to preserve those 'core' labour standards, which the ILO deems fundamental to human dignity. In 1993, this concern led the International Confederation of Free Trade Unions (ICFTU) to call for the inclusion of a labour clause within the programme of the World Trade Organisation (WTO) that would aid the preservation of these basic rights. The leaders of the many institutions promoting a labour clause argue that if international trade and the defence of labour standards are not linked with an immediate attack on the worst forms of child labour, there may occur a

---

[117] International Labour Organization, *Child Labour—Targeting the Intolerable—The Problem*, Geneva, 1996.

global devaluation of employment conditions with an immediate attack on the worst abuses. Many governments have embarked on a review and updating of national legislation on child labour and have adopted practical policies and programmes on child labour.

The Child Labour Deterrence Act 1992 (Harkin-Brown Bill)
An initiative to legislate on import ban on child labour products was first introduced by Senator Tom Harkin in the US Senate in 1988. The underlying concerns of the Child Labour Deterrence Act were to ensure that competition was based upon 'the quality of our goods, not the misery and suffering of those who make them and that the adult workers in the US and other developed countries should not have their roles imperiled by imports produced by child labour in developing countries'. This clause was dropped in the 1994 text of the bill. It was said that the original bill was put forward primarily to protect US trade interests. Later, the bill was amended and was given a humanitarian look. This Act links the granting of trade privileges to foreign countries with their respect for minimum workers' rights.

Social Labelling—The Rugmark Scheme—The 'Kaleen' Scheme
During the economic crisis of the 1980s, when the Indian government was desperate for foreign exchange, the carpet industry proved to be a godsend export. Earnings from carpets boomed but so did the number of children working on looms—from 10,000 in 1975 to 420,000 in 1989. The first response was the launch in 1989 of the South Asian Coalition on Child Servitude (SACCS) consisting of sixty non-governmental organizations and campaign groups, which aimed at building a national and international campaign on child labour, especially in the carpet industry.

Eventually in 1994, the Indo German Export Promotion Programme, the SACCS (which claimed an increase in members to 200 NGOs), the UNICEF, and a few carpet exporters came together to term the trademark 'Rugmark'. 'Rugmark' is a trademark certifying that a child has not produced a carpet. The Rugmark Foundation that introduced this label also acts as a monitoring system guaranteeing that child labour is not used in the manufacturing units from where a particular carpet is produced. Under the current procedures, carpet exporters must apply for the logo. If, upon inspection, the Foundation finds that the exporter *does not* employ child labour, it gives the latter the logo.

But even this strategy has serious problems. Firstly, Rugmark's success depends upon the honesty and efficiency of its inspection. Besides 'zeroing in' on a single industry such as carpets can simply push children from that industry into others like textiles and clothing, household services, or construction with virtually no impact on the total number of child workers.

The existence of Rugmark introduces an inevitable bias in favour of large factories. Regular inspections required for effective enforcement are feasible only when production is concentrated in large establishments. It is unlikely that tiny operations located in remote villages will be able to obtain the Rugmark logo even if they never used child labour.

Nevertheless, Rugmark has been a significant success story so far. It is said that the network of controls is so efficient that those opposing Rugmark have identified so far only one falsely-labelled carpet. Exporters, who contribute a fee of 25 per cent of the carpets' export value, pay for the inspection system. Meanwhile, importers of Rugmark carpets agree to contribute one per cent of the export values to a fine administered by UNICEF.

Rugmark needs to broaden its areas of operation. But the Rugmark initiative is a ray of hope. The Rugmark Foundation has recently extended its jurisdiction to Nepal. The Government of India has also set up an inspection and certification system for the carpet industry known as *Kaleen*, which literally means carpet.

Applicable International Law on Bonded Children

The practice of bonded child labour violates the following international human rights conventions; India is a party to all of them, and as such is legally bound to comply with their terms.

1926: CONVENTION ON THE SUPPRESSION OF SLAVE TRADE AND SLAVERY

This Convention requires signatories to 'prevent and suppress the slave trade' and 'to bring about, progressively and as soon as possible, the complete abolition of slavery in all forms'. It also obligates to 'take all necessary measures to prevent compulsory or forced labour from developing into conditions analogous to slavery'.[118]

1956: SUPPLEMENTARY CONVENTION ON THE ABOLITION OF SLAVERY, THE SLAVE TRADE, AND INSTITUTIONS AND PRACTICES SIMILAR TO SLAVERY

The supplementary Convention on slavery offers further clarification of prohibited practices and refers specifically to debt bondage and child servitude

---

[118] Convention on the Suppression of Slave Trade and Slavery was signed at Geneva on 25 September 1926; Protocol amending the Slavery Convention done at New York, was entered into force on 7 December 1953; Supplementary Convention on the Abolition of Slavery, the Slave Trade and Institutions and Practices similar to Slavery, was entered into force on 30 April 1957.

as institutions similar to slavery. It requires State parties to take all practicable and necessary legislative and other measures to bring about progressively and as soon as possible the complete abolition of . . . debt bondage . . . [and] any institution or practice whereby a child or young person under the age of 18 years, is delivered by either or both of his natural parents or by his guardian to another person, whether for reward or not, with a view to the exploitation of the child or young person or his labour.[119]

The Convention defines debt bondage as follows:

Debt bondage, that is to say, the status or condition arising from a pledge by a debtor of his personal services or those of a person under his control as security for a debt, if the value of those services as reasonably assessed is not applied towards the liquidation of the debt or the length and nature of those services are not respectively limited and defined.[120]

1989: CONVENTION ON THE RIGHTS OF THE CHILD

Articles 32, 35, and 36 mandate protections that are particularly relevant for the bonded child labour.

Conclusion

In 1986 and 1987 the Government of India adopted a new set of policies towards working children. The policy of the government is to ban the employment of children below the age of fourteen years in factories, mines, and other hazardous employment in accordance with the provisions of the Constitution and to regulate the working condition of children in non-hazardous occupations and processes. The government would also endeavour to provide voluntary part-time non-formal education for working children rather than press for compulsory universal primary education.[121] Besides, the present CLPRA 1986 does not deal with the causes in the political economy, which give rise to child labour, nor does it provide for any mandatory time frame for the gradual prohibition of child labour This policy now has to change. No longer can the dual policy of prohibition and regulation along with non-formal, part-time education continue. A firm and a clear policy stand has to be taken that the place of children is at school and not in the workplace. Basic, full-time, formal primary education for all children is a keystone of these rights, and in some ways a condition for the exercise of other rights.

[119] Supplementary Convention on the Abolition of Slavery.
[120] Ibid.
[121] Myron Weiner, *The Child and the State in India*, Oxford University Press, Delhi, 1991.

Several socio-economic and political factors are responsible for the existence and perpetuation of child work. Although poverty and inequality are the main factors influencing the number of child workers, they are not the only causes. Child labour is not purely an economic question and we have to opt for a model that will continuously generate employment, but 'poverty can no longer be an excuse for child labour'. Poverty has not prevented governments of other developing countries from expanding mass education or making primary education compulsory. In many countries, the diffusion of mass literacy preceded the Industrial Revolution and governments often introduced compulsory education when levels of poverty were high. Poverty as one of the causes has to be addressed.

The governments of all developed countries and many developing countries have removed children from the labour force and required that they attend school. They believe that employers should not be permitted to employ child labour, and parents, no matter how poor, should not be allowed to keep their children out of school. Modern states regard education as a legal duty, not merely a right—parents are required to send their children to school, children are required to attend school, and the state is obligated to enforce compulsory education. Compulsory primary education is the policy instrument by which the state effectively removes children from the labour force. The State thus stands as the ultimate guardian of children, protecting them against both parents and would-be employers.[122] Therefore, poverty cannot prevent India from providing education to all children. The ninety-third constitutional amendment, despite its inadequacies,[123] can be a good beginning. This amendment has inserted Article 21A,[124] which provides for free and compulsory education to all children of the age of 6–14 years in such manner as the state may by law determine. This can be interpreted to mean that any work whether hazardous or non-hazardous that blocks children's access to education violates Article 21A. Every State has to enact a comprehensive legislation to implement the provisions of the Constitution and to provide adequate budget.

In our country law has a crucial role to play in social transformation. It is evident that legislation is one of the main weapons and the process is still incomplete. Child labour is a complex issue. It needs a multi-sectoral, integrated approach. It is not only the concern of the Ministry of Labour or the

---

[122] Myron Weiner, *The Child and the State in India*, Oxford University Press, Delhi, 1991.

[123] See the Chapter on Education.

[124] Constitution of India, Article 21A: 'The State shall provide free and compulsory education to all children of the age of six to fourteen years in such manner as the State, by law may determine.'

Department of Women and Child Development or Family Welfare the Ministry of Human Resource, Finance, Health, Social Justice and Empowerment and Agriculture, all have to work together. A legal strategy could be a combination of several legislations. The related Acts and the rules made thereunder need to be reviewed and amended to conform and be linked to the child labour legislation.

'Recently, the Study Group on Women and Children of the Second National Commission on Labour appointed by the Ministry of Labour, Government of India, recommended a draft for discussion. The draft Bill is known as The Child Labour (Prohibition and Education) Bill, 2001. The Bill intends to ensure that no child would be deprived of a future by being deprived of an education and having to spend his childhood working. It recognizes every child out of school as a child labour or a potential child labour. It seeks to tackle the problem of child labour by ensuring universal education. It also seeks to ensure that children do not work in situations where they are exploited and deprived of a future.' The Commission felt that the Child Labour Legislation should not only be regulatory but also developmental.

The main focus should now be on enforcement and implementation. Compulsory education laws normally precede child labour laws and their enforcement. It has been experienced that enforcing compulsory education laws, though by no means simple, is easier than enforcing child labour laws and factory laws. The enforcement of compulsory education laws was facilitated by the system of compulsory birth registration. Of course, the societal coalitions have proved to be crucial in introducing and extending compulsory education laws and banning the employment of children. Church groups, religious leaders, trade unionists, schoolteachers and educational officials, philanthropists, and social reformers have played significant roles.[125]

Modern States regard education as a legal duty and not merely a right.[126] The notion of the duty denies parents the right to choose. Parents are told by the State that no matter how great their need is for child labour or income, they must relinquish their child to school for a part of the day. The notion of duty also applies to the State. Education needs more of our funds, it also needs our creative thinking about how to develop schools relevant to the

---

[125] Myron Weiner, *The Child and the State in India*, Oxford University Press, Oxford, 1991.

[126] The Constitution of India, Article 51A: A parent or guardian has a fundamental duty to provide opportunities for education to his child or, as the case may be, ward between the age of six to fourteen years.

—93rd Constitution Amendment Act

needs of actual and potential child workers. Schools must be able to draw and retain children. Schools must teach useful skills that are seen as relevant by both children and parents.

It is also clear that any programme of eliminating child labour has to provide reasonable alternatives for the child workers it ousts, out of the workplace they had entered due to extreme poverty. The Convention on the Rights of the Child explicitly specifies in Article 28 that parties must promote and encourage international cooperation in support of developing countries' efforts to ensure access to education for all children.

The best guarantee that the government will take its responsibilities seriously is when all sectors of society become involved in the genuine national movement. As the implications of child rights and the principle of the Convention on the Rights of the Child start to permeate society, attitudes, assumptions, and values will correspondingly change. And with greater community awareness comes greater involvement, leading to a powerful, if informal, labour inspectorate—of families and neighbours, strangers and friends. Such a development represents the best chance of protecting all children, but especially those farthest from official scrutiny, who are working in the informal sector and in rural areas.

5
Right to Protection Against Sexual Abuse and Exploitation

Introduction

Child sexual abuse and exploitation is not new, the extent of the problem is—children are sold, rented out, and sexually abused by adults everywhere. While it is almost impossible to obtain accurate figures, it is a fact that millions of girls and boys worldwide are being used in prostitution, pornography, trafficking, and other forms of sexual abuse and exploitation. There is no uniformly accepted definition of child abuse. There have been a number of definitions of the phrase 'child sexual abuse'. It could be defined as an activity relating to sex organs engaged in for sexual gratification, which takes advantage of, violates, or deceives children or young people. Furthermore, their plight has a multiplier effect since research has shown that frequently abused and exploited adolescents are abusers and exploiters themselves as adults.

Child Sexual Abuse (CSA) has been defined as any kind of physical or mental violation of a child with sexual intent usually by a person who is in a position of trust or power vis-à-vis the child. CSA is also defined as any sexual behaviour directed at a person under sixteen, without informed consent.

The Standing Committee on Sexually Abused Children[1] has defined Child Sexual Abuse as: 'Any child below the age of consent may be deemed to have been sexually abused when a sexually mature person has by design or by neglect of their usual societal or specific responsibilities in relation to the child engaged or permitted engagement of that child in activity of a sexual nature, which is intended to lead to the sexual gratification of the sexually mature person. This definition pertains whether or not it involves genital or physical contact, whether or not initiated by the child and whether or not there is a discernible harmful outcome in the short run.'

[1] SCOSAC 1984.

The Children's Act 1989 of Great Britain defines 'sexual abuse' as the involvement of dependent, developmentally immature children and adolescents in sexual activities they do not normally comprehend, to which they are unable to give informed consent, or that which violate the social taboos of family roles. This definition introduced the concepts of 'informed consent' and 'dependent'. It is the dependent nature of child and young people that make child sexual abuse a particular problem.

In Australia, child sexual abuse refers to a variety of behaviour ranging from enthusiasm to intercourse, from intimate kissing and cuddling to penetration with an object. The penetration may be oral, vaginal, or anal.[2] In 1988, a National Seminar on Child Abuse in India[3] recognized the need for defining afresh the term 'child abuse' in the Indian context. The committee concerned evolved the following definition:

Child Abuse and Neglect (CAN) is the intentional, non-accidental injury, maltreatment of children by parents, caretakers, employers or others including those individuals representing government/non-government bodies which may lead to temporary or permanent impairment of their physical, mental, psycho-social development, disability or death.

The problem of child sexual abuse is, for feminists, the problem of masculine sexuality. *Saakshi*[4] defines child sexual abuse as any behaviour directed at a person under sixteen, without that person's informed consent.[5] According to *Saakshi* child sexual abuse is the physical or mental violation of a child with sexual intent, usually by an older person, who is in some position of power and/or trust *vis-à-vis* the child. Child sexual abuse includes an adult exposing his or her genitals to a child or persuading the child to do the same; an adult touching a child's genitals or making the child touch the adult's genitalia; an adult involving a child in pornography; an adult having oral, vaginal, or anal intercourse with a child; any verbal or other sexual suggestions made to a child by an adult; and so on. Sexual abuse of children can take place in the family, in the neighbourhood, in school, in institutions, and on the street. The abuser, generally a male, usually violates a relationship of trust with the child, taking advantage of his power and position.[6]

The United Nations has defined child sexual abuse as contacts or interactions between a child and an older or more knowledgeable child or adult

---

[2] See Australian Report Commissioned by the Law Reform Commission of Victoria.
[3] National Institute of Public Cooperation and Child Development, New Delhi, 2–24 June 1988.
[4] A Non-governmental Organization, New Delhi.
[5] See Child Sexual Abuse—A draft manual, Saakshi, Unpublished.
[6] Saakshi, *Child Sexual Abuse: Beyond Fear Secrecy and Shame*, New Delhi, 1999.

(a stranger, sibling, or person in a position of authority, such as a parent or a caretaker), when the child is being used as an object of gratification for the older child's or adult's sexual needs. These contacts or interactions are carried out against the child, using force, trickery, bribes, threats, or pressure.[7]

Some other definitions define it as any kind of physical or mental violation of a child with a sexual intent, usually by an older person who is in possession of trust or power *vis-à-vis* the child. The list is not exhaustive.

Child Sexual Abuse becomes Exploitation when a Third Party Benefits through a Profit

Commercial sexual exploitation of children commonly refers to using a child for sexual purposes in exchange for cash or favours in kind between the client/customer and the intermediary or agent who profits from such trade in children. Those who profit may be from a wide range of persons, including parents, family members, procurers/agents, community members—largely men, but also women.[8] It includes child prostitution through trafficking, child sex tourism, and child pornography.

Child Sexual Abuse and Exploitation (CSA&E) covers the sexual maltreatment of both children and young people. The sexual exploitation of children is a multi-billion-dollar industry of international proportions. It is an abuse of power and violation of human rights and, in many cases, a contemporary form of slavery. The perpetrator can be anyone who exploits the child's vulnerability to gain sexual gratification. CSA&E involves mental, physical, and emotional abuse of a child through overt and covert sexual acts, gestures, and disposition when informed consent or resistance by the child victim to such acts is not possible. It can also include activities which do not involve direct touching. Sexual abuse and exploitation takes different forms such as:

- Child labourers and young domestic workers are frequently used for the *sexual gratification* of the employers and other adults.
- Children are sexually abused within the family. *Rape* within a family has its own alarming numbers.
- With the advent of HIV/AIDS, there is an increased demand for younger *child prostitutes.*
- Children are used as attractions in *sex tourism.* Children are victims of a globally organized sex trade. In some countries, this helps in bringing the much-needed foreign exchange.

[7] UNICEF, 2001.
[8] Ibid.

- Children are abused within the context of cultural or traditional practices such as *child marriages*.
- Children in institutions are vulnerable to *sexual abuse* from those who are supposed to take care of them.
- Children in situations of conflicts, displaced, migrant, and refugee children are particularly vulnerable to all forms of *sexual exploitation*.
- Child pornography is reaching alarming proportions especially with the help of hi-tech mediums.

Disabled children with problems of communication and comprehension are particularly vulnerable to sexual abuse.

Sexual abuse and exploitation include:

- Fondling, touching, and kissing;
- Exhibitionism and voyeurism;
- Oral, anal, or vaginal sexual intercourse;
- Photography/filming children for sexual purposes;
- Persuading a child to touch or fondle the sexual parts of any other person (child or adult); and
- Masturbating (using the child as a sexual object).[9]

There are occurrences of sexual abuse and exploitation of children within families and homes. The law generally presumes that guardians of the child are innocent and it takes a lot of professional commitment to establish an offence against such guardians.

Impact of Sexual Abuse/Exploitation

The sexual exploitation of children not only has damaging and long-term impact on the victim, but also affects the families, communities, and society at large. Like any crime that continues to go unchecked, the sexual exploitation of children—both within the homes and as an organized trafficking racket—directly suggests the health of a society as a whole.

Children who have been sexually abused suffer severe traumas or damage which can be physical, mental, emotional, or psychological. The trauma may last a lifetime if the process of healing does not take place. Sexually transmitted diseases or HIV or pregnancy at an early age can be some of the disastrous outcomes of CSA. With the family support system getting destroyed, the child can face social isolation and social stigmatization. Very often, the child is blamed for being sexually exploited, for 'affecting the honour of the

---

[9] *Child Sexual Abuse—A Draft Manual*, Saakshi, New Delhi, (Unpublished).

family'. The child is made to feel guilty for what happened and a deep sense of worthlessness develops. Children may also feel powerless, angry, frightened, and lonely. Depression, isolation, and self-destructiveness are also some of the short-term and long-term impacts of sexual abuse.

PART A: CHILD SEXUAL ABUSE IN INDIA

Introduction

The incidence reported against children (classified on the basis of crime heads) and the percentage of variation in the registered cases during 1999 over 1995 and 1998 are presented in Table 5.1.

Table 5.1: Reported Crimes Against Children (1995–9) in India

Sr. No.	Crime Head	1995	1996	1997	1998	1999	Percentage Variation 1999 over 1995	1999 over 1998
1.	Child rape	4067	4083	4414	4153	3153	(–) 22.5	(–) 24.1
2.	Kidnapping and Abduction	726	571	620	699	791	8.95	13.2
3.	Procurement of minor girls	107	94	87	171	172	60.7	0.6
4.	Selling of girls for prostitution	17	6	9	11	13	(–) 23.5	18.2
5.	Buying of girls for prostitution	19	22	13	13	5	(–) 73.7	(–) 61.5
6.	Child Marriage Restraint Act	57	89	78	56	58	1.8	3.6

Source: Crime in India, 1999.

Child Rape

Child rape continues to be reported significantly from various states and Union territories. Table 5.2 provides the detailed information on child rape victims and their proportion in the total rape victims during the years 1995–99.

212 Child Rights in India

Table 5.2: Victims of Child Rape (1995–9)

Sl. No.	Year	Age Group Below 10 years	Age Group 10–16 years	Percentage of child rape victims to total rape victims
1.	1995	747	3320	29.5
2.	1996	608	3475	27.5
3.	1997	770	3644	28.8
4.	1998	646	3507	27.4
5.	1999	731	2422*	20.4
6.	Percentage change in 1999 over 1998	13.2	(–) 30.9	(–) 25.5
7.	Percentage change in 1999 over 1995	(–) 2.1	(–) 27.0	(–) 30.8

*Age Group 11–15 years

Source: Crime in India, 1999.

It is a matter of grave concern that of all victims in rape cases, children alone accounted for 20.4 per cent. During 1999 there was an increase of 13.2 per cent in cases of child rape in the age group below ten years and a decline of 30.9 per cent in victims in the age group of 11–15 years was reported compared to 1998. The cases of rape of children below the age of ten years were more than those of 1992 for every succeeding year thereafter.[10]

Child Marriage is a form of Sexual Abuse of Children

Ameena, a child bride married to a sixty-year-old man, was rescued by an alert flight attendant who noticed her sobbing during a flight between Hyderabad and New Delhi.[11] The bridegroom was arrested and sent to prison for marrying a minor without consent and later released on bail.

In Rajasthan on *Akshay Tritiya* day which is popularly known as *Akha Teej*, hundreds of child marriages are openly performed. *Akha Teej* is regarded as the most auspicious day for celebrating marriages. On this day even

---

[10] See Crime in India, 1999.

[11] Later the battles for Ameena's custody were fought as much in news reports, opinion columns, and letters to the editor of newspapers as in courts. Questions were raised especially about Ameena's age, the validity of her marriage, and the applicability of secular laws to minority communities.

infants, who have just been born or are only a few years old and cannot even sit or walk, are married. The child brides or the bridegroom do not understand the solemnity of these ceremonies, but for elders it is the safest and most tested way of keeping property and money within the family and of

Table 5.3: Age at First Marriage by State, 1998–99

State	Median age at first marriage	Median age at first cohabitation with husband
India	16.4	17.0
North	17.97	18.48
Delhi	19.0	19.3
Haryana	16.9	17.9
Himachal Pradesh	18.6	18.8
Jammu and Kashmir	18.2	18.4
Punjab	20.0	20.1
Rajasthan	15.1	16.4
Central	14.85	16.15
Madhya Pradesh	14.7	16.0
Uttar Pradesh	15.0	16.3
East	16.4	17.03
Bihar	14.9	16.6
Orissa	17.5	17.6
West Bengal	16.8	16.9
North-east	19.4	20.01
Aruanchal Pradesh	18.7	18.8
Assam	18.1	18.2
Manipur	21.7	21.8
Meghalaya	19.1	19.3
Mizoram	22.0	22.0
Nagaland	20.1	20.2
Sikkim	19.8	19.8
West	19.07	19.37
Goa	23.2	23.2
Gujarat	17.6	18.2
Maharashtra	16.4	16.7
South	17.7	17.88
Andhra Pradesh	15.1	15.4
Karnataka	16.8	17.0
Kerala	20.2	20.3
Tamil Nadu	18.7	18.8

Source: National Family Health Survey, 1998–99.

preserving the 'chastity' of their daughters. These types of marriages are greatly prevalent in Rajasthan, but in other states also there are several incidents of child marriages. In rural India, the girls are married off at 12–14 years even before they are physically, psychologically, and emotionally mature.

The National Family Health Survey (NFHS) statistics on the median age of marriage are given in Table 5.3 in the previous page. The actual figures are probably much higher as correct information is not often available. One of the major reasons for this incorrect information is that registration of marriages is not compulsory in many states and even where this is compulsory, this is not done because of several socio-cultural practices.

From the above table, it is apparent that the median age of first cohabitation with the husband is as low as 16 years in some States. The percentage of Indian girls getting married by thirteen years of age is 15.4 per cent, by the age of fifteen, 33.3 per cent get married. So almost one-third of the female population is married even before they reach the legal age of getting married. By eighteen years of age, this figure reaches 64.6 per cent, at 20 it is 79.4 per cent, at 22 it increases to 87.9 per cent, and at 25 it is 93.7 per cent.[12] Early marriage is a form of sexual abuse of the girl child as they have to become mothers. Early motherhood denies the girl an opportunity for development and incrseases the risk of higher numbers of low-birth-weight babies, child deaths and disabilities, maternal deaths, gynaecological problems, and an increased number of pregnancies to replace the lost children. Early marriage also deprives the girls of the opportunities of schooling; they are made to assume domestic and childcare responsibilities early, which hampers their intellectual and personality development.[13] The age at marriage is, therefore, indicative of the status of women.

Child Sexual Abuse in Institutions

There has been a significant increase in the number of cases of child sexual abuse in institutions. The sexual assault case of a deaf and mute girl in the Observation Home, Umerkhadi, Mumbai (OHU), referred to as 'Billa No. 31' in all available documents pertaining to her case, is an example of lapses that occur in dealing with such cases under the present system.[14]

The medical examination for investigation of sexual assault ordered by

[12] National Family Health Survey, 1998-1999.

[13] Shanti Ghosh, 'Girl Child: A Lifetime of Deprivation and Discrimination', *The Indian Journal of Social Work*, Vol. II, No. 1, Tata Institute of Social Sciences, Mumbai, Jan. 1991.

[14] Report of the Investigation done by the Forum Against Child Sexual Exploitation (FACSE) team.

the superintendent on 22 September 1997 conducted by the doctor on duty at OHU was inconclusive because it was incomplete. No attempt was made to collect any forensic evidence other than from the clothes she was wearing. The doctor appeared to be unaware of the procedures to be followed while investigating a case of sexual assault. There was no facility to help the victim to cope with the physical and emotional trauma. There was a lapse of twenty days between the date of assault and the report to the police. There was no efficient and timely communication mechanism. There was infact suppression of evidence.

Many such cases have come to light. There is no procedure laid down to deal with such cases of abuse within the institutions. In several cases the 'carers', i.e. those who are supposed to take care of the children in the institutions are the abusers. There are several cases which go unreported. Doctors who are the first to come in contact with such victims are not trained to deal with such cases. Often doctors are not equipped to examine rape victims. The trauma caused to the child victim of sexual assault finds no mention in any report. The medical reports are incomplete and vague in many cases. The medical or psychiatric assessment needs to be sensitively carried out. The staff in the institutions are not equipped or trained to deal with such cases.

From the police point of view, child rape and indecent assault are peripheral crimes. The police also have practically no training in dealing with cases of child sexual abuse. Besides, investigation of such cases requires a different kind of expertise which is lacking. There is a wide communication gap between the child's statement and the recordings of the police and the language of the courts. There is a stereotype pattern of investigation which is followed without any sensitivity.

A survey by Samvaad[15] of 348 girl students from schools and colleges shows that approximately 24 per cent had experienced sexual abuse at least once in their lives. Twenty-one per cent were less than ten years of age, 14 per cent were between ten and fourteen years of age and 54 per cent were fifteen years of age at the time of abuse.

A research study by the Special Cell for Women and Children of the Tata Institute of Social Sciences, Mumbai,[16] revealed that a total of 1176 cases of child sexual abuse were registered during 1990–95 in Mumbai and a total of fifty-seven reported cases (in Mumbai during 1994–5) on sexually abused girls below the age of ten years were studied from police records.

[15] An NGO in Bangalore.
[16] Nahida Shaikh, T. Panchal, *Documentation of Police Cases of Sexually Abused Girls in Mumbai City between 1994–95 by the Special Cell for Women & Children*, Tata Institute of Social Sciences, Mumbai, 1997.

Some of the findings of this study were significant:
- The offender is often known to the child and her family.
- A large number of children (40.4 per cent) have been abused or assaulted in the offender's house. In 35 per cent cases the child was sexually abused in public places such as a garden, creek, building halls, common areas in chawls,[17] public toilets, etc.
- Only serious cases have been reported to the police.
- More than half the accused arrested were not granted bail. Out of the twenty-two accused who were granted bail, fifteen were below the age of eighteen years and hence the bail was granted through the juvenile courts.
- The age of consent of abuse is around three years and it shows increased vulnerability at around seven years of age.
- Men of all ages can be abusers. In this study, the ages of the accused were in the range of twelve years to sixty-two years. The data also showed that seventeen of the abusers were below eighteen years of age.
- About 30.4 per cent of the offenders (that is seventeen out of fifty-seven cases) were aged less than eighteen years.
- A large number of cases in the study show that the offender was a neighbour of the child. Sometimes, the offenders were older children in the community. Some of the offenders were in fact popular among children.
- Sexual abuse could involve both touching as well as non-contact abuse.
- Statements taken by investigating officers mostly revolve around one episode of child sexual abuse and no history is therefore looked at or questioned.

The Present Legal Regime

At present there is no comprehensive law on child sexual abuse. The Constitution of India contains provision for the protection of children. Under the Constitution, it is the duty of the state to secure that children of tender age are not abused and forced by economic necessity to enter vocations unsuited to their age and strength [Article 39(e)] and to ensure that children are given opportunities and facilities to develop in a healthy manner and in conditions of freedom and dignity [Article 39(f)]. According to Article 23 of the Constitution, trafficking in women for immoral purposes is prohibited. The Constitution directs the State to enact special legislations and policies for

---

[17] Cluster of tiny homes.

protecting children and youth against exploitation of moral and material abandonment.

In India, legal intervention is presently in the form of investigations which start with registration of offences under the earlier Juvenile Justice Act 1986 or the present Juvenile Justice (Care and Protection of Children) Act 2000 or the Indian Penal Code or the Prevention of Immoral Traffic Act 1956 (amended in 1986).

The Juvenile Justice Act 1986 (JJ Act 1986)

JJ Act 1986 was enacted to provide for the care, protection, treatment, development, and rehabilitation of neglected or delinquent children. The Act did not directly deal with child sexual abuse but the definition of a neglected juvenile included a juvenile who lived in a brothel or with a prostitute or frequently went to any place used for the purpose of prostitution or was found to associate with any prostitute or who was being or was likely to be abused or exploited for immoral or illegal purposes. Such neglected children were produced before a Juvenile Welfare Board who would, after an inquiry, send the child to a juvenile home for care, protection, and rehabilitation.

Under the Juvenile Justice Act 1986, a prostitute's child was automatically a neglected child. The magistrate had the power to segregate the prostitute from her child and place the child in a corrective institution. Besides, under the Act, while males above eighteen years were considered adults, the age was reduced to sixteen years for females. The Juvenile Welfare Boards generally were not equipped to deal with cases of child sexual abuse. The observation homes could not provide special care and treatment for such victimized children.

Juvenile Justice (Care and Protection of Children) Act 2000

Since the Juvenile Justice Act 1986 has been replaced by the Juvenile Justice (Care and Protection of Children) Act 2000, such children are now being produced before the Child Welfare Committees which have replaced the Juvenile Welfare Boards.[18] In practice, at present, it appears that there has been a change only in the nomenclatures. The actual functioning of the earlier Boards and the present Committees remain almost the same.

The Indian Penal Code

There is, at present, neither a comprehensive law nor a policy to deal with child sexual abuse. The Indian Penal Code deals with the sexual abuse of

---

[18] See the Chapter on Juvenile Justice.

children in the form of rape. Section 375[19] defines rape. Section 376[20] of the Indian Penal Code provides for the punishment of rape which shall not be less than seven years but which may be for a term that may extend to ten years, unless the woman raped is his own wife and is not under twelve years

[19] IPC, Section 375: A man is said to commit 'rape' who, except in the case hereinafter excepted, has sexual intercourse with a woman under circumstances falling under any of the six following descriptions:

First—Against her will.

Secondly—With her consent, when her consent has been obtained by putting her or any person in whom she is interested in fear of death or of hurt.

Fourthly—With her consent, when the man knows that he is not her husband, and that her consent is given because she believes that he is another man to whom she is or believes herself to be lawfully married.

Fifthly—With her consent, when, at the time of giving such consent, by reason of unsoundness of mind or intoxication or the administration by him personally or through another of any stupefying or unwholesome substance, she is unable to understand the nature and consequences of that to which she gives consent.

Sixthly—With or without her consent, when she is under sixteen years of age.

Explanation—Penetration is sufficient to constitute the sexual intercourse necessary to the offence of rape.

Exception—Sexual intercourse by a man with his own wife, the wife not being under fifteen years of age, is not rape.

iii) on a woman in his custody or in the custody of a police officer subordinate to him, or
  b) being a public servant, takes advantage of his official position and commits rape on a woman in the custody of such public servant or in the custody of a public servant subordinate to him; or
  c) being on the management or on the staff of a jail, remand home, or other place of custody established by or under any law for the time being in force or of a woman's or children's institution takes advantage of his official position and commits rape on any inmate of such jail, remand home, place, or institution; or
  d) being on the management or on the staff of a hospital, takes advantage of his official position and commits rape on a woman in that hospital; or
  e) commits rape on a woman knowing her to be pregnant; or
  f) commits rape on a woman when she is under twelve years of age; or
  g) commits gang rape.

Shall be punished with rigorous imprisonment for a term which shall not be less than ten years but which may be for life and shall also be liable to fine;

Provided that the court may, for adequate and special reasons to be mentioned in the judgment, impose a sentence of imprisonment of either description for a term of less than ten years.

Explanation-1: Where a woman is raped by one or more in a group of persons acting in furtherance of their common intention, each of the persons shall be deemed to have committed gang rape within the meaning of this subsection.

of age, in which case, he shall be punished with imprisonment for a term which may extend to two years or with fine or both.

The other provisions of IPC, that are invoked are related to unnatural practices like Section 377.[21] This is generally invoked when boy children are

---

Explanation-2: 'Women's or children's institution' means an institution, whether called an orphanage or a home for neglected women or children or a widow's home or by any other name, which is established and maintained for the reception and care of women or children.

Explanation-3: 'Hospital' means the precincts of the hospital and includes the precincts of any institution for the reception and treatment of persons during convalescence or of persons requiring medical attention or rehabilitation.

[20] IPC, Section 376-A: Intercourse by a man with his wife during separation.

Whoever has sexual intercourse with his own wife who is living separately from him under a decree of separation or under any custom or usage without her consent shall be punished with imprisonment of either description for a term which may extend to two years and shall also be liable to fine.

IPC, Section 376-B: Intercourse by public servant with woman in his custody.

Whoever, being a public servant, takes advantage of his official position and induces or seduces, any woman, who is in his custody as such public servant, or in the custody of a public servant subordinate to him, to have sexual intercourse with him, such sexual intercourse not amounting to the offence of rape, shall be punished with imprisonment of either description for a term which may extend to five years and shall also be liable to fine

IPC, Section 376-C: Intercourse by superintendent of jail, remand home, etc.

Whoever, being the superintendent or manager of a jail, remand home, or other place of custody established by or under any law for the time being in force or of a women's or children's institution takes advantages of his official position and induces or seduces any female inmate of such jail, remand home, place, or institution to have sexual intercourse with him, such sexual intercourse not amounting to the offence of rape, shall be punished with imprisonment of either description for a term which may extend to five years and shall also be liable to fine.

IPC, Section 376-D: Intercourse by any member of the management or staff of a hospital with any woman in that hospital.

Whoever, being on the management of a hospital or being a staff of a hospital takes advantage of his position and has sexual intercourse with any woman in that hospital, such sexual intercourse not amounting to the offence of rape, shall be punished with imprisonment of either description for a term which may extend to five years and shall also be liable to fine.

[21] IPC, Section 377: Whoever voluntarily has carnal intercourse against the order of nature with any man, woman or animal, shall be punished with imprisonment for life, or with imprisonment of either description for a term which may extend to ten years, and shall also be liable to fine.

Explanation: Penetration is sufficient to constitute the carnal intercourse.

sexually abused. Sections 366(A)[22] and 366(B)[23] relate to export and import of girls for prostitution. Under Sections 366-A and 366-B, the girl should be below eighteen years and she should be intentionally induced by the accused to go from any place or to any act that is likely to force her into prostitution.

The Prevention of Immoral Traffic Act 1986 (PITA)

Under Section 8, children, both girls and boys, are given protection from sexual abuse. There are also provisions against brothel keepers and keeping minor girls. Discretionary powers have been given to magistrates for interim placement of children who are housed in institutions.

Child Marriages

Child marriages are dealt by the Child Marriage Restraint Act (CMRA) 1929 and by the various personal laws. The Indian Majority Act 1875 lays down the age of majority as eighteen years [Section 3]. But in case of marriage, dower, divorce, and adoption, personal laws of parties regulate the age of majority. In 1929, the pressure exerted by social reformers had forced the British government to pass laws relating to child marriages. Taking into consideration the popular traditions and practices, the British government enacted the Child Marriage Restraint Act 1929, popularly known as the Sharda Act. The Child Marriage Restraint Act 1929 was an Act to restrain the solemnizaton of child marriages. It was applicable to all Indians, i.e. Hindus, Muslims, and Christians. It prescribed the minimum age for marriage for both boys and girls. In 1929, the minimum age of marriage for girls was fifteen and for boys it was eighteen. This position was maintained by the Hindu Marriage Act 1955 which prescribed the same minimum age of marriage. This Act prohibited the solemnization of child marriages but it did not declare these marriages either void or illegal. The punishment under the

---

[22] IPC, Section 366-A: Whoever, by any means whatsoever, induces any minor girl under the age of eighteen years to go from any place or to do any act with intent that such girl may be, or knowing that it is likely that she will be, forced or seduced to illicit intercourse with another person shall be punishable with imprisonment which may extend to ten years, and shall also be liable to fine.

[23] IPC, Section 366-B: Importation of girl from foreign country.

Whoever imports into India from any country outside or from the state of Jammu and Kashmir any girl under the age of twenty-one years with intent that she may be, or knowing it to be likely that she will be, forced seduced to illicit intercourse with another person.

Act was very mild. This was a weak legislation and could not achieve the desired results.[24] Child Marriages were deeply entrenched in the society as a custom and the Sharda Act failed to make any dent in this practice.

The Child Marriage Restraint (Amendment) Act 1978 was passed to provide more teeth to the Act and to raise the minimum age of marriage. This amended Act 1978 raised the minimum age of marriage by three years. It is now eighteen years for girls and twenty-one for boys.[25] Child marriage means a marriage to which either of the contracting parties, i.e. parties whose marriage is or is about to be solemnized [CMRA 1929, 2 Section (b)] is a child.[26]

Injunctions to Restrain Child Marriages

On the basis of the information received by the court through a complaint or otherwise that a child marriage has been arranged or is about to be solemnized, the civil courts under their ordinary civil jurisdiction can, after issuing a show cause notice, grant an injunction prohibiting such marriage [CMRA 1929, Section 12]. If such an injunction is disobeyed and the marriage is performed, the court has the power to punish the offenders with a sentence of simple imprisonment of up to three months or with a fine of up to one thousand rupees or with both. [CMRA 1929, Section 12(5)]. Besides, in cases of contempt, the courts have wider power including attachment of property. This power to issue injunction is an important tool under the Act to prevent child marriages, but rarely used.

Age of Marriage under Various Personal Laws

The personal laws in India are based on religion. Marriages among the Hindus[27] are regulated by the provisions of the Hindu Marriage Act 1955. A valid marriage between two Hindus can take place where the bridegroom has completed the age of twenty-one years and the bride has completed the age of eighteen years, apart from other conditions like not having a living

---

[24] S. Saxena, 'Child Marriages in Rajasthan: A Challenge to Child Marriage Restraint Act', A.I.R. Journal, 2000.

[25] CMRA 1929, Section 2(a): defines a child as a person who, if a male, has not completed twenty-one years of age, and if a female, has not completed eighteen years of age.

[26] CMRA 1929 Section 2(b): 'child marriage' means a marriage in which either of the contracting parties is a child.

[27] The Act applies to any person who is a Hindu by religion in any of its forms or developments (including a Virashaiva or a Lingayat or follower of the Brahma, Prarthana, or Arya Samaj), to any person who is Buddhist, Jain, or Sikh by religion and to any person who is not a Muslim, Christian, Parsi, or Jew by religion.

spouse, not being of unsound mind, etc. Thus, neither party to a marriage amongst Hindus can any longer be of a child's age, that is, of less than eighteen years of age which is the age of majority. Any marriage made in contravention of the age limits has not been declared to be void or violable under other provisions of the Act, but such marriages have been made punishable with simple imprisonment up to fifteen days and fine up to one thousand rupees or with both. Both the bride and bridegroom are punishable if they marry before their eligible age. Since marriage can be solemnized only between two major persons, there is no question of obtaining consent of the guardian of the persons for the purpose of marriage under the Act. But if the marriage of a girl has been solemnized before she attained the age of fifteen years, she can repudiate the marriage after attaining fifteen years but before attaining the age of eighteen years whether or not the marriage has been consummated. She can also seek divorce thereafter from her husband through the court.

In Muslim law, it is essential that parties at the time of marriage should have attained puberty, which is a biological fact to be ascertained by evidence. Puberty is generally taken to come at the age of fifteen years. According to the Hanafi School of Law, the earliest stage of puberty is twelve years for boys and nine years for girls. The marriage of a person below the age of puberty is to be solemnized by a guardian and such marriage is not void. A marriage arranged by the father or parental grandfather binds the minor. The minor cannot annul such marriage on attaining puberty if the guardian had acted in the interest of the minor. If a guardian other than the father or grandfather arranges the marriage, the minor can exercise the 'option of puberty' and repudiate the marriage within a reasonable time if it is not consummated.

The Christian Marriage Act 1872

A minor has been defined as a person who has not completed the age of twenty-one years and who is not a widower or widow. A minor under the Act can marry with the consent of the father and, if he is dead, with the consent of the guardian, and if there is no guardian, with the consent of the mother.

The Parsi Marriage and Divorce Act 1936

A valid marriage amongst Parsis can take place between a boy who has completed the age of twenty-one years and a girl who has completed the age of eighteen years. Since only major persons can marry under the Parsi law, there cannot be any child marriage amongst Parsis.

The Special Marriage Act 1954

The age of marriage under this Act is twenty-one years for males and eighteen years for females. Any marriage solemnized in contravention of the age requirement will be null and void and can be nullified by the court.

The Foreign Marriage Act 1969

Under this Act a valid marriage can be effected in a foreign country or in a foreign ship in foreign territorial water between a boy who has completed the age of twenty-one years and a girl who has completed the age of eighteen years at the time of the marriage.

Validity of Child Marriages

The CMRA 1929 is applicable to all communities and child marriages are not void under the CMRA 1929. The marriages if performed under the personal laws are not void. The marriages are void only under the Special Marriage Act 1954 and the Parsi Marriage and Divorce Act 1939, but under all the other personal laws, i.e. under the Hindu Marriage Act 1955, Christian Marriage Act 1872, and the Muslim law, the marriages are valid. Marriage below the age of consent is valid under Christian law provided it is with the consent of the guardians. Under Muslim law, every Muslim of sound mind, who has attained puberty may be validly contracted in marriage by their guardians.[28] The persons concerned, as provided under Sections 3, 4, 5, and 6 of the Act, can be punished but the marriage remains valid. If such child marriages had been rendered void, the sufferer would have been the bride as a stigma of 'already once married' would have been attached to her and because the marriage would be illegal she would not receive any maintenance. It is also to be noted that women are not punished under the CMRA 1929. Perhaps because of the then social notions, it was presumed that the woman had little say in finalizing and performing marriages. Secondly, the main objective of the Act was preventive rather than punitive.

Repudiation of Child Marriages

The Hindu Marriage Act 1955 gives an option to the girl to opt out of a child marriage and repudiate it if her marriage was performed when she was below fifteen years. However this has to be done before she attains the age of

---

[28] Baillie, *Digest of Muhammedan Law*, London, Pt 1(1865), Pt II(1869) p. 50. Under the Shafei, Ithna Ashari and Ismaili laws, the father or father's father can act as the marriage guardian for a minor. In so far as Hanafi law is concerned, the list is not so restricted and includes other relations.

eighteen years. The boys are not given such an option. Under Muslim law, a parent or guardian can validly arrange for the marriage of the child but the child has the option to repudiate the marriage on attainment of puberty. In the absence of evidence, puberty is generally assumed to be at fifteen years.[29] A minor whose marriage has been contracted by any guardian other than the father or father's father has the option to repudiate the marriage on attaining puberty. The mere exercise of the option of repudiating such a marriage on attaining puberty does not act as dissolution of the marriage unless the act of repudiation has the approval of the court.[30]

Inadequacies in Law

The Child Marriage Restraint Act 1929 is openly flouted with thousands of child marriages being performed.* The provision of appointing child marriage prevention officers is not being implemented. During 1999, the police disposed of fifty-eight cases out of sixty-eight including pending cases for investigation from previous year. In forty-five cases, the police submitted charge sheets. Of the 244 cases for trial, forty-nine cases were decided by the courts, but of which only sixteen ended in convictions.[31] The age of sexual consent whether a girl is married or not should be eighteen years. The Child Marriage Restraint Act 1929 needs to be made more stringent. Perhaps, the representatives of the local self-governments or *panchayats*[32] could be given the responsibility of enforcing this legislation.

Under the current laws, if a child is sexually abused, a case can be filed for statutory rape or 'outraging the modesty of the woman' in the case of girls and for 'unnatural sexual offence' in the case of boys. The ordinary criminal laws are totally inadequate to protect the children who are victims of sexual abuse. These legislations do not include the common forms of child sexual abuse, nor their impact on the children.

---

[29] Ibid. The lowest age of puberty according to its natural signs is twelve in males and nineteen in females. When the signs do not appear both the sexes are held to be adult when they have completed their fifteenth year. See Fatwa Alamgiri, Vol. V, p. 93; *Md Idris v State of Bihar*, 1980 Cr LJ 764.

[30] Baillie, *Digest of Muhammedan Law*, London, Pt 1(1865), Pt II (1869) p. 51. It has been held that no formal decree is required to confirm the exercise of option of repudiation by a spouse. However, an order of judge is necessary to give it the force of law. See *Mafizuddin Mondol v Rahima Bibi* (1933) 58 Cal LJ 73, 1934 AC 104; *Pirmahommad v State of Madhya Pradesh* AIR 1960 MP 24.

[31] Crime in India, 1999.

[32] Village councils.

The discretionary power given under Section 376 of the IPC to decrease the sentence of the accused has been used in many cases to the detriment of the victims. For instance, in *Raju v State of Karnataka*,[33] considering the young age of the accused persons, one being twenty-four years and the other being twenty-one years, and the long lapse of time during which they suffered disrepute, sentence was reduced from seven years of rigorous imprisonment to three. In a case reported in 1987, an eleven-year-old girl was raped and she was pinned down to the floor and gagged. The session's court convicted the accused with five years' imprisonment. In an appeal, to enhance the sentence, the Madhya Pradesh High Court held that 'increasing cases of personal violence and crime rate cannot justify a severe sentence on young offenders'.[34] There are several such insensitive judgments.

The restrictive interpretation of 'penetration' in the Explanation to Section 375 is an obstacle to cases of CSA. Explanation to Section 375 does not treat forced sexual intercourse by a husband against the wife (above fifteen years) as an offence. Section 376-A also has the same reasoning.

The classification of penetrative abuse of a child below the age of twelve as unnatural offence under Section 377 or as outraging the modesty of a woman under Section 354 only depending on the type of penetration is wrong. It ignores the 'impact' of the abuse on the child and focuses more on technicalities. There is no provision to deal with the trauma of the child.

The Indian Penal Code needs to be reviewed. The existing definitions of rape and molestation should be suitably amended to adequately address the various types of sexual assault on children. Infact, sexual assault on children should be made a specific offence requiring stringent punishment.

Clearly, there is an urgent need for recognition of children's human rights and their need for legally mandated protection. The legal notion of sexual abuse of children is outdated. There are no procedural provisions concerned with ensuring successful prosecution of protecting the best interests of the child. The existing laws do not really provide relief to a child who has been sexually abused because of their built-in problems of a limited perspective and insensitive procedures.[35]

The Juvenile Welfare Boards are not equipped to deal with children who are victims of sexual abuse. The observation homes set up under the Juvenile Justice Act 1986 do not provide special care and treatment for victimized

---

[33] 1994 (1) SSC 453.
[34] *Vinod Kumar & Anr. v State of Madhya Pradesh*, 1987 CrLJ 1541.
[35] P.D. Mathew, 'Sexual Abuse of Children and the Law', *Legal News And Views*, May 1996.

children. The structures under the new Juvenile Justice (Care and Protection of Children) Act 2000 have still to be put in place.

The testimony of the child victim is not recorded sensitively by the police/judge/prosecutor/magistrate. The recording of the statements of child victims need a special provision in the CrPC. There is no such provision at present. Trained personnel should interview the victimized children. The language of the child has to be understood by the legal system. Under the present system, the natural habitat of the victim is generally disturbed which is a source of trauma to the child. The delays in the system at every stage further add to the trauma of the child victim. There are several cases pending in the courts as the trial goes on for years. In several cases the girls have become adults by the time the final judgment came through. The investigation of trial of sexual offences have to be made time bound. Special courts need to be set up.

The minor child is required to give his/her evidence in the presence of the accused as well as several 'strangers' in the court. In the jurisprudence of fair trail in India, exceptions of hearsay evidence are accepted in cases of dying declaration, murder victims, etc. Therefore, in case of child victim's testimony, such an exception could be made possible. A guardian ad litem or a representative of the child's interest could be appointed to help the child in court proceedings. It will be their job to look after the best interests of the child and convey it to the court. Section 155(4) of the Indian Evidence Act permits the person accused of rape or attempt to ravish to prove that the prosecutrix was of generally immoral character. During cross-examination in a prosecution for sexual assault, the previous sexual history/character of the victim is sought to be adduced to establish consent or otherwise. The Indian Evidence Act 1872 needs to be further amended to lay down that no corroboration of the evidence of child victim is required to prove the guilt of the accused. In a recent Supreme Court judgment, the court took a very positive stand by confirming the decision of the High Court by convicting the accused even though the prosecutrix could not be examined as she did not understand the sanctity of oath and affirmation.

There is a need for a special provision relating to medical examination of child victims in the CrPC. The absence of a proper medical report in the case of a sexual assault goes against the assaulted child. The mental health of the victim needs to be attended to as the trauma has to be reduced. It is experienced that limiting the exposure of the child to the courtroom and providing therapy for traumatized children produce more complete testimony. Such protective provisions for victims of child sexual abuse are possible under

Article 15(3) of the Constitution of India, which guarantees special protection to children.

Judicial Trends

Judgments Relating to Child Marriages

SMT SUSHILA GOTHALA V STATE OF RAJASTHAN AND OTHERS[36]

This petition was a public interest litigation. The petitioner had approached the court under Art 226 of the Constitution of India for issuance of direction to the respondents to stop immediately the menace of child marriage in Rajasthan in an effective manner, and further for a direction to punish the officer who is responsible for not prohibiting the child marriage, as per the provisions of the Child Marriage Restraint Act 1929. On the occasion of *Akha Teej*[37] every year, child marriages are performed in contravention of the Act as it is considered as an auspicious day for performing marriages.

The writ petition was disposed of with the observations that this social evil can be eradicated only if the people of Rajasthan themselves revolt against this age-old custom, which is primitive in nature and cannot be justified by any civilized society. The court further held that as per Section 13 of the Act, if the child marriage prevention officers have not been appointed, the government should consider the feasibility of making the provisions of the Act more stringent, and punishment for contravention of the Act should be severe.

WILLIAM REBELLO V AGNELO VAZ AND ANOTHER[38]

An application was filed for dispensing with the age limit of the marriage and to give necessary directions to the civil registration authority to register the marriage of the applicants. As Applicant No. 1 was not 21 years of age and could not marry, the court was requested to remove the impediment as both the parents had given consent for such marriage. In the application, it was also contended that as a result of a friendship between Applicants No. 1 and 2, Applicant No. 2 had become pregnant and the pregnancy was twenty weeks old.

The application for the removal of the impediment was entertained under the provisions of Article 5 of the Portuguese Civil Code and the trial

---

[36] AIR 1995 Rajasthan 90.
[37] The festival of *Akha Teej* is observed every year in the state of Rajasthan. It falls sometimes in the month of April and sometimes in the month of May.
[38] AIR 1996 Bombay 204.

judge, on the basis of the submissions made, considered the application and thought it fit to remove the impediment and accordingly allowed the application.

P. Venkataramana v State[39]

The question placed before the Full Bench was 'whether a Hindu marriage governed by the provisions of the Hindu Marriage Act 1955, where the parties to the marriage or either of them are below their respective ages as set out in Clause (iii) of Section 5 to the Hindu Marriage Act, is void ab initio and is no marriage in the eye of law'.

It was held that clause (iv) inserted in Subsection (2) of Section 13 clearly indicates the mind of the legislature that the violation of clause (iii) of Section 5 is not to render the marriage either void or voidable; but in case the bride was below the age of fifteen years at the time of solemnization of the marriage and she has repudiated the marriage after attaining the age of eighteen years, a decree for divorce can be obtained whether the marriage was consummated or not. If the marriage performed in contravention of clause (iii) of Section 5 was void ab initio, there was no necessity to insert clause (iv) in Subsection (2) of Section 13. It may be pointed out that, by insertion of this clause (iv), the legislature has given to the Hindus an option of what is known in Mohammedan law as *Khyar-ul-bulugh* (option of puberty). But the legislature has not proceeded on the footing that the marriage between the spouses, when it is performed in violation of clause (iii) of Section 5, is void ab initio. This amendment reinforces and confirms the view that we are taking on a pure interpretation of the different provisions of the Hindu Marriage Act 1955 even as it stood prior to its amendment by the Marriage Laws (Amendment) Act 1976.

It was held for these reasons that the decision of the Division Bench of this High Court in *P.A. Saramma v Ganapatulu*[40] does not lay down the correct law and that any marriage solemnized in contravention of clause (iii) of Section 5 is neither void nor voidable, the only consequence being that the persons concerned are liable for punishment under Section 18 and further if the requirements of clause (iv) of Subsection (2) of Section 13, as inserted by the Marriage Laws (Amendment) Act 1976 are satisfied, at the instance of the bride, a decree for divorce can be granted. Barring these two consequences, one arising under Section 18 and the other arising under clause (iv) of Subsection (2) of Section 13, after the enactment of the Marriage Laws

---

[39] AIR 1977 AP 43 (FB).
[40] AIR 1975 AP 193.

(Amendment) Act 1976, there is no other consequences whatsoever resulting from the contravention of the provisions of clause (iii) of Section 5.

Judgments on Other Non-commercial Forms of Child Sexual Abuse

DELHI DOMESTIC WORKING WOMEN'S FORUM v UOI[41]

The Supreme Court laid broad parameters in this case in assisting rape victims. The Court indicated the inherent defects in the present system as:

- Complaints are being handled roughly and not given due attention;
- The victims are, more often than not, humiliated by the police;
- The experience of furnishing evidence in court has been negative and destructive.

The court suggested the following guiding principles:

- The complainant of sexual assault is to be provided with legal representation; it being important to secure continuity of assistance by ensuring that the same person who looked after the complainant's interest in the police station represents her up to the end of the case.
- Legal assistance is to be provided at the police station as the victim would be in a state of distress.
- The police should be under a duty to inform the victim of her right to representation before any questions are asked of her and the police report should state so.
- Victims who do not have their own lawyers should be provided with a list of advocates at the police station.
- The Court upon application shall appoint the advocate by the police at the earliest convenient moment.
- In all rape trials anonymity of victims must be maintained as far as necessary.
- It is necessary having regard to the directive principles contained under Article 38(1) of the Constitution that victims are awarded compensation by the court on conviction of the offender.

NARAYANAMMA v STATE OF KARNATAKA[42]

The Supreme Court did not enhance the sentence of three years rigorous imprisonment passed by the trial court. It was held that merely because the prosecutrix was simple enough to repose confidence in the accused persons and stayed with them in a room in a hotel, it cannot be held that she was a consenting party.

[41] 1995 (1) SCC 14, 18 to 21.
[42] 1994 (1) SSC 728.

Ghanshyam Mishra v The State[43]

The High Court in this case had enhanced the sentence as the perpetrator of the offence had taken advantage of the teacher-student relationship he shared with the victim.

Tukaram & Another v The State of Maharashtra (Mathura's Case)[44]

Mathura, a girl aged between 14 and 16 years, was raped by two policemen attached to Desaigunj police station where she had gone along with others for recording a complaint. The sessions court held that the prosecution had failed to prove its case, and that Mathura was a 'shocking liar' whose testimony is riddled with falsehood and improbabilities and that, of her own free will, she had surrendered her body to a police constable. The medical examination showed old injuries on the hymen, and no semen stains were traced.

In an appeal, the High Court while convicting the accused observed: 'Mere passive or helpless surrender of the body and its resignation to the other's lust induced by threats or fear cannot be equated with the desire or will, nor can it furnish an answer by the mere fact that the sexual act was not in opposition to such desire or violation. On the other hand, taking advantage of the fact that Mathura was involved in a complaint filed by her brother and that she was alone at the police station at the dead of the night, it is more probable that the initiative for satisfying sexual desire must have proceeded from the accused and that the victim Mathura must not have been a willing party to the act of sexual intercourse. Her subsequent conduct in making a statement immediately not only to her relatives but also to the members of the crowd leave no manner of doubt that she was subjected to forcible sexual intercourse.'

The Supreme Court set aside this conviction on the grounds that sexual intercourse is not proved to amount to rape in the present case and that no offence is brought home. It further held that there were no circumstances available which made out a case of fear on the part of the girl and there was no finding that she was put into fear of death or hurt. Therefore, Section 375(3) of the Indian Penal Code does not apply. This judgment was severely criticized by women's organizations and led to the amendments of rape laws in India.

[43] AIR 1957 Orissa 78.
[44] 1979 2 SCC 143; AIR 1979 SC 185.

Gorakh Daji Ghadge v The State of Maharashtra[45]

This was a case where a father had raped his thirteen-year-old daughter in their home. The Mumbai High Court held that seminal emission is not necessary to establish rape. What is necessary to establish rape is that there must be penetration. The High Court has also dealt with the father-daughter relationship and stated that: 'Crimes in which women are victims need to be severely dealt with and in extreme cases such as this when the accused, who is the father of the victim girl, has thought it fit to 'deflower' his own daughter of tender years to gratify his lust, then only a deterrent sentence can meet the ends of justice.'

State of Punjab v Gurmit Singh

This case was with regard to the gang rape of a girl victim under sixteen years of age. The Supreme Court in this case settled several important points of law. First, it stated that the courts cannot overlook the fact that in case of sexual offences, the delay in lodging an FIR can be due to a variety of reasons, partly because of the reluctance of the prosecutrix and her family members to go to the police and complain about an incident which concerns the reputation of the prosecutrix and the honour of her family. Secondly, it also held that there is no requirement of law to insist upon corroboration of the statement of the prosecutrix for conviction of an accused and that corroborative evidence is not an imperative component of judicial credence in every case of rape.

While dealing with the importance of in-camera trial in rape cases, the Supreme Court observed that a trial in camera would not only be in keeping with the self-respect of the victim of the crime and in tune with the legislative intent, but it is also likely to improve the quality of the evidence of a prosecutrix because she would not be so hesitant or bashful to depose frankly as she may be in an open court under the gaze of the public.

Yashwant Rao v State of MP[46]

There was a rape of a minor girl aged around seven or eight years. It was held that there was no legal compulsion to look for corroboration of the evidence.

The trends of these decisions reflect that the approach and the attitude towards the rights of the child are gradually progressing beyond mere technicalities. But, there is still a long way to go. In one of the most outstanding

---

[45] 1980 CRLJ 1380.
[46] 1993 (Suppl 1) SCC 520.

cases of CSA, the Delhi High Court held that when a father in perverted company sexually molested and abused his daughter over a period of time, his acts amounted to acts against the order of nature, and charges could be framed under Section 377 of the IPC along with Sections 354 and 100 of the IPC, though not under Section 376. This decision was reached after considering comparable legislation of Western Australia, Canada, Washington State, Massachusetts law, Michigan Statute, British law, etc. The Court, after observing on the inadequacies of our archaic system of examination in court, laid down specific guidelines and directions for the trial judge to follow while hearing the case to avoid harassment, anxiety, and embarrassment to the child psyche. In another recent case of sexual violation of a four-year-old child who was said to have been molested, ravished, raped, and sodomized, the Supreme Court imposed a life sentence upon both the accused for the offence of culpable homicide not amounting to murder. The Supreme Court set aside the Delhi High Court order of acquittal, holding that the report of the doctor who conducted the autopsy with meticulous precision and the evidence of the investigating officer about recovery of articles, require to be believed unless shown to be unreliable.

The trial of sexual abuse cases is conducted in such an insensitive manner that a sexually abused child, rather than being treated for her own trauma, has to fight the adversarial system and end up in being further traumatized. The child has to be cross-examined by the defence lawyer who may use different strategies to get the answers desired. Lack of proper understanding of the law among the judges and insensitivity to child rights has resulted in the accused being discharged in several child sexual abuse cases.

The judges do not at all consider the issue of the child's trauma. Besides, the offence of sexual assault are generally tried by the criminal justice system under three different sections, viz., rape, attempt to rape, and molestation depending upon the proximity of molestation.

Law Reform

The need for a law on child sexual abuse was brought to the attention of the Supreme Court in the case of *Sakshi v Union of India & Ors*.[47] The petitioners submitted that the expression 'sexual intercourse' as contained in Section 375 of the Indian Penal Code should include all forms of penetration as the restrictive interpretation of penetration as existing in Section 375 defeated the very purpose and intent of the provision for punishment for rape under Section 376. The Indian Penal Code, the Indian Evidence Act, and the

---

[47] (1999) 6 SCC 591.

Criminal Procedure Code should be accordingly amended. Pursuant to the order passed by the Supreme Court in this matter, the Law Commission of India reviewed the laws related to child sexual abuse and recommended amendments to the Indian Penal Code in its 172nd report.*

Recommendations of the 172nd Law Commission Report

PROPOSED AMENDMENTS TO THE INDIAN PENAL CODE 1860(IPC)

- *Substitution of the existing Section 375 of the IPC recommended*: The existing Section 375 defining rape be substituted by the definition of sexual assault.[48] It has been attempted to include the common forms of child sexual abuse in this definition. The exception regarding marital rape has been retained.

[48] Sexual Assault: Sexual assault means—
(a) Penetrating the vagina (which term shall include the labia majora), the anus, or urethra of any person with:
 (i) any part of the body of another person or
 (ii) an object manipulated by another person
(b) Manipulating any part of the body of another person so as to cause penetration of the vagina (which term shall include the labia majora), the anus, or the urethra of the offender by any part of the other person's body;
(c) introducing any part of the penis of a person into the mouth of another person;
(d) engaging in cunnilingus or fellatio; or
(e) continuing sexual assault as defined in clauses
(a) to (d) above
in circumstances falling under any of the six following descriptions:
First—Against the other person's will;
Secondly—Without the other person's consent;
Thirdly—With the other person's consent when such consent has been obtained by putting such other person or any person in whom such other person is interested, in fear of death or hurt;
Fourthly—Where the other person is a female, with her consent, when the man knows that he is not the husband of such other person and that her consent is given because she believes that the offender is another man to whom she is or believes herself to be lawfully married;
Fifthly—With the consent of the other person, when, at the time of giving such consent, by reason of unsoundness of mind or intoxication or the administration by the offender personally or through another of any stupefying or unwholesome substance, the other person is unable to understand the nature and consequences of that to which such other person gives consent; and
Sixthly—With or without the other person's consent, when such other person is under sixteen years of age.
Explanation: Penetration to any extent is penetration for the purposes of this section.

- *Section 376 has been redefined to provide for punishment for sexual assault.*[49]
- *Punishment for sexual assault has been enhanced*: The minimum punishment has been recommended as five years by amending Sections 376B, 376C, and 376D.[50]

Exception: Sexual intercourse by a man with his own wife, the wife not being under sixteen years of age, is not sexual assault.

[49] Section 376. Punishment for sexual assault— (1) Whoever, except in the cases provided for by subsection

(2) commits sexual assault shall be punished with imprisonment of either description for a term which shall not be less than seven years but which may be for life or for a term which may extend to ten years and shall also be liable to fine unless the person subjected to sexual assault is his own wife and is not under sixteen years of age, in which case, he shall be punished with imprisonment of either description for a term which may extend to three years and shall also be liable to fine.

If the sexual assault is committed by a person in a position of trust or authority towards the person assaulted or by a near relative of the person assaulted, he/she shall be punished with rigorous imprisonment for a term which shall not be less than ten years but which may extend to life imprisonment and shall also be liable to fine.

Provided that the court may, for adequate and special reasons to be mentioned in the judgment, impose a sentence of imprisonment for a term of less than minimum punishment prescribed in this subsection.

(2) Whoever:
(a) being a police officer commits sexual assault:
   (i) within the limits of the police station to which he is appointed; or
   (ii) in the premises of any station house whether or not situated in the police station to which he is appointed; or
   (iii) on a person in his custody or in the custody of a police officer subordinate to him; or
(b) being a public servant, takes advantage of his official position and commits sexual assault on a person in his custody as such public servant or in the custody of a public servant subordinate to him; or
(c) being on the management or on the staff of a jail, remand home, or other place of custody established by or under any law for the time being in force, or of a women's or children's institution takes advantage of his official position and commits sexual assault on any inmate of such jail, remand home, place, or institution; or
(d) being on the management or on the staff of a hospital, takes advantage of his official position and commits sexual assault on a person in that hospital; or
(e) commits sexual assault on a woman knowing her to be pregnant; or
(f) commits sexual assault on a person when such person is under sixteen years of age; or
(g) commits gang sexual assault;
shall be punished with rigorous imprisonment for a term which shall not be less than ten years but which may be for life and shall also be liable to fine:

- *Insertion of a new section dealing with unlawful sexual contact*: A new Section 376E has been recommended to be added to the IPC, which deals with unlawful sexual contact. This section is intended to cover those forms of child sexual abuse wherein the abuser touches the victim with sexual intent either directly or indirectly with any part of the body or with an object. It also includes inciting or inviting or counselling and using undue influence with sexual intent to touch directly or indirectly with the part of the body or object.[51] Many common forms of sexual abuse occur in this manner. Complaints under this proposed offence have to be instituted by the aggrieved person or by his/her father, mother, and brother or by his/her father's or mother's brother or sister or by any other person related to him/her by blood or adoption.[52]

Provided that the court may, for adequate and special reasons to be mentioned in the judgment, impose a sentence of imprisonment of either description for a term of less than ten years.

Explanation 1—Where a person is subjected to sexual assault by one or more in a group of persons acting in furtherance of their common intention, each of the persons shall be deemed to have committed gang sexual assault within the meaning of this subsection.

Explanation 2—'Women's or children's institution' means an institution, whether called an orphanage or a home for neglected women or children or a widows' home or an institution called by any other name, which is established and maintained for the reception and care of women or children.

Explanation 3—'Hospital' means the precincts of the hospital and includes the precincts of any institution for the reception and treatment of persons during convalescence or of persons requiring medical attention or rehabilitation.

[50] The modified Sections 376A, 376B, and 376D of the IPC shall read as follows:

'376B. Sexual intercourse by public servant with person in his custody—Whoever, being a public servant, takes advantage of his/her official position and induces or seduces any person, who is in his custody as such public servant or in the custody of a public servant subordinate to him, to have sexual intercourse with him/her, such sexual intercourse not amounting to the offence of sexual assault, shall be punished with imprisonment of either description for a term which shall not be less than five years and which may extend to ten years and shall also be liable to fine.

Provided that the court may, for adequate and special reasons to be mentioned in the judgment, impose a sentence of imprisonment for a term of less than five years.

[51] 376E. IPC: Unlawful sexual contact: (1) Whoever, with sexual intent, touches, directly or indirectly, with a part of the body or with an object, any part of the body of another person, not being the spouse of such person, without the consent of such other person, shall be punished with simple imprisonment for a term which may extend to two years or with fine or with both.

(2) Whoever, with sexual intent, invites, counsels, or incites a young person to touch, directly or indirectly, with a part of the body or with an object, the body of any person, including the body of the person who so invites, counsels, or incites, or touches, with

- *Deletion of Section 377 of the IPC*: The controversial Section 377 IPC relating to unnatural offences, which was generally used in cases of boy child sexual abuse cases as there was no other adequate provision, to be deleted.[53]
- *Section 509 of the IPC to be amended*: The punishment for insulting the modesty of any woman by word, gesture, or act is to be enhanced from one year to three years.[54]
- *Insertion of new Section 166A IPC*: If any public servant knowingly disobeys any direction of the law requiring his attendance at any place or regarding the conduct of any investigation will be punished.[55]

---

sexual intent, directly or indirectly, with a part of the body or with an object any part of the body of a young person, shall be punished with imprisonment of either description which may extend to three years and shall also be liable to fine.

(3) Whoever, being in a position of trust or authority towards a young person, or is a person with whom the young person is in a relationship of dependency, touches, directly or indirectly, with sexual intent, with a part of the body or with an object, any part of the body of such young person, shall be punished with imprisonment of either description which may extend to seven years and shall also be liable to fine.

Explanation: 'Young person' in this subsection and Subsection (2) means a person below the age of sixteen years.'

[52] Insertion of Section 198B to the CrPC:
No court shall take cognizance of an offence punishable under Subsections (2) and (3) of Section 376E of the Indian Penal Code (45 of 1860) except upon a police report of facts which constitute such offence or upon a complaint made by the person aggrieved by the offence or by his/her father, mother, brother, sister, or by his/her father's or mother's brother or sister or, by any other person related to him/her by blood or adoption, if so permitted by the court.

[53] Section 377, IPC deserves to be deleted in the light of the changes effected by us in Sections 375 to 376E. We leave persons having carnal intercourse with any animal to their just deserts.

[54] Section 509, IPC—'Word, gesture, or act intended to insult the modesty of a woman: Whoever, intending to insult the modesty of any woman, utters any word, makes any sound or gesture, or exhibits any object intending that such word or sound shall be heard, or that such gesture or object shall be seen, by such woman, or intrudes upon the privacy of such woman, shall be punished with simple imprisonment for a term which may extend to three years and shall also be liable to fine.'

[55] 166A. Whoever, being a public servant:
(a) knowingly disobeys any direction of the law prohibiting him from requiring the attendance at any place of any person for the purpose of investigation into an offence or other matter, or
(b) knowingly disobeys any other direction of the law regulating the manner in which he shall conduct such investigation, to the prejudice of any person, shall be punished with imprisonment for a term which may extend to one year or with fine or with both.'

Proposed Amendments to the Criminal Procedure Code 1973 (CrPC)

- *Sections 160(3) and 164(4) and proviso of Section 160(1) to be amended*: In cases of sexual assault and unlawful sexual contact, the statement of the victim is to be recorded by a female police officer and in case a female police officer is not available, by a female government servant or in the alternative by a female authorized by an organization interested in the welfare of women and children. If none of them are available, the officer in charge of the police station will have to record the statement after giving the reasons in writing.[56] The recording of the statement of any woman or a male less than sixteen years (instead of fifteen years at present) has to be done at the place of residence in the presence of a relative, friend, or a social worker.

- *Insertion of Section 164A to the CrPC*: The medical examination of the victim of sexual assault should be by a registered medical practitioner with the consent of the victim. If the victim is a female, the medical examination has to be done by a female medical officer. The proposed amendment gives a format of the medical examination report. The details to be provided include name, address, age, injury marks, victim's mental condition and a reasoned conclusion.[57]

---

[56] Section 160(3) CrPC: Where the statement of a female is to be recorded either as first information of an offence or in the course of an investigation into an offence and she is a person against whom an offence under Sections 354, 375, 376, 376A, 376B, 376C, 376D, 376E, or 509 of the Indian Penal Code is alleged to have been committed or attempted, the statement shall be recorded by a female police officer and in case a female police officer is not available, by a female government servant available in the vicinity and in case a female government servant is also not available, by a female authorized by an organization interested in the welfare of women or children.

Subsection 160(4): Where in any case none of the alternatives mentioned in Subsection (3) can be followed for the reason that no female police officer or female government servant or a female authorized by an organization interested in the welfare of women and children is available, the officer in charge of the police station shall, after recording the reasons in writing, proceed with the recording of the statement of such female victim in the presence of a relative of the victim.

The proviso to Subsection (1) of Section 160 CrPC be substituted to read as follows: 'Provided that no male person under the age of sixteen years or woman shall be required to attend at any place other than the place in which such male person or woman resides. While recording the statement, a relative or a friend or a social worker of the choice of the person whose statement is being recorded shall be allowed to remain present. The relative, friend, or social worker so allowed to be present shall not interfere with the recording of statement in any manner whatsoever.'

[57] Section 376-A, 376-B, 376-C, 376-E CrPC (1) Where, during the stage when any

- *Insertion of Section 53A in the CrPC*: This proposed amendment relates to the medical examination of the accused of sexual assault by a registered medical practitioner. The report should include the name, address, age, marks of injury, who brought him, the duration of the medical examination, and any other details and a reasoned conclusion.[58]

---

offence under Section 376, Section 376A, Section 376B, Section 376C, Section 376D, or Section 376E is under investigation and it is proposed to get the victim examined by a medical expert, such examination shall be conducted by a registered medical practitioner, with the consent of the victim or of some person competent to give such consent on his/her behalf. In all cases, the victim should be sent for such examination without any delay. Provided that if the victim happens to be a female, the medical examination shall be conducted by a female medical officer, as far as possible.

(2) The registered medical practitioner to whom the victim is forwarded shall without delay examine the person and prepare a report specifically recording the result of his examination and giving the following details:
 (i) the name and address of the victim and the person by whom he/she was brought,
 (ii) the age of the victim,
 (iii) marks of injuries, if any, on the person of the victim,
 (iv) general mental condition of the victim, and
 (v) other material particulars, in reasonable detail.
(3) The report shall state precisely the reasons for each conclusion arrived at.
(4) The report shall specifically record that the consent of the victim or of some person competent to give such consent on his/her behalf to such examination had been obtained.
(5) The exact time of commencement and completion of the examination shall also be noted in the report, and the registered medical practitioner shall, without delay, forward the report to the investigating officer, who shall forward it to the magistrate referred to in Section 173 as part of the documents referred to in Clause (a) of Subsection (5) of that section.
(6) Nothing in this section shall be construed as rendering lawful any examination without the consent of the victim or any person competent to give such consent on his/her behalf.

[58] Section 53A CrPC: (1) When a person accused of any of the offences under Sections 376, 376A, 376B, 376C, 376D, or 376E, or of an attempt to commit any of the said offences, is arrested and an examination of his/her person is to be made under this section, he/she shall be sent without delay to the registered medical practitioner by whom he/she is to be examined.
(2) The registered medical practitioner conducting such examination shall without delay examine such person and prepare a report specifically recording the result of his examination and giving the following particulars:
 (i) the name and address of the accused and the person by whom he was brought, the duration of the medical examination,

- *A proviso to be added to Section 273 CrPC*: While taking evidence of a sexual assault victim who is below sixteen years of age, appropriate measures have to be taken so as to avoid confrontation by the accused.[59]

PROPOSED AMENDMENTS TO THE INDIAN EVIDENCE ACT 1872 (IEA)

Sections 114A and 146 of the IEA to be amended: In a prosecution for sexual assault and unlawful sexual contact or an attempt to commit such offences, if the victim states in her evidence that she did not consent, the court shall so presume. This will be a rebuttable presumption of law.[60] It has also been proposed that in such cases, the evidence of the character or the past sexual history of the victim will not be relevant.[61]

Recommendations not Accepted by the Law Commission

There are certain recommendations which were made in the petition by *Sakshi* but were not accepted by the 172nd Law Commission Report and

---

(ii) the age of the accused,
(iii) marks of injury, if any, on the person of the accused, and
(iv) other material particulars, in reasonable detail.
(3) The report shall state precisely the reasons for each conclusion arrived at.
(4) The exact time of commencement and completion of the examination shall also be noted in the report, and the registered medical practitioner shall, without delay, forward the report to the investigating officer, who shall forward it to the magistrate referred to in Section 173 as part of the documents referred to in Clause (a) of Subsection (5) of that section.

[59] 'Provided that where the evidence of a person below sixteen years, who is alleged to have been subjected to sexual assault or any other sexual offence, is to be recorded, the court may take appropriate measures to ensure that such person is not confronted by the accused while at the same time ensuring the right of cross-examination of the accused.'

[60] Section 114A IEA: Presumption as to absence of consent in certain prosecutions for sexual assault: In a prosecution for sexual assault under Clause (a) or Clause (b) or Clause (c) or Clause (d) or Clause (e) or Clause (g) of Subsection (2) of Section 376 of the Indian Penal Code (45 of 1860) where sexual intercourse by the accused is proved and the question is whether it was without the consent of the other person alleged to have been sexually assaulted and such other person states in his/her evidence before the court that he/she did not consent, the court shall presume that he/she did not consent.

Explanation: 'Sexual intercourse' in this section and Sections 376C and 376D shall mean any of the acts mentioned in Clauses (a) to (e) of Section 375. Explanation to Section 375 shall also be applicable.

[61] Section 53A IEA 1973: In a prosecution for an offence under Sections 376, 376A, 376B, 376C, 376D, or 376E, or for attempt to commit any such offence, where the question of consent is in issue, evidence of the character of the victim or of his/her previous sexual experience with any person shall not be relevant on the issue of such consent or the quality of consent.

which need to be incorporated in the laws relating to CSA to make the law more effective and child friendly. They are as follows:

- Exception to Section 375 not deleted [sexual intercourse by a man with his own wife (above sixteen years) is not sexual assault]. Marital rape has still not been recognized in the Indian legal system.
- Second proviso to Section 376(1) and the proviso to Section 376(2) (which confer a discretion upon the court to award a sentence lesser than the minimum punishment) are not deleted. The discretion still remains.
- Definition of 'consent' has not been considered. It is important to define as to what consent is in rape cases. In Mathura's case, the court regarded absence of marks of injury as consent. Such interpretations need to be prevented in future.
- No mandatory provision has been laid down for investigation of offences of rape and other sexual offences by women police officers only.
- While granting bail to a person accused of sexual assault, one of the conditions which should be imposed by the court shall be that such person shall not be in the proximity of the person. No provision has been made relating to this aspect.
- No provisions have been made for non-interference with or disturbance of the natural habitat of the person sexually assaulted by or through the criminal justice process and for the investigation of trial of sexual offences to be time bound and to be concluded within six months.
- The expression 'social worker' is not defined.
- There is no presumption in respect of the age of victim. The age of the victim will have to be proved. As mentioned earlier, the age of proof is a very cumbersome process, at present, as many children do not have documentary evidence and the medical evidence has to be relied on.
- There is no provision for safe environment in which the child can recover. (Recording of evidence of minor by video tape/circuit television or appropriate breaks not provided for).

In Section 146 of the Indian Evidence Act, the following clause shall be added after Clause (3):

'(4) In a prosecution for an offence under Sections 376, 376A, 376B, 376C, 376D, or 376E, or for attempt to commit any such offence, where the question of consent is in issue, it shall not be permissible to adduce evidence or to put questions in the cross-examination of the victim as to his/her general immoral character, or as to his/her previous sexual experience with any person for proving such consent or the quality of consent.'

- There is no provision for trial by special courts (this suggestion was considered impractical by the Law Commission).

International Legal Initiatives

The United Nations Convention on the Rights of the Child (CRC), which has been ratified by several countries including India, gives a common, cross-national, comprehensive foundation standard for all the world's children. Article 11 prohibits the illegal transfer of children abroad. Article 19 refers to the State's obligation to protect children from all forms of physical or mental violence, injury or abuse, negligent treatment, maltreatment, or exploitation including sexual abuse perpetrated by parents or others responsible for their care. Article 34 enjoins the State parties to protect the child from all forms of sexual exploitation and abuse.

Some International Best Practices

WORKING TOGETHER TO DEAL WITH CHILD SEXUAL ABUSE

Interdisciplinary and inter-agency work is an essential process in the task of attending to protect children from abuse. Local systems for inter-agency cooperation have been set up throughout England and Wales. The experience gained by professionals in working and training together has succeeded in bringing about a greater mutual understanding of the roles of the various professions and agencies and a greater ability to combine their skills in the interest of abused children and their families. In every local authority area there is a close working relationship between social services departments, the police service, medical practitioners, community health workers, the education service, and others who share a common aim to protect the child at risk. Cooperation at the level of individual cases is supported by joint agency and management policies for child protection, consistent with their policies and plans for related service provision. There is a recognized joint forum for developing, monitoring, and reviewing child protection policies. This forum is the *Area Child Protection Committee (ACPC)* in the UK. Similar multidisciplinary forum in USA is the *Child Protection Services. The Dutch Child Protection Boards*[62] are a public service under the control of the Ministry of justice in Netherlands. The Boards receive reports from mental health agencies, schools, the confidential doctors, the police, and so on, and investigate whether the rights of the child are being violated and how that violation

---

[62] L. Bette Bottoms and Gail S. Goodman (eds), *International Perspectives on Child Abuse and Children's Testimony*, Sage Publications Inc., New York, 1996.

influences the child's normal development. They also seek to determine the causes of the violation and the measures necessary to restore the rights of the child.[63] Investigations are carried out by social workers, but contrary to usual practice in the United States and the United Kingdom, the social workers of the Child Protection Boards usually do not interview a child about alleged sexual abuse.

Mandatory Reporting Laws

In India, under the present legal system there are no mandatory reporting systems of cases relating to child sexual abuse. The United States has detailed statutory provisions to deal with the issue of detection and prevention. All their states have enacted child abuse reporting statutes by 1967, with the following basic elements:

- A definition of conditions worthy of reporting,
- List of persons that required reporting,
- The degree of certainty required warranting reporting the suspected abuse,
- Penalties imposed for failure to report, and
- Delineation of the reporting procedures.

TV Link Courts (Closed-Circuit Television)

A child is competent to testify if it can understand the question and give rational answers. The right to confrontation requires the accused to see the witness and vice versa. In case of child sexual abuse, the child victim is the main witness. In *Coy v Lowa*, 487 US1012 (1988), the court held that there could be exceptions to this rule where it is required to further an important public policy such as the protection of children. In *Maryland v Craig*, 497 US805 (1990), a closed-circuit TV was used at the stage of recording the testimony of an alleged victim of child abuse as the child was under serious emotional distress and found it difficult to communicate. The Supreme Court of the USA has held that, 'The State's interest in the physical and psychological well-being of child abuse victims may be sufficiently important to outweigh a defendant's right to face-to-face confrontation since the State has a competing interest in protecting minor victims of sex crimes from further trauma and embarrassment.'[64]

---

[63] T. Veldkamp, 'De toekomst van de kinderbescherming [The Future of child protection]', In A. Groen and A. van Montfoort (eds), *Kinderen Beschermen en jeugd hulp verlenen* [*Protecting and helping children*], Arnhem, the Netherlands: Gouda Quint, 1993, pp. 93–113.

[64] L. Bette Bottoms and Gail S. Goodman, *International Perspectives on Child Abuse and Children's Testimony*, Sage Publications, New Delhi, 1996.

Under Sections 32 and 32A of the Criminal Justice Act 1988, in the UK in the Crown Court or in the youth courts, a child may, at the discretion of the court, give evidence in chief by means of a video and/or be questioned during the trial via a live CCTV link. These provisions apply to child witnesses under the age of fourteen years in the case of offences of violence or cruelty, and to child witnesses under seventeen years of age in the case sex offences. The provisions apply to any child witness (with prosecution and defence), other than the accused if she is a child. Underrepresented defendants are also prohibited, under Section 34A of the 1988 Act, from cross-examining child witnesses, or a witness who is to be cross-examined following the admission of video evidence. Other measures such as the use of screens or the removal of wigs and gowns, can be used at the court's discretion on a non-statutory basis.

Legislation allowing the use of closed-circuit television for child witnesses has been enacted in most Australian states. For example, the Evidence (Closed-Circuit Television) Act 1991 provides that a court may order the use of closed-circuit television. The legislation provides that the court is not to make an order if it considers that to do so would be unfair to any disability in the child as well as the importance of the matters on which the child is called upon to give evidence. It can be seen that closed-circuit television is not an automatic right, with the court needing to be satisfied in each case that its use would be an advantage over the ordinary method of testifying.

LEGAL INTERVIEWING

Experts in the field of children must conduct legal interviewing of the child victim. Different strategies may be utilized in different circumstances to obtain an appropriate response from the child.[65] These include:

- Open questions, i.e. questions that allow the child to narrate their own point of view.
- Closed questions, i.e. questions that can be answered only with a 'yes' or 'no'.
- Choice questions, i.e. questions that suggest one of two given possibilities.
- Hypothetical questions, i.e. questions that raise a topic introduced by the interviewer.

A specially trained and skilled interviewer interviews a child and it is this interviewer who interprets the child's narrative and presents it before the

---

[65] Maharukh Adenwalla, *Child Sexual Abuse and the Law*, India Centre for Human Rights and Law, Mumbai, 2000.

court. It is the interviewer and not the child who gives evidence and faces cross-examination under the law of Israel. Under Texan law an out of court statement of a child witness is admissible as evidence without producing the child for cross-examination if, the totality of the circumstances render the statement reliable, and the facts of a particular case indicate that use of out-of-court testimony is necessary to protect the child. Under the Magistrate's Courts Act, a child is not to be normally called as witness for the prosecution; any statement made in writing by a child should be treated as admissible in evidence in any matter in which his/her oral testimony would be admissible. The Report of the Advisory Group on Video Evidence in 1989 recommended that both examination-in-chief, i.e. the interview, and cross-examination should be video-recorded and produced before the court as evidence. Though, under the British law, the procedure adopted is the replacing of examination-in-chief by the video-recorded interview of the child.

ASSISTANCE TO VICTIMS

Payment of compensation may be awarded to the victim in both civil and criminal proceedings. Compensation is necessary as often the harm suffered by the child limits his/her ability to acquire an education and earn living. The payment of compensation is in addition to penal sentences in criminal proceedings. Criminal Inquiries Compensation Boards have been constituted under the Children's Act 1989 (United Kingdom) for payment of compensation to victims of child abuse who have sustained physical injury as a result of a crime of violence. The Juvenile Justice Coalition and the Victim Assistance Programme have been set up under the American law to assist victims of child sexual abuse. The Juvenile Justice Coalition include, service providers, mental health professionals, doctors, and lawyers. They assist the child in dealing with legal procedures. The Victim Assistance Programme assists sexually abused children after the indictment has been obtained. In the Delhi Domestic Working Women's Forum case,[66] the Supreme Court has directed the establishment of Criminal Injuries Compensation Board for awarding compensation to rape survivors. These Boards have to be set up immediately.

DELAYED DISCOVERY STATUTE

A provision requires to be incorporated under the law to extend the limitation period for survivors of child sexual abuse. Extension of statue of limitation will ensure that crimes against children can be initiated even several

---

[66] (1995),1 SCC 14.

years after the offence has been committed. The period of limitation runs form attaining majority or from the child victim becoming aware of the incident. Victims of child sexual abuse often suffer from repressed memory or post-traumatic stress disorder. The law perceives these as constituting 'insanity' and therefore, the period of limitation will run once the disability is removed. Under the Alaskan law, a criminal prosecution for sexual offences against a victim less than eighteen years of age may be commenced at any time. The law prevailing in New Hampshire allows a criminal prosecution to be brought up to twenty-two years after the victim has attained eighteen years of age. Under the California Code of Civil Procedure, the Delayed Discovery Statute applies to perpetuators of the offence as well as liable third parties, i.e. a person entity who owes a duty of due care to the victim. Several adult survives of child sexual abuse will benefit from such a statute.

WITNESS SUPPORT SYSTEM

In the UK, child witnesses are entitled to assistance to prepare for the court experience.[67] The child witness supporter should ask children if they would like the parent or carer, or some other supportive adult who is close to the child, to be present during preparation sessions. Such people can play a critical role in the child's ability to cope with the court case and in reinforcing messages.

CHILD WITNESS CODE[68]

In the US, there is a Child Witness Code. The code draws heavily on the existing law in the United States and several other countries. The purpose of this code is to ascertain the truth, reduce trauma to children, create conditions that will allow children to provide reliable and complete evidence, increase the number of children who are able to testify in legal proceedings, and protect the rights of persons accused of crime.

The salient features of the code are:

- The court shall give docket priority for a speedy trial to any criminal case involving a child victim.
- Programmes designed to prepare children to testify serve the interests of justice and are encouraged.

---

[67] *Preparing Young Witnesses for Court—A handbook for child witness supporters*, National Society for the Prevention of Cruelty to Children (NSPCC) and Childline, 1998.

[68] L. Bette Bottoms and Gail S. Goodman (eds), *International Perspectives on Child Abuse and Children's Testimony*, Sage Publications Inc., New York, 1996.

- Waiting area for child witnesses.
- The court shall appoint a guardian ad litem for a child who has been a victim of, or a witness to, a crime to protect the best interests of the child.
- A child satisfying a judicial proceeding or deposition shall have the right to be accompanied by up to two persons of the child's own choosing.
- Every child, irrespective of age, is qualified to be a witness unless the child lacks the ability to communicate, remember, distinguish truth from falsehood, or appreciate the duty to tell the truth in court.
- Interpreter for child.
- While testifying, a child shall be allowed to have a comfort item of the child's own choosing such as a blanket, toy, or doll.
- Rearranging courtroom.
- Leading questions can be asked during direct examination.
- Live link television testimony.
- Closing the courtroom.
- Videotape deposition.
- Screens and other devices to shield the child from the defendant.
- Protection of child's privacy and safety.
- Child hearsay exception.
- Multidisciplinary team investigation and interviewing.
- Videotaping and audiotaping investigative interviews.

The Indian legal system needs to adopt some of these international best practices in the interest of the child and to make the legal system more children friendly.

Role Played by NGOs and the Government in Child Sexual Abuse Cases

Interventions in CSA cases are generally in the form of bringing cases of such abuse to the notice of the police and the court, helping the police and the courts in investigating these cases sensitively. Forum Against Child Sexual Abuse (FACSE) is a group of interested activists. The group has brought to light several cases of child sexual abuse. Trauma counselling is also provided by the Forum to the victims of child sexual abuse and exploitation in institutions.

The Maharashtra State Monitoring Committee on Juvenile Justice set up by the Mumbai High Court[69] has also investigated and sent reports to the

---

[69] See the decision in the case of *Krist Pereira v the State of Maharashtra & Ors*, Crim. Writ Petition No. 1107 of 1996, Mumbai High Court.

Mumbai High Court on cases of child sexual abuse. The Court has issued directions to the authorities concerned to follow up these cases.

The legal processes involved in the entire prosecution of child sexual abuse have to be seen in the best interest of the child right from the stage of the decision to file a complaint, to the registration of the FIR and filing a charge sheet, and making the decision to commence trial proceeding and of course the trial in the courts. There is thus a need to amend both the substantive and procedural laws to ensure successful prosecution and protect the best interest of the child. Law reform alone cannot bring about justice to the child. Inter-agency structures and systems need to be worked out laying great emphasis on prevention. Undoubtedly, the most effective prevention measure is awareness of such possible abuse and of how to deal with it amongst the various service providers—doctors, teachers, lawyers, judges, police, volunteers, parents, and social workers so that they can significantly reduce the risk of abuse and respond appropriately, if it does occur.[70]

PART B: COMMERCIAL SEXUAL EXPLOITATION AND TRAFFICKING OF CHILDREN

Introduction

The nightmare of child abuse takes a more alarming turn when placed in the context of organized exploitation for commercial gain. Sexual exploitation of children involves the use of children for sexual activities for material gains to the children themselves or others. Child prostitution is a term in popular usage but is inaccurate because it implies consent. And a child does not consent. Sexual exploitation of a child occurs at an age when consent has no meaning. He/she is rather victimised into sexual slavery for profit. Child sexual exploitation involves power relations and social structures.

Cutting across class, caste, and gender there is an emerging scenario of child vulnerability *per se*. The groups at risk and the areas prone to commercial sexual exploitation of children can be identified as follows:[71]
Children in general are at risk but the high-risk groups of children can be identified as:

- Children living in brothels;
- Children living in communities where religious and cultural norms

---

[70] Asha Bajpai, 'The Sexual Abuse and Exploitation of Children', *One India, One People*, Sept., 1999.
[71] Report on the Six Regional Consultations on Sexual Exploitation and Trafficking of Children, sponsored by the department of women and child development, Government of India, and UNICEF, India.

force them into prostitution, such as *jogins, devadasi, basavis, bedias, bancharas, dommaras, venkatasanis,* etc.;
- Street children, slum children, and children without shelter;
- Children of alcoholic parents and drug traffickers;
- Children who have been sexually abused, raped, molested, and stigmatized;
- Child widows and those deserted by husbands;
- Children employed as domestic help;
- Children born to AIDS victims;
- Children detained in custodial and educational institutions away from families;
- Children affected by terrorism and natural calamities;
- Children of families affected by displacement and sickness in industries;
- Children affected by transitory poverty in families;
- Children in refugee camps;
- Children of bonded labourers;
- Children of low-skilled or un-employed labour;
- Children of broken and disturbed families, and
- Migrant children

The vulnerable areas are:

- State and national highways;
- Areas from where locals displaced due to big projects and ventures are forced to migrate and settle without proper rehabilitation, e.g. tribal areas;
- Areas experiencing closure or failure of industry;
- Residential schools, childcare institutions, and jails where children are illegally detained;
- Beauty parlours, massage homes, health clubs, and casinos;
- Areas prone to natural disasters such as floods and drought;
- Inhospitable terrain such as deserts and mountainous areas and arid zones;
- Quarry and construction sites;
- Industries involving child labour; and
- Coastal belt, especially tourist resorts where children become victims of paedophiles.

The origin of child sexual exploitation lies only in the circumstances in which a young victim is gainfully subjected to sell his/her body to satiate the sexual urges of another person. The sexual exploitation of children does not occur in a vacuum but involves a more widespread exploitation, sexual or otherwise. Sexual exploiters include not only 'users' but also 'suppliers', viz. pimps, brothel owners, parents etc., and the 'protectors', viz. government officials, local politicians, police, etc. Poverty and ignorance are the underlying causes of this worldwide phenomenon, as families rely on their youngest members to contribute to the household income.

The propelling factor which actualizes commercial sex exploitation of children is the role played by traffickers. The traffickers, through various modus operandi, take the children through unknown and unfamiliar routes to make retracing practically impossible, and they cut off the children from their roots and alienate and isolate them. 'Trafficking' as a phenomenon has been defined by the UN General Assembly in 1994 as: the illicit and clandestine movement of persons across national and international borders, largely from developing countries, with the end goal of forcing women and girl children into economically oppressive and exploitative situations for the profit of recruiters, traffickers, and crime syndicates as well as other illegal activities such as forced domestic labour, false marriage, clandestine employment, and forced adoption'. The element of migration, with or without consent, to an alien exploitative environment is an essential component of the concept of trafficking. Globalization, liberalization, and feminization of poverty have only aggravated the situation. Though there are no comprehensive and absolutely reliable statistics to that effect, it is a known and acknowledged fact that trafficking women and girls for labour and commercial sexual exploitation is on the rise in India. This includes not merely cross-border trafficking but also transportation of victims from less developed rural areas to urban markets where there is a rising demand. There are now many routes by which children are being moved from one country to another by criminal networks. Children are trafficked (on the supply side) for prostitution, begging, organ transplant, pornographic and other unlawful sexual activities, child brides, camel races, and for supposedly good jobs that lead to prostitution. The demand for children to be trafficked comes from the clients, pimps, procurers, brothel owners, police, guardians, and parents. There is a pervasive and powerful alliance, always adult-dominant, in society which originates, perpetuates, and proliferates this demand. Perfect market conditions exist in the sex trade, where there is unfailing supply of children to meet the burgeoning demand. The definition of trafficking by the UN General Assembly clearly indicates that trafficking has the distinct components of recruitment, movement through transportation, forced or slavery-like labour, and third-party profit.

250 *Child Rights in India*

At the time of recruitment, it is possible that all or some of the members of the family are instrumental, or at least aware of the trafficking. In fact, this assumes importance from the point of view of action. The issue is of the person in authority taking advantage of the vulnerability of the individual to be trafficked. The traffickers are generally more than one individual and often change hands to avoid getting caught during transit. Different kinds of traffickers have been identified, like nexus-organized crime gangs, police, pimps, and even politicians. Unfortunately, peer trafficking too occurs in cases where children themselves are used to force or entice other children.

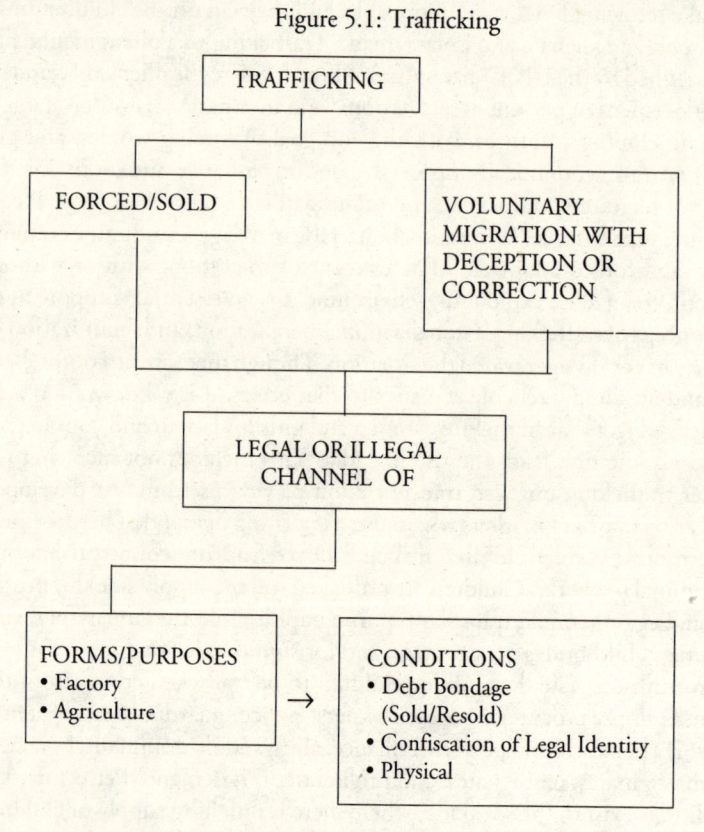

Figure 5.1: Trafficking

```
                    ┌──────────────┐
                    │ TRAFFICKING  │
                    └──────┬───────┘
              ┌────────────┴────────────┐
      ┌───────┴───────┐         ┌───────┴──────────┐
      │ FORCED/SOLD   │         │ VOLUNTARY        │
      │               │         │ MIGRATION WITH   │
      │               │         │ DECEPTION OR     │
      │               │         │ CORRECTION       │
      └───────┬───────┘         └────────┬─────────┘
              └────────────┬─────────────┘
                    ┌──────┴───────────┐
                    │ LEGAL OR ILLEGAL │
                    │ CHANNEL OF       │
                    └──────┬───────────┘
              ┌────────────┴─────────────┐
      ┌───────┴────────┐        ┌────────┴──────────────────┐
      │ FORMS/PURPOSES │   →    │ CONDITIONS                │
      │ • Factory      │        │ • Debt Bondage            │
      │ • Agriculture  │        │   (Sold/Resold)           │
      │                │        │ • Confiscation of Legal   │
      │                │        │   Identity                │
      │                │        │ • Physical                │
      └────────────────┘        └───────────────────────────┘
```

Source: Global Alliance Against Traffic in Women[72]

[72] 'Global Alliance Against Trafficking in Women', *Human Rights and Trafficking in Persons: A Hand Book*, Bangkok, Thailand, 2001.

The transportation routes normally used are the existing roads, railway lines, river routes, and open borders. Needless to say, those earning third-party profit are the least affected by the altered social situation. Figure 5.1 in previous page illustrates the different aspects of trafficking in a flow diagram.

Sex Tourism

The rapid growth of tourism during the 1970s and 1980s has coincided, in several countries, with the emergence or expansion of the child sex industry. The World Tourism Organization has defined sex tourism as 'trips organised with the primary purpose of effecting a commercial sexual relationship by the tourist with the residents at the destination'. Sex tourism is attaining global dimensions through the Internet. The advent of sex tourism in India has rung the death knell for the thousands of children who are being forced into sexual slavery.

Child Pornography

Child pornography which is the audio-visual material using children in a sexual context is another form of commercial sexual exploitation of children and is in great demand. India and other South Asian countries are slowly replacing South East Asia as the venue of choice for foreigners as there are fewer laws against child sexual abuse and South Asian children can be bought more cheaply.[73] Sex offenders commit crimes in other countries and return to their own, confident that the law enforcement agencies of the third world countries will not be able to catch up with them.

Sexually explicit material exists on the Internet. Such material includes text, pictures, and chat, and includes bulletin boards, news groups, and other forms of Internet communication, and extends from the modestly titillating to the hardest core. The two main ways in which children may potentially be harmed by child pornography are by being exposed to pornography and by being filmed or photographed or made the subjects themselves in some other way. Teenagers are particularly at risk because they often use the computer unsupervised and because they are more likely than younger ones to participate in online discussions regarding companionship, relationship, or sexual activity. These risks include exposure to inappropriate material of a sexual or violent nature, or encountering email or bulletin-board messages that are demeaning or belligerent. Another risk is the possibility that, while

---

[73] Child Prostitution—The Ultimate Abuse, Report on The National Consultation on Child Prostitution, 18–20 Nov. 1995, New Delhi, Organized by the Young Men's Christian Association (YMCA), End Child Prostitution in Asian Tourism (ECPAT), and UNICEF.

online, the child may provide information or arrange an encounter that could risk his or her safety or the safety of other family members. In a few cases pedophiles have used online services and bulletin boards to gain a child's confidence and then arrange a face-to-face interview.

The advances in computer technology, including the use of camcorders, VCRs, home-editing desks, computer-generated graphics, and editing have made the creation and distribution of pornography easier, cheaper, and more difficult to detect. It has developed into a multi-billion-dollar industry which can be run from within the exploiter's home. Every photograph or videotape of child pornography is evidence of that child's abuse. The distribution of that depiction repeats the victimization over and over again, long after the original material was created.

The Indian Scenario

India has the dubious distinction of being the source, transit, and destination country—all in one. There are various forms of trafficking within the Indian context, even though trafficking has most often been linked to prostitution. The issues of forced marriage for labour and other forms of forced labour in agriculture as well as industry, domestic service, begging, camel jockeying, organ transplant, etc., cannot be ignored. Entry and consolidation of major crime syndicates in the sphere of trafficking makes it difficult to probe and intervene into specific cases. Evidence of trafficking for forced begging, marriage, and labour in informal work ghettoes are on the rise within the Indian context. There are some evident forms of trafficking with religious or community sanction—the *Bassani*s, *Jogini*s, *Bhogam Vandhi*s, and *Venkatesini*s in Andhra Pradesh; the *Murali*s, *Aradhini*s, and *Tamasha* girls in Maharashtra; the *Thevadiyar*s in Tamil Nadu; the *Bedia*, *Bachhda* and *Sansi* communities in Madhya Pradesh; and the *Nat* community in Uttar Pradesh. The community justifies and legitimizes the practice and, ultimately, many of the victims get trafficked into prostitution.

In India, traditional systems of children in prostitution varied as the *devdasi* or the *Jogini*, and the trafficking system that moves young girls across South Asia and into urban centres reveal the active exploitation and the socio-economic realities that make such exploitation possible. In the last few years, increasing number of instances of commercial sexual exploitation of children have also come to light in popular tourist destinations like Goa.

A survey sponsored by the Central Social Welfare Board (CSWB) in 1991 in six metropolitan cities of India indicated that the population of women and child victims of commercial sexual exploitation would be between

70,000 to 100,000. It also revealed that about 30 per cent of them are below eighteen years of age. The major contributory factors for the commercial sexual exploitation of women and children are poverty and unemployment or lack of appropriate rehabilitation. Seventy per cent of them are illiterates; 43 per cent of them desire to be rescued. Most of those who want to leave have given the reasons like desire to save their children from commercial sexual exploitation, protection of the future of their children, fear of diseases, etc. The others continue to be exploited due to absence of alternative sources of income, social non-acceptability, family customs, poverty, ill health, and their despondence.

Indian Laws Dealing with Commercial Sexual Exploitation of Children and Trafficking

According to Article 23 of the Constitution of India, trafficking in women and children for immoral purposes is prohibited. Articles 39(e) and (f) of the directive principles of State policy state that it is the duty of the state to secure that the tender age of children are not abused and forced by economic necessity to enter vocations unsuited to their age and strength and directs the state to ensure that the children are given opportunities to develop in a healthy manner and in conditions of freedom and dignity.

Trafficking was first dealt with by The Suppression of Immoral Traffic in Women and Girls Act 1956 (SITA), which was passed on 31 December 1956. The legislation was enacted in pursuance of the UN Convention of 1950.[74] This Act had several loopholes. Some of the drawbacks were:[75]

- The Act did not conform fully to the international convention on the subject.
- The definition of prostitution was unsatisfactory.
- No provision for dealing with policing and punishment of criminals who have set up interstate and international networks to procure children.
- No specific provisions to deal with prostitution of children.
- No provision for dealing with sexual exploitation of boys.
- Lesser sentence compared to that in the Indian Penal Code to offenders who induct children and women into prostitution.

[74] UN Convention for the Suppression of Traffic in Persons and of Exploitation of the Prostitution of Others. This was approved by the General Assembly resolution 317(iv) of 2 December 1949. In 1950, the Government of India ratified this Convention.
[75] Sheela Barse, *A Critique of the Suppression of Immoral Traffic in Women and Girls Act 1956*, Neer Gaurav Research and Development Foundation, Mumbai, India.

- Customer not made accountable.
- Protective homes set up under the Act were mainly custody homes and not properly staffed.
- No provision for the children of prostitutes.
- No accountability placed on the superintendent of the protective homes.

The Immoral Traffic (Prevention) Act 1956 (ITPA or PITA)

The Suppression of Immoral Traffic in Women and Girls Act 1956, proved to be inadequate to combat the increasing commercialization of trafficking. Parliament amended the law in 1970 and later in 1986. The suppression of Immoral Traffic in Womens and Girls Act 1956 was amended by:

- The Suppression of Immoral Traffic in Women and Girls (Amendment) Act 1978 (46 of 1978) w.e.f. 2 October 1979, and
- The Suppression of Immoral Traffic in Women and Girls (Amendment) Act 1986 (44 of 1986) w.e.f. 26 January 1987.

As a result of substitution of the words 'Immoral Traffic (Prevention) Act' for the words 'Suppression of Immoral Traffic in Women and Girls Act' made by Section 3 of the amending Act No. 44 of 1986, the principal Act was shorttitled as the Immoral Traffic (Prevention) Act, (104 OF 1956). This Act does not make prostitution *per se* a criminal offence or punish a person because the person prostitutes himself or herself. The purpose of the enactment is to inhibit or abolish commercialized sexual abuse and exploitation and the traffic in persons as an organized means of living. The object is attempted to be achieved by two major strategies, namely, by punishing those who are guilty of such conduct and by rescuing and rehabilitating the victims of such exploitation.[76]

Prostitution under this Act means the sexual exploitation or abuse of persons for commercial purposes and the expression 'prostitute' should be construed accordingly.[77] This definition is wider and includes sexual exploitation and abuse of any person—female, eunuch, or male—for commercial purposes. The Act has introduced the concept of child[78] victims as against

---

[76] N.R.M. Menon, *Prevention of Immoral Traffic and Restoration of Human Dignity*, Select Materials on Public Legal Education, Legal Services Clinic, National Law of India University, Bangalore, 1991.

[77] The Immoral Traffic (Prevention) Act, 1986, Section 2(f).

[78] 'Child' means a person who has not completed the age of sixteen years—Sec. 2(aa) ITPA 1986.

minors[79] and majors[80] and imposes higher degree of criminality to sexual exploiters of children.

By the use of presumptions, the burden of the prosecution is lightened by the ITPA 1986. There are certain presumptions under the Act in favour of the child victims. These are:

- If a child is found in a brothel or under suspicious circumstances in the custody of a person, other than the parent or lawful guardian who is unable to explain satisfactorily the presence of such a child, that person shall be presumed to have procured the child for the purposes of prostitution.
- A report in a newspaper on the use of certain premises as a brothel is deemed to be sufficient proof of the landlord, occupier, or tenant knowingly allowing such use.
- If a child is found accompanying, in suspicious circumstances,[81] a person who is neither its parent or lawful guardian and who is leaving the country, that person is committing the offence of immoral trafficking.

Rescue and Rehabilitation of Children and Minors under the ITPA, 1986

Where a magistrate has reason to believe from information received from the police or from any other person authorized by the state government that any person is living on, or is carrying on, or is being made to carry on prostitution in a brothel, he may direct a police officer not below the rank of a sub-inspector to enter such brothel and to remove such person and produce him before him [Section 16]. A minor or a child rescued under this Act is treated as a neglected child [Section 2(l)] under the Juvenile Justice Act 1986 now the Juvenile Justice (Care and Protection of Children) Act, 2000, and has to be produced before the Juvenile Welfare Board [Section 4(1)], now the Child Welfare Committee for reception and rehabilitation, and placing in safe custody. There is a provision for providing for intermediate custody in a shelter home or corrective institution [Section 2(b)] after rescue pending detailed inquiry.

[79] 'Minor' means a person who has completed the age of sixteen years but has not completed the age of eighteen years—Sec. 2(cb) ITPA 1986.

[80] 'Major' means a person who has completed the age of eighteen years—Sec. 2(ca) ITPA 1986.

[81] Suspicious circumstances in this section includes situations in which (i) the mother tongue of the accused is different from that of the child or the language is different from that generally spoken in the locality, (ii) where the child is wrongfully confined without access to others, and (iii) where the child is married to a foreigner.

Laws relating to Obscenity and Pornography

Young Persons (Harmful Publications) Act 1956

In this Act [Section 2(c)], young person means a person under the age of twenty years. It is an offence to sell, let, hire, distribute, or publicly exhibit harmful publications [Section 3(1)].

Information Technology Act 2000

Under Section 67 of the Information Technology Act 2000, publication and transmission of pornography is an offence.

Regulation of Cyber Cafes

Attempts to regulate cyber pornography are being made. For instance, the Government of Maharashtra and the Mumbai police have attempted to bring cyber cafes within the purview of the Rules for Licensing and Controlling Places of Public Amusement (Other than Cinemas) and Performances for Public Amusement Including Cabaret Performances, Melas and Teammates Rules 1960 ('the Amusement Rules') framed under Section 13 of the Mumbai Police Act 1951.

Judgments on Trafficking

Vishal Jeet v Union of India[82]

This was a public interest litigation wherein the Supreme Court issued directions that all State governments must direct their law-enforcing authorities to take appropriate speedy steps against the evil and directed to set up advisory committees with experts from all fields to make suggestions regarding measures for eradicating child prostitution, for care and rehabilitation of rescued girls, for setting up of rehabilitative homes, and for a survey of the *devadasi* and *Jogin* traditions.

Dhananjaya Chatterjee v State of West Bengal[83]

It was a case of rape and murder of a helpless and defenceless schoolgirl of eight years by a security guard. Death sentence imposed by the trial court was subsequently confirmed by the High Court. It was held that the offence was not only inhuman and barbaric, but a totally ruthless crime of rape followed by cold-blooded murder and it was an affront to human dignity.

---

[82] *Vishal Jeet v Union of India*, AIR 1990 SC 1412.
[83] [1994(2) SCC 220].

The Public at Large v State of Maharashtra and Others[84]

This petition arose due to *suo motu* notice taken by the court of a newspaper article which indicated that minor girls were illegally confined and forced to be sex workers. The respondents were directed by the court to show cause as to why action had not been taken under Sections 336 and 366 of the Indian Penal Code, and Sections 5 and 6 of the Suppression of Immoral Traffic in Women and Girls Act 1956. The Court passed directions as under:

- To frame a proper scheme so that the women including minors who are produced for sexual slavery are released from the confinement of their procurers;
- For implementing this scheme, a proper cell, also involving social workers, be created so that by regular checking, minors and others can be released and rehabilitated in the society; and
- Considering the spread of the dreaded disease of AIDS, the State of Maharashtra shall frame a proper scheme with the active assistance of the Municipal Corporation of Greater Mumbai for carrying out HIV tests for the willing sex workers so that the disease may not spread like wildfire in the city.

On the basis of the directions passed by the court, raids were carried out and about 473 minor girls and child sex workers were rescued by the police and kept in the custody of juvenile homes, etc. The respondents pointed out in their affidavit that a majority of the girls had come to Mumbai from the neighbouring states of Karnataka, Kerala, Tamil Nadu, Andhra Pradesh, etc., and the North-eastern states of Assam, etc., and also from countries like Nepal and Bangladesh. The court constituted a committee for the rehabilitation of the rescued girls. The court gave the following directions:

- The respondents, State government, to see that strict vigilance is maintained in the areas where sex workers normally operate and to rescue the child sex workers. Further, adequate steps should be taken to see that those who indulge in trafficking of women should be suitably punished. For this purpose, appropriate directions should be issued to the investigating agencies to take immediate steps. Sometimes, it is noticed that a police officer who detects this type of activity does not take immediate action on the ground that such duty is assigned to some other officer. In the view of the Court, this was not the proper approach because all police officers are bound to take immediate action in those

[84] 1997 (4) Bom CP 171.

cases where cognizable offences are committed. They may not investigate those cases but they can certainly report them to the proper officer and during such time take preventive measures. Section 107 of the Indian Penal Code 1860 provides that the a person abets the doing of a thing if he intentionally aids, by any or illegal commission, the doing of that thing.

- It is high time that the state governments take serious steps to prevent forcible pushing of women and young girls into prostitution and to prevent the trafficking in women, i.e. buying and selling of young girls. These girls may be victims of kidnapping, they may be victims of various deprivation, they may be victims of circumstances beyond their control. For this purpose, regular raids should be carried out in the area where sex workers operate. On numerous occasions, it is reported in newspapers that persons from social organizations who dare to rescue these girls are manhandled, beaten, or threatened. To prevent such situations, for the time being the government must have a squad of police officers who can take immediate action.
- The State government shall set up an advisory committee, if not already set up, within four weeks from the date of the order in terms of Direction No. 2 of Paragraph 15 of the judgment of the Apex Court in the case of Vishal Jeet[85] to comply with the objects set out therein and to further take steps to implement the suggestions made by the advisory committee.
- The State is to set up homes for rehabilitation of rescued sex workers including children so as to enable these rescued sex workers to acquire alternative skills in order to enable them to have alternative source of employment. In a civilized state, it is the duty of the State to take preventive measures to eradicate child prostitution without giving room for any complaint of culpable indifference. One should not forget that these rescued girls are also fellow human beings who require some support and treatment for getting out of the immoral activities.
- To regularly carry out AIDS awareness programmes in the areas where sex workers normally operate.
- The State government is to submit periodic reports, by taking out notice of motion, either through the learned advocate-general or the learned government pleader, stating what steps are taken pursuant to the aforesaid directions and how many girls are rescued from the clutches of middlemen, whether medical treatment is given, and whether

---

[85] AIR 1990 SC 1413.

rehabilitation facilities are made available to them. Even recent newspaper reports indicate that pimps or middlemen are raising their muscle strength to prevent NGOs from receiving illegally confined girls.
- The State government is further to place before the court the compliance report of these directions.

Public at Large v State of Maharashtra and Others[86]

This petition was relating to the rehabilitation of rescued girls. After hearing the various parties and the representations on behalf of various women's social organizations, consensus on the following points was arrived at:

- There was unanimity on the point that the rescued girls should not be subjected to HIV test.
- If HIV tests have already been carried out on some of the girls, their identity should not be disclosed and they should not be informed of the result of the test.
- All the rescued girls must be subjected to medical examination for finding out their age and also given treatment if they are suffering from any other diseases.
- If the girls are found to be adult and are not covered by the Juvenile Justice Act, and if they do not desire to remain in the present institutes, they must be allowed to leave the said homes.
- The other State governments should be contacted and if those state governments were ready and willing to make arrangements for reception of these girls, the chairman, Juvenile Justice Board would pass necessary orders. The police should give them necessary escort and the girls must be handed over to the respective States on receipt of the request made by such states.
- Rehabilitation of these girls is possible if they are segregated in groups of ten or fifteen and thereafter counselling work is done.
- Parents of four minor girls who have been traced and who have been pleading that the police have wrongly taken them in custody should be released.
- Until the girls are sent back to their respective States, the State government will direct adequate number of probation officers to carry out the counselling job. The management in charge will permit the police to record statements of the girls. The police should trace the belongings of the girls and restore the same to them.

[86] Writ petition No. 112 of 1996.

State v Shri Freddie Peats and Others[87]

The accused Freddie Peats, then sixty-six years old, claimed to be a man of God ('Father' Peats), a medical doctor and social worker who ran a 'boarding' or 'orphanage' for boys generally from broken homes and deprived families. Peats used to sexually abuse and assault the boys. On his arrest there were 2305 photographs found in his flat. These photographs recorded different acts of sexual assault, abuse, exploitation, repulsive remarks, and other brute and silent violence against the children and their privacy. These photographs covered a period of about seventeen years and were of boys from the neighbourhood and from schools all over Goa. Some of them were of foreign visitors. Apart from photographs, there were negatives, drugs, syringes, torture paraphernalia, several passports, and bankbooks. In many photographs, the man in the criminal act of sexual assault on children was Peats himself.

The sessions court held Freddie Peats guilty of offences punishable under Sections 292, 293, 342, 355, 328, 337, 323, and 337 of the Indian Penal Code; Sections 20 and 43 of the Juvenile Justice Act; Section 9 of the Immoral Traffic (Prevention) Act 1956; Section 27 of the Drugs and Cosmetics Act 1940. Freddie Peats was ordered life imprisonment and fine. He appealed against the order but the appeal was dismissed.

Due to the intervention of child rights activist Sheela Barse, the trial in the Freddy Peats Case followed some child friendly procedures like the following:

- Trial was held in camera in the chamber of the sessions judge. Similarly, examination of child victim/witnesses were also conducted in camera so that the witnesses are not 'awed' by the court atmosphere.
- All persons in the trial were in informal dress.
- No police officer was present inside the chamber or at the place where the trial was conducted.
- While recording evidence, the child was directed to face the judge so that he will not have occasion to look at the accused and be frightened.

Similar procedures need to be followed in other CSA trials under the present legal system.

Prerna v State of Maharashtra and Ors[88]

Prerna, the petitioner is a registered organization which works in the red light areas of Mumbai and Navi Mumbai with the object of preventing the

---
[87] Sessions case No. 24/1992, Criminal Appeal No. 4/1996.
[88] Criminal Writ Petition No. 788 of 2002, Mumbai High Court.

trafficking of women and children and rehabilitating the victims of forced prostitution. This petition was filed in public interest to protect children and minor girls rescued from the flesh trade against the pimps and brothel keepers keen on re-acquiring possession of the girls. On 16 May 2002, the social service branch of the Mumbai police raided a brothel at Santacruz. Four persons who are alleged to be brothel keepers/pimps were arrested. Twenty four females were rescued. On conducting an ossification test, ten of them were found to be minors. In this case the Mumbai High Court passed the following directions which are of great significance for the children rescued from the brothels:

- No magistrate can exercise jurisdiction over any person under eighteen years of age whether that person is a juvenile in conflict with law or a child in need of care and protection, as defined by Sections 2(1) and 2(d) of the Juvenile Justice (Care and Protection of Children) Act 2000. At the first possible instance, the magistrate must take steps to ascertain the age of a person who seems to be under eighteen years of age. When such a person is found to be under eighteen years of age, the magistrate must transfer the case to the Juvenile Justice Board if such a person is a juvenile in conflict with law, or to the Child Welfare Committee if such a person is a child in need or care and protection.
- A magistrate before whom persons rescued under the Immoral Traffic (Prevention) Act 1956 or found soliciting in a public place are produced should, under Section 17(2) or the said Act, have their ages ascertained the very first time they are produced before him. When such a person is found to be under eighteen years of age, the magistrate must transfer the case to the Juvenile Justice Board if such person is a juvenile in conflict with law or to the Child Welfare Committee if such a person is a child in need of care and protection.
- Any juvenile rescued from a brothel under the Immoral Traffic (Prevention) Act 1956 or found soliciting in a public place should only be released after an inquiry has been completed by the probation officer.
- The said juvenile should be released only to the care and custody of a parent/guardian after such parent/guardian has been found fit by the Child Welfare Committee, to have the care and custody or the rescued juvenile.
- If the parent/guardian is found unfit to have the care and custody of the rescued juvenile, the procedure laid down under the Juvenile Justice (Care and Protection of Children) Act 2000 should be followed for the rehabilitation of the rescued child.
- No advocate can appear before the Child Welfare Committee on

behalf of a juvenile produced before the Child Welfare Committee after being rescued under the Immoral Traffic (Prevention) Act 1956 or found soliciting in a public place. Only the parents/guardian of such juvenile should be permitted to make representations before the Child Welfare Committee through themselves or through an advocate appointed for such purpose.
- An advocate appearing for a pimp or brothel keeper is barred from appearing in the same case for the victims rescued under the Immoral Traffic (Prevention) Act 1956.

Law Reform

The enforcement of law in India has been weak in dealing with abusers, exploiters, and traffickers of children. There have been several gaps in implementation. Some of them are:

- Under the Immoral Traffic Prevention Act 1986, 75 per cent of those arrested are females. It is evident that the spirit of the Act has not been followed as the victims are being harassed.
- There have been several instances of occurrences of sexual abuse and exploitation of children within families and homes. The law generally presumes that guardians of the child are innocent and it takes a lot of professional commitment to establish such an offence against such guardians.
- Law relating to paedophiles is inadequate. Therefore, the police is generally ineffective when it comes to registering the crimes, especially when it actually comes to registering the cases against foreign tourists where passport officers and international links are involved. The judiciary and the police are not aware of the laws and rights of the children.
- The laws governing prostitution are biased against the prostitute. Under the Prevention of Immoral Traffic Act 1986, the customer is not an offender. For a fixed sum of money, a man is able to obtain women or girls to satisfy his sexual needs, with or without her consent. In other words, what constitutes rape outside the brothel is converted to prostitution inside the brothel and both children and women are deprived of their rights.
- To prevent secondary victimization during interrogation/examination by investigating agencies as well as during court procedure, where a child is made to recall minute details of the sexual acts and experience,

and is grilled in getting proof, a model code of conduct[89] should be evolved. There should be a standardized questionnaire for examination of the prosecutrix, indicating the parameters for supervision.

- Examination of the victim/witnesses should be in the presence of social workers/women police/parents or others who have the trust or confidence of the child. Examinations should also be done in a familiar atmosphere and not in police stations.
- Age and other tests of the rescued victim should also be done in the presence of child-supporting individuals and preferably in the homes where the children are lodged after rescue. The homes should therefore, be provided with these facilities.
- Questioning should be done mostly by women police officers.
- The mental health aspects of the children have to be kept in mind. There should not be too much pressure on the child to speak all the details of the traumatic incident.
- Adopting a multidisciplinary approach to the crime should be attempted by co-opting additional members into the investigating team so as to include doctors, social workers, co-opting mental health exerts counsellors, or anyone who would be useful in the overall rehabilitation of the child.
- Investigation should necessarily be conducted into the trafficking angle in all cases of missing persons, procurement of minor girls, buying and selling, child marriages, and all cases of kidnapping and abduction.
- Police officers should not be in uniform while examining the child and specially trained child-friendly police officers should examine the child.
- The venue of the trial should be a safe place other than the usual court buildings.
- Law and order and 'VIP' duties are of high priority for police, whereas child sexual abuse cases are low priority crimes. This should be rectified.
- Criminal Compensation Injuries Board should be set up.
- Special courts, within a certain time frame, should handle all cases involving sexual abuse of children.

---

[89] Report on the Six Regional Consultations on Sexual Exploitation and Trafficking of Children, sponsored by department of women and child development, Government of India, and UNICEF, India.

- The burden of proof should be shifted to the accused.
- Formation of a nodal cell at the State level to deal with interstate and inter-country dimensions of abuse may be tried.
- The age of the child in applicable Acts varies. The JJ Act defines child as below eighteen years of age. The Child Marriage Restraint Act also specifies eighteen years as the cut-off age for restraining child marriage. Section 375 IPC identifies wife as not being under fifteen years of age and Section 376(2)(f) as not under twelve years of age. The PITA sees a female child as not exceeding sixteen years of age, while a minor is up to eighteen. The age of the child should be uniformly defined as upto eighteen years. There should be a proper mechanism to determine the age of the child.
- The laws governing prostitution are biased against the prostitute. Under the Prevention of Immoral Trafficking Act, the customer is not an offender. Under the Indian Penal Code, transmitting a sexually transmitted disease is an offence. The prostitute can be isolated compulsorily if she is found to have AIDS. The rescue operations have led to a spate of glaring human rights abuses of the prostitutes including right to freedom from violence, right to shelter and residence, right to seek legal help, right to family, right to information and right to representation.
- The Prevention of Immoral Traffic Act 1986, to be more effective, needs the following measures:
  – Notification of Public place.
  – Closure of brothels keeping minors.
  – Setting up of special courts for speedy trials.
  – Rescue operations to be more humanely and sensitively carried out along with a rehabilitation plan protecting the human rights of the prostitutes.
  – Age verification of the rescued children to be immediately carried out. Infact it should be linked to the rescue operations.

Monitoring of Cyber Pornography

Recently a committee appointed by the Mumbai High Court[90] laid down several restrictions on cyber cafes to provide for an adequate degree of supervision and control so that minors are protected from being exposed to pornographic sites on the Internet in the cyber cafes. The committee has given recommendations to make a child-friendly or child-safe 'cyber zone'

---

[90] *Jayesh Thakker & Another v State of Maharashtra & Others and Internet Users Association of India (Intervenors), Suo Motu,* Writ Petition 1611 of 2001, Mumbai High Court.

where minors could safely access and use the Internet for information, education, communication, and entertainment. The committee's recommendations include:

- A suggested definition of cyber cafes to be included in the Rules under the Mumbai Police Act.
- Procedures for licensing cyber cafes.
- Regulations requiring cyber cafe operators to demand photo ID cards (of any kind) from all users.
- Requiring that minors be restricted to using machines in the common open space of cyber cafes (i.e. not in cubicles).
- Requiring that these machines be fitted with software filters.
- Email and website information to be provided by the Internet service providers informing the public about the hazards and possible solutions.
- Setting up a hotline to the cyber crime investigation cell.
- Taking steps to increase awareness about cyber crime in general.

Extra-Territorial Jurisdiction

Recently, several instances of child sexual abuse and exploitation have come to light in India involving foreigners. The objective of extra-territorial jurisdiction is to apply the domestic criminal law to crimes committed by nationals in other territories. Jurisdictional lines must not be allowed to come in the way of apprehending and convicting adults who prey upon children. There is an urgent need for such legislation to effectively tackle sex tourism and trafficking of children for commercial sexual exploitation. Under the Swedish Penal Code, a Swedish citizen who has committed an offence outside of Sweden, which is an offence in Sweden and in the country in which it was committed, is liable under the Swedish law and can be tried by the Swedish court. The Crimes (Child Sex Tourism) Amendment Act 1994 is an Australian law that prohibits and criminalizes sexual acts overseas with children under sixteen years of age. Australian courts have adopted the procedure of video-link evidence whereby the court is able to hear evidence directly from witnesses who are in overseas locations.

International Instruments

The United Nations Convention on the Rights of the Child (CRC), which has been ratified by several countries including India, gives a common, cross-national, comprehensive foundation standard for all the world's children. Article 6 enjoins all State parties to take appropriate measures to suppress all forms of traffic in women and exploitation of prostitution of women. Article

11 prohibits the illegal transfer of children abroad. Article 19 is also relevant. It refers to the States' obligation to protect children from all forms of physical or mental violence, injury or abuse, neglect or negligent treatment, maltreatment, or exploitation including sexual abuse perpetrated by parents or others responsible for their care. Articles 34 and 35 lay down the obligations of the State to protect the child from all forms of sexual exploitation and sexual abuse. For these purposes, State parties shall, in particular, take all appropriate national, bilateral, and unilateral measures to prevent:

- The inducement or coercion of a child to engage in any unlawful sexual activity.
- The exploitative use of children in prostitution or other unlawful sexual practices.

On the exploitative use of children in pornographic performance and materials, Article 35 enjoins the State parties to take all appropriate national, bilateral, and multilateral measures to prevent the abduction or the sale of or traffic in children for any purpose or in any form. Article 39 ensures that States take all appropriate measures to promote the physical and psychological recovery and social reintegration of a child victim from any form of neglect, abuse, torture, or any other form of cruel, inhuman, or degrading treatment or punishment or armed conflict.

The UN Convention on the Rights of the Child

This is the principal legal reference in the combat against the sexual exploitation of children. Many other international instruments also address the issue and offer international legal protection against abuses of human rights.

The Convention for the Suppression of Trafficking in Persons and of the Exploitation of the Prostitution of Others 1949

The preamble to the Convention states that prostitution and the accompanying evil of the traffic in person for the purpose of prostitution are incompatible with the dignity and worth of the human person and endanger the welfare of the individual, the family and the community.

The salient features of the Convention are as follows:

- Any person, who in order to gratify the passions of another, procures, entices, or leads away for the purpose of prostitution another person, even if with such person's consent, or exploits the prostitution of another person, even if with such person's consent, is liable for punishment [Art. 1].

- Any person who keeps or manages or knowingly finances a brothel or knowingly lets or rents a building or other place or any part thereof for the prostitution of another is liable for punishment [Art. 2].
- The above offences shall be regarded as extraditable offences in any extradition treaty entered into between state parties to this Convention [Arts. 8 and 9].
- Each State party to this Convention shall establish or maintain a service to coordinate and centralize results of investigation of offences under the Convention, and such service should compile all information for facilitation of prevention and punishment of offences, and such service should be in close touch with corresponding services of other state parties [Art. 14].
- The service so established should furnish particulars of an offence or an attempt to commit such offence to services established by other state parties. The information so furnished should include the description of the offender, fingerprints, photographs, method of operation, police record, and record of conviction [Art. 15].
- The State parties should take measures for the prevention of prostitution and for the rehabilitation and social adjustment of the victims of prostitution [Art. 16].
- The State parties shall undertake with immigration and emigration authorities such measures as are required to check the traffic in persons of either sex for the purpose of prostitution [Art. 17].
- The State parties shall, pending the completion of the procedure for repatriation, make suitable arrangements for the temporary care and maintenance of destitute victims of international traffic. Repatriation should take place only with the consent of the victim or the person claiming such victim and after agreement is reached with the state of destination [Art. 19].
- The state parties are to communicate to the Secretary General of the United Nations such laws and regulations that have been promulgated in their respective states, and each year thereafter, such laws and regulations that have been promulgated and measures taken by the State parties concerning the applicability of the Convention [Art. 21].

The International Covenant on Civil and Political Rights (ICCPR) 1966

This Convenant lays down that every child, without any discrimination, has the right to such measures of protection as are required by his status as a minor on the part of his family, society, and the state.

The Convention on the Elimination of all Forms of Discrimination Against Women (CEDAW)

This enjoins State parties to take all appropriate measures, including legalization, to suppress all forms of traffic in women and exploitation of prostitution of women.[91]

India has ratified all the above instruments and therefore is bound to make laws in consonance with the above provisions.

The United Nations Convention Against Torture and Other Cruel, Inhuman or Degrading Treatment or Punishment 1984

The Monitoring Body under this Convention is the Committee Against Torture. The Convention states that there should be no expulsion or return of a person to another State if there are substantial grounds for believing that she would be in danger of torture. The alleged victims of torture have the right to complain to and have her case promptly and impartially examined by competent authorities. Complainant and witnesses shall be protected against any consequential ill treatment or intimidation. There is also a provision for redress and right to compensation.

ILO (International Labour Organization) Convention No. 29 on Forced Labour[92] 1930

Under this Convention, the States have to suppress use of forced or compulsory labour within the shortest possible period. The officials shall not constrain any person to work for private individuals, companies, or associations. The monitoring body, as of all ILO Conventions, is the Committee of Experts on the Application of Conventions and Recommendations.

The Universal Declaration of Human Rights 1948

Though not a legally binding document, this sets the stage for most of the international instruments. Article 4 of the Declaration states that no one shall be held in slavery or servitude. Slavery and the slave trade shall be prohibited in all its forms. Article 5 provides that no one shall be subjected to torture or to cruel, inhuman, or degrading treatment or punishment.

The Tourism Bill of Rights and the Tourist Code 1985

This was adopted by the World Trade Organization (WTO). It enjoins that the States should prevent any possibility of using tourism to exploit others

---

[91] CEDAW, Article 6.

[92] Under this Convention, 'forced or compulsory labour' means all work or service which is exacted from any person under the menace of any penalty and for which the said person has not offered himself voluntarily.

for prostitution purposes. The Tourist Code enjoins tourists to refrain from exploiting others for prostitution purposes.

These Covenants and Conventions which India has ratified, unless they infringe on the fundamental rights, do not need legislative measures to enforce them in the courts of India.

The SAARC Regional Convention on Combating the Crime of Trafficking in Women and Children for Prostitution

The Male Declaration adopted by SAARC member states at the close of the Ninth SAARC Summit called for a Regional Convention on Combating the Crime of Trafficking. Some of the significant features of this Convention agreed to by the parties are as follows:

- Trafficking in women and children for prostitution is a crime against human dignity and as such effective measures, including legal, socio-economic, and administrative, to be taken to effectively prevent trafficking in women and children.
- To specify in their national legislation, the procurement, enticing, or taking away of another person for the purposes of prostitution and exploitation even with consent, as a serious offence.
- To provide in their national legislations, punishments for any person who keeps or manages or knowingly finances or takes part in the financing of a brothel or rents out a building or a place or any part thereof for the purposes of prostitution.
- In a spirit of cooperation among themselves, the parties agree to assist and coordinate the various aspects of trafficking in women and children inside and outside their countries.

Optional Protocol to the Convention on the Rights of the Child on the Sale of Children, Child Prostitution, and Child Pornography (2000)

The important articles of this protocol (adopted by the UN General Assembly) are as follows.

- To prohibit sale of children, child prostitution, and child pornography[93]
    - Sale of Children has been defined as any act or transaction whereby a child is transferred by any person/s to another for remuneration or other consideration[94]

[93] Optional Protocol to the CRC Article 1.
[94] Optional Protocol to the CRC Article 2.

– Child Prostitution has been defined as use of a child in sexual activities for remuneration or other consideration.
– Child Pornography has been defined as any representation of a child engaged in real or simulated explicit sexual activities or any representation of the sexual parts of a child for primarily sexual purposes.
- Criminal or penal law to be made to cover sale of children including offering, delivering, or accepting a child for purposes of sexual exploitation, transfer of organs for profit of forced labour.[95]
- To protect rights of child victims in criminal justice process keeping the best interest of the child in view.
– Protection of rights of child victims in the criminal justice process: In recognizing their special needs, especially as witness; in keeping them informed at all times of all things; providing support services; protecting privacy and identity of the child; providing for their safety and that of their family where appropriate; and avoiding unnecessary delay in granting compensation.
– *Best interests of the child* shall be a primary consideration.
- To ensure appropriate training for persons working with child victims.

The ILO Convention No. 182 Concerning the Prohibition and Immediate Action for the Elimination of the Worst Form of Child Labour

This Convention includes:

- Use of child for prostitution, production of pornography, or pornographic performances.
- Use, procuring, or offering of a child for illicit activities, in particular for the production and trafficking of drugs.

An accompanying Recommendation[96] defines 'hazardous work' as 'work which exposes children to physical, psychological or sexual abuse'. Paragraph 11 recommends how countries may cooperate with each other to deal with criminals and criminal networks, such as those involved in the trafficking of children and child pornography.

International Initiatives to Prevent Child Pornography on the Internet

In the Netherlands the hotline for child pornography on the Internet was created by the Foundation for Internet Providers, Internet users, the

---

[95] Optional Protocol to the CRC Article 3.
[96] Paragraph 4 of the recommendation.

National Criminal Intelligence Service, the National Bureau against Racial Discrimination, and a psychologist. Like other national hotlines that are starting to be set up, it operates by asking Internet users to report any child pornography that they find. The Netherlands hotline tries to have a preventive attitude towards the problem, in that once a site is reported, the web site provider will ask the issuer of the material, if he can be traced, to remove it from the Internet, and will report that person to the police if he or she fails to do so.

Singapore has attempted to regulate the content of the Internet as far as possible, through a Class Licence Scheme, where Internet service providers and Internet content providers are required to block out objectionable sites as directed by the Singapore Broadcasting Authority. Schools, libraries, and other providers of Internet access to children are required to institute a tighter level of control, although options as to how this could be implemented have not yet been identified.

In China, Internet users must register with the police, and it is reported that a company in Massachusetts, United States, is investing in technology designed to allow the Government of China to censor the Internet.

The Internet Society of New Zealand and the Internal Affairs Department set up a joint working group to tackle pornography on the Internet in December 1996. This followed several high-profile raids and monitoring exercises by the authorities. The society is also developing a code of practice for Internet service providers.

The United Kingdom police were involved in Operation Starbust, an international investigation of a paedophile ring thought to be using the Internet to distribute graphic pictures of child pornography, and the biggest operation so far carried out in the United Kingdom. Nine British men were arrested as a result of the operation which involved other arrests in Europe, America, South Africa, and the Far East. The Operation identified thirty-seven men worldwide.

Government/NGO Interventions in the Area of Exploitation and Trafficking in India

The National Plan of Action for Children (1992) includes children of prostitutes in the category of children in especially difficult circumstances, but does not suggest any goals or activities for them. Based on a Supreme Court judgment in July 1997, a committee was formed to make an in-depth study of the problems of prostitution, child prostitutes, and children of prostitutes, with the secretariat of the department of women and child development

(DWCD) as its chairperson. The report of this committee[97] includes a plan of action to combat trafficking and commercial sexual exploitation of women and children, aiming at bringing to the mainstream and reintegrating these women and child victims in the society. The Plan includes action points such as prevention of trafficking, awareness generation and social mobilization, health care services, education and childcare, housing shelter and civic amenities, economic empowerment, legal reforms and law enforcement, rescue and rehabilitation, and so on. It recommends setting up of night-care shelter, education support programme, institutionalization, *Anganwadi*-cum-day-care centres or *Balwadi*, non-formal education, formation of self-help groups by women victims, and community education based on experience of the Devadasi Rehabilitation Programme in Karnataka and Prerana in Mumbai. The DWCD has prepared guidelines for proposals for projects to combat trafficking of women and children through prevention, rescue, and rehabilitation in destination and source areas, including trafficking under sanction of tradition.

NGO initiatives in India have been restricted primarily to networking, lobbying/advocacy, and welfare services to the victims and their children. There are some organizations which have tackled the issue of trafficking for prostitution but in a different perspective, like sensitizing and taking preventive measures among caste-based communities of prostitutes, through programmes for their children, specially the girl child. There are many such organizations like Abhivday Ashram, Morena, Sanlaap in Kolkata, Satya Sohan Ashram, Sagar, and Vimochana at Athni. Vocational training is imparted along with education to the girl child so that she does not become a prey to the traffickers. They also conduct community sensitization programmes. *Sangram* in Sangli, Maharashtra, conducts awareness generation programmes among the community where the devadasi practice is common. *Gram Niyojan Kendra* runs awareness generation and skill-training programmes in Rajasthan and UP.

Organizations such as *Prerana* in Bombay and Joint Women's Programme in Delhi and Allahabad run *balwadis* and health care centres for children of prostitutes. Intervention by NGOs and women's groups on the issue of trafficking take the following forms:

- Advocacy for the rights of those who are trafficked for the purpose of prostitution
- Advocacy for the rights of migratory labour or for those who are trafficked for labour

[97] Department of Women and Child Development, Government of India, 1998.

- Networking for united action to prevent trafficking by like-minded groups
- Lobbying for changes in legislation
- Advocacy for rights of women in prostitution
- Providing welfare services for health, education, and childcare
- Running of shelter/safe homes
- Facilitation of rehabilitation and repatriation
- Providing information about laws, policies, and programmes.

There are some networks and organizations that work in the areas of trafficking. There include the following.

End Child Prostitution in Asian Tourism (ECPAT)

This has been monitoring and acting against sex tourism in Asia and, in recent times, elsewhere. ECPAT promotes transactional governmental cooperation and extraterritorial legislation, which allows governments to bring their nationals to trial for crimes committed in other countries, and draws public attention to the arrest, detention, and conviction of paedophiles engaged in sex tourism. ECPAT also engages the interest and commitment of world tourism authorities, travel agents, holiday guide publishers, and tour promoters in actively working against sex tourism.

Action Against Trafficking and Sexual Exploitation of Children (ATSEC)

This is a network that deals with cross-border activities between West Bengal and Bangladesh to facilitate advocacy, research, social mobilization, technical assistance, and programme support at the national and regional levels. It also aims to develop capacity of the government and non-government organizations to plan and implement advocacy programmes.

The Network Against Child Sexual Exploitation and Trafficking (NACSET)

This is a network against commercial sexual exploitation and trafficking. As the prevention of trafficking and CSE is a major orientation and thrust of NACSET, it has given adequate importance to approaching organizations which can play a crucial role on this front. For example, village-based organizations engaged in water conservation, drought relief, soil conservation work in the perennially drought-prone areas along with women's organizations and youth organizations are encouraged to join the network. NACSET believes effective prevention can be achieved primarily by expanding in this manner to all the relevant organizations and social forces.

Action Aid

Action Aid is working to curb the trafficking of women and children The Action Aid India campaign, aimed at promoting coordinated action against trafficking, looks closely at interventions at the grass roots and links it to policies and action at state, national, and international levels. Prevention at source is attempted by using strong systems and a community-based approach through exact mapping and tracking of the vulnerable areas from where trafficking takes place. A comprehensive analysis of the situation on the ground with respect to trafficking has been carried out. In the course of conducting sensitization and training exercises, a training manual has been developed for use by those doing prevention work. An assessment tool has been designed to go with the training manual. Rehabilitation and reintegration of trafficked persons is attempted through interventions which are sensitive to the situation of the trafficked persons and in keeping with their aspirations. Support has been given to create an organization of trafficked persons themselves to have self-regulatory boards to prevent children from being trafficked into prostitution.

SOS Movement

The Save Our Sisters (SOS) Movement, recently launched by Save the Children India, Mumbai, has a major goal to seek out the feasibilities of establishing working partnerships among NGOs working at the city, state, and national levels, corporate sector, media, government, and the judiciary to combat the problem. Its objectives are grouped under advocacy, prevention, rehabilitation, and legislation. It has started holding regional workshops, developing awareness booklets, collecting resource material for a Central Resource and Documentation Centre, conducting a survey of various rehabilitation homes for the reused children in Maharashtra, mapping of the traffick-prone areas, and so on.

Campaign Against Child Trafficking (CACT)

The CACT has been initiated by Terre des Hommes aiming at developing a national strategy for combating child trafficking using three broad dimensions for addressing the problem: awareness generation, legal interventions, and projects at the grass roots creating and strengthening a region-specific intervention through database and building local strategies; and building partnership with the appropriate groups like decision-makers, media, and citizens to ensure implementation of international conventions, initiating national legislative processes, and aiding its conversion into enforceable law.

Sanlaap

As an obvious outcome a major focus of *Sanlaap's* activities is centred in and on the red-light areas of Kolkata and its suburbs. *Sanlaap* is particularly engaged in lobbying with the government, judiciary, and police to get access to the rescued children commercially abused in prostitution, who are in custody, and the children of the prostitutes, to support them with necessary counselling and care. An effort is also made to rehabilitate the young girls trafficked from suburban and rural areas of West Bengal, Nepal, and Bangladesh.

Whose Child Next?

Children across the country are being sexually abused and exploited. When it happens in homes, in schools, etc., it is called abuse. When it happens outside and payment is involved, it is called prostitution. Clearly, both are issues of child protection The legal system has so far failed to respond to this grim situation, as the existing law is grossly inadequate. There is an immediate need to prevent secondary victimization of the child by the legal system. Children and young people have to be offered more effective protection by the legal process. Joint investigation and action teams are required in each area for dealing and monitoring cases of child sexual abuse and exploitation. A range of multi-agency services are required to reflect the diversity of children and young people's situations taking a holistic approach to meeting their rights. And above all the status of the girl child has to be enhanced.

The Blue Sky—Handling Child Sexual Abuse in Future[98]

When I began to dream about what would make the legal system better for children—I became a little carried away, a phenomenon often referred to as 'blue sky' in certain training circles. This is when one just allows one's imagination to run riot. I began to think that the Indian Penal Code, the Criminal Procedure Code, and the Indian Evidence Act have been amended so that young children are presumed to be competent witnesses and video-recorded testimony of child victim of sexual abuse are admissible as evidence in the special courts that deal exclusively with cases of child

---

[98] Adapted from the Memorandum of Good Practice, London Home Office, HMSO, 1988; and the author's observations during the visit to the Area Child Protection Committee of the Northumbria Police, UK, in 1999.

sexual abuse and exploitation. The special courts have powers to grant protection orders in cases where there is a reasonable apprehension that a child is in a vulnerable position and is likely to be abused or exploited. A case of an eight-year-old girl child who was sexually abused was brought to the author's notice, who immediately contacted the Joint Investigating Team (JIT) of the area. The team had a police officer, a medical doctor, a psychiatrist, an educational psychologist, a social worker, a lawyer, a child welfare officer from the department of women and child development, and a schoolteacher. Each member of the team had training in child rights and experience and attitude of dealing with children. The JIT immediately swung into action. A sensitive and trained doctor did the medical examination in a very child-friendly clinic after explaining to the child and taking her consent. Once it was clear that a criminal offence was committed and the abuser was living with the family, the abuser was taken away from the family setting. After joint consultations, the JIT prepared an action plan after taking an overview of the cognitive, sexual, physical and other developments, and the child's attentive span. After consultation it was decided that as the child knew the schoolteacher in the JIT and the schoolteacher also knew the mother tongue of the child, she would be a suitable and sympathetic interviewer for the video interview. The venue of the interview was a specially designed room attached to the paediatrician's clinic. It resembled a playroom of a child. Toys and games were available in the room. The child was made comfortable in the room and she was allowed to be accompanied by her mother. After the initial rapport building, the child was allowed to talk in her own pace. The interviewer listened to the child and adjusted her language according to the child's limited vocabulary, language, and style, particularly in relation to sexual activity. Since the child was mature enough to understand the concept, she was given an explanation of the purpose of the video recording. The JIT took careful notes of any available information during the interview. No leading questions were asked during the interview. The child was given breaks for play and refreshments. Once the interview was recorded, it was sealed by the JIT to be produced before the court. The court did not go into the competency of the witness and the trained sensitive judge of the special court, who had undergone a training on child rights, carefully saw the video recording. During cross-examination, the child gave the evidence from outside via a television link. The accused was convicted and sentenced. Suddenly came the harsh sound of reality. It was a dream—a dream which must come true in the interest of the child and to meet the ends of justice. Law reformers and policy makers should realize this.

6

Juvenile Justice: Administration and Implementation

Introduction

Care of the child is primarily the responsibility of parents and elders in the family. In traditional India, the child in need of care and protection was looked after in the joint family, caste group, village community, and religious institutions. To be born in a happy and comfortable home is a privilege that not many children are destined to enjoy. With the spread of urbanization and industrialization, breakdown of family structures and religious sanctions, population explosion, prospects of adventure and excitement in cities, the conditions of children deteriorated.

The vast majority of the children are impoverished. This has given rise to children in especially difficult circumstances (CEDC) who are vulnerable, marginalized, destitute, and neglected, and are quite frequently deprived of their basic rights to family care, protection, shelter, food, health, and education. According to an estimate, there are around 340 million deprived children in India. The vulnerable group of deprived children can be categorized as:

- orphans, abandoned and destitute, working and street children, victims of natural calamities, emergencies or man-made disasters, children with disability, aids affected children, children engaged in substance abuse, children of sex workers, juvenile offenders or children in conflict with law, children of families 'at risk' like refugees, migrant and construction workers, chronically and terminally ill, prisoners or lifers, single parents and the girl child.

Among the vulnerable groups of children, India has the largest population of street children in the world.[1] At least eighteen million children live or work on the streets of urban India. According to a UNICEF definition,

[1] Human Development Report, UNDP, 1993.

street children are those for whom the street, (in the widest sense of the word) more than their family, has become their real home, a situation where there is no protection, supervision, or direction from responsible adults.

Another group of vulnerable children is that of the child labourers. Today India has the largest population of employed children. These children are exposed to physical and mental abuse, besides hazardous work and unsafe working conditions. Underage sex workers are those who have been forced into prostitution. Torture and exploitation are a cruel reality these children have to face. Many of them are also badly affected by drug abuse and are

Figure 6.1: Children in Especially Difficult Circumstances (CEDC)

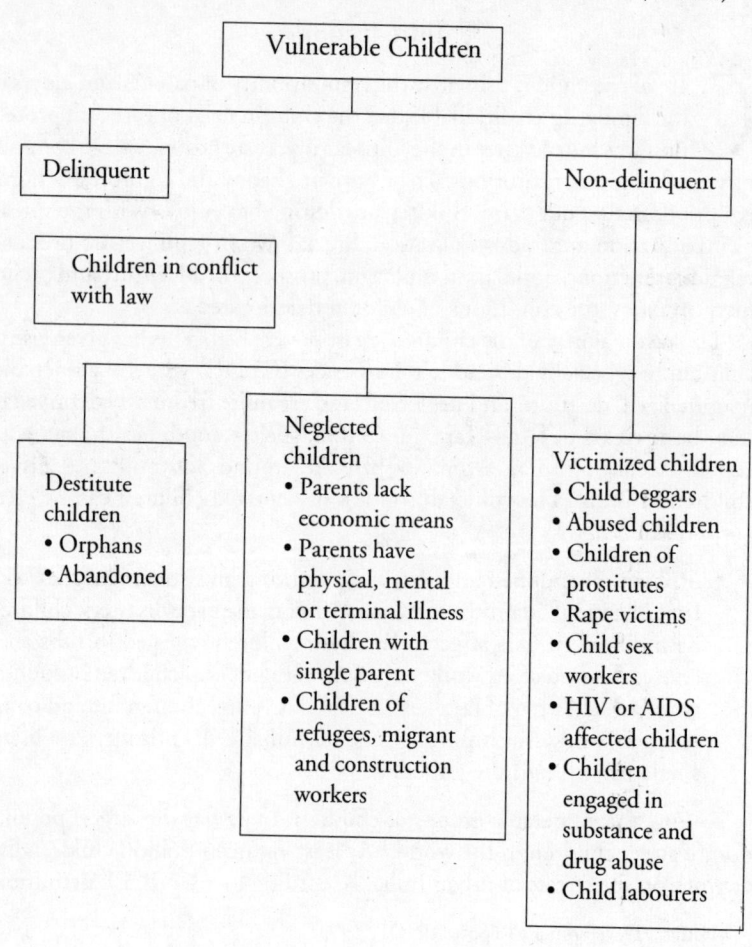

```
                    Vulnerable Children
                    /                \
              Delinquent          Non-delinquent
                 |
         Children in conflict
            with law
```

Destitute children
- Orphans
- Abandoned

Neglected children
- Parents lack economic means
- Parents have physical, mental or terminal illness
- Children with single parent
- Children of refugees, migrant and construction workers

Victimized children
- Child beggars
- Abused children
- Children of prostitutes
- Rape victims
- Child sex workers
- HIV or AIDS affected children
- Children engaged in substance and drug abuse
- Child labourers

being used by organized crime in drug trafficking and peddling. Most Indian children are disabled because of poverty and it is correlated. Protein malnutrition, iodine deficiency, and Vitamin A deficiency are the major causes of mental retardation and blindness.

Exodus to cities like Mumbai has led to expansion of slums and pavement dwellings. Children of such migrant workers suffer from abuse, neglect, and exploitation. Children also become orphans and destitute due to natural calamities like floods, droughts, earthquakes, and environmental disasters. Children are also the most innocent victims of terrorism, armed conflicts, and other political reasons. India is a country that traditionally idolizes sons. Girl children, especially in rural areas, remain deprived of adequate access to basic health care, nutrition, and education.

Children in especially difficult circumstances (CEDC) can be further classified as shown in Figure 6.1 in the previous page.

Delinquency

Delinquency is any act, course of conduct, or situation, which might be brought before the court and adjudicated whether in fact it comes to be treated there, or by some other resources or indeed remains untreated. The juvenile delinquent or a child in conflict with law, is thus a person who has been adjudicated as such by a court of proper jurisdiction though he may be no different, at any rate, up and until the time of court contact and adjudication, from masses of children who are not delinquents. Juvenile delinquency is an act or omission by a child or young *fantasy*, which is punishable by law under the legal system. A Brazilian activist had rightly said, 'A juvenile delinquent is nothing more than a poor child caught red-handed in the struggle for survival.'

Studies indicate that juvenile delinquency is a result of the interactions of contextual, individual, and situational factors.[2] Some of these factors within a family are:

- living with criminal parents,
- harsh discipline,
- physical abuse and neglect,
- poor family management practices,
- low levels of parent involvement with the child,
- high levels of family conflict,
- parental attitudes favorable to violence, and
- separation from family.

[2] Rolf Loeber, David Farrington (eds), *Serious and Violent Juvenile Offenders*, Sage Publications Inc., 1998.

These have all been linked to later delinquency. Academic failure, low commitment to schooling, truancy, and early school leaving also predict delinquency. Delinquent siblings, delinquent peers, and gang membership also predict delinquency, though the effects of these factors appear to be the greatest in adolescence. Finally, poverty, community disorganization, availability of drugs, and neighbourhood adults involved in crime are also linked to increased risk for later violence.

Profile of Juveniles Apprehended during 1999 in India[3]

Of the total 18,460 juveniles who were involved in various offences during 1999:

- 55.9 per cent involved in various crimes were between 12–16 years and 22.3 per cent were in the age group of 16–18 years.
- 78.2 per cent were either illiterate (6,345) or had education up to primary level (8,087).
- Children living with parents (13,638) and guardians (2,847) constituted 89.3 per cent of the juveniles apprehended.
- The share of 'homeless' children who were involved in crimes was just 10.7 per cent.
- The large majority of juveniles (77.3 per cent) belonged to families whose annual income was up to Rs 25,000. Juveniles from upper middle income (Rs 200,001 to 300,000) was 1.0 per cent and from upper income (above Rs 300,000) was 0.5 per cent.

Figure 6.2 presents a classification by attributes of juveniles apprehended during 1999.

Of the total number of 18,460 arrested and sent to court in 1999:[4]

- 1656 juveniles were sent home after advice or admonition.
- 5298 were released on probation and placed under the care of parent or guardians.
- 768 were released on probation and placed under the care of a fit institution.
- 1281 were sent to special homes.
- 832 paid fine.
- 3358 were acquitted or otherwise disposed of.
- 5267 were pending disposal.

Figure 6.3 depicts the nature of disposal of juveniles arrested and sent to courts during 1999.

[3] Crime in India 1999.
[4] Ibid.

Figure 6.2: Classification by Attributes of Juveniles
Apprehended during 1999

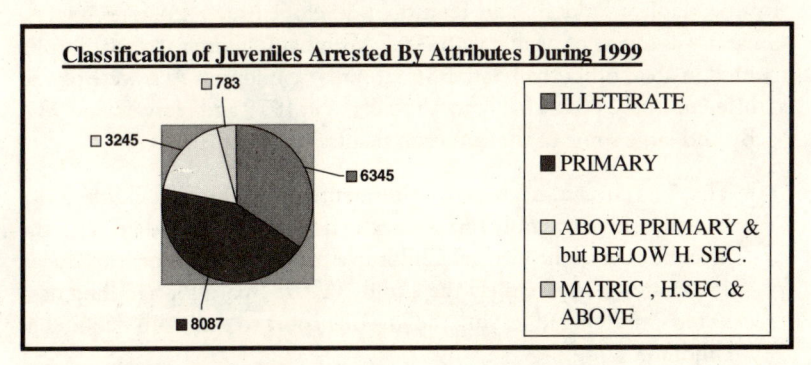

Classification of Juveniles Arrested By Attributes During 1999

- 783
- 3245
- 6345
- 8087

■ ILLETERATE

■ PRIMARY

☐ ABOVE PRIMARY & but BELOW H. SEC.

☐ MATRIC , H.SEC & ABOVE

Source: Crime in India 1999

Figure 6.3: Disposal of Juveniles Arrested and Sent to
Courts during 1999

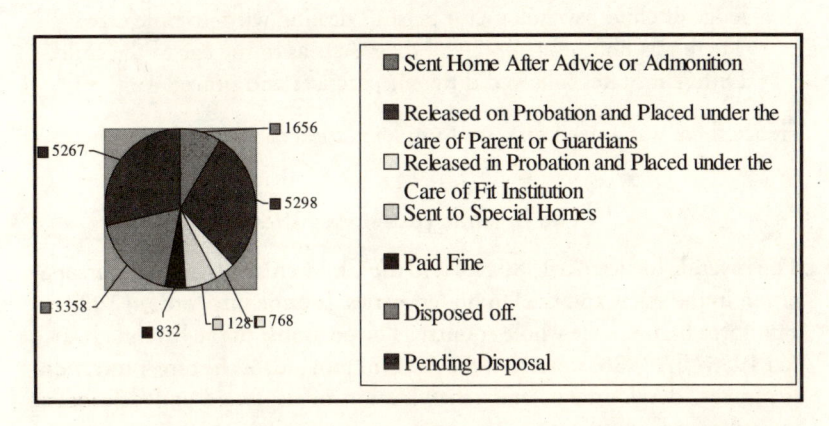

- 1656
- 5267
- 5298
- 3358
- 832
- 128
- 768

■ Sent Home After Advice or Admonition

■ Released on Probation and Placed under the care of Parent or Guardians

☐ Released in Probation and Placed under the Care of Fit Institution

☐ Sent to Special Homes

■ Paid Fine

■ Disposed off.

■ Pending Disposal

It is significant to note that a large number of juveniles are sent home, i.e. back to the same family and neighbourhood that have most likely contributed to their delinquent behaviour. Therefore, families, schools, and neighbourhoods are the primary socializing agents to bring up children into non-delinquent individuals and need to be strengthened. Another area of concern is the large number of cases pending disposal.

After independence many of the then States like Uttar Pradesh, Hyderbad, Mysore, West Bengal, and Saurashtra also developed their separate Acts whereas the centrally governed States (Union territories) were covered under the Central Children Act 1960 which was amended in 1978. In 1969, Assam, Madhya Pradesh, and Rajasthan developed their separate Acts. As Gujarat was a part of Maharashtra, the Mumbai Children Act was implemented in areas other than Saurashtra. Similar Children's Acts were passed at different times. Himachal Pradesh passed it in 1979 and Haryana in 1984.

By and large some of the common features of these Acts were:

- The Acts covered neglected, delinquent, and victimized children.
- Initially, there was only one agency to deal with the children, viz., the juvenile court. The Central Children Act for the first time introduced a separate agency, namely the Child Welfare Board for handling neglected children and leaving the juvenile court to deal with delinquent children.
- Appointment of a separate probation officer to deal with the child and proper aftercare services for his/her rehabilitation in the society were provided for in the Acts of all the States, though in practice they were hardly taken care of by the States.
- There were no provisions for special qualification, training or knowledge of child psychology for persons dealing with juvenile cases.
- There was no uniformity in all these Acts as to the age of the child.
- Different States followed different practices and procedures.

Hence there was a need for a uniform legislation for the entire country.

The Juvenile Justice Act 1986

The Juvenile Justice Act 1986 replaced the Children's Acts, formerly in operation in the states and the Union territories. It came into force in 1987 on a uniform basis for the whole country. The preamble of the Juvenile Justice Act 1986 (JJA 1986) states that the Act is to provide for the care, protection, treatment, development, and rehabilitation of neglected and delinquent juveniles and adjudication of certain matters relating to disposition of delinquent juveniles.

The objectives of the Juvenile Justice Act 1986 were the following:

- To lay down a uniform framework for juvenile justice in the country so as to ensure that no child under any circumstances is lodged in jail or police lock-up.
- To provide for a specialized approach towards the prevention and treatment of juvenile delinquency.

- To spell out the machinery and infrastructure required for the care, protection, treatment, development, and rehabilitation of various categories of children coming within the purview of the juvenile justice system.
- To establish norms and standards for the administration of juvenile justice.
- To develop appropriate linkages and coordination between the formal system of juvenile justice and voluntary agencies.
- To constitute special offences in relation to juveniles.
- To bring the operation of the juvenile justice system in conformity with the United Nations Standard Minimum Rules for the Administration of Juvenile Justice.

Under the J J Act 1986, juvenile means a boy who has not attained the age of sixteen years or a girl who has not attained the age of eighteen years [Section 2(h)]. The juveniles are further classified into neglected juveniles and delinquent juveniles. A neglected juvenile [Section 2(i)] is a very wide term and includes a juvenile who is found begging [Section 2(a)], or who has no home and is a destitute, or who has unfit parents, or who lives in a brothel or with a prostitute, or who leads an immoral life, or a juvenile who is being abused or there is a possibility that in future he may be abused for immoral purposes. A delinquent juvenile[5] is one who has committed an offence under any law of the land and comes in conflict with law. The Juvenile Welfare Board deals the neglected juvenile whereas the delinquent juveniles are brought before the juvenile court.[6]

Machinery for Implementing the Act

The Act has provided for the classification and separation of delinquents on the basis of their age, the kind of their delinquency, and the nature of offences committed by them. The four types of institutions under the Act are as follows:

- *Observation Homes*: These are for temporary reception of juveniles during the pendency of any inquiry regarding them under this Act [Section 11].
- *Juvenile Homes*: A neglected juvenile is sent for accommodation, maintenance, and facilities for education, vocational training, and rehabilitation [Section 9].

---

[5] JJ Act 1986 Section 2(e): 'Delinquent juvenile' means a juvenile who has been found to have committed an offence.
[6] JJAct 1986 Section 2(i): 'Juvenile court' means a court constituted under Sec. 5.

- *Special Homes*: A delinquent juvenile is sent for accommodation, maintenance, and facilities for education, vocational training, and rehabilitation [Section 10].
- *After-care Organizations*: These are for the purpose of taking care of juveniles after they leave juvenile homes or special homes and for the purpose of enabling them to lead an honest, industrious, and useful life [Section 12].

Procedure in Case of a Neglected Juvenile

The procedure in brief [Sections 13 and 14] can be represented as shown in Figure 6.4.

Procedure in Case of a Delinquent Juvenile

The procedure in brief [Sections 18, 19, and 20) can be represented as shown in Figure 6.5.

Factors for Consideration while Making an Order

The following factors are to be taken into consideration while making an order under the Act [Section 33]:

- The age of the juvenile,
- The state of physical and mental health of the juvenile,
- The circumstances under which the juvenile lives,
- The report made by the probation officer,
- The religion of the juvenile, and
- Any other circumstances to be taken into consideration in the welfare of the juvenile.

Special Offences in Respect of Juveniles

Chapter VI of the Juvenile Justice Act 1986 provides for punishment for certain special offences in respect of the juvenile [Sections 41, 42, 43, 44, and 45]. These offences and their corresponding punishments are listed below:

Special offences	Punishment
1. Cruelty to juveniles (assault, abandoning, etc.)	1. Imprisonment up to six months or fine or both
2. Employment of juveniles for begging	2. Imprisonment up to three years and fine
3. Giving intoxicating or narcotic drugs or psychotropic substances to a juvenile	3. Imprisonment up to three years and fine
4. Exploitation of juvenile employees	4. Imprisonment up to three years and fine

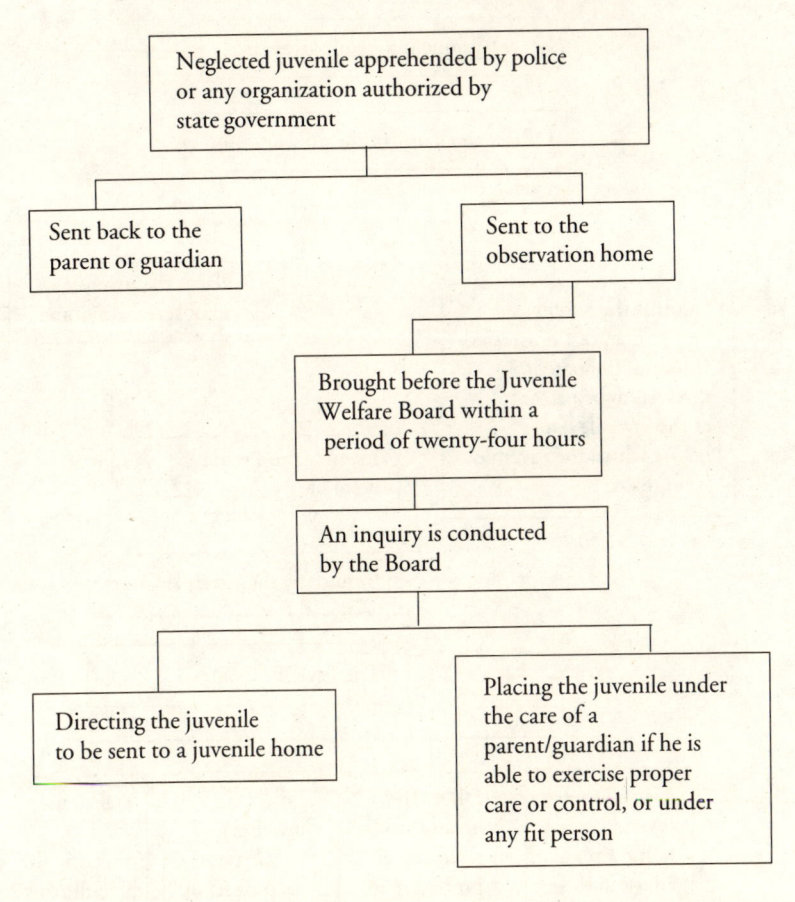

Figure 6.4: Procedure in Case of a Neglected Juvenile

```
Neglected juvenile apprehended by police
or any organization authorized by
state government
        │
   ┌────┴────┐
Sent back to the      Sent to the
parent or guardian    observation home
                           │
                  Brought before the Juvenile
                  Welfare Board within a
                  period of twenty-four hours
                           │
                  An inquiry is conducted
                  by the Board
                    ┌──────┴──────┐
         Directing the juvenile    Placing the juvenile under
         to be sent to a juvenile  the care of a
         home                      parent/guardian if he is
                                   able to exercise proper
                                   care or control, or under
                                   any fit person
```

Sanctions by the Juvenile Court [Sec. 21]

The court may order any of the following dispositions after explaining to the juvenile and the parent or guardian under whose care the juvenile has been placed, the terms and conditions of the order:

- Direct the juvenile to be released on probation of good conduct and placed under the care and custody of any parent, guardian, or other fit person executing a bond with or without surety as required by the court for the well-being and good behaviour of the juvenile for a period not exceeding three years;
- Direct the juvenile to be released on probation of good conduct and

Figure 6.5: Procedure in Case of a Delinquent Juvenile

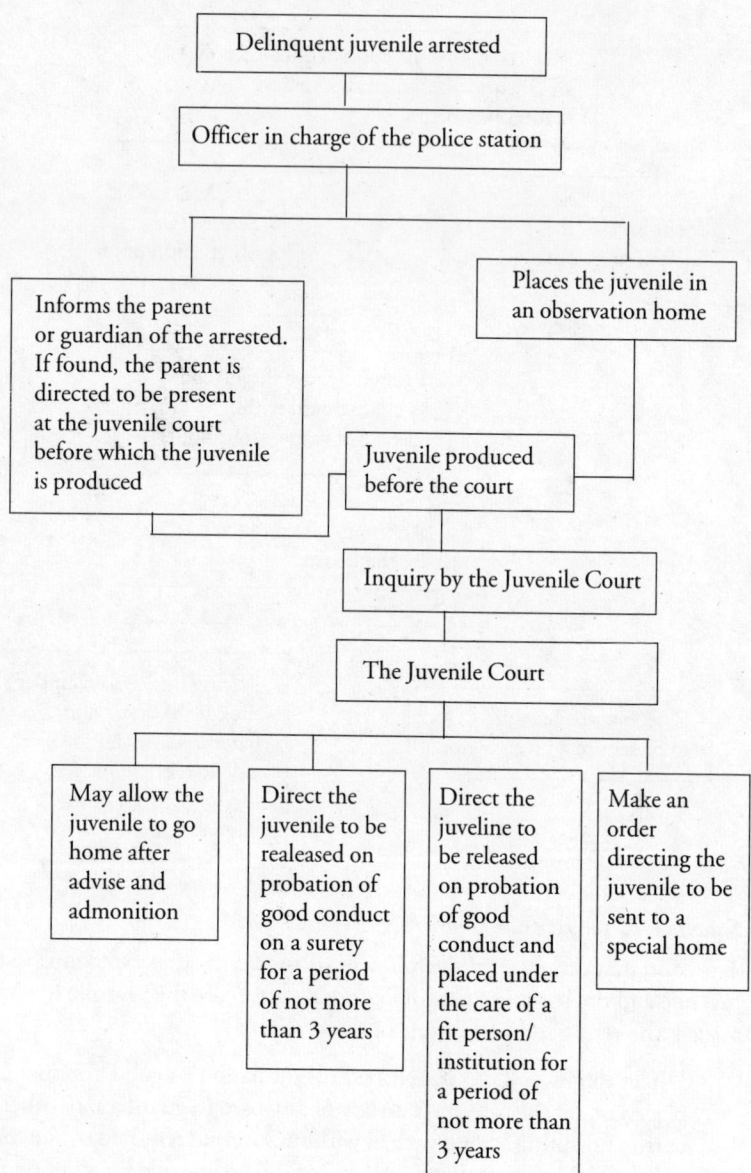

```
                    ┌─────────────────────────────┐
                    │ Delinquent juvenile arrested│
                    └─────────────────────────────┘
                                  │
                    ┌─────────────────────────────────────┐
                    │ Officer in charge of the police station │
                    └─────────────────────────────────────┘
                          │                       │
┌──────────────────────────────┐        ┌──────────────────────────┐
│ Informs the parent           │        │ Places the juvenile in   │
│ or guardian of the arrested. │        │ an observation home      │
│ If found, the parent is      │        └──────────────────────────┘
│ directed to be present       │                  │
│ at the juvenile court        │        ┌──────────────────────────┐
│ before which the juvenile    │        │ Juvenile produced        │
│ is produced                  │        │ before the court         │
└──────────────────────────────┘        └──────────────────────────┘
                                                  │
                              ┌──────────────────────────────────┐
                              │ Inquiry by the Juvenile Court    │
                              └──────────────────────────────────┘
                                                  │
                              ┌──────────────────────────────────┐
                              │ The Juvenile Court               │
                              └──────────────────────────────────┘
```

| May allow the juvenile to go home after advise and admonition | Direct the juvenile to be realeased on probation of good conduct on a surety for a period of not more than 3 years | Direct the juveline to be released on probation of good conduct and placed under the care of a fit person/ institution for a period of not more than 3 years | Make an order directing the juvenile to be sent to a special home |

placed under the care of any fit institution for the good behaviour and well-being of the juvenile for any period not exceeding three years;
- Order the juvenile to pay a fine if over fourteen years of age and earning money; or
- Order the juvenile to be released on probation of good conduct and placed under the supervision of a probation officer for any period not exceeding three years.

If none of the above alternatives were feasible, the court could order the juvenile to be sent to a special home, established or recognized within the State. A delinquent boy above fourteen years of age or a delinquent girl above sixteen years of age must be sent to a special home for a minimum period of three years. The juvenile delinquents below the age specified above should be sent to a special home till they cease to be children.

There are provisions relating to appeal by an aggrieved person against an order made by a competent authority under the Act. Only one appeal to the court of sessions has been permitted [Section 37] but in majority of the cases, the children have no resources for appeal and so there are not many appeals against the orders of the juvenile courts.

Administration and Implementation of the Juvenile Justice Act 1986

The history of the implementation of the Juvenile Justice Act 1986 is a history of hopes unrealized and promises unfulfilled. The judges, the law enforcers, the police, the probation officers, and other staff, have not carried the spirit of the Act.

One of the objectives of the Act was to lay down a uniform framework and to ensure that no child is lodged in jail or police lock-up. The Act has fulfilled the long-felt need of bringing about a uniform legislation for the whole of India. Though the Act is a Central legislation but the implementation is left to the state governments. Section 1(3) also makes provision for appointing different dates for bringing into force the different provisions of the Act. It can be done on different dates by different states. Therefore, even in the new millennium there are States which have still to set up the machinery under the Act. In practice, there are the following areas of concern in the administration and implementation of the Act:

- Arbitrary detention is illegal under Articles 21 and 22 of the Constitution of India. Articles 50, 56, and 57 of the Code of Criminal Procedure

(CrPC) mandate that no person can be detained in custody without knowing the grounds of arrest and that a detainee must be presented before a magistrate within twenty-four hours of his arrest. Section 160 of the Criminal Procedure Code prohibits the detention of males under the age of fifteen or females of any age for the purpose of investigation or questioning by the police. Article 9 of the International Covenant on Civil and Political Rights and Article 37 of the UN Convention on Rights of Child prohibit arbitrary detention. Both the Beijing Rules and the UN Rules for juveniles deprived of their liberty state that the human rights of juveniles should be protected and respected while in custody. India has ratified both these instruments. The Juvenile Justice Act 1986 also prohibits the detention of juveniles in either police stations or jails. But in spite of all these mandates, there have been several instances where children have been taken overnight for interrogation by the police and tortured and later released next morning. There is no record of their arrest. It is alleged that this normally happens when big thefts occur. Secondly, there have been complaints that the police do not produce the child within twenty-four hours after they have been arrested. Then, pressure is put on the child to tell the judge the wrong time of the pick-up. Many children prefer to go to adult lock ups rather than observation homes. Therefore, when picked up by the police, they say that they are eighteen years so that they are taken to the lock-up where they will be released earlier rather than being confined to institutions. The magistrate does not send them for age verification. In rural areas, if the child is well built, he is treated like an adult offender and taken to the police station. If later on his parents manage to come with evidence of age (which is very rare) he is released, otherwise the procedures of ordinary criminal law are followed.

- Juvenile courts are generally situated at district headquarters. Many children and their parents have to travel long distances at considerable trouble and expense to reach the courts on the date of the hearing and after reaching there they may have to return due to adjournments. The juvenile court has all the semblance of an adult criminal court. The juvenile courts use the word 'arrest', 'charge sheet', 'offence', 'offender', 'criminal', 'bail', 'bond', etc. The police, judge, magistrate, advocate, lawyer, public prosecutor, stamp fee, etc. are very much present in the juvenile justice system. The juvenile courts set up under J J Act can be called 'special courts' but the personnel in these courts are not aware of the specialized approach The atmosphere in the juvenile court is generally very intimidating. The judges sit in the front of the table and the child stands like an 'accused' in front of them. The child is not made comfortable or made to sit down. The child is petrified and does not know what is happening to him or what is going to happen when he appears before them. Therefore, the adult criminal justice system, terminology, functioning style, and attitudes are prevalent in practice. On days the juvenile courts do not sit, children in many States are taken to the premises of the ordinary courts for remand. In many instances, the police have arrested a juvenile without enough evidence. The bail application formats in some of the juvenile courts are in English. Petitions in juvenile court also have to bear a nominal stamp fee. In the juvenile courts, the court fee, the application, and the bail procedure are a source of harassment to the poor parents. The Mumbai High Court in a recent judgment has suggested the waiver of court fees. Cases are piling up in the juvenile courts mainly due to delay in filing charge sheets by the police, non-appearance of the investigating officer, etc.[7]

- Juvenile Courts have turned into second-class criminal courts. To a large extent differences are due to court organization and resources. The lack of clear laws, rules, and standards articulating how the court process is supposed to work has also contributed to the problem. The best interests principle requires an individual assessment in each case. But the caseload of the judges and probation officers is so high in the juvenile courts, especially in metropolitan cities like Mumbai that there is no time for such assessment.[8] The assistant public prosecutor is present but there is nobody to present the interests of the child before the courts. A duty counsel has been recently appointed in the juvenile court in Mumbai but there is a need to appoint such duty counsels in all the juvenile courts to represent the interests of children.

- The definition of juvenile delinquency is very legalistic and, restrictive and as a matter of fact, it does not take into consideration all actions that lead to the act of 'offence' but these acts are by themselves not an offence. Exclusion of these acts has a far-reaching consequence and may often make the whole juvenile justice system meaningless. For example, absenteeism, act of defiance to lawful authority, all these can be symptoms of a child gradually turning into a criminal unless treated early. But unfortunately, due to restrictive and legalistic definition of juvenile delinquency, these symptoms are neglected so long as the child does not

---

[7] Asha Bajpai, *A Pilot Study of Children and Courts in Mumbai*, Sponsored by Board of Research Studies, TISS, Mumbai, 2000.

[8] Asha Bajpai, *Juvenile Justice in Maharashtra—Administration and Implementation*, A study sponsored by UNICEF, 1998 (unpublished).

completely turn criminal by committing an act of crime.[9] The Indian Penal Code defines offences with an adult perspective. As far as children are concerned the offences cannot be the treated similarly as is the practice today. All borderline sub-delinquency and pre-delinquency acts can be included, for instance, in a school code non-formal authorities be given the power to take correctional steps.[10] The juvenile justice system should be the last resort and petty acts should not come before the courts. Such acts can be dealt within the community.

- An issue to be noted here is the motivation of the personnel involved in the system. There are several pressures at work that influence their behaviour, like the poor pay, the inadequate staff, the desire to succeed, the need to release acute feelings of frustration, and other overwhelming emotions.

- The investigating officer, under the present system, is a police officer and he has practically no experience of dealing with CEDC. Besides, dealing with children is not considered as *mainstream work*. It is a low-priority job. Their priority is *bandobust*, law and order, and investigating the so-called high-profile crimes like dacoities, extortions, and murders. Many a times, the cases in the juvenile courts are adjourned, as the investigating officer is absent. The repatriation orders for children are pending for months and years because the police is busy with law and order, VIP *bandobust*, duties during festivals like *Ganpati, Navratri*, etc. Many investigating officers are unaware of either the objectives of the Juvenile Justice Act or its provisions, or whether the children are neglected or delinquent, or whether they are lost or vulnerable. The policemen, at the grass roots like the *havaldar* and the constable are unaware of this law. A very senior police official commented that as far as children are concerned, we are aware of only three things— they should not be handcuffed, police should not be in uniform, and they should be produced before the juvenile court. This is the level of awareness at the highest level. The juvenile justice law forms almost negligible portion of the police-training curriculum. *The investigation of these issues requires a different kind of expertise which is absolutely lacking.* There is now a stereotype pattern of investigation which is carried on without any sensitivity or follow-up.

---

[9] N.L. Mitra, *Juvenile Delinquency and the Indian Justice System*, Deep And Deep Publication, New Delhi, 1988, p. 34.
[10] Ibid.

- A child in extremely difficult circumstances, who is already a victim of his circumstances, when he comes in conflict with the prevalent system, is subjected to secondary, in fact multiple, victimization. The detention, investigation, trial, and institutionalization processes further contribute to his victimization. The insensitive and untrained functionaries concerned, which include the police, the Juvenile Welfare Boards, the juvenile courts, the children's homes, further perpetuate the trauma. The core staff like caretakers, cooks, and guards who are directly in contact with the children are not trained at all. The delays in the system at every stage further add to the trauma of the child. The issue of the child's trauma is not at all considered by the legal system. The insensitivity of the functionaries has led to the children being scared of the system. A terrified child stands before the court or the board, not knowing what is happening. Some children are seen clinging to the table at the Juvenile Welfare Board for support but are rudely told to take their hands off the table. Children are also sometimes labelled by the insentive staff as 'thief', 'criminal', 'insects', etc.[11]
- The JJA classifies children into neglected and delinquent, with the intention of providing different structures to deal with them. One with a 'welfare approach' and the other with a 'justice approach'. The term 'juvenile' has a stigma attached to it. It is very difficult to differentiate between a neglected juvenile and a delinquent juvenile. One is the cause of the other. Neglect leads to delinquency and vice versa. The categorization is therefore, vague and artificial. Besides, in the observation home both categories of children are kept together for long periods of time and both are dealt with similarly.
- The Juvenile Welfare Board is the backbone of the entire juvenile justice system as they handle 80 per cent of the children. The members are part-time honorary workers, whereas this is a full-time job which requires total commitment.
- The Juvenile Justice Act 1986 does not directly deal with child sexual abuse but the definition of a neglected juvenile includes a juvenile who lives in a brothel or with a prostitute or frequently goes to any place used for the purpose of prostitution or is found to associate with any prostitute or who is being or is likely to be abused or exploited for immoral or illegal purposes. Such neglected children are produced before a

---

[11] Asha Bajpai, *Juvenile Justice in Maharashtra, Administration and Implementation*, A study sponsored by UNICEF, 1998.

Juvenile Welfare Board who may, after an inquiry, send the child to a juvenile home for care, protection, and rehabilitation. Under the Juvenile Justice Act 1986, a prostitute's child is also automatically regarded a neglected child. The magistrate has the power to segregate the prostitute from her child and place the child in a corrective institution. Besides, under this Act while males above eighteen years are considered adults, the age is reduced to sixteen years for females. The juvenile welfare boards are generally not equipped to deal with cases of child sexual abuse. The observation homes cannot provide special care and treatment for such victimized children.

- The J J Act binds itself only to matters regarding the relationship between the government and the children. Parents, relatives, school, and community do not have any role in the care and nurture of the child.

Problems with Institutional Care

The current legal response is 'institutionalization' in several cases. The J J Act 1986 does not clearly specify that institutionalization should be the last resort and that non-institutional, family-based, preventive services should be explored and made mandatory. Although the Juvenile Justice Act does not mention about non-institutional services, there are some non-institutional services that are presently being carried out in some parts of the country. Some juvenile welfare boards have taken the initiative of linking non-institutional services.

Non-institutional Services

Non-institutional services have the following major objectives:

- To ensure the child's right to a family.
- To strengthen the family as a unit and prevent family disintegration.
- To develop preventive, supportive, community-based, family-oriented outreach programmes for the CEDC.
- To provide the necessary support and strength to families 'at risk' in order to prevent abandonment and institutionalization of the child due to social and economic circumstances.
- To arrange for substitute family care when the child's own family of origin cannot look after him due to special circumstances.
- To work towards de-institutionalizing the child and reinstate/rehabilitate him in his own biological family or a substitute adoptive or foster family.
- To mobilize resources within the local community so that the innate capacities of the people are developed, leading to their participation.

Non-institutional services include adoption,[12] foster care,[13] sponsorship,[14] daycare/night shelter,[15] family assistance,[16] school social work,[17] and community centres.[18] It has been observed that:

- The need for non-institutional services is greater among families 'at risk' who belong to the lower socio-economic strata.
- Children in nuclear families are more vulnerable to the effects of family disintegration than extended families/joint families.
- Families are willing to help children of relatives and friends, or children from the same socio-economic strata if support is provided to them.
- In child welfare interventions, if the family as a unit is assisted rather than the child in isolation, the process of rehabilitation can be more effective.
- The rehabilitation and integration of the institutionalized child into the mainstream of society is difficult because of the deprivation and

---

[12] Adoption provides substitute family care for abandoned, destitute, and orphan children. No child should be deprived of care by biological parents solely because of economic reasons. Such families should be given economic support. But when the biological parents relinquish a child permanently due to circumstances beyond their control, or the child is declared a destitute, adoption is the best non-institutional service. First option should be in-country and after all possible efforts have failed, the child can be given in inter-country adoption. After adoption the child severs all ties with his natural parents and should get all the rights of a natural child in the adoptive family.

[13] Foster care provides temporary substitute care for children. When the family is undergoing a temporary crisis (like a death of a parent or sudden illness) children experience a lot of stress and tension. They may need to be removed from their natural home to prevent their neglect. These unfortunate children can be placed in foster families till the crisis is over. Unwed mothers or single parents could also be helped by this scheme by giving financial support.

[14] This programme provides supplementary support to families who are unable to meet educational and other needs of their children. Sponsorship enables the family to send the child to school, provide medical aid, and at the same time, remain with the birth family.

[15] Here the child is placed in a substitute family only during the day or night. This kind of service would enable working mothers or single parents to keep the child within the family and continue their work.

[16] This scheme provides the families with opportunities for self-employment so that they become financially independent. This is especially useful for families to help them to overcome temporary crisis situations like unemployment or serious family illness.

[17] These are multipurpose counselling centres and are very effective in controlling juvenile delinquency and family breaks.

[18] Supportive services in government and municipal schools through a school counsellor or a social worker are very effective in preventing drop-outs and providing counselling and other support services.

psychological trauma experienced in early childhood, which are sometimes irreversible.
- De-institutionalization with careful supervision of children as part of an early rehabilitation plan has proved to be an effective strategy.

Institutional care is expensive and includes infrastructure costs. This is not cost-effective and hence it is important to promote more cost-effective and child-friendly, non-institutional care.[19] The closed institutions are shrouded in their own mysterious goings-on. Children are at the mercy of caretakers who are untrained. Stories of beatings, sodomy, rape, and corruption filter through the homes. In this age of satellite communication, children at the institutions are learning to make brooms and chalks.[20] After-care homes in practice are absolute failures; they have turned into boarding and lodging places. There is no system of investigation or monitoring. The visitors' body does not exist and the advisory board is only on paper.[21] Appointments of staff to these institutions are done by the government which is itself a defaulter in the system.[22] Training is on *ad hoc* basis. The core staff who are actually in direct contact with the children untrained. There are no ongoing intensive training programmes. The issue of missing and runaway children is very important as the major chunk of neglected children fall in this category. The parents of missing children have to run from pillar to post to trace their children. There is a need for a centralized agency that can give information relating to missing children.

- The classification committee is not there in majority of the institutions. In some institutions, where it is present, it has become a mere formality.
- In case of children of substance abuse there is a need for specialized treatment and approach which is lacking.
- Children who are utilized in the workshops in the institutions and for selling the products sold are not paid any remuneration.
- The inspection of the institution is mostly a formality looking into written records, weights, quantity, etc., rather than looking at the quality of childcare and the interests of children.
- There is no interim/ periodical assessment and review of children who

---

[19] Nilima Mehta, *Non-Institutional Services for Children in Especially Difficult Circumstances*—A Manual supported by UNICEF, Maharashtra, and compiled for the directorate of women and child development, Government of Maharashtra, July 1996.

[20] Asha Bajpai, *Juvenile Justice in Maharashtra, Administration and Implementation*, A study sponsored by UNICEF, 1998.

[21] Ibid.

[22] Ibid.

are in the institutions. Once committed by the court, the child remains in the institution till his period is over.
- No child is informed of his rights, especially the right to free legal aid.
- There is no proper facility for development of character and abilities.
- Escape of children is treated as on offence and punished.

Government Schemes and NGO Interventions in the Juvenile Justice System

There are several Central and State government schemes and NGO interventions in the administration and implementation of the Juvenile Justice Act 1986. The interventions are in the areas of preventive, institutional, non-institutional, as well as rehabilitative work. Observation homes, juvenile homes, special homes, and aftercare homes are run by the government as well as by the NGOs. The government also provides grant-in-aid to the NGOs to run the homes. The services provided by these homes might include medical treatment, education, accommodation, vocational training, recreation, and job placement. The intake of children depends on the age and 'category' of the child. Some of these 'categories' are: street children, orphans, semi-orphans, girl children, non-court committed, court committed, children from broken families, children of unwed mothers, and school dropouts.

The interventions seem to be concentrated within urban areas, prime cities, and in certain geographical areas. The NGOs appear to be working in an individualized, small-scale manner and their efforts are thus fragmented and confined to certain areas and to certain specified categories of children. It is alleged that some of the NGOs are 'choosy' about the children. Some of them want only 'good children'. A major area of concern is that there are inadequate homes for the disabled children and children affected by HIV/AIDS.

There are network organizations as well working with street children and other underprivileged children for their survival, protection, and development. A good example of evolving partnerships to reach out to children is the Childline intervention, a national twenty-four-hour, free phone emergency outreach service, which tries to link children in need of care and protection to long-term services. Any child/adult concerned can call 10-9-8 (1098) free of charge. This includes regular follow-up. It is a project of the ministry of social justice and empowerment, Government of India, in partnership with NGOs, the UNICEF, and the corporate sector.

The SOS Children's Villages of India are an example of a good NGO intervention which needs to be emulated. These villages provide a home to orphaned and abandoned children. Children in SOS Villages grow up as children in an ordinary family. They live with a mother, brothers and sisters in a family home Siblings are not separated. An SOS Village is made up of ten to twenty houses, run by a team of efficient child care workers, who support and help the mothers in caring for the emotional and educational well-being of the children entrusted to their care. This type of child care is recommended as this is the closest alternative to a family and is in an integrated setting that balances the needs and develops relationships between the child, mother, family, and community. Institutional care provided by the government should be on the lines of a SOS Village.

What Needs to be Done

While planning child welfare interventions, services have to be in the context of the socio-economic, political, cultural realities, so that there is a *child-in-situation* approach rather than a *child-removed-from-situation* approach. The following issues are required to be taken care of by the government, the lawmakers, the NGOs, and the society at large:

- The entire juvenile justice system should be 'child-friendly' with a focus on the empowerment of the child.
- The juvenile court remains the venue with the most hope of rehabilitating society's troubled families and youths. To function well, it needs qualified and committed staff, funds, and effective dispositional options along with community support.
- Children are to be made aware of their rights.
- A grievance mechanism is to be provided in all institutions or homes wherein children can have access.
- Clear rules are to be laid down to deal with the staff who physically and sexually abuse children.[23] Health, nutrition, education, and vocational training facilities are to be updated for CEDC.
- All accredited journalists, public interest litigation lawyers, researchers, academicians, and legal aid organizations need to be given the right to visit any institution and interview any inmate.
- Social audits by independent bodies are to be made mandatory for the institutions wherein CEDC are lodged.
- Media should be friendly towards child rights and highlight pending cases, missing children, facilities in homes, and children's grievances and views.
- Trained social workers are to be attached to the courts as per the J J Act.

[23] In one case of sexual abuse in an institution in Mumbai, nobody knew whom to complain to.

- Institutionalization should be the last resort. Closed institutions should be gradually eliminated. Only open institutions with family-type environment should be allowed in future. Partnership between government-run institutions and voluntary organizations is essential so that there is no situation of either/or, but a relation of complementarity between institutional and non-institutional services. Existing institutional infrastructure should be utilized as a base for initiating the non-institutional services so that there is a gradual phasing out of institutional care. A linkage should be established between both the approaches.
- Non-institutional services should be given statutory recognition. The Juvenile Justice Act 1986 should clearly mention that institutionalization should be the last resort and the courts should opt for rehabilitation within the families and the communities. The functionaries and staff of the institutions, when reoriented and sensitized to the needs of children and the advantages of non-institutional services, would support the de-institutionalization of the child in a phased manner.
- The J J Act should contain special provisions to reflect the new approaches relating to child care. The J J Act should be liberally constructed so that each child under the jurisdiction of the juvenile court shall receive, preferably in the child's own home, the care, guidance, and control that will serve the child's welfare and its best interests. The court's intervention should build on the family strengths and be responsive to the family needs.
- The J J Act should be suitably amended to provide that representatives of all non-institutional services are present at the entry point, i.e. at the Juvenile Welfare Boards and, Juvenile Courts to prevent institutionalization of children.
- Rights of the girl child relating to arrest, interrogation, and release should be protected.
- Standards should be set for quality services in childcare standards for recreation, rehabilitation, and counselling. Standards of childcare should be laid down as per the Convention on the Rights of the Child. Inspection should be done on the quality of these services provided to the children.
- Only violent, serious offences are to be regarded as 'offence' as far as children are concerned. Needy, dependent, neglected children and children in especially difficult circumstances are to be kept out of the judicial system. Schemes and welfare measures for their protection and

empowerment need to be formulated. Families of such children are to be empowered.
- There should be a separate and exclusive investigating agency for children.
- Appointments of personnel in the juvenile justice system should be made by an independent body. Schemes for rewards and incentive along with punishment should be formulated for the personnel. Accountability of functionaries is to be taken into consideration.
- Quality education and vocational training for children should be arranged in consonance with the present market requirements.
- Mentally and physically disabled children are to be provided with special residential facilities and education.
- Special treatment for victimized and sexually abused children should be provided.
- Grants to organizations should depend on the ratings of the quality of services provided to children and not on the number of children as is being done now.
- There should be reservation of seats in higher education and jobs for children from the institutions.
- More involvement of the community, NGOs, and child welfare agencies should be encouraged.
- Training of all the functionaries to be made continuous and ongoing. Special focus should be on the core staff who directly deal with the children, like attendants, caretakers, security staff, cooks, probation officers, and superintendents.
- Inspection and monitoring of the institutions and organizations are to be conducted by an independent agency.
- There should be periodic evaluation of programmes thar are conducted in the institutions.
- A separate department for missing/runaway children with extensive links with the print and television media should be organized.
- The juvenile should participate in decision-making process in the issues affecting him/her.
- Judges should visit the place of detention for necessary observations and review of their orders.
- Records relating to children have to be properly maintained.
- Interaction and sharing of expenses between juvenile court and juvenile welfare board and institutions should be encouraged.
- A guardian *ad litem* or a representative of the child's interest could be appointed to help the child in court proceedings. It will be his job to

look after the best interest of the child and convey the same to the court. Legal aid and legal representation should be provided to the child. The medical and psychiatric assessment and treatment need to be humanely and more sensitively carried out.

The Juvenile Justice (Care and Protection of Children) Act 2000[24] (J J Act 2000)*

The ratification of the Convention on the Rights of the Child 1989 by India in 1992 and the changing social attitudes towards criminality by children reflected in Supreme Court decisions like Amrutlal Someshwar Joshi,[25] Ramdeo Chauhan,[26] and Arnit Das,[27] and the need for a more child-friendly juvenile justice system were some of the factors that led to the passing of the Juvenile Justice (Care and Protection of Children) Act 2000.

The preamble to the Act states that it is an Act to consolidate the law relating to juveniles in conflict with law and children in need of care and protection, by providing for proper care, protection, and treatment, by catering to their development needs, and by adopting a child-friendly approach in the adjudication and disposition of matters in the best interest of children and for their ultimate rehabilitation through their various established institutions under this enactment.

In this Act, 'juvenile' or 'child' means a person who has not completed eighteenth year of age [Section 2(k)] whereas the 'juvenile in conflict with law' means a person who is alleged to have committed an offence [Section 2(I)]. Thus there are two distinct categories of children under this Act:

- 'juvenile' for children in conflict with law and
- 'child' for children in need of care and protection [Section 2(d)].

The Act expands the definition of the 'neglected juvenile' by adding new categories of children. This category of children includes: mentally and physically disabled children; sick children or children suffering from terminal diseases or incurable diseases having no one to support or look after them; children who are abused or tortured or likely to be abused or tortured; children likely to be inducted in drug abuse, and children victimized by armed conflict or natural calamity.

---

[24] Received the assent of the president on 30 December 2000.
[25] (1994) 6 SCC 488.
[26] (2000) 7 SCC 455.
[27] (2000) 5 SCC 488.

Chapter II of the Act deals with juvenile in conflict with law. Chapter III provides for children in need of care and protection, and Chapter IV deals with rehabilitation and social integration of both the categories of children. Chapter V is for miscellaneous measures.

Provisions Relating to Juveniles in Conflict with Law

Constitution of Juvenile Justice Boards

The State government is empowered to constitute Juvenile Justice Boards to deal with juveniles in conflict with law [Section 4(1)]. The Board shall consist of a Bench of a metropolitan magistrate or a judicial magistrate of the first class and two social workers of whom at least one has to be a woman [Section 4(2)]. The magistrate appointed to the Bench shall have special knowledge or training in child psychology or child welfare and he shall be designated as the principal magistrate. The social workers appointed to the Bench shall be actively involved in health, education, or welfare activities pertaining to children for at least seven years [Section 4(3)].

Production of the Juvenile in Conflict With law

A juvenile in conflict with law has to be produced before the Juvenile Justice Board. When the Board is not sitting, such a juvenile may be produced before an individual member [Section 5(2)]. The order made by the Board shall not be invalid in the absence of any member during any stage of the proceedings provided there are at least two members, including the principal magistrate, present at the time of the final disposal of the case [Section 5 (3)]. If there is any difference of opinion among the members of the Board, the opinion of the majority shall prevail and where there is no majority, the opinion of the principal magistrate shall prevail [Section 5(4)].

Apprehension of Juveniles in Conflict with Law

As soon as a juvenile in conflict with law is apprehended by the police, he shall be placed under the charge of the special juvenile police unit [Section 2(d) (4)] or the designated police officer who shall immediately report the matter to a member of the Board [Section 10].
After the juvenile is placed under the charge:

- the officer in charge of the police station or the special juvenile police shall inform the parent or guardian of the juvenile, if found, and direct him to be present at the Board;
- the probation officer [Section 2(s)] has to obtain information regarding the antecedents and family background and other matters [Section 13].

When such a juvenile who is accused of a bailable or non-bailable offence appears before the Board, such a person shall be released on bail with or without surety unless there are reasonable grounds for believing that the release is not in the interest of the juvenile [Section 12(1)]. The Board shall hold an inquiry, which has to be completed within a period of four months from the date of its commencement unless there are special circumstances to be recorded in writing [Section 14].

Orders that may be passed regarding the juvenile in conflict with law [Section 15]

The scope of the orders have been widened. The Board shall have to obtain the social investigation report on juvenile either through a probation officer or a recognized voluntary organization and, after taking into account the findings, pass an order Where a Board is satisfied that a juvenile has committed an offence, it can pass the following orders:

- Allow the juvenile to go home after advice and admonition and counselling.
- Direct the juvenile to participate in group counselling and similar activities.
- Order the juvenile to perform community service.
- Order the parent of the juvenile or the juvenile himself to pay a fine, if he is over fourteen years of age and earns money, or in the interest of the juvenile, impose necessary conditions and order that the juvenile remain under the supervision of a probation officer for a period not exceeding three years.
- Direct the juvenile to be released on probation of good conduct and placed under the care of any parent, guardian, or other fit person [Section 2(1)] after executing a bond with or without surety for any period not exceeding three years, or in the interest of the juvenile, impose necessary conditions and order that the juvenile remain under the supervision of a probation officer for a period not exceeding three years [Section 15(3)].
- Direct the juvenile to be released on probation of good conduct under the care of any fit institution for a period not exceeding three years, or in the interest of the juvenile, impose necessary conditions and order that the juvenile remain under the supervision of a probation officer for a period not exceeding three years.
- Make an order directing the juvenile to be sent to a special home till he ceases to be a juvenile. In case of a juvenile over seventeen years, the period in a special home should not be less than two years.

It has been specifically provided that no juvenile in conflict with law shall be sentenced to death or imprisonment, or committed to prison in default of payment of fine or in default of furnishing security. The Act also states that if none of the above provisions are suitable or sufficient, the Board may order the juvenile in conflict with law to be kept in a place of safety and report it to the state government who may provide for protective custody [Section (1)(2)]. The Board also has powers to make an order directing that the relevant records of conviction shall be removed after the expiry of the period of appeal or a reasonable period [Section 19(2)].

Homes To Be Established Under The Act

Observation homes and special homes have to be established under this Act for the juveniles in conflict with law by the state government in or under an agreement with voluntary organizations in every district or a group of districts [Section 9(1)].

The observation homes are for the temporary reception of any juvenile in conflict with law during the pendency of any inquiry regarding them under this Act. The observation home will have a reception unit where the juvenile who is not placed under the charge of a parent or guardian will be initially kept for preliminary inquiries, care, and classification. The classification has to be done according to the age groups such as 7–12 years, 12–16 years, and 16–18 years. While doing such classification, due consideration has to be given to physical and mental status and degree of offence committed, for further induction of the juvenile into observation home [Section 8(4)].

Provision in Respect of Escaped Juveniles

Any police officer can take charge without warrant of a juvenile in conflict with law who has escaped from a special home or an observation home or from the care of a person under whom he was placed under this Act. The juvenile should be sent back to the home or person from where or whom he has escaped and no proceedings should be instituted against him for such escape. The Board that passed the order in respect of the juvenile should be informed [Section 22].

Prohibition of Publication of Name, etc., of Juvenile Involved in any Proceedings under the Act

There is a prohibition on publication of any report in any newspaper, magazine, news-sheet, or any other visual media of any inquiry regarding a juvenile in conflict with law under this Act. Unless it is in the interest of the juvenile, the name, address, or any other particulars that will lead to the identification of the juvenile cannot be published [Section 21].

PENALTIES AND PUNISHMENT OF SPECIAL OFFENCES AGAINST THE JUVENILE UNDER THE ACT

There are certain special offences under the Act, which are cognizable:

Special Offences

Offences	Punishment
Assaulting, abandoning, exposing, or willfully neglecting the juvenile or causing or procuring him to be assaulted, abandoned, exposed, or neglected in a manner that is likely to cause such juvenile mental or physical suffering by a person who has actual charge of the juvenile [Section 23]	Imprisonment for a term which may extend to six months or fine or both
Employment or use of juvenile or the child for the purpose of begging or causing him to beg [Section 24(1)]	Imprisonment for a term which may extend to three years and fine
Abetment of the above offence by a person who has actual charge of the juvenile [Section 24(2)]	Imprisonment for a term which may extend to one year and fine
Giving or causing to give a juvenile or a child intoxicating liquor in a public place or any narcotic drug or psychotropic substance except upon the order of a duly qualified medical practitioner or in a case of sickness [Section 25]	Imprisonment for a term which may extend to three years and fine
Ostensibly procuring a juvenile or the child for the purpose of any hazardous employment, keeps him in bondage and withholds his earnings or uses such earning for his own purpose [Section 26]	Imprisonment for a term which may extend to three years and fine

Provisions Relating to Children In Need Of Care and Protection

Chapter III of the JJ Act 2000 deals with the provisions relating to children in need of care and protection. The important provisions of the Act in this respect are:

Setting up of Child Welfare Committees (CWC)

To dispose of cases for the care, protection, treatment, development, and rehabilitation of children in need of care and protection and to provide for their basic needs and protection of human rights [Section 31(1)], Child Welfare Committees have to be formed by the State government for every district or a group of districts. The Committee shall consist of a chairperson and four other members, of whom at least one shall be a woman. One member of the CWC has to be an expert on matters concerning children. The CWC will function as a Bench of magistrates. The appointment of any member of the Committee can be terminated after holding an inquiry by the State government, if:

- He has been found guilty of misuse of power vested under this Act.
- He has been convicted of an offence involving moral turpitude.
- He fails to attend the proceedings of the Committee for consecutive three months or three-fourths of the sittings in a year, without any valid reason.

Production Before CWC [Section 32]

Any child in need of care and protection may be produced before the CWC by any one of the following persons:

- Any police officer or special juvenile police unit or a designated police officer;
- Any public servant;
- Childline, a registered voluntary organization or such other voluntary organization or an agency as may be recognized by the State government;
- Any social worker or a public spirited citizen authorized by the state government; or
- The child himself/herself.

On receipt of a report from any of the above persons who is authorized to produce the child, or the CWC on its own can hold an inquiry and complete it within four months and pass an order to send the child to the children's home or shelter home till suitable rehabilitation is found or till he attains the age of eighteen years. The primary objective of the children's home or shelter home will be restoration of and protection to the child.[28] There are also provisions for inspection committees and persons and institutions for monitoring and evaluating and social auditing of children's homes.

Provisions Relating to Rehabilitation and Social Reintegration

Chapter IV of the Juvenile Justice Act 2000 provides for the rehabilitation and social reintegration of the child in the children's home or special home. The Act provides for non-institutional services like:

- adoption,
- foster care [Section 42(a)],
- sponsorship [Section 43(1)], and
- sending the child to an after-care organization [Section 44].

Adoption has to be resorted to for the rehabilitation of orphaned, abandoned, and neglected children. The children's homes or the institutions run by State governments for orphans will be recognized as adoption agencies under the Act, both for scrutiny and placement of such children for adoption in accordance with the guidelines issued for adoption by the State government [Section 41(4)]. The Juvenile Justice Board is empowered to give the child in adoption after the following formalities are complied with [Section 41(3)]:

- Two members of the Child Welfare Committee have declared the child legally free for placement in case of abandoned children;
- Till two months period for reconsideration by the parent is over in the case of surrendered children; and
- The consent of the child who can understand and express has been obtained.

The Board can allow a child to be given in adoption to a single parent and also to parents who have a child of the same sex irrespective of the number of living biological sons or daughters [Section 41(5)].

Appeals, Revisions and Confidentiality

The J J Act 2000 also has provisions for appeal to the court of sessions [Section 52]. The High Court has the power to call for the record of the proceedings of the court of sessions or the competent authority [Section 53]. All the reports of the social worker and the competent authority have to be kept confidential [Section 51].

---

[28] J J Act 2000, Section 39. For the purpose of this section, restoration of child means restoration to parents, adopted parents, or foster parents.

Creation of a Fund [Section 61]

The State government can create a fund for the welfare and rehabilitation of the juvenile or child.

Advisory Boards [Section 62]

There is a provision for the creation of Central, State, District and City Advisory Boards for advising the government on matters relating to the children under this Act.

Significant Changes Brought about by the Juvenile Justice Act 2000

The Juvenile Justice Act 2000 has brought in some significant changes in an attempt to make the system more child-friendly. These are:

- The Act defines a child as a person who has not completed eighteen years of age. There is now no discrimination in ages between boys and girls and the age conforms to the CRC.
- Use of distinct terms such as 'juvenile' for children in conflict with law and 'child' for children in need of care and protection has been introduced.
- Juvenile Justice Board is to replace juvenile courts and Child Welfare Committees to replace the existing Juvenile Welfare Boards.
- The Juvenile Justice Act 2000 empowers the Board to give a child in adoption.
- The Juvenile Justice Act 2000 requires that the child's consent be taken into account before the adoption is completed.
- The new J J Act allows parents to adopt a child of the same sex irrespective of the number of living biological sons or daughters.
- Rehabilitation and social integration of a child is an important part of the Act.
- Non-institutional services are provided as alternatives to institutionalization.
- Non-governmental organizations have been involved in the Act.
- There is a provision for juveniles being placed under the charge of special juvenile police unit.
- The Act provides for reception, classification, and pre-trial detention of juveniles.
- New dispositional alternatives such as group counselling and community service have been provided to the Juvenile Justice Boards.

- There are provisions for children's home or shelter home for children in need of care and protection.
- Provision for monitoring and evaluation of children's home and shelter homes by the Central and State governments has been incorporated.
- Restoration of child to the family is now considered as prime objective of any children's home or shelter home.

Critique of the Juvenile Justice (Care and Protection of Children) Act 2000

- The Act has expanded the definition of the child in need of care and protection very significantly. It could lead to undue interference in the lives of several poor children and their families by the 'system'. Adequate safeguards need to be provided or there should be two distinctly separate legislation.
- The Act fails to expressly lay down the age of innocence, i.e. the minimum age below which this Act would not be applicable.
- The Act retains a high degree of dependence on adult criminal justice agencies like the police, the magistrate, and the lawyers, and also on procedures.
- The problem of special care and needs of the disabled children have been ignored. The education, training, and recreation of children have not been provided for. Besides basic or school education, even higher education and training of these children have to be considered. Open school and open university education system should be made accessible to these children.
- The health and nutrition of the children have to be provided for. Permanent posts of residential nurse and doctors are very important.
- The Child Welfare Committees will be playing a very important role under the new Act. It should have been specifically provided that these posts should no longer be on honorary, part-time, or voluntary basis.
- The Act has not taken into account the orders and directions of the Supreme Court and the various High Courts on the issues relating to juvenile justice, for instance, orders relating to repatriation and duty counsels, determination of the age of the child, etc.
- Training of personnel and functionaries working in the system is required for the implementation of the Act in its true spirit.
- There is no concept of parental responsibility in the Act.
- The Act fails to provide for procedural guarantees like right to counsel and right to speedy trial.

- The dispositional alternatives provided for a child in need of care and protection are very limited considering the wide scope of the Act. These should be increased.
- The Act is silent on inter-country adoption. The Act empowers the Juvenile Justice Board to give a child in adoption whereas it is the Child Welfare Committee that deals with children in need of care and protection.
- The provision on adoption in the new J J Act could lead to problems because of prohibition of adoption by the personal laws of certain communities. Muslims, Christians, Parsis, and Jews are not covered by any law on adoption. It is not clear whether the new J J Act can give them rights not conferred upon them by any law directly. The Hindus are governed by the Hindu Adoption and Maintenance Act 1956 which is a special law on adoption whereas the J J Act 2000 is a general law on adoption. It is unclear as to which law would have precedence. Usually, a special law overrides a general law.
- Standards of quality care have not been laid down.
- There is no linkage between the J J Act 2000 and the other related legal provisions relating to children, for instance, child labour, primary education, sexual abuse, adoption, disabilities, and health.
- There is a need for a provision relating to the kind of inspections required for the smooth functioning of the homes. The inspections should include physical facilities, cleanliness, nutrition, behavioural problems and disabilities, disciplinary practices, and physical and emotional health of the staff and children.
- Section 16 of the Act provides for segregation of a juvenile who has attained the age of sixteen years and has committed a serious offence. This has to be removed as segregation and solitary confinement will violate the right to development of the child.
- Punishment for cruelty to a juvenile or child, or exploitation of juvenile employees as provided in Sections 23, 24, 25, and 26 is imprisonment for a term which may extend to six months, or fine, or both. This is a serious offence and the punishment should be enhanced. There should also be a provision for compensation to be paid to the victim.
- All institutions/homes established under this Act should obtain a certificate of recognition from the Board of Control established under the Orphanages and Other Charitable Homes Act 1960.
- Section 8 should provide a time limit within which the preliminary inquiries are completed. Under the 1986 Act, it was observed that under the 1986 Act, it was observed that children remained in observation homes for long periods of time.

- Many States have still not complied with the provisions of the 1986 Act. A mandatory time frame should be set up to comply with the provisions of the 2000 Act.

Trends of Judicial Response to Juvenile Justice

Krishna Bhagwan v State of Bihar[29]

FACTS

Krishna Bhagwan was convicted of murder by a session's judge and sentenced to life imprisonment. No plea was taken that he was a 'child' under the Children Act at the time of committing the offence. If it was done, the session's judge could not have tried him. The plea of age was taken for the first time in the High Court. The Bench, which heard it, placed it before a larger bench. It referred two questions for answer. First, whether the Children Act would be applicable if the convict was a child (a boy below sixteen years) at the time of the offence but has crossed that age at the time of the sentence? Secondly, whether the plea of age can be taken at the time of the appeal and what procedure should be adopted to determine the age of the convict at the time of the offence?

HELD

The High Court stated that the various provisions of the Children Act and the Juvenile Justice Act showed that extraordinary procedure has been prescribed for enquiring into offences committed by a child. The basic approach is curative and reformative, not punitive.

Answering the first question, the High Court quoted Sections 3 and 56 of the J J Act and stated that even if a child accused has ceased to be a child, the inquiry may be continued and orders may be made as if the accused had continued to be a juvenile. The lawmakers were aware of the possibility that while undergoing trial, a child accused may cease to be a juvenile. They introduced a 'deeming fiction' which requires the courts to treat the accused as a child. This provision is made, treating children as a class, as they are of tender age and immature mind. Even if the crime is abhorrent, there shall be no imprisonment or death sentence. They shall be kept only in safe custody.

Regarding the question whether the question of age can be raised at the appellate stage, the High Court held that it could be done at the appellate stage, in the case of children. But the Court should be alert to the misuse of such a plea when a convict is sentenced.

[29] AIR 1989 Patna 217.

Sanjay Suri v Delhi Administration[30]

FACTS

A news report described the ill treatment meted out to minors in the Tihar Jail in Delhi in connivance with the jail staff. The writers of this report then moved the Supreme Court seeking the relief on behalf of the child prisoners. The Court then appointed the district judge to make an inquiry and report to it. His report 'disclosed a shocking state of affairs', according to the judgment. Adult prisoners subjected children to sexual assault. They feared that if their names were disclosed, they would be victimized.

HELD

The court passed several orders based on the report. Some juvenile undertrial prisoners were ordered to be released immediately. Some convicted minors were freed on parole for one month. The judgment stressed the need to generate a sense of humanism in jail administration.

The court passed certain orders to protect children. It called upon the magistrates and trial judges to specify the age of the person ordered to be detained. 'We call upon the authorities in the jails throughout India not to accept any warrant of detention as a valid one unless the age of the detainee is shown therein,' the judgment emphasized. Thus, the jail authorities can refuse to honour a warrant if the age of the person remanded to jail custody is not indicated. The warrant may be returned to the issuing court for rectifying the defect. The age is to be shown so that the detainee could be directed to an adult prison or a juvenile jail. The youth shall not be assigned any work in the same area where regular prisoners are made to work. Care should be taken to ensure that there is no scope for their meeting and having contact. Wardens should be shifted every three years. The visitors' board should consist of a cross-section of society, the judgement said.

Jayendra v State of UP[31]

FACTS

The offence was committed in 1974. Jayendra was convicted by the trial court which was confirmed by the Allahabad High Court. Under Section 2 of UP Children's Act, a child was defined one who is below sixteen years. Section 27 of the Act said that notwithstanding anything to the contrary in law, no court shall sentence a child to imprisonment for life or to any term of imprisonment. If a child was found to have committed an offence punishable with imprisonment, the court may order him to be sent to an approved

---

[30] AIR 1986 SC 414.
[31] AIR 1982 SC 685.

school till the age of eighteen years. However, the High Court sent the convict to jail. This was challenged before the Supreme Court.

HELD

The Supreme Court called for a report from the doctor in charge of the jail hospital as regards the age wherein the age of the convict based on various tests was found to be about twenty-three years at the time of the report (in 1981). That would mean that in 1974, at the time of offence, he was about sixteen years and four months old. The judgment stated that in the normal course, the Court would have sent the convict to an approved school but in view of the fact that he was by now twenty-three years old, it could not be done. Therefore, the conviction was upheld but the sentence of imprisonment was quashed. The Court directed the immediate release of the youth.

Munna v State of UP[32]

FACTS

A public interest petition was filed both in the Allahabad High Court and the Supreme Court when reports of sexual abuse in Kanpur Central Jail appeared in newspaper based on a social activist's findings. The High Court asked the sessions judge of Kanpur to visit the jail and find out whether boys below sixteen are detained in the Central Jail and whether they are maltreated. The jail authorities meanwhile released a large number of boys. Therefore, when the sessions judge visited the jail, there were only some six children there. But there were eighty-four undertrials who were between sixteen and twenty-one years of age. The judge also reported that there was general ignorance about the UP Children's Act among the jail authorities. There were parallel proceedings on the same issue in the High Court and the Supreme Court.

HELD

The High Court orders are not available, but the Supreme Court passed certain general directions regarding children in jails. The Supreme Court stated that if the allegations were true, it showed 'to what utter depths of depravity man can sink'. A court cannot abdicate its constitutional duty of ensuring human dignity to the juvenile undertrial prisoners. Declaring that the court must investigate into the allegations, it said that even if it was found that the youths were guilty, they could not be maltreated. 'They do not shed their fundamental right when they enter the jail. Moreover, the object of

[32] AIR 1982 SC 806.

punishment being reformation, we fail to see what social objective can be gained by sending juveniles to jails where they would come into contact with hardened criminals and lose whatever sensitivity they may have to finer and nobler sentiments,' the Court said.

Bhoop Ram v State of UP[33]

FACTS

The appellant and five others were convicted by the sessions judge of Bareilly for murder and other offences and were sentenced to life imprisonment. The appellant appealed to the Supreme Court arguing that he should have been treated as a 'child' within the meaning of Section 2(4) of the Children Act and sent to an approved school for detention till he attained the age of eighteen years instead of being sentenced to life imprisonment. He said he was less than sixteen years when the offence was committed, and showed his school certificate as evidence. The sessions judge had rejected the certificate as evidence and stated that since he was below eighteen years he was given life sentence and not the capital punishment. When the appeal was heard, the Supreme Court asked the sessions judge to have the convict examined by the chief medical officer of the State to ascertain his age. The medical report, after radiological and physical tests, showed that the convict was above sixteen years at the time of commission of the offence. The sessions judge rejected the school certificate as 'it is not unusual that in schools, ages are understated by one or two years for future benefits'. It was argued by the convict that the Court should go by the school certificate and the opinions of the medical officer and sessions judge about the age were subjective.

HELD

The Supreme Court ordered his immediate release as it ruled that at the time of the commission of the offence the man was below sixteen years according to the school certificate. It followed an earlier Supreme Court order in similar circumstances (AIR 1982 SC 685). This is because the convict should have been sent to an approved school in the first place. Since there was miscarriage of justice, the conviction was sustained, but the sentence was set aside. The Supreme Court held that the school certificate should be taken as valid, as there was no material evidence contradicting the age given in it. The medical opinion cannot replace the fact given in the certificate. The sessions judge went by his surmise that many parents give false age to gain

[33] AIR 1987 SC 1329.

benefits. The medical opinion cannot be foolproof. Therefore, the convict should have been treated as a 'child' under the Act, said the Supreme Court while quashing the sentence and releasing him.

Sheela Barse v Secretary, Children's Aid Society[34]

FACTS

The petitioner, a freelance journalist, sent a letter to the Bombay High Court making certain allegations about the observation homes managed by the Children's Aid Society. The society was regarded as a public trust and given state funds. The letter was treated as a writ petition and the High Court passed certain orders. The main grievances in her letter-petition were:

- Delay in restoration of children to their parents,
- Non-application of mind in the matter of taking children into custody and directing production before the juvenile court,
- Absence of proper follow-up action after admission of the children in the homes, and
- Detention being illegal, it amounts to harassment of children.

The society denied the allegations in the High Court, producing documents as evidence. The High Court accepted some charges and rejected others. It then passed seven procedural directions. The petitioner was not satisfied with them and appealed against the High Court.

HELD

The Supreme Court held that children should not be made to stay in the observation homes for too long. As long as they were there, they should be kept occupied. The occupations should be congenial and intended to bring about adaptability in life, self-confidence, and development of human values. Dedicated workers must be found and, after training, they alone should be employed in the children's homes. The juvenile court has to be manned by a judicial officer with some special training.

Krist Pereira v The State of Maharashtra and Others[35]

FACTS

This was a public interest litigation, which was filed after the death of a child in a remand home in Bhiwandi under mysterious circumstances. The Mumbai High Court constituted a committee of experts to examine the

---

[34] AIR 1989 SC 1278.
[35] Criminal writ petition No. 1107 of 1996, Mumbai High Court.

conditions in different juvenile remand homes, children's homes, and special homes in the State of Maharashtra and to make appropriate recommendations for improving their standards. The report of the committee brought to light the extremely distressing and pathetic conditions prevailing in the various homes in the state.

HELD

The High Court constituted a State Committee on Juvenile Justice which shall be consulted in matters of appointments as well as removal of personnel in the remand homes. The other significant directions were:

- Establishment of more juvenile and special homes,
- Establishment of rehabilitation committees in districts,
- Appointment of at least one social worker in each juvenile court,
- Appointment of duty counsellors and visitors,
- Superintendent of institutions to be given powers to suspend caretakers and other members of the staff for misbehaviour, and
- Training programmes for judges and other staff.

Arnit Das v State of Bihar[36]

FACTS

According to the FIR,[37] one Abhishek was shot dead on that day. On 13 September 1998, the petitioner was arrested in connection with the said offence. On 14 September 1998 the petitioner was produced before the additional chief judicial magistrate, Patna, who after recording his statement under Section 164 of the Code of Criminal Procedure remanded him to juvenile home, Patna. The petitioner claimed to have been born on 18 September 1982 and therefore a juvenile entitled to protection of the Juvenile Justice Act 1986. The petitioner's claim was disputed on behalf of the prosecution. The additional chief judicial magistrate (ACJM) directed an inquiry to be held under Section 32 of the J J Act. A medical board referred the petitioner to examination. On receipt of the report of the medical board and on receiving such other evidence as was adduced on behalf of the petitioner, the ACJM concluded that the petitioner was above 16 years of age on the date of the occurrence and therefore, was not required to be tried by a juvenile

---

[36] AIR 2000 SC 2264.
[37] On 5 October 1998 Crime No. 574/98 under Section 302 IPC was registered at police station Kadamkuan, Patna.

court. The sessions court in appeal and the High Court in revision had upheld the finding. The petitioner had filed this petition seeking leave to appeal. The leave was granted.

ISSUES

Two questions were considered by the Supteme Court:

- By reference to which date, the age of the petitioners is required to be determined for finding out whether he is a juvenile or not. Is it the date of offence which is crucial for determining the age of the person claiming to be juvenile or is it the date on which the person is brought before the competent authority.
- Whether the finding as to age, as arrived at by the courts below and maintained by the High Court, can be sustained.

HELD

So far as the present context was concerned, it was held that the crucial date for determining the question whether a person is juvenile is the date when he is brought before the competent authority. So far as the finding regarding the age of the appellant was concerned it was based on appreciation of evidence and arrived at after taking into consideration the material available on record and valid reasons being assigned for it. The finding arrived at by the learned ACJM had been maintained by the sessions court in appeal and the High Court in revision. The Supreme Court found no case for interfering with that finding. The appeal in this case was dismissed.

The age of the child is a matter of great concern. The issue has come up before the courts several times and in practice there are children lodged in adult jails because they had no evidence to prove their age. In such cases it is recommended that the benefit of doubt should always be in favour of the child.

In another case of *Raj Singh v State of Haryana*,[38] the Supreme Court held that the trial of the delinquent juvenile in the court of sessions stands vitiated as at the time of occurrence of the offence, the accused was a juvenile. In the case of *Arnit Das v State of Bihar* the Supreme Court overruled this judgment and held that the 'date of commission of the offence is irrelevant for finding out whether the person is a juvenile'. And that 'the crucial date for determining whether a person is a juvenile is the date when he is brought before the competent authority'. The decision in the Arnit Das case is being criticized as the concern of the Court in this decision seems to be more on the offence than on the best interest of the child. Many juveniles continue to

---

[38] 2000(6)SCC 759.

languish in jails for long periods of time because their age is not determined. The Magistrates who are not empowered to exercise the powers of the Juvenile Justice Boards should send the accused who claims or appears to be a juvenile for immediate determination of age.

International Law and the Administration of Juvenile Justice

There have been several international developments in the administration of juvenile justice. It was not until the International Covenant on Civil and Political Rights 1966 that specific provisions regulating the administration of juvenile justice were enshrined in a global treaty. The provisions on the administration of juvenile justice in the International Covenant are very specific. Article 10(2)(b) provides for the separation of accused juveniles from adults and for their speedy adjudication; Article 14(4) provides that the trial procedures for juveniles should take into account the age of juveniles and the desirability of promoting their rehabilitation.[39] These are provisions which, although useful, are limited as they only focus on narrow and specific aspects of juvenile justice. As an increasing number of States began to develop separate juvenile justice systems, the need became apparent on the international level for a complete framework which States could utilize for guidance in establishing and operating their own national juvenile justice systems. In 1980, the Sixth United Nations Congress on the Prevention of Crime and the Treatment of Offenders called for the preparation of minimum rules regulating the administration of juvenile justice.[40] In 1985, the General Assembly adopted the United Nations Standard Minimum Rules for the Administration of Juvenile Justice, known as the Beijing Rules.[41] They provide, as intended, a framework within which a national juvenile justice system should operate and a model for States of a fair and humane response to juveniles who may find themselves in conflict with the law.

The Beijing Rules

The Beijing Rules, which are divided into six parts, cover the whole range of juvenile justice processes:

- General Principles;
- Investigation and Prosecution;

[39] See Article 6(5) International Covenant on Civil and Political Rights in Van Beuren International Documents, 1993.
[40] UN Doc. Resolution 4, Sixth United Nations Congress on the Prevention of Crime and the Treatment of Offenders.
[41] UN Doc A/RES/40/33.

- Adjudication and Disposition;
- Non-institutional Treatment;
- Institutional Treatment and Research and Planning; Policy Formulation; and
- Evaluation.

The Beijing Rules are not a treaty and they as an entire body of rules are non-binding *per se*. But some of the rules have become binding on State parties by being incorporated into the Convention on the Rights of the Child. Others can be treated not as establishing new rights but as providing more details on the contents of existing rights.

The Beijing Rules provide that:

- A comprehensive social policy is in place to ensure the well-being of juveniles.
- Reaction to juvenile offenders is always to be in proportion to the circumstances of both the offenders and the offence.
- Police officers who deal extensively with juveniles shall be specially instructed and trained.
- Detention pending trial is to be used as a measure of last resort and for the shortest possible period of time.
- The placement of a juvenile in an institution is always to be a disposition of last resort and for the minimum necessary period.
- Necessary assistance such as housing, vocational training, and employment is to be provided to facilitate the rehabilitative process.[42]

THE DEFINITION OF JUVENILE UNDER BEIJING RULES

In international law the definition of child is generally directly or indirectly related to age. The term juvenile, however, does not necessarily correspond to the concept of 'child'. According to Rule 2(2)(a) of the Beijing Rules, 'A juvenile is a child or young person who under the respective legal system may be dealt with for an offence in a manner which is different from an adult.' It is the manner in which a child is treated for an offence which dictates whether a child is also a juvenile.

The definition of a juvenile is critical because the standards incorporated into the Beijing Rules, many of which are improvements on existing standards, only apply to juveniles and not to all children. Hence the definition enshrined in the Beijing Rules contains a gaping hole, because it allows the national legal system to define juvenile. In essence, the Beijing Rules say no

---

[42] N.L. Mitra, *Policy and Law in Juvenile Justice*, National Law School of India University, Bangalore, 1999.

more than that if a person is treated as a juvenile, he or she is a juvenile. The reason for the special protection and entitlements of children is because of their age and vulnerability, not because of the system of trial.

Although the Beijing Rules were drafted by States so as to be applicable within the widest range of legal systems, this definition of a juvenile severely limits the application of the Rules. In some jurisdictions children who are accused of serious offences are treated as if they were adults and in such cases the Beijing Rules would not apply.[43] The drafters of the Beijing Rules did try partially to overcome this handicap by encouraging States to make efforts to extend the principles enshrined in the Beijing Rules to all juveniles in welfare and care proceedings but this does not affect children accused of serious offences. The Convention on the Rights of the Child has transformed some of the Beijing principles into binding law.

Basic Principles of International Law for a Juvenile Justice System in the Best Interest of the Child

International law incorporates a number of basic principles upon which a juvenile justice system should be based. They are based on the various covenants, conventions, and guidelines. They are broadly as follows:

- The well-being of the child in the administration of justice needs to be maintained.[44]
- Criminal responsibility should be related to age at which the children are able to understand the consequences of their action.[45]
- Diverting children from formal trial procedures.[46]
- Juveniles to be brought as 'speedily as possible' to adjudication.[47]
- The arrest, detention, or imprisonment should only be imposed on children as a measure of last resort.[48]

---

[43] In the United States, children who are accused of murder may be tried as adults.
[44] Both the Beijing Rules and the Convention on the Rights of The Child emphasize this.
[45] Article 40(3)(b) of the UNCRC and Rule 4 of Beijing Rules.
[46] Article 40(3)(b) of the UNCRC and Rule 11.1 of the Beijing Rules.
[47] Article 10(2)(b) of the International Covenant on Civil and Political Rights and Rule 20 of the Beijing Rules.
[48] Rule 30 of the Rules for the Protection of Juveniles Deprived of Their Liberty. See also United Nations Standard Minimum Rules for Non-custodial Measures. Tokyo Rules adopted by GARes. 45/110 on 14 December 1990. [17(1)(c) of the Beijing Rules, 37(b) of UNCRC, and Rules for the Protection of Juveniles Deprived of Their Liberty].

- The rights of children prior to the determination of charges include the duty to inform parents or guardians[49] and all children should be presumed innocent until proven guilty according to law.[50]
- The Convention on the Rights of the Child, the International Covenant on Civil and Political Rights, the regional human rights treaties, and the Beijing Rules provide the rights of children during the determination of criminal charges. They provide that the principles of natural justice are equally applicable to children. Right to counsel is important for children.[51]
- Specific forms of punishment like corporal punishment and imposition of death penalty are prohibited for children.[52] The children should be provided with alternatives to institutional care.[53]

Standards for the Prevention of Juvenile Delinquency

The United Nations Guidelines for the Prevention of Juvenile Delinquency, known as Riyadh Guidelines were adopted in 1990.[54] The guidelines focus on early protection and preventive intervention paying particular attention in situations of social risk. The term 'social risk' denotes children who are demonstrably endangered and in need of non-punitive measures because of the effects of their circumstances and situation on health, safety, and education as determined by a competent authority.

The underlying principle of the Riyadh Guidelines is that the prevention of juvenile delinquency should utilize both the child's family and the school. The principal aim of the Guidelines is to help socialize and integrate children through the family and through the active involvement and support of the community.

The Guidelines also recommend that children should use schools as resource and referral centres for the provision of counselling, particularly for children with special needs and for the dissemination of information on the prevention of drug, alcohol, and substance abuse.[55]

---

[49] Articles 9(4) and 15(1) of the International Covenant on Civil and Political Rights.
[50] Articles 40(2)(b)(1) of the UNCRC and Article 14(2) of the International Covenant on Civil and Political Rights.
[51] A UN study found that the right to counsel can become more important because of the informality of juvenile proceedings.
[52] Article 37(a) of the UNCRC, Article 7 of the ICCPR, and Rule 111 of the Beijing Rules.
[53] Article 40(4) of the UNCRC.
[54] Adopted by the General Assembly on 28 March 1991; UN Doc. A/RES/45/112.
[55] Guidelines 25 and 26.

A Comparative Survey of the Juvenile Justice Systems in Various Countries and the Developments

A survey of the Juvenile Justice Systems in some other countries reveal the following rrends.

Prevention of Institutionalization

The traditional approach of institutionalization of CEDC deprives the child of basic human rights. The child is also separated from his/her family environment. These children are thus deprived of their family environment and experience several negative experiences in large, depersonalized institutions. Institutions generally tend to be destructive, unhealthy, and debilitating places. Some of the end products of such institutions are seen in the aftercare homes. Many of them have psychological and behavioural problems and inadequate skills, and feel unable to fit into the community. They have been stigmatized as 'losers'.

Of course, not all juvenile institutions are harsh, brutal, and cruel. But, they all, by nature, deprive children of their freedom to a greater or lesser degree and they are undesirable alternatives to keeping children in their own homes or communities whenever possible. Secondly, institutionalization is an expensive alternative.

Article 9 of the United Nations Convention on the Rights of the Child states that the child should ideally be brought up in a family environment that is secure and nurturing, and protects its rights. If the biological family is unable to look after the child, then there should be a substitute or alternative family for long-term or short-term care. These alternatives are the non-institutionalization services. They are the programmes for the rehabilitation and care of children outside the institution. They have to be integrated, community-based, family-oriented, and preventive.

The main objective of non-institutional services is that every child has a right to a family and therefore it is necessary to ensure the child's rights within a family. This can be achieved by strengthening the family as a unit, by providing counselling and support services. When the child's own family of origin cannot look after him, substitute foster care should be arranged. The final objective is to work towards de-institutionalization of the child.

There are several countries that have statutes for preserving and strengthening the families and thus preventing delinquency and institutionalization. The new child welfare provisions reveal language that essentially covers the entire range of governmental and legal actions aimed at families. Generally, institutionalization is resorted to in three instances.

- When a youth has committed an especially heinous crime,

- When a youth is a chronic and serious offender, or
- When a youth is dangerous to himself or others.

Rehabilitation within the Families and Communities

It is believed that the families of juveniles are necessarily dysfunctional because juvenile crime results from individual family and environmental factors. It is unwise to attempt to prevent juvenile crime by removing juveniles from conditions in which they will eventually return.

Because families and communities contribute significantly to juveniles' troubling behaviour, family counselling remains the most effective method for healing juvenile offenders.[56] Efforts conducted in community settings have been extremely effective in reducing institutionalization and attenuating the criminal activity of even serious offenders.

Public policy goals demand that policy makers consider the human benefits of avoiding institutionalization. Even if the costs and general efficacy of the punitive, out-of-home-community and rehabilitative, in-home-community options were equivalent and if States ignored the rights and treatment needs of children, basic values would dictate a preference for in-home rehabilitation. Obvious social benefits are derived from programmes that reduce crime because of the high human costs of victimization. Wise public policy demands supporting family integrity, minimizing restrictions on liberty and intrusions on the privacy of youth and their families.

De-institutionalization

Children are entitled to a decent, stable home environment. This entitlement is a human right memorialized in several International Declarations and Conventions. The significance of the family is reflected in the United Nations Declaration of 1994 as the International Year of the family. The year 1994 highlighted the importance of the family and its role in promoting healthy behaviour.[57] The United Nations Convention on the Rights of the Child 1989, also affirms this right.

In addition to recognizing the rights of duties of children and families, the United Nations also adopted the Riyadh Guidelines, which aimed at delinquency prevention. These guidelines demonstrate the international

---

[56] See Levesque and Tomkins, *Revisioning Juvenile Justice*, Journal of Urban and Contemporary Law, Vol. 48:87. Washington University School of Law, 1995.

[57] See United Nations Convention on the Rights of the Child, 1989. The Convention establishes children's right to a family environment, 'a full and decent life' and 'a standard of living adequate to the child's physical, mental, spiritual, moral, and social development' (at preamble, Art. 23, Art. 27).

community's renewed focus on families and communities and its continued belief that young people should be institutionalized only as a last resort. The International Covenant on Civil and Political Rights explicitly protects families and proposes a justice system that contains special procedures for juveniles designed to promote their rehabilitation.

Examples of these approaches and trends can be seen in The Uniform Juvenile Court Act adopted by Georgia, North Dakota, and Pennsylvania that aim to achieve the foregoing purposes in a family environment wherever possible; separating the child from his parents only when necessary for his welfare or in the interests of public safety. The State of Oregon has, however, incorporated the Uniform Act's focus on Community Empowerment and has become a model. The objectives of Oregon's Community Juvenile Services Acts are as follows:

- The family unit shall be preserved.
- Intervention shall be limited to those actions, which are necessary and utilize the least restrictive and most effective and appropriate resources.
- The family shall be encouraged to participate actively in whatever treatment is afforded to a child.
- Treatment in the community rather than commitment to a State Juvenile Training School shall be provided whenever possible.
- Communities shall be encouraged and assisted in the development of alternatives to secure temporary shelter for children who are not eligible for secure detention.

The above programme had improved juvenile justice by decreasing the number of 'at risk' youth who enter the system. [See US Department of Justice Office of JJ and Delinquency Prevention OJJDP, *The Juvenile Justice Bulletin*, 1990.] The focus however has typically been on community involvement by providing more shelter, specialized foster care, runaway projects, and services for street youth.[58]

Maine's Family Support Services Act 1994, Oklahoma's Family Support Act 1993, and Louisiana's Community and Family Support Act 1995, all stress on providing in-home, family-based services for children and preventing or delaying 'out of home placement' of children with severe development disabilities, and providing social services to stabilize family life and to preserve family units.

[58] Juvenile Justice: A New Focus on Prevention. Hearing before the sub-committee of the Senate Committee on the Judiciary on Juvenile Justice, 102nd Congress Session 32, 36 (1992) [testimony of Thomas R. English, Executive Director of the Oregon Council on Crime and Delinquency].

This new international ethos in juvenile justice should be reflected in the approaches to the Juvenile Justice legislations. The Juvenile Justice legislation should provide that the Act be liberally constructed so that each child under the jurisdiction of the juvenile Court shall receive, preferably in the child's own home, the care, guidance and control that will best serve the child's welfare and its best interests.[59] The goals of family preservation statutes must attempt to pre-empt juvenile and family problems, strive to serve the best interests of children and the community by improving parenting skills, and providing services in the least restrictive environment. The ultimate goal should be family preservation, reunification, or permanent alternative placement.

Mission of Juvenile Courts for the Twenty-first Century

The interpretations, procedures, and perceptions of juvenile justice system (gauged from the empirical study, observations and interviews) have transformed the juvenile court from its original model as a social service agency into a deficient, second-rate, marginalized criminal court. Families have been completely left out of the present juvenile justice system. The conditions that required treatment was poor parental guidance care as well as social harms associated with poverty and these were completely overlooked. The principle of best interest of child is not prevalent at all. The court orders do not mention these words nor any reasons for these orders. The following important issues are to be taken care of in order to improve the system:

- Juvenile Courts have to be revitalized with the most expansive vision and based upon a deeper understanding of the psychological and social forces which bring children into court. There has to be a juvenile court that is sensitive to the developmental needs of juveniles in each case, flexible enough to respond to new discoveries in social science research, and willing to invest in and experiment with promising new interventions for offenders. Juvenile Courts should be vital community resources. A developmental perspective may be usefully employed in formulating legal responses.[60]

---

[59] IOWA Code Ann. (1994). The Nebraska Juvenile Court Code states: 'to achieve its purpose in the juveniles' own home whenever possible, separating the juvenile from his or her parent when necessary for his or her welfare or in the interest of public safety and when temporary separation is necessary, to consider the developmental needs of the individual juvenile in all placements and to ensure every reasonable effort to reunite the juvenile and his or her family.'

[60] See Scott and Grisso 'The Evolution of Adolescence: A Developmental Perspective

- Interventions in the juvenile courts should have educational, mental health, and social service components. It has been found that multi-systemic therapy shows promise with young offenders.[61]
- Personnel in the juvenile courts are the key. Unless the juvenile court can identify and train good people, juvenile justice systems will not realize their potential. (Law students could be good resource). Judges in juvenile courts should be especially trained to recognize the educational, social, and treatment needs of children and families in crisis.
- The needs of the children and families who appear in juvenile courts have to be addressed. The orders cannot be passed in isolation; knowing and tapping the available services for such children should be the first priority.
- It is significant to note that there is too much reliance on plea bargaining. When a child is in an institution or before strangers, he is asked to choose between going to trial and pleading guilty. The deal is almost impossible to resist. A child's response to such an offer may not be voluntary. In a juvenile court, plea bargaining is particularly destructive. Children who are scared cannot understand the various forces at work. This negotiation does not further the interest of the child but furthers the interest of the system.[62] Pressures are generally applied by probation officers to encourage children to plead guilty. Children who are not guilty and who have to plead to something that he did not do, undermine the entire system. In future, plea bargaining need not be done without a representative of the child's best interest.
- Juvenile courts cannot possibly succeed without a level of professionalism and experience that would require for any important endeavour.

---

on Juvenile Justice Reform', *The Journal of Criminal Law and Criminology*, Volume 88, Number 1, Fall, 1997.

Developmental models help to understand how we become the people we are. According to Professor Erikson's model, each period of life has its 'own particular challenges and hurdles and from the way each child resolves or facts to resolve these may come an enduring set of responses in the future. Each stage brings with it a new social role, a new set of tasks to be mastered, new patterns of interaction, and new emotions. Erikson's theory relates to identity development.

[61] See David Tate et al, 'Violent Juvenile Delinquents: Treatment Effectiveness and Implications for Future Action,' *50 AM PSYCHOLOGIST*, 777, 779 (1995). This therapy is directed at solving the youth's multiple problems in many contexts—family, peers, schools, and neighbourhood.

[62] Thomas F. Geraghty, 'Justice for Children: How do we get there?' *The Journal of Criminal Law and Criminology*, Vol. 88, Fall, 1997.

- Institutionalization should be the last resort. Children need not spend their formative years in an environment with no positive role models and no useful education or training (they still learn to make brooms today!) other than an intensive immersion in the ways of crime brutality. Community-based support programmes for children and families should be encouraged.
- A Juvenile Court of the twenty-first century must have interdisciplinary connections with a variety of professions: law, medicine, psychiatry, psychology, and child welfare administration and management.
- There should be speedy disposal of cases involving children in order to ensure that the developmental needs of the child are addressed and the child continues to live in his growth and development.
- Community-based correction includes activities and programmes within the community that have effective ties with local environment with employment, education, and social and clinical service delivery systems including drug abuse prevention services.
- Computerized facilities should be introduced for recording social histories and court records. Investigating social histories offer valuable perspectives. It is important to keep records of repeat offences. The traditional confidentially of juvenile court records and proceedings must be replaced by greater transparency and openness.
- The basic human rights of the child must be protected in the juvenile court. In *re Gault*,[63] the Supreme Court of the USA laid down the following basic rights in a Juvenile Court:
  - Notice of charges
  - Right to counsel
  - Right to confrontation and cross-examination
  - Privilege against self-incrimination
  - Right to a transcript of proceedings
  - Right to appellate review
- The juvenile court should be able to supervise the control over services that are provided for the child. A court should be able to hold a State agency responsible for the treatment of children.
- Juvenile treatment and correctional facilities are unlikely to perform well without the oversight of an independent ombudsman, as the children in their care are powerless.

---

[63] In *re Gault*, 38 US 1 (1967).

- Standards should be set for institutions dealing with children.
- And finally, best interest of the child in juvenile justice must integrate and link the conduct of all who work in juvenile courts—prosecutors, defence lawyers, judges, mental health professionals, NGOs, and probation officers.

7

Right to Development

Elementary Education—The Right of Every Child

Right to education of every child is clearly a human right. Education is important as it enables the child:

- To develop and realize her/his full potential as a human being
- To develop the ability to think, question, and judge independently
- To develop a sense of self-respect, dignity, and self-confidence
- To develop and internalize a sense of moral values and critical judgment
- To learn to love and respect fellow human beings and nature
- To develop civic sense, citizenship, and values of participatory democracy
- To enable decision making.

Education is a human right with immense power to transform. On its foundation rest the cornerstones of freedom, democracy, and sustainable human development. Education is desired for itself as it opens up a vast world of opportunities and ideas to the educated person. It is also of great instrumental value in the process of economic growth and development. Education plays a critical role in demographic transition; female education, in particular, is seen to be important in the process of economic growth and development.[1] Education also plays a critical role in the process of lowering fertility and mortality. Primary schooling is associated with better health outcomes. There is a strong correlation between literacy and life expectancy. The returns to education are large and positive. Schooling has been seen to have a positive impact on agricultural output. In political and social terms too, schooling creates an educated population and a more constructive citizenry. Education empowers and empowerment affects larger social processes.[2] In recent decades, the importance of education has been reflected

---

[1] The State of the World's Children, 1999, UNICEF.
[2] M. Swaminathan, and V. Rawal, *Primary Education for All*, India Development Report, 2000, p. 68.

in increased budgetary allocations to basic education, compulsory schooling legislation, and widespread media attention to education and development issues.

Millions of young people around the world grow up unable to build decent lives for themselves because they are denied their right to education. The State of the World's Children, 1999 points out that 130 million children in the developing world are denied this right—almost two thirds of them are girls.[3] Denying girls their right to a quality education effectively denies them all other human rights and minimizes the chances of successive generations—particularly the chances of their daughters—to develop to their fullest potential.

Thus, as the world has become more complex, school systems have expanded in both size and complexity and the challenges they face. People see growing disparities and gaps—in costs, quality, achievement, and certification—and this has led to a 'crisis of confidence' in public schooling throughout much of the world.

Basic education consists of a combination of indispensable competencies, knowledge, skills, and an attitude that serves as the foundation of any individual's lifelong learning. Although there will be differences in what constitutes 'basic education' from society to society, there are some fundamentals that are common across cultural, social, and political boundaries. Key competencies include reading, writing, and numeracy. Without these competencies it is difficult for an individual to pursue learning in modern times. Knowledge should be both theoretical and practical. An example is the area of basic science. Its content, for instance, is likely to vary according to the particular context, but it must provide learners with the basic scientific concepts and experience that will allow them to function on a daily basis in such areas as food, nutrition, water, and sanitation. Skill provides an individual with the ability to use knowledge effectively and easily. There are many different types of skills. Survival skills are those that are basic to survival, such as finding food and seeking protection. Life skills enable an individual to have access to a better life. These might include skills for work, problem-solving skills, communication, analysis, and logic. Attitudes are feelings about or positions towards certain purposes or aspects of life. These include self-esteem, tolerance, cooperation, and civic responsibility. Thus, basic education is a broad and complex concept. Although there is general agreement as to what the components are, there is plenty of room for each country and community to configure these components in ways that are most relevant to

---

[3] The State of the World's Children, 1999, UNICEF.

them. In operation, basic education occurs in a wide range of contexts and is not limited by structure, content, or participants.[4] Basic education meets the fundamental learning needs of children, youth, and adults, going beyond the confines of formal primary education. This expanded vision of basic education encompasses all ages and all modalities, focuses on learning and acquiring specific competencies rather than on institutional forms, and promotes a unified basic education system with mutually supportive and complementary components.

Primary education for children is the most important component of basic education, if only because the human life cycle requires that the basic competencies and life skills be acquired at an early age. The formal primary school is the principal vehicle for primary education, but other complementary non-formal and flexible approaches are needed to make primary education universal. Other programmes which support progress towards that goal, but which are also important in their own right, are 'second chance' primary education for youth and adults, adult education and literacy, early childhood programmes, and parents' education.

The absence of primary education of an acceptable quality remains a serious problem in most parts of the developing world. Early childhood development (ECD) and adult basic education serve as supporting efforts to primary education. The relative emphasis and mix of activities will vary from country to country.[5]

Elementary Education in Five-Year Plans in India

Five-year plans are an important development strategy in India. Five-year plans have repeatedly promised to take the nation towards achieving universalization of elementary education. Expenditure on education in the five-year plans has shown a rapid rise since the inception of the first five-year plan in the country, but an analysis of intra-sectoral allocation of resources during the plan period shows a lopsided emphasis on elementary education. In the first five-year plan, 56 per cent of the total plan resources to education were allocated to elementary education. The relative importance given to elementary education declined to 35 per cent in the second plan, to 34 per cent in the third plan, and gradually to 30 per cent in the sixth plan. It was only during the seventh and eighth plans that significant efforts were made to increase the allocation substantially, though the allocation in the eighth plan was still

---

[4] www.unicef.org visited on 4 July 2002.
[5] Ibid.

less than the corresponding one in the first plan in percentage terms. Elementary education was given a boost in the seventh plan. It also received a favourable response in the eighth plan.[6] Figure 7.1 illustrates the share of elementary education expenditure in the five-year plans. Elementary Education was also included in the National Programme of Minimum Needs in the five-year plans, and this inclusion has significant implications for allocation of resources. This was expected to ensure favourable treatment in the allocation of resources and to protect it from reallocation of approved outlays away from elementary education. Education is also made an important component of the 'national human development initiative' in the union budget 1999–2000.[7]

The need for strengthening the resource base for education is obvious. Given the constitutional directive and other considerations, the government should continue to take complete responsibility of financing elementary education. In the trends on foreign aid for education a clear shift can be noted. The 1990s was a decade that marked a new phase of developments in education in general and primary education in particular. In case of foreign aid, the international assistance for primary education in India on a large scale has been the most significant development.[8] The situation of elementary education is indeed improving (as in most other countries). The pace of improvement, however, is slow. The primary education system in the country is one of the largest in the world. An idea about the scale of the primary education system in the country can be had from Table 7.1.

Table 7.1: Expansion of Primary Education in India

No. of Schools	1950–51	1990–91	1996–97	Annual Rate (%) 1990s	Growth
Primary	21,000	560,935	598,400	1.08	110.3
Upper Primary	13,000	151,456	176,700	2.60	41.1
Enrolment (in million)					
Primary		19.2	97.4	110.3	2.09	19.2
Upper Primary		3.1	34.0	41.1	3.21	3.1

Source: Selected Educational Statistics, MHRD, GOI, 1997.

[6] Jandhyala B.G. Tilak, *Financing of Elementary Education in India*, National Institute of Educational Planning and Administration, Ministry of Human Resource Development, Government of India, New Delhi, April 2000.
[7] Ibid.
[8] Ibid.

Right to Development 331

Figure 7.1: Share of Elementary Education Expenditure in the Five-Year Plans

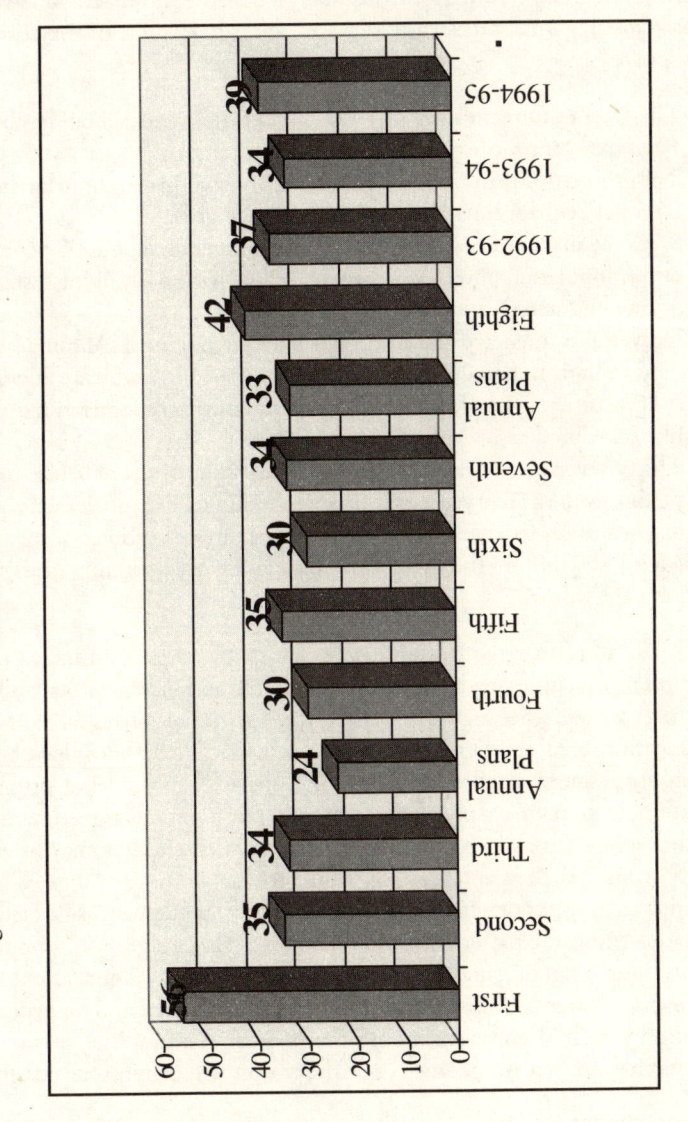

Plan	Share
First	56
Second	35
Third	34
Annual Plans	24
Fourth	30
Fifth	35
Sixth	30
Seventh	34
Annual Plans	33
Eighth	42
1992-93	37
1993-94	34
1994-95	30

Source: Report of the NDC committee on Literacy, Planning Commission, New Delhi.

The Indian population is characterized by a low overall rate of literacy. The total literacy rate in India in 2001 is 65.38 per cent consisting of 75.85 per cent men and 54.16 per cent women.[9] There are, however, wide variations across regions, states, castes, classes, and sexes. Some of the current statistics are:

- The gross enrolment ratio in 1999–2000 for primary school has been 100.9 per cent for boys and 82.9 per cent for girls.
- The gross enrolment ratio in 1999–2000 for secondary school has been 65.3 per cent for boys and 49.1 per cent for girls.
- With the massive expansion in provision of schools, about 95 per cent of the population now have a primary school within a walking distance of one kilometer.
- Universal elementary education has not been attained. About a hundred million Indian children are not in school and many are at work. A large proportion of them belong to marginalized/deprived families like scheduled castes and scheduled tribes.
- Thirty-seven per cent of children who join school drop out before completing even the five years of primary schooling. Girls are denied equal opportunities to attend and complete primary education.
- About 460 million Indians cannot read and write including nearly 58 per cent women.[10]

The spread of primary education has been a spatial spread, an increase in infrastructure facilities, wider coverage of children and increased availability of primary schools. (See Figure 7.1). Nevertheless, the national goal of primary education for all children continues to be elusive. Three factors have been commonly acknowledged to be important obstacles to universal primary education. First, there is a problem of poverty. The poor, it is argued, cannot afford to send their children to school. In some cases, children may be employed as child workers and may contribute to the family's earnings. While it is children of the poor who work, there are important demand-side factors which determine the pattern of child labour use. Also, a significant proportion of children not in school is also not working. So child labour cannot entirely explain low school attendance. There is a growing demand for primary education for children, even among the poorest communities. Evidence suggests that poverty of income is not the reason why parents fail to enrol

---

[9] *UNICEF in India 1999–2002—Challenges and Opportunities*, UNICEF.
[10] The PROBE Team, *Public Report on Basic Education*, Oxford University Press, New Delhi, 1999.

their children in school, or keep them there. More importantly, the costs of education may be too high for poor parents. Even in government schools with no tuition fees, there are other costs such as those of uniforms or textbooks. The Public Report on Basic Education (PROBE) survey found, for example, that on an average, the expenditure on fees, books, slates, and uniforms for a child was Rs 318 a year.[11] This is a high level of expenditure relative to income for many households such as that of an agriculture labourer. There have been several instances where children have been seen returning from the so-called 'free primary education' because they could not afford to wear proper uniforms or they did not appear for the exams because they did not have money to buy the answer sheets for writing the examinations. The costs of schooling deter poor parents. In such cases, free schooling including books, uniforms, stationery, transportation, and incentives such as free meals are needed to overcome the problem of non-attendance.

A second reason pertains to the quality of schooling and school infrastructure. In India, school infrastructure is woefully inadequate. For many children, the absence of a functioning school in the neighborhood is the main determinant of non-attendance. The problems of physical distance from a school are exacerbated by problems of social distance for children from underprivileged households.[12] Given that the average quality of schooling is very low, a frequently cited argument is that education of such poor quality is of little use. The low quality of education is blamed for low school enrolment and the high dropout rate. While these statements are valid, it is wrong to argue, as is often done, that without an improvement in quality, nothing much can be gained. While quality is very important, the case for universal education cannot be separated from that for raising quality. To put it differently, the struggle for more schools and for universal education must be made together with the struggle for better quality.

Lastly, there are problems of motivation, both among parents and children. These may be due to a range of factors including long years of deprivation, an environment in which there is no tradition of literacy, inadequate information about the returns to schooling, nutrition deprivation of children, low quality of school education, and so on. Empirical studies, however, indicate a high level of motivation among poor parents. Parents are willing to take on extra work to see that their children go to school. In other words, there is demand for schooling even among poor parents and poor children.

[11] The PROBE Team, *Public Report on Basic Education*, Oxford University Press, New Delhi, 1999.
[12] Ibid.

Apart from this, children were not in school for other reasons like lack of time in the morning and inability to help with homework. Further, the initial enthusiasm for school often waned with the children's negative experience of school such as the absence of classroom activity and physical punishments.[13] Disciplinary practices are certainly a deterrent to schooling. Some teachers, most of them being overenthusiastic and some with uncontrollable anger, punish the children physically as well as mentally. A Division Bench of the Delhi High Court commented: 'Brutal treatment of children can never inculcate discipline in them. Obedience exacted by striking fear of punishment can make the child adopt the same tactics when he grows up for getting what he wants.'[14] The High Court banned corporal punishment in Delhi schools. Other deterrents include rigid admission and examination schedules, formalities, and procedures.*

Laws Relating to Child Education in India

Evolution of Laws

The Indian Education Commission appointed in 1882, contained the proposal for adopting a law for universal compulsory education or at least for children employed in factories was mooted. This was also rejected due to financial and administrative difficulties. The first experiment of making primary education compulsory took place in 1893 when the ruler of the state of Baroda, Maharaj Sayajirao Gaekwad, introduced compulsory education in the Amreli division of his state; since the results were promising, he extended it to the entire state in 1906.[15]

Gopal Krishna Gokhale made the first definite demand for the official introduction of primary education in March 1910 when he moved a resolution in the Imperial Legislative Council, which was later withdrawn. Even as late as 1913, the British government was not prepared to accept the principle of compulsion, but wished to expand primary education on 'a voluntary basis'. However, in 1918, with the efforts of Vithalbhai Patel, Bombay passed a Primary Education Act permitting municipalities to introduce compulsory education in their areas. Within a few years, other provinces also passed laws aimed at compulsory education. By the early 1930s, the principle of compulsory education was written into state law. But these laws,

---

[13] Ibid.

[14] 'HC Bans Corporal Punishment for School Children': The Tribune, Vol. 120, No. 333, City Ed., Chandigarh, 2 December 2000, p. 1.

[15] A. Mehendale, 'Compulsory Primary Education in India: The Legal Framework', from the Lawyers Collective. April 1998, pp. 4–5.

however, were not implemented satisfactorily due to many reasons like technical flaws, lack of experience, unwillingness to make use of the power of prosecution under the Acts, etc.[16]

Constitution of India

In 1950, after independence, the Constitution of India in Article 246 dealt with the subject matter of laws made by the Parliament and by the legislatures of States. Education, including technical and medical education, is placed in List III, i.e. the Concurrent List of the Seventh Schedule of the Constitution of India.[17] Thus, the Parliament as well as the individual State legislatures can make laws on the subject of education. Such a scheme of distribution of legislative powers under the Constitution is a necessary component of a federal political structure.

The Constitution, in Article 45, made compulsory education a matter of national policy. The Constitution, in Article 45, lays down as a directive principle that every child up to the age of fourteen shall receive free and compulsory education. Articles 39f, 46, and 47 lend further support to this constitutional directive. The founding fathers of the Constitution clearly intended to ensure that every child, irrespective of social or economic status of his/her parents, received care and education from birth up to the age of fourteen years. This goal was to have been achieved 'within a period of ten years from the commencement of this Constitution'.

Article 28 of the Constitution is also relevant to education of children. It provides freedom as to attendance at religious instruction or religious workshop in certain educational institutes. The provision in this Article protects the child from any information of religious instruction through educational institutions. Article 29 of the Constitution provides the right to admission to educational institutes (receiving state aid) without discrimination on the basis of religion, race, caste, and language. A related directive has been given in Article 41 of the Constitution, which states that the state shall, within the limits of its economic growth and development, make effective provisions for securing the right to work.

The Constitution of India lays down that the State legislature may by law endow the panchayats [Article 243g] and municipalities [Article 243w] with

---

[16] Ibid.

[17] Education was a state subject whereby the state legislature had the exclusive jurisdiction of legislating in matters pertaining to education. In 1976, with the Constitution (Forty-second Amendment) Act, education became a concurrent subject. As a result of this amendment, no part of the subject of education now belongs to the exclusive state list.

such powers and authority as may be necessary to enable them to function as institutions of self-government. Such a law may contain provisions for the devolution of powers and responsibilities with respect to:

- The preparation of plans for economic development and social justice.
- The implementation of schemes for economic development and social justice as may be entrusted to them, including those in relation to the matters listed in the schedules.

The Eleventh Schedule[18] of the Constitution recognizes the powers, authorities, and responsibilities of the panchayats in matters pertaining to education, including primary and secondary schools, technical training and vocational education, and adult and non-formal education.[19] The Twelfth Schedule[20] of the Constitution covers the powers, authorities, and responsibilities of the municipalities, which includes promotion of cultural, educational, and aesthetic aspects.[21] Thus, among the local bodies the panchayats have been given clear-cut powers for undertaking activities for the promotion of elementary education, whereas for the municipalities, this has not been spelt out clearly.[22] The seventy-third and seventy-fourth constitutional amendments have given a statutory basis to district planning by providing for a District Planning Committee to consolidate the plans prepared by panchayats and municipalities and to prepare a draft development plan for the district as a whole.

The Constitution (Eighty-third Amendment) Bill provided to make free and compulsory education to all citizens of the age group of 6–14 years, a fundamental right by inserting Article 21A in the Constitution. Under this bill, Article 45 of the Constitution had to be omitted and in Article 51A of the Constitution, after clause (j) the following clause will be added, namely: clause(k) to provide opportunities for education to a child between the age of six and fourteen years of whom such citizen is a parent or guardian. This Bill was replaced by the Constitution (Ninety-third Amendment Bill) 2001 which was passed by the Lok Sabha in November 2001. It has also received the presidential assent.

---

[18] Added by the Constitution (Seventy-third Amendment) Act 1993.

[19] Entries 17,18, and 19 respectively.

[20] Twelfth schedule has been inserted by the Constitution (Seventy-fourth Amendment) Act 1993.

[21] Entry 13.

[22] 'Frequently asked questions on the Fundamental Right to Education', compiled by Centre for Child and the National Law School of India University, Bangalore, August 1998.

The significant provisions of the ninety-third amendment are:

- The amendment makes education a fundamental right for children in the age group 6–14 years.[23]
- The state shall endeavour to provide early childhood care and education for all children until they complete the age of six years.[24]
- It shall be the fundamental duty of the parents and guardians to provide opportunities for education to their children or, as the case may be, wards between the age of six and fourteen years.[25]

This amendment has made the right to free and compulsory education for the children a fundamental right. The fundamental right to free education will have paramount importance as it means that the State is now under the legal obligation to provide free and compulsory education to all children between 6–14 years of age. If the State fails to fulfil its obligations, any person can seek constitutional remedies against the State for the violation of fundamental rights.[26] Universal free and compulsory education should have become a reality in India by 1960. Article 45 of the Indian Constitution says: 'The State shall endeavour to provide, within a period of ten years from the commencement of this Constitution, for free and compulsory education for all children until they complete the age of 14 years.' But that constitutional obligation was time and again deferred—first to 1970 and then to 1980, 1990, and 2000. Realizing the sluggish attitude and delaying tactics in implementing the Constitutional commitment, the Supreme Court of India, in the Unnikrishnan judgment in 1993, said: 'It is noteworthy that among the several articles in Part IV only Article 45 speaks of time limit, no other article does. Has it not significance? Is it a mere pious wish, even after 44 years of the Constitution?' The Tenth Five-year Plan visualizes that India would achieve universal elementary education by 2007. However, the Union Human Resource Development Minister recently announced that India would achieve this target by 2010.

---

[23] Ninety-third Constitutional Amendment: After Article 21 of the Constitution the following article shall be inserted, namely: 'Article 21A. The State shall provide free and compulsory education to all children of the age of six to fourteen years in such manner as the State may, by law, determine.'

[24] For Article 45 of the Constitution, the following shall be substituted: 'Article 45. The State shall endeavour to provide early childhood care and education for all children until they complete the age of six years.'

[25] In Article 51A of the Constitution, after clause (j) the following clause shall be added, namely: '(k) who is a parent or guardian to provide opportunities for education to his child or, as the case may be, ward between the age of six and fourteen years.'

[26] Constitution of India, Articles 226 and 32.

Critique of the Ninety-third Constitution Amendment Act

The amendment seeks to make free and compulsory education a fundamental right only for the children in the age group of 6–14 years and not for the children in the age group of 0–6 years. However, in the Unnikrishnan judgment (1993), the Supreme Court of India gave the clear verdict that education is a fundamental right for all children up to fourteen years. Therefore, this provision dilutes the judgment and can be termed regressive. In fact it should provide free and compulsory education to all children till the age of eighteen years. India has ratified the Convention on the Rights of the Child wherein the child is defined as a person below eighteen years of age.

In the amendment, the provision for early childhood care and education (ECCE) for the age group of 0–6 years has been included in the directive principles of state policy. The directive principles are not enforceable. The age group of 0–6 years, should be a part of the fundamental right to education as it influences the most vital period of the child's development. Without the ECCE, the effort to provide free and compulsory education to children in the age group of 6–14 years cannot be successful.

The new Article 21A states, 'The State shall provide free and compulsory education to all children of the age of six to fourteen years in such manner *as the state may, by law, determine* (emphasis added).' This discretion will enable the government to justify cheap, low cost alternatives in the name of education as the enjoyment of this right would depend upon the whims and fancies of the government. The government might resort to second-class alternatives like single-teacher schools, education guarantee scheme, para-teachers, etc. There have been alarming arbitrary trends of promoting a large variety of non-formal education centres. The non-formal stream is considered equivalent to school education. Adult literacy classes have been considered as school education. The term 'education' needs to be defined and qualified. It should be made the commitment of the Government of India to provide quality education to all children, without any discrimination.

This Act compels the parents to send their children to school by including it as a fundamental duty (Article 51A). There is an apprehension that the government would use this provision randomly against poor parents to shirk its responsibility of imparting free and compulsory education.

There is a provision for 'free and compulsory' education to all children. The word 'free' is not defined. Presently, it is claimed that government schools are giving free education to the students as they do not charge any fee. However, the poor parents have to bear other expenses pertaining to school uniforms, books, examination fees, etc. This implies that the parents still have to pay for the education. Thus the concept of free education is certainly a misnomer or a myth. Therefore, a clear definition of the expression 'free education' should be inserted to make this amendment meaningful.

The amendment is silent on the role of private schools which can still charge exorbitant fees, as they appear to be out of the purview of the Act.

There have been strong demands from various child rights activists, educationists, and NGOs that the Act is amended to:[27]

- Include free and compulsory education as a fundamental right up to the age of eighteen years. The state cannot abdicate its responsibility of imparting free and compulsory education by transferring it to the parents under the alibi of a fundamental duty.
- Lay down that there should be an unambiguous provision of imparting equitable quality education for all children. There should not be any cheap, alternative education for the poor children.
- Allocate all necessary resources to achieve this right from the Consolidated Fund of the Union and states.
- Determine, by law, appropriate means to verify whether children upto eighteen years are enjoying this right. In other words there should be a monitoring mechanism.
- Extend this right to all educational institutions, whether under state or non-state auspices.
- Establish accountability for implementing this law. Failure to provide conditions for the exercise and enjoyment of this right shall be an offence punishable by law.
- Provide special opportunities for the girl child, disabled and other disadvantaged and vulnerable groups.*

State Laws on Primary Education

Every State legislature has to bring a new Bill or amendments in the existing laws for making education a fundamental right as per the 93rd amendment. A number of legislations have been passed on free and compulsory education in India before and after Independence. Between 1918–21, Primary Education Acts were passed in 8 provinces. All the Acts were applicable to both the sexes except in the Central Provinces where the Act was essentially for boys. After Independence, States have enacted legislations making elementary education compulsory. In the 1960s, most states framed their own laws

---

[27] Campaign Against child Labour, National Alliance for the Fundamental Right to Education, Bharatiya Jan Vigyan, and Forum for Crèche and Childcare Services, and other networks working on education have suggested many of the above amendments to the ninety-third Constitutional Amendment Bill.

on the model of the Delhi School Education Act 1960. The provisions of the Acts are similar to the provincial laws enacted during the British rule.[28] Compulsory education laws in India do not make education compulsory; they merely establish the conditions under which State governments may make education compulsory in specified areas. All these laws permit local authorities to introduce compulsory education.[29]

All the State Acts indicate that no fee shall be levied for any child attending an approved school under the management of the State government or local authority, or a school board. Education is not provided free of cost at schools managed by private bodies. In addition, the concept of 'free education' implies merely non-payment of fees and does not include expenses such as transport, school uniforms, examination fees, etc. Thus 'free education' is not actually free and families have to incur costs on education in addition to losing out on the meagre wage that the child may have otherwise brought home.[30]

The State Acts have provided for attendance authorities. The attendance authorities are persons appointed under the various State Primary Education Acts to ensure that children attend school as per the provisions of the Acts. The Acts state that the state government may appoint as many persons as it thinks fit to be attendance authorities. It may also appoint as many persons as are considered necessary, to assist the attendance authorities in the discharge of their duties. There is a reliance on the bureaucracy to enforce the laws. In case the child is not sent to school, the attendance authority has to hold an inquiry. If no 'reasonable excuse' exists for non-attendance, an order against the parent has to be passed in a prescribed form. In the event of failure on the part of parents to send their children to school, judicial proceedings are to be initiated. In certain State rules as of Karnataka, exemption from school attendance is granted when the child's assistance is specially required by the parent or guardian to help his vocation. Thus, laws and rules themselves leave enough scope for defeating the object of child's right to education.[31]

All the state Acts clearly indicate that parents are duty-bound to send the child to an approved school, unless a reasonable excuse for non-attendance exists. In case parents are unable to send their children to school, they are liable to be penalized. Compelling parents without providing any facilities for schooling or supportive measures for ensuring that children complete at

[28] A. Mehendale, 'Compulsory Primary Education in India: The Legal Framework', from the *Lawyers Collective*, April 1998, p. 5.
[29] Ibid.
[30] Ibid., pp. 6–7.
[31] Ibid., p. 7.

least the minimum level of schooling, is meaningless. There is a legitimate fear that penal provisions can be used as a weapon to cause further harassment to poor families, already struggling for survival. All the Acts state that children of school-going age should not be employed. Any employer engaging a child who should be in school can be penalized under the State Acts. However, child labour is rampant and it is evident that these provisions as also laws prohibiting child labour are not enforced. It is absurd to equate parents with employers.

All the State statutes on free and compulsory education do not impose any duty on the States to provide adequate and quality educational facilities. There is absolutely no mention of the quality of education in any of them. There is also no mention of the obligation towards others.

Common features of some of the State Primary Education Acts from the States of Delhi, Karnataka, Assam, Andhra Pradesh, Rajasthan, Madhya Pradesh, Punjab, West Bengal, Maharashtra, etc., are the following:

- The age group is generally 6–11 years or 6–14 years.
- Parents are duty-bound to send their child to an approved school unless there is a reasonable excuse.
- All the State Acts indicate that no fee shall be levied for any child attending an approved school under a State government or local authority but there is no definition of the word 'fee'. There is a need to define 'free education'. The word 'free' should include fees as well as all ancillary expenses.
- Children of school-going age should not be employed. Such employer will be penalized. However, this is not enforced in practice as there are hardly any convictions.
- Many State Acts come into effect by notification. Since there is no time limit within the Acts, the States may notify as and when it pleases them.
- Reliance is placed on the bureaucracy as the implementing authority. There is a provision of attendance authorities.
- Exemption from school attendance is allowed if the child's assistance is required by parents/guardians.
- No duty is imposed on the State to provide adequate and quality educational facilities.
- There is no mention of quality of education, child rights, and citizenship education.

The history of compulsory primary education worldwide shows that legislation cannot play a positive role in ensuring universal education unless the social conditions are favourable. So, a strategy of mass mobilization and supportive services to bring children to school and a social recognition of the value of education is required for effective implementation of laws. When the legal basis of primary education is voluntary, enrolment in primary schools shows a rapid increase only up to a certain point. When this point is reached, enrolment slows down and almost reaches a standstill; rapid advance beyond this point is possible only if compulsion is introduced.

Compulsion has to be accompanied with measures to strengthen the socio-economic conditions of families. If families have the means to meet their basic necessities, primary education itself being a fundamental necessity, the notion of compulsion in universalizing education will become redundant.[32]

The effectiveness of law as a means to achieve 'education for all' has been limited. The State has not displayed the political will to create conditions for the implementation of laws dealing with the prohibition of child labour, extending school facilities for all, improving the quality of education, etc. Secondly, the law itself is outdated and divorced from ground realities. Thirdly, there is very poor implementation of the education laws.

The enforcement of compulsory education laws in several developing countries was facilitated by the system of compulsory birth registration. Of course, the societal coalitions have proved to be crucial in introducing and extending compulsory education laws and banning the employment of children. Church groups, religious leaders, trade unionists, school teachers and educational officials, philanthropists, and social reformers have played significant roles.

Modern States regard education as a legal duty and not merely a right. The notion of the duty denies parents the right to choose. Parents are told by the State that no matter how great is their need for child labour or income, they must relinquish their child to school for a part of the day. The notion of duty also applies to the State. Education needs more of our funds, it also needs our creative thinking about how to develop schools relevant to the needs of actual and potential child workers. Schools must teach useful skills that are seen as relevant by both children and parents. The debate needs to shift to the rights of the child *vis-à-vis* the duty of the State.

Educational Policy and Planning in India

National Policy of 1968

The National Policy of 1968 marked a significant step in the history of education in post-independence India. It aimed to promote national progress,

[32] Ibid., pp. 7–8.

a sense of common citizenship and culture, and to strengthen national integration. It laid stress on the need for a radical reconstruction of the education system, to improve its quality at all stages, and gave much greater attention to science and technology, the cultivation of moral values, and a closer relation between education and the life of the people. Since the adoption of the 1968 Policy, there has been considerable expansion in educational facilities all over the country at all levels. More than 90 per cent of the country's rural habitations now have schooling facilities within a radius of one kilometer. There has been sizeable augmentation of facilities at other stages also. Perhaps the most notable development has been the acceptance of a common structure of education throughout the country and the introduction of the 10+2+3 system by most States. In the school curricula, in addition to laying down a common scheme of studies for boys and girls, science and mathematics were incorporated as compulsory subjects and work experience assigned a place of importance.

National Policy on Education (NPE) 1986

The National Policy on Education 1986 was the second policy on education since independence. It was regarded as a landmark. It redefined educational priorities and made a fresh attempt to cope with with the three strands that have influenced educational policy in India, viz., issues relating to quantity, quality, and equity. The policy gave the highest importance to universal primary education (UPE).

The activities which foster and promote the all-round balanced development of the child in the age group of 0–6 years in all dimensions—physical, mental, social, emotional, and moral—have been collectively described in NPE 1986 as early childhood care and education (ECCE). Both these components, care and education, are essential, since either by itself is inadequate. ECCE is the birthright of every child.

The National Policy on Education 1986 has explicitly recognized the importance of early childhood care and education (ECCE) as a crucial input not only for human development but also for universalization of elementary education and women's development. It has, therefore, emphasized the need for large-scale investment in the development of the young child, both through the government and through voluntary organizations. It has recommended a holistic approach of providing ECCE programmes which should aim at fostering nutrition, health, and social, physical, mental, moral, and emotional development of the child. In this context the policy has clearly recommended that ECCE programmes should be 'child-oriented, focused around play and the individuality of the child. Formal methods and introduction of the three Rs will be discouraged at this stage'.[33]

Consistent with the thrust of the national policy, early childhood education programmes are being qualitatively and quantitatively strengthened both in the voluntary and in the government sectors. While early childhood education per se is being provided to children in the 3–6 age group under these schemes, there exist wide diversities in terms of curriculum, infrastructure, financial allocations, staff quality, clientele, etc. These diversities are evident not only in different schemes but often within the same scheme from one region to another.

Often, what is practised in the name of pre-school education is not necessarily what has been envisaged in the national policy. Most ECCE programmes, based on curriculum, have become a downward extension of primary schools, wherein the basic philosophy and methodology of early childhood education are being generally ignored. The staff, in many cases, are not adequately qualified or trained in early childhood education and does not have the basic knowledge of child development. Particularly in urban settings, pre-schools are generally located in cramped, poorly ventilated areas, sometimes even in *barsatis*[34] on roof tops, with no safe, open space for children to play in. In rural areas, in addition to other constraints, the availability of suitable manpower is the major issue. Facilities in terms of equipment and material form another significant area of diversity. In view of the present scenario, provision of early childhood education of a good quality cannot be ensured. In this context a persistent recommendation emerging from major seminars/conferences over the years has been that there should be some system of licensing or accreditation of pre-schools/ECCE programmes. There is, therefore, a need to formulate certain prerequisites and standards which would ensure some uniformity within the diversities with respect to different aspects/components of an early childhood education programme.

With the specific objective of laying down these minimum prerequisites, the department of pre-school and elementary education developed a document—Minimum Specifications for Pre-schools. An effort was made to specify these, keeping in mind the contextual realities of our country. While the minimum was specified as 'essentials', the 'desirables' were also included, provision of which would certainly enhance the quality of any ECCE programme. These specifications were categorized into several groups. The

---

[33] Department of pre-school and elementary education, ministry of human resources development, Government of India.

[34] *Barsati* means a one-room set of accommodation constructed adjacent to the entrance to the roof of any building.

physical structure and facilities included details about the location, play areas, facility for drinking water, sanitary facilities, sleeping facilities, and storage space. Under equipment and material, details about the outdoor equipment, material for large muscle development, indoor equipment/material, and first-aid kit were provided. Also the safety precautions, age of admission, and admission procedure were given. Under the pre-school staff, the staff structure and adult-child ratio, qualifications of the teacher, qualifications of the helper, and salary structure were detailed out. The timings and content and methodology of the pre-school programme were also listed. It finally included the kind of records and registers to be maintained, viz., the admission records, the progress records, teachers' diary, and other registers. All this was specified in detail with a view to bringing uniformity all across.

Following the policy statement in 1986 on improving learning conditions, a number of national-level programmes were launched which have continued to contribute to improvement of school conditions in the 1990s. For instance, Operation Blackboard (OB), launched in 1987 and continued and expanded in the 1990s, is one major programme under which learning conditions have been created and expanded to improve the quality of schooling at the primary stage. OB has a wide coverage throughout the country. Some of the responses to policy changes in the years since the national policy chartered a new course of community-based education for development are being highlighted later in this chapter. These include initiatives of the Central and State governments, as well as independent initiatives from educational institutions and voluntary organizations.[35]

Judgments

Before the Constitution (Ninety-third Amendment) Act 2001, the right to education was prescribed by Articles 41, 45, and 46 of the Constitution, all of which were drective principles of State policy, but the courts have interpreted the right to education as a fundamental right by incorporating it within the fundamental rights in Article 21. The trend has been to hold that the right to life under Article 21 and the dignity of the individual cannot be assured unless it is accompanied by the right to education and that the provisions in Parts III and IV of the Constitution are supplementary and complementary to each other.

[35] M.S. Yadav and Meenakshi Bhardwaj, *Learning Conditions for Primary Education*, National Institute of Educational Planning and Administration, ministry of human resource development, Government of India, April 2000.

A.V. Chandel v Delhi University[36]

This was the first case where the courts demonstrated the new trend of interpreting the right to education as a fundamental right. The Delhi High Court observed that 'Fundamental Rights (also called human rights or basic rights) are of two kinds: (1) the classical rights and (2) the economic (and social) rights. Article 41 of the Constitution of India, therefore, provides that "the State shall, within the limits of its economic capacity and development, make effective provision for securing the right to work, to education, etc." even in the narrower sense, right to education would appear to be a fundamental right which can be spelt out if sub-clause (a), (b), and (c) of Article 19(1) is read with Article 21 independent of Article 41 and the Delhi University Act.'

Bandhua Mukti Morcha v Union of India[37]

Right to education is implicit in and flows from the right to life guaranteed under Article 21 (related to the dignity of the individual).

Mohini Jain v State of Karnataka[38]

In this petition under Article 32 of the Constitution of India, Mohini Jain has challenged the notification of the Karnataka government permitting the private medical colleges in the State of Karnataka to charge exorbitant tuition fees from the students other than those admitted to the 'Government seats'. It was held and declared that charging of capitation fee by the private educational institutions as a consideration for admission is wholly illegal and cannot be permitted.

Unnikrishnan J.P. and Others v State of Andhra Pradesh[39]

The main question under consideration in this landmark case was whether the right to primary education as mentioned in Article 45 of the Constitution of India is a fundamental right under Article 21 of the Constitution of India. It was held that right to education is not stated expressly as a fundamental right in Part III. This court has, however, not followed the rule that unless a right is expressly stated as a fundamental right, it cannot be treated as one. Freedom of press is not expressly mentioned in Part III, yet it has been read into and inferred from the freedom of speech and expression. The right

---

[36] AIR 1978 Del 308.
[37] AIR 1984 SC 802.
[38] AIR 1992 SC 1858.
[39] AIR 1993 SC 2178.

to education, which is implicit in the right to life and personal liberty guaranteed by Article 21 must be construed in the light of the directive principles in Part IV of the Constitution.

A true democracy is one where education is universal, where people understand what is good for them and the nation, and know how to govern themselves. The three Articles 45, 46, and 41 are designed to achieve the said goal among others. It is in the light of these articles that the content and parameters of the right to education have to be determined. Right to education, understood in the context of Articles 45 and 41, means:

- Every child/citizen of this country has a right to free education until he completes the age of fourteen years, and
- After a child/citizen completes fourteen years, his right to education is circumscribed by the limits of the economic capacity of the State and its development.[40]

University of Delhi v Ram Nath[41]

Education seeks to build up the personality of the pupil by assisting his physical, intellectual, moral, and emotional development. Article 21 of the Constitution has been used by the Courts to make right to education a fundamental right much before the (Ninety-third Constitution Amendment) Act 2001. The word 'life' in Article 21 has been interpreted in the widest possible manner. It does not simply mean physical life, but also covers other expressions of life. It is something more than a mere biological existence of a human body. Life also includes education, personality, and whatever is reasonably required to give expression to life, its fulfilment, and its achievements.

Government Schemes and Programmes in the Field of Elementary Education in India

Sarva Siksha Abhiyan (SSA)

The *Sarva Shiksha Abhiyan* mission has been established with the prime minister as the chairperson and the Union Minister of Human Resource

---

[40] This position has been reiterated in the following judgments after the Unnikrishnan case: *Murlidhar Kesekar v Vishwanath Barde* (1995) Supp (2) SCC 549; *Ganapathi Nath Middle School v M.D. Kannan* (1996) 6 SCC 464; *K. Krishnamacharyulu v Sri Venkateswara Hindu College of Engineering* (1997) 3 SCC 571; *State of Himachal Pradesh v Himachal Pradesh State Recognized and Aided Schools Managing Committee* (1995) 2 SCC 534; *N. Kunchichekku v State of Kerala* (1995) Supp. 2 SCC 382.

[41] (1964) 2 SCR 703 at p. 710: (AIR 1963 SC 1873 at p. 1875, para 6).

Development as the vice-chairperson. The *Sarva Shiksha Abhiyan* (SSA) is being projected as a historic stride towards improving the performance of the school system and to provide community-owned, quality elementary education. SSA lays a special thrust on making education at the elementary level useful and relevant for children by improving the curriculum and through effective teaching methods. The components of SSA include appointment of Block and Cluster Resource Centres for academic support, construction of school buildings and classrooms, and integrated education. The programme envisages bridging the gender and social gaps. States will be encouraged to enlarge the accountability framework by involving NGOs, teachers, activists, women's organizations, etc.

Operation Blackboard[42]

The centrally sponsored scheme of Operation Blackboard was launched in 1987 to address the task of providing basic educational facilities to all primary schools. The scheme, with active collaboration of the governments in States and Union territories, aimed at providing the following essential facilities in each primary school of the country:

- For the construction of buildings, the State governments were expected to utilize resources available under the ongoing rural employment programmes, provided by the Finance Commission or any other source. In 1990, it was decided that the central assistance under the rural employment scheme, *Jawahar Rozgar Yojana (JRY)*, would supplement the State resources on buildings. In 1993, construction of school buildings was made a high-priority item under the newly-introduced employment assurance scheme (EAS) in selected blocks and in 120 backward districts identified under the JRY. These funds were made available by the ministry of rural areas and employment. Separate district-specific projects had to be formulated for the purpose.
- Provision of at least two teachers, one of them a woman as far as possible, in every primary school (Teacher Component).
- Provision of essential teaching-learning material including blackboards, maps, charts, a small laboratory, and some equipment for work experience (Equipment Component).
- The scheme was planned to be implemented in a phased manner 20 per cent of the blocks and municipal areas were to be covered in 1987–88,

[42] M.S. Yadav, Meenakshi Bhardwaj, *Learning Conditions for Primary Education*, National Institute of Educational Planning and Administration, ministry of human resources development, Government of India, New Delhi, April 2000.

30 per cent in 1988–89, and 50 per cent in 1989–90. On review, the scope of OB was modified and enlarged in 1992 to include the following sub schemes:
- Continuation of ongoing OB to cover all the remaining primary schools especially those in SC/ST areas;
- Expanding the scope of OB to provide three teachers and three rooms to primary schools wherever enrolment warranted them; and
- Expanding OB to upper primary schools.

The District Primary Education Projects (DPEP)[43]

In the 1990s there was the emergence of large multi-state programmes for Education for All (EFA) under the banner of the District Primary Education Programme. DPEP promotes and supports the development of participatory processes in planning and management, increased gender awareness, and enhanced teacher effectiveness through inputs into teacher training and decentralized management. The programme covers several districts in various States, which include districts where the female literacy rate is less than the national average. A joyful learning methodology is used by teachers that have helped to attract and retain children, including girls, in school.

Bal Mitra Shala—A Child-friendly School

It is a part of the strategy of *Shikshak Samakhya*, the teacher empowerment programme, that has rejuvenated primary schools in the state of Madhya Pradesh. The word 'strategy' is carefully chosen: This is a different model of teacher education, a change in classroom process and practice, and a very effective motivation programme; but it is much more than the sum of these parts. For almost the first time, the education system—the planners and the administrators—have placed their faith in the teachers at the grass roots. And they have been rewarded by the most heartening success stories.

The Education for All (EFA) assessment process in India was set in motion around the middle of 1999. The basic framework for the review process was given by the UNESCO. The framework consisted of eighteen indicators ranging from literacy rate and enrolment figures to allocation of finances for primary education. Information on these indicators was to form the overall framework for assessing the progress made. In India, a National Assessment Group was set up at the ministry of human resources development to coordinate the effort. The EFA projects have been in operation, gradually expanding to cover half the country. Rajasthan initiated a fairly

[43] Ibid.

large programme of EFA under the name *Lok Jumbish*. These EFA initiatives coupled with various centrally sponsored schemes have undoubtedly made the 1990s the most intensive period of development of primary education in India. Besides, there have been mass literacy campaigns stretching across the country through the National Literacy Mission.[44]

There are also certain state-specific projects to improve learning conditions in primary schools. The Shiksha Karmi Project in Rajasthan, and Primary and Elementary Education Projects in Maharashtra are some of the programmes implemented during the 1990s with a focus on improving quality of primary schooling by creating supportive learning conditions.

NGO Interventions in Elementary Education

Pioneering initiatives by NGOs have drawn attention to new models of classroom pedagogy, teacher training, school management, and so on. NGOs have played a crucial role in advocating for the right to education to be a fundamental right and helping to foster public participation in schooling matters. NGO interventions are generally concerned with activities relating to primary education, literacy, non-formal education, education for street children, child labour, education for groups with physical or mental disability, education for the marginalized or socio-economically deprived groups, education for the girl child, networking, and advocacy.

National Alliance for the Fundamental Right to Education (NAFRE)

The National Alliance for the Fundamental Right to Education is a direct consequence of attempts to generate a campaign to support the constitutional amendment to make education a fundamental right. Pratham, is a Mumbai-based NGO involved in the issue of universalization of primary education, initiated the idea of a national alliance and invited a few major NGOs and funding agencies to create such an alliance. The main points of agreement of the alliance are:

- Education is a fundamental right of every child. Children must be in school, not at work.
- The right to education of every Indian child should be realized by year 2005. This is possible.
- Quality and equitability of education must improve throughout India.

---

[44] Disha Nawani, *Role and Contribution of NGOs to Basic Education*, National Institute of Educational Planning and Administration, Ministry of Human Resource Development, Government of India, New Delhi, April 2000.

- Government cannot successfully implement the right to education on its own. People's participation is essential. Mechanisms have to be developed at the school and in administration through models, statutes, and mutual cooperation to encourage effective participation of people.
- In spite of differing views on various specific issues, anyone participating in the Alliance must actively work to make sure that all children are in school and learning.
- Factors impeding universalization of elementary education are more social, political, and cultural in nature. Improvement of pedagogical techniques and their wide, effective dissemination is essential to make school learning effective. This is also a way to involve more teachers and parents and to overcome the impediments.
- Replicable large-scale work is important.
- All sections of the civil society have to work together. Empowerment of teachers and parents are key issues.
- In order to ensure that all children are in school, it is essential to counter gender bias at all stages and levels.
- The Alliance will not work in a manner that may undermine, nationally or internationally, the gains of the last fifty years and the long history of social reform and struggle for self-reliance.

The multi-pronged work of the Alliance will be to:

- Act as a platform to voice various opinions about specific issues so that more and more people who are normally away from such debates learn about them and participate in creating a broader consensus.
- Work with all levels of government, the Parliament, the people, the media, and industry/business to make fundamental right to education and related matters a national priority.
- Monitor the status of education while also encouraging, creating, and catalyzing large-scale replicable models of realization of the fundamental right.
- Work to gather and disseminate factual information about education, not only to opinion-makers and policy makers but also to the parents of children whose future is at stake.

Citizens' Initiative on Elementary Education

Citizens' Initiative on Elementary Education (CIEE) is a national body that seeks to make quality education for every child a reality. It believes that reform of the educational system is possible through the active participation of all people—parents, children, teachers, and all other concerned citizens. CIEE started when a group of concerned citizens came together and formulated a charter of demands on education. The citizens' charter represents aspirations of the people with regard to the educational system. CIEE's concern in Karnataka is on children's low learning levels, the lack of relevance of school to daily life, poor participation of people, and the absence of accountability in the system. Hence, CIEE's focus in Karnataka is to bring about accountability, equity, and quality. Education is hardly ever discussed as a developmental issue, and hence there is a total lack of information about its status among the people. CIEE, Karnataka, initiated a discussion on education with the people by gathering information on the government school in their area—on the school infrastructure, school management, the teachers, and students—and then presenting it to them at a *Shikshana Grama Sabha*. The *Grama Sabha*[45] has been legitimiszed as a means of ensuring direct democracy (as opposed to respresentative democracy) through the tribal self-rule and the seventy-third constitutional amendment. 'In spirit, the *grama sabha* means that all citizens of the village or urban community come together to collectively decide on matters concerning them. In practice, this has been often reduced to a few powerful people making decisions and seeking acceptance at the *grama sabha*. Rarely have *grama sabha*s taken to discussing developmental matters and almost never education. It was for their immense potential for enabling educational reform that the *Shikshana Grama Sabha*s were held. In the *Grama Sabha*s, information is presented in a simple manner motivating people to engage in action for change. Rather than merely stating problems, solutions are sought from the people. Children's issues, specifically education, are being brought into the political agenda of communities and local governments for the first time. To keep the enthusiasm generated by the *Shikshana Grama Sabha*s alive and to encourage the local community to increase its level of ownership of schools, Citizens' Action Groups (CAGs) have been formed at the village level. Village-level CAGs are being federated into CAGs at the level of village panchayat to support one another's activities and thus gain greater stability.

Prerna

Prerna, a Mumbai-based NGO, working towards organizing services for commercial sex workers and their children, has attempted to teach children of the sex workers of the Kamathipura area. The institutional programme

---

[45] Common assembly of a village.

helps tremendously in the long term. The children too, placed in a new environment, envisage options other than getting into prostitution, or becoming bar dancers and 'agents' or errand boys of customers in the case of boys. The ambitions and dreams of the children soar high; the students spoke about becoming teachers, policemen, and so on.

The Avehi-Abacus Project

Avehi-Abacus is a curriculum enrichment programme for schools. The underlying objective, that finds reflection both in the curriculum and their methodology of Abacus, is to develop childrens' skills of thinking, analysing, and making choices; to inculcate the values and habits of mind that will enable them to live with others in harmony, without being either perpetrators or victims of exploitation or oppression. The focus on the 'content' of the education is deliberate. It is based on the preparation of the role of education as an initiator of social change. While supplementing and enriching the 'mainstream' school curriculum, the programme also attempts to provide children with an interlinked and interdependent entity. Given the belief that any effective change, particularly a change in the system of education, can take place only through a gradual process, curriculum enrichment was seen as a necessary first step in the process of creating an alternative curriculum.[46] The Avehi-Abacus programme for children works in two distinct ways:

- In the formal school system, it works as a foundation course from Classes III to VII. It fills in some of the gaps in the existing curriculum, particularly in the general and social sciences. It provides links between what is taught in different subjects and helps children relate what is learnt in school to their own life situation.
- In the non-formal system, Avehi-Abacus serves as a post-literacy programme for children between the ages of eight and twelve. It provides new information and skills and supplements the regular curriculum.

In both the contexts, the programme works in a way that will develop childrens' skills of thinking, analysing, and making choices. The emphasis is on values that will help them live and work together in a spirit of understanding and harmony.

[46] Simandhini Dhuru, The Avehi-Abacus Project, The Indian Child 2001, CRY, Mumbai, 2001.

Schoolnet India Limited

Schoolnet India Limited was born in 1998 as a social initiative to propagate life-long learning. Schoolnet primarily aims at enhancing the quality and delivery of education across the entire spectrum and learning segments. Schoolnet believes in preparing the child of today for the world of tomorrow through various activities and programmes in schools across the country. The focus is to achieve equity of access in education for children who are less empowered. This includes disadvantages arising out of gender, learning disabilities, economic and physical conditions. Schoolnet India Limited hopes to bring about learning interventions at every stage of the knowledge cycle, from the first unsteady steps of a child in kindergarten to a self-reliant individual.[47]

The Global Context of Basic Education

During the last twenty years, significant progress has been made in the state of education worldwide. The average literacy rate for all developing countries rose from 43 per cent in 1970 to 65 per cent in 1990. The average net primary school enrolment rate for school-age children of all developing countries rose from 50 per cent in 1970 to 76 per cent in 1990. This both relative and absolute increase in primary school enrolment took place in the context of economic recession, external debt burden, and high population growth rates in many developing countries.

The issues of completion, dropouts, quality, and learning achievement are critical areas of concern in all developing countries. Some 30 per cent of those children who enrol in primary schools in developing countries do not complete primary education, and those who complete their primary education do not acquire adequate knowledge and skills to improve their lives or to continue learning. The Latin American, the Caribbean, and the East Asian regions have achieved some degree of success in providing access to primary education for most children, but high rates of repetition and low levels of learning achievement underline the need, even in these regions, to address great disparities in the quality of available educational opportunities. Issues of quality, disparities in opportunities, and Early Childhood Development (ECD) also are critical in most countries of the Middle East and North Africa. Above all, access to a learning place with a trained teacher and learning materials is still beyond the reach of some 132 million out-of-school children in developing countries.

---

[47] www.schoolnetindia.com.

The gender gap in education adds another dimension to the inadequacy and inefficiency of the existing systems of education. In 1990, two-thirds of the 948 million adults who were illiterate were women, and 77 million of the estimated 132 million out-of-school children were girls (see Table 7.2). In the forty lowest-income countries, the gap in primary school enrolment rates between boys and girls averages twenty percentage points. The situation is most pronounced in South Asia, sub-Saharan Africa, and some countries of the Middle East and North Africa, especially in the rural areas of these regions. Selected educational and economic indicators of various regions, as presented in the table, show that during the period 1986–92, sub-Saharan Africa had the lowest gross primary school enrolment rate, with a difference of nineteen percentage points between boys' and girls' enrolment and an extremely high (3 per cent) population growth rate. Likewise, South Asia had a low gross enrolment rate, a high gender gap (twenty-five percentage points) and a high population growth rate (over 2 per cent). Per capita gross national product (GNP) was low in both regions, as was the share of public expenditure on education as a percentage of GNP.

Table 7.2: Out-of-School Children (6–11 yrs) by Region and Gender

Regions	1980 Total (million)	Percentage of total children	No. of girls (million)	Percentage of total girls	1990 Total (million)	Percentage of total children	No. of girls (million)	Percentage of total girls
Sub-Saharan Africa	26	43	15	49	41	50	22	54
South Asia	59	40	38	53	48	27	32	38
East Asia	55	25	32	30	26	14	14	16
Middle East	9	33	6	43	9	24	5	31
Latin America and Caribbean	9	17	5	18	8	13	4	13
Total developing	158	27	96	38	132	21	77	29

Source: UNESCO 1993, Trends and Projections of Enrolment by Level of Education, by Age and by Sex, 1960–2025, Paris.

The right to basic education has been a key element of almost every international declaration on human rights since the UN was established.

The UN Declaration of Human Rights (1948), the 1959 Declaration of the Rights of the Child, the 1966 International Covenant on Economic, Social, and Cultural Rights, the 1989 Convention on the Rights of the Child, the 1990 World Declaration on Education for All, the 1990 World Declaration on the Survival, Protection, and Development of Children, the 1995 Beijing Declaration, and the 1996 Amman Affirmation, all express a commitment to education as a right. Constitutions and laws in most countries recognize the child's right to education.

Universal Declaration of Human Rights 1948

The Article 26 [UDRA 1948] was proclaimed by the General Assembly as a 'common standard of achievement for all peoples and all nations' to the end that every individual and every organ of society, keeping this declaration constantly in mind, shall strive by teaching and education to promote respect for these rights and freedoms and by progressive measures to secure the universal and effective recognition and observance. The Article provides that:

- Everyone has the right to education. Education shall be free, at least in the elementary and fundamental stages. Elementary education shall be compulsory. Technical and professional education shall be made generally available and higher education shall be equally accessible to all on the basis of merit.
- Education shall be directed to the full development of human personality and to the strengthening of respect for human rights and fundamental freedoms. It shall promote understanding, tolerance, and friendship among all nations, racial or religious groups, and shall further the activities of United Nations for the maintenance of peace.
- Parents have the prior right to choose the kind of education that shall be given to their children, inherent dignity of the equal and inalienable right of all members of the human family being the foundation of freedom. Justice and peace in the world is well recognized. People of the United Nations have reaffirmed their faith in the fundamental human rights and in the dignity and worth of human person, and have determined to promote social progress and better standards of life in larger freedom. All human beings are born free and equal in dignity and rights. They are endowed with reason and conscience and they should act towards one another in a spirit of brotherhood. Article 2 of the Universal Declaration of Human Rights which is the International Bill of Human Rights states that everyone is entitled to all the rights and

freedoms set forth in this declaration, without distinction of any kind such as race, colour, sex, language, religion, political or other opinion, national or social origin, property, birth or other status.

International Covenant on Economic, Social, and Cultural Rights 1976

Article 13(1) of the Covenant provides that the State parties recognize the right of everyone to education. Article 13(2) recognizes that with a view to achieving full realization of the right to education, primary education should be made compulsory and available free to all and the development of a system of schools at all levels should be actively pursued. The article also respected the liberty of parents or legal guardians to choose their childrens' schools other than those established by public authorities and to ensure religious and moral education of their children. Article 13(3) recognizes the liberty of individuals and bodies to establish and direct educational institutions which shall conform to such minimum standards as may be laid down by the State. Article 14 provides that each party to the Covenant, if it has not been able to secure within its jurisdiction free, compulsory, primary education within a period of two years, shall adopt a detailed plan of action for its progressive implementation.

India is a signatory to the Universal Declaration of Human Rights and has acceded to the International Covenants on Civil and Political Rights and on Economic, Social, and Cultural rights on 10 April 1979. The civil and political rights were made subject to immediate realization, while the other group of economic, social, and cultural rights were sought to be progressively realized. Delicate balance between the political and civil rights and social and economic rights has been sought to be achieved in the Indian Constitution. Likewise, balance has been tried to be maintained between the individual rights and social needs. The holistic approach made in our Constitution to both categories of human rights, i.e. (i) political and civil Rights and (ii) social and economic Rights, is highly appreciable.

Political and civil rights are guaranteed in one form or the other under Chapter III of our Constitution. They are made fundamental and are enforceable though they are subjected to reasonable restrictions. Principles have been laid down in Chapter IV of the Indian Constitution under the directive principles of State policy, though not enforceable by any court of law. Nevertheless, they are fundamental in the governance of the country and it shall be the duty of the State to apply these principles in making laws.

Convention on the Rights of the Child 1989

Nearly every country in the world has ratified the Convention on the Rights of the Child. Articles 28 and 29 of the Convention on the Rights of the Child 1989 deal with the right to education. Article 28(1) enjoins the State parties to make primary education free and compulsory to all and take measures to encourage regular attendance at schools and the reduction of dropout rates. It also states that particular steps should be taken to make educational and vocational information and guidance available and accessible to all children. Article 29 specifies that the education of the child shall be directed to development of mental and physical abilities and overall all-round development.

Starting from a child-rights perspective, there are a number of overarching principles that relate to education. In the CRC:

- Education is a right.
- Education is also an enabling right, a right that facilitates children and adults access many of their other rights throughout their lifetimes. In this regard, education has an important role to play in empowerment because it supports democratic action, is a means to promote child rights and social rights, and can equip individuals and groups with the skills to move on in their lives. Thus, education is a very profound right.
- Education must be available without discrimination.
- Children have a right to quality education that will serve as the basis for lifelong learning.
- Education must address the best interests and ongoing development of the complete child. This means that, in addition to being child-centred, education is much more than attention to cognitive development. It is also concerned with the child's social, emotional, and physical development. It also calls for more than the conventional integrated approach. Rather education must be conceptualized from the child's point of view and with an understanding of the interrelated nature of the child's needs, which vary according to the level of individual development.
- Education must accord dignity to every child. Thus, respect, as a value is critical.

In Article 28, the CRC established the right of all children, without discrimination, to education. The Convention also provides a framework by which the quality of that education must be assessed. If children are required to sit in overcrowded classrooms or classrooms with no teachers, their learning and developmental needs are clearly not being fulfilled. Article 29 guides us, therefore, towards a more child-centred model of teaching, one in which students participate actively, with proper classrooms and teachers, and developing the self-esteem that is essential for learning and decision making throughout life.[48] The CRC also establishes the indivisibility of rights. That is, we must address all rights equally, and it is here that there are significant further implications that go to the very core of the conduct of educational activities. In addressing education in a CRC framework, it means going far beyond Articles 27, 28, 29, and 32. Every other article needs to be considered in relation to those articles that specifically address the right to education. Furthermore, an added challenge is considering how education can and must address a child's right to protection.

There must be an enabling legislative framework that does more than paying lip service to guaranteeing children their right to education. It must facilitate these necessary changes in the education system, both at the macro and micro levels. The CRC calls for free compulsory education. It is recognized that this might not be possible immediately, especially as universality is not yet a reality in many countries, but plans must be put in place and immediate action initiated toward this end. In the short run, it is essential that any cost of education be equitable.

World Declaration on Education for All 1990

Article 1 of this Declaration states that every person—child, youths, and adult—shall be able to benefit from the educational opportunities designed to meet their basic learning needs. These needs comprise both learning tools (literacy, oral expression, numeral proficiency, and problem solving) and basic learning content (knowledge, skills, values, and attitudes) required by human beings to be able to survive, to develop their full capacities, to live and work in dignity, to participate fully in development, to improve the quality of their lives, to make informed decisions, and to continue learning. The declaration recognized the diversity, complexity, and changing nature of the basic learning needs of children, youth, and adults necessitating broadening and constantly redefining the scope of basic education to include the following components:

- Learning begins at birth.
- The main delivery system for the basic education of children outside the family is primary schooling.
- The basic learning needs of youth and adults are diverse and should be met through a variety of delivery systems.

[48] The State of the World's Children 1999, UNICEF.

- All available instruments and channels of information, communication, and social action could be used to help convey essential knowledge and inform and educate people on social issues.[49]

Meeting these basic learning needs involves action to enhance the family and community environments for learning.[50]

Jomtien Declaration 1990

In 1990, some 1500 participants from 155 nations and dozens of non-governmental organizations (NGOs) and development agencies met in Jomtien, Thailand, to adopt the World Declaration on Education For All (EFA). This Declaration and its framework for action were remarkably insightful documents; they analysed the challenges and opportunities facing the last decade of the twentieth century and proposed that countries set targets for the year 2000 based on an 'expanded' vision of universal basic education. These were:

- expansion of early childhood care and development (ECCD) activities;
- universal access to, and completion of, primary education;
- improvement in learning achievement;
- reduction of the adult illiteracy rate to one half of its 1990 level;
- expansion in basic education and training in other essential skills required by youth and adults; and
- increased acquisition of the knowledge, skills, and values required for better living and sustainable development (World Conference on Education For All, Framework for Action, 1990).

Jomtien emphasized not only access to education, but equity and learning achievement through broadening the means and scope of basic education. According to the 1990 Jomtien Declaration, 'Active and participatory approaches are particularly valuable in assuring learning acquisition and allowing learners to reach their fullest potential.' Encouraging the use of interactive, learner-centred methods is a priority in the promotion of quality basic education. These methods should be used deliberately to support learning aims that relate to the knowledge, skills, and attitudes of peace education. Research supports the idea that cooperative and interactive learning methods promote values and behaviours.

A child-friendly education system requires the development of child-friendly, child-centred systems. Schools, which are effective vehicles of

---

[49] Article 5.
[50] Framework for Action to Meet Basic Learning Needs: Guidelines for Implementing the World Declaration on Education for All (Paragraph 10).

learning, provide a healthy environment (physically and psychologically), and should be based on the principles of CRC. Child-friendly education systems recognize and respect children's rights and responsibilities, provide the enabling environment to realize these rights, and help ensure such an environment in the community and household.

More specifically, a child-friendly education system reflects and realizes the rights of every child; cooperates with other partners to promote and monitor the well-being and rights of all children; defends and protects all children from abuse and harm (as a sanctuary), both inside and outside the school.

The goals for children and development for the decade adopted at the World Summit for Children in September 1990 endorsed the Jomtien goals, emphasizing the priority to universal access to primary education, completion of the primary stage by at least 80 per cent of the children and reduction of the gender gap.

World Education Forum, Dakar, Senegal, 2000

One hundred eighty-two countries attended the World Education Forum 2000 at Dakar in Senegal. The Dakar Framework of Action has been adopted by all of them. The Framework of Action:

- recognizes the right to education as a fundamental human right,
- reaffirms commitment to the expanded vision of education as articulated in Jomtien, and
- calls for renewed action to ensure that every child, youth, and adult receive education by 2015.

THE EDUCATION FOR ALL 2000 ASSESSMENT (EFA 2000)

The EFA Framework for Action provides for an end-of-decade assessment of progress.[51] The assessment is now well under way, with strong UNICEF support; many countries are already working on reports, and eleven Regional Technical Advisory Groups have been established. While the world as a whole has made some progress in achieving the Jomtien vision—and some countries quite remarkable success—the following two general trends have been disappointing.

---

[51] The EFA Forum Secretariat, based at the United Nations Educational, Scientific, and Cultural Organization (UNESCO), is coordinating this assessment, with technical input from a Technical Advisory Group consisting of representatives of the five partner agencies (UNESCO, the United Nations Development Programme, the United Nations Population Fund, UNICEF, and the World Bank).

EARLY CHILDHOOD CARE FOR SURVIVAL, GROWTH AND DEVELOPMENT

The decade has seen a slight growth in formal pre-school enrolments. More significant is the expansion of structured but less formal learning opportunities for young children through home-based and community-based programmes and parental education. However, very few countries have access to good data on such programmes, and official data are usually limited to formal pre-schools.

GETTING CHILDREN INTO SCHOOL AND KEEPING THEM THERE

The number of school-age children enrolled in schools has increased both globally and for every region in the developing world. But the global goal of EFA by the year 2000 will not be achieved—between 130 million and 150 million children of school-going age, two-thirds of them girls, are not in school. The growth in enrolment in some regions has barely kept pace with population growth, and some countries show an actual decline in enrolment rates.

The EFA Declaration identified girls' education as 'the most urgent priority', and this was underlined in the Amman Affirmation, using the term 'priority of priorities'.

The World Bank has expanded substantially its involvement in education over the decade, and regional development banks are showing increased interest in this sector. UNICEF, which supports education in over 140 countries, continues to be one of the key agencies financing programmes at the country level. The decade has also witnessed new partnerships at the regional level, with the Association for the Development of Education in Africa encouraging collaboration between government ministries and development agencies.

New forms of collaboration have developed around the United Nations System-wise Special Initiative on Africa, especially for low-enrolment countries. Sector-wise approaches are also being tried as countries and agencies begin to apply to education the lessons learned in health. In the best of cases, these mechanisms lead to greater donor collaboration, strong government ownership of the reform process, and more effective and efficient investments. The United Nations Development Assistance Framework (UNDAF) presents another opportunity for coordinated work in assessing, planning, and implementing reform programmes.

Of particular importance has been the larger role that families, communities, local governments, and NGOs are playing in education. Through decentralization, more authority for providing education is often being devolved to local actors. This should not absolve national governments from their primary responsibility in this regard, but rather build important linkages between schools and communities and supplement national resources with local support.

Children in Emergency Situations

Another area of major international concern is the education of children in emergencies. Emergencies include natural disasters such as floods and earthquakes, and human-made crises such as civil strife and war, the latter also called 'complex emergencies'. Persistent poverty, the increasing number of children living on streets, and the HIV/AIDS pandemic are silent, chronic emergencies. All emergency situations have an adverse impact on education. Children, for example, especially girls, drop out of school during natural disasters and war. During droughts parents may not be able to pay the required school fees. Poverty and fighting disable students, hamper their ability to learn. War is a major psychosocial stressor with long-lasting effects that influence learning.[52]

The Convention on Human Rights and the Convention on the Rights of the Child, among others, declare education to be an inalienable right. It is also an enabling right, in that it assists children and adults to access their other rights. It is the right of every child regardless of the circumstances in which she or he is thrust. Children in emergency situations must be able to participate in quality primary education that includes the same 'core' of skills, knowledge, competencies, values, and attitudes that constitute a basic education, and to which the world committed in 1990 at the Jomtien Conference on Education for All (EFA). In emergency situations, whether caused by human or natural forces, education serves many purposes. It plays a critical role in normalizing the situation for the child and in minimizing the psychosocial stresses experienced when emergencies result in the sudden and violent destabilization of the child's immediate family and social environment. It is essential in assisting children to deal with their future more confidently and effectively, and can be instrumental in making it possible for them to develop a peaceful society. Furthermore, educational activities that include parents and other community members can play an important part in rebuilding family and community cohesiveness. The increasing use of children as fighters in conflict is most alarming. While stopping this trend will require coordinated effort, education must play a key role in demobilization. As with other educational responses in emergencies, this must have

---

[52] www.unicef.org.

two aspects: the basic care that is every child's right, and a component tailored to the particular circumstances. The challenge is to tailor a programme that allows children to reassume the childhood that has been stolen from them.

Some International Initiatives

School Clusters in Cambodia

In mid-1993, UNICEF, in cooperation with the Cambodian government, established the cluster schools in seven target areas of rural, urban, and minority populations. The major objective of the clusters was to remove imbalances in school quality by sharing resources, administration, and often, even teachers, to improve the weaker schools without diminishing the stronger ones. Government policy nationalized their development in 1995. Experience has shown that parents move their children to cluster schools because they realize that these schools offer good teachers, new or refurbished buildings, and better equipment. Surveys indicate that enrolment rates in these schools are substantially higher than the national and provincial averages and dropout rates are much lower, especially in urban areas.[53]

Parent-training Programme in Turkey

A parent-training programme in Turkey[54] has become a model of non-formal, multipurpose education designed to keep children in school and learning. Group discussions are held on such topics as childrens' health, nutrition, creative play activities, and mother-child interactions. In follow-up studies of the first pilot project, significant differences were found in cognitive development between children whose mothers had undergone the training and those who had not. As expected, children in these families stayed in school longer. Since expanded, the programme is conducted in cooperation with the Turkish Ministry of Education and has served more than twenty thousand mother-child pairs.

Wake Up, Brazil, It's Time for School!

Brazil offers an important example of mobilization and partnership that embrace the whole society beyond the education sector and the traditional education constituency. In 1993, Brazil's nationwide mobilization effort culminated in a 'National Week on Education for All', resulting in a ten-year

---

[53] The State of the World's Children 1999, UNICEF.
[54] Ibid.

plan that led to concrete government action on many fronts. In 1995, the new Brazilian government expanded actions that included transferring federal funds to local schools and municipalities, improving the national testing of students' 'learning achievement', and using television as the medium for a national distance-learning teacher education programme. The government's most important role has probably been to mobilize the whole nation behind the universal education campaign.[55]

Right to Play and Recreation[56]

The Convention on the Rights of the Child guarantees the right to play and recreational activities to all children. The Convention on the Rights of the Child in Article 31 acknowledges the importance of play and recreation. The article recognizes the right of the child to engage in play and recreational activities appropriate for the age of the child and to encourage the provision of appropriate and equal opportunities for cultural, artistic, recreational, and leisure activity. However, millions of children are denied this right, never experiencing this vital aspect of their development because of war, disease, and poverty, or because the importance of play has not been recognized or accepted, or because of misconceptions relating to play.

Play is an important vehicle for young people's development and an introduction to lifelong active living.[57] The involvement of children and youth in enjoyable physical recreation activities is a cornerstone of their health and well-being. Children and youth develop physically and socially through involvement in sport, and research shows a connection between physical fitness, academic ability, and positive behaviour generally. The healthy stress of the competitive situation, and participation with their peers, can help young people gain self-confidence and mature emotionally. Also, there is much evidence that participation in physical recreation programmes can have a very positive influence on children and youth at risk and that such programmes, if adapted to their needs, have the potential of engaging otherwise 'hard-to-reach' youth.

Natural outdoor play environments offer important opportunities for children to begin to value the environment. Through play, children explore cause and effect and gradually build a knowledge base that cannot be taught through structured learning activities. Play is a vehicle for the development of creativity and flexibility, invaluable qualities in human development.

[55] The State of the World's Children 1999, UNICEF.
[56] www.UNICEF.org visited on 5 July 2002.
[57] www.SCY.org visited on 5 July 2002.

Play can be a vehicle for children to pass on their culture for sharing between generations, and for children to communicate their feelings and ideas to adults. Through play, young children learn to become active participants in community. Play days and play festivals are a major form of celebration of culture and community around the world. Play has therapeutic value and is also a way for children to gain a sense of control over difficult circumstances as witnessed in hospital settings and in war zones.

Play is fundamental to all aspects of child development and is a key component in preserving community and culture, in the broadest sense.[58] Play is valuable in children's physical exercise and growth and in their development of motor skills. Children playing together present rich opportunities for social, moral, and emotional development and hence for the development of their personality and their ability to handle stress and conflict. It is in free play that children learn to understand and cooperate with others.

The importance of play to children is strongly supported by researchers from a range of disciplines including psychology, education, philosophy, anthropology, and recreation. In spite of this, society as a whole continues to view play as a frivolous pastime, at best useful for children to 'let off steam'. The reasons for this misunderstanding are many and varied. One reason is our difficulty in clearly defining play. Play is not synonymous with recreation, although there are many opportunities for play in recreation programmes and environments, and it does not include everything children do in their leisure time. Play is not created by adults for children but children initiate themselves. Play is spontaneous, self-motivated, controlled by the child.[59]

For reasons already outlined, specialists in children's play theory see play as fundamental to human development. *A concerted effort on the part of governments, organizations, and communities should be made to promote the fact that play and learning are not competing ideologies.* Parents and other decision makers must ensure a balance in children's lives both to avoid unhealthy levels of stress and to allow opportunities for informal play.

Schools, communities, and parents must work together to ensure a balance in children's lives through offering engaging and healthy alternatives to sedentary and isolated activities.

There are a number of issues that create barriers to children's play opportunities. While ensuring that safety is not compromised, there is a need for a paradigm shift in the way we think about playgrounds. Children need a wider range of play possibilities, which would be ensured through a much

---

[58] www.ccy/scy visited on 5 July 2002.
[59] Ibid.

greater variety of play material and by involving children in the planning process. Special consideration should be given to access for children with disabilities. Children play everywhere. Spontaneous or free play is important for children in both the natural and built environment. Open space is diminishing due to competition for urban land and commercial priorities for its use, and the built environment, such as, shopping malls, hotels, etc., do not always anticipate or plan for children playing.

Decision makers and planners should apply a 'child-friendly lens' to policy affecting young people in public space and involve children themselves as much as possible. Examples of things that may be considered are:

- preservation of undeveloped land,
- parks that are close to schools and jointly planned with schools,
- community gardens where children and youth can care for plants, and
- parks and open space that offer children and youth opportunities for climbing, challenge, and adventure. Planners should ensure a wide range of environments to encourage many kinds of children's play and ensure they are well situated, safe, and well maintained. A field action project[60] converted a dumping space into playground for children. Such initiatives have to be taken on a mass scale.

The challenge before us now is to make every child feel part of something special. To encourage policy planners to think creatively about how they can use sport as a tool in their policies. To build partnerships among governments, civil society, and the private sector to ensure the widest and most effective use possible of that tool. Child advocates must be vigilant in their protection of this right, for the twenty-first century offers serious threats to this seemingly natural and simple aspect of human development.[61]

Future Challenges

The changing concept of development, from a narrow preoccupation with national income to a broader concern with people's well-being and their capacity to better themselves and to improve their environment, casts a new light on the importance of education. Human development—interpreted as widening human choices in economic, political, social, and cultural terms—assigns a critical role to education. The new vision of human development will remain an empty rhetoric until education enables people to understand and exercise the choices that are promised by this new vision.

[60] A project of Tata Institute of Social Sciences, Mumbai.
[61] Visit www.scyofbc.org.

The recognition of the central importance of education in promoting human development has led to three areas of agreement on educational priorities. First, it is recognized that priority must be given to basic education since it is the foundation of a national educational system and because basic education contributes most substantially to overall economic and social development, including the reduction of poverty, fertility, and child mortality. Second, it is recognized that the core of basic education is primary education for children since they embody the future of a society. Third, the education of girls and women has emerged as the most precious investment that a society can make in its future. The beneficial impacts of education, especially of the education of girls, on social development are well recognized. The number of years of schooling of girls has been found to be closely related to the reduction of child mortality and morbidity, the improvement of family health and nutrition, and the slowing of population growth. The International Conference on Population and Development, held in Cairo, Egypt, in September 1994, again highlighted the central role of the education of girls and women in lowering population growth, promoting women's status in society, and contributing to sustainable human development. A challenge before India as well as before other developing countries is the education of the girl child. In a culture that idolizes sons and dreads the birth of a daughter, to be born a female comes perilously close to being less than human. The girl child has to be made a priority in educational policies. There is a draft bill pending in the Indian Parliament called the Girl Child (Compulsory Education and Welfare) Bill 2000. This Bill is to provide for free and compulsory minimum education for the girl child and other welfare measure to be undertaken by the State for her proper development and for matters connected therewith. In this bill the girl child has been defined to be below sixteen years.[62] The draft bill enjoins the government to provide to every girl child:

- Compulsory and free education up to the matriculation or secondary level;
- Study materials, such as, books, note books, stationery, etc., free of cost;
- Free hostel facilities wherever necessary;
- School uniforms, shoes, socks, free of cost;
- Scholarships to the deserving girl child for her school education and higher education in university/college including medical and technical education;
- Nutritious free food to all the girl students in schools, colleges, institutes, and universities; and

[62] Section 2(b): 'girl child' means any woman who is below the age of sixteen years.

- Free medical aid and health care to every girl child throughout the country.

Government shall formulate a scheme for providing training to the girl child in the following vocations: home science; tailoring; doll making; cookery; food preservation; embroidery and painting; knitting and weaving; interior decoration; architecture; midwifery; and nursing. The scheme may also incorporate any vocation other than those referred to above, from time to time, for imparting training to the girl child in such vocation. Proper and gainful employment to every girl child shall be arranged after completion of her education or training in any vocation.[63]

Under the draft bill, it shall be the duty of the head of each family or *Karta* of the family, male or female, to send every girl child of the family to school, college, or such other institutions for receiving education or training, as the case may be, from the normal age of schooling of such girl child. Whoever contravenes the provisions shall be punishable with imprisonment which may extend to two years, or with fine which may extend to two thousand rupees, or with both.[64]

The draft bill itself reflects the outdated notions of certain stereotype attitudes towards the girl child and their status and role in society. Such attempts are doomed to be futile. Punishing the family members for not sending the girl child to school will not solve the problem. A few scattered experiments providing integrated services for children below the age of twelve under a single roof have had a positive impact on the enrolment and retention of girls in school.

Universal primary education is widely recognized as one of the most effective instruments for combating child labour. It is believed that no country can successfully eliminate child labour without first enacting and implementing compulsory education legislation. Quality basic education, particularly at the primary level, not only improves the lives of children and their families but contributes to the future economic growth and development of a country. Education and child labour laws should not only reinforce but also complement one another. Education laws and policies can reinforce child labour laws by keeping children in schools and away from the workplace. Child labour laws, in turn, can be a useful tool for retaining children in school, helping Governments achieve their universal basic education objectives. International Standards on child labour have made this link by encouraging countries to make admission into the workforce conditional on completion of compulsory education. ILO Convention No. 138

---

[63] Section 7 of the draft bill.
[64] Section 8 of the draft bill.

establishes the minimum age for employment at not less than the age for completing compulsory schooling and in no event less than fifteen years.

Education must be available to all children without discrimination. It should reach out to those who have been traditionally unreached including girls, the poor, working children, children affected by emergencies and HIV/AIDS, the disabled, and those with nomadic lifestyles. This right is one that transcends access alone and includes quality. Education must be provided from a rights perspective, recognizing the indivisibility of rights and the need for educational processes to respect all rights. Education can also be an 'enabling right'—a right that facilitates access to other rights throughout a lifetime.

In order for the world to survive and prosper in the new century, people will need to learn more and learn differently. A child entering the new century is likely to face more risks and uncertainties and will need to gain more knowledge and master more skills than any generation before. The challenges the world faces at the onset of the twenty-first century are an impressive lot: urbanization and globalization, population expansion and environmental deterioration, terrorism, sexism, fundamentalism, and authoritarianism—with the addition of ethnic conflict and political instability, corruption, disease, and poverty. But the end of the twentieth century has also brought with it technological and scientific development, at a faster rate than at any previous period in human history, in health, in agriculture, in industrial production, and notably in the fields of communication, mass media, and information. As the twenty-first century begins, the opportunities to learn have expanded in more ways than most people can imagine.

Schools will remain the most effective and efficient way to transmit the knowledge and skills, and promote the values, needed for the future. They must continue to be expanded in quantity and improved in quality. But given the increasing complexity of the world, and the increasing amount of learning that takes place outside of the classroom, a single focus on schools and even on the basic education system is no longer enough. Strengthening the other critical environments in which children learn—the family, the community—must also become a major and more explicit focus of development.

Filling the gap between the kind of education now being provided by most school systems and the kind needed for the twenty-first century requires significant changes in the way policy makers make policies, planners plan systems, teachers teach, communities participate, learners learn, and development agencies function. It requires, most of all, a broadening of thinking and attention away from an almost exclusive focus on the more formal structure and output orientation of 'schooling' to greater concern for the more broadly defined process of 'learning'.

A new approach is needed where it is recognized that building and supplying more schools (with teachers, new curricula, and texts), though important tasks in themselves, do not automatically lead to more positive learning outcomes and that learning takes place not only in schools (in fact, not even mostly in schools) but also in other environments—in families and communities, with peers and through the media, in the playgrounds and other public places.

The basic right of the child is not only to education as in Article 28 of the CRC, but to learning and to the opportunity to learn, to have access to enabling and supportive learning environments, which will help children gain both access to other rights and to the knowledge, skills, competencies, attitudes, and values needed for continuing lifelong learning.

The 'expanded vision' of basic education which the Jomtien Declaration promotes includes universalizing access and promoting equity; focusing on learning acquisition; broadening the means and scope of basic education; enhancing the environment for learning; and strengthening partnerships within a supportive policy context, through mobilizing resources and strengthening international solidarity.

Learning should be to develop one's personality and be able to act with greater autonomy, judgment, critical thinking, and personal responsibility; to develop all aspects of one's potential—memory, reasoning, aesthetic sense, spiritual values, physical capacities, and communication skills; to make one healthy and enjoy play and sports; to value one's own culture; to possess an ethical and moral code; to speak for and protect oneself; to make one resilient.

A pragmatic and realistic approach has to be taken. Insistence on certificates, admission deadlines, etc., have to be overlooked. The education system must also be geared towards inculcating democratic and gender-sensitive values in the youth. The disciplinary practices in school must be reviewed and modified with the child's dignity and human rights in mind. The role of media is very crucial. NGOs and voluntary organizations working for children also need to take up the responsibility of creating bridges between what is taught to the child and the cultural practices of the child. Popular knowledge systems require to be re-appraised and modernized so that the best in our traditional knowledge systems can be combined with modern scientific learning. Universal education for children can only be possible when parents themselves are educated. Therefore, compulsory elementary education can be a success only when it is linked to universal adult education programmes.

Public expenditure on education as a percentage of GNP declined from 2.9 to 2.5 per cent between 1980 and 1994 in the least developed countries, and it remains below 3.0–3.4 per cent (on an average) in Asia. The correlation between public expenditure and enrolment rates is far from consistent, but low public expenditure is a common feature of almost all low-enrolment countries. It is vital to continue to advocate and to support education ministries in their own advocacy for a greater share of public expenditure. This should be complemented by wider public advocacy, greater transparency and better data on the education system in general and education expenditure in particular.

Partnerships and networks are needed at all levels of the system. The promotion of such partnerships at the community level often produces little success if the major sectoral and political forces of society do not support them, and likewise, sectoral collaboration at the top of the system does not necessarily translate into easy networking in fractious, heterogeneous communities. Mobilization and advocacy, at all levels, are essential. Policy makers, teachers, and parents, for example, must all understand the importance of good quality schooling and the indicators of successful learning.

It is important to obligate the State, the trustee of the nation, to provide education for all. Too often, compulsory education is seen as a legal framework that places parents and children in the negative role of criminal or victim. It is not to make children and families obligated to something they cannot achieve, but rather to place the burden on the States, to require the states to make quality primary education accessible to every child. Only after that is it appropriate to place the burden of proof on children and families. This will require dialogue and, sometimes, pressure, and advocacy for the border between family responsibility and State responsibility is not one that is well defined and may vary according to the context.

All advanced industrial countries and those contemporary developing countries that have made education compulsory regard education not as a right but as a duty. When education is made a duty, parents, irrespective of their economic circumstances and beliefs are required, by law, to send their children to school. It is also the legal obligation of the State to provide an adequate number of schools appropriately situated and to ensure that no child fails to attend school.[65]

[65] Myron Weiner, *The Child and the State in India*, Oxford University Press, Delhi, 1991.

If the right to education is to become meaningful, the process of education has to be one that equips children to face the challenges of life as they grow up to become adults. Seen in the context of the larger society, it has not only to prepare children for the challenges of tomorrow, but also to act as an agent of change, something that empowers them to play an active role in the creation of the world of tomorrow. The close links between basic education and key civic, economic, and social goals of communities lend a special urgency to the effort to fulfil the promise of basic education for all.

There is now an urgent need to bring comprehensive State laws, to provide adequate budget and to have a strong political will and commitment to ensure elementary education to every child in India.

8

Right to Survival: Health, Nutrition, and Shelter

The right to survival of a child includes:

- Access to health care services for children in emergency situation and for prevention of disease, through the existing health care network;
- Providing shelter;
- Providing nutritional facilities for children in need of care and protection; and
- Providing an identity.

Right to Health

In 1946, the World Health Organization (WHO) defined health in its Constitution as 'a state of complete physical, mental, and social well-being and not merely the absence of disease or infirmity'. The Constitution proclaimed that the enjoyment of the highest attainable standard of health is one of the fundamental human rights of every human being without distinction of race, religion, political belief, and economic or social condition. The Constitution also recognized that the health of all people is fundamental to the attainment of peace and security and is dependent upon the fullest co-operation of individuals and States. This was the vision shared by all the member States including India.

This vision was translated into a conceptual framework in the 'Health for All By 2000' Declaration of Alma Ata in 1978 (which meant the attainment by all citizens of the world by the year 2000 of a level of health that would permit them to lead socially and economically productive lives). The Alma Ata Declaration strongly reaffirmed that health, which is a state of complete physical, mental, and social well-being, and not merely the absence of disease or infirmity, is a fundamental human right and that the attainment of the highest possible level of health is a most important worldwide social goal whose realization requires the action of many other social and economic sectors in addition to the health sector. It also stated that primary health care (PHC) was the key to attaining health for all as part of overall development. It defined PHC as, 'essential health care made universally accessible to individuals and families in the community by means acceptable to them, through their full participation and at a cost that the community and the country can afford'. PHC is the first level of contact of individuals, the family and community bringing health care as close as possible to where people live and work.

The call for 'Health for All' was a call for social justice. It was not a single finite goal, but a strategic process leading to progressive improvement in the health of people. Despite many gains in the realm of health (increase in life expectancy, decreasing mortality, decline in infectious diseases, reduction in child mortality and morbidity, etc.), progress towards Health for All in many countries has been hampered due to slow socio-economic development, lack of political commitment, failure to achieve equity in access to all PHC elements, inappropriate allocation and use of resources, low status of women, etc. Thus Health for All still remains an unfulfilled dream. Recognizing this, the World Health Organization has renewed the health-for-all strategy and has given a call for Health for All in the twenty-first century.

International Human Rights Law

The right to health requires countries to do more than merely provide for comprehensive systems of health care delivery and insurance. It obligates them to undertake measures aimed at promoting individual and community health and at preventing diseases, to remove other external causes of morbidity and mortality, to eliminate health inequalities, and to improve the conditions that may hamper achievement of the highest attainable level of health. The right to health is interdependent with many other human rights. The human right to health includes:[1]

- The human right to the highest attainable standard of physical and mental health, including reproductive and sexual health.
- The human right to equal access to adequate health care and health-related services, regardless of sex, race, or other status.
- The human right to equitable distribution of food.
- The human right to access to safe drinking water and sanitation.
- The human right to an adequate standard of living and adequate housing.

[1] www.pdhre.org

- The human right to a safe and healthy environment.
- The human right to safe and healthy workplace, and to adequate protection for pregnant women in work proven to be harmful to them.
- The human right to freedom from discrimination and discriminatory social practices, including female genital mutilation, prenatal gender selection, and female infanticide.
- The human right to education and access to information relating to health, including reproductive health and family planning to enable couples and individuals to decide freely and responsibly all matters of reproduction and sexuality.
- The human rights of the child to an environment appropriate for physical and mental development.

The right to health is solidly embedded in international human rights law. It is explicit in Article 25 of the Universal Declaration of Human Rights (UDHR) adopted by the United Nations General Assembly in 1948. According to Article 25, everyone has the right to a standard of living that is adequate for the health and well-being of himself and his family including food, clothing, shelter, housing, etc. Article 25 lays special emphasis on motherhood and childhood. Again in the International Covenant on Economic, Social, and Cultural Rights (ICESCR), which came into force in 1976, Article 11 states that the State parties to the present Covenant recognize the right of everyone to an adequate standard of living for himself and his family including adequate food, clothing, and housing. Of special importance is Article 12 of the ICESCR, which formulates the right to health as an autonomous right. The Convention on the Rights of the Child 1989 addresses the issue of health in Articles 24 and 27. Article 24 says that the state parties recognize the right of the child to the enjoyment of the highest attainable standard of health and shall take appropriate measures to combat disease and malnutrition through the provision of adequate nutritious food, clean drinking water, and health care. Article 27 of the CRC says that in case of need, the State parties shall provide material assistance and support programmes, particularly with regard to nutrition, clothing, and housing. The Convention on the Elimination of All Forms of Discrimination Against Women (CEDAW) provides that the States shall eliminate discrimination against women in health care and ensure, on the basis of equality of men and women, access to health care services, including those related to family planning and further ensure appropriate services in connection with pregnancy. It has to be ensured that women in rural areas have access to adequate health care facilities, including information counselling and services in family planning [CEDAW, Articles 10, 12, and 14]. The Convention on the Elimination of All Forms of Racial Discrimination Against Women enjoins the States to eliminate racial discrimination and to guarantee the right of everyone, without distinction as to race, colour, or national or ethnic origin, to equality before law, the right to public health, medical care, social security, and social services.

Numerous subsequent international and regional human rights treaties have given further definition to the right to health. Other international instruments recognizing the right to health include various conventions adopted within the context of the International Labour Organization (ILO) and, at the regional level, the European Social Charter (ESC), the African Charter on Human and Peoples Rights (ACHPR), and the Additional Protocol to the American Convention on Human Rights in the Area of Economic, Social, and Cultural Rights. The European Convention on Human Rights and Biomedicine also proclaims a right to equitable health care.

The heads of States and Governments gathered in Rome at the World Food Summit at the invitation of FAO, reaffirmed on 13 November 1996 the right of everyone to have access to safe and nutritious food, consistent with the right to adequate food and the fundamental right of everyone to be free from hunger. They considered it intolerable that more than 800 million people throughout the world, and particularly in developing countries, do not have enough food to meet their basic nutritional needs. They pledged their political will and their common and national commitment to achieving food security for all and to an ongoing effort to eradicate hunger in all countries. They formally renewed their commitment to the right to adequate food and recommended that the content of this right be defined more clearly and ways to implement it be identified.

The concept of nutrition rights originated in the context of the Convention on the Rights of the Child (CRC) and was developed by the United Nations Children's Fund (UNICEF) which defined nutrition rights as the combination of access to food, health, and necessary care. These three components are necessary to guarantee adequate nutrition to children. More and more NGOs are resorting to an explicit rights approach, especially in their work related to the Committee on the Rights of the Child, the committee which monitors State compliance with the CRC. On the international level, the World Alliance on Nutrition and Human Rights, a network of experts in the fields of nutrition and human rights, is strongly promoting the rights approach to the food and nutrition aspects of its work. Other organizations are involved in issues such as breastfeeding, access to health facilities, and especially, child malnutrition are increasingly working on a rights basis.

Health for All in the Twenty-first Century

Health for All remains the cornerstone of World Health Organization's institutional vision. Health for All in the Twenty-first Century is a continuation of the Health for All process. As a result the Fifty-first World Health Assembly has recognized 'Health for All in the Twenty-first Century' as a framework for the development of future policy.

World Health Declaration[2]

The Member States of the World Health Organization (WHO) reaffirmed their commitment to the principle enunciated in its Constitution that the enjoyment of the highest attainable standard of health is one of the fundamental rights of every human being; in doing so, the dignity and worth of every person is affirmed. The Declaration recognized that the improvement of the health and well-being of people is the ultimate aim of social and economic development.

International Campaigns on Health

People's Health Assembly

The People's Health Assembly, an international multi-sectoral initiative, aims at bringing together individuals, groups, national and international organizations, networks, and civil society movements that have been long involved in the struggle for health. The goal of People's Health Assembly is to re-establish health and equitable development as top priorities in local, national, and international policy making, with primary health care as the strategy for achieving these priorities.

Global Health Assembly

The Global Health Assembly was convened during 4–8 December 2000 at Dhaka, Bangladesh. Ninety-two countries sent 1453 participants to the Assembly which was the culmination of eighteen months of preparatory action around the globe. The preparatory process elicited unprecedented enthusiasm and participation of a broad cross-section of people who have been involved in thousands of village meetings, district-level workshops, and national gatherings. At the Assembly, they reviewed their problems and difficulties, shared their experiences and plans, and formulated and endorsed the People's Charter for Health. The Charter is now the common tool of a

---

[2] Article 23 of the Constitution of World Health Organization.

worldwide citizen's movement committed to making the Alma Ata dream a reality.

Massive Effort Campaign Against the Diseases of Poverty

The Massive Effort Campaign is a campaign to break the vicious cycle of poverty and disease. For the first time in history, the international community got together the financial means, the medications, and the know-how to take a stand against a small number of diseases that cause tremendous suffering and economic loss. This Massive Effort Campaign against the diseases of poverty, which unites partners in unique ways, is moving the world from word to action that can facilitate sustainable development, stimulate economic growth, ensure greater global public health security, and, most importantly, save human lives. This is a multi-sectoral initiative involving health networks, NGOs, ethical organizations, corporates, etc., to develop an integrated approach that combines preventive, curative, promotive and rehabilitative aspects to address the diseases of poverty, namely, malaria, tuberculosis, and HIV/AIDS. In recent times, the efforts to control communicable diseases are directed towards HIV/AIDS. The campaign seeks to bring about a policy change for concerted efforts to tackle the diseases of poverty. In India, the campaign is in its initial phase. The campaign planning has started off with a preparatory meeting of activists, corporates, social action groups, media persons, etc.[3]

Law and Policy on Health in India

The Constitution of India envisages the establishment of a new social order based on equality, freedom, justice, and dignity of the individual. It aims at the elimination of poverty, ignorance, and ill health, and directs the State to regard the raising of the level of nutrition and the standard of living of its people and the improvement of public health as among its primary duties. The provision of health care services is the responsibility of the State governments. The Ministry of Health and Family Welfare at the Centre is responsible for policy formulation and allocation of funds for certain health programmes.

The Constitution of India provides in Articles 39(e) and (f) that the State shall, in particular, direct its policy towards securing the health of children.

[3] The National Centre for Advocacy Studies hosted the meeting in Pune, Maharashtra. The Catholic Health Association of India in Secunderabad hosted the second planning meeting. In this meeting a National Campaign Team was constituted, and it was decided to launch the campaign in March 2002.

Further, in Article 47 of the Constitution, the State is directed to raise the level of nutrition and the standard of living of its people and the improvement of public health as among its primary duties and, in particular, the State shall endeavour to bring about prohibition of the consumption except for medicinal purposes of intoxicating drinks and of drugs which are injurious to health. Unfortunately, in the Constitution of India, health is not a fundamental right of citizens and, therefore, cannot be justiciable in courts. The provision of health care is contained in the directive principles and it is a duty of the State to raise the level of nutrition and the standard of living and to improve public health. Article 21 of the Constitution of India deals with 'Right to Life' which is a fundamental right and justiciable in courts. The Supreme Court has observed 'that the right to life includes the right to live with human dignity and what goes along with it, namely, the bare necessaries of life such as adequate nutrition, clothing and shelter.'[4]

There are several legislations dealing with the various issues of health. Until 1983, India did not have a formal National Health Policy. The health sector was developed through the discussions of the Central Council of Health and Family Welfare, the Planning Commission, and the occasional committees constituted by the Central government.

National Health Policy 1983

In its first National Health Policy 1983, India was committed to attaining the goal of 'Health for All by the Year 2000.' through the universal provision of comprehensive primary health care services. The main focus was the formulation of an integrated and comprehensive approach towards future development of health services. The Policy aimed at a thorough overhaul of the existing approaches to education and training of medical and health personnel and reorganization of health infrastructure. It envisaged the complete integration of all plans for health and human development with the overall national socio-economic development process integrating all health-related sectors. With multi-sectoral approach, the Policy sought to provide universal, comprehensive primary health care services relevant to the actual needs and priorities of the community at a cost which the people can afford, ensuring that the planning and implementation of the various health programmes are through the organized involvement and participation of the community, adequately utilizing the services being rendered by private voluntary organizations active in the health sector. Accordingly, the goals were set to achieve 'Health for All by 2000'.

---

[4] *Francis Coralie Mullin v The Administrator, Union Territory of Delhi and others* (1981) 1 SCC 608.

In the realm of primary health care, the Policy recognized the need for comprehensive primary health care with special emphasis, besides curative aspect of health, on preventive, promotive, and rehabilitative aspects of health. It also focused on decentralized primary health care with people's involvement in the identification of their health needs and priorities and in the implementation and management of the various health programmes.

Government initiatives in the pubic health sector have recorded some noteworthy successes over time. Smallpox and Guinea worm disease have been eradicated from the country; polio is on the verge of being eradicated; leprosy, kala-azar, and filariasis can be expected to be eliminated in the foreseeable future. There has been a substantial drop in the Total Fertility Rate (TFR) and Infant Mortality Rate(IMR). The success of the initiatives taken in the public health field are reflected in the progressive improvement of many demographic/epidemiological/infrastructural indicators over time[5] as may be seen from Table 8.1.

Table 8.1: Achievements Through The Years: 1951–2000

Demographic Indicator	1951	1981	2000
Life Expectancy	36.7	54	64.6
Crude Birth Rate	40.8	33.9	26.1
Crude Death Rate	25	12.5	8.7
Infant Mortality Rate (IMR)	146	110	70

Source: Sample Registration System (SRS), SRS Bulletin Vital Statistics, Registrar General of India (RGI).

In respect of TB, the public health scenario has not shown any significant decline in the pool of infection amongst the community, and there has been a distressing trend in the increase of drug resistance to the type of infection prevailing in the country. A new and extremely virulent communicable disease, HIV/AIDS, has emerged on the health scene since the declaration of the NHP 1983. As there is no existing therapeutic cure or vaccine for this infection, the disease constitutes a serious threat, not merely to public health but to economic development in the country. The common waterborne infections—gastroenteritis, cholera, and some forms of hepatitis—continue to contribute to a high level of morbidity in the population, even though the mortality rate may have been somewhat moderated.

Another area of grave concern in the public health domain is the persistent incidence of macro and micro-nutrient deficiencies, especially among

[5] www.who.int/archives/who50/en/health4all.htm

women and children. In the vulnerable subcategory of women and the girl child, this has the multiplier effect through the birth of low-birth weight babies and serious ramifications of the consequential mentally and physically retarded growth.[6]

National Health Policy 2002

NHP 1983, in a spirit of optimistic empathy for the health needs of the people, particularly the poor and underprivileged, had hoped to provide 'Health for All by 2000', through the universal provision of comprehensive primary health care services. NHP 2002 has attempted to set out a new policy framework for the accelerated achievement of public health goals in the socio-economic circumstances currently prevailing in the country.

NHP 2002 has been formulated taking into consideration the ground realities in regard to the availability of resources. In the period when centralized planning was accepted as a key instrument of development in the country, the attainment of an equitable regional distribution was considered one of its major objectives. Despite this conscious focus in the development process, the attainment of health indices has been very uneven across the rural-urban divide.

NHP 2002 also envisages giving priority to school health programmes which aim at preventive health education, providing regular health check-ups, and promotion of health-seeking behaviour among children. The school health programmes can gainfully adopt specially designed modules in order to disseminate information relating to 'health' and 'family life'. This is expected to be the most cost-effective intervention as it improves the level of awareness, not only of the extended family, but the future generation as well.

It is widely accepted that school and college students are the most impressionable targets for imparting information relating to the basic principles of preventive health care. The policy will attempt to target this group to improve the general level of awareness in regard to 'health-promoting' behaviour.

Social, cultural, and economic factors continue to inhibit women from gaining adequate access even to the existing public health facilities. This handicap has an adverse impact on the health, general well-being, and development of the entire family, particularly children. This policy recognizes the catalytic role of empowered women in improving the overall health standards of the community including children.[7]

---

[6] Jan Swasthya Sabha. *Whatever happened to Health for All by 2000?* National Co, Chennai, 2000.

[7] www.mohfw.nic.in Draft National Health Policy, 2001.

Efforts made over the years for improving health standards have been partially neutralized by the rapid growth of the population. Government has separately announced the 'National Population Policy 2000'. The principal common features covered under the National Population Policy 2000 and NHP 2002 relate to the prevention and control of communicable diseases giving priority to the containment of HIV/AIDS infection, the universal immunization of children against all major preventable diseases, addressing the unmet needs for basic and reproductive health services, and supplementation of infrastructure. The synchronized implementation of these two Policies—National Population Policy 2000 and National Health Policy-2002—will be the very cornerstone of any national structural plan to improve the health standards of children in the country.

The National Population Policy 2000 (NPP 2000)

The NPP 2000 recognizes the link between high infant mortality and excessive population growth. The policy statement commits the nation to a reduction of the infant mortality rate to under 30 per 1000 by the year 2010. This necessitates a rapid reduction in neonatal deaths which form a major component of infant mortality. The Policy also aims to achieve 80 per cent deliveries in institutions and 100 per cent deliveries by trained personnel by the year 2010. In pursuance of the National Population Policy 2000, the government has constituted the National Technical Committee on Child Health with a view to harnessing professional inputs regarding implementation of programmes for child survival with special focus on newborn health.

Children's Health Scenario in India

Children in India suffer from various health problems since early childhood. Some come across fatal diseases and problems even before birth leading to shortened and unhealthy lives. The principal findings of the mid-decade review[8] highlighted many aspects:

- Remarkable progress has been made in the eradication of polio and the goal of polio eradication by 2000. The number of cases reported fell from 28,264 in 1987 to 1,005 in 1995. Nationwide immunization days were declared in December 1995 and January 1996.
- There was an improvement in the management of diarrhoea at home.

[8] *India Report on the World Summit for Children 2000*, Department of Women and Child Development, Ministry of Human Resource Development, Government of India.

Oral Rehydration Therapy (ORT) became popular in 80 per cent of the villages under the Child Survival and Safe Motherhood Programme and many families had access to Oral Rehydration Salts (ORS) through depots.
- Malnutrition as manifested in underweight and stunted children continued to be a major problem. It was particularly acute amongst infants and pre-school children in the poorest socio-economic groups.
- Deliberate discrimination against girl children took several forms: nutritional denial such as inadequate breastfeeding and early weaning; insufficient or delayed medical care; lack of attention, causing emotional deprivation; and insufficient investment in resources. All these have been documented as leading to excess mortality in the female child.
- The Infant Mortality Rate (IMR) fell from 80 per 1000 in 1991 to 74 per 1000 in 1995. The infant mortality rate is a sensitive indicator of the socio-economic development of a country. IMR has two distinct components, viz., the neonatal mortality (deaths during first month of life) and post-natal mortality (deaths from one month to twelve months of life). India has made significant progress in reducing infant mortality (deaths less than one year) in recent decades. Infant mortality rate (IMR) per 1000 live births has declined from 146 in 1951 to 72 in 1998, a reduction of over 50 per cent. Twenty States and Union territories now record IMR of less than 60 per 1000.[9] Most of the decline in IMR has been due to reduction in the post-neonatal mortality. The decline in mortality of infants under one month of age has been unsatisfactory. Thus, of the 25 million infants born in India every year, 1.2 million die in the first month of life. India's share of the global burden of neonatal deaths is the highest for any single country.[10]
- At present the Under-5 mortality rank of India in the world is forty-nine.[11] The Under-5 mortality rate (viz., probability of dying between birth and exactly five years of age, per 1000 live births) has improved from 109.3 in 1990 to 94.9 in 2000.[12] The Infant Mortality Rate (viz., the probability of dying before the first birthday) in India has declined from 80 to 70 per 1000 live births over the period 1991–2000 and

---

[9] *Newborn Health Key to Child Survival*, Child health division, Department of Family Welfare, Ministry of Health and Family Welfare, Government of India, 2001.
[10] Ibid.
[11] *The State of the World's Children 2001*, UNICEF.
[12] *India Report on the World Summit for Children 2000*, Department of Women and Child Development, Ministry of Human Resource Development, Government of India.

fourteen of India's States and six Union territories had achieved the goal of IMR of 60 per 1000 by the year 2000.[13] A difference of one was noted in the IMR of male and female children with the rate for males and females being 69.8 and 70.8 respectively. Similarly, the Child Mortality Rate (viz., the probability of dying between the first and the fifth birthday) has declined from 33.4 in 1991 to 29.3 per 1000 live births in 1998.[14] The Under-5, Infant and Child Mortality Rates reflect a country's level of socio-economic development and quality of life, and are used to monitor and evaluate health programmes and policies.
- Vitamin-A Deficiency is one of the major public problems in India, a rough estimate showing 30,000 to 40,000 children losing their sight every year. This deficiency is also aggravated by infections, which reduce the absorption and utilization in the body.

Rights of Unborn Child and Rights during Early Childhood

The Right of a Child to be Born

FEMICIDE

Femicide, which includes female infanticide, sex-selective abortions, sex selection of embryos and other methods of averting the natural formation of a female foetus (sperm separation), takes place everyday in every corner of this country. During the late 1970s, cases of abortion of female foetuses were reported from many of the major cities of India. The practice continues to this day, with the more invasive techniques of sex determination, such as amniocentesis and chronic villus sampling, replaced by ultrasonography.In the states of Punjab and Haryana in north-western India, there are today mobile ultrasound units, which regularly visit rural areas. Abortion of female foetuses is no longer an urban phenomenon in these parts of India.

According to the 1991 census the overall sex ratio of the country was 929 women per 1000 men. This sex ratio is becoming more skewed day by day. Medical and scientific procedures are becoming more efficient and it has consequently it is becoming easier to get rid of a female child. With a population count of 1,027 million, the census[15] also showed the male population as 531 million and female population as 496 million. The sex ratio of 933

[13] Ibid.
[14] Ibid.
[15] Census of India, 1991.

females per 1000 males showed an overall improvement of 6 points from the sex ratio of 927 per 1000 males in 1991. But a matter of deep concern is the decline in the sex ratio of population in the 0–6 age group or the child sex ratio from 945 in 1991 to 927 in 2001. The child sex ratio had earlier declined by seventeen points from 962 in 1981 to 945 in 1991. This problem is now not limited only to metropolitan regions but has spread to even smaller towns. This poses a challenge to the already dwindling sex ratio as may be seen from the data presented in Table 8.2.

Table 8.2: Sex Ratio Trends: Implications for Girls[16]

Sex Ratio (per 1000) in	1991	2001
Total Population	927	933
Child Population	945	927
Population aged seven and above	923	935

Amniocentesis was brought into India in 1975, as a measure of detecting genetic disorders and abnormalities. Unfortunately, this invention of medical science has resulted in 'quickening the pace of death of the female child from the born to the unborn stage'.[17] It is being used to get rid of the girl child before birth. Amniocentesis in India has become synonymous with the sex determination test, which has led to sex-selective abortions. The advancement of science and invention of sophisticated equipment has now made it easy to know the sex of the foetus much in advance of birth and to facilitate decision whether to abort or not, even in case of healthy foetus, to get rid of the unwanted female. Amniocentesis involves removing amniotic fluid from the pregnant woman after twenty weeks of pregnancy. The test can reveal any genetic abnormality as well as the sex of the foetus.

Legal Provisions Relating to Female Foeticide, Amniocentesis, and Abortion

There are provisions under the Indian Penal Code 1860 for foeticde and infanticide. Amniocentesis or sex-selective abortion is a crime under the Indian Penal Code (IPC). The IPC lays down stringent penalties if miscarriage is caused without the consent of the woman. The Prenatal Diagnostic Techniques (Regulation and Prevention of Misuse) Act 1994 is aimed at

[16] *India: Social and Economic Statistics*, UNICEF in India, 1999–2002: Challenges and Opportunities.
[17] Anand Grover, 'Amniocentesis or female foeticide', *The Lawyers*, March 1986, 3.

banning selective abortion of females. The Medical Termination of Pregnancy Act 1971 permits termination of pregnancies before twenty weeks under certain circumstances.[18] The relevant provisions of IPC are as follows:

Section	Offence	Punishment
312	Causing miscarriage voluntarily.	Imprisonment for three years or fine or both.
	If the woman be quick with child (quick with child is not defined under the Act but it can be interpreted to mean a child capable of being born alive).	Imprisonment for seven years and fine.
313	Causing miscarriage without the woman's consent.	Imprisonment for life or imprisonment for ten years and fine
314	Death caused by an act done with intent to cause miscarriage	Imprisonment for ten years and fine.
	If the act is done without the woman's consent.	Imprisonment for life or as above.
315	Act done with intent to prevent a child being born alive or to cause it to die after its birth.	Imprisonment for ten years or fine or both.
316	Causing death of a quick unborn child by an act amounting to culpable homicide.	Imprisonment for ten years and fine.
318	Concealment of birth by secret disposal of dead body.	Imprisonment for two years or fine or both.

The Prenatal Diagnostic Technique (Regulation and Prevention of Misuse) Act 1994 (PNDT Act 1994)

The objective of the Act is to provide for the regulation of the use of prenatal diagnostic techniques [19] for the purpose of detecting genetic or metabolic

---

[18] Asha Bajpai, *The Girl Child and the Law: Rights of the Child*, NLSIU/UNICEF, 1990.

[19] PNDT Act 1994, Section 2(j): 'Prenatal diagnostic techniques' include all prenatal diagnostic procedures and prenatal diagnostic tests.

disorders or chromosomal abnormalities or certain congenital malformation or sex-linked disorders and for the prevention of the misuse of this techniques for the purpose of prenatal sex determination leading to female foeticide.[20]

The Regulation of Prenatal Diagnostic Techniques

The Act provides for regulation of genetic counselling centres [PNDT Act 1994, Section 2c], genetic laboratories, and genetic clinics set up to conduct or associate with or help in conducting activities relating to prenatal diagnostic techniques. Every such centre, laboratory, or clinic shall be registered [PNDT Act 1994, Section 18] under the Act by the appropriate authority.[21]

Section 3 provides that no place including a registered genetic counselling centre or genetic laboratory or genetic clinic shall be used or caused to be used by any person for conducting prenatal diagnostic techniques except for the purposes specified under the Act. Medical practitioners, gynaecologists, and pediatricians cannot conduct prenatal diagnostic techniques at a place other than one registered under the Act.

The Act allows prenatal diagnostic techniques to be conducted only for the purposes of detection of any of the following abnormalities, namely: chromosomal abnormalities, genetic metabolic diseases, haemoglobinopathies, sex-linked genetic diseases, congenital anomalies, or any other abnormalities or diseases specified by the Central Supervisory Board [PNDT Act 1994, Section 4(2)].

Prenatal diagnostic techniques can be conducted only if one of the following conditions is satisfied [PNDT Act 1994, Section 4(3)]:

- The pregnant woman is above thirty-five years;
- She has undergone two or more spontaneous abortions or foetal loss;
- She has been exposed to teratogenic agents such as drugs, radiation, infection, or chemicals;
- The woman seeking the use of prenatal diagnostic techniques has a family history of mental retardation or physical deformities and spasticity or any other genetic disease, or
- Any other condition as may be specified by the Central Advisory Board [PNDT Act 1994, Section 7].

[20] The Preamble to the Prenatal Diagnostic Techniques (Regulation And Prevention of Misuse) Act 1994.

[21] The appropriate authority shall have the power to grant, suspend, or cancel registration, enforce standards, and investigate complaints, and also power to search and seize records.

The prenatal diagnostic procedures[22] can be carried out only after the following conditions are satisfied:
- All known side effects and after-effects of the procedures are explained to the pregnant woman;
- The consent of the woman undergoing the procedures has been obtained after explaining to her in the language in which she understands; and
- A copy of the written consent has been given to the pregnant woman.

No person conducting prenatal diagnostic procedures shall communicate to the pregnant woman or her relatives the sex of the foetus in any manner. The Act specifically provides that no genetic counselling centre or genetic laboratory or any person shall conduct any prenatal diagnostic techniques including ultrasonography for the purpose of determining the sex of the foetus [[PNDT Act 1994, Section 6].

The above prerequisites are mandatory and any violation of the same would entail punishment as prescribed under the Act. Every offence under this Act is cognizable, non-bailable, and non-compoundable [PNDT Act 1994, Section 27].

OFFENCES AND PENALTIES UNDER THE PNDT ACT

Offences	Penalties
No person, organization, genetic counselling centre, genetic laboratory, or genetic clinic shall issue or cause to be issued any advertisement regarding facilities of prenatal determination of sex available at such centre, laboratory, or clinic or any other place.	Punishable with imprisonment for a term which may extend to three years and with fine which may extend to ten thousand rupees [PNDT Act 1994, Section 22 (1)].
No person or organization shall publish, distribute or cause to be published or distributed any advertisement regarding facilities for prenatal determination of sex.	Punishable with imprisonment for a term which may extend to three years and with fine which may extend to ten thousand rupees [PNDT Act 1994, Section 22(2)].

[22] PNDT Act 1994, Section 2(i): 'Prenatal diagnostic procedures' means all gynaecological or obstetrical or medical procedures such as ultrasonography, foetoscopy, taking or removing samples of amniotic fluid, chronic villi, blood, or any tissue of a pregnant woman conducted to detect genetic or metabolic disorders or chromo-sexual abnormalities or congenital anomalies or haemoglobinopathies or sex-linked diseases.

Any medical geneticist, gynaecologist, registered medical practitioner, or any person who owns a genetic counselling centre, laboratory, or clinic or is employed in them and renders his professional or technical services and contravenes the provisions of this Act or rules made thereunder.	Punishable with imprisonment for a term which may extend to three years and with fine which may extend to ten thousand rupees and on any subsequent conviction with imprisonment which may extend to five years and with fine which may extend to fifty thousand rupees [PNDT Act 1994, Section 23(1)]. The name of the registered medical practitioner convicted for the above offence can be removed from the State Medical Council for a period of two years for the first offence and permanently for the subsequent offence [PNDT Act 1994, Section 23(2)].
If a person is compelled to undergo diagnostic techniques for purposes other then those specified in the Act.	Punishable with imprisonment for a term which may extend to three years and with fine which may extend to ten thousand rupees and on any subsequent conviction with imprisonment which may extend to five years and with fine which may extend to fifty thousand rupees[PNDT Act 1994, Section 23(3)].
Contravening any other provision of the Act or rules.	Punishable with imprisonment for a term which may extend to three months or with fine which may extend to one thousand rupees or with both and in the case of continuing contravention with an additional fine which may extend to five hundred rupees for every day during which such contravention continues after conviction for the first such contravention [PNDT Act 1994, Section 25].
When any offence under this Act is committed by a company.	Every person who at the time, the offence was committed was in charge of and was responsible for the conduct of business and was aware of the offence shall be deemed to be guilty and proceeded against and punished accordingly [PNDT Act 1994, Section 26].

Cognizance of Offences under the Act

A court of a metropolitan magistrate or a judicial magistrate of first class shall take cognizance of any offence under this Act on a complaint made by:

- The appropriate authority concerned or any officer authorized in this behalf by the Central government or the state government, or
- A person including a social organization who has given notice of not less than sixty days to the appropriate authority [PNDT Act 1994, Section 28(1)].

Presumption in the Case of Conduct of Prenatal Diagnostic Techniques

Unless the contrary is proved, the court shall presume that the pregnant woman has been compelled by her husband or relatives to undergo prenatal diagnostic technique and such a person shall be liable of abetment of offence under Section 23(3) of the PNDT Act.

Authorities under the Act

The two main authorities under the Act are:

- The Appropriate Authority, and
- The Advisory Committee.

Implementation of the PNDT Act 1994

The PNDT Act came into force on 1 January 1996. From the declining sex ratio, it is apparent that to a large extent, the PNDT Act is not implemented by the Central government or by the State governments. The situation of femicide continues to worsen despite the introduction of the PNDT Act. Unfortunately, in most of the States appropriate authorities are not actively functioning and in fact there are over 200 applications for registration of genetic clinics pending with the appropriate authority in the State of Tamil Nadu alone. The net result is that the genetic clinics are functioning in full swing without authorization and this delay in the process of applications has given a leeway for many such clinics to operate without bothering even to apply for registration. In many of these clinics, doctors who do not have the requisite qualifications are performing these procedures. In almost all the States appropriate authorities have not been set up at district levels and in some States at the State level. There are hardly any complaints made by the appropriate authority to the concerned magistrate for the violations under the Act, nor have any proceedings been initiated for cancellation of registration of these clinics.[23]

---

[23] Petition of CEHAT to the Supreme Court of India. See www.cehat.org.

A writ petition was filed under Article 32 of the Constitution of India by the Centre for Enquiry Into Health and Allied Themes (CEHAT), Mahila Sarvangeen Utkarsh Mandal (MASUM), and Dr Sabu M. George.[24] According to the petitioners, the PNDT Act for all its intents and purposes was a toothless piece of legislation. The problem was the interpretation of this Act by the ultrasonologists, the abortionists, the doctors, and most importantly, the government. Despite the intent and purpose of the Act being wide and all-encompassing, it was being interpreted to exclude prenatal sex selection. Thereby there were widespread advertisements by various clinics providing prenatal sex selection. It was further alleged that a narrow interpretation of the Act was being forwarded which gives a licence to all doctors to conveniently adopt this technique without the fear of the law. This technique has been condemned by the Beijing Convention as violation of human rights and ethical medical practices, and India is a signatory to the same as early as from 1995 and the same is binding on India.

The petitioners further contended that by ultrasonography and amniocentesis, the sex of the foetus is determined during the pregnancy of the woman and the foetus is aborted if found to be a female. These tests were carried out even by compounders and doctors without the necessary qualifications. At times the ultrasonologist and abortionist is one and the same person, but no one really cares as families want to get rid of their female child and the medical professionals (abortionists) want to make money. Another method which has increasingly become popular is sperm separation or Ericsson's technique. In this technique men's sperms are taken and tested in a laboratory to separate the XX and XY sperms and only XY sperms which can produce boys are used to artificially inseminate the women. Thus, sex selection takes place prenatally, in this instance, even before conception. The latest genetic technique, which is primarily used for sex determination, is Prenatal Genetic Diagnosis (PDG).

After filing of this petition, the Court issued notices to the concerned parties on 9 May 2000. It took nearly one year for the various States to file their affidavits in reply/written submissions. Prima facie, it appeared that despite the PNDT Act being enacted by the Parliament five years back, neither the State governments nor the Central government has taken appropriate actions for its implementation. The Supreme Court therefore issued the following directions for the proper implementation of the Act:

- The Central government is directed to create public awareness against the practice of prenatal determination of sex and female foeticide

[24] In the Supreme Court of India, extraordinary original jurisdiction. Writ Petition [C] No. 2000

through appropriate releases/programmes in the electronic media. This shall also be done by the Central Supervisory Board (CSB) as provided under Section 16(iii) of the PNDT Act.
- The Central government is directed to implement with all vigour and zeal the PNDT Act and the Rules framed in 1996. Rule 15 provides that the intervening period between two meetings of the Advisory Committees constituted under Subsection (5) of Section 17 of the PNDT Act to advise the appropriate authority shall not exceed sixty days. It would be seen that this rule is strictly adhered to.
- Meeting of the CSB will be held at least once in six moths [refer proviso to Section 9(1)]. The constitution of the CSB is provided under Section 7. It empowers the Central government to appoint ten members under Section 7(2)(e), which includes eminent medical practitioners, eminent social scientists, and representatives of women welfare organizations. It is hoped that this power will be exercised so as to include those persons who can genuinely spare time for the implementation of the Act.
- The CSB shall review and monitor the implementation of the Act [refer Section 16(ii)].
- The CSB shall issue directions to the Appropriate Authorities in all states and Union Territories to furnish quarterly returns to the CSB giving a report on the implementation and working of the Act. These returns should inter alia contain specific information about:
  — Survey of bodies specified in Section 3 of the Act.
  — Registration of bodies specified in Section 3 of the Act.
  — Action taken against non-registered bodies operating in violation of Section 3 of the Act, inclusive of search and seizure of records.
  — Complaints received by the appropriate authorities under the Act and action taken pursuant thereto.
  — Number and nature of awareness campaigns conducted and results flowing therefrom.
- The CSB shall examine the necessity to amend the Act keeping in mind emerging technologies and difficulties encountered in implementation of the Act and to make recommendations to the Central government [refer Section 16].
- The CSB shall lay down a code of conduct under Section 16(iv) of the Act to be observed by persons working in bodies specified therein and to ensure its publication so that public at large can know about it.
- The CSB will require medical professional bodies/associations to create awareness against the practice of prenatal determination of sex and female foeticide and to ensure implementation of the Act.

394 Child Rights in India

This judgment has been hailed as a positive step in the implementation of the PNDT Act.

ABORTIONS

In the USA, the entire issue of abortion had been the centre of intense debate. It is viewed as part of the rights of women to abort. In the leading decision on *Roe v Wade*[25] the US Supreme Court recognized the constitutional right of a woman to decide as to whether or not to terminate the pregnancy. This decision was altered in *Webster v Reproductive Health Service*[26] that allowed the State to impose greater restrictions on the availability of abortion and of doctor-patient communication with respect to abortion. In India, the Medical Termination of Pregnancy Act 1971 deals with the issue of abortion.

Medical Termination of Pregnancy Act 1971 (MTP Act 1971)

Under the Medical Termination of Pregnancy Act 1971, in India all abortions carried out require the consent of the woman and all abortions after twenty weeks are illegal. Pregnancies under the Medical Termination of Pregnancy Act are allowed to be medically terminated [Section 3]. The conditions under which abortions can be conducted under the Act are depicted in Figure 8.1.

Figure 8.1: Termination of Pregnancy under MTP Act 1971

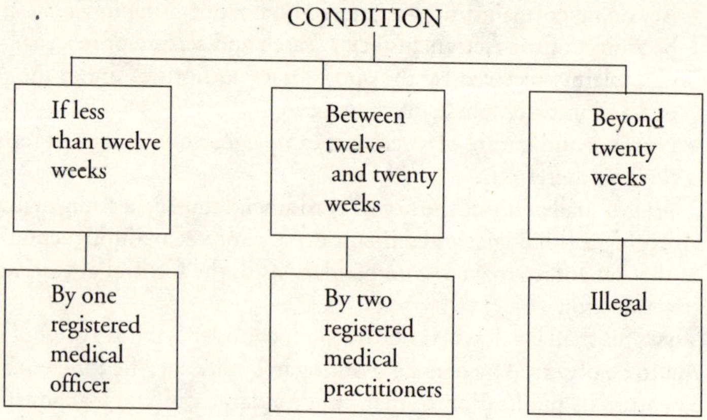

```
                        CONDITION
          ┌────────────────┼────────────────┐
   If less           Between            Beyond
   than twelve       twelve             twenty
   weeks             and twenty         weeks
                     weeks
      │                 │                 │
   By one           By two             Illegal
   registered       registered
   medical          medical
   officer          practitioners
```

---
[25] 410 US 13 (1973).
[26] Delivered on 3 July 1989.

If any of the above conditions are satisfied, the termination of pregnancy is allowed with the consent of the woman, as a health measure, on humanitarian grounds, and on eugenic grounds. The pregnancies can be terminated only at government hospitals or at other places approved by the government[27] under the following circumstances:[28]

- Pregnancy would involve a risk to life of the pregnant woman or cause a grave injury to her physical or mental health.
- If there is substantial risk that the child, if born, would suffer from such physical or mental abnormalities as to be seriously handicapped.
- If the pregnancy is alleged to have been caused by rape, the anguish caused by such pregnancy shall be presumed to cause a grave injury to the mental health of the pregnant woman.
- Where any pregnancy has occurred as a result of failure of any device or method used by any married woman or her husband for the purpose of limiting the number of children, the anguish caused by such unwanted pregnancy may be presumed to constitute a grave injury to the mental health of the pregnant woman.
- In case of a minor below eighteen years or a lunatic, the pregnancy shall be terminated with the consent in writing of her guardian.

The MTP Act 1971 also plays a 'guilty' role by sanctioning abortions up to twenty weeks. A woman can be brought into the acceptable categories defined in Section 4 of the MTP Act. On finding of a female foetus, she can easily have her pregnancy terminated. The 1994 Act permits diagnostic tests to find out whether there is any chromosomal abnormality, congenital anomaly, sex-linked genetic disorder, or any other abnormality justifying termination of the pregnancy. Such tests would disclose the sex of the foetus. These techniques are thus largely misused to determine the sex and not the abnormalities. It is not out of curiosity but with the object of destroying the female foetus. The constitutional validity of sex determination followed by abortion is doubtful. In law, an unborn child can be considered a person as such within the meaning of Articles 14, 15, and 21 of the Constitution and with several statutory rights. Abortion being resorted to in the case of female children only would make them violate Articles 14 and 15. The right to an abortion is essential to a woman to ensure her control over her reproductive process. But the decisions as to whether she wants the child or not must be taken regardless of the sex of the unborn child. But in practice, in a majority of the cases, the issue is not of the reproductive rights of the woman or her

[27] MTP Act 1971, Section 4.
[28] Ibid., Section 3.

choice but of the sex of the unborn child. Abortion preceded by sex determination is totally illegal and a criminal act on the part of the doctor.[29] To overcome this, doctors specify any of the grounds available under the Medical Termination of Pregnancy Act 1971 for carrying out abortions. There is no method to check that the reasons specified are true. These certificates have to be forwarded to the government. The government being concerned only with its family planning programme 'targets' is thus a willing party to this legalized female foeticide.[30]

Amendments to the Medical Termination of Pregnancy Act 1971, and the Prenatal Diagnostic Techniques (Regulation and Prevention of Misuse) Act, 1994

The Parliament of India recently approved the amendments to the above two existing laws, one amending legislation on abortion, and other imposing a ban on sex selection and prenatal sex determination.

The Medical Termination of Pregnancy (Amendment) Bill 2002 (MTP 2002)

The Medical Termination of Pregnancy (Amendment) Bill 2002, was approved by the Parliament of India on 5 December 2002, to amend the MTP Act 1971. Complications of illegal and unsafe abortions in India remain a major factor in high rates of maternal mortality. The MTP Act 1971, legalized termination of pregnancy on various socio-medical grounds. The amended Act is aimed at eliminating abortion by untrained persons and in unhygienic conditions, thus reducing maternal morbidity and mortality. The main objective of the recent amendments to the MTP Act is to reduce the rate of unsafe abortions by making legal abortion more widely accessible.

Some of the important amendments are:

- Substituting the word 'lunatic' by the words 'mentally ill person' [Section 2(b)]
- Lack of access to MTP services at the primary health care level has been cited as an important reason for the high rate of unsafe and illegal abortions. One of the most important provisions of this amendment therefore is the decentralization of authority for approval and registration of MTP centres from the state to the district level. Section 4 has

---

[29] Anand Grover, 'Amniocentesis or female foeticide', *The Lawyers*, March 1986, p. 6.
[30] Peter Borne (ed.), *Medicine, Medical Ethics and the Value of Life*, John Wiley & Sons, London, p. 145.

been amended with a view to delegating powers to the Government to approve places for medical termination of pregnancy and constituting District Level Committees to be headed by the Chief Medical Officer/ District Health Officer.[31]

- Section 5 of the amended Act Prescribes punishment by rigorous imprisonment of not less than two years, extending up to seven years:
  - to clinics which are not authorized to conduct abortions; and
  - to persons who are not registered medical practitioners with requisite experience or training for terminating pregnancy.[32]

The Pre-natal Diagnostic Techniques (Regulation and Prevention of Misuse) Amendment Bill 2002 (PNDT 2002)*

Parliament approved the PNDT Bill 2002 on 20 December 2002, and is now called the Pre-Conception and Pre-Natal Diagnostic Techniques (Prohibition and Sex Selection) and 2002. As mentioned earlier, the 2001 Census data revealed an alarming decline in the child sex ratio in India.

---

[31] For section 4 of the principal Act, the following section shall be substituted namely: no termination of pregnancy shall be made in accordance with this Act at any place other than- a) a hospital established or maintained by Government, or b) a place for the time being approved for the purpose of this Act by Government or a District Level Committee constituted by that Government with the Chief Medical Officer or District. Health Officer as the Chairperson of the said Committee: provided that the District Level Committee shall consist of not less than three and not more than five members including the Chairperson as the Government may specify from time to time.

[32] In section 5 of the principal Act (a) for subsection (2) and the Explanation thereto, the following shall be substituted, namely: '(2) Notwithstanding anything contained in the Indian Penal Code, the termination of pregnancy by a person who is not a registered medical practitioner shall be an offence punishable with rigorous imprisonment for a term which shall not be less than two years but which may extend to seven years under that Code, and that Code shall, to this extent, stand modified.

32(3) Whoever terminates any pregnancy in a place other than that mentioned in Section 4, shall be punishable with rigorous imprisonment for a term which shall not be less than two years but which may extend to seven years.

32(4) Any person being owner of a place which is not approved under clause (b) of section 4 shall be punishable with rigorous imprisonment for a term which shall not be less than two years but which may extend to seven years.

Explanation 1: For the purposes of this section, the expression "owner" in relation to a place means any person who is the administrative head or otherwise responsible for the working or maintenance of a hospital or place, by whatever name called, where the pregnancy may be terminated under this Act.

Explanation 2: For the purposes of this section, so much of the provisions of clause (d) of section 2 as relate to the possession, by registered medical practitioner, of experience or training in gynecology and obstetrics shall not apply'.

According to the statement of objects and reasons of the PNDT Bill 2002, the prenatal diagnostic techniques are being misused on a large scale to detect the sex of the foetus and to terminate the pregnancy if the unborn child is a female. It further states that the proliferation of these technologies may, in future, precipitate a catastrophe in the form of severe imbalance in the male-female ratio. It was therefore necessary to enact and implement, in letter and spirit, a law to ban pre-conception sex selection techniques and the misuse of prenatal diagnostic techniques for sex-selective abortions, to provide for the regulation of the techniques only for appropriate scientific use for which they are intended, and to include technologies such as pre-conception sex selection.

Some of the important amendments in the PNDT Act 2002 are:

- The original law targeted only post-conception medical techniques like sonography and amniocentesis, useful for the detection of genetic or chromosomal disorders or congenital malformations. Since pre-conception was not covered by any law, several clinics were openly offering sex selection services. The amendment expands the ban on sex determination tests to include pre-conception sex selection techniques. It makes the use of techniques like pre-implantation genetic diagnosis, which allows doctors to detect an embryo's genetic disorders and also identify its sex, illegal if used for sex selection.
- Maintenance by doctors of written records of procedures carried out.
- Vesting in authorities, at the State, district, and sub-district level, powers equivalent to those of Civil Courts to ensure compliance with the law.
- Follow-up of reports on violation and misconduct;
- The amended Act asks the state authorities to create public awareness about the issue.
- It also provides for the possibility of further amendments, which may be needed to deal with changes in technology and social conditions.
- It makes it compulsory for any laboratory or clinic, which has techniques that could be used for sex selection, to be registered.
- It increases the punishment for violation of the law.
- The state's monitoring authorities will have to include non-government entities like women activists and doctors.

Parliament's approval of the above two bills to amend the existing laws on abortion and banning sex determination are positive steps but these have to be complemented by addressing the social and cultural biases against the girl child and enhancing her status.

Rights during Early Childhood

Registration of Birth

This is another right of the child immediately after birth. Under Article 7 of the Convention on the Rights of the Child, the child shall be registered immediately after birth and shall have a name and the right to acquire a nationality. The Registration of Births and Deaths Act 1969 provides for the regulation of registration of births[33] in India. It has been made the duty of the following persons to give the information to the registrar of births orally or in writing [Section 8]:

- In respect of births in a house, by the head of the household and in his/her absence the oldest adult male member;
- In respect of birth in a hospital, health centre, maternity or nursing home, etc., the medical officer in charge;
- In respect of births in a jail, the jailor in charge;
- In respect of birth in a hostel, boarding house, lodging house, or public place, the person in charge;
- In respect of any newborn child deserted in a public place, the headman of the village or the officer in charge of the police station;
- In respect of births in plantation [Section 9], the superintendent of the plantation;

It has been made the duty of the midwife or any other medical or health attendant at a birth or any other person specified by the State government to notify the birth to the registrar [Section 10]. If the birth of any child has been registered without a name, the parent or guardian of such a child has to give the name to the registrar either orally or in writing and then the registrar will enter the name [Section 15]. In case of a child born outside India, within sixty days from their date of arrival in India, the parents should get the birth of the child registered under this Act [Section 20]. If any person fails to give the information or issue any certificate which he is bound to do under the Act, without any reasonable cause, he shall be punishable with a fine which may extend to fifty rupees [Section 23].

This Act is difficult to enforce. Registration of births is not a widely prevalent practice in India. Easy access and facilities for registration are required. The panchayats and the local bodies set up under the seventy-second and seventy-third constitutional amendments may be utilized to perform the functions of registration.

---

[33] The Registration of Births and Deaths Act 1969, Section 2(a).

Immunization

Immunization remains the single most feasible and cost-effective way of ensuring that all children enjoy their rights to survival and good health. In the developing world, immunization saves the lives of 2.5 million children every year. Because of its recognized power and efficacy, renewed efforts are being made globally to mobilize more resources for another push to ensure that all children are protected by immunization and that new vaccines for other common killer diseases are developed. The series of immunizations known as DPT can prevent diphtheria, pertussis (whooping cough), and tetanus, but these three diseases still kill 600,000 children and afflict millions of others every year in developing countries. To be fully protected, children must receive three doses of the vaccine, administered at the ages of one month, one and a half month, and three months. The percentage of children receiving the final dose (DPT3) is, therefore, a revealing and vital gauge of how well countries are providing immunization coverage for their children.[34] Immunization also consists of one dose of BCG, three doses of OPV, and one dose of measles vaccinations to be given to infants. This prevents infants and young children from contracting six common, vaccine-preventable diseases, namely, measles, neonatal acute paralytic poliomyelitis, and childhood tuberculosis. Also, pregnant women are given tetanus toxoid injections.[35]

There has been a steady rise in coverage of children under the immunization programme. Percentage of fully immunized one-year-old children during 1997–9 are seventy-two for TB, sixty-nine for DPT, sixty-nine for polio, and fifty-five for measles. Seventy-three per cent of pregnant women were given tetanus injections. The figures of 2000 reported by the government are as high as 96 per cent for BCG, 89 per cent for DPT, and 80 per cent for measles. This has been the result of the Child Survival and Safe Motherhood programmes at both urban and rural levels. India launched its Expanded Immunization Programme (EPI) in 1978–9. This was changed to Universal Immunization Programme (UPI) with the support of the UNICEF, the World Health Organization (WHO) and the Indian Academy of Pediatrics (IAP) with the objective of increasing the coverage levels by districts, improving the quality of services, and achieving self-sufficiency in vaccine production as well as indigenous manufacture of cold chain equipment. India has also been known for its countrywide initiative to wipe

---

[34] The Progress of Nations 2000, UNICEF.
[35] *An Update on Measles Immunization*, National Immunization Programme, Government of India.

out polio. Fixed-day drives of Pulse Polio Immunization (PPI) cover a maximum of 127 million children on single-day sessions twice a year.

However, the evaluation of routine immunization by the UNICEF in 1998-9 has not given a very happy picture. It revealed a national average of only 48.5 per cent cases having cards, though as many as 78.6 per cent had the services provided within the community. The urban coverage was naturally higher than the rural. There is still much to be achieved towards having a universal coverage.

Vaccination Act 1880

The Vaccination Act 1880 gives power to prohibit inoculation and to make the vaccination of children compulsory in certain municipalities and cantonments. According to the Act. in any place to which the Act applies, inoculation is prohibited. There is also a provision for the vaccination of unprotected children. An unprotected child is a child who has not been protected from smallpox by having had that disease either naturally or by inoculation or by having been successfully vaccinated and who has not been certified under this Act to be unsusceptible to vaccination. Various other provisions are made relating to vaccination, such as the procedures to be adopted when vaccination is unsuccessful or when vaccination is successful or when the child is unfit for vaccination. The Act also provides for the giving of certificates. This is an outdated legislation not in tune with the present-day health scenario.

Nutrition

It is well established that the good health of the mother has a distinct and direct bearing on that of the child, effecting the store of nutrients in the foetus, a full-term well-developed baby at birth, a risk-free delivery, and breast milk of good quality during the lactation period. Pregnancy is a period demanding a support system that ensures additional dietary allowances, systematic antenatal care, life free from stress and risk, and a positive attitude from family and society. This is extremely important as it has long-term effects on the birth and development of the child.[36]

The three indices of nutritional status, viz., weight for age, height for age, and weight for height still indicate a high prevalence of malnutrition among children under three years of age. The rate of malnutrition is decreasing at only one per cent per year. Malnutrition is much higher in rural areas and

---

[36] M. Swaminathan, *The Continuum of Maternity and Childcare Support*, Paper presented at the Sixth Conference of the Indian Association for Women's Studies, Mysore, 31 May–2 June 1993.

in children from disadvantaged groups in urban areas.[37] The nutritional status of Indian children in 1999 based on a UNICEF study in presented in Table 8.3.[38]

Breastfeeding is recognized as the single most important strategy in infant survival. The superiority of breast milk over any other food in promoting the optimum growth of the newborn and in combating infections has been clearly established. The WHO recommends that breastfeeding should begin as early as possible, be maintained exclusively for the first 4–6 months of life, and continued with supplementary feeds at least upto the second year of life. Of late, much concern is being expressed worldwide over the declining trend in breastfeeding, largely attributed to the aggressive marketing strategies

Table 8.5: Nutrition Status in 1999

Categories	Percentages
Infants with low birth weight	23
Breastfeeding	
Exclusive breastfeeding 0–3 months	55.2
Breast milk with complementary feeding 6–9 months	33.5
Breast milk continued 12–15 months	88.9
Children 0–3 years underweight	
Moderate and severe (below 2SD)	47.0
Severe (below 3SD)	18.0
Children 0–3 years	
Moderate and severe wasting (below 2SD)	15.5
Moderate and severe stunting (below 2SD)	45.5
Anaemic children less than 3 years	74.3
Children 12–35 months who received at least one dose of Vitamin-A	29.7

Note: Standard Deviation (SD) score or Z-score is a statistical unit. Although the interpretation of a fixed percent -of- median value varies across age and height and generally the two scales can be compared, the approximate percent of the median values for –1 SD and –2 SD are 90% and 80% of median respectively. (Bulletin of the World Health Organization, 1994, 72:273–83.)

    Wasting means underweight
    Stunting means no growth

[37] *India Report on the World Summit for Children 2000*, Department of Women and Child Development, Ministry of Human Resource Development, Government of India.
[38] *India: Social and Economic Statistics*, UNICEF in India 1999–2002: Challenges and Opportunities.

adopted by manufacturers of baby food. The World Health Assembly, on 21 May 1981, adopted an International Code of Marketing of Breast Milk Substitutes[39] for the proper nutrition and health of world's children. The aim of the Code is to contribute to the provision of safe and adequate nutrition for infants by the protection and promotion of breastfeeding and by ensuring the proper use of breast milk substitutes, when these are necessary, on the basis of adequate information and through appropriate marketing and distribution.[40] The Code also lays down in Article 4 that governments should have the responsibility to ensure that objective and consistent information is provided, on infant and young child feeding for use by families and those involved in the field of infant and young child nutrition. This responsibility should cover the planning, provision, design, and dissemination of information or their control. India was a signatory to this International Code and the Government of India responded through the ministry of health by adopting the 'Indian National Code for Protection and Promotion of Breastfeeding' in 1983.

In India, however, breastfeeding is deep-rooted culturally, and studies in the country record the fact that breastfeeding is universal and is accepted as a natural function. But in spite of this, studies reveal declining trends in urban areas. There was evidence of malnutrition and mortality in children because of artificial milk-food substitutes in the absence of strong legal interventions.[41] Artificial milk substitutes were being promoted through the health care system and aggressive advertising and marketing. The Infant Foods, Breast Milk Substitutes and Feeding Bottles Act 1992 (IMS Act 1992) sought to provide for the prohibition of advertisements, incentives, donation, and promotion of artificial milk-food substitutes and to promote, protect, and support breastfeeding.*

The objectives of IMS Act are:

- To regulate the production, supply and distribution of infant milk substitutes,[42] feeding bottles,[43] and infant foods,[44] and
- To promote breastfeeding and to ensure the proper use of infant foods.

[39] 20 ILM 1004 (1981).
[40] International Code of Marketing of Breast Milk Substitutes, Article 1.
[41] Chidananda Reddy, 'The Infant Government's Anti-Infant Policy', *The Lawyers*, June 1990.
[42] IMS Act 1992, Section 2(g): 'infant milk substitute' means any food being marketed or otherwise represented as a partial or total replacement for mother's milk, whether or not it is suitable for such replacement.
[43] IMS Act 1992, Section 2(c): 'feeding bottle' means any bottle or receptacle used for the purpose of feeding infant milk substitutes, and includes a teat and a valve attached or capable of being attached to such bottle or receptacle.
[44] IMS Act 1992, Section 2(f).

Prohibitions under the Act

Under the IMS Act, there are certain prohibitions in relation to infant milk substitutes, feeding bottles, and infant foods. The prohibitions are:

- It prohibits any person from taking part in publication of any advertisement [IMS Act 1992, Section 2(a)] or taking part in the promotion or use or sale or giving an impression or creating a belief that the milk substitutes are equivalent to or better than mother's milk [IMS Act 1992, Section 3].
- It prohibits any person from giving incentives or inducement or any other articles as gifts for the use or sale of infant milk substitutes or feeding bottles or contacting any pregnant woman or the mother of an infant for giving the above incentive or inducement [IMS Act 1992, Section 4].
- Donations or distribution of infant milk substitutes or feeding bottles can be done only to an orphanage or through the health care system [IMS Act Section 5(a)].
- Any informational or educational equipment or material relating to infant milk substitutes or feeding bottles cannot be donated or distributed except through the health care system [IMS Act 1992, Section 5(b)].

Provisions as to Information to be Included on the Containers, Labels, etc. [Section 6]

The Act lays down that every container [IMS Act 1992, Section 2(b)] or any label [IMS Act 1992, Section 2(c)] affixed to the container must clearly and conspicuously indicate an important notice giving the following particulars:

- a statement 'MOTHER'S MILK IS BEST FOR YOUR BABY' in capital letters;
- a statement that infant milk substitute or infant food should be used only on the advice of a health worker as to the need for its use and the proper method of its use;
- a warning that infant milk substitute or infant food is not the sole source of nourishment of an infant;
- the instructions for its appropriate preparation and a warning against the health hazards of its inappropriate preparation;
- the ingredients used;
- the composition or analysis;
- the storage conditions required;
- the batch number, date of manufacture, and the date before which it

is to be consumed, taking into account the climatic and storage conditions of the country; and
- such other particulars as may be prescribed.

The Act also prescribes that the container or label should not have the following [Sec 6(2)]:
- pictures of an infant or a woman or both;
- pictures or other graphic material or phrases designed to increase the saleability of infant milk substitutes;
- the word 'humanized' or 'materialized' or any other similar word; or
- such other particulars as may be prescribed.

Particulars to be Provided on Educational and Other Materials Relating to Feeding of Infants [Section 7]

The following clear information should be included on every educational or other audio or visual material dealing with the feeding of an infant and intended to reach pregnant women or mothers of infants:
- the benefits and superiority of breastfeeding;
- the preparation for, and the continuance of breastfeeding;
- the harmful effects on breastfeeding due to the partial adoption of bottle feeding;
- the difficulties in reverting to breastfeeding of infants after a period of feeding by infant milk substitute;
- the financial and social implications in making use of infant milk substitutes and feeding bottles;
- the health hazards of improper use of infant milk substitutes and feeding bottles; and
- such other matters as may be prescribed.

Directions Regarding Health Workers and the Health Care System [Section 8]

The health care system cannot be used for the display or distribution of placards or posters relating to the promotion or use or sale of infant milk substitutes or feeding bottles or infant foods. There are two exceptions to this direction:
- donation or distribution to orphanages, and
- dissemination of scientific, educational, and factual information and materials to health workers.[45]

---

[45] IMS Act 1992, Section 2(e): 'health worker' means a person engaged in health care for mothers, infants, or pregnant women.

Only a health worker shall demonstrate feeding with infant milk substitutes or infant foods to a mother of an infant and also clearly explain the hazards of its improper use [IMS Act 1992, Section 8(3)]. Any person who works in the health care system cannot be paid for promoting the use or sale of such substitutes or bottles or foods by the producer, supplier, and distributor of these products [IMS Act, Section 8(2)]. No commission or remuneration to the employees can be fixed based on the volume of sale [IMS Act, Section 9(2)]. Only an institution or an organization engaged in health care for mothers can distribute infant milk substitutes or feeding bottles to a mother who cannot resort to breastfeeding [IMS Act 1992, Section 8(4)].

Standards of Infant Milk Substitutes, Feeding bottles, or Infant Foods

Infant milk substitutes or infant foods or feeding bottles should conform to the standards laid down under the Prevention of Food Adulteration Act 1954 or the Bureau of Indian Standards Act 1986[46] or these should have the approval of the Central Government [IMS Act 1992, Section 11].

Powers Relating to Enforcement of the Act

Sections 12–20 of the Act lay down the provisions relating to the enforcement of the Act. The provisions of the Code of Criminal Procedure 1973 relating to search and seizure are applicable. Any food inspector appointed under Section 9 of the Prevention of Food Adulteration Act 1954 or any authorized officer not below the rank of a Class I officer can enter and search at any reasonable time any premises or any place if there are reasons to believe that any provision under this Act have been violated.[47] The food inspector has the following powers:

- He can take any sample and send the sample for analysis.
- He can inspect any place where any article of food is manufactured or stored for sale.
- He can seize or carry away or keep the article under safe custody.
- If the article of food is unfit for human consumption, he may destroy it after giving notice.
- He can break open any package or door if the person in charge refuses to open the package.
- He can seize the books of accounts or other documents and return within a period of thirty days.

---

[46] The Bureau of Indian Standards Act 1986, Section 3.
[47] The IMS Act 1992, Section 12.

- He can seize the milk substitute or feeding bottle or infant food or container [IMS Act 1992, Section 13].

PENALTIES UNDER THE ACT

Contravention of Sections 3, 4, 5, 7, 8, 9, 10, or 11(2) under the Act[48] will entail imprisonment for a term which may extend to three years or with fine which may extend to five thousand rupees or with both. For contravening Section 11(1) [IMS Act 1992, Section 20(2)], the punishment is imprisonment for a term not less than six months but which may extend to three years and with fine which may not be less than two thousand rupees. The court may for special reasons to be mentioned in the judgment, impose a sentence of imprisonment for a term which shall not be less than three months but which may extend to two years and with fine which shall not be less than two thousand rupees. Where an offence under this Act has been committed by a company, every person who at the time when the offence was committed was in charge of the company shall be deemed to be guilty of the offence [IMS Act 1992, Section 22].

COGNIZANCE OF OFFENCES UNDER THE ACT

The offences under this Act[49] are bailable and cognizable [IMS Act 1992, Section 23]. A complaint in writing can be made by:

- a person authorized under the Prevention of Food Adulteration Act 1954,[50]
- an officer authorized by the government,
- a representative of such voluntary organizations that are engaged in the field of child welfare, development, and child nutrition.

Rights of the Child and Working Mothers

Even though the government has passed the legislation of Infant Foods, Breast Milk Substitutes and Feeding Bottles Act 1992 regulating the sale and marketing of infant foods and feeding bottles, attention has not been paid to the role of mothers as working women. Women with full-time jobs face difficulties while breastfeeding. The primary needs, both nutritional and

---

[48] The IMS Act 1992, Section 20(1): (1) Any person who contravenes the provisions of Sections 3, 4, 5, 7, 8, 9, 10, or Subsection (2) of Section 11 shall be punishable with imprisonment for a term which may extend to three years, or with fine which may extend to five thousand rupees, or with both.
[49] The IMS Act 1992, Section 21.
[50] The Food Adulteration Act 1954, Section 20.

psychic, of the mother-child dyad at this stage are in close proximity and constant interaction. This can be achieved by a working mother only by either abstaining from full-time work away from home or by keeping the infant near the workplace in a crèche or day-care centre. Keeping in mind the inherent health hazards and standards of hygiene involved in group care of young children, the possible health hazards in a workplace environment, the difficulties of transportation to and from the workplace, and the child's need for close one-to-one interaction, the women either leave their jobs or have a tendency to wean the child away from breastfeeding. Provisions need to be made looking into the role of the mother as working woman so that it does not affect the development of children adversely.

The major law addressing this issue is the Maternity Benefit Act 1961 (MBA), which applies to women working in establishments whether factories, mines, plantations, offices, shops, and circuses. Moreover, the State government has powers to extend the application of the Act to any other establishment—agricultural, commercial, etc., after taking the approval of the Central government and giving a notice of two months. The Employees State Insurance Act 1948 (ESI Act), which applies to factories, shops, hotels, restaurants, newspapers, and road and motor establishments, provides similar benefits to certain categories of employees not falling within the purview of the Maternity Benefit Act. This means that a woman cannot claim benefits under the ESI Act and the MBA simultaneously. This automatically restricts the scope of the Act to large establishments, leaving out those who are employed in small establishments, self-employed, contractual workers, casual labour, temporary and seasonal workers, family labour, etc. with the exception of bidi workers, who are covered by a separate Act.

Relevant Provisions of the Maternity Benefit Act 1961

The Maternity Benefit Act 1961 prohibits employment of women in any establishment[51] for a period before and after childbirth,[52] and provides for payment of maternity benefits to them. The Act provides that a woman (who has actually worked for a period of not less than eighty days immediately preceding the date of her expected delivery [Maternity Benefit Act 1961, Section 5(2)] shall be entitled to maternity benefit for a period not exceeding three months (usually six weeks preceding and including the day of delivery and six weeks immediately following that day) [Maternity Benefit Act 1961, Section 5(3)]. This obviously restricts exclusive breastfeeding to a period

[51] Maternity Benefit Act 1961, Section 3(e).
[52] Ibid., Section 3(b): 'child' includes a still-born child.

ranging from six weeks at worst to ten weeks at best, since most women would prefer to take some part of the leave before childbirth.

Under Section 10 of the Maternity Benefit Act 1961 a woman is also entitled to an additional period of leave with wages up to a maximum of one month if she is suffering from illness arising out of pregnancy, delivery, premature birth, or miscarriage. This clause is intended to safeguard the mother's health but cannot be used to extend the period of breastfeeding. Section 11 provides for two nursing breaks of fifteen minutes duration each in the course of the mother's working day. If the crèche is not attached to the workplace she can take not less than five or not more than fifteen minutes time for travel. This assumes that the mother has access to a crèche or some other facility near enough for her to avail of the nursing breaks.

Qualitatively, the law practically debars healthy mothers from exclusively breastfeeding their infants for more than six to ten weeks and more or less compels them to resort to supplementary milk foods, thus running counter to the intention of the Act regulating the sale of infant foods and breast milk substitutes, and illustrating the manner in which a haphazard approach leads to laws which cancel each other out.

Hence, the single most important step from the point of view of promotion of breastfeeding is the amendment of the Maternity Benefit Act along lines more sensitive to the needs of mother and child, as suggested below:

- Maternity leave as such should be calculated from the day of childbirth and should be for a period of four months.
- Mothers may have the option of extending leave for a further period, at first on half pay and then without pay but without loss of other service benefits, seniority, etc.
- Leave from two to four weeks may be taken during the final stages of pregnancy as medically advised and should not be treated as maternity leave.
- Women should not be transferred or subjected to other punitive actions or suffer loss of benefits during the basic maternity leave period of four months.
- Nursing breaks should be of minimum forty minutes duration each—twenty minutes for feeding and twenty minutes for travel and may be allowed till the child reaches the age of twelve months.

The last rule should be applicable only:

- When there is a crèche facility, statutory or otherwise, at or near the workplace, defined as ten minutes travel time each way.

- When there is any arrangement, individual or organized, by which the mother can go to the child or the child can be brought to the mother within this period. In the latter case, nursing space should also be provided.

The above legislation is applicable only to the organized sector. The low level of utilization of home-based women bidi workers under the Beedi and Cigar Workers [Conditions of Employment] Act 1966, which attempts to imitate the organized sector legislation, illustrates the futility of enforcing such laws in the unorganized sector. In the unorganized sector, maternity benefits must become the direct responsibility of the State, as well as autonomous boards and corporations that stand in an employer relationship to women artisans and labourers. As far as funding is concerned, devices can be found to oblige employers to share the financial burden.[53] Labour welfare funds can also be drawn upon for this purpose, as in the case of *bidi* workers.

Day Care and Crèche Facilities

The provisions for crèches for children of working mothers is obligatory under certain labour laws in the organized sector. Laws with reference to crèches exist primarily in relation to the organized sector. The Factories Act 1948, the Mines Act 1950, and the Plantations Act 1951 make it obligatory for the employer to provide crèches for children aged 0–6 years wherever more than a stipulated minimum of women are employed in factories, mines, and plantations. Modelled on those of industrialized countries, these laws have not been amended to keep pace with the changing economic situation and are largely irrelevant to the present-day working conditions, besides being applicable to only a small minority of working women. This becomes evident when it is noted that similar legislation has not been passed for the benefit of women working in the tertiary sector (services, trades, and professions) in whose numbers there has been a spectacular increase in the last three decades. Provisions in relation to crèches in various legislations in India are summarized in Table 8.4.

Analysis of the laws reveal several lacunae, chief among which is the insistence on a minimum number of women workers for the law to become applicable. This not only makes it easy for evasion by various simple strategies, but even assuming no evasion is attempted, this makes it of limited applicability, since it omits certain categories of workers such as those employed in small establishments, temporary and casual workers, contract workers, etc.

---

[53] Shram Shakti Report, National Commission On Self-employed Women and Women in the Informal Sector, 1988.

Table 8.4: Legislation relating to Crèches

	Factories Act 1948 (Section 48)	Plantation Labour Act 1951	Beedi and Cigar Workers (Conditions of Employment) Act 1966	Contract Labour (Regulation and Abolition) Central Rules 1971
No. of women workers	More than thirty	More than fifty	More than fifty	More than twenty
No. of children (including women workers employed by the contractor)	—	More than twenty	—	—
Age of children	Till six years	Below six years	Below six years	Below six years
Provision	A suitable room or rooms for the use of children	A suitable room for the use of children of such workers	A suitable room or rooms for the use of children	Two rooms to be provided for children. One playroom and the other as a bedroom
Authority to make rules	The state government may make rules relating to location and standards of construction	The state government may make rules prescribing location, standards of construction, equipment, and amenities	The state government may make rules prescribing location and standards in respect of construction, accommodation, furniture, and so on	The chief labour commissioner may prescribe the standard of construction and maintenance of crèches

Further, if one considers childcare as a fundamental right of women and children, the question of stipulating numbers or their use and misuse becomes irrelevant. Within the broader framework of the Constitution, which allows equality to all citizens with no discrimination, every child has a right to holistic care and development and every mother the right to demand such facilities irrespective of what she contributes to the national statistics. Another shortcoming is the placing of administrative as well as financial responsibility on employers, who may lack the willingness and expertise to run crèches, rather than on professionals or agencies specialized for the purpose. This only results in reducing attention to the quality and nature of daycare, focusing instead on numerical targets.

Laws in the Unorganized Sector

There are about 120 million women in the unorganized sector needing childcare support, as a majority of young children are unsupervised or are cared by older siblings. In the unorganized sector, the Contract Labour Act 1970 and the Interstate Migrant Workers Act 1980, which is an upgraded version of the former, as well as the Bidi and Cigar Workers Act 1966 attempt to legislate for the provision of crèches. These laws follow the same pattern in relation to crèches as in the case of factories, mines, and plantations, laying down a minimum number of women to be employed for the rules to become operative, though this is extremely impractical in the case of industries such as construction and quarrying for which the former are intended as against home-based workers in the latter case. In the case of agricultural labour, only a few States like Kerala and Maharashtra have made provision for crèches. These laws suffer from the same fundamental defects noted already, in addition to being unsuited to the unorganized sector and more difficult to implement. The women in the service sector like hospitals, schools, communications, etc., need to be brought within the purview of these benefits. The focus should be on the developmental rights of children and not on the number of female employees. Childcare is not only the responsibility of the mothers. The criteria for providing crèches should be where there are employees, whether male or female, who have children.

Government Programmes and Schemes for Child Health and Development

A number of childcare programmes for improving the health status of children are being implemented.

Maternal and Child Health (MCH)

The major programme in the country for pregnant women is the network of maternal and child health (MCH) centres which aim to provide comprehensive health care to mothers and children. The numerous services include antenatal health care and checks, nutritional supplements like vitamin tablets, prevention of anaemia through folic acid tablets, immunization against tetanus, screening of at-risk pregnancies, midwifery through birth attendants, nurses, and health personnel for both home and hospital deliveries, post-natal care, education of mothers, and other elements.

Integrated Child Development Services Scheme (ICDS)

Another major scheme being implemented for pregnant women from the poorer sections of the society is the ICDS, one of whose objectives is to provide supplementary nutrition to pregnant and lactating women as well as antenatal care and referral services.

The objectives of ICDS Scheme (introduced in 1974) are sixfold which include supplementary nutrition, health check-up, referral, immunization, nutrition education, and pre-school education. The scheme is funded by the Government of India and has a complicated administrative set-up with the focal point at the village level being the *Anganwadi*. The positive features of the scheme are:

- Children in the 0–6 year age group are covered and a holistic approach to growth and development is attempted by means of health, nutrition, and pre-school education. An effort is made to distinguish between the needs of children of 0–2 years and the older group, and to reach pregnant and lactating women directly.
- There are high chances of sustainability since the scheme is indigenously funded and forms only a negligible (0.13 per cent) of the gross domestic product.
- The major successes have been in immunization, growth monitoring, and supplementary feeding.

Day Care Programmes and Schemes

The major scheme for day care in the unorganized sector is the Scheme of Assistance for Crèches for Working/Ailing Mothers, launched in 1974, which is intended to provide day care for the children (0–6 years) of women labourers below poverty line. In practice, however, the scheme has not developed or rendered services along the lines originally envisaged. The quantitative coverage after almost four decades is abysmally inadequate. In terms of nature of coverage, available evidence points to a strange situation. In most parts of the country (Kerala and Tamil Nadu being exceptions) the crèches do not even work for the whole day and are often unrelated to the work timings of the mothers. The reasons for this are partly financial, since the scheme only allows for crèche workers to be paid a pittance, far below the minimum wages for unskilled labour. The crèches also often fail to take into consideration the work status of the mothers, sometimes admitting the children of housewives as well as working mothers. Most of them seem to function like private nursery schools for the children of the poor and lower middle class. In terms of quality, again, the programme is mostly either custodial or heavily oriented to formal education, with little emphasis on play, stimulation, or development of children.

The Reproductive and Child Health Programme 1996 (RCH)

A number of earlier programmes like the Maternal and Child Health (MCH) and Child Survival and Safe Motherhood (CSSM) followed a top-down approach to achieve health goals and so did not reflect use needs and preferences. Realizing this, the government took a bold step to reorient the health programmes to make them more client oriented with an emphasis on the quality of services and care. This brought about a paradigm shift in the health policies, which is reflected in the RCH. This new programme integrates all family welfare and women and child health services with the explicit objective of providing beneficiaries with need-based, client-centred, demand-driven, high-quality, integrated RCH services. The strategy for the RCH programme shifts the policy emphasis from achieving demographic targets to meeting the health needs of women and children.

NGO Initiatives

NGOs are involved in advocacy and networking and providing childcare services. The Forum for Childcare and Crèche Services (FORCES) is a network of over a hundred organizations involved in the provision of childcare services. Many of these groups provide day-care services for marginalized sections like construction workers, whereas others are trade unions and workers associations involved in policy issues concerning the child.

The proposal for the Maternity and Childcare Code (MCC Code) was first put forward in Shram Shakti, the report of the National Commission on Women in the Unorganized Sector. Childcare services were viewed as an essential support service for women especially from this sector. After a review of already existing laws, schemes, and programmes, the need for a holistic view to childcare including health, welfare, and development services were felt. To achieve this, formulation of a single, comprehensive maternity and childcare (MCC) code was required. The objectives of the code are:

- It aims to translate the right of women and children into action in the context of their life cycle.
- It will facilitate inter and intra-sectoral convergence of programmes.
- It will enhance the implementation of social policies and programmes through appropriate infrastructure development.
- It will bring in more coordination between NGOs and government, giving enough scope for development of innovative models for different groups concerned.
- Focusing on the groups of mothers and children will create an opportunity for allocating substantial funding, viewing these groups as important human resources.

The code would cover: children with special needs, children of sex workers, children of families at risk, HIV-affected children, victims of natural/man-made disasters, children from deprived groups, children of women prisoners, children in adoptive families and foster care, children of migrants, children of pavement dwellers, children with disability, children of single parents, and victims of abuse.

Special Health Issues Relating to Children

Children Affected by HIV/AIDS

THE EPIDEMIOLOGICAL SITUATION WORLDWIDE

The global epidemic appears to have started in mid-1970s. By 1980, an estimated 100,000 people worldwide had become infected by HIV. During the 1980s, the pandemic expanded rapidly, reaching most countries and affecting a total of about ten million people. By January 1993, approximately 19.5 million people had become HIV infected of whom 1.2 million were children. According to the Global AIDS Policy Coalition,[54] between thirty-eight and 110 million adults and at least ten million children are likely to have been HIV infected by the year 2000.[55] Another report states that as

---

[54] An independent research and analysis centre based at the Harvard School of Public Health.
[55] J.M. Mann and A. Petitgirand, 'Aids and Children—Dangers and Opportunities'. *Children Worldwide*, Vol. 20, No. 2–3/93, International Catholic Child Bureau.

of now, there are 34.3 million people in the world living with HIV/AIDS, including 1.3 million children under fifteen years of age.[56] The overwhelming majority of these children were born to mothers with HIV, acquiring the virus in the womb, around the time of being born (during labour or childbirth), or during breastfeeding. With their right to survive, grow, and develop threatened from their very beginnings, most of these children would live shortened lives, dying before they are in their teens.

THE EXISTING SITUATION IN INDIA[57]

An alarming 3.5 million individuals have been affected by AIDS in India. Also, more than one per cent antenatal women were suffering from HIV thus implying that these many children would contract the disease even before birth. The disease is taking epidemic proportions and much needs to be done to check the fast growing spread. It is a dreaded disease and more than awareness, the attitude towards it is still a big problem. In such a scenario, a child, with its own limitations of understanding, facing the rejection of elders and society at large, has to go through a lot of emotional hurt. Also the onus of the problem does not lie on any specific institution—the government, AIDS societies, NGOs, or people.

There are many categories of children living with AIDS who may have family/community support or may not have it. They include:

- Children who are confirmed as infected by HIV
- The infections may be through mother to child
- Needing blood transfusion due to illnesses
- Drug abuse—IVD users
- Sexually abused
- Affected by the epidemic: where parents or siblings are HIV positive
- Vulnerable to HIV (in high-risk communities)
- Living under the shadow of the epidemic, being born, growing, and becoming sexually active in a world having added risk of infection.

Impact on Children Living with Aids

Children with HIV/AIDS in a developing or poor country face many more problems than the children of developed countries due to lack of funds and

[56] Joint United Nations Programme on HIV/AIDS, Report on the Global HIV/AIDS Epidemic, June 2000, UNAIDS, Geneva.
[57] K. Kapadia, Former Director, CCDT, Mumbai, *Work with Children Infected and Affected by HIV/Aids*, Synopsis of the Paper presented at Training programme on Child Rights at Nagpur, 2001.

proper health care services. This is reflected in the length of survival of an infected child from these countries. Very often, they are seen only as added burdens on already scarce resources. Many a times, a child affected with the infection does not get the required attention from the family or immediate social circle due to lack of funds on their part. Heavy health care costs and lack of government support create difficult situations. Children also are seen not getting enough nutrition to fight against the disease.

On the other hand, the children having infected parents or siblings have other types of problems. They do not get outside support to take care of their parents. Very often, they have to take the burden of taking care of their parents and other younger siblings. This might also affect their education. The parents' capacity to earn reduces leading to malnourishment of children. They might also have to resort to income earning due to financial pressures. While the death of male members and increase of women-headed households create a negative impact on their growth, the death of both parents leads to being an orphan with no one to take care of them and their siblings. These children might have to take help of their grandparents or might also suffer from loss of inheritance or might be forced to migrate. All these situations create a lot of emotional and physical vulnerability for children.

The 'Rights' Approach to Children Infected and Affected by HIV/AIDS

India is a signatory to the Rights of the Child. However, children are suffering from discrimination, exploitation, and abuse. Infected children face several denials or limitation of their rights. Some of the violations of their rights are:[58]

- Right to education
- Health and social services—as a result of inadequate or inaccessible health services
- Treatment, care, education, and social programmes
- Societal and family abandonment and rejection
- Children and mothers being forced to live on the streets
- Lack of nutrition to fight against infection
- Children's proneness to infection/epidemics related to their own communities
- Right to family being affected from challenge to immediate family environment and support through sickness, disability, and premature death from AIDS of one or both parents

[58] Ibid.

- Reduced ability of infected parents to sustain their livelihood and care for them
- School dropout due to need for caring for parents and younger siblings and need to earn
- Right to information, education, and services
- Understanding of circumstances that make them especially vulnerable to sexual exploitation and abuse.

Based on the Convention on the Rights of the Child, the following standards should be established and affirmed for children living with HIV/AIDS:

- Children have a right to survival and development. Therefore, realization of all rights must be protected from the impact of HIV/AIDS. Children have a right to health services/non-discrimination in health services. The medical personnel including doctors need to be sensitized on this issue.
- Children have a right to information and opportunities to develop life skills. Therefore, children should have access to HIV/AIDS prevention education, information, and the means for prevention, including attention to the ability to negotiate safer sex practices. Media should be encouraged to disseminate information of social and cultural benefits to children, taking into account their linguistic needs.[59]
- Voluntary testing and counselling must be available in antenatal clinics to provide information on what women can do if they are HIV positive and given their situation, what acceptable alternatives to breastfeeding exist.
- Children have a right to a safe and supportive environment free from exploitation and abuse. Therefore, special measures should be taken by governments to prevent and minimize the impact of HIV/AIDS caused by such factors as sexual abuse and trafficking, forced prostitution, sexual exploitation, use of illicit drugs, and harmful traditional practices. Sexual exploitation of girls of all ages was fuelled by the AIDS fear and was taking a heavy toll. Sexual abuse within the family also needed to be addressed. Educating the parents and reaching out directly to the children were essential in preventing the exploitation.[60]
- Children have a right to be protected from discrimination and exploitation, irrespective of their own HIV/AIDS status or that of members

---

[59] Sandie Blanchet, *The Rights Approach to HIV/AIDS*, Presentation at the Media Workshop on HIV/AIDS and Child Rights, Gujarat, 13–14 August 1999, supported by UNICEF, Gujarat.

[60] Ibid.

of their families. In relation to HIV/AIDS, to which a strong stigma was attached, protection from non-discrimination was particularly important. No discrimination should be suffered by children on any grounds, including in education, leisure, recreation, sports, and cultural activities because of their HIV/AIDS status. Children have a right to access health and social services on an equitable basis, irrespective of their own HIV/AIDS status or that of members of their families. All infected children should be provided with adequate HIV/AIDS treatment and care. Attention must be paid to ensure that orphans receive adequate support services.
- Children have a right to be heard and to have their aspirations, views and needs reflected in decisions affecting them and their future.
- Children's right to privacy and confidentiality should be protected. The identity of the child and of his family should always be protected in the media.

National Policy on AIDS

During the Eighth Five Year Plan (1992–7), the National AIDS Control Organization was established under the ministry of health and family welfare to implement the programme which consists of five components: strengthening of management capacity for prevention and control of HIV/AIDS; improving public awareness; improving blood safety and rational use of blood; building surveillance and clinical management capacity; and controlling sexually transmitted diseases. In Thailand, a high-level commitment of the government, a multi-pronged approach to HIV/AIDS awareness, and a 100 per cent condom policy had considerably brought down the rate of spread of the disease. The issues that needed to be examined in this connection are: respect for the rights of sex workers; their empowerment so that they have a choice and they do not have to resort to prostitution; and above all improving the status of the girl child.[61]

Children and Disability

In India, estimating the number of disabled people is not an easy task as it varies a great deal depending upon the definitions, the methodology, the source, and the appropriate use of scientific instruments in measuring the

[61] Doris Grote, *HIV/AIDS Situation in India and in Gujarat*, Presentation on HIV/AIDS at the Media Workshop on HIV/AIDS and Child Rights, Gujarat, 13–14 August 1999, supported by UNICEF, Gujarat.

degree of disability to identify the same. However, the National Sample Survey Organization (NSSO) in 1991 took a countrywide sample survey revealing that about 1.9 per cent of the total population of the country, i.e. 16.15 million people have physical and sensory disabilities. According to the report of the Rehabilitation Council of India on Manpower Development 1996, estimated on the basis of the NSSO report, the following are the population of children with disabilities in the educable age group of 5–14 years:

- Locomotor handicap   8.94 million
- Hearing handicap   3.24 million
- Speech handicap   1.96 million
- Visual handicap   4.01 million
- Mental retardation   9.00 million
- Cerebral palsy   3.00 million

Legislations and Policies of Government of India pertaining to Disability

THE NATIONAL POLICY ON EDUCATION (NPE) 1986

The NPE is implemented to achieve the goal of providing education to all including the disabled. The objective of the policy is to integrate the physically and mentally handicapped with the general community as equal partners to prepare them for normal growth and to enable them to face life with courage and confidence. It envisages that wherever possible, education for children with motor and other mild handicap will be with others. Special schools with hostels will be provided as far as possible at district headquarters for severely handicapped children.

THE PLAN OF ACTION 1986

The Plan of Action 1986 also stresses that as education of handicapped in special schools is very expensive, it will be ensured that only those children whose needs cannot be met in common schools be enrolled in special schools. Once the communication and reading and writing skills are acquired they will be integrated in regular schools. The Central Scheme for integrated education revised in 1989 proposes to provide educational opportunities for the disabled in regular schools. The State governments in India have adopted the scheme and established cells for monitoring the same with relevance to the current policy guideline on education.

PROGRAMME OF ACTION 1992

This programme stresses on the implementation of the project 'Integrated Education for Disabled'. The innovative multi-category training of resource teachers has been institutionalized in the regional institutions of the National Council of Educational Research and Training (NCERT).

The Rehabilitation Council of India Act 1992

This Act was passed by the Parliament to regulate the manpower development programmes in the field of education of children with special needs. Earlier, the government in 1986 decided to set up a Rehabilitation Council under the Ministry of Social Justice and Empowerment as an autonomous body. Later, it got the assent from the President and became an Act in 1992, and the Council came into force with effect from June 1993. The major objectives of the RCI Act are:

- To regulate the training policies and programmes in the field of rehabilitation of people with disabilities.
- To standardize training courses for rehabilitation professionals/personnel dealing with people with disabilities and ensure uniformity in various training centres throughout the country.
- To prescribe minimum standards of education and training institutions in the field of rehabilitation uniformly throughout the country.
- To recognize institutions/universities running degree/diploma/certificate courses in the field of rehabilitation of the disabled and to withdraw recognition, wherever the facilities are not satisfactory.
- To recognize and equalize foreign degree/diploma/certificate in the field of rehabilitation awarded by universities/institutions.
- To maintain a Central Rehabilitation Register of persons possessing the recognized rehabilitation qualification.
- To collect information on a regular basis, on education and training in the field of rehabilitation of people with disabilities from institutions in India and abroad.
- To encourage continuing rehabilitation education by way of collaboration with organizations working in the field or rehabilitation of persons with disabilities.

The RCI has so far developed more than fifty courses and recognized more than a hundred institutions to offer special education and rehabilitation manpower development programmes in India. Out of these courses, nine are pertaining to visual impairment. Recently, RCI introduced a fully sponsored manpower development scheme so as to enable universities and colleges in the country to conduct need-based courses. This scheme will enable the most difficult regions in the country to initiate teacher preparation programmes in education of children with special needs. The enactment of RCI

Act 1992 goes a long way in accrediting special education manpower development programmes in the country.

THE PERSONS WITH DISABILITIES (EQUAL OPPORTUNITIES, PROTECTION OF RIGHTS, AND FULL PARTICIPATION) ACT 1995 (PD ACT 1995)

This Act came into force on 7 February 1996. It is a comprehensive legislation and the main purpose of the Act is to define the responsibilities of the Central and State governments with regard to the services for disabled persons. The Act also ensures full life to disabled individuals so as to make full contribution in accordance with their disability conditions. Blindness [Section 2(b)], Low visions [Section 2(u), Leprosy-cured [Section 2(n), Hearing impairment [Section 2(l)], Locomotor disability [Section 2 (o)], Mental illness [Section 2(q)], and Mental retardation [Section 2(r)] are the seven disability conditions covered under the Act. Person with disability means a person suffering from not less than 40 per cent of any disability as certified by a medical authority [Section 2(f)].

IMPORTANT PROVISIONS OF THE ACT

Chapter II of the Act deals with the Central Coordination Committee and the Central Executive Committee to be set up by the Central government under the Act. And Chapter III provides for the setting up of the State Coordination Committees and the State Executive Committees by the State governments.

Chapter IV deals with prevention and early detection of disabilities through surveys, investigations, and research conducted concerning the cause, occurrence, and prevention of disabilities. Provisions are also made for creating awareness and training and taking measures for prenatal, peri-natal and postnatal care of the mother and child [PD Act 1995, Section 25].

Chapter V deals with Education. As per the Act, the Central and State governments shall ensure that every child with disability has access to free and adequate education till the age of eighteen years. It also indicates that integrated education and special schools will have to be set up to meet the educational needs of children with disabilities. Introduction of non-formal education, functional literacy schemes, provision of aids and appliances, education through open schools and universities, etc., are also stressed in the Act. It also indicated that the government should create adequate teacher-training facilities to prepare teachers for special and integrated schools. Development of research on assistive devices and other areas of disability and financial incentives to universities for taking researchers are also envisaged in the Act [Sections 26–30].

Chapter VI of the Act provides for employment of the disabled. The appropriate governments have been enjoined upon:

- to identify posts in establishments reserved for persons with disabilities [PD Act 1995, Section 32],
- to reserve one per cent posts each for persons with blindness or low vision, hearing impairment, and locomotor disability or cerebral palsy [PD Act 1995, Section 33]. If vacancies are not filled, they have to be carried forward.
- to create a special employment exchange [PD Act 1995, Section 34].
- to develop schemes for ensuring employment [PD Act 1995, Section 38].
- to reserve 3 per cent seats in all educational institutions [PD Act 1995, Section 39].
- to keep vacancies reserved in poverty alleviation schemes [PD Act 1995, Section 40].
- to give incentives to employers to ensure 5 per cent of the workforce to be composed of persons with disabilities [PD Act 1995, Section 41].

Chapter VII is for affirmative action for the disabled. Under this the government shall prepare schemes for providing aids and appliances to persons with disabilities, schemes for preferential allotment of land at concessional rates to the disabled [Sections 42 and 43].

To provide equal opportunities and full participation to the disabled, as far as it is economically possible, the roads, buildings, constructions, structures, transport and employment should be so adapted that they are accessible to the persons with disabilities [Sections 44-7]. The Act also provides for certification of institutions for the disabled.[62]

Chapter XIII deals with social security and rehabilitation of persons with disabilities. There is a provision for unemployment allowance to be paid to the disabled. But these social security measures have to be undertaken within the economic capacity of the State governments.[63]

Government and NGO Schemes and Initiatives for the Disabled

There are presently two types of educational programmes available in India for different categories of handicapped children:

- Integrated Education Programme for children with mild disability in a regular school set up under the Scheme of Integrated Education for Disabled Children (IEDC) formulated by the Ministry of Human

[62] PD Act 1995, Chapter X, Sections 50-5.
[63] PD Act 1995, Chapter XIII.

Resources Development being implemented through SCERT[64] and NGOs at the state level.
- Special School Programme for the severely disabled children in a special school formulated under the Ministry of Social Justice and empowerment, being implemented through State governments involving NGOs.
- Apart from this, children with disability within the age group of 14–35 are given the opportunity to education through the National Open School (NOS), an autonomous body under the Ministry of Human resources development, Government of India, through the support of study centres. Such children can complete education as parallel to formal education.

The children are getting opportunity for education through the aforesaid programmes by the following educational intervention in accordance with their entry age:

Age Group	Programme
0–2 years	Parent-infant training
2–5 years	Pre-school
5–8 years	Preparatory classes
8–14 years	Remedial teaching through non-formal education set-up

BHARATHI BRAILLE FOR VISUALLY IMPAIRED CHILDREN

According to the National Sample Survey Organization (1991) there are 4.005 million blind persons above the age of four years. As per the Sixth Survey of Education, 8633 blind children are enrolled in integrated education programmes. The Special Schools in India are serving approximately 30,000 blind children. Therefore, the number of children in schools is not exceeding 40,000 which is less than 1 per cent of the NSSO statistics of 4.01 million persons with visual impairment. The coverage of visually impaired children in rural areas is even less—not even 0.5 per cent. The coverage of girls with visual impairment is 39.1 per cent whereas they constitute 54 per cent of the population of persons with visual impairment.[65]

Work for children with visual impairment in India is more than a century old. Miss Anne Sharp founded the first school for the blind in Amritsar in

---

[64] State Council for Education, Research, and Training.
[65] L. Kashyap and J. Modi, *Status of the Disabled in India 2000*, A paper presented at the Maharashtra State-Level Workshop on the Convention on the Rights of the Child, 18–19 January 2001.

1887. Indians also started other schools later. But India did not have a code for the Indian languages. The different languages followed in India made the task even more complicated. However, the decision of UNESCO in 1947 to follow a phonetic-based Braille code paved the way for the evolvement of the Braille code in India. The phonetic-based Braille codes were evolved for use in India in 1951. This enabled the growth of a large number of educational institutions in the country for persons with visual impairment.

Scheme of Integrated Education for Disabled Children

The Government of India launched a centrally sponsored scheme of integrated education for disabled children in 1974. At that time the scheme was under the direct control of the Ministry of Social Welfare. The scheme promoted implementation of integrated education for disabled children of all categories and the institutions are eligible for 100 per cent financial assistance from the central grant. The scheme was revised during the last two decades. In 1982, it was transferred to the Department of Education. The following assistance as per the scheme are provided:

- Appointment of a resource teacher for every 8–10 disabled children enrolled in the school.
- Stationary allowance of Rs 400 per child per annum.
- Uniform allowance of Rs 50 per child per annum.
- Transport allowance of Rs 50 per child per month.
- Reader allowance of Rs 50 per month for children with visual impairment.
- Escort allowance for severely handicapped children with lower extreme disabilities @ Rs 75 per child per month.
- Actual cost of equipment subject to a maximum of Rs 2000 per student for a period of five years.

Though this scheme has enabled the development of hundreds of integrated education programmes in the country, its mass expansion is limited as the State governments are yet to accept responsibility for the same.

The National Institute for the Visually Handicapped was established in the year 1979. This gave recognition to the services for these children. The institute concentrated on Braille production, employment, training of staff, etc. Later, regional training centres were also initiated by this institute.

THE EFA CAMPAIGN AND DISABLED CHILDREN

The commitment of the Government of India in 1993 to special education became multifold with the inclusion of disabled children in the campaign for

Education For All (EFA). The inclusion of education of disabled persons in the EFA statement has given special impetus to the services for this population. The EFA statement reads as follows: Expansion of early childhood care and development activities, especially for poor, disadvantaged, and disabled children, through a multi-pronged effort involving families, communities, and appropriate institutions.

NATIONAL AND COLLABORATIVE EFFORTS FOR PRIMARY PREVENTION OF HEARING IMPAIRMENT

The NSSO data of 1991 survey showed that there are 3,242,000 persons with hearing impairment in India. According to the India Human Development Report 1999, there are 27.9 children per million in the age group of 0–4 and 76.3 children per million in the age group of 5–12 years. The main causes of hearing impairment are infections, neglect, and ignorance. Among the underlying causes are low socio-economic conditions, inadequate health care, and nutrition. The prevention of hearing impairment has to be done at three levels: first to prevent its occurrence; second, in case of occurrence, to check its further progress; and third to rehabilitate the persons with hearing impairment.

National Measures for Immunization are taken under the Expanded Programme of Immunization to prevent some of the childhood diseases which may lead to the onset of hearing impairment. The National Iodine Deficiency Disorder Control Programme is also carried out as iodine deficiency leads to diseases like goiter, mental retardation, and hearing impairment. The Child Survival and Safe Motherhood Programme also aims at prevention of early infections which might have hearing impairment as a side effect. The National Nutrition Policy aims at providing supplementary nutrition to children below six years of age, pregnant women and women in 15–41 years' age group. The National Programme to Overcome the Problems of Ignorance deals with increasing awareness about the prevalence, causes, and prevention measures of hearing impairment.

NATIONAL MEASURES FOR EARLY IDENTIFICATION

Primary health centres have been set up by the government for primary health care. Thes centres have trained *gram sevikas, anganwadi* workers, multipurpose workers, and *vikalanga bandhus,* nurses, etc. Though these organizations are available for early detection of hearing impairment, there is no other national measure/policy for this purpose.

MEASURES FOR EDUCATION OF THE HEARING IMPAIRED

About two decades ago, the age of detection of hearing impairment was over five years. These children attending normal school was a rarity and the percentage of these children getting educated was only 1.5 as the number of special schools was only 143. The scenario of education has not changed despite the government's policy of Integrated Education for the Disabled (IED) initiated by the NCERT in 1974 under the Ministry of Human Resource Development. There are now about 540 to 550 special schools and the percentage of children attending these schools has gone upto three. Apart from this the National Open School (NOS) was started in 1988. Language exemption is made (so that the hearing impaired can study only one language).

Children as Victims of Drugs

Children, because of their tender age, are particularly prone to be swayed into addiction under unhealthy influences and to be used as an instrument in drug trafficking. There is a widespread use of illicit drugs among street children. Even amongst children in institutions, use of drugs is increasing. There are innumerable documented instances to show that children of the poor are introduced and addicted to drugs only to be manipulated as tools in drug trafficking by organized criminal syndicates. If a child is less than seven years of age, Section 82, Indian Penal Code is applicable and the act committed by the child is not treated as an offence. If the child is above seven years and below twelve years, depending on his/her maturity of understanding, the criminal liability will be decided [Section 83 IPC]. If above twelve years, the child will be dealt under the Juvenile Justice System. The Narcotic Drugs and Psychotropic Substances Act 1985 declares illegal the production, possession, transportation, purchase, and sale of any drug enumerated in the schedule to the Act. A general rule of penal policy envisaged under the Act is that an offender, be he an addict or a trafficker, is subject to punishment which includes imprisonment as well as fine. Under the Juvenile Justice (Care and Protection of Children) Act 2000, it is an offence to give or cause to be given to any juvenile or child, any intoxicating liquor or any drug or psychotropic substance except upon the order of a duly qualified medical practitioner or in case of sickness. The punishment for this offence is imprisonment for a term which may extend to three years and fine [The Juvenile Justice (Care and Protection of Children Act) 2000, Section 25].

The interventions of the NGOs in this area include running detoxificatioin centres, advocacy, developing community mobilization strategies, and networking.

Children's Right to Shelter/Housing

Here are a few recent reports on some instances that affected the child's right to shelter/housing:

- The settlement of Babrekar Nagar was razed to the ground in 1997. An area of around 30 hectares belonging to the Collector and 10 hectares belonging to the Maharashtra Housing and Area Development Authority (MHADA) was cleared . . . 12,842 families were displaced which amounted to approximately 26,000 children exposed to violence and the traumatic experience of an eviction.
- Children in eighteen villages of Tamil Nadu were uprooted by the State Industries Promotion Corporation of Tamil Nadu (SIPCOT). Among the approximately 36,000 people to be involuntarily evicted with no place to go, are 13,000–14,000 children. These children will lose stability of a house and the rural surroundings, because it will be very hard for the immigrants once in the city of Chennai (the most likely place to go for most of them once evicted) to find, build, and keep a stable home. Certainly, a large number of them will, from sheer necessity, end up in the streets, on pavements, or in a slum.
- The Sanjay Gandhi Nagar Demolition is one of the largest ever demolition conducted in urban India. The Sanjay Gandhi National Park, Mumbai, has an area of 103.09 square kilometres and contains about 86,000 huts, i.e. about 450,000 people. An environmental group, viz., Bombay Environmental Action Group filed a petition before the Mumbai High Court for clearing Sanjay Gandhi National Park. Fifty-six thousand families, i.e. about 300,000 people have been evicted without being provided with an alternative site. Only those families having their names included in the electoral roll of 1 January 1995 are entitled to a patch of land admeasuring 15' x 10' for which they have to pay a sum of Rs 7000 per family. The alternative site is offered outside the city limits, i.e. in an adjoining district and about 13 km away from the railway station. Many do not have the financial capacity to pay Rs 7000 and others apprehend that this relocation will severe them from their means of livelihood and will disturb their children's schooling.

Seven per cent of the city's population live on pavements. This amounts to a staggering figure of 980,000 people who are homeless and of whom almost an astounding 40 per cent are children. Civic authorities confronted with issues of health and sanitation, waste management, obstruction to vehicular and pedestrian traffic see eviction as the solution. At periodic intervals, they have carried out demolitions in an organized and planned fashion. The impact of forced evictions on the weaker sections of the pavement communities and especially the children is severe. Next to the loss of livelihood, home, and identity, the event can cause great psychological damage, trauma, and a permanent loss of a sense of security.

Street children are an extremely vulnerable group because of the way they are forced to live, homeless, out on the streets. Their mobility is high, they are without any parental guidance and without any form of family love or affection, and hence are subjected to the grimness of an existence not suitable for their physical and emotional stage of development. They have to work to make a living and are constantly exposed to the dangers and the unhealthy life of the city and the streets. Due to their distrust and even hatred against all forms of authority (created by their daily experiences with them) it is hard to reach this specific group of children. While engaged in various trades and services which directly/indirectly benefit the city dwellers, they do not have sufficient access to even the basic services required for their healthy growth and development.

The significance of such forced demolitions cannot be understated, and the impact of this on families and especially the children cannot be forgotten. Majority of the people said that they come to large cities in search of work and to support their families. In such an event, it often happens that needs of children often go neglected. The right to development and survival of children in such situations is often not appropriately met.

The above case studies[66] present the displacement of children and the consequent gross violation of their basic human rights to housing and to live in dignity. The right to housing is defined as follows: 'The human right to a place to live is an inalienable right closely linked to the right to live, in all of its spiritual and material aspects. All children, women and men have the right to a safe and decent place to live in peace with dignity. . . . The right to a place with dignity is not limited exclusively to a physical structure, a house. It is conceived in a broader sense that integrates housing—shelter and habitat—environment as a whole. This includes the cultural, historic, social, economic, political, legal, environmental, physical, and territorial dimensions.'[67]

---

[66] 'The Child in Search of the State', Alternate Report to the India Country Report on the implementation of the Right to Housing as enshrined in the Convention on the Rights of the Child' submitted by Human Rights Foundation (HRF), LAYA's and Youth for Unity and Voluntary Action (YUVA), Sept. 1998.

[67] The Habitat International Coalition in coordination with other international voluntary organizations and community-based organizations have defined this right.

In its essence, housing as a living impulse creates roots entailing security. The house is to be seen as the home—the one stable point in the child's life where she/he can return to, where she/he will find love and peace: 'Nurturing families, in all their forms, are the primary institution and the best environment for protecting and promoting the rights and well-being of children. Whenever possible, children must be able to live with their families in adequate, secure housing.[68] Adequate housing includes legal security of tenure, including protection from forced eviction and displacement; availability of services, materials, facilities, and infrastructure; affordability, habitability, accessibility, and location. Essential to the survival of families is their capacity to support themselves in ways which do not undermine family life. When families are unable to provide adequately for their children, States have the obligation to assist and support them.'[69]

The Constitution of India and the Right to Housing

Environmentally, housing is as important as pure drinking water, because many diseases including respiratory and ophthalmic, etc., are the result of overcrowding, poor ventilation and generally unsatisfactory conditions of housing environment. It is the poor, and especially the women and children among them, who live in the slums and are at the receiving end of a dehumanizing mode of development and planning. In Mumbai alone, there are 2,335 pockets of slums containing 902,015 structures and it is estimated that more than fifty-five million people are slum dwellers.[70] Article 21[71] of the Constitution of India deals with the right to life and includes the right to housing and shelter. In the case of *Francis Coralie Mullin, Petitioner v The Administrator, Union Territory of Delhi and others*[72] it was held that the right to life enshrined in Article 21 cannot be restricted to mere animal existence. It means something much more than just physical survival. The right to life includes the right to live with human dignity and all that goes along with it, namely, the bare necessaries of life such as adequate nutrition, clothing, and

---

[68] In the words of the Expert Seminar on Children's Rights and Habitat organized by the UNICEF, the United Nations Centre for Human Settlement (UNCHS)/Habitat in February 1996.

[69] The Child in Search of the State, Alternate Report, CRC, HRF, LAYA, YUVA, Sept. 1998.

[70] This approach has already been adopted in the Urban Basic Services Programme and the same is incorporated in the Prime Ministers Integrated Urban Poverty Eradication Programme (PMIUPEP).

[71] Article 21: Protection of life and personal liberty.

[72] AIR 1981 SC 746.

shelter over the head, and facilities for reading, writing, and expressing oneself in diverse forms, freely moving about and mixing and commingling with fellow human beings. Article 39(f) of the Constitution of India also deals with the necessity of the appropriate conditions for the overall development of children.

In the case of *Prabhakaran Nair v State of Tamil Nadu*,[73] the Supreme Court held that shelter is one of our fundamental rights. Again in *M/s Shantistar Builders v Narayan Khimalal Totame*,[74] the Supreme Court dealt with the concept of suitable accommodation. 'Basic needs of man have traditionally been accepted to be three—food, clothing, and shelter. The right to life is guaranteed in any civilized society. This right would take within its sweep the right to food, the right to clothing, the right to decent environment and a reasonable accommodation to live in. The difference between the need of an animal and a human being for shelter has to be kept in view. For the animal it is bare protection of the body; for a human being it has to be a suitable accommodation which would allow him to grow in every aspect—physical, mental, and intellectual. The Constitution aims at ensuring fuller development of every child. That would be possible, only if the child is in a proper home . . .'

Despite the constitutional provisions and the provisions in the Covenant on Economic, Social, and Cultural Rights and the Convention on the Rights of the Child, demolitions are conducted all over the country by the State and under orders of the higher judiciary, viz., the Supreme Court and the High Courts. The Supreme Court has in *Almitra H. Patel v Union of India and Others*[75] stated that providing a slum dweller with alternative accommodation is like rewarding a pickpocket. There has been a marked change in the attitude of the courts during the last decade, the concentration being on clearing cities of its 'dirt' and on assisting the rich and the middle class to lead a comfortable life.

Violation of the Rights of the Child under the Convention on the Rights of the Child (CRC)

Children's housing rights imply more than the mere concept of a shelter. Adequate housing is of particular importance for children whose physical and intellectual development is closely linked to the environment where they grow up and the living conditions they confront. Article 27 of the Convention on the Rights of the Child addresses the right of the child to adequate

---
[73] AIR 1987 SC 2117.
[74] AIR 1990 SC 630.
[75] (2000) 2 SCC 678.

shelter. Homeless children, migrant children, runaway and abandoned children are all children whose right to shelter is violated.

The right to privacy [Art 16 CRC] and the right to a secure and permanent home are often the most important aspects for privacy. Though urban slum pockets often face the problem of overcrowded homes, such homes at least provide some kind of personal space and protection, which is very necessary for the child's overall development. A home for most children is primarily the existence of a warm, intimate, social climate. Such a climate is vital not only for the quality of life of children but also future adult lives. All children have the right to live with their closest relatives in an atmosphere characterized by love and understanding and the State has the obligation to support parents in child raising. To fulfil this obligation, right to housing is one necessary condition.[76]

Children's right to adequate housing cannot be interpreted in a narrow or restrictive sense but is rather understood to encompass living in security, peace, and dignity. This concept is interrelated to and interdependent with nearly every other right in the CRC

The gross violation of the right to housing of a child has an adverse impact on the other rights to shelter, nutrition, clean water, sanitation, education, health, and a safe environment as listed below:

- The right to privacy, family, and home [CRC, Article 16.1]. The right to information, access, and support of health, hygiene, and sanitation [CRC Article 24.2(e)];
- The right to appropriate measures to combat disease and malnutrition;
- The right to the highest attainable standard of health and the right to appropriate measures to combat disease and malnutrition;
- The right to provisions of primary needs such as clean drinking water [CRC Article 24.2(c)];
- The right to protection from the illicit use of narcotic drugs and psychotropic substances [CRC Article 33];
- Right to education [CRC Articles 28.1, 2, and 3];
- The right to play, recreation, and cultural life [CRC Article 31];
- The right to a name and nationality [CRC Articles 7.1 and 2].
- The right to an identity [CRC Articles 8.1 and 2];
- The right to be cared for by a (legal) guardian [CRC Articles 18.1, 2, and 3];

[76] M. Subramaniam, *Civil Rights of Children and the CRC*, A Paper presented at the Maharashtra State-level Workshop on the Convention on the Rights of the Child. 18–19 January 2001.

- The right to survival and development [CRC Article 6.2];
- The right to protection from the law against interference and attacks [CRC Article 16.2];
- The right to protection from physical and mental violence [CRC Articles 19.1 and 2];
- The right to protection from economic exploitation [CRC Articles 32.1 and 2];
- The right to protection from sexual exploitation and abuse [CRC Article 34].

Recommendations for the Protection of the Rights of the Child[77]

The following recommendations should be followed in order to avoid violation of the rights of the child in forced eviction cases:

- The state should not undertake forced evictions unless it can provide adequate rehabilitation.
- A grievance redressal mechanism must be set up for cases of any violation of human rights.
- In the event of an eviction becoming unavoidable either due to risk to the settlement or for a stated development purpose:
  - Evictions must be announced at least one month before the actual demolition.
  - Assistance must be offered to those who need it the most, like elderly people, women, and families with (young) children.
  - Arrangements for proper and complete resettlement must be made. Transit accommodation must be created for the interim period prior to resettlement.
  - The government must be responsible for providing food supplements, education, health care, and leisure to the affected children.
  - There must be extra care for the children of working parents during the transit period so that these children can feel safe and secure while their parents go out to work.
  - The resettlement must be within the vicinity of the old one, so that the social structure of the child's life like school, friends, playgrounds, and simple familiarity is not disrupted.
  - All the children evicted must be registered and given new identification cards.

[77] 'The Child in Search of the State', Alternate Report to the India Country Report on the implementation of the Right to Housing as enshrined in the Convention on the Rights of the Child' submitted by Human Rights Foundation (HRF), LAYA's and Youth for Unity and Voluntary Action (YUVA), Sept. 1998.

– All the above-mentioned provisions and services should be continued once the people have been resettled and not end after the transit period.[78]

Institutionalized mechanisms for participatory planning including participation of children in the process of need assessment, planning, implementation, evaluation, and monitoring in urban and rural human settlement programmes should become an essential prerequisite to child-centred habitat.[79]

The government has given a low priority to provision for shelter as reflected in the declining direct public investment on housing in the successive five-year plans, from 16 per cent in the first to 1.5 per cent of the outlay in the seventh plan. In the Eighth Five-Year Plan, though emphasis has been placed on social housing schemes and the public sector outlay has increased from Rs 1,491 crore in the seventh plan to Rs 4,823 crores in the eighth plan, it fails even to propose any viable alternative for providing and improving the housing condition of the homeless people in the country.

Children are the worst affected because of lack of housing policy. While it is certain that commercial interests and market forces will not care for the interests of the poor and the children in the present context of globalization, liberalization, structural adjustments, and privatization of essential services, the struggle for ensuring the housing rights of the poor and marginalized sections like the children is one of the most crucial needs.

Campaigns and Initiatives

The Committee for Right to Housing (CRH) was a precursor to the Campaign for Housing Rights. It emerged in 1985 as a direct response to the Supreme Court judgment of July 1985 which sought to re-empower the government/Bombay Municipal Corporation to continue with demolitions/evictions of slums and pavement dwellers. CRH was a collective of sixteen voluntary organizations working with slum and pavement dwellers of Mumbai. Simultaneously, at the national level, the National Campaign for Housing Rights (NCHR) was initiated in 1986 with the support of various individuals, organizations, mass-based groups, and trade unions.

Campaign for Housing Rights has been one of the most planned and organized advocacy efforts that succeeded in developing a public argument for advocating the fundamental rights of millions of homeless people to have adequate housing. The campaign helped channelling and coordinating the

[78] Ibid.
[79] Ibid.

efforts of hundreds of social action groups, voluntary organizations and individuals at the national, regional, and grass-roots level to bring forth housing into the centre stage of public advocacy and policy priorities. National Campaign for Housing Rights (NCHR) began in August 1986, emerged as an all-India organization with a fairly widespread membership and units in more than twenty states. The problem of housing in India was analysed and addressed by the campaigners in a holistic manner, taking it as an issue related to human rights, socio-economic rights, environment, gender equality, distributive justice, and paradigms of development.

Towards Right to Survival for All

Right to survival is a prerequisite for the realization of all other rights including social, economic, cultural, civil, and political rights. Right to health is a right to life, right to live with dignity, and right to livelihood. But poverty, undernourishment, ill health, rural-urban divide, regional variations and disparities among different socio-economic groups, etc., contribute to an uneven attainment of health of the people. In the Constitution of India, health is still not recognized as a fundamental right of citizens. The fundamental right to health would mean making the right to health care a legally enforceable entitlement. In the Alma Ata declaration, provision of universal, comprehensive primary health care was seen as the key to attaining health for all as part of overall development. Poverty contributes to undernourishment and ill health, and ill health perpetuates poverty. Thus there is a need to see health as being central to sustainable human development and formulating a national health policy with a detailed plan and timetable for realization of the core right to health care. Investment in health is one of the major steps towards poverty alleviation, and improved health is a key factor for human development. Health has to become an integral part of development agenda.[80] Therefore, there is a need for renewed campaign initiatives to make health a fundamental human right, to take the Health for All strategy to the new millennium, to force the government to commit for Health for All in the Twenty-first Century. All health networks, NGOs, people's organizations, social action groups, etc., must come together to realize the vision of Health for All in the Twenty-first Century into a reality, through networking, grass-roots mobilization and policy advocacy.

[80] Ashish Bose, 'Health for All: Broken Promises', *Economic and Political Weekly*, 36.11: 905–7, 2001.

The campaign must strive for the following charter of demands:[81]

- Making basic health care a fundamental, constitutional right of every citizen
- Ensuring provision of basic prerequisites for a healthy life
- Allocation of 5 per cent of GDP towards health
- Ensuring comprehensive primary health care to all
- Provision of good-quality secondary and tertiary services
- A comprehensive policy on education of professionals in the health sector
- Social and self-regulation of the private medical sector
- Rational and people-centred drug policy
- Support to traditional healing systems
- Democratization of the process of health policy making
- Ecological and social measures to check resurgence of communicable diseases
- Child-centred health initiatives
- Special measures relating to occupational and environmental health
- Comprehensive measures to promote mental health
- Special measures to promote the health of physically and mentally disadvantaged and disabled
- Universal availability of birth control measures.

Besides, India is also a signatory to the Universal Declaration of Human Rights 1948 and the International Covenant on Economic, Social, and Cultural Rights 1966, which declare and establish housing as a universally recognized fundamental human right. In spite of these proclaimed stands, the Indian government is yet to recognize the right to housing as a fundamental right. Lobbying for an amendment to Articles 19 and 21 of the Constitution of India declaring housing an explicit fundamental right, there is a need to advocate and campaign for a comprehensive people's bill of housing rights with the perspective of child rights.

---

[81] Anand Phadke, 'Towards health care for all', Indian Academy of Social Sciences, Allahabad, 1999, pp. 33–8.

9

Making Child Rights a Reality

The Paradigm Shift

Children have a special place in all the wisdom and traditions of the world. Sri Ramana Maharishi, looking at a child in the prayer hall, reportedly remarked: 'One can attain the bliss of *Brahman* only when the mind becomes pure and humble, like the mind of this child.' The gospel according to St Luke says that people brought their babies to Jesus, asking him to place his hands on them in blessing. When his disciples tried to prevent the people from approaching their teacher, Jesus said, 'Let the children come to me, do not stop them because the Kingdom of God belongs to them.' Rabindranath Tagore had stated: 'Every child when born brings with it the hope that God is not yet disappointed with man.' There is thus a societal recognition of the fact that all children constitute the most fundamental and valuable resource of any society and any developmental activity has to include the child rights perspective. Development projects and priorities must be made accountable to the rights of the child.

The importance of the 1989 Convention on the Rights of the Child (CRC) is now widely accepted and recognized. The CRC has been described as nothing short of 'the cornerstone of a new moral ethos for children', and an instrument stressing that 'respect for and protection of children's rights is the starting point for the full development of the individual's potential in an atmosphere of freedom, dignity and justice'. Once ratified, the CRC makes it a binding duty for the States to implement its provisions by adopting relevant legislative and administrative measures. Further, governments must report on the measures adopted and progress made in advancing children's rights in their countries in the form of a report submitted to the Committee on the Rights of the Child [1] appointed by the United Nations under

---

[1] India Report on the World Summit for Children, Department of Women and Child Development, Ministry of Human Resources Development, Government of India, 2000.

Article 43 of the Convention.[2] The Government of India submitted its first Country Report on the Convention of the Rights of the Child in February 1997. The report reviewed the situation of children in the country with reference to the articles of the Convention. The priority issues that the Country Report focused on included the measures of implementation, civil rights and freedom, and special measures of protection. The first India Country Report on the CRC stated that:

> Unless the life of the child in the family and community improves, all development efforts would be meaningless. There is, therefore, a need to raise awareness and create an ethos of respect for the rights of the child in society to meet his or her basic developmental needs. Advocacy and social mobilization are two crucial processes which are being emphasized to achieve this end. With India's ratification of the UN Convention on the Rights of the Child, the 'rights approach' to child development is gradually gaining importance and will henceforth form the basis of Government's strategy towards child development.[3]

There has been a paradigm shift in approaches towards children The shift in focus is from the welfare to the developmental approach (Table 9.1).

Table 9:1: Approaches Towards Children

Earlier approach	Present approach
Needs	Rights
Welfare	Development
Institutional and residential care	Non-residential and family-based alternatives
Custodial care	Holistic development
Segregation and isolation	Inclusion in mainstream
Beneficiary and recipient	Participant and partner

The Government of India is in the process of framing the second India Country Report to the UN Child Rights Committee. The Country CRC Report preparation process is underway since August 1999. There have been consultation workshops—a mix of community-based NGOs and those with

---

[2] The Committee comprises ten members elected by the State parties for the term of four years. The Committee meets three times every year. See M. O'Flaberty, *The United Nations and Human Rights*, Sweet and Maxwell, 1996, p. 180.

[3] India Country Report on the Convention on the Rights of the Child, Government of India, 1997.

experience of national/global meetings on child rights and child representatives. There is a provision in the CRC for Non-Governmental Organizations in member countries to propose and undertake to submit Alternate Reports to those of the national governments. The first Alternate Report suggested that the Indian child is deprived and vulnerable in more ways than one.[4] Wide consultations are on amongst the NGOs for framing the Second Alternate Report.

As far as India is concerned, the UN Committee on the Rights of the Child observed that the State party should establish a statutory, independent National Commission for Children with the mandate of, inter alia, regularly monitoring and evaluating progress in the implementation of the Convention at the federal, State, and local levels.[5] Further, such a commission should be empowered to receive and address complaints of violations of child rights, including those with respect to the security forces. Subsequent to the observations of the UN Committee, the Union Minister of Human Resource development agreed to set up a National Commission for Children.

Since signing its agreement to the Convention, the Indian government has made several attempts to bring the country up to the standard, such as organizing reviews of the existing laws pertaining to children, increasing publicity around children's issues by organizing conventions with key functionaries and the public, and so forth. A Children's Code Bill 2000 (CCB 2000) has been drafted for the setting up of a National Commission for Children (NCC) which is likely to be placed before Parliament any time.[6] A draft National Policy and Charter for Children (NPC 2001) has been drawn up. Policy documents like the ninth five-year plan and population and health policies have reiterated the government's commitment to protecting the child.

Initiatives by the Government of India

The Children's Code Bill 2000 provides for the constitution of a National Commission for Children for the better protection of child rights and for promoting the best interests of the child within the larger context of promoting and upholding values to strengthen the family, society, and the nation. Under the Bill 'Child rights' means and includes the rights relating

---

[4] The Alternate Report on the Convention on the Rights of the Child, Working Group on the Convention on the Rights of the Child, India, May 1998.
[5] UN Committee Report, para 19.
[6] The Draft National Commission for Children Bill 2000, prepared by a Special Expert Committee chaired by Justice V.R. Krishna Iyer, was presented to the Prime Minister.

to survival, protection, development, and participation as elaborated in the Convention on the Rights of the Child 1989 and the Constitution of India. The Code Bill declares the UNCRC as acceded by the Government of India to be part of the law of India and enforceable by all the courts in India. The bill makes it a duty and the responsibility of the government to respect and ensure that the rights of the child are protected and guaranteed to every child within the territory of India, irrespective of nationality, race, colour, sex, religion, language, birth, political or other opinion, ethnic, economic or social status, or property or disability. The bill enjoins that every child should be protected against all forms of discrimination, exploitation, punishment, or abuse on any ground.

Some of the salient features of the Children's Code Bill 2000 are:

- Constitution of a National Commission for Children[7]
  The National Commission for Children constituted by the Central Government shall consist of:
    – a chairperson who has been a judge of the Supreme Court of India;
    – a vice-chairperson appointed from amongst the members;
    – one member who is an eminent educationist, preferably in the field of primary education;
    – one member who is an eminent expert in child health;
    – one member with proven commitment and contribution in the area of social action in childcare, child welfare, or child rights with experience of at least five years;
    – one member who has been active in the field of juvenile justice or care of neglected or marginalized children for at least five years;
    – one member with proven commitment and contribution in the field of child labour; and
    – one member who is an eminent child psychologist or sociologist.

The proposed Commission will also include a member secretary of the Commission, with a rank not lower than that of joint secretary/additional secretary to the Government of India who shall exercise such powers and discharge such functions of the Commission as may be delegated to her/him.

The chairperson, vice-chairperson, and other members shall be appointed by the President of India by warrant under his hand and seal.[8] Every appointment is to be made after obtaining the recommendations of a Committee on Appointments consisting of the Prime Minister as the chairperson

---

[7] The Children's Code Bill 2000, Section 3.
[8] The Children's Code Bill 2000, Section 4.

and the Speaker of the House of the People, Minister in-Charge of the Ministry of Human Resource Development dealing with women and children in the Government of India, leader of the Opposition in the House of the People, and leader of the Opposition in the Council of States as members.

- The functions of the Commission

  The functions include the following:[9]
  - Oversee proper implementation of the existing laws for children.
  - Review and recommend revision of existing laws to bring them in harmony with the provisions of Part III (Fundamental Rights) and Part IV (Directive Principles of State Policy) of the Constitution of India and the National Policy for Children.[10]
  - Monitor all sectorial policies, welfare programmes, and any other proactive interventions in respect of children and periodically recommend best practices for effective implementation.
  - Enquire *suo motu* or on a petition presented to it by a victim or any person on behalf of the victim, into a complaint of:
    † Violation of laws pertaining to children or child rights or their abetment.
    † Negligence in the prevention of such violation by a public servant.
  - Conduct research and undertake appropriate measures for awareness generation in respect of children's issues, especially children in difficult circumstances, street children, and the special circumstances of the girl child, document the same, and make appropriate recommendations for rectifying the problems.
  - Initiate and encourage study, research, and documentation about child abuse and offences committed against the child, and make appropriate recommendations, including those about legal processes to develop a child-friendly jurisprudence which will respond to the best interests of the child.
  - Study treaties and international instruments on child rights and make recommendations for their effective implementation.
  - Scrutinize, evaluate, and monitor steps taken by the government for the welfare of children and to recommend suitable measures for achieving the goals laid down in Part III and Part IV of the Constitution of India, the National Policy for children, and the National Plan of Action for Children.

[9] The Children's Code Bill 2000, Section 13.
[10] 'National Policy for Children' means the National Policy for Children, 1974, and would include any future amendments to it.

- Visit, under intimation to the State government or appropriate authority, any jail, lock-up, State home, or any other place of residence or institutions meant for children, under the control of the government or other authority, including institutions run by social organizations, where children are detained or lodged for purposes of treatment, reformation, or protection; to study the living conditions of the inmates and make recommendations thereon.
- Propose, evolve, promote, and help consolidate and multiply creative interventions, through collaboration and dynamic partnership between agencies of the State and voluntary organizations, in keeping with the social and cultural roots of the children.
- Intervene in any complaint/proceedings involving any allegation of violation of child rights pending before a court with the approval of such court.
- Identify all harmful and dehumanizing practices pertaining to the child, especially the girl child, whether within the family, the community, the educational institution, the place of work, or in any institution for children run by the State or the voluntary sector, and take appropriate action.
- Spread awareness of child rights and duties among various sections of society including children themselves, and the need to promote awareness of the safeguards available of these rights and inculcation of duties through publications, the media, seminars, and other available means; and such other functions as it may consider necessary for the promotion of child rights.

While inquiring into complaints under this Act, the Commission shall have all the powers as that of a civil court trying a suit under the Code of Civil Procedure 1908, and in particular in respect of the following matters, namely:[11] summoning and enforcing the attendance of witnesses and examining them upon oath; discovery and production of any document; receiving evidence on affidavits; requisitioning any public record or copy thereof from any court or office; issuing commissions for the examination of witnesses or documents and in any other matter which may be prescribed.

All proceedings before the Commission shall be deemed to be judicial proceedings within the meaning of Sections 193 and 228, and for the purposes of Section 196, of the Indian Penal Code, and the Commission shall be deemed to be a civil court for all the purposes of

---

[11] National Commission for Children, Draft Bill, 2001, Section 14.

Section 195 and Chapter XXVI of the Code of Criminal Procedure 1973.

- Procedure of the Commission

  The procedure to be followed by the Commission while inquiring into complaints as laid down in the code is as follows:[12]
  - The Commission, while inquiring into the complaints against offences against children or of violations of child rights, shall call for information or report from the Central government or any State government or any other authority or any subordinate organization within a specified time limit and if the information or report is not received within the time stipulated by the Commission, it may proceed to inquire into the complaint on its own.
  - Where the inquiry discloses commission of a violation of child rights of a serious nature and in contravention of provisions of law notified by the Commission or the Central government, it may:[13]
    † recommend to the government or the authority concerned the initiation of proceedings for prosecution or such other action as the Commission may deem fit against the person or persons concerned;
    † approach the Supreme Court or the High Court concerned for such directions, orders, or writs as that Court may deem necessary;
    † recommend to the government or authority concerned for the grant of such immediate relief to the victim or the members of his family as the Commission may consider necessary.

There is also a provision for the formation of State Commissions for Children to be constituted by the State governments on similar lines as the National Commission for Children.[14]

- Children's Courts

  The National Code Bill has provided for the formation of Children's Courts[15] for the purpose of providing speedy trial of offences against children or of violation of children's rights. For every Children's Court, the State government shall, by notification, specify a public prosecutor or appoint an advocate who has been in practice for not less than seven

---

[12] Children's Code Draft Bill 2000, Section 18.
[13] Children's Code Draft Bill 2000, Section 19.
[14] The Children's Code Draft Bill 2000, Section 21.
[15] The Children's Code Draft Bill 2000, Section 29, The National Commission for Children Bill 2001 (NCC).

years, as a special public prosecutor for the purpose of conducting cases in that Court.[16]

Revised Draft National Policy and Charter for Children 2001 (NPC 2001)

The National Policy for Children 1974 has become outdated as several social, political, economical, and global developments have taken place since 1974. The Draft National Policy and Charter for Children 2001 (NPC 2001) affirms that children's rights—economic, social, cultural, and civil are fundamental human rights and must be protected through combined action of the state, civil society, communities, and families in their obligations in fulfilling children's rights by inculcating a sense of values directed towards the same end through the maximum extent of its available resources.

The following rights have been laid down in the Draft National Policy and Charter for Children 2001.

RIGHT TO SURVIVAL

Under this right, in particular, the State and the community will undertake all appropriate measures to address the problems of infanticide and feticide, especially of the female child and all other emerging manifestations which deprive the girl child of her right to survival (Article 1, Draft National Policy and Charter for Children 2001).

RIGHT TO HEALTH

The State shall take measures to ensure that all children enjoy the highest attainable standard of health, and provide for preventive and curative facilities at all levels especially immunization and prevention of micronutrient deficiencies for all children. This right includes: primary health facilities and specialized care and treatment for all children of families below the poverty line; adequate prenatal and postnatal care for mothers along with immunization against preventable diseases; measures to provide for a national plan that will ensure that the mental health of all children is protected; and steps to ensure protection of children from all practices that are likely to harm the child's physical and mental health (Article 2, Draft NPC 2001).

RIGHT TO NUTRITION

The state shall take steps to provide all children from families below the poverty line with adequate supplementary nutrition and undertake adequate

---

[16] The Children's Code Bill 2000, Section 30, The National Commission for Children Bill 2001 (NCC).

measures for ensuring environmental sanitation and hygiene (Article 3, Draft NPC 2001).

Right to a Standard of Living

The State recognizes every child's right to a standard of living that fosters full development of the child's faculties. In order to ensure this, the State shall, in partnership with the community, prepare a social security policy for children, especially for abandoned children and street children, and provide them with infrastructural and material support by way of shelter, education, nutrition, and recreation (Article 4, Draft NPC 2001).

Right to Play and Leisure

The State and the community should recognize the right of all children to play and leisure and ensure means to provide for recreational facilities and services for children of all ages and social groups (Article 5, Draft NPC 2001).

Right to Early Childhood Care

The State shall, in partnership with the community, provide early childhood care for all children and encourage programmes which will stimulate and develop their physical and cognitive capacities and aim at providing a childcare centre in every village where infants and children of working mothers can be adequately cared for. The State will make special efforts to provide these facilities to children from Scheduled Castes/Scheduled Tribes and marginalized sections of society (Article 6, Draft NPC 2001).

Right to Education

The State recognizes the right to elementary education for all children. Education at the elementary level shall be provided free of cost and special incentives should be provided to ensure that children from disadvantaged social groups are enrolled and retained in school and participate in schooling. At the secondary level, the State shall provide access to education for all and provide supportive facilities for children from the disadvantaged groups. The State shall, in partnership with the community, ensure that all educational institutions function efficiently and are able to reach universal enrolment, universal retention, universal participation, and universal achievement. The right of all children to education in their mother tongue has been recognized under this article. The State shall formulate special programmes to spot, identify, encourage, and assist the gifted children for their development in the field of their excellence (Article 7, Draft NPC 2001).

Right to be Protected from Economic Exploitation

The State shall provide protection to children from economic exploitation and from performing tasks that are hazardous to their well-being. The State shall ensure that there is appropriate regulation of conditions of work in occupations and processes where children perform work of a non-hazardous nature and that the rights of the child are protected. The State shall move towards a total ban on all forms of child labour (Article 8, Draft NPC 2001).

Right to Protection

All children have a right to be protected against neglect, maltreatment, injury, trafficking, sexual and physical abuse of all kinds, corporal punishment, torture, exploitation, violence, and degrading treatment. The state shall take legal action against those committing such violations against children even if they be legal guardians of such children. The State shall, in partnership with the community, set up mechanisms for identification, reporting, referral, investigation, and follow-up of such acts, while respecting the dignity and privacy of the child (Article 9, Draft NPC 2001). The State shall take strict measures to ensure that children are not used in the conduct of any illegal activity, namely, trafficking of narcotic drugs and psychotropic substances, begging, prostitution, pornography, or armed conflicts. The State, in partnership with the community, shall ensure that such children are rescued and immediately placed under appropriate care and protection. The State and community shall also ensure protection of children during the occurrence of natural calamities (Article 10, Draft NPC 2001).

Right to Protection of the Girl Child

The State and the community shall ensure that offences committed against the girl child, including child marriage, forcing girls into prostitution and trafficking are speedily abolished. The State shall, in partnership with the community, undertake measures, including social, educational, and legal, to ensure that there is greater respect for the girl child in the family and society (Article 11, Draft NPC 2001).

Right of Adolescents to Education and Skill Development

The State and the community shall take all steps to provide the necessary education and skill to adolescent children so as to equip them to become economically productive citizens. Special programmes will be undertaken to improve the health and nutritional status of the adolescent girl. (Article 12, Draft NPC 2001).

Right to Equality

The State and the community shall ensure that all children are treated equally without discrimination on grounds of the child's or the child's parents' or legal guardian's race, colour, caste, sex, language, religion, political or other opinion, national, ethnic or social origin, disability, birth, political status, or any other consideration (Article 13, Draft NPC 2001).

Right to Life and Liberty, Name and Nationality

Every child has a right to life, liberty, and a name, and to acquire a nationality (Article 14, Draft NPC 2001).

Right to Freedom of Expression

All children shall be given every opportunity for all-round development of their personality, including creativity of expression (Article 15, Draft NPC 2001).

Right to Freedom to Seek and Receive Information

Every child shall have the freedom to seek and receive information and ideas. The state and the community shall provide opportunities for the child to access information that will contribute to the child's development (Article 16, Draft NPC 2001). The State and the community shall undertake special measures to ensure that the linguistic needs of children are taken care of, and encourage the production and dissemination of child-friendly information and material in various forms. The State and the community shall be responsible for formulating guidelines for the mass media in order to ensure that children are protected from material injurious to their well-being.

Right to Freedom of Association and Peaceful Assembly

All children enjoy freedom of association and peaceful assembly, subject to reasonable restrictions and in conformity with social and family values (Article 17, Draft NPC 2001).

Right to a Family

In case of separation of children from their families, the State shall ensure that priority is given to reuniting the child with the parents. In cases where the State perceives adverse impact of such a reunion, the State shall make alternative arrangements immediately, keeping in mind the best interests and the views of the child. All children have a right to maintain contact with their families, even when they are within the custody of the State for various reasons. The State shall undertake measures to ensure that children without families are either placed for adoption, preferably intra-country adoption, or foster care, or any other family substitute services. All children shall have the right to meet their parents and other family members who may be in custody (Article 18, Draft NPC 2001).

Responsibilities of the Parents

The State recognizes the common responsibilities of both parents in rearing the children (Article 19, Draft NPC 2001).

Rights of Refugee Children

The State shall ensure that all refugee children, with or without parents, receive due care and protection (Article 20, Draft NPC 2001).

Rights of Children with Disabilities

The State and the community recognize that all children with disabilities have a right to lead a full life with dignity and respect. All measures would be undertaken to ensure that children with disabilities are encouraged to be integrated into the mainstream society and actively participate in all walks of life (Article 21, Draft NPC 2001). State and community shall also provide for their education, training, health care, rehabilitation, and recreation in a manner that will contribute to their overall growth and development. State and community shall launch preventive programmes against disabilities and early detection of disabilities so as to ensure that the families with disabled children receive adequate support and assistance in bringing up their children. The State shall encourage research and development in the field of prevention, treatment, and rehabilitation of various forms of disabilities.

Rights of Children from Marginalized and Disadvantaged Communities

The State and the community shall respect the rights of children from all marginalized and disadvantaged communities, to preserve their identity, and will encourage them to adopt practices that promote the best interest of children in their communities (Articles 22 and 23, Draft NPC 2001).

Rights of Child Victims

The State shall, in partnership with the community, draw up plans for the identification and rehabilitation of child victims and ensure that they are able to recover, physically, socially, and psychologically, and reintegrate into society (Article 24, Draft NPC 2001).

Right to Child-Friendly Procedures

All matters and procedures relating to children, viz., judicial, administrative, educational, or social, should be child-friendly. All procedures laid down under the juvenile justice system for children in conflict with law and for children in need of special care and protection should also be child-friendly (Article 25, Draft NPC 2001).

Major Concerns and Obstacles in Realizing the Rights of the Child

A large number of children in India still live much below the standards set by the Constitution, national and international law. They suffer an array of threats to their development, well-being and survival. They suffer from poverty, diseases, famine, and war, and they also suffer from acts and omissions by their own caretakers, guardians, and parents. Primary education is far from universal. Over seventy-two million children in the age group of five to fourteen years in India are deprived of basic education and have no opportunity of going to school.[17] India continues to have the highest numbers of child labourers globally. There are thousands of child labourers, working in agriculture, animal husbandry, manufacturing, entertainment, and household work. They live below poverty line with insufficient food and shelter, and having no access to health care. There are an estimated 500,000 street children nationwide exposed to violence and exploitation.[18] The continued neglect of the environment in urban slums poses one of the greatest threats to progress on infant and child mortality and improving the nutritional status of children living in disadvantaged areas. According to the National Family Health Survey, India accounts for one-third of the world's children who suffer malnutrition.[19] In India, 15 per cent of children have serious emotional disturbances.[20] In addition, children are discriminated against because of their class, caste, or religion. There is no adoption law for children of other religious groups besides Hindus. The continuously declining sex ratio has been a major cause of concern among the socially conscious demographers and policy makers. Girls are consistently denied equal opportunities to attend and complete primary schooling. Hundreds and thousands of girls are trafficked and used for prostitution in brothels in cities. The

---

[17] UNESCO Report 2000.
[18] Achievements, Challenges, Aims and Strategies, UNICEF.
[19] Indian Express, 22 December 2000.
[20] World Health Report 2001.

phenomenon of sale of children is universal. Children are not only sold and exploited at national level but they are also trafficked across frontiers far and wide. Children are also victims of wars, riots, natural calamities, poverty trap and debt burdens, and globalization. An obstacle in realizing the rights of the child is the debt burden facing third-world countries like India. It is estimated that nearly 700 million people live in the forty-two heavily indebted countries. New technology, changing economic structures and policies need to be reviewed. Some of the major obstacles in realizing the rights of the child are described here:

Low Level of Awareness of Rights and Laws

The UN Committee on the Rights of the Child observed under para 24: In the light of Article 42, the Committee notes low level of awareness of the Convention amongst the general public, including children, and professionals working with children. The Committee is concerned that the State party is not undertaking adequate dissemination and awareness-raising activities in a systematic and targeted manner. The laws relating to children are not even known to law enforcement and implementation authorities. These laws do not form a part of the curriculum of several traditional law schools and police and judicial training.[21] In most cases, the deprived children do not even know that their rights are being violated, as they are not aware of their rights.

The Menace of HIV/AIDS

The HIV/AIDS pandemic has become an increasing threat to the life of children in India. It is a huge obstacle in the way of the child's right to survival and development. The access to basic social services, especially school and health care, is very difficult.

Child Sexual Abuse and Exploitation—Insensitive and Inadequate Legal Interventions

There is no comprehensive legislation on child sexual abuse. Definition of child abuse has many grey areas. The definition is not flexible enough to encompass a wide range of cultural contexts. There is no legal intervention to tackle detection and reporting of the phenomenon itself. In the last few years an increasing number of cases on child sexual abuse have been brought to light. The number of cases registered by the police has gradually increased. Children are often hired out or sold by their families. Some young girls are

---

[21] In the Maharashtra Judicial Officers Training Institute (JOTI), as per the orders of the Mumbai High Court in Criminal Writ Petition No 1107/1992, a two-day training programme on child rights has been introduced in the training courses since 2001.

deceived into fake marriages and sold in city brothels. The practices of rescue and rehabilitation of sex workers in India violate numerous human rights provisions of international law like the right to equality, right to freedom of movement and residence, right to development, right to physical and mental health, right to shelter and residence, and right to seek legal help. The child in prostitution is a victim of pedophiles who pose as tourists and of traffickers who force them into the flesh trade. Child prostitution is not simply a social crime that is led by supply but also a serious economic crime that is driven by demand.

Poor Care and Services for Disabled Children

There is a poor level of access to care and service for children with physical and mental disabilities. Disabled and abandoned children are in many instances put to work as beggars or they languish in remand homes with no special facilities for them.

The Concept of Legitimacy in Indian Laws

An area of concern is the perpetuation of the offensive term 'illegitimate' in the legal system in referring to a child born to parents not married to each other. An innocent child is still stigmatized by this reference. Statutes need to be amended to remove such age-old terms which are offensive in our present-day society.[22] The modern law has tried to improve the position of illegitimate children by raising their status to legitimate children in certain matters. But a vast majority of children still remain unaffected. 'To be designated as an illegitimate child in preadolescence is an emotional trauma of lasting consequence.'[23]

In Indian law, or in the personal law of any community of India, legitimization by subsequent marriage of parents is not recognized. All laws in India make a distinction between legitimacy and illegitimacy. The Hindu Marriage Act 1955 (as amended by the Marriage Laws (Amendment) Act 1976)[24] and the Special Marriage Act 1954 confers a status of legitimacy on the child of annulled, voidable, and void marriage.[25] But on such children an inferior status has been conferred in as much as it has been laid down that

[22] From Washington, Supreme Court Judge Charles Smith in *Guard v Beeston* (1997) 940 P. 2d 642, 668.

[23] *Mississippi Code of 1972* (as amended). From the Alaska Supreme Court in *BEB v BEB* (1999) 979, P. 2d 514, 517.

[24] Section 16, as amended by the Marriage Laws (Amendment) Act 1976. Before the amendment, the status of legitimacy could be conferred only on the children of those void marriages which were declared null and void.

[25] Section 26: the language of Section 16, Hindu Marriage Act 1955 and this section is identical.

such children can inherit the property of the parents alone, and of none else.[26] However children of bigamous Hindu marriages can inherit the property of their father (Section 16 HMA). Such a child cannot get any right to inherit the property of other parental relatives or be a 'coparcener'. This is done by the introduction of the doctrine of fiction in the Hindu Marriage Act 1955. On the other hand, a child born to a mother with whom the father has not gone through a form of marriage cannot inherit from him.

The Special Marriage Act (SMA) 1954 also recognizes the right of the children born of void marriages to inherit from both the parents (Section 26, SMA 1954). Parsi, Muslim, and Christian children, if illegitimate, cannot inherit from their father according to their personal laws. Section 21 of the Indian Divorce Act 1869 applicable to Christians, however, provides that children of such marriages shall be entitled to succeed to the estate of the parents only when the marriage is annulled (a) on the ground that another spouse was living at the time of the marriage but that the subsequent marriage was contracted in good faith and with full belief of the parties that such other spouse was dead, or (b) on the ground of insanity of any of the parties. Section 21 does not make any provision for the children when the marriage is annulled on any other ground, e.g. on the ground of the parties being within the degree of prohibited relationship or on the ground of any of the parties being idiot. When compared with the provisions of Section 16 of the Hindu Marriage Act 1955 or Section 26 of the Special Marriage Act 1954 the provisions of Section 21 of the Indian Divorce Act 1869 are obviously discriminatory and since the Indian Divorce Act 1869 applies to the parties solely on the ground of their professing Christian religion, the discrimination would appear to be based on religion and thus violative of Article 15 of the Constitution. Similarly, the provisions of Section 3 of the Parsi Marriage and Divorce Act 1939 thus appear to be much less comprehensive than the analogous provisions in Section 26 of the Special Marriage Act and Section 16 of the Hindu Marriage Act and would, therefore, result in denial of equality before the law and equal protection of the laws[27] to children of different religions.

Under the Muslim law a status of legitimacy may be conferred on a child by acknowledgement of paternity. The Muslim doctrine applies to cases where the legitimacy of a child is uncertain. If he is known to be an illegitimate child, the doctrine does not apply. In other words, it applies only to cases where either the fact or the exact time of the alleged marriages is a matter

---

[26] Proviso to Section 16, Hindu Marriage Act 1955.
[27] Paras Diwan, *Law of Adoption, Minority, Guardianship and Custody*, Universal Law Publishing Co. Pvt. Ltd., Delhi, 2000.

of uncertainty that is neither proved nor disproved.[28] It is required that the acknowledgment must be not merely as a child but as a legitimate child, the age of the child and the person acknowledging should be such as to admit being the father of the child, the child must not be known to be the child of another and the acknowledgement must not be repudiated by the child.[29]

Under the scheme of the Indian Succession Act 1925, illegitimate children cannot be deemed to be included within the ambit of the expressions used in describing the heirs of Class I of the Schedule to the said Act. These expressions have to be taken to refer to legitimate 'son' and 'daughter' born out of the union of a subsisting marriage. The Act does not expressly equate illegitimate children to legitimate children. In the matter of inheritance and succession under the Act, the two do not stand on par but stand apart. The Act in terms separates and distinguishes the two and excludes the illegitimate from any right to intestate succession except to the extent expressly enacted in the proviso to Section 3(1)(j) of the Act. For the purpose of succession to the property of a male Hindu dying intestate, the Hindu Succession Act 1956 clearly intends only a legitimate relationship with the father unlike with the mother with whom a special fictional legitimacy and consequent heritability flowing therefrom is established. This outdated concept of legitimacy as far as children are concerned should be abolished.

Child Labour

Child labour denies a child the 'right to childhood'. Any work done by children that harms them, exploits them either physically, mentally, or morally, or blocks their access to education can be termed as child labour. Domestic child workers are one of the most exploited children and they are also the most difficult to protect. Children who are even below ten work as domestics. They are victims of all kinds of exploitation. They are vulnerable to sexual exploitation and in many cases they are starved, beaten up, and tortured by the sadistic employers. It is a severe form of slavery. They are not included in the hazardous forms of child labour under the Child Labour (Prohibition and Regulation) Act 1986.

Institutionalization

In practice, institutions have become 'hostels' where children are being placed for food, clothing, shelter, and education due to inability of their parents

---

[28] Baillie 406; *Hedaya*, 439; *Md Allabad v Muhammad* (1888) 10 All 289.
[29] Baillie 408; *Hedaya*, 408; *Habibur Rehman v Altaf Ali* (1921) 48 IA 114.

to look after them. Such institutionalized children suffer from the 'Institutional Child Syndrome' and are victims of excessive routinization and regimentation, physical and sexual abuse and trauma, low self-esteem, segregation and isolation from society, and low education and skills. They do have difficulty in joining the mainstream and adjusting in society. Institutionalization seems to be the rule rather than an exception. Non-institutional and family-based alternatives are not adequate. Failure to secure a uniform law on adoption in spite of several attempts is a major setback. There are still disparities in the interpretation and implementation of adoption procedures which causes undue delays. The general impression is that legal adoption is time consuming and tedious. Unethical practice of buying and selling babies violates the child's dignity and sense of self-worth.

Child Custody

There does not seem to be any consideration of the concept of the best interest of child in lower courts. The records of the lower courts do not reveal the reasons why a particular order was given by a judge.[30] Children are 'dragged' in the courts dealing with matrimonial disputes as ancillary to the main matter. The trauma of the child in a matrimonial dispute is not considered. The child's interest needs to be represented and protected in such matters.

Violation of the Right to Survival

In cities like Mumbai, nearly 70 per cent of the population reside in slums and on pavements under the most difficult circumstances. These slum dwellers include children and they are constantly under the threat of forced eviction. Demolitions and forced evictions from homes disrupt the social structure of the child's life to survival including the right to shelter, nutrition, school, playground, and friends.

Child Marriages

There are still thousands of child marriages reported throughout the country. Early marriages are a form of child sexual abuse and a violation of a child's freedom to enjoy childhood. Child Marriages Restraint Act 1928 is very weak and dilatory and is not being implemented.

Child Witnesses

Under the prevailing Indian law, a child victim of sexual abuse or a witness of any crime is required to give evidence before the court in the presence of

---

[30] Asha Bajpai, Children and Courts, unpublished study supported by the Board of Research Studies, Tata Institute of Social Sciences, 2000.

the accused and face cross-examination of the prosecution Hearsay evidence is inadmissible under the present criminal justice system. Delay in prosecution and trials in cases involving children have a devastating effect on the child as it prolongs the child's trauma. There is secondary victimization of the child by the legal system.

Mental Health of Children

In India 15 per cent of children have serious emotional disturbances.[31] The facilities for healing are inadequate and majority of the children are never identified. The legal system has no provision to consider the mental health perspective or to deal with the trauma of children who come in contact with the system either as victims or as offenders.

Challenge of New Technology

The digital revolution, the global spread of computers and the Internet, the electronic revolution has made pornography more accessible to children. Statistics reveal that pedophiles (adults engaged in sexual crimes against children) have an access to the children through the means of Internet. Research has established that online pornography plays an accessory role in negative social issues such as child abuse, youth crime, promiscuity, and sexually transmitted diseases.[32]

Status of the Girl Child

Child marriages, amniocentesis, female feticide, child trafficking, child sexual exploitation and abuse, infant and maternal mortality rates, dowry demands and deaths, are all evils linked in some way or the other to the low status of the girl child in India. There appears to be an utter powerlessness of the girl child against the ideological onslaught of patriarchal forces perpetuated through customs and traditions, proverbs and myths, folklore and folk songs. In a culture that idolizes sons and dreads the birth of a daughter, the girl child suffers special disadvantages. Today the 'rejection' of the unwanted girl can begin even before her birth; prenatal sex determination tests followed by quick abortions eliminate thousands of female foetuses. This has led to the growing disparity between male and female infant mortality rates. It is a matter of deep concern that there is a decline in sex ratio of population in the 0–6 age group (called the child sex ratio) from 945 in 1991 to 927 in 2001. These 'unwanted' and 'unwelcome' girls are born in indifference and reared in neglect. A girl is likely to be breastfeed less often and for shorter

---

[31] World Health Organization Report, 2001.
[32] See http://netsafety.nic.in/internet.htm visited on 22 August 2002.

periods than a boy is. A number of studies indicate that in children under the age of five, girls suffer from malnutrition more often than boys do. Not only are more girls malnourished, the degree of their malnutrition is also greater. The root cause is not so much as the lack of food but as the lack of 'value' attached to the girl child. Eating less than her brother, a girl does twice as much work, not only at home but also in the fields. The temporary nature of the girl's membership in her family coupled with her low economic worth ensures a minimum investment in her development. The girl child's labour is as continuous as it is unrecognized, unpaid, and unrewarded. She is denied education and training and this denies her many basic skills or information that would equip her to earn a living wage or fight for her rights either within the home or outside it. Child marriages though prohibited by law are still prevalent. Although the family and the larger economic order exploit the labour of young children of both sexes in different ways, girls are worse off. Their work is either not visible enough or is accorded such low value that they are viewed merely as an economic liability. The girl child's status should be enhanced by empowering her through education and providing her with skills to make herself reliant and economically independent.

Poverty and Exclusion among Urban Children

Cities represent some of the most serious obstacles to children's development and the enjoyment of their rights. Children from cities face chronic poverty, marginalization, violence, and exploitation. They lack a secure home, access to health services, shelter, and education and have no space for play. They have to face air pollution, high noise levels, and difficulty in sleeping.[33]

Non-participation of Children

Unfortunately, children's participation at any level is considered least important in India. As a cultural practice children are always told to obey elders without questioning. Children are always told not to express their opinions in front of the elders. They are always told that they do not have the capacity to think on their own and they are not capable of taking any decision on their own. This culture also reflects in the education system. The same culture persists in the society where efforts to understand children's views even on the issues of their concern are never taken into consideration. Against a historical and cultural legacy of 'children being seen and not heard', children's voices have been unheard, silenced, ignored, or at best interpreted. Children and young people have been largely ignored as active participants in

[33] UNICEF, 'Poverty and Exclusion Among Urban Children', *Innocenti Digest*, No. 10, November 2002, Florence, Italy.

decision-making processes. However, in recent years evidence of children's 'invisibility in decision making processes' has begun to accumulate from different sectors of the world community.'[34] Such awareness is acting as a catalyst for change.

Non-enforcement of Laws

Legislation is one of the main weapons for empowering children and providing them with justice. If laws could guarantee their own enforcement there would never be any injustice. On paper there are laws and policies but there is a need for mechanisms and structures to ensure that the rights of the child do not remain on paper and get translated into action.

Lack of Coordination

Although community resources are available on the ground, the judiciary and the police are not aware of them as there is no coordination or sharing of information among government, law enforcers and implementers community, and civil society resources.

Action Plan and Strategies for Realizing the Rights of the Child

Eliminating the obstacles will help realize the rights of the child. The action plan has to be multifaceted and multidimensional and with diversity of approaches as the solutions are complex and deep-rooted. Several underlying issues need to be addressed, the child's perspective, context, and environment must be incorporated. There are several challenges ahead.

Awareness Campaigns

A campaign to promote awareness of the Convention, the constitutional provisions and the situation of children in India must be launched. The campaign should focus on information dissemination on child rights at the state and national levels. It should also demand the implementation of the commitments made by the Government of India. The campaign must undertake initiatives at national level through awareness building, networking, and child-centred policy advocacy, for building a conducive institutional environment wherein all the internationally agreed and accepted child rights are fully practised and promoted. One of the objectives of the campaign must be to mobilize public opinion for the protection and promotion of child rights through information dissemination, awareness, and

---

[34] Oxfam, 1985, Save the Children, 1995; Johnson, Hill and Ivan-Smith, 1995; Quortrup, 1996, Butler and Williamson, 1994.

sensitization activities. School children, children in institutions, law enforcers, teachers, doctors, lawmakers, policy planners should all be made aware of the rights of the child.

Enactment of Legislation and Law Reform

Legislation is one of the main weapons for empowering children and providing them with justice. The Indian legal system has to evolve a great deal in securing the rights of the child. Firstly there has to be some synchronization of the upper age limit for childhood if the rights of childhood have to be realized. The Convention on the Rights of the Child creates, for the first time, a balanced and clearly articulated framework for determining the rights that a child has under international law. Even with its inherent problem of enforcement, the Convention can be a catalyst for legal reform since it sets out the rights a child should be able to claim at some point in the national legal system. This multilateral treaty has given a new dimension to the concept of child rights that must be appreciated at the national level if domestic legal systems are to incorporate this holistic perception of rights. The criticism in South Asia that legal systems are irrelevant to social problems results from the practice of engaging in ad hoc law reform without any attention to creating adequate support systems for implementation. The balanced and holistic approach to child rights in the Convention encourages law reform to be integrated with basic changes in government policy and other initiatives, so that there is a concerted effort to impact on social practice and the lives of citizens.[35] Any reform in law should be strategic and aimed at systemic change.

Amendments to the Draft National Commission of Children Bill and National Policy for Children

There has to be an agreed policy framework for children. Formulation of civil codes is also essential as standards can be set in respect of children based on international standards. The NCC Bill is based on the National Policy for Children of 1974, which is outdated. Activists are completely rejecting the draft National Policy 2001 as it seems to be a mechanical 'cut and paste' job from the United Nations Convention on the Rights of the Child (UN CRC). The policy does not lay down directions either for legal reforms or for programme content. It seems to be without a definite action plan, timeframes, and targets. The very meaning of 'child rights' adopted in the NCC Bill is inadequate as it includes only the rights elaborated in the CRC and

---

[35] Savitri Goonesekere, *Children, Law and Justice: A South Asian Perspective*, UNICEF, Sage Publication, New Delhi, 1998, pp. 92–3.

the Constitution of India and does not include the several landmark judgments of the Supreme Court and the High Courts which expanded child rights in this country.

The main weakness of the proposed National Commission for Children is that it is structured on the lines of other statutory Commissions, such as the National Human Rights Commission (NHRC) and the National Commission for Women (NCW) whose directives are only recommendatory in nature and the bodies lack any powers to enforce their own recommendations. The implication is that the Commission can call for records, summon, and record evidence and submit its report to the government. But if the government refuses to send a report or appear before it, there is nothing that the Commission can do except chastise the government. It has been noted that even the strictures and awards of compensation by the NHRC are only recommendatory and very rarely have its directions ever been carried out by the State governments.

Further, the same bureaucracy and police who are often the main violators and abusers of children's rights conduct the inspections, inquiries and investigations. Very often, inspections and inquiries are reduced to 'calling for reports' from Central or State agencies and if the Commission is satisfied 'either that no further inquiry is required or that the required action has been initiated or taken by the concerned government or authority, it may not proceed with the complaint and inform the complainant accordingly'. It is not obliged to hear the versions of all concerned, such as the child, children's groups, parents, others in the community, etc. The inquiries should be carried out by trained and sensitized investigators, either by the commission's own investigators or by an independent body with persons from civil society as members, who may be assisted by a government official.

There is no prescribed time frame within which the NCC should initiate enquiries upon receiving complaints and also complete enquiries and investigations.

There is a need to include the provision for mandatory enforcement of the orders of the Commission and the Commission should be given powers to initiate contempt proceedings against those not complying with its orders within a time frame.

There is also no time frame within which State governments are to compulsorily set up State Commissions for children. Also, the word 'may' instead of 'shall' for setting up the State Commissions will mean that this bill will go the way of the NHRC Act under which State Human Rights Commissions are yet to be set up. The bill also does not define the roles, responsibility and jurisdiction between the National Commission and the State

Commissions, with respect to one another. There should be some coordination or linkages between the National and State Commissions

The proposed NCC Bill also allows the Commission to visit, 'under intimation to the State government' any institution meant for children under the control of the government . . . to study the living conditions of the children there. The prior intimation to the State government to inspect a State institution is not going to serve the purpose. Surprise inspections should be allowed, not merely to study living conditions, but to investigate into cases of child abuse, both physical and sexual, which occur all too frequently in such institutions. The views of the children in institutions should also be taken into consideration during these inspections. The inspections should be on the standards of quality care in the institutions and should be done with the participation of the children in institutions.

Retired judges of the Supreme Court and High Courts who are to head the National and the State Commissions should have a proven record of promoting child rights and that all other members should also have at least five years experience in the field of child rights

There is no provision for any form of participation by children in the NCC Bill. This is not in conformity with the CRC's right to participation. Some activists have suggested that there should be an 'advisory body' of children (consultative body may be more appropriate) whose opinions are taken and valued before any decisions or actions are taken by the NCC.[36]

The mode of appointment of the members of the Commission in the draft Bill is through a panel consisting of politicians alone, including the prime minister, speaker, home minister, leaders of the Opposition in both houses, etc. This generally leads to political appointments. An expert panel of child rights activists and professionals should make the appointments.

The NCC should be so structured at Central, State, district, *taluka*, and *panchayat* levels that anyone, even a child or children's group, should have access to it and be able to interact and influence its functioning right from the *panchayat* level upwards.

Special courts for children, and not merely designated courts that function as children's courts, should be set up at taluka level, possibly as mobile courts, so that children and others can easily access them for settling cases. Children now have to travel long distances to reach courts. Mobile Children's Courts will give them greater access to justice.

Adequate funds should be exclusively earmarked for the activities of the Commission and 75 to 80 per cent of the funds should be used for its

[36] HRARF and the CRY consultations.

activities. Expenditure administration, salaries, and establishment should be less than 25 per cent.*

Amendment to the Child Labour (Prohibition and Regulation) Act 1986

CHILD LABOUR

The UN Committee on the Rights of the Child in it concluding observations, in the twenty-third session recommended under para 67 that the Child Labour (Prohibition and Regulation) Act 1986, should be amended so that household enterprises, government schools and training centres are no longer exempt from prohibitions on employing children and coverage is expanded to include agriculture and other informal sectors. The Act should also address issues related to rehabilitation, education, and family income generation schemes. There should be stricter law enforcement in the cases of child labour with more incentives for exemplary enforcement personnel. Besides, there is a need for a legislative ban on employment of children below a certain age. The invisible hidden child labour in the unorganized informal sector should be brought within the purview of the Act. This includes such activities as domestic work and agricultural employment. More emphasis should be laid to the plight of domestic child labour. Domestic child labour should be brought immediately within the list of prohibited occupations in the Child Labour (Prohibition and Regulation) Act 1986 and recognized as a hazardous form of child labour. A mandatory registration of the child domestic worker and the employers, development of helplines and outreach programmes is required to protect the child domestic workers. There is need for legislation that will protect their rights. Illegal or undocumented child labourers should get greater protection. The Government of India should ratify the International Labour Organizations Convention 182 concerning the prohibition and immediate action for the elimination of the worst forms of child labour.[37] The Government should also ensure compliance of the Supreme Court ruling on child labour. The district-level vigilance committees should be strengthened to identify and eliminate bonded child labour. The provision mentioned in the education policies, if implemented, will reduce children dropping out of schools and becoming child labourers. There should be stricter law enforcement in the cases of child labour with more incentives for exemplary enforcement personnel. The Factories Act should be amended to cover all factories or workshops

[37] AIR 1997 SC 699.

employing child labour. The 'Beedi Act' should be amended so that exemptions for household-based production are eliminated. Employers should be required to have, and produce on demand; proof of age of all children working on their premises. Our national government has projected the National Child Labour Programme (NCLP) as a major instrument and flagship programme for the elimination of child labour system. However, the experience so far shows that NCLP itself needs a substantial modification and upscaling to be able to make any significant change in child labour situation in the country.

Law Reform for Juvenile Justice

The concept of juvenile justice is composed of two important ideas, namely fairness or justness to children and an alternative justice system. A new Juvenile Justice (Care and Protection of Children) Act 2000 has been passed. The Act needs amendments. This new Act should include procedural guarantees such as right to counsel, right to speedy disposal of cases, and right to child-friendly proceedings. In most of the advanced countries, one of the most resorted to dispositional alternative is the compulsory education order. This alternative has to be incorporated under the Act. Children must be allowed to participate in the running of the homes. The education of these children should be in keeping with the market trends. The inspection of the institutions should be carried out with some special issues in mind. Inspections should consider quality care standards and view of children. Homosexual behaviour is largely common in institutions, older ones molesting some younger children. The staff of some institutions also abuse the resident children. The Juvenile Justice Act 2000 should provide for complaints and prosecution mechanisms for cases of custodial abuse of children. These mechanisms should be constituted along the lines described in the National Police Commissions recommendations. Complaints against law enforcement personnel should be promptly and thoroughly investigated. Such an agency should be directly accessible to all children, especially the street children, who are generally the victims of police abuse. There should be compensation provided for children who have been victims of custodial and institutional abuse, as per the Supreme Court decision in the case of *Nilabatti Behara v State of Orissa*.[38] Government schemes relating to child development, education, and child labour should reach the children in institutions. Recruitment and personnel policies of the staff in these homes need to be

[38] AIR 1993 SC.

immediately reviewed so that committed and sensitized people are involved in looking after children.

Non-institutionalization

The traditional approach of custodial care in an institution is undergoing a change and all child welfare activities must try and ensure that the physical, social, emotional, and educational needs of the child are met in a secure, nurturing family environment. The emphasis in future should be on non-institutionalization and improving the quality of childcare in residential institutions, ensuring participation of children and simultaneously developing family-based alternatives. There should be a genuine attempt to develop a consolidated and comprehensive package of the various schemes and grants of the various Ministries to develop non-institutional services and prevent institutionalization so that more and more children are rehabilitated through family-based alternatives. The family should be strengthened as a unit to prevent family disintegration and institutionalization of the child. The right to family and home would include the right to shelter.

Organizations working with children in need of care and protection and with families at risk should expand their activities to initiate preventive, community-based, family-oriented, non-institutional services for the vulnerable child. There should be uniform social and legal practices governing adoption throughout the country. A uniform law on adoption needs to be secured so that the children of all religious communities can be adopted.

New Laws Relating to Child Sexual Abuse and Exploitation

Procedural innovations, such as the exceptions to the rule of hearsay, use of expert testimony, mandatory reporting laws, delayed discovery statute, expeditious hearings, and appointment of guardian *ad litem* need to be introduced. Recommendations of the 172 Law Commission Report of the Ministry of law, justice, and company affairs should be accepted and the Indian Penal Code, Indian Evidence Act, and the Criminal Procedure Code should be accordingly amended to ensure successful prosecution in cases of child sexual abuse and to protect the best interest of the child. Advocacy and lobbying should continue for further amendments and recommendations.

Child prostitution has to be a priority concern. Rehabilitation is very important to children rescued from the trade. A more critical area is the formulation of a well-thought-out policy that would clearly focus on prevention of child postitution. The problem of child prostitution has to be addressed not merely through rehabilitation but with greater emphasis on prevention. There are backward villages and districts that are the source areas for traffickers. The brothels in the cities are a symptom of that problem. NGOs working towards rural development should target such poor families that are forced to send their children to earn. The poverty alleviation and development programmes should target such families that are at risk.[39] It is necessary that integration be established between various agencies, NGOs at the grass roots and state/city-level NGO networks to ensure a substantial impact on the problems of children in prostitution.

To address the issue of trafficking, the Immoral Traffic (Prevention) Act 1956, needs to be examined in order to curb child prostitution and strengthen law enforcement mechanism as well, as to increase rehabilitation and reintegration schemes. There is a need for development of bilateral and interstate control and reintegration and advocacy programmes to prevent the exploitation of children in forced prostitution and trafficking. Immediate steps should be taken to enforce extraterritorial laws and initiate appropriate action to ensure that no offending foreign tourist escapes punishment by leaving the country. Appropriate legislation be immediately initiated to make sexual abuse and commercial sexual exploitation of children a very serious crime and to impose very severe and deterrent punishment on the offenders, both Indian and foreign. The laws should be gender-neutral and ensure that procedures are simplified and child-friendly, responses are appropriate, timely, and sensitive to victims. There should be victim support services to protect the victims from discrimination and reprisals and also to protect those who expose violations and vigorously pursue enforcement. A mechanism to monitor implementation and enforcement should be laid down. In case of sex tourism, extradition and other arrangements must be promoted to ensure that a person who exploits a child for sexual purposes in another country (the destination country) is prosecuted either in the country of origin or in the destination country. There should be a provision for confiscation or seizure of assets and profits and other sanctions against those who commit sexual crimes against children in destination countries. Relevant sharing of data should be there among different countries.

Custody and Guardianship

In custody battles between parents the trauma of the child has to be taken into consideration. It is absolutely necessary that experienced and able judges preside over custody and guardianship disputes. They should be

---

[39] Gerry Pinto, Agenda for the NGOs, presentation at the National Consultation on Child Prostitution November 18-20, 1995, New Delhi, organized by YMCA, ECPAT and UNICEF.

trained in handling such sensitive matters and be child-friendly. Besides the judges, the other staff and personnel of the courts should also be sensitized to be child-friendly.

Education Law Reform

This fundamental human right has to be addressed as this would give children hope for the future and skills to ensure that they have options in life besides living on streets, labouring under exploitative, hazardous, or abusive conditions, or a life of crime. Education is an enabling right that contributes to opening the space for the fulfilment of all other rights—to health, nutrition, leisure, and participation. Many human rights can only be accessed through education which operates as a multiplier enhancing the enjoyment of all individual rights and freedoms.[40] Education has to be made accessible, flexible, and innovative. High priority must be given to the quality and relevance of curricula and teaching styles of primary education. Secondly, it is the families who decide whether or not to send their children to school and the education system should be supported by national programmes that provide resources for incentives, income generation and other means that enable families to value, demand and benefit from education for their children. Women's educational level is one of the most significant variables affecting maternal mortality rates. Mother's education is an important predictor of children's educational attainment. This is especially so for the girl children's educational opportunities. A mother with even a few years of formal education is considerably more likely to send her children to school. Research in many countries indicates that each additional year of formal education completed by a mother translates into her children remaining in school for an additional one-third to one-half year.[41] Nearly 56 per cent women are unlettered in India. Only 43.6 per cent girl children are taking admission in primary schools. The dropout rate has been higher for girls. It was 42.3 per cent for Classes I–V and 58 per cent for Classes I–VIII in 1999–00.[42] Macro-policies aimed at increasing access and enrolment in general, including universal primary education policies, compulsory education, and the encouragement of private religious bodies and NGOs in educational provision, all clearly contribute to increasing school enrolment including those of girls. However, experience shows that more gender-

[40] Katarina Tomasevski, The Right to Education—a discussion source: International Development Corporation Agency www.sida.org.
[41] Advocacy Internet Vol. 4, issue no. 03, May–June 2002, Online at www.ncasindia.org.
[42] Planning Commission of India, 2001.

specific policies often need to be promoted at the national level, including those which support initiatives such as open admissions, automatic promotions, and flexible school scheduling and examination systems. There is an urgent need to introduce health education.

The ninety-third Constitutional amendment has been passed to make education a fundamental right. The mere passing of the amendment does not by itself ensure that millions of children would get education automatically. Every State will now have to enact a comprenensiove law to implement the provision in the amendment. There is now a need for a strong political will and commitment to ensure provision of free, equitable, and quality education for all children All resources that are necessary to achieve this right to education should be allocated from the Consolidated Fund of the Union and the states. Accountability should be assigned to designated officers to enforce this right.

Amendment to the Child Marriage Restraint Act 1929

The Act should be amended and made more stringent. Registration of marriages should be made compulsory. The enforcement of this law should be taken up on a priority scale. Medical and community facilities are to be provided to help children and their families. Emphasis should be placed on family-based and community-based rehabilitation rather than state institutionalization. Such marriages are prejudicial to the developmental needs of very young parents and their children. A change in the legal value system on the age of marriage must also be reflected in the age for expression of sexual consent in the laws regulating rape and other sexual offences.[43] This will require reform in the penal codes as well.

Children Affected and Infected by HIV/AIDS

HIV/AIDS should be included in Reproductive Child Health Programmes. Rehabilitation options should be worked out through child-centred policies, special support programmes, and placement of affected children in adoptive homes and acceptance by children's homes. HIV/AIDS should be viewed in the context of total quality of health, education, care, and support services. Knowledge is power over AIDS. AIDS awareness programmes must be undertaken on a massive scale.

Children with Disabilities

More institutions should be set up or the capacity increased in the existing institutions for the education and rehabilitation of children with disabilities

---

[43] Savitri Goonsekere, *Children, Law and Justice: A South Asian Perspective*, Sage Publications, India, 1998.

and to improve access to services for those children living in homes and rural areas. Awareness campaigns, which focus on prevention, inclusive of education, family care, and promotion of the rights of children with disabilities, need to be undertaken. The carers who have to look after disabled children should be given special assistance in terms of financial support and their right to employment.

Improving the Status of the Girl Child

A holistic approach is required in improving the girl child's overall status. Extending the reach of the health and education infrastructure—both quantitatively and qualitatively—and deploying the media wisely are essential if we are to create a climate in which girls can develop to their full potential. The ICDS network is clearly one effective response to the problem of early neglect of the girl child. Through its immunization, nutritional supplementation, and pre-school education components, it can offset the discrimination girl faces at home and can lay the foundation for healthy physical and mental development. It is also necessary to enlarge the scope of the ICDS to address the needs of the 6–14 years children. This is an important period in a girl's life when major biological, psychological, and social changes take place and the girl child is seriously affected by the absence of suitable legislative protection. The girl child has hardly any time to play or to be a child. She requires freedom from domestic drudgery and in many cases freedom from the tyranny of her family. She requires both physical and mental solace to grow. Laws must be enacted to ensure provision of crèches and *balwadis* in the countryside where women work on land. Medical services and welfare services must be expanded. As with the right to be born, their right to remain alive can only be enforced if parents, family, and society at large value their daughters.

Right to Participation

Participation of children has been described as the present-day 'buzzword'.[44] Human rights instruments on children's rights stress 'participation' as a core value along with survival, protection, and development. The concept of participation rights involves a value system on the child's personal autonomy that has to be worked out within the important relationship with the child, the parents, and the state. Participation rights require the recognition of many civil rights already incorporated into national Constitutions. Since participation rights give a new priority to constitutionally guaranteed civil

---

[44] Hank Van Beers, 'A Plea for a Child-Centred Approach to Research and Street Children, *Childhood*, Vol. 3, No. 2, 1996, pp. 90–105.

rights, the Convention can help to strengthen the enforcement of these rights and foster perception that children must have these rights.

These rights reflect a growing awareness of the need to listen to children's views, and to facilitate their participation in decisions which affect them. In recent years there have been significant developments in national and international policies in relation to children and young people. National laws in Norway and the United Kingdom, which also had their roots in a strong concept of parental rights, have already articulated this change in new legal concepts. Children are no longer seen merely as recipients of adult care and protection, but are recognized as actors in their own lives, as individuals whose views and options should be exposed and seriously listened to. Article 12[45] of the United Nations Convention on the Rights of the Child 1989 clearly establishes that the children have a right to be involved in decisions which affect them.

This right extends from decisions affecting them as individuals to decisions which affect them as a body. Yet making a reality of children's participation presents an enormous challenge to society. Participation rights may be the most difficult to recognize because they can be perceived as a challenge to parental and state authority. There is now a recognition that children's participation creates a new challenge for social development (Save the Children Alliance 1995).

Children who participate effectively will be aware of societal processes, their rights and responsibilities, will be sensitive towards rights violations of others in the society, will develop capacity to think, question, and judge and will accordingly be prepared to take action for bringing about change in the society. This will facilitate a process of empowerment of the child's mind. There should be programmes aiming at empowering children through creating awareness about children's rights and responsibilities in relation to their environment. *Meljol* is a programme in Mumbai on child participation. *Meljol* believes that child participation will lead to a child-friendly society. To address this issue, *Meljol* has come out with a series of interactive and child-friendly programmes like Aflatoon value education books which emphasize the concept of learning through doing. These programmes aim at empowering children through creating awareness about children's rights and responsibilities in relation to their environment. In *Meljol Aflatoon* clubs children themselves take up various issues—imparting these programmes with the help of teachers, making teaching-learning process more interactive through these programmes, and trying to integrate these programmes into

---

[45] CRC Article 12.

the regular education system for the benefit of all. The Aflatoon programmes in twelve municipal schools that reaches out to 14,000 children across Mumbai are an example of children's participation. These children belong to the lowest socio-economic strata of Mumbai, residing mostly in slums and low-cost housing colonies. These children work against addictions like *gutkha*, alcohol, etc., and other social evils.[46] Bal Sansad, (Children's Parliament), Bal Melas (Children's fair), Panchayat Toofan,[47] Shishu Panchayt,[48] and Bal Mazdoor Unions (Child Workers' Unions) are all examples of children's participation.

The Committee on the Rights of the Child recommended that India should develop skills-training programme in community settings for teachers, social workers, and for local officials in assisting children to make and express their informed decisions and to have these views taken into consideration.

Child Witness Code

Testimony from children is often essential to prove that abuse occurred, to identify the perpetrator of abuse, and to prove other crimes. Thus children often have to testify in legal proceedings. The courtrooms in India are not designed with children in mind and the formal nature of proceedings that occur there cause fear and anxiety that interferes with some children's ability to provide full and accurate testimony. Testifying in courts also is very stressful for many children. A child witness code is required to ascertain the truth, reduce trauma to children, create conditions that will allow children to provide reliable and complete evidence, increase the number of children who are able to testify in legal proceedings, and also to protect the rights of persons accused of crimes.

Role of Courts

Courts can play a very important role in promoting the rights of children. Public interest litigation has been used beneficially to realize the protection rights of children. Courts have ensured the implementation of progressive

---

[46] V. Mahabale, *Right to Participation—An Experience by Meljol*, A Paper for the Maharashtra State-Level Workshop on the Convention on the Rights of the Child, 18–19 January 2001.

[47] A programme that is promoted by The Concerned for Working Children, an NGO in Karnataka, in collaboration with Panchayati Raj Institutions.

[48] Children's Village Level Committee assessed the situation of children in their village by interacting with other children and adults in their village. The Committee worked out a list of priorities and presented them to the adult *Panchayat* in the village and insisted on the compliance of these priorities.

laws and interpretation of restrictive laws in the best interest of the child. Courts have used innovative methods to ensure justice to the child. In the Bhiwandi remand home case in Mumbai,[49] the courts permitted the inspection of institutions and then formulated an expert committee to visit all the children's institutions in Maharashtra and submit a report. A Committee has been formed to monitor institution. In another matter relating to custody, the judge played an important role in putting the child at ease. A Division Bench of the Mumbai High Court comprising Justice A.P. Shah and Justice J.A. Patil also gave directions for incorporating training programmes on child rights for judicial officers of the State of Maharashtra. A child-centred approach stimulated by the standards of the Constitution and CRC can help create spaces for providing justice to the child even within the constraints of the existing laws and to promote the realization of the rights.

Representation of the Child's Interest in Courts

The child's future is at stake but his/her interests are never separately represented in Indian courts. The child's interests are considered to coincide with the parents or as the court thinks fit relying on the probation or welfare officer's report, or counsellor's report. There is a need to introduce the concept of guardian *ad litem* or child's legal counsel or a child's representative, involved throughout the court proceedings in which children are involved. This is especially required as child-friendly court procedures and personnel have yet to be evolved. To protect the children best, independent child advocates must be appointed by the courts. These advocates will not only represent the children but also hear their problems and concerns, work with their families, and prepare them for the court proceedings. Because child's own interests may be in conflict with the courts' judgment, specially trained child advocates are required to play the roles of fact finder, legal representative, case monitor, mediator, and information and resource persons.

Legal Aid and Services

Under Section 12(c) of the Legal Services Authorities Act 1987, a child who has to file or defend a case shall be entitled to free legal services. Legal aid and legal literacy programmes can be used to further childrens' rights. These programmes need to be linked to community awareness programmes Legal counselling could be included in these programmes. Clinical legal education programmes focusing on children's issues need to be developed in law schools. Law school curriculums should also include child rights and laws.

---

[49] *Krist Pereira v State of Maharashtra and Others*, Criminal Writ Petition No. 1107/1996.

Non-formal dispute resolutions like *Lok Adalats* could also be used to settle disputes involving children in a manner which is informal and which has a non-adversarial environment. The *Panchayati Raj* institutions can be involved in these services. These programmes could also involve paralegal training programmes among adult social workers.

There is scope for NGOs to play a role as paralegal professionals in juvenile justice boards, child welfare committees, and to assist specific groups such as street children, child labourers, disabled children, etc.

Enforcement of International Law

International human rights treaties, conventions, covenants, and declarations are powerful tools to realize the rights of the child. India has ratified the United Nations Convention on the Rights of the Child. Article 73 of the Constitution of India states, 'Subject to the provisions of the Constitution, the executive power of the Union, shall extend—

- to the matters with respect to which Parliament has power to make laws; and
- to the exercise of such rights, authority and jurisdiction as are exercisable by the Government of India by virtue of any treaty or agreement. . . .' This power covers the Conventions ratified by the country or any decision made at any international conference, association or other body.

Therefore, international conventions like the CRC can be enforced in Indian courts without a statute. This was clearly laid down in the case of *Mayanbhai Ishwarlal Patel v Union of India*.[50] Again in the case of *Vishaka v State of Rajasthan*[51] the Supreme Court reiterated the principle that in the absence of a domestic law the contents of international conventions and norms are significant for the interpretation of fundamental rights. Any international convention consistent with the fundamental rights and in harmony with its spirit must be read into the provisions of the convention. Therefore, the provisions of the Convention on the Rights of the Child which India has ratified can be enforced without a statute if they are in consonance with the fundamental rights.

Role of Media

The work of the media affects children's lives. It influences decisions made about them and the way in which they are regarded by the rest of the society. The media can inform the public about child rights, draw attention to

[50] AIR 1969 SC 783.
[51] (1997) 7 SCC 323.

violations, give children a voice, expose shortcomings in the system, highlighting the achievements of children—their aspirations and the risks they face. The media has a responsibility to ensure that children are not inadvertently exposed while reporting on them. In the context of HIV/AIDS, this right is crucial to prevent children from discrimination. The functions of the media should be to inform, to educate, and to entertain in that order.

Community Participation

Protecting children is as much a part of community responsibility as that of the system. Community participation could be included in the areas of decision making, priority setting, planning, implementation, services delivery system, evaluation of programmes, consolidation of benefits of development, and sharing of financial responsibility.

Role of NGOS

NGOs have significant roles and crucial tasks in the struggle for the realization of the rights of children and in elaboration and further development of the standards and rights affirmed by the national and international laws, developing more effective implementation by monitoring resource allocation, child development programmes and projects and undertaking evaluation thereof, helping develop participatory, community-level structures for delivering resources and services to meet the basic needs of children. Advocacy and lobbying will also be necessary in support of proposals for law reform and standard setting. Rights are of limited value unless they can be effectively asserted. NGOs have an important role to ensure effective assertion of rights. The Mathura rape case involving the rape of a girl in custody led to the reform in rape laws. Additional tasks include critiquing national reports prepared by governments and, where appropriate, preparing alternative NGO reports on the subject. NGOs will also have to play important roles to ensure effective assertion of the rights of the child. At the regional level NGOs will also need to explore ways of using regional human rights machinery and instruments to address regional specificities and disparities and developing regional positions and strategies regarding issues relating to children.[52] At the international level, NGOs' vital role will include identifying specific areas for international cooperation and technical assistance to realize the rights of the child. The challenge for child rights NGOs lies in applying a participatory empowerment approach to the development of the rights of the child.

[52] Clarence Dias, *The Child in the Developing World: Making Child Rights a Reality*, Report of the Seminar on Rights of the Child, sponsored by National Law School of India University and UNICEF, NLSIU, Bangalore, 1990.

Training, Sensitization, and Capacity Building

It is an important part of the strategy to protect the rights of the child. Effective child protection and development depend on skills, knowledge, and judgment of all professionals, personnel, and staff working with children. It is important that people in direct contact with children receive training to raise their awareness of the issues and concerns of laws and rights relating to children. The various agencies involved in the childcare system need to be trained to protect the interests of the child. The Juvenile Justice Boards and Child Welfare Committee members, the bar, school teachers, government officials from various ministries like the Ministry of Human Resources, Development, Department of Women and Child Development, Ministries of labour, finance, social justice and empowerment, and the Planning Commission. The functionaries of the children's institutions including the superintendents, the probation officers, the caretakers, cooks, teachers, and medical officers, all need to receive training to sensitize and humanize them. Bureaucracy needs to be sensitized. Training of law-enforcing agencies, police, judiciary, lawyers, doctors and paramedics, and NGOs is necessary. The police force needs to be trained to handle the needs of child victims which requires awareness of law, methodologies of handling child victims, administration, and reaching out to NGOs. Border police, registration officials, visa and passport and immigration authorities should all be provided with detailed guidelines to deal with children. Railway police and authorities should be sensitized, including all senior government servants, and IAS and IPS officers for empathy building and replacing hostile attitudes.

Determination of Best Interest of the Child

This principle applies not only to courts but also in all decisions relating to children including parents, local and administrative authorities, and children themselves. To determine the best interest of the child the least detrimental solution must be found. Considerations must be weighed against each other. The best interest of the child should be a paramount consideration in anything related to the child. Today, the best principle universally applies not only in the context of legal and administrative proceedings or in other narrowly defined contexts of custody and guardianship in family law but in relation to all actions concerning children.

Working Together Approach

The 250-plus legislations relating to children have to be harmonized and interlinked. For instance, the Juvenile Justice (Care and Protection of Children) Act 2000 need to be linked to the Probation of Offenders Act 1958, the

Orphanages and Other Charitable Homes (Supervision and Control) Act 1960, the Child Labour (Prohibition and Regulation) Act 1986, the Primary Education Acts, the Adoption laws, the Child Marriage Restraint Act 1929, and the Persons with Disabilities (Equal Opportunities, Protection of Rights and Full Participation) Act 1995. The different ministries dealing with different issues and concerns of children have to work in coordination. The ministries of labour, social justice and empowerment, finance, and human resources development deal with different legislations. Each of these legislations cannot work in isolation. Multidisciplinary and interdisciplinary teams and partnerships have to work together. A partnership between many actors and stakeholders can work together to realize the rights of the child. The judiciary, different ministries, bureaucrats, medical professionals,

Figure 9.1: Working Together Approach

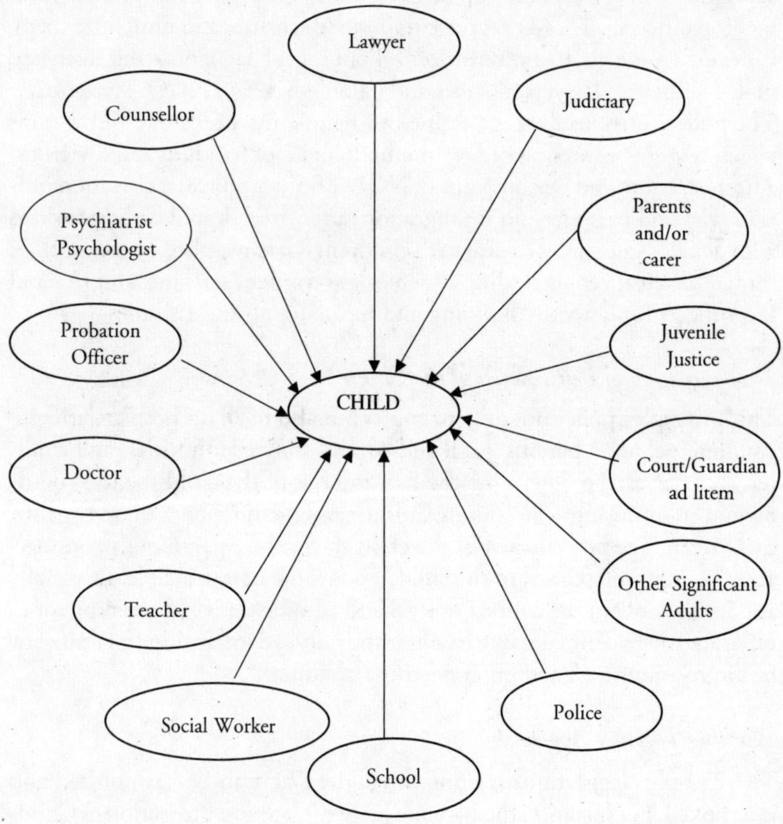

agencies and NGOs, legal activists, police, teachers, lawyers, counsellors, parents, mental health professionals and all those citizens who are concerned with the rights of the child need to have a coordinated and a partnership approach. Figure 9.1 in previous page depicts a graphic presentation of the Working Together Approach for the protection of child rights.

Monitoring Bodies and Ombudsperson

Passing of orders by the courts or child-friendly laws is not the end of the matter. These laws and orders have to be monitored and violators held accountable. Directions of the courts should not remain on paper as far as children are concerned. For compliance of court orders, the Mumbai High Court, in the case of *Krist Pereira v State of Maharashtra and Others*,[53] constituted a permanent body called the Maharashtra State Monitoring Committee consisting of a retired judge of the High Court, two secretaries including the secretary of women and child development, and three experts in the field out of whom two should be female members. The Committee makes appropriate recommendations to the State government for proper functioning of the juvenile justice system. In *Prerana v State of Maharashtra*,[54] the court constituted a Monitoring and Guidance Committee under the deputy secretary, women and child development, and whose members consist of representatives of non-governmental organizations specializing in different fields. The Committee has been authorized to supervise the functioning of the rehabilitation home and ensure proper rehabilitation of the rescued girls. This is one of the effective methods of implementing court orders. Besides, there are legislations wherein there are provisions for monitoring bodies, boards of control, and advisory bodies. These bodies should be activated and strengthened.

Another strategy is the appointment of the ombudsperson for children. Such an ombudsperson first appeared in the early 1980s in Sweden and Norway.[55] In order to be really the voice of children the ombudsperson must be an independent body and be able to express freely his/her opinion on actions undertaken by the public administration, reprimanding—where necessary—the lack of a system. The ombudsperson should be able to promote authoritatively the best interests of children. If children are to be given valuable help, they must be clearly told whom to get in touch with and must be given the appropriate means to do so. The ombusdperson must direct the

---

[53] Criminal Writ Petition No. 1107 of 1996, Mumbai High Court.
[54] Criminal Writ Petition No. 1332 of 1999, Mumbai High Court.
[55] Dominick Luquer and Massimo Toschi, *New Tools for the Protection of Children in Europe*, European Conference Report, Milano, 1997.

child to a kind of help tailored to meet his or her needs and then to monitor the specific handling of the case and the quality of the service offered to the child. It is of utmost importance for the ombudsperson to have a direct link with the children and to become for them *the* ultimate point of reference.

The ombudsperson must imperatively be free from any bond and external influence, in order to keep his/her distance. There are two essentials models: a public and a private one. In the first one, the office of the ombusperson is situated at a governmental or, even better, at a parliamentary level. In Norway and Flanders—the Parliament is accountable for the seriousness of the office: it acknowledges children as a special category of citizens and allows this function to be performed in the most democratic way. This is known as the Scandinavian model. The second model is the non-governmental one, found in the Anglo-Saxon tradition. In this case, the ombudsperson's office is run by a private initiative, by non-governmental organizations acting generally through 'class actions'.[56] To begin with, the chosen model of ombudsperson needs to have an official status, in order to be able to express publicly the specific reasons of children and to guarantee the respect of their needs. The 'acknowledgement' is also necessary to guarantee the stable and permanent nature of this office.

Conclusion

A wide range of stakeholders and reform agents need to be brought together including relevant actors from outside the legal, judicial, and human rights area, to jointly address issues in a strategic way. Given the diversity and the disparities in the country, perhaps regional networks or strategic alliances on specific issues may be more workable. Initiatives have to be taken by various people's organizations, community leaders, advocacy groups, child rights activists and public interest professionals, civil society, and governments working towards the goal of translating the dream of child rights into reality. Socio-eco-political-legal change cannot be sustained in isolation. Alliances have to be built with other movements for change such as women's rights, environment, labour, housing, health, education rights, and with organizations, individuals, parents, and other civil society organizations involved in child rights issues. Interventions should be made at the level of government programmes and policy directives towards establishing an agenda to ensure the rights of the child.

[56] Tosh Luquer, European Conference Report, New tools for the protection of children in Europe: a comparison of experiences of National Ombudspersons for Children, Milano, 1997.

Children can no longer be considered as passive recipients of services. Governments and civil society must accept children as partners and facilitate their participation in matters which affect their lives The challenge is, therefore, to change the mindset that children can no longer be objects of charity, philanthropy, and welfare. They have rights and the government, civil society, and NGOs are obliged to provide for them. There must be legislative, administrative, and judicial support to implement the policies, plans, and legislations in the interest of the child. The ideals and norms set forth in our Constitution, national laws and case laws, international conventions, regulations, policies, and practices have addressed norms and issues relating to children and have contributed considerably towards the betterment of children. We also need other means like political, psychological, managerial, economic, social, and financial to implement the best interest of the child. Public interest litigation has been used beneficially to realize the protection of rights of children. The Supreme Court of India has in recent years used the directive principles so as to expand fundamental rights to include socio-economic rights.

The major significance of the Convention on the Rights of the Child is that it represents a commitment to improving the situation of children in India. Thus, it can be used by public advocates to force the government to take action on child issues. As the government has already agreed that these standards should be met, advocates need to bring instances of the violation of children's rights to the attention of the government and the public, and demand change. However, the efforts have not been utterly inadequate. Although law in the form of international conventions or national legislation can contribute considerably towards the child rights what matters is how laws are actually implemented, what is done to reach the ideals contained in these laws. Ways must be found, therefore, to enforce the implementation and to ensure that children experience true childhood.

There is a dire need for correcting legal perspectives both substantive and procedural, and to foster, adopt, and create child-centred approaches and institutions. Accountability has to be fixed for non-implementation of legislation. Legal education and research should include child rights advocacy. All this requires reallocation of resources for children. It is essential that the children are placed high on the political agenda of development. Bodies like the Planning Commission has to provide adequate financial allocation for children and greater economic aid to villages. It is also imperative that such resource allocation be accompanied by the creation of participatory delivery mechanisms and structures for the effective utilization of these resources. Quality control and a set of indicators need to be developed to assess the implementation of child rights. Besides the parents, teachers and other adult community have to be educated on the rights of the child. And giving children a voice, a forum empowering their opinion may accelerate the progress towards realizing the rights of the child. India should develop resources—intellectual, ideological, and institutional and ecological—for sustained child rights advocacy. Realization of the rights of the child calls for a well-defined, child-friendly, national movement involving individuals and masses, peoples and societies, families and communities, states and nations. We all have an obligation to give a *first call on resources for children*. And above all create and sustain an environment in which children's rights can be realized. Such a child-friendly movement will include families, schools, media, workplaces, homes, communities, neighbourhoods, cities, and nations. And finally, good governance has a central role to play to ensure that children are at the centre of development agenda that guide policy decisions and budgetary allocations as well as monitor progress. Good governance and the full enjoyment of children's right are mutually reinforcing.[57]

---

[57] UNICEF, Poverty and Exclusion Among Urban Children, *Innnocenti Digest*, No. 10, Nov. 2002, Florence, Italy.

Select Bibliography

Adenwalla, Maharukh (2000), *Child Sexual Abuse and the Law*, India Centre for Human Rights and Law, Mumbai.

Agnes, Flavia (1999), *Contesting Rights Over Children, Custody and Guardianship in Matrimonial Disputes*, Manushi, No. 114, Sept.–Oct.

Amato, P.R. and S.J. Rezac (1994), 'Contact with non-residential parents, interparental conflict, and children's behavior', *Journal of Family Issues*, No. 15, pp. 191–207 (an independent research and analysis centre based at the Harvard School of Public Health).

Annoswamy, David J. (1996), *The French Legal System and its Indian Connection*, Institute of Compartive Law, National Law School of India University, Bangalore, India.

Awards Digest: Journal of Labour Legislation, Vol. XX, Nos 7–12.

Baillie, Digest of Muhammedan Law, London, Pt. 1 (1865), Pt. II (1869) p. 50.

Baillie, Digest of Muhammedan Law, London, Pt. 1 (1865), Pt. II (1869) p. 51.

Bajpai, Asha (1990), *The Girl Child and the Law: Rights of the Child*, NLSIU/UNICEF.

——— (1996), *Adoption Law and Justice to the Child*, National Law School of India University, Bangalore, India.

——— (1998), Juvenile Justice in Maharashtra—Administration and Implementation, a study sponsored by UNICEF (unpublished).

——— (1998), The Legal System and the Principle of the Best Interest of the Child, Empirical Study, Mumbai (Unpublished).

——— (1999), *The Sexual Abuse and Exploitation of Children*, One India, One People Foundation, Sept.

——— (1999), *Towards Equity and Empowerment of Children, 1989–1999: A Decade of Family Court*, Family Court Bar Association, Mumbai.

——— (2000), A Pilot Study of Children and Courts in Mumbai, sponsored by the Board of Research Studies, TISS, Mumbai (unpublished)..

——— (2001), Recommendations given to the National Commission for Women, New Delhi, for amending the Child Labour (Prohibition and Regulation) Act 1986.

Barse, Sheela (1996), *A Critique of the Suppression of Immoral Traffic in Women & Girls Act 1956*, Indian Laws on Prostitution and Sexual Offences, Neer Gaurav Research & Development Foundation, Mumbai, India.

Select Bibliography

Barse, Sheela (ed.) (1996), *Indian Laws on Prostitution and Sexual Offences*, Neergaurav Research and Development Foundation, Mumbai, India.

——— (ed.) (1996), *The Report of International Conference on Child Sex Abuse, Victim Protection Investigation and Trial Procedure*, 22–24 February, Neergaurav Research and Development Foundation, Mumbai. India.

Bequele, Aseefa and Jo Boyden (eds) (1988), *Combating Child Labour*, Geneva: International Labour Office.

Blanchet, Sandie (1999), *The Rights Approach to HIV/AIDS*, Presentation at the Media Workshop on HIV/AIDS and Child Rights, Gujarat: 13–14 August (supported by UNICEF, Gujarat).

Bose, Ashish (2001), 'Health for All: Broken Promises', *Economic and Political Weekly*, Mumbai, 36.11: 905–7.

Bottoms L. Bette and Gail S. Goodman (eds) (1996), *International Perspectives on Child Abuse and Children's Testimony*, Sage Publications, New Delhi.

Boyden, Jo and William Myers (1995), *Exploring Alternative Approaches to Combating Child Labour: Case Studies from Developing Countries*, Innocenti Occasional Papers, Child Rights Series No. 8, Florence: UNICEF International Child Development Centre.

Britannica Inc. (1991), *The New Encyclopaedia Britannica*, Vol. I, Fifteenth Edition.

Bueren Van, G. (1995), *The International Law on the Rights of the Child*, Martinus Nijhoff Publishers, Netherlands.

Bulsara, Sohra Jamshedjee (1937), 'The Laws of the Ancient Persians', in *Digest of a Thousand Points of Law*, Bombay: Hosing Ankleshwaria, 7.

Campaign Against Child Labour (1995), Child Labour in India—A Dossier, Compiled by Campaign Against Child Labour, Sponsored by UNICEF, Maharashtra State Office, Mumbai, India.

Campaign Against Child Labour, CACL Update, 3 February 1998, CACL, Central Secretariat, Karnataka, India.

Campaign Against Child Labour, CACL Update, 6 February 1998, CACL, Central Secretariat, Karnataka, India.

Centre for Child and National Law School of India University (compiled by) (1998), *Frequently Asked Questions on the Fundamental Right to Education*, Bangalore, August.

Child Prostitution—The Ultimate Abuse, Report on The National Consultation on Child Prostitution, 18–20 November 1995, New Delhi, Organized by YMCA, ECPAT, and UNICEF, UNICEF, India Country Office, 1995.

Chowdhry, D. Paul (1988), *Inter-Country Adoption, Social and Legal Aspects*, Indian Council For Child Welfare, New Delhi.

Cohen, C.P. (1989), *United Nations Convention on the Rights of the Child*, 28 International Legal Materials (ILM), 1448, American Society of International Law, Washington.

Select Bibliography

Delupis, I. (1975), *International Adoptions and the Conflict of Laws*, Uppsala: Almqvist & Wiksell.

Dhuru, Simandhini (2001), *The Avehi–Abacus Project*, The Indian Child 2001, Child Relief and You (CRY) Documentation Centre, Mumbai.

Dias, Clarence (1991), 'The Child in the Developing World: Making Rights a Reality: Report of a Seminar on Rights of the Child, Bangalore: National Law School of India University.

Diwan, Paras (1992), *Modern Hindu Law*, Allahabad, India: Allahabad Law Agency.

——— (1993), *Law of Adoption, Minority, Guardianship and Custody*, Wadhawa and Company, Allahabad, India.

——— (2000), *Law of Adoption, Minority, Guardianship of Custody*, Universal Law Publishing Co. Pvt. Ltd., Delhi, India.

Luquer, Dominick and Toschi, Massimo (1997), 'New Tools for the Protection of Children in Europe', European Conference Report, Milano.

Frazer, T.G. (1922), *The Golden Bough*, New York: Macmillan.

Geraghty, Thomas F. (1997), 'Justice for Children: How do we get there?' *The Journal of Criminal Law and Criminology*, Vol. 88, Fall.

Ghosh, Shanti (1991), 'Girl Child: A Lifetime of Deprivation and Discrimination', *The Indian Journal of Social Work*, Vol. II, No. 1, Mumbai: Tata Institute of Social Sciences, Jan.

Global Alliance Against Trafficking in Women (2001), *Human Rights and Trafficking in Persons: A Hand Book*, Bangkok.

Goonsekere, Savitri (1998), *Children, Law and Justice: A South Asian Perspective*, UNICEF and Sage Publications, India.

Government of India (1987), National Policy on Child Labour.

——— Ministry of Welfare (1989), *Guidelines to Regulate Matters Relating to Adoption of Indian Children*. Resolution Nos 13–33/85-CHR(AC), New Delhi.

——— (1991), Registrar General of India, Census of India.

——— (1997), India Country Report on the Convention on the Rights of the Child.

——— (1999), Crime in India, Ministry of Home Affairs.

——— (2000), India Report on the World Summit for Children, Department of Women and Child Development, Ministry of Human Resource Development.

——— (2000), Ministry of Law, Justice and Company Affairs, 172nd Law Commission Report on Review of Rape Laws.

——— (2001), Newborn Health Key to Child Survival, Child Health Division, Department of Family Welfare, Ministry of Health and Family Welfare.

——— (2001), Registrar General of India, Census of India.

Grote, Doris (1999), 'HIV/AIDS Situation in India and in Gujarat, Presentation on HIV/AIDS', Media Workshop on HIV/AIDS and Child Rights, 13–14 August, supported by UNICEF, Gujarat.

Grover, Anand (1986), *Amniocentesis or female foeticide*, The Lawyers, March, Lawyers Collective, Mumbai, India.

482 Select Bibliography

Gupta, Meena (1994), *Special Problems of Enforcement of Child Labour Laws and Regulations*, Awards Digest, Journal of Labour Legislation, National Institute of Labour, Vol. XX, Nos 7–12.

Hammerberg, T. (1993), 'Making Reality of the Rights of the Child', *Legal Perspectives*, File No. 33, Legal Resources for Social Action, Chengalpattu, Tamil Nadu, India, p. 9.

HMSO, London Home Office (1988), Memorandum of Good Practice (Adaptations from).

Hobbs, Sandy, Jim Mckechnie, and Michael Lavalette (1999), *Child Labour: A World History Companion*, Bodmin, Cornwall, Great Britain: MPG Books Limited.

Huard, L.A. (1956), *The Law of Adoption, Ancient and Modern*, Vanderbilt Law Review, 9. 743–63, Vanderbilt University, USA.

Human Rights Foundation (HRF), LAYA's and Youth for Unity and Voluntary Action (YUVA) (1988), *The Child in Search of the State, Alternate Report to the Implementation of the Right to Housing as enshrrined in the Convention on the Rights of the Child (CRC)*, Mumbai, India.

Human Rights Watch Children's Rights Project (1996), *The Small Hands of Slavery: Bonded Child Labour in India*, Human Rights Watch, USA.

Interim Fact-Finding Report (1999)—Task Force Against Domestic Child Labour, Mumbai.

International Covenant on Civil and Political Rights in Van Bueren International Documents, 1993.

International Labour Organization (1996), Child Labour: Targeting the Intolerable—The Problem, Geneva.

Jandhyala, B.G. Tilak (2000), *Financing of Elementary Education in India*, New Delhi: National Institute of Educational Planning and Administration, Ministry of Human Resource Development, Government of India, April.

Kabuta (1989), 'Protection of Children's Rights', *International Review of Criminal Policy*, Vols. 39–40, No. 108, United Nations, Geneva.

Kapadia, Kamini (2001), 'Work with Children Infected and Affected by HIV/AIDS', Synopsis of Paper presented at Training Programme on Child Rights at Nagpur (unpublished).

Kashyap, L. and J. Modi (2001), 'Status of the Disabled in India—2000', A paper presented at the Maharashtra State Level Workshop on the Convention on the Rights of the Child, 18–19 January.

Kocourek, I. and P. Wigmore (1947), 'Evaluation of Law, Sources of Ancient and Primitive Laws', *Encyclopaedia Brittanica*, Vol. II.

Law Reform Commission of Victoria (commissioned), Australian Report.

Levesque, Roger J.R. and Alan J. Tomkins (1995), 'Revisioning Juvenile Justice: Implications of the New Child Protection Movement', *Journal of Urban and Contemporary Law*, Vols. 48–97, Washington, USA: Washington University School of Law.

Loeber, Rolf and David Farrington (eds) (1998), *Serious and Violent Juvenile Offenders*, Sage Publications Inc., USA.

Mackenzie, A. Donald (1985), *India—Myth and Legend*, London: Mystic Press.

Mann J.M. and A. Petitgirand (1993) 'Aids and Children: Dangers and Opportunities', *Children Worldwide*, Vol. 20, Nos 2–3, International Catholic Child Bureau. Mathew 1: 18–23, The New Testament.

Mehendale, A. (1998), 'Compulsory Primary Education in India: The Legal Framework', *Lawyers Collective*, April.

Mehta N. and K. Telang (2001), *A Paper on Family Environment and Alternate Care*, The Maharashtra State Level Workshop on the Convention on the Rights of the Child, January.

Mehta, Nilima (1996), *Non-Institutional Services for Children in Especially Difficult Circumstances*—A Manual supported by UNICEF, Maharashtra, and Compiled for the Directorate of Women and Child Development, Government of Maharashtra, July.

——— (1999), *The Adoption Agenda in India*, Horizons, Gender Just Laws Bulletin, India Centre for Human Rights and Law, Mumbai, Vol. 2, No. 2, July.

Menon, N.R.M. (1991), *Prevention of Immoral Traffic and Restoration of Human Dignity*, Select Materials on Public Legal Education, Legal Services Clinic, NLSIU, Bangalore.

Mitra, N.L. (1988), *Juvenile Delinquency and the Indian Justice System*, New Delhi: Deep And Deep Publication.

——— (1999), *Policy and Law in Juvenile Justice*, National Law School of India University, Bangalore.

Narayan, Ashok (1988), *Child Labour Policies and Programmes. The Indian Experience*, New Delhi: Government of India, Ministry of Labour.

National Centre for Advocacy Studies (2002), *Advocacy Internet*, Vol. 4, No. 03, May–June, Pune, India.

National Family Health Survey (1998–99), Indian Institute of Population Sciences, Mumbai, India.

National Society for the Prevention of Cruelty to Children (NSPCC) (1998), *Preparing Young Witnesses for Court—A Handbook for Child Witness Supporters*, London: The Young Witness Pack, NSPCC National Centre.

Nawani, Disha (2000), *Role and Contribution of NGOs to Basic Education*, New Delhi: National Institute of Educational Planning and Administration, Ministry of Human Resource Development, Government of India, April.

O'Flaherty, M. (1996), *The United Nations and Human Rights*, London: Sweet and Maxwell.

Panchal, T. and Shaikh Nahida (1997), *Documentation of Police Cases of Sexually Abused Girls in Mumbai City between 1994–95*, Study by the Special Cell for Women & Children, Tata Institute of Social Sciences, Mumbai, India.

Patkar, Pravin, Priti Patkar, and Monica Sakhrani, *Trafficking & Commercial Sexual Exploitation: International Conventions*, Anti-Trafficking Centre, Prerna, Mumbai, India.

Phadke, Anand (1999), *Towards Health Care for All*, Allahabad: Indian Academy of Social Sciences.

Pillai, M.P.P. (1990), *The Law of Adoption in India: Need for a Fresh Approach*, Rights of the Child, NLSIU.

Pinto, Gerry (1995), 'Agenda for the NGOs', presentation at the National Consultation on Child Prostitution organized by YMCA, ECPAT, and UNICEF, New Delhi, 18–20 November.

Premi, Mahendra (2001), 'The Missing Girl Child', *Economic and Political Weekly*, 26 May.

Presser, S.B. (1972), 'The Historical Background of the American Law of Adoption', *Journal of Family Law*, 11443–516, USA.

RALLY (1998), *The Hidden 'Live-In' Slaves, The Domestic Workers*—May Day Message 1998 (Excerpts), April.

Reddy, Chidananda (1990), 'The Infant Government's Anti-Infant Policy', *The Lawyers*, Mumbai, June.

Report of Expert Seminar on Children's Rights and Habitat organized by UNICEF (1996), UNCHS/Habitat in February.

Rustomfram, H. (1995), 'The Silent Scream—Commercial Sexual Abuse of The Child', from *Lawyers Collective*.

Saakshi (1999), *Child Sexual Abuse: Beyond Fear Secrecy and Shame*, New Delhi.

Saha, A.N. (1988), *B.B. Mitra's Guardians and Wards Act*, 13th Edition, Calcutta: Eastern Law House.

Saxena, S. (2000), 'Child Marriages in Rajasthan: A Challenge to Child Marriage Restraint Act', *All India Reporter Journal*, Nagpur, India.

Scott and Grisso (1997), 'The Evolution of Adolescence: A Developmental Perspective on Juvenile Justice Reform', *The Journal of Criminal Law and Criminology*, Vol. 88, No. 1.

Sekar, Helen R. (1992), Child Labour Prohibition and Regulation Act 1986: A Critique, *Awards Digest, Journal of Labour Legislation*, March–June.

——— (1994), *Child Labour Legislation in India: A Study in Retrospect and Prospect*, Noida, U.P., India: V.V. Giri National Labour Institute.

——— (2001), *Ensuring Their Childhood*, V.V. Giri National Labour Institute, Noida, U.P., India.

Seligman, Edwin R.A. (ed.) (1957), *Encyclopedia of Social Sciences*, New York: Macmillan.

Sharing (2000), A newsletter produced by the Indian Association for Promotion of Adoption and Child Welfare, Vol. II, No. 1, July–October.

Sharma, K. (1999), 'Child Labour in India', *Lawyers Collective*, November.

SHRAM SHAKTI Report (1988) (National Commission On Self-Employed Women And Women In The Informal Sector).

Singh, Abhimanyu (2000), *Participatory Micro-Planning for Universal Primary Education*, New Delhi: National Institute of Educational Planning and Administration, Ministry of Human Resource Development, Government of India, April.

Subramaniam, M. (2001), Civil Rights of Children and the CRC, A paper presented at the Maharashtra State-Level Workshop on the Convention on the Rights of the Child, 18–19 January.

Swaminathan, M. (1993), The Continuum of Maternity and Childcare Support, A paper presented at the Sixth Conference of the Indian Association for Women's Studies, Mysore, 31 May–2 June.

Swaminathan, M. and V. Rawal (2000), *Primary Education for All*, India Development Report.

Tate, David et al. (1995), Violent Juvenile Delinquents: Treatment, Effectiveness and Implications for Future Action, 50 AM PSYCHOLOGIST. 777, 779.

Telang, K. (2001), 'Editorial', *Sharing*, A Newsletter of Indian Association for Promotion of Adoption and Child Welfare, April–June, Vol. II, No. 4.

The Holy Koran, Revised and Edited by the Presidency of Islamic Researchers, IFTA, Call of Guidance, 123.

The PROBE Team (1999), *Public Report on Basic Education*, New Delhi: Oxford University Press.

The Report of the Committee on Child Labour 1979.

The Report of the Gurupadswamy Committee on Child Labour 1976.

The Report of the National Commission on Labour 1969.

The Report of the Sanat Mehta Committee 1984.

Times of India, News Service (2000), *Centre to Decide Soon on Judges Panel*, May 11.

Tomasevski, Katarina, The Right to Education, a discussion, source: International Development Corporation Agency, www.sida.org

The Tribune, 'HC Bans Corporal Punishment for School Children', Vol. 120, No. 333, City Ed., Chandigarh, Dec. 2, 2000, p. 1.

UNAIDS (2000), *Report on the Global HIV/AIDS Epidemic*, Joint United Nations Programme on HIV/AIDS, Geneva.

UNICEF (1994), *The Right to be a Child*, New Delhi, India.

——— (1997), *The State of the World's Children*, New York, USA.

——— (1999), *The State of the World's Children*, New York, USA.

——— (2000), Achievements, Challenges, Aims and Strategies.

―――― (2000), *The Progress of Nations*, New York, USA.
―――― (2001), *The State of the World's Children*, New York, USA.
―――― (2002), 'Poverty and Exclusion Among Urban Children', *Innocenti Digest*, No. 10, November 2002, Italay.
UNICEF, India Country Office, New Delhi (2001), *India: Social and Economic Statistics UNICEF in India 1999–2002: Challenges and Opportunities*.
United Nations Development Programme (1993), Human Development Report.
United Nations Office, United Nations Centre for Human Rights (1996), *The Rights of the Child*, Human Rights Fact Sheet Series (1990) Fact Sheet No. 10, Geneva, Switzerland.
United Nations Organization (1990), Rules for the Protection of Juveniles Deprived of Their Liberty (Beijing Rules).
Van Bueren, G. (1989), 'Special Features of the Assistance and Protection of Children as Victims of Armed Conflict', in *Assisting the Real Victims of Armed Conflict and Other Disasters*, (ed.) Frits Karlshoven, Dordrecht.
Varma, A.P. (1994), 'Child Labour in India: An Overview', *Awards Digest: Journal of Labour Legislation*, Vol. XX, Nos 7–12, July–Dec 1994, National Labour Institute, New Delhi: Deep Printers.
Veldkamp, T. (1993), 'De toekomst van de kinderbescherming [The Future of child protection]', in *Kinderen Beschermen en jeugd hulp verlenen [Protecting and helping children]*, A. Groen and A. van Montfoort, Arnhem, the Netherlands: Gouda Quint.
Vidhyasagar, R. (1998), *Child Labour in India: An Analysis of 1991 Census*, Mimeo.
Vikas Adhyayan Kendra (1996), *Facts Against Myths*, Vol. III, Mumbai, India.
Walker, Brooks, Wrightsman (1999), *Children's Rights in the United States*, New Delhi: Sage publication.
Weiner, Myron (1991), *The Child and the State in India*, New Delhi: Oxford University Press.
Working Group on the Convention on the Rights of the Child (1998), *The Alternate Report India*, Butterflies, New Delhi, May 11.
World Book Inc, *The World Book Encyclopaedia*. Chicago, Illinois 1988. A Vol. I, p. 66.
World Health Report (2001), World Health Organization, Geneva.
Yadav, M.S. and Meenakshi Bhardwaj (2000), *Learning Conditions for Primary Education*, National Institute of Educational Planning and Administration, Ministry of Human Resource Development, Government of India, April.

WEB SITES VISITED

www.cehat.org
www.SCY.com
www.mohfw.nic.in
www.netsafety.nic.in

www.pdhre.org
www.scyofbc.org
www.unicef.org
www.who.int/archives/who50/en/health4all.htm
www.ncasindia.org
www.cry.org
www.unesco.org

Other Relevant Web Sites

www.unhchr.ch
www.amnesty.org
www.article 19.org
http:ffhumanrights.britishcouncil.org
www.nhrc.nic.in
www.schoolnetindia.com

Index

abandoned children 125
  adoption of 55
abortions 394, 395–6
  legal provisions relating to 386–98
  sex-selective 385
  Supreme Court of USA on 394
  see also female foetus
Academy for Mobilizing Rural Urban Action through Education (AMMRAE) 192
Action Against Trafficking Sexual Exploitation of Children (ATSEC) 273
Action Aid, on action against trafficking in women and children 274
Additional Protocol to the American Convention on Human Rights in the Area of Economic, Social and Cultural Rights 377
adoption(s), of children 33–91, 305
  abandoned children 125
  and adoptive families/parents 55, 74–5, 79
  concept of 39, 40
  among Christians 39–40
  courts' jurisdiction in cases relating to 146–7
  definition of 33
  Dharamputra custom of, among Parsis 37
  doctrine of relation back 56, 57
  documents needed for 52–61
  freedom of religion and right to 77
  in Hindu mythology 34–6
  of Indian children by foreign parents 51, 61–3
    malpractices in 48–9
  in-country 41, 73
  inter-country 41, 42, 47–9, 51, 54–61, 73, 79
    in United Kingdom 83–4
  laws in India 30, 42–7, 463, 474
    under Juvenile Justice Act 2000 308
  in Maharashtra 90
  Maharashtra Adoption Bill 1995 90
  among Muslims 37–9, 77n
  non-governmental organizations (NGOs) work on 73
  Palukaputra custom of, among Parsis 37
  among Parsis 36–7
  practice 52–61
    in developing countries 82–3
    in Netherlands 84
    in Sweden 71
    in United States of America 84, 85
  status of 40–2
  through agencies 41, 48–50
  by widows 56–7
Adoption of Children Bill 1980 37

adult literacy 338
African Charter on Human and
    People's Rights (ACHPR) 377
AIDS/HIV situation, in India 381,
    383, 416
    National Policy of 1968 on 419
    United Nations on children
        with 418–19
Alma Ata Declaration on Health for
    All 374, 435
alternative dispute resolution (ADR)
    techniques, in custody disputes
    142
Amman Affirmation 1996 356
amniocentesis, legal provisions relating
    to 385, 386–98
Anganwadi centres 28, 272, 413
Appellate Courts, powers of, in United
    Kingdom 139–41
Apprentice Act 1961 8, 163
Area Child Protection Committee
    (ACPC), UK 241
Association for the Development of
    Education in Africa 362
Avehi-Abacus Project 353

Bal Asha Trust 68
Bal Majdoor Union 186
Bal Mitra Shala (child-friendly school)
    349
Balwadis 191, 272
beedi manufacturing units, child labour
    in 187
Beedi and Cigar Workers (Conditions
    of Employment) Act 1966 163,
    410
    crèche facilities under 412
begar 172
Beijing Declaration 1995 356
Beijing Rules 316–19
    definition of juvenile under
        318–18, 288

Bharathi Braille, for visually impaired
    children 424–5
bigamy case, judgment on 89
Bombay Children Act 1948 69
Bombay Zoarastrian Jasham Committee
    37
bonded child labour 155–6, 158
    court rulings related 183–4
    debt bondage 203
    laws related to 172–80
        enforcement of legislation
        178–80
    NGOs intervention in 185–92
    rehabilitation of 177
Bonded Labour System (Abolition) Act
    1976 172, 177, 184
    enforcement of 180
Braille Code, use of, for blind children
    in India 425
breastfeeding, of child 402–3, 409
Bureau of Indian Standards Act 1986
    406

Cable Television Network (Regulation)
    Act 1995 9
California Code of Civil Procedure,
    USA 245
Campaign Against Child Trafficking
    (CACT) 274
Campaign for Housing Rights
    434
Census of India 2, 30
    on sex ratio 397
Central Adoption Resource Agency
    (CARA) 50, 72, 73, 75, 81
Central Children Act 1960 282
Central Social Welfare Board (CSWB),
    survey on commercial sexual
    exploitation 252–3
child/children, -care programme, by
    government 412–14
    by NGOs 414–15

concept of 254–5
definition of 2–5, 60
in emergency situations 370
and education for 363
in especially difficult circumstances (CEDC) 277, 279, 290, 297, 320
homes/shelter for 305
labour *see* child labour
in need of care and protection 299, 3–4–5
-parent relationship 145–7
population, projected 2
sex workers, rescue/rehabilitation of 257, 259
welfare 296, 320
as witnesses 243, 244, 454–5
in sexual abuse cases in United Kingdom 245
child labour 148–206, 278, 453, 461–2
in Africa 150
in agricultural sector 151–3, 155
in Andhra Pradesh 154
in Asia 150
in Brazil, legislation on 198–9
carpet industry 201
causes and consequences of 154–5
in developing countries 150
domestic servants 156–7, 188, 461
and education 188–9, 191, 369
and employment in fireworks units 181–3
exploitation and trafficking of, NGOs intervention in 271–5
in 'hazardous' employment 174–5
in Hong Kong, elimination of 198
ILO policy on 198
international legislation on 198–9

judicial responses to cases on 180–3
and labour causes, WTO and 200–1
laws, to prohibit and regulate, in India 158–68, 369
in Latin America 150
national policy on 168–72
in unorganized sector 173
Child Labour Deterrence Act 1992 (Harkin-Brown Bill) USA 201
Child Labour in Hazardous Employment (Abolition, Rehabilitation and Welfare) 2000 draft bill on 175–6
Child Labour (Prohibition and Education) Bill 2001 205
Child Labour (Prohibition and Regulation) Act 1986 3, 8, 14, 157, 163–8, 171, 172, 183, 189, 190, 203, 474
amendment to 461–2
need for legal reforms 9n, 173–8
penalties for offences under 166–7
prosecution and convictions under 178–80
Child Labour Technical Advisory Committee 165, 167
Child-line India Foundation (CIF) 28, 295, 304
Children's Act 1980, UK 61n
Children's Act 1989, UK 139, 140, 208, 244, 309
Children's Code Bill (Draft) 31, 439–40, 444n
Child Marriage Restraint Act (CMRA), of 1926 4
of 1928 14, 30, 454
of 1929 3n, 5, 7, 220, 221, 223, 224, 227, 264, 474
amendment to 466

(Amendment) Act of 1978 221
child marriage(s) 30, 210, 213–14, 220–7, 454
  age at, among Christians 222
    among Hindus 221–2
    among Muslims 222
    among Parsis 222–3
  minimum age for boys and girls 5
  under different personal laws 221–4
  judgments relating to 227–32
  repudiation of 223–4
  as sexual abuse of child 212–14
Children (Pledging of Labour) Act 1933 8, 172–3, 178
Child Protection Services, USA 241
Child Sexual Abuse and Exploitation (CSA & E) 209
child sexual abuse/exploitation 211–47
child prostitutes 155, 156, 209, 247, 252, 278, 451, 463–4
  commercial, high-risk groups 247–8
  impact of 210–11
  in institutions 214–16
  international legislation, initiative against 241–6
  judgments in cases related to 229–32, 256–62
  legal intervention/laws in 216–20, 243–4, 450–1, 463–4
    need for reforms in 232–41
  NGOs and government on cases relating to 246–7
  molestation of child 225
  right to protection against 207–76
  and trafficking, commercial 247–75
  in United Kingdom 243
  United Nations definition of 249
  in United States 242
  victims of 225–6
  witness code, for child testifying in 469
  see also Child Witness Code, USA
Child Survival and Safe Motherhood Programmes (CSSM) 400, 414, 426
Child Welfare Board 282
Child Welfare Committees 217, 255, 261, 262, 304, 307
Child Witness Code, USA 245–6
Child Workers Opportunities Project (CWOP) 190–1
Christian Adoption Bill 1988 40
Christian Marriage Act 1872 222, 223
Christians, adoption practice among 39–40
  age at marriage among 222
  on legitimacy of child 452
Citizen's Action Group (CAGS) 352
Citizen's Initiative on Elementary Education (CIEE), Karnataka 351–2
Civil Procedure Code 1908 9, 24, 128, 442
Code of Hammurabi 34
Committee on Child Labour 1979 163n
Committee on the Rights of the Child 1n, 2n, 437, 469
Committee for Rights to Housing (CRH) 434
Communicable diseases, prevention and control of 383
Community and Family Support Act 1995, Louisiana, USA 322
Community Juvenile Services Acts, Oregon, USA 322
Constitution of India, Article 14 of 122
  Article 15 of 59, 87, 122, 129

Article 21 of 66, 157, 184, 204, 287, 336, 338, 345–7, 380
Article 22 of 287
Article 23 of 172, 184, 216, 253
Article 24 of 180–1
Article 25 of 88
Article 28 of 335
Article 29 of 335
Article 32 of 182
Article 37 of 89
Article 39 of 182, 253, 335, 379
Article 41 of 335, 345–7
Article 44 of 88–9
Article 45 of 182, 335, 337, 345–7
Article 46 of 335, 345–7
Article 47 of 335, 380
Article 51 of 205n, 336
Article 73 of 23, 471
Article 225 of 68
Article 226 of 68, 123, 227
Article 246 of 335
Article 253 of 23–4, 78n
Seventh Schedule of 66
Eleventh Schedule of 336
Twelfth Schedule of 336
Ninety-Third Amendment to 5, 31, 337–9, 345, 347
    judgments relating to 345–7
Constitution of India, on child employment 158
on education 335–9
(Eighty-third Amendment) Bill, on free and compulsory education 336
fundamental rights under 6
on healthcare 374, 435
on health and nutrition 379–80
on political and civil rights 357
right to housing 430–1
Contract Labour Act 1970 412
Convention on the Abolition of Slavery, Slave Trade and Institutions and Practices Similar to Slavery 1956 202–3
Convention on the Elimination of all Forms of Discrimination Against Women (CEDAW) 268, 376–7
Convention on the Elimination of all Forms of Racial Discrimination Against Women 377
Convention on Protection of Children and Cooperation in Respect of Inter-Country Adoption 78–82
Significance to India 80–2
Convention on the Rights of the Child on the Sale of Children, Child Prostitution and Child Pornography, 2000 269–70
Convention on the Suppression of Slave Trade and Slavery 1926 202–3
Convention for the Suppression of Trafficking in Persons and of the Exploitation of the Prostitution of Others 1949 266–7
Council of Europe, on protection of children 23
Court of Appeals, USA 136
Covenant on Economic, Social and Cultural Rights 431
Covenant on the Rights of the Child 376, 377
crèche facilities, for children 410–12
government programme for 413–14
Crimes (Child Sex Tourism) Amendment Act 1994, Australia 265
Crime Against Torture 268
Criminal Inquiries Compensation Boards, UK 244
Criminal Justice Act 1988, UK 243

Criminal Procedure Code (Cr.PC)
1973 5, 9, 24, 128, 226, 233,
237, 238, 275
　on detention of children 288
　proposed amendments to 237–9
custody, and guardianship of
　　children 92, 464–5, 463
　dissolution of marriage and, of
　　children 106–13
　　in France 133–4
　father as natural guardian 128–9
　in family courts/legal proceedings
　　106–13, 141, 146–7
　　　grandparents 130
　Hizanat, right of mother 103–6
　Ithana Ashari law, on mother's right
　　to 104
　laws on 94–113, 128–31, 134–7
　　international laws on 75–82,
　　　131–41
　　in Japan 132–3
　during matrimonial proceedings
　　99–100
　judicial decisions on, in divorce
　　cases 113–23
　mothers' right to 103–6
　tender years doctrine and 124–5,
　　127, 136, 142
　trial courts on 127–8
　in United Kingdom, laws on 137–41
　in United States, laws on 134–7
　visitation right of mother 123
　welfare doctrine/principle in cases
　　of 126–30, 140, 143–4, 147
　Writ of Habeas Corpus, in cases of
　　123–4
Custody of Children Act 1891, UK
　138

Declaration of the Rights of the Child,
　of 1924 15, 16
　of 1959 16, 76, 77n

Declaration of Social and Legal
　　Principles 76
Declaration of the World Summit for
　　Children 78
Delhi schools, ban on corporal
　　punishments in 334
Delhi School Education Act 1960 340
devdasi system/tradition 252, 256
Devadasi Rehabilitation Programme,
　　Karnataka 272
Department of Women and Child
　　Development (DWCD) 271–2
Directive Principles of State Policy
　　6–7, 181, 380
disabled children 419–27, 451, 466–7
　access to free and adequate
　　education for 422
　hearing impairment 426
　legislation and government policies
　　pertaining to 420–7
　NGOs initiatives for 423–7
　rights of 448
　sexual abuse of 210
disadvantaged and marginalized
　　communities, rights of children
　　from 448
displaced children, eviction and
　　428–9, 433–4
Dissolution of Muslim Marriage Act
　　1939 3n, 108
District Primary Education Projects
　　(DPEP) 349
Draft National Policy and Charter for
　　Children 2001 31
drug trafficking, child victims of
　　427
Drugs and Cosmetics Act 1940 260
Dutch Child Protection Boards,
　　Netherlands 241

Early Childhood Development (ECD)
　354

early childhood care and education
(ECCE) programme 338, 343–4
early childhood care and development
(ECCD) 360
Early Childhood Care for Survival,
Growth and Development 362
education, access to 354, 465
  campaign in Brazil 364–5
  and child labour 341
  compulsory and free primary, for
    children 204, 205, 342, 372
  cost of 333
  elementary/basic, under Five-Year
    Plans 329–34, 347–50
  right of child to 14, 327–34,
    466
  gender gap in 355
  judgments relating to 345–7
  laws on 334–42
  law reform 465–6
  literacy rate 332
  NGOs intervention in
    elementary 350–4, 362
  policy and planning on 329–34,
    342–5
  primary 12, 339–42, 368, 371
  primary schools in Madhya Pradesh
    349
  resource allocation for 329–30
  school enrolment 354
    of women/girls 332, 465
    for working children 176
Education for All (EFA) project
  349–50, 361–2
  and disabled children 425–6
Employees State Insurance Act 1948
  (ESI Act) 408
Employment of Children Act 1938
  161–2, 163, 181
  (Amendment) Act 1951
    162
  (Amendment) Act 1978 163

End Child Protection in Asian
  Tourism (ECPAT) 273
estoppel, principles of 86
European Convention on Human
  Rights 1950 23–4
European Convention on Human
  Rights and Biomedicine 377
European Social Charter (ESC) 377
European Union (EU), Generalized
  System of Preferences (GSP) of
  199
Expanded Immunization Programme
  (EPI) 400

Factories Act 461
  of 1881 159
  of 1891 159
  of 1911 159
  of 1922 (Amendment) 159–60
  of 1926 (Amendment) 160
  of 1934 (Amendment) 161
  of 1948 4, 165n, 162, 174, 410
  of 1954 (Amendment) 162
family, environment, right to 33
  importance of, and healthy
    behaviour 321
  right to, child's 40
family courts 142
  on custody of children 106–13,
    131
  in Japan 132–3
Family Courts Act 107, 108, 112
Family Law Act 1975, Australia 131–2
Family Support Act 1993, Oklahoma,
  USA 322
Fatwai Alamgiri 103, 104, 105n
female/girls, age at marriage 214
  agriculture labour by 152
  education of 332, 465
  foetuses, abortion/pregnancy
    termination of 395, 455

foeticide, legal provisions relating to 386–98
infanticide 385
see also girls
femicide 385–6
Finance Commission 348
Foreign Marriage Act 1969 223
Forum Against Child Sexual Abuse (FACSE) 246
Forum for Childcare and Crèche Services (FORCES) 414
Fundamental Rights 66–7, 346

General Agreement on Tariffs and Trade (GATT) 197
genetic counseling centers 388, 389, 391
Geneva Declaration of the Rights of the Child 1924 75
Girl Child (Compulsory Education and Welfare) Bill 2000 368–9
Global AIDS Policy Coalition 415
Global Alliance Against Traffic in Women 250n
Global Consultation on Water and Sanitation 1990 12
Global Health Assembly 378–9
government, policy and legislation pertaining to disabled children 420–7
programmes and schemes for children 27–8, 192–3
for child health and development 412–14
Guardian and Wards Act (GWA) of 1890 7, 39, 43, 45–8, 54, 60, 62, 66, 67, 69, 94–9, 102, 103, 108, 114–16, 119, 122, 125, 127, 130
guardianship, adoption and 48, 92
adoption by Muslims, Christians, Parsis and Jews 59

appointment of, by courts 95, 96
custody of children and 54, 464–5
dominant position of father in 93–4
judgment on case of minor child 66–8, 122–3
law of, in British India 94
mother as natural 125, 127, 128
Guardianship of Infant Act 1925, repeal of, UK 137
Guardianship of Minors' Act 1971, UK 137, 138
Gurupadasmamy Committee on Child Labour 1976 163n

Hadis, on custody and guardianship of children 101
Hague Conference on Private International Law 78
Hanafi School of Law, on age at marriage 222
Hanafis, mother's right to custody of minor children (*hizanat*) among 104, 105
health, access to 374
of children in India 383–5
immunization programme 383, 400–1, 413
malnutrition among children 384, 401, 403
mental health of children 455
policy and law in India 379–85
primary health centers 374, 381, 426
right to 374–8
'Health for All by Year 2000', Declaration 374, 375, 380, 435
Hedaya 105n, 38
High Courts, Allahabad 311
Bombay 313
see also Mumbai
Delhi 27, 186, 232, 334, 346

496 Index

Gujarat 123, 188
Madhya Pradesh 225
Mumbai 66, 68, 69, 231, 246–7, 261, 289, 313, 428, 475
Hindu Adoption and Maintenance Act (HAMA) 1956 7, 36, 42–4, 46, 47, 54–7, 59, 60, 72, 87, 130, 308
Hindu Minority and Guardianship Act (HMGA) 1956 3, 7, 43, 59, 93, 94, 98–101, 119, 122–4, 127–30
   natural guardians under 98–9
Hindu Marriage Act 1955 112, 120, 220, 221, 223, 228, 451, 452
   governing children 9, 99, 100
Hindu Succession Act (HAS) 1956, governing Hindu children 9, 43, 45, 453
Hindus, adoption practice among 44, 54–5
   age at marriage among 221–3
   guardianship under ancient law 92–3
   personal law of 60, 209, 210
homeless children 428
   see also street children
human development, concept of 367–8
Human Rights Law, international 375–8
Human Rights Watch Children's Rights Project 158n, 178n

illegitimate child(ren), and adoption 55, 58, 83
   custody of 114–15
   guardians of 46, 98
   position of, in India 451–3
Immoral Traffic (Prevention) Act (ITPA) 1956 and 1986 9, 254, 255, 260–2, 464

India Human Development Report 426
Indian Academy of Pediatrics (IAP) 400
Indian Adoption Bill 39n
Indian Association for the Promotion of Adoption and Child Welfare (IAPA) 74
Indian Contract Act 1870 4
Indian Council for Child Welfare 49, 61
Indian Council for Social Welfare 49, 61, 69, 70
Indian Council of Social Work (ICSW) 67
Indian Education Commission 1882 334
Indian Evidence Act 1872 5, 9, 24, 226, 232, 275
   proposed amendment to 239–41
Indian Majority Act 1875 3–5, 220
Indian Mines Act 1923 160
Indian Penal Code (IPC) 1860 4, 5, 9, 24, 217–20, 225, 232, 236, 257, 258, 260, 275, 386, 427, 442
   on criminal responsibility and children 3
   proposed amendments to 233–6
Indian Posts (Amendment) Act 1931 160
Indian Succession Act 1925 (ISA) 43, 46
   governing Christian children 9
   governing Parsi children 9
   on inheritance and succession 453
Industrial Revolution 204
Infant Foods, Breast Milk Substitutes and Feeding Bottles Act 1992 (IMSA) 8, 403–7
infant milk substitutes, directions and standards for 405–7

Infant Mortality Rate (IMR) 14, 381, 384–5
Information Technology Act 2000 256
Integrated Child Development Services (ICDS) 28, 413, 467
Integrated Education for Disabled Children (IED) 425, 427
International Code of Marketing of Breast Milk Substitutes 403
International Confederation of Free Trade Unions (ICFTU) 200
International Conference on Population and Development, Cairo 368
International Covenant on Civil and Political Rights 1966 (ICCPR) 22–3, 267, 288, 316, 319, 322
International Covenant on Economic, Social and Cultural Rights 1966 22, 194, 356, 357, 376
India signatory to 436
International Labour Organization (ILO) 161, 199, 377
Bureau of Statistics 150
Conventions 159, 180, 193, 369, 461
on forced labour 194, 268
on Prohibition and Immediate Action for the Elimination of the Worst Form of Child Labour 195–6, 270
on prohibition of night work by children 162
on the Rights of the Child 1989 193
Minimum Age (Industry) Convention 1919 194, 195
Programme on the Elimination of Child Labour (IPEC) 200
report on child labour 149
international law/legislation, comparative study of 82–7
initiatives, against sexual abuse and exploitation 241–6
legal policies for adoption of children 75–82
on rights of child 14–24
international movements, against child labour 199–200
International Programme on Elimination of Child Labour (IPEC) 193
International Year of the Child (IYC) 77n
Interstate Migrant Workers Act 1980 412

Jawahar Rozgar Yojana (JRY) 348
Jogini system/tradition 252, 256
Joint Women's Programme, Delhi 272
Jomtien Conference on Education for All (EFA) 363
Jomtien Declaration 1990 360–1, 371
juvenile(s), age of, in jails 315–16
apprehended for offences in India 280–2
in conflict with law 299, 300–4
definition of, under Beijing Rules 317–18
delinquent 279–80, 284, 286, 293, 294, 319
judicial decisions of cases under 309–16
justice, international law and administration of 316–23
observation/remand homes for 302, 314
Juvenile Courts 285, 287–9, 323–5
on basic rights, in USA 325
Juvenile justice, administration and implementation 277–326

law reform for 462
legislation 323
Maharashtra State Monitoring Committee on 246, 475
NGOs intervention in 295–6
system 290, 427
Juvenile Justice Act 1986 3, 72, 217, 225, 255, 260, 264, 291, 292, 282–7, 297, 309
   administration and implementation of 287–95
Juvenile Justice (Care and Protection of Children) Act 2000 3, 4, 8, 14, 24n, 31, 43, 46, 47, 60, 217, 226, 261, 299–309, 462
   critique of 307–9
   on drugs 427
   and Probation of Offenders Act 1958 473
Juvenile Justice Boards 24, 46, 261, 300–2, 305, 306, 308
Juvenile Justice Coalition, USA 244
Juvenile Welfare Boards 217, 225, 255, 283, 291, 292

Kafala, concept of, under Islamic law 77n
Karnataka Shops and Commercial Establishments (Amendment) Bill 1997 192
Khyar-ul-bulugh (option of puberty) 228
Koran, injunction on orphans 38
   law of custody and guardianship of children under 101, 102n

laws, reforms in 72–4, 262–5
Law Commission of India 5, 58, 59n, 127, 233
   recommendations of report of 233–9, 463
   Report of 31, 128

Law Commission, UK 140
League of Nations 15, 75n
Legal Services Authorities Act 1987 470–1
Legitimacy, concept of, in Indian laws 451–3
Lok Jumbish 350

Maharashtra, *Bal Sangopan Yojana (BSY)* programme in 74
Mahila Sarvangeen Utkarsh Mandal (MASUM) 392
Maine's Family Support Services Act 1994, USA 322
Malikis, mother's right of *hizanat* among 104, 105
Marriage Laws (Amendment) Act 1976 228–9, 451
Massive Effort Campaign, against diseases of poverty 379
Maternal and Child Health (MCH) programme 413, 414
Maternal Mortality Rate (MMR) 14
Maternity Benefit Act 1961 (MBA) 408–10
Mathura rape case, NGOs role in 472
Matrimonial Causes Act 1959, Australia 131
media, role of, and children 471–2
Medical Termination of Pregnancy Act 1971 (MTP Act) 8, 394–7
Medical Termination of Pregnancy (Amendment) Bill 2002 396–7
Meljol, Mumbai 468–9
Merchant Shipping Act 1958 162
Mines Act 1901 159, 174
   (Amendment) Act 1938 161
   of 1950 410
   (Amendment) Act of 1952 4, 5, 171

Ministry of Health and Family Welfare 379
Monitoring and Guidance Committee 475
Motor Transport Workers Act 1961 162
Mumbai Police Act 1951 256, 265
Muslim Personal law, on age at marriage 222, 223
  on custody and guardianship 101–6
  governing children 9
  on legitimacy of child 452–3
  right of father to custody of minor children 105, 106
Muslim Personal Law (Shariat) Application Act 1937 102
MV Foundation 188n

Narcotic Drugs and Psychotropic Substances Act 1985 427
National AIDS Control Organization 419
National Alliance for the Fundamental Right to Education (NAFRE) 350–2
National Association of Adoptive Families (NAAF), Mumbai 74
National Campaign for Housing Rights (NCHR) 1986 434–5
National Child Labour Projects 192, 462
National Commission for Children, proposed 439–44
  Bill, amendments to 458–61
National Commission on Labour 1969 163n
  Study Group on Women and Children of 205
National Commission for Women (NCW) 459

National Commission on Women in the Unorganized Sector 410n, 414
National Council of Educational Research and Training (NCERT) 421, 427
National Family Health Survey, on age at marriage 214
  on malnutrition of children 449
National Health Policy of 1983 380–2
  of 2001 10, 13–14
  of 2002 382–3
National Human Rights Commission (NHRC) 459
National Initiative for Child Protection (NICP) 28, 75
National Institute of Social Defence (NISD) 28, 75
National Institute for the Visually Handicapped 425
National Iodine Deficiency Disorder Control Programme 426
National Literacy Mission 350
National Measures for Immunization 426
National Nutrition Policy 1993 10, 13, 426
National Open School 424, 427
National Plan of Action for Children 1992 10, 12–13, 78n, 271
National Plan for the Girl Child (1991–2000) 12
National Plan for SAARC Decade for the Girl Child 1991–2000 10, 12
National Policy and Charter for Children (NPC 2001) draft 444–9
National Policy on Child Labour 1987 101, 102, 168–72

National policy for Children, India 1974 101–11, 14, 41, 80
  amendments to 458–61
National Policy on Education 1986 (NPE) (modified in 19920) 10–12, 343–5
National Population Policy 2000 (NPP) 10, 13, 383
National Programme of Minimum Needs 330
National Programme to Overcome the Problem of Ignorance 426
National Sample Survey Organization (NSSO), estimate on blind children 424
  on children with disability 429
  on children with hearing impairment 426
  estimate on child labour 151
National Technical Committee on Child Health 383
neglected children 284, 285, 291–2, 299
  foster care scheme 41, 73, 74, 293
  non-institutional services to 292–4, 297
Network Against Child Sexual Exploitation and Trafficking (NACSET) 273
nutrition 401–7
  deficiency among children and women 381–2
  rights, concept of 377
  status in India 402

Oklahoma Supreme Court, USA 136
ombudsperson, appointment of, for children 475–6
Operation Blackboard (OB) 1987 345, 348–9
Organization of African Unity (OAU), on protection of children 23
Organization of American States (OAS), on protection of children 23
Orphanages and Other Charitable Homes (Supervision and Control) Act 1960 7, 308, 474

paedophiles, laws relating to 262
Parsis, adoption among 36–7
  age at marriage among 222
Parsis Marriage and Divorce Act 1936 3n, 9, 108
  on custody of children 100
  on legitimacy of child 452
People's Charter for Health 378
People's Health Assembly 378
People's Union for Civil Liberties 188
Persons with Disabilities (Equal opportunities, Protection of Rights and Full Participation) Act 1995 14, 422–3, 474
Plan, Eighth Five-Year, on AIDS 419
  On social housing schemes 434
Plan of Action 1986, for disabled children 420
Planning Commission, NDC Committee on Literacy 331n
Plantations Labour Act 1951 162, 171, 410
play and recreation, right to 365–7
polio eradication 383
pornography, child 210, 251–2
  internet, in New Zealand 271
  laws relating to, in obscenity and 256
  monitoring of cyber café 264–5
  in Netherlands, regulation on 270–1
  prevention of, on internet 270–1
  in United Kingdom, regulation on 271

Portuguese Civil Code, Article 5 of 227
poverty, and child labour 154–5, 204
  and ill health 435
Pratham, NGO, on primaru education 350
Pre-Conception and Pre-Natal Diagnostic Techniques (Prohibition and Sex Selection) Act 2002 397
Prenatal Diagnostic Technique (Regulation and Prevention of Misuse) Act 1994 8, 386–94
  Amendment Bill 2002 397–8
Prenatal Genetic Diagnosis (PDG) 392
Prerana (NGO), Mumbai 191, 272, 352–3
Prevention of Food Adulteration Act 1954 406
Prevention of Illicit Traffic in Narcotic Drugs and Psychotropic Substances Act 1988 9
Prevention of Immoral Traffic Act 1956 (PITA) (amended in 1986) 217, 220, 264
Primary Education Acts 334, 339, 340, 474
Primary and Elementary Education Projects, Maharashtra 350
Probation of Offenders Act 1958 7, 473
Programme of Action 1992, for disabled children 420–1
Project for the Rehabilitation and Prevention of Working Children from Abattoirs, in Parbhani (Maharashtra) 191–2
prostitution, children of 217, 291, 292
  definition of 254
  laws governing 262, 264

Public Report on Basic Education (PROBE), survey by 333

Rajasthan, mass child marriages in 212–13, 227
rape, of child 211–12, 225, 231
  IPC definition of 233
  Mathura rape case, NGOs role in 472
  and punishment 9, 218
refugee children 80
  rights of 448
Registration of Births and Deaths Act 1969 399
Birth of a child 399
Rehabilitation Council of India Act 1992 421–2
Rehabilitation Council of India on Manpower Development 1996 420, 421
Reproductive and Child Health Programme 1996, government scheme of 28, 414
right(s), of child, against economic exploitation 148–206, 446
  to basic education 355
  to development 327–73
  to early childhood care 445
  to education 336, 337, 373, 445
  to equality 447
  to a family 447
  to freedom of association and peaceful assembly 447
  to freedom of expression 447
  to freedom of religion 88
  to health 444
  of inheritance 86
  international laws/legislations on 14–24, 450
  to life 66, 447
  NGOs work on 32, 472

to nutrition 444
obstacles in realizing 449–76
to parental care 92–147
to participation 467–9
to play and recreation, United Nation's 365–7, 445
to protection 446
to shelter and housing 428–35
to survival 374–436, 444, 454
in Third World 32
and working mothers 407–12
Riyadh Guidelines 319, 321
Royal Commission on Labour (1931) 160
Rudd-ul-Muhtar 103
Rugmark Foundation 201, 202
'Rugmark' scheme 201–2
rural areas, schooling in 343

SAARC Regional Convention on Combating the Crime of Trafficking for Prostitution 269
SAARC Summit on Children 12
Saakshi 208, 239
Samvad, survey on sexual abuse 215
Sanat Mehta Committee 1984 163n
Sanlaap, action on children of prostitutes 275
Sapinda relationship 45
Sarva Siksha Abhiyan (SSA) 347–8
Save the Children India, Mumbai 274
Save the Children International Union 75n
Save Our Sisters (SOS), Movement 73n, 274
  children's village 295–6
Scheme of Assistance for Crèches for Working/Ailing Mothers 413
Scheme of Integrated Education for Disabled Children (IEDC) 423
school(s), attendance 340

for the blind 424–5
drop-outs 33
enrolment 152, 332, 342, 372, 465
  in Cambodia 364
  global 355, 362
  health programmes 382
  quality of 333
Sachoolnet India Limited 354
sex, determination tests 395
  ratio, in India 30–1, 385–6
  decline in 397–8, 455
  selection, of foetus 392
  tourism 251, 265, 464
Shah Bano case 88
Sharda Act see Child Marriage Restraint Act
Shariat, on types of guardians for children 102–3
Shias, *hizanat* of minor children among 105–6
  on right of mother to custody of children 104, 105
Shiksha Karmi Project, Rajasthan 350
Shaikshana Grama Sabhas 352
Shops and Establishment Acts 5
Shram Shakti, report of 410n, 414
Sihikshak Samakhya 349
slums, children living in 428–32
  demolition and eviction of 454
social rights, of children under UN Convention 17–18
Solnit, Albert 135
South Asian Coalition on Child Servitude (SACCS) 185, 201
Special Marriage Act 1954 223
  on custody of children 99, 100
  on legitimacy of children 451, 452
Special School Programme, for disabled children 424
Standing Committee on Sexually Abused Children 207

State of the World's Children 1999 328
street children, in India 277–8, 428, 429
succession laws, in India 58
Suppression of Immoral Traffic in Women and Girls Act 1956 (SITA) 253–5, 257
  amendments to 254
Supreme Court 26–7, 68
  directions, for adoption of children 51–2
  on children in jails 311, 312
  on children in observation homes 313
  on forced labour 184
  on in-country adoption 80–1
  on inter-country adoptions 80–1
  judgment, on adoption cases 49
  on bigamy case 89
  on child employment 176n
  on child custody cases 114–16, 120, 121, 146
  on education as fundamental right of children 338
  on interpretation of fundamental rights 471, 477
  on maintenance to minor child 118
  on mother as also natural guardian 115, 125
  on problems of prostitution 271
  on sale of land of minor by mother 121
  on Shah Bano case 88
  on trafficking in children 256
  on trial of delinquent juvenile 315
Swedish Penal Code 265

Tata Institute of Social Sciences, Special Cell for Women and Children, study on child sexual abuse 215
Tea Districts' (Emigration Labour) Act 1932 160
Total Fertility Rate (TFR), drop in 381
Tourism Bill of Rights and the Tourist Code 1985 268–9
Tribunal de Grande Instance, France 133
Turkey, Parent-training Programme in 364

Uniform Civil Code 87–9
Uniform Marriage and Dovorce Act (UMDA) 1979, USA 137
United Nations 208
United Nations Children's Fund (UNICEF) 74, 193, 199, 202, 295, 364, 377, 400, 401, 402
  definition of street children 277–8
  support to education 361, 362
United Nations Commission on Human Rights 76, 363
United Nations Committee on the Rights of the Child 18, 450
United Nations Congress on the Prevention of Crime and the Treatment of Offenders 316
United Nations Convention Against Torture and Other Cruel, Inhuman or Degrading Treatment or Punishment 1984 268
United Nations Convention on All Forms of Discrimination Against Women 15, 17
United Nations Convention on the Rights of the Child (CRC) 1989 1, 2, 5, 11, 12, 15, 17–21, 24, 27, 80, 176, 195, 199, 203, 206, 241, 265–6, 288, 317–21, 338,

358–9, 363, 365, 399, 437, 438, 440, 458, 460, 461
ratification by India 23, 299, 436
on right to participation 468, 471, 477
violation of 431–3
United Nations Declaration on the Rights of Child 1959 41, 356, 358
United Nations Development Assistance Framework (UNDAF) 362
UNESCO 349
United Nations General Assembly 194, 376
United Nations Guidelines for the Prevention of Juvenile Delinquency (Riyadh Guidelines) 319
United Nations Instruments Relating to Adoptions 76–9
United Nations intervention, strategies and movements 193–203
United Nations Standard Minimum Rules for the Administration of Juvenile Justice (Beijing Rules) 316
Universal Declaration of Human Rights (UDHR) 1948 16, 21–2, 194, 268, 356–7, 376
India as signatory to 357
universal primary education, in India 332, 333, 343, 369
see also education

Uttar Pradesh Children's Act 311

Vaccination Act 1880 401
Victim Assistance Programme, USA 244
Virginia High Court, USA 136
Virudha Sambandha rule 44n

World Alliance on Nutrition and Human Rights 377
World Bank, on education 362
World Conference on Education for All 1990 12, 356, 359–60
World Declaration on Survival, Protection and Development of Children (1990) 12, 356
World Education Forum, Dakar, Senegal 2000 361
World Food Summit 1996 377
World Health Organization (WHO) 374, 400, 402
definition of health by 374
Health for All 378
World Summit on Children 1990 12, 23, 361
World Tourism Organization 251
World Trade Organization (WTO) 268
labour clauses within 200

Young Persons Harmful Publications Act 1956 7, 256

Addendum

Page 4: Table 1.2

Age prescribed for majority under various laws. The following additions would make the table more comprehensive:

Legislation	Provision
Child Labour (Prohibition and Regulation) Act, 1986	Child means any person who has not completed fourteen years of age[1]
Indian Majority Act, 1875	Unless a particular personal law specifies otherwise, every person domiciled in India is deemed to have attained majority upon the compution of 18 years of age. If a guardian has been appointed by a Court of Wards, the age of majority is 21 years[2]
Immoral Traffic (Prevention) Act, 1986	Child is a person who has not completed the age of 16 years[3]
	Minor is a person who has completed the age of 16 years but has not completed the age of 18 years[4]
The Plantation Labour Act, 1951	Child means a person who has not completed his fourteenth year[5]

[1] Child Labour (Prohibition and Regulation) Act, 1986, Section 2(ii).
[2] Indian Majority Act, 1875, Section 3.
[3] Immoral Traffic (Prevention) Act, 1956, Section 2(aa).
[4] Immoral Traffic (Prevention) Act, 1956, Section 2(cb).
[5] The Plantation Labour Act, 1951, Section 2(a).

	Adolescent means a person who has completed his fourteenth year but has not completed his eighteenth year[6]
Beedi and Cigar Workers (Conditions of Employment) Act, 1966	No child shall be required or allowed to work in any industrial premises[7]
Motor Transport Workers Act, 1961	No child shall be required or allowed to work in any capacity in any motor transport undertaking[8]
Merchant Shipping Act, 1951	No person under 15 years of age shall be engaged or allowed to work in any capacity in any ship, except a. in a school ship, or training ship, in accordance with the prescribed conditions; or b. in a ship in which all persons employed are members of one family; or c. in a home trade ship of less than two hundred tons gross; or d. where such person is to be employed on nominal wages and will be in the charge of his father or other adult near male relative[9]
The Protection of Women from Domestic Violence Act, 2005	'child' means any person below the age of eighteen years and includes any adopted step or foster child[10]

Page 10: Under the heading 'Policies and Action Plans' add the following two bullet points:

- National Charter for Children 2004[11]
- National Plan of Action 2005[12]

[6] The Plantation Labour Act, 1951, Section 2(c).
[7] Beedi and Cigar Workers (Conditions of Employment) Act, 1966, Section 24.
[8] Motor Transport Workers Act, 1961, Section 21.
[9] Merchant Shipping Act, 1951, Section 109.
[10] The Protection of Women from Domestic Violence Act, 2005.
[11] For details please refer to the Introduction to the Second Edition.
[12] Ibid.

Page 21: Add the following new paragraph.

To help stem the growing abuse and exploitation of children worldwide, the United Nations General Assembly in 2000 adopted two Optional Protocols to the Convention to increase the protection of children from involvement in armed conflicts and from sexual exploitation. The two Optional Protocols to the CRC, to provide legal protection for children against the worst forms of exploitation, are:

(i) The Optional Protocol on the involvement of children in armed conflict
(ii) The Optional Protocol on the sale of children, child prostitution and child pornography

The Optional Protocol on the involvement of children in armed conflict establishes 18 as the minimum age for compulsory recruitment and requires States to do everything they can to prevent individuals under the age of 18 from taking a direct part in hostilities.

The Optional Protocol on the sale of children, child prostitution, and child pornography draws special attention to the criminalization of these serious violations of children's rights and emphasizes the importance of fostering increased public awareness and international cooperation in efforts to combat them.

The Optional Protocols must always be interpreted in the light of the original treaty as a whole, in this case guided by the principles of non-discrimination, the best interests of the child, and child participation. Both these protocols have been signed and ratified by India. The Government of India now has to take affirmative steps to comply with them.

Page 23, para 3: Under the sub heading 'Regional Instruments for the Protection of Children' the matter should read as follows:

'There are several regional human rights instruments for the protection of children adopted by the South Asian Association for Regional Cooperation (SAARC), the Council of Europe, the Organization of American States (OAS), and the Organization of African Unity (OAU).'

The following new paragraph should be added:

SAARC CONVENTION ON PREVENTING AND COMBATING TRAFFICKING IN WOMEN AND CHILDREN FOR PROSTITUTION, 2002

This convention has been ratified by all the SAARC countries, including India. Its adoption on 5 January 2002 at the Eleventh SAARC Summit held in Kathmandu was a timely initiative and significant milestone in combating and preventing trafficking.[13]

It is an important step forward especially since it recognizes the need for extra-territorial application of jurisdiction. Significantly, it includes a provision that the Convention shall be effective and the States Party to the Convention bound to prosecute or extradite offenders, even in the absence of extradition treaties between the states concerned.

Page 23: last para. After the first sentence add the following:

While ratifying, India made the following declaration:[14]

While fully subscribing to the objectives and purposes of the Convention, realising that certain rights of the child, namely those pertaining to the economic, social, and cultural rights can only be progressively implemented in the developing countries, subject to the extent of available resources and within the framework of international cooperation; recognizing that the child has to be protected from exploitation of all forms including economic exploitation; noting that for several reasons children of different ages do work in India; having prescribed minimum ages for employment in hazardous occupations and in certain other areas; having made regulatory provisions regarding hours and conditions of employment; and being aware that it is not practical immediately to prescribe minimum ages for admission to each and every area of employment in India—the Government of India undertakes to take measures to progressively implement the provisions of Article 32, particularly paragraph 2 (a), in accordance with its national legislation and relevant international instruments to which it is a State Party.

Page 60. Bullet point 7 should be replaced with the following:

After codification of the law, the father alone has the right to give the child in adoption, but only with the consent of the mother.[15] It has to be noted that the mother may give the child in adoption only if the father is dead or has completely renounced the world or has ceased to be a Hindu or has been declared by a court of competent jurisdiction to be of unsound mind.[16] The wife can never on her own adopt a child. She is only the consenting party along with her husband.

An unmarried woman, or if she is married, her marriage has been dissolved, or she is a widow, or her husband has completely and finally renounced the world, or has ceased to be a Hindu or has been declared by

---

[13] See http://www.fwld.org.np/csaarc.html.
[14] http://www.unhchr.ch.html/menu3/b/treatyu15_asp.htm.
[15] Hindu Adoptions and Maintenance Act, 1956, Section 9 (2).
[16] Ibid., Section 9(3).

a court of competent jurisdiction to be of unsound mind, can also adopt a son or daughter.[17]

Page 224

The Prevention of Child Marriage Bill 2004, is under consideration by the Government. For details see the Introduction to the Second Edition.

Page 233

The Offences against Child Bill 2006, is under discussion. For details see the Introduction to the Second Edition.

Page 299

The Juvenile Justice (Care and Protection of Children) Amendment Act 2005, has introduced several amendments to the Act. For details see the Introduction to the Second Edition.

Page 334

For further details on corporal punishment, see the Introduction to the Second Edition, under the sub heading 'Class Room Violence on School Children'.

Page 339

The Right to Education (Draft) Bill 2005 is under consideration. For details see the Introduction to the Second Edition.

Page 397

The Pre-natal Diagnostic Techniques (Regulation and Prevention of Misuse) Act 1994 (PNDT) now stands amended and renamed as 'The Pre-Conception and Pre-natal Diagnostic Techniques (Prohibition of Sex Selection) Act 2003 (PCPNDT) with effect from 14 February 2003. For details see the Introduction to the Second Edition.

Page 403

Infant Milk Substitutes, Feeding Bottles and Infant Foods (Regulation of Production, Supply and Distribution) Amendment Act 2003 has amended the IMS Act. For details see the Introduction to the Second Edition.

Page 461

The Commission for the Protection of Child Rights Act 2005 is now law. See the Introduction to the Second Edition for details.

---

[17] Hindu Adoption and Maintenance Act, 1956, Section 8.